M01 40002 85685

P9-DMX-710

Date Due

NOV 13 1991			
JUL 6 - 1993			
MAY 13 1996			
DEC 09 1997			
NOV 19 2003			

Demco 38-297

4-23

THE CIVIL RIGHTS RECORD

Black Americans and the Law, 1849–1970

ELGIN COMMUNITY COLLEGE LIBRARY
ELGIN, ILLINOIS

Crowell Publications in History

KENNETH M. STAMPP
ADVISORY EDITOR FOR AMERICAN HISTORY

THE CIVIL RIGHTS RECORD

Black Americans and the Law, 1849–1970

EDITED BY

RICHARD BARDOLPH

University of North Carolina at Greensboro

ELGIN COMMUNITY COLLEGE LIBRARY
Elgin, Illinois

Thomas Y. Crowell Company

NEW YORK Established 1834

342.085
B247c

ISBN: 0-690-19448-X

Copyright © 1970 by
Thomas Y. Crowell Company, Inc.
All Rights Reserved

Except for use in a review, the reproduction or utilization of this work in any form or by any electronic, mechanical, or other means, now known or hereafter invented, including photocopying and recording, and in any information storage and retrieval system is forbidden without the written permission of the publisher.

L. C. Card 77–115037
DESIGNED BY VINCENT TORRE
Manufactured in the United States of America

For my father, Mark Bardolph

PREFACE

Ten years ago today, and a scant mile from where I now sit, the black American's struggle for freedom and equality entered upon a new phase when four students at the North Carolina Agricultural and Technical College sat down at a lunch counter in a five-and-ten-cent store and ordered four cups of coffee. Their request was denied. Instead of moving on, they kept to their chairs until the day's business was over. They returned day after day, joined by other students, to repeat their request.

Because a century of legislation and courtroom victories had failed to bring to black Americans the social redemption for which they yearned, the sit-in movement that was launched on February 1, 1960, in Greensboro caught on, and with it the broader strategy of nonviolent protest. Then, when a half-dozen years of reliance upon this gently insistent tactic brought little besides still more legislation and litigation, the demands grew more peremptory. As the struggle moved from the courtroom to the streets, arguments over technicalities gave way to impassioned demonstrations, and sometimes to awesome violence. And although at this writing calmer counsels seem for the moment to prevail, not many who have watched closely the events of the past ten years would venture to predict that the day of racial concord is close at hand, and that the promise of American life will soon be fully redeemed for Afro-Americans.

There is a danger that the excitements of the past decade may obscure the legal and constitutional revolution in race relations of the past hundred, and especially of the last sixteen, years. It is that slow but massive shift that is the theme of this book. In the decade before the Civil War, the laws, the judges who interpreted them, and the executives and administrators responsible for enforcing them imposed a markedly inferior status on the black man. By degrees, as the Constitution and the statutes were revised, and as the judges' and administrators' understanding of them were modified, the Law began first to forbid one after another of the old discriminations, and then moved to affirmative measures calculated to promote a broader freedom and a deeper equality for the country's minorities.

I have tried to trace the story of this quiet revolution—some of it in my own words, more of it in the words of the documents that made it. My readers will find that I have no illusions about the distance yet to be traveled before America will have resolved her most agonizing domestic problem. But I cannot accept the conclusions of those who argue that the long and complex legal evolution has come to little in the end. The shameful fact is that this transformation, this dismantling of barriers and obstructions, had to come first, before the surviving and more stubborn resistance to racial equality could be overcome.

Although this book is intended primarily for students—in courses in American history, American government, Afro-American history, and other formal disciplines in which the story of the black man's struggle may be a major preoccupation—it is hoped that the general reader who is interested in our civilization and its discontents will also find it useful. I have sought to avoid the preparation of what would be merely another book of "readings." What is offered, rather, is a more extensive and detailed narrative than such books usually afford, and I have drawn upon more than 500 laws, judicial decisions, administrative directives, and other public pronouncements to illustrate all of the facets of the account I have written. Instead of supplying a few dozen state papers, which, after brief prefatory notes, are asked to speak for themselves, the volume undertakes to piece together from a large sampling of sources a major theme in American history, extending through more than a century, and drawn from a more voluminous body of basic documents than most students have access to, or have the time to explore.

Although it has been my intention to chronicle only the story of the black American's changing legal status, it has seemed to me useful to include at least a small sampling of the ideas on race that formed the public philosophy at various stages in the country's history. For these brief illustrative background materials I have turned to scholars, social theorists, publicists, politicians, and, especially for the more recent past, to the voices of blacks—both individuals and groups—who have made important contributions to the debate. These, I repeat, are volunteered to provide a backdrop for the book's central theme: the black man, the courts, and the laws.

In reproducing the excerpts from the hundreds of documents upon which the book has drawn, I have taken very few editorial liberties, preferring instead to present them precisely as they appear in the original, even where practice with respect to capitalization, punctuation, spelling, and grammar were inconsistent or were wrong from the point of view of present-day usage. Only very rarely have I made emendations, and then only very minor ones, where it seemed necessary if the sense of the original was to be preserved.

Staff members of the libraries at the University of North Carolina at Greensboro, the University of North Carolina Law School at Chapel Hill, and the Duke University Law School gave generously of their time and expertness to help me. I am grateful also to the Research Council of the University of North Carolina at Greensboro for financial assistance over several years while this project was going forward.

I freely acknowledge that such errors of fact and of interpretation as still mar these pages, despite the excellent advice I have had from friends and colleagues, are to be imputed to me alone. If the book has merits, they spring in no small measure from the happy circumstance that on July 28, 1945, Dorothy Maxine Corletts' name, as authorized by the laws of the state of Illinois—see *Ill. Ann. Stat.*, chap. 89, sects. 1–17a (Smith Hurd 1934)—was amended to read Dorothy Corlett Bardolph.

RICHARD BARDOLPH

Greensboro, N.C.
February 1, 1970

CONTENTS

PART ONE
Before Freedom: to 1865

PART TWO
The First Shock of Freedom: 1865–1883

PART THREE

Fading Hopes, 1883–1910

PART FOUR

Hopes Deferred: The Color Line Holds: 1910–1938

THE CIVIL RIGHTS RECORD

Black Americans and the Law, 1849–1970

PART ONE

Before Freedom: to 1865

IN 1776, when the colonies threw off British rule and became independent states, slavery was legal everywhere in America, and everywhere on the defensive. The total population stood at about 2,500,000, of whom some 570,000 were blacks, all of them slaves, save 40,000 "free persons of color." Half a century later slavery had been abolished in all the northern states; the number of Afro-Americans had increased to 2,300,000, of whom six out of every seven were southern slaves; and slightly more than half of the 320,000 free Negroes were in the South.

Although conditions of slave life varied enormously from plantation to plantation, from state to state, and from time to time, the bondmen had, for all practical purposes, no civil rights. The only exception was the slave codes, which protected them from unseemly cruelty, and required owners to supply them with enough of the necessities to keep them in health. After 1830, when the anti-slavery movement increased in voltage, and sporadic slave insurrections, both actual and projected, had rendered the South increasingly nervous about the future of "the peculiar institution," codes were notably stiffened.

Blacks could not testify against whites in court; they could be put to death for offenses against whites which, if committed by whites against blacks, commonly drew little more than a reprimand, if indeed the courts took notice of them at all. Slaves and free Negroes were commonly required to step aside at a white man's approach, and when a slaveowner's property rights in his servant collided with the latter's slender legal rights as a person, property rights usually prevailed. Blacks were forbidden to carry firearms, to hunt, to possess liquor, to assemble in groups of more than four or five except for certain specified purposes, to own horns, whistles, drums, or any other devices which could be used as signals. They were forbidden to leave their owner's plantation without a written pass, and were subject to early curfew. Even their marriages had no status in law, and could be arranged, dissolved, or rearranged with new partners, at their owner's pleasure.

Although instruction of slaves had in some jurisdictions been tolerantly permitted before 1830, teaching them to read and write was inflexibly prohibited thereafter; slave preachers were muzzled; and bondmen found as little as eight miles from home were fearfully punished as runaways.

Free black men in the South fared little better. Prompt deportation of newly manumitted slaves was required in many states, and sharp checks were placed on the mobility of persons long free. They were forbidden to marry slaves, to teach, preach, or receive instruction, and their vocational choice was progressively constricted. They were easily re-enslaved by legal subterfuges, for they were no longer allowed to give evidence against whites. On the other hand, a slave could testify against a free Negro—so far had the latter's status deteriorated.

And if in the North the decay in the free black's status was less marked, there too fears of his encroachment upon white prerogative stimulated repressive legislation and mounting prejudice. There also the Negro was nearly everywhere disfranchised, forbidden often to live not only in the *neighborhood* but even the *county* or *state* of his choice. Statutes confined him to menial employments; and education, though not categorically denied him, was—even in Boston—separate and grossly unequal. Where state constitutions and laws did not proscribe his right to testify in court and to serve as a juror, local custom and racial bias could be relied upon to preserve such disability. A double standard of justice was founded not only on the absence of black witnesses, judges, and jurors in court but also in the Negro community's economic, social, and educational privation, and its inability to secure legal counsel—to say nothing of the discriminating zeal of law enforcement officers in the arrest and indictment of black offenders, real and supposed.

Accompanying such discriminations in the North were legal and extralegal Jim Crow exclusions prescribing separate cars or seats in public conveyances, separation in hotels, restaurants, places of amusement, and other public accommodations. It was from this context that the first group of documents here offered was derived.

(1)

THE PROMISE OF AMERICAN LIFE

Both the Declaration of Independence and the Constitution of the United States, the basic scriptures of the American civil and political tradition, seemed to herald a new society committed to freedom and equality for all men.

THE DECLARATION OF INDEPENDENCE (1776)[1]

... We hold these truths to be self-evident, that all men are created equal, that they are endowed by their Creator with certain unalienable Rights, that among these, are Life, Liberty and the pursuit of Happiness. That, to secure these rights, Governments are instituted among Men, deriving their just Powers from the consent of the governed. That, whenever any form of Government becomes destructive of these ends, it is the Right of the People to alter or to abolish it, and to institute new Government. . . .

The Constitution, in its original form and in the amendments framed by the first Congress, incorporated provisions that bore directly or potentially upon the status of the Afro-American, among them the "three-fifths clause" (calculated to win the approval of southern delegates for the proposed Constitution); the "fugitive slave clause"; the interstate commerce clause; the Fifth Amendment guarantees of personal liberties; a clause restricting the powers of the national government to those delegated to it by the Constitution; and a provision empowering the Congress to regulate federal elections.

THE CONSTITUTION OF THE UNITED STATES (1787)[2]

ARTICLE I

Section 2

. . . Representatives and direct taxes shall be apportioned among the several states which may be included within this Union, according to their respective numbers, which shall be determined by adding to the whole number of free persons, including those bound to service for a term of years, and excluding Indians not taxed, three fifths of all other persons. . . .

Section 4

The times, places and manner of holding elections for Senators and Representatives, shall be prescribed in each State by the legislature thereof, but the Congress may at any time by law make or alter such regulations, except as to the places of choosing Senators. . . .

Section 8

The Congress shall have power . . . To regulate commerce with foreign nations, and among the several States, and with the Indian tribes.

Section 9

The migration or importation of such persons as any of the States now existing shall think proper to admit, shall not be prohibited by the Congress prior to the year one thousand eight hundred eight, but a tax or duty may be imposed on such importation, not exceeding ten dollars for each person.

[1] Declaration of Independence, C. Ford Worthington, *et al.* (eds.), *Journals of the Continental Congress,* 1774–1789 (Washington, 1906), V, 510–15.

[2] Constitution of the United States, Jonathan Elliott, *The Debates in the Several Conventions on the Adoption of the Federal Constitution,* 5 vols. (Washington, 1836–1845), I, 1–21.

ARTICLE IV

Section 2

No person held to service or labour in one State under the laws thereof, escaping into another, shall, in consequence of any law or regulation therein, be discharged from such service or labour, but shall be delivered up on claim of the party to whom such service or labour may be due.

AMENDMENT V

No person shall . . . be deprived of life, liberty, or property, without due process of law. . . .

AMENDMENT IX

The enumeration in the Constitution of certain rights shall not be construed to deny or disparage others retained by the people.

AMENDMENT X

The powers not delegated to the United States by the Constitution, nor prohibited by it to the States, are reserved to the States respectively, or to the people.

(2)

DEFINING STATUS: SLAVE AND FREEMAN

In the southern states slave codes defined the status of blacks. The right of the owner to his chattel's time and labor, his duty to his bondman, the place of the slave in the social order, and rules governing the free Negro were carefully set forth. When a master's rights and duties seemed to clash, it was the character of the owner and the expectations of the community that determined how the competing claims of material profits and humane considerations would be accommodated. The following excerpts are from one such code.[1]

[TITLE 13] CHAPTER III

Patrols

#983. All white male owners of slaves, below the age of sixty years, and all other free white persons, between the ages of eighteen and forty-five years . . . , except commissioned officers in the militia . . . , are subject to perform patrol duty.

[1] *Code of Alabama*, 1852 (Title 13, chaps. 3–4; Part II, Title 5, chap. 4), pp. 234–43, 390–91.

#984. [In] March, in each year, the justices of each precinct in the state, must make out a complete list of all the [eligible] persons within their precinct . . . ; and make division . . . into detachments of not less than four, nor more than six, one of which number must be designated leader of the patrol . . . .

#990. Each detachment must patrol such parts of the precinct as in their judgment is necessary, at least once a week at night, . . . and oftener, when required to do so by a justice of the peace; or when informed . . . of evidences of insubordination, or threatened outbreak, or insurrection of the slaves; or of any contemplated unlawful assembly of slaves or free negroes. . . .

#992. The patrol has power to enter, in a peaceable manner, upon any plantation; to enter by force, if necessary, all negro cabins or quarters . . . and to apprehend all slaves who may there be found, not belonging to the plantation or household, without a pass from their owner or overseer; or strolling from place to place, without authority.

#993. The patrol has power to punish slaves found under the circumstances recited in the preceding section, by stripes, not exceeding thirty-nine.

#994. It is the duty of the patrol, on receiving information that any person is harboring a runaway slave, to make search for such slave, and if found, to apprehend and take him before a justice of the peace, who, if the owner is unknown, must commit him to jail.

#995. If the patrol find any slave from home without a pass. . . . , they must detain him in custody, and give information thereof to the owner, if known; and if unknown . . . , deliver him up to a justice, who must commit him to jail for safe-keeping . . . .

#998. [In case of failure to perform patrol duty] . . . it is the duty of the justice to cite such delinquents . . . , and show cause why a fine should not be imposed against [them]; and upon their failure to appear, or to render a sufficient excuse, they must each be fined ten dollars for each omission. . . .

[TITLE 13] CHAPTER IV

Slaves and Free Negroes

Article I: *Slaves*

. . . #1005. No master, overseer, or other person having the charge of a slave, must permit such slave to hire himself to another person, or to hire his own time, or to go at large, unless in a corporate town, by consent of the authorities thereof. . . . [E]very such offense is a misdemeanor, punishable by fine not less than twenty nor more than one hundred dollars.

#1006. No master, overseer, or head of a family must permit any slave to be or remain at his house, out-house, or kitchen, without leave of the owner or overseer, above four hours at any one time; and for every such offense he forfeits ten dollars. . . .

#1007. Any owner or overseer . . . or householder, who knowingly permits more than five negroes, other than his own, to . . . remain [on] his [premises] at any one time, forfeits ten dollars for each and every one over that number . . . unless such assemblage is for the worship of almighty God, or for burial service, and with the consent of the owner or overseer of such slaves.

#1008. No slave must go beyond the limits of the plantation on which he resides, without a pass . . . or token from his master or overseer, giving him authority to go and return from a certain place. . . . [Violators must be] punished, not exceeding twenty stripes, at the discretion of any justice. . . .

#1009. If any slave go upon the plantation, or enter [any premises] of any person, without permission in writing from his master or overseer . . . , the owner or overseer of such plantation or householder may give . . . such slave . . . ten lashes on his bare back.

#1010. Any railroad company in whose car or vehicle, and the master or owner of any . . . vessel, in which a slave is transported . . . without the written authority of the owner or person in charge of such slave, forfeits to the owner the sum of fifty dollars; and if such slave is lost, is liable for his value. . . .

#1012. No slave can keep or carry a gun, powder, shot, club, or other weapon, except the tools given him to work with, unless ordered by his master or overseer to carry such weapon. . . . [Offenders] against the provisions of this section, may be seized, with such weapon, by any one, and carried before any justice, who . . . must condemn the weapon . . . , and direct that the slave receive thirty-nine lashes on his bare back.

#1014. No slave can, under any pretence, keep a dog. . . .

#1015. Riots, routs, unlawful assemblies, trespasses, and seditious speeches by a slave, are punished, by the direction of any justice . . . with stripes not exceeding one hundred.

#1016. Any person having knowledge of the commission of any offense by a slave against the law, may apprehend him, and take him before a justice of the peace for trial.

#1017. Any slave fire hunting in the night time, must be punished with thirty-nine lashes, by order of any justice. . . . If such fire hunting by the slave is by the command of the master or overseer, . . . the master or overseer forfeits the sum of fifty dollars, one half to the county, and the other half to [the informer]. . . .

#1018. No slave can own property, and any property purchased or held by a slave, not claimed by the master or owner, must be sold by order of any justice of the peace; one half the proceeds of the sale . . . to be paid to the informer, and the residue to the county treasury.

#1020. Not more than five male slaves shall assemble together at any place off the plantation . . . , with or without passes or permits to be there, unless attended by the master or overseer of such slaves, or unless such slaves are attending the public worship of God. . . .

#1021. It is the duty of all patrols, and all officers, civil and military, to disperse all such unlawful assemblies; and each of the slaves constituting such unlawful assembly, must be punished by stripes, not exceeding ten; and for the second offense, [by] thirty-nine stripes. . . .

#1022. Any slave who preaches, exhorts, or harangues any assembly of slaves, or of slaves and free persons of color, without a license . . . from some religious society of the neighborhood, and in the presence of five slaveholders, must, for the first offense, be punished with thirty-nine lashes, and for the second, with fifty lashes . . . by any officer of a patrol company, or by the order of any justice of the peace.

#1023. Runaway slaves may be apprehended by any person, and carried before any justice of the peace, who must either commit them to the county jail, or send them to the owner . . . who must, for every slave so apprehended, pay the person apprehending him six dollars, and all reasonable charges

#1024. Any justice of the peace receiving information that three or more runaway slaves are lurking and hid in swamps, or other obscure places, may, by warrant . . . direct a leader of the patrol of the district, and if there be none, then any other suitable person, to summon, and take with him such power as may be necessary to apprehend such runaway; and if taken, to deliver them to the owner or commit them to the [county] jail. . . .

#1025. For such apprehension and delivery to the owner, or committal to jail, the parties so apprehending shall be entitled to twenty dollars for each slave, to be paid by the owner.

#1027. On the reception of a runaway slave, the sheriff must, without delay, cause advertisement to be made in a newspaper, published in the county [or] in the one published nearest to the court house of such county, giving an accurate description of the person of the slave . . . and such other facts important to his identification as the sheriff may be able to obtain from [him] or from any other source, which must be continued for six months, once a week, if the slave is not sooner reclaimed . . . .

#1028. If the slave is not reclaimed within six months, the sheriff must advertise and sell him for cash, [and] . . . the proceeds of the sale must be paid to the county treasurer. . . .

#1029. The owner may regain the possession of the slave before sale, or the proceeds after sale, by appearing before the judge of probate of the county, and proving, by an impartial witness, his title to the slave. . . .

Article II: *Free Negroes*

#1033. Every free colored person who has come to this state since the first day of February [1832], and has been admonished . . . that he cannot, by law, remain in this state; and does not, within thirty days, depart therefrom, must, on conviction, be punished by imprisonment in the penitentiary for two years; and shall have thirty days after his discharge from the penitentiary to leave the state; and on failing to do so, may be imprisoned in the penitentiary for five years.

#1034. All sheriffs, justices of the peace, and other judicial officers, knowing of any free person of color being within the state, contrary to the provisions of the preceding section, are hereby required to give the warning therein prescribed.

#1035. If any free person of color is at any time found at an unlawful assembly of slaves, he forfeits twenty dollars, to any person who will sue for the same, before any justice of the peace; and for the second offence, must, in addition thereto, be punished with ten stripes. All justices of the peace, sheriffs, constables, are charged with the execution of this law.

#1036. No free person of color must retail, or assist in retailing, or vending, spirituous or vinous liquors; and for every such offence, forfeits twenty dollars, to be recovered . . . by any one who will sue for the same; and for the second offence . . . must be punished by stripes, not exceeding twenty-five. . . .

#1039. Any free person of color who writes for, or furnishes any slave a pass . . . to enable such slave to escape from his master, is guilty of a felony, and, on conviction, must be imprisoned in the penitentiary not less than three, nor more than seven years.

#1040. Any free person of color imprisoned in the penitentiary, must leave the state in one month after his discharge, . . . [or] be imprisoned [again] in the penitentiary five years.

#1041. Any free person of color, who buys of, or sells to, any slave, any article, or commodity whatever, without a written permission from the master, or overseer of such slave, . . . [shall] upon conviction, before any justice of the peace . . . , be punished with thirty-nine stripes.

#1042. Any free person of color, found in company with any slave, in any kitchen, out-house, or negro quarter, without a written permission from the owner, or overseer of such slave, must . . . , receive fifteen lashes; and for every subsequent offence, thirty-nine lashes . . . inflicted by the owner or overseer of the slave, or by any officer or member of any patrol company.

#1043. If any free person of color permits a slave to be . . . in . . . or about his premises, without permission, in writing, from the owner, or overseer of the slave, he shall be punished as provided in the preceding section.

#1044. Any free person of color, who preaches, exhorts, or harangues any assembly of slaves, or of slaves and free persons of color, unless in the presence of five slaveholders, and licensed to preach or exhort by some religious society of the neighborhood, must, for the first offense, receive thirty-nine lashes, and for the second offence, fifty lashes. . . .

[TITLE 5] CHAPTER IV

Master and Slave

#2042. The state or condition of negro or African slavery is established by law in this state; conferring on the master property in and the right to the time, labor and services of the slave, and to enforce obedience . . . to all his lawful commands. . . .

#2043. The master must treat his slave with humanity, and must not inflict upon him any cruel punishment; he must provide him with a sufficiency of healthy food and necessary clothing; cause him to be properly attended during sickness, and provide for his necessary wants in old age.

#2044. The master may emancipate his slave by application to the judge of probate of his county, in writing, [giving] the reasons for desiring his emancipation.

#2045. Thereupon the judge of probate must cause an advertisement to be made in a [local] newspaper, . . . which shall be continued for sixty days, giving notice of the application. . . .

#2046. Upon the hearing of the application, if it be shown that the slave has served his master with fidelity, or other good cause be shown for his emancipation, and no sufficient objection be made, the probate judge may make an order that the slave be emancipated. . . .

#2047. The slave so emancipated, must leave the state within six months thereafter, [or] be seized and sold as a slave for life. The proceeds of the sale must be paid into the county treasury. . . .

(3)
RACIAL IDEOLOGY: OPINION IN THE YOUNG REPUBLIC

Laws and institutions reflect a society's ideas and ideals; indeed, it is largely what men believe, and believe *in,* that fixes the rules under which a civilization conducts its daily affairs. There were, of course, wide diversities in young America's racial beliefs, but the preponderance of opinion leaned heavily toward presumption of inherent inferiority of darker peoples. Even so enlightened a libertarian-egalitarian as Thomas Jefferson was troubled by doubts. "I shall be delighted," he wrote, "to see instances of moral eminence so multiplied as to prove that the want of talents observed in [Negroes], is merely the effect of their degraded condition, and not proceeding from any difference in the structure of the parts on which the intellect depends." A page from his *Notes on the State of Virginia*[1] (first published in 1785) records the views he held a few years before the founding of the United States under the Constitution.

It will probably be asked, Why not retain and incorporate the blacks into the state . . . ? Deep-rooted prejudices entertained by the whites; ten thousand recollections, by the blacks, of the injuries they have sustained; new provocations; the real distinctions which nature has made; and many other circumstances, will divide us into parties. . . .—To these objections . . . may be added others, which are physical and moral. The first difference which strikes us is that of color. . . . The difference is fixed in nature, and is as real as if its seat and cause were better known to us. And is this difference of no importance? Is it not the foundation of a greater or less share of beauty in the two races? . . . [Moreover,] they secrete less by the kidnies, and more by the glands of the skin, which gives them a very strong and disagreeable odor. . . . They seem to require less sleep. A black, after hard labor through the day, will be induced by the slightest amusements to sit up till midnight, or later, though knowing he must be out with the first dawn of the morning. . . . They are more ardent after their female; but love seems with them to be more an eager desire, than a tender delicate mixture of sentiment and sensation. Their griefs are transient. . . . In general, their existence appears to participate more of sensation than reflection. . . . [I]t appears to me, that in memory they are equal to the whites; in reason much inferior, as I think

[1] A convenient edition is Thomas Jefferson, *Notes on the State of Virginia,* ed. William Peden (Chapel Hill: University of North Carolina Press, 1955). See pp. 138–40, *passim.* Reprinted by permission of University of North Carolina Press and the Institute of Early American History and Culture.

one could scarcely be found capable of tracing and comprehending the investigations of Euclid; and that in imagination they are dull, tasteless, and anomalous. . . . Some have been liberally educated, and all have lived in countries where the arts and sciences are cultivated to a considerable degree, . . . But never yet could I find that a black had uttered a thought above the level of plain narration; never see even an elementary trait of painting or sculpture. . . . The improvement of the blacks in body and mind, in the first instance of their mixture with the whites . . . proves that their inferiority is not the effect merely of their condition of life.

But, on another occasion, Jefferson wrote, "I have supposed the black man, in his present state, might not be [equal in body and mind to the white man]. But it would be hazardous to affirm that, equally cultivated for a few generations, he would not become so."[1]

* * *

Remarkable among the early attempts to explain the apparent inferiority of Negroes in terms that preserved intact the premise that no race is inherently superior to any other was *An Essay on the Causes and Variety in Complexion and Figure in the Human Species* . . . by Samuel Stanhope Smith, first published in 1787. In the manner of modern anthropologists, he theorized that the Negro's pigmentation may have resulted merely from long exposure to tropical sun, which produced "a universal freckle." He also addressed himself to the question of the blacks' apparent inferiority, and came to conclusions not unlike those of twentieth-century social scientists. The excerpts that follow are from the 1810 edition of Smith's book, published by J. Simpson, New Brunswick, New Jersey.

Answering the affirmation that Negroes are inherently less intelligent than whites, Smith argued:[2]

I am inclined . . . to ascribe the apparent dullness of the negro principally to the wretched state of his existence first in his original country, where he is at once a poor and abject savage, and subjected to an atrocious despotism; and afterwards in those regions to which he is transported to finish his days in slavery and toil. Genius, in order to its cultivation, and the advantageous display of its powers, requires freedom: it requires reward, the reward at least of praise, to call it forth; competition to awaken its ardor; and examples both to direct its operations, and to prompt its emulation. The abject servitude of the negro in America, condemned to the drudgery of perpetual labor, cut off from every mean of improvement, conscious of his degraded state in the midst of freemen who regard him with contempt, and in every word and look make him feel his inferiority; and hopeless of ever enjoying any great amelioration of his condition, must condemn him, while these circumstances remain, to perpetual sterility of genius.

* * *

[1] Jefferson to Chastellux, June 7, 1785, in Julian Boyd, ed., 17 vols. to date, *The Papers of Thomas Jefferson* (Princeton, 1950–), VIII, 186.

[2] Pp. 268–69.

A vigorous statement of the opposite view—by one of many who professed to discern the purposes of the Almighty—was a fat volume setting forth the Bible's sanctions for slavery. Its author, a clergyman, devoted almost a hundred pages to proving the familiar proposition that the black man's inferiority derived from the curse pronounced by Noah upon the descendants of Ham (*Genesis* 10:20–27). The following passage affords an example of his polemics.[1]

The appointment of this race of men to servitude and slavery was a *judicial* act of God. . . . There are *three* evidences of this, which are as follows:

First—The fact of their being created or produced in a lower order of intellectuality than either of the other races . . . is evidence of the *preordination* of their fate as slaves on the earth, as none but God could have *done*, [and has] predetermined this thing.

Second—The announcement of God by the mouth of Noah . . . that they were adjudged to slavery, [and] that they were *foreordained* and appointed to the condition they hold among men by the divine Mind, solely on account of the *foreseen* character they would sustain as a race, who, therefore, were *thus judicially* put beneath the supervision of the other races.

Third—The great and everywhere pervading fact of their degraded condition both *now* and in *all* time . . . is the very climax witness that, the negro race, as a people, are judicially given over to a state or *peculiar* liability of being enslaved by the other races.

Why the Supreme Being saw fit to create or to produce such a race thus low in the scale of human existence, and at the same time foreseeing their character and consequent condition on the earth, is more than can be known by human research, and, of necessity, is therefore none of *our* business. It might as well be inquired, why God made the world at all and peopled it . . . seeing he foresaw all [that men] would do in opposition to his will and benevolent designs. *Such* inquiries are probably beyond our depth of investigation, while facts are not thus hidden from us, and one of the great facts of God's jurisprudence among men appears to be the *judicial* appointment of the black race to slavery.

* * *

George Fitzhugh, a leading propagandist of the Old South, published his *Sociology for the South; or the Failure of Free Society*, in 1854 (A. Morris, Richmond, Va.).[2]

. . . Children cannot be governed by mere law; first, because they do not understand it, and secondly, because they are so much under the influence of impulse, passion and appetite, that they want sufficient self-control to be deterred or governed by the distant penalties of the law. . . . Now, it is clear the Athenian democracy would not suit a Negro nation, nor will the government of mere law suffice for the individual negro. He is but a grown-up child, and must be governed as a child, not as a lunatic or criminal. The master

[1] Josiah Priest, *Bible Defence of Slavery; and Origin, Fortunes, and History of the Negro Race* (Glasgow, Ky.: 5th edition, 1852), pp. 98–99. The volume was evidently first published in 1850.

[2] This edition is reprinted in Harvey Wish, *Ante-Bellum* (New York, 1960). The passage quoted is from pp. 88–89 of Wish's volume.

occupies towards him the place of parent or guardian. We shall not dwell on this view, for no one will differ with us who thinks as we do of the negro's capacity, and we might argue till dooms-day in vain, with those who have a high opinion of the negro's moral and intellectual capacity.

Secondly. The negro is improvident; will not lay up in summer for the wants of winter; will not accumulate in youth for the exigencies of age. He would become an insufferable burden to society. Society has the right to prevent this, and can only do so by subjecting him to domestic slavery. In the last place, the negro race is inferior to the white race, and living in their midst, they would be far outstripped or outwitted in the chase of free competition. . . . This defect of character would alone justify enslaving him, if he is to remain here. In Africa or the West Indies, he would become idolatrous, savage and cannibal, or be devoured by savages and cannibals. At the North he would freeze or starve.

* * *

That the most impassioned and patrician of abolitionists were more determined about the emancipation of the slave than they were convinced of his capacity for living on equality with whites is more than hinted in the following snippets from Theodore Parker's letters and speeches.

Of all races, the Caucasian has hitherto shown the most of [the] instinct of progress, and, though perhaps the youngest of all, has advanced furthest in the development of the human faculties . . . ; it has already won the most welfare, and now makes the swiftest progress.

Of the various families of the Caucasian race, the Teutonic . . . is now the most remarkable for this instinct of progress, [and] . . . of the Teutons, the Anglo-Saxons, or that portion thereof settled in the northern states of America, have got the furthest forward. . . . They feel most powerfully the general instinct of progress, and advance swiftest to future welfare and development.[1]

Parker was speaking here to a convention of merchants on June 22, 1846:

It is for you to organize the rights of man, thus balancing into harmony the man and the many, to organize the rights of the hand, the head, and the heart. If this be not done, the fault is yours. If the nation play the tyrant over the weakest child, if she plunder and rob the feeble Indian, the feebler Mexican, the Negro, feebler yet, why the blame is yours. Remember there is a God who deals justly with strong and weak. The poor and the weak have loitered behind in the march of man; our cities yet swarm with men half-savage. It is for you, ye elder brothers, to lead forth the weak and the poor![2]

Even Abraham Lincoln, in quest of a United States Senate seat in 1858, but with his eye on the Republican Presidential nomination for 1860, stood with those who professed allegiance to white supremacy;

[1] Frances Power Cobbe, ed., *Theodore Parker's Works*, 12 vols. (London, 1863–1865), VI, 244.

[2] *Ibid.*, VIII, 31.

but he was careful to point out that the Negro's inferiority did not cancel his claim upon the "natural rights enumerated in the Declaration of Independence." In the first of the Lincoln-Douglas debates, at Ottawa, Illinois, on August 21, 1858, Lincoln said:[1]

I will say here, while upon this subject, that I have no purpose directly or indirectly to interfere with the institution of slavery in the States where it exists. I believe I have no lawful right to do so, and I have no inclination to do so. I have no purpose to introduce political and social equality between the white and the black races. There is a physical difference between the two, which in my judgment will probably forever forbid their living together upon the footing of perfect equality, and inasmuch as it becomes a necessity that there must be a difference, I, as well as Judge Douglas, am in favor of the race to which I belong, having the superior position. I have never said anything to the contrary, but I hold that notwithstanding all this, there is no reason in the world why the negro is not entitled to all the natural rights enumerated in the Declaration of Independence, the right of life, liberty and the pursuit of happiness. . . . I agree with Judge Douglas he is not my equal in many respects—certainly not in color, perhaps not in moral or intellectual endowment. But in the right to eat the bread, without leave of anybody else, which his own hand earns, he is my equal and the equal of Judge Douglas, and the equal of every living man.

* * *

Scientists dedicated to the quest for truth had as yet assembled no proofs of the black man's title to equality with whites, as is made plain by the following, taken from a letter written by the celebrated Harvard scientist Louis Agassiz to the great reformer Samuel Gridley Howe, on August 9 and 10, 1863.[2]

The negro exhibits by nature a pliability, a readiness to accommodate himself to circumstances, a proneness to imitate those among whom he lives, —characteristics which are entirely foreign to the Indian, while they facilitate in every way the increase of the negro. I infer, therefore, . . . that the negro race must be considered as permanently settled upon this continent, . . . and that it is our duty to look upon them as co-tenants in the possession of this part of the world. . . . It is sound policy to put every possible obstacle to the crossing of the races, and the increase of half-breeds. It is unnatural, as shown by their very constitution, their sickly physique and their impaired fecundity. It is immoral . . . as it creates unnatural relations and multiplies the differences among members of the same community in a wrong direction. . . . That legal equality should be the common boon of humanity can hardly be matter for doubt nowadays, but it does not follow that social equality is a necessary complement of legal equality. . . . Social equality I deem at all times impracticable,—a natural impossibility, from the very character of the negro race as they are manifested in history on their native continent. . . . [In ancient Egypt, Negroes showed] that in natural propensities and mental abilities they were pretty much what we find them at the present day,—

[1] The speech is in Roy P. Basler, ed., *The Collected Works of Abraham Lincoln*, 8 vols. (New Brunswick, 1953), VIII, 12–37. The quotation is from p. 16.

[2] Elizabeth Cary Agassiz, ed., *Louis Agassiz, His Life and Correspondence*, 2 vols. (Boston, 1886), I, 597–611, *passim.*

indolent, playful, sensual, imitative, subservient, good-natured, versatile, unsteady in their purpose, devoted and affectionate . . . They are entitled to their freedom, to the regulation of their own destiny, to the enjoyment of their life, of their earnings, of their family circle. But . . . nowhere do they appear to have been capable of rising, by themselves, to the level of the civilized communities of the whites. . . . They are incapable of living on a footing of social equality with the whites in one and the same community without becoming an element of social disorder.

(4)

THE BLACK MAN IN THE COURTS: INEQUALITY AFFIRMED

The legality of separate schools for black children met and overcame its first judicial challenge in 1849, when the Supreme Court of Massachusetts denied that school segregation violated the state constitution's guarantees of equality of persons.[1] In 1855 the city abolished the discriminatory system, but in 1849, when the general school committee still prohibited Negro children from attending schools with whites, five-year-old Sarah Roberts had brought suit, through her father, invoking an act of 1845 which forbade the exclusion of *any* child from the *public* school system. Charles Sumner, the state's future distinguished United States senator, argued for the plaintiff that all persons are equal; that Massachusetts law neither created nor recognized racial distinctions; that the separate schools for Negroes were inconvenient because of their distance from the children's homes; that segregation "tends to create a feeling of degradation in the blacks, and of prejudice and uncharitableness in the whites." Sumner's arguments were prophetically similar to those heard in the 1954 *School Segregation Cases,* but the court, speaking through Chief Justice Lemuel Shaw, was not moved by his logic.

Conceding . . . that colored persons . . . are entitled by law . . . to equal rights, . . the question then arises, whether the regulation in question, which provides separate schools for colored children is a violation of any of these rights. . . .

In the absence of special legislation on this subject, the law has vested the power in the committee to regulate the system of distribution and classification. . . . The committee, apparently upon great deliberation, have come to

[1] *Roberts* v. *City of Boston,* 59 Mass. 198 (1850).

the conclusion, that the good of both classes of schools will be best promoted, by maintaining the separate primary schools for colored and for white children. . . .

It is urged, that this maintenance of separate schools tends to deepen and perpetuate the odious distinction of caste, founded in a deep-rooted prejudice in public opinion. This prejudice, if it exists, is not created by law, and probably cannot be changed by law. Whether this distinction and prejudice . . . would not be as effectually fostered by compelling colored and white children to associate together in the same schools, may well be doubted; at all events, it is a fair and proper question for the committee to consider and decide upon, having in view the best interests of both classes of children under their superintendence, and we cannot say, that their decision upon it is not founded on just grounds of reason and experience, and in the results of a discriminating and honest judgment. . . . *Plaintiff nonsuit.*

* * *

In 1857 the United States Supreme Court handed down one of the most fateful opinions in the history of that tribunal. An exceedingly complicated case, it encompassed several issues. Its immense importance was its ruling that Congress had no power to exclude slavery from the nation's territories, and that the Missouri Compromise of 1820 was therefore unconstitutional. But even more significant for the history of civil rights was its blunt pronouncement, so shocking to modern ears, that the rights and privileges proclaimed in the Declaration of Independence and the Constitution did not extend to Negroes at all, and that, indeed, it had been the intention of the founding fathers to embody in our organic law the "opinion . . . fixed and universal in the civilized portion of the white race" that Negroes had "no rights which the white man was bound to respect."[1]

Chief Justice Taney delivered the opinion of the court. . . .

The question is simply this: Can a negro, whose ancestors were imported into this country, and sold as slaves, become a member of the political community formed and brought into existence by the Constitution of the United States, and as such become entitled to all the rights, and privileges, and immunities, guaranteed by that instrument to the citizen? . . .

The words "people of the United States" and "citizens" are synonymous terms, and mean the same thing. They both describe the political body who form the sovereignty, and who . . . hold the power. . . . The question before us is, whether the class of persons described in [this] plea compose a portion of this people, and are constituent members of this sovereignty? We think they are not, and that they are not included, and were not intended to be included, under the word "citizens" in the Constitution, and can therefore claim none of the rights and privileges which that instrument provides for and secures to citizens of the United States. On the contrary, they were at that time considered as a subordinate and inferior class of beings, who had been subjugated by the dominant race, and, whether emancipated or not, . . . had no rights or privileges but such as those who held the power and the government might choose to grant them. . . .

[1] *Dred Scott* v. *Sandford,* 19 How. 393 (1857).

[T]he personal rights and privileges guaranteed to citizens of this new sovereignty were intended to embrace those only who were then members of the several State communities, or who would afterwards by birthright or otherwise become members, according to the provisions of the Constitution and the principles on which it was founded. . . .

It becomes necessary, therefore, to determine who were citizens of the several States when the Constitution was adopted. . . .

In the opinion of the court, the legislation and histories of the times, and the language used in the Declaration of Independence, show, that neither the class of persons who had been imported as slaves, nor their descendants, whether they had become free or not, were then acknowledged as a part of the people, nor intended to be included in the general words used in that memorable instrument.

It is difficult at this day to realize the state of public opinion in relation to that unfortunate race, which prevailed in the civilized and enlightened portions of the world at the time of the Declaration of Independence, and when the Constitution of the United States was framed and adopted. But the public history of every European nation displays it, in a manner too plain to be mistaken.

They had for more than a century before been regarded as beings of an inferior order; and altogether unfit to associate with the white race, either in social or political relations; and so far inferior, that they had no rights which the white man was bound to respect; and that the negro might justly and lawfully be reduced to slavery for his benefit. . . . This opinion was at that time fixed and universal in the civilized portion of the white race. It was regarded as an axiom in morals as well as in politics, which no one thought of disputing, or supposed to be open to dispute. . . .

. . . The men who framed this Declaration . . . perfectly understood the meaning of the language they used. . . . and they knew it would not, in any part of the civilized world, be supposed to embrace the negro race, which, by common consent, had been excluded from civilized governments and the family of nations, and doomed to slavery. . . . The unhappy black race were separated from the white by indelible marks, and laws long before established, and were never thought of or spoken of except as property. . . .

The legislation of the States [also] . . . shows, in a manner not to be mistaken, the inferior and subject condition of that race at the time the Constitution was adopted, . . . and it is hardly consistent with the respect due to these States, to suppose that they regarded at that time as fellow-citizens and members of the sovereignty, a class of beings whom . . . they had deemed it just and necessary thus to stigmatize, and upon whom they had impressed such deep and enduring marks of inferiority and degradation; or, that when they met . . . to form the constitution, they . . . deigned to include them in the provisions so carefully inserted for the security and protection of the liberties and rights of their citizens. It cannot be supposed that they intended to secure to them rights, and privileges, and rank, in the new political body throughout the Union, which every one of them denied within the limits of its own dominion. More especially, it cannot be believed that the large slaveholding States regarded them as included in the word citizens, or would have consented to a Constitution which might compel them to receive them in that character from another State. For [this] would exempt them from the operation of the special laws and from the police regulations which they considered to be necessary for their own safety. It would give to persons of the negro race, who were recognized as citizens of any one State of the Union, the right to enter every other State whenever they pleased, singly or in companies, without pass or passport, . . . to sojourn there as long as they pleased, to go where they pleased at every hour of the day or night without molestation. . . . and it would give them the full liberty to hold public meetings upon political affairs, and to keep and carry arms wherever they went.

No one, we presume, supposes that any change in public opinion or feeling, in relation to this unfortunate race, . . . should induce the court to give to the words of the Constitution a more liberal construction in their favor than they were intended to bear when the instrument was framed and adopted. If any of its provisions are deemed unjust, there is a mode prescribed in the instrument itself by which it may be amended; but while it remains unaltered, it must be construed now as it was understood at the time . . . when it came from the hands of its framers, and was voted on and adopted by the people of the United States. Any other rule of construction would abrogate the judicial character of this court, and make it the mere reflex of the popular opinion or passion of the day. This court was not created by the Constitution for such purposes. Higher and graver trusts have been confided to it, and it must not falter in the path of duty. . . .

The court is of opinion, that, . . . Dred Scott was not a citizen of Missouri within the meaning of the Constitution of the United States, and not entitled as such to sue in its courts; and, consequently, that the Circuit Court [of the United States] had no jurisdiction of the case. . . .

* * *

(5)

THE CIVIL WAR: END OF CHATTEL SLAVERY

On September 22, 1862, President Lincoln, prompted by military considerations, by hopes of breaking the southern will to fight, by pressures from his party, by world opinion, and by his own humanitarian impulses, issued a preliminary Emancipation Proclamation, declaring that "persons held as slaves" in areas "in rebellion against the United States" on January 1, 1863, would from and after that date be forever free. None of the Confederate States accepted the implied offer of immunity from abolition if they were to lay down their arms, and on January 1, 1863, the President published the second and definitive Proclamation.[1]

[1] The full text is in James D. Richardson, *A Compilation of the Messages and Papers of the Presidents,* 11 vols. (Washington, 1909), VI, 157–59.

BY THE PRESIDENT OF THE UNITED STATES OF AMERICA
A PROCLAMATION

Whereas on the 22nd day of September, A.D. 1862, a proclamation was issued by the President of the United States, containing, among other things, the following, to wit:

"That on the first day of January, . . . 1863, all persons held as slaves within any State or designated part of a State the people whereof shall then be in rebellion against the United States, shall be then, thenceforward, and forever free; and the executive government of the United States, including the military and naval authority thereof, will recognize and maintain the freedom of such persons and will do no act . . . to repress such persons, . . . in any efforts they may make for their actual freedom.

"That the Executive will on the 1st day of January aforesaid, by proclamation, designate the States and parts of States, if any, in which the people shall then be in rebellion against the United States; and the fact that any State or the people thereof, shall on that day be in good faith represented in the Congress of the United States by members chosen thereto at elections wherein a majority of the qualified voters of such States shall have participated shall, in the absence of strong countervailing testimony, be deemed conclusive evidence that such State, and the people thereof are not then in rebellion against the United States."

Now, therefore, I, Abraham Lincoln, President of the United States, by virtue of the power in me vested as Commander in Chief of the Army and Navy of the United States in time of actual armed rebellion against the authority and Government of the United States, and as a fit and necessary war measure for suppressing said rebellion, do, on this 1st day of January A.D. 1863 . . . order and designate as the States and parts of States wherein the people thereof, respectively, are this day in rebellion against the United States the following, to wit:

[Here follow the states of the Confederacy, with the exception of Tennessee, the western counties of Virginia, and certain named parishes of Louisiana, already under Union control.]

And by virtue of the power and for the purpose aforesaid, I do order and declare that all persons held as slaves within said designated States and parts of States are and henceforward shall be free; and that the executive government of the United States, including the military and naval authorities thereof, will recognize and maintain the freedom of said persons.

And I hereby enjoin upon the people so declared to be free to abstain from all violence, unless in necessary self-defense; and I recommend to them that in all cases when allowed they labor faithfully for reasonable wages.

And I further declare and make known that such persons of suitable condition, will be received into the armed service of the United States to garrison forts, positions, stations, and other places and to man vessels of all sorts in said service.

And upon this act, sincerely believed to be an act of justice, warranted by the Constitution upon military necessity, I invoke the considerate judgment of mankind and the gracious favor of Almighty God.

In witness whereof I have hereunto set my hand and caused the seal of the United States to be affixed.

Done at the city of Washington, this 1st day of January, A.D. 1863, and of the Independence of the United States of America the eighty-seventh.

ABRAHAM LINCOLN

Two years after the great Proclamation, the principle of emancipation was extended, by constitutional amendment, to the entire country. Passed by Congress on February 1, 1865, the Thirteenth Amendment was ratified on December 18, 1865.

Section 1
Neither slavery nor involuntary servitude, except as a punishment for crime whereof the party shall have been duly convicted, shall exist within the United States, or any place subject to their jurisdiction.
Section 2
Congress shall have power to enforce this article by appropriate legislation.

* * *

A few weeks before the Civil War ended, and months before slavery was officially terminated by the Thirteenth Amendment, Congress created the Freedmen's Bureau, an agency to help the former slaves in the immediate transition from slavery to freedom.

FIRST FREEDMEN'S BUREAU ACT[1]

(March 3, 1865) Section 1
Be it enacted . . . That there is hereby established in the War Department, to continue during the present war of rebellion, and for one year thereafter, a Bureau of Refugees, Freedmen, and Abandoned Lands, to which shall be committed, as hereinafter provided, the supervision and management of all abandoned lands, and the control of all subjects relating to refugees and freedmen from rebel States, or from any district or county within the territory embraced in the operations of the army, under such rules and regulations as may be prescribed by the head of the bureau and approved by the President. The said bureau shall be under the management and control of a commissioner to be appointed by the President. . . .
Section 2
. . . The Secretary of War may direct such issues or provisions, clothing and fuel as he may deem needful for the immediate and temporary shelter and supply of destitute and suffering refugees and freedmen, and their wives and children . . . .
Section 3
. . . The President may, by and with the advice and consent of the Senate, appoint an assistant commissioner for each of the states declared to be in insurrection . . . who shall . . . aid in the execution of the provisions of this act. . . .
Section 4
. . . The commissioner, under the direction of the President, shall have authority to set apart, for the use of loyal refugees and freedmen, such tracts of land within the insurrectionary States as shall have been abandoned, or to which the United States shall have acquired title by confiscation or sale, or otherwise; and to every male citizen, whether refugee or freedman, as aforesaid, there shall be assigned not more than forty acres of such land, and the person to whom it was so assigned shall be protected in the use and enjoy-

[1] *Acts and Resolutions*, 38th Cong., 2d sess., p. 96.

ment of the land for the term of three years at an annual rent not exceeding six per centum upon the value of such land as it was appraised by the State authorities in the year eighteen hundred and sixty for the purpose of taxation. . . . At the end of said term, or at any time during said term, the occupants of any parcels so assigned may purchase the land and receive such title thereto as the United States can convey, upon paying therefor the value of the land as ascertained and fixed for the purpose of determining the annual rent aforesaid.

PART TWO

The First Shock of Freedom: 1865–1883

At the close of the Civil War, the population of the United States stood at about 35 million, and of these, slightly more than 4.75 million—13 percent—were Afro-Americans. In 1883, blacks, still accounting for about 13 percent of the American people, numbered about 7 million, in a total population of about 54 million. Throughout this eighteen-year chapter of their history, approximately 91 percent of all Negro Americans were massed in the South, the overwhelming majority of them (about 90 percent in 1865 and perhaps 85 percent in 1883) on the land. In the North, the relatively small black population was nearly equally divided between town and country in 1865, but the drift during these years was toward the cities, and in 1883 the major fraction living in cities and towns was approaching two-thirds of the whole northern Negro group.

The period that spanned the gap between the close of the war and the *Civil Rights Cases* of 1883 defines a distinctive era in the history of black Americans. It opened with the collapse of the slave system, and closed with a Supreme Court decision that killed federal legislation designed to confer upon a lately emancipated people the political, civil, and social status that only free whites had hitherto enjoyed.

In the years between—as many of the statutes and judicial opinions reproduced in the following pages fully attest—no significant liberalization in thinking about race had as yet occurred. In some senses it had even moved to a more reactionary position, especially among intellectuals and the leaders of what might later have been called the opinion industry, for ancient prejudice, superstition, and folklore now seemed to have irrefutable scientific support in the implications that social theorists chose to extract from the new Darwinian biology. For them, darker peoples were, by nature's intention, the unfit whom the fitter whites were to vanquish and displace.

Meanwhile the victorious North, through the Radical Republican faction in Congress, imposed what seemed to southerners a drastic social revolution which they could not and would not accept. Federal constitutional amendments and statutes to elevate the ex-slave toward freedom and equality with southern whites evoked resistance too formidable for the federal government to put down except at fearful

ELGIN COMMUNITY COLLEGE LIBRARY
ELGIN, ILLINOIS
342.73
B

cost. So, in 1877, wearied by its efforts, the nation backed down and restored self-rule to the South, including the responsibility for adjusting race relations on her own terms with no effective restraints from Washington.

The occasion for calling off the Reconstruction program was the election of 1876 and its immediate aftermath. Although the accumulated failures and resentments of the previous decade were, of course, more important, the bitterly contested presidential election supplied a convenient pretext for conciliating the South and restoring harmony to the sections. Hardly anyone now disputes that the Republican presidential ticket was defeated in 1876, and that the subsequent decision of the Electoral Commission (which Congress had created to resolve the controversy over the electoral votes of Florida, Louisiana, and South Carolina), to award the presidency to the Republicans, was little short of theft. And since the South was the chief loser by the decision, northern Republicans, tired of the Reconstruction program anyhow, saw their opportunity to purchase the South's acquiescence in the selection of Hayes by offering the former Confederate states what they wanted even more than they wanted a Democratic administration in Washington: home rule. The result was the "Compromise of 1877": withdrawal of federal troops from the South, the end of Radical Reconstruction, and the inauguration of a conciliatory policy toward that section, in exchange for the South's acceptance of a Republican president and for her pledge that she would deal fairly with the Negro.

The latter's prospects began to deteriorate at once but at first it was only slowly. The really determined drive to impose upon him a clearly inferior legal and social status got fully under way only after 1883, when the United States Supreme Court, in the *Civil Rights Cases,* seemed to say (as Congress had seemed to intimate six years earlier) that the former slave was no longer the nation's problem but the South's, a problem to be disposed of by the individual southern states as they might choose.

(1)

RACIAL IDEOLOGY: ANGLO-SAXON MASTER-RACISM

Popular conceptions about race were still, in the dozen years after Appomattox—and long beyond—a major obstacle to any attempts to improve the black man's status. The assumption that he was in every respect hopelessly inferior to whites persisted during these years among all but a tiny minority of Americans, though a growing number, at least in areas where blacks were not numerous, might have had some misgivings about the almost universal disposition to withhold from them the ordinary privileges and immunities of the American birthright. Indeed, by the end of this brief period of thirteen years, the belief in the Afro-Americans' inborn incapacities was strongly reinforced by the vogue of Social Darwinism and of the Social Gospel. The popular Josiah Strong, a Congregational clergyman and one of the most influential and articulate spokesmen of the dominant social and religious outlook in the 1880's, confidently proclaimed that racial inequality was just one more majestic demonstration of the wonder-working providence of God, who had decreed that the baser races be gradually extinguished to give place to the Anglo-Saxon super race.

The following pages are from Strong's book. Although it was published two years after the close of the period under review, the selection here given was first presented as a lecture three years earlier, and in fact expresses a point of view already widely current then among intellectuals—the editors, writers, clergymen, jurists, and educators who, mediately if not immediately, mold the public mind.[1]

Every race which has deeply impressed itself on the human family has been the representative of some great idea—one or more—which has given direction to the nation's life and form to its civilization. Among the Egyptians this seminal idea was life, among the Persians it was light, among the Hebrews it was purity, among the Greeks it was beauty, among the Romans it was law. The Anglo-Saxon is the representative of two great ideas, which are closely related. One of them is that of civil liberty. Nearly all of the civil liberty of the world is enjoyed by Anglo-Saxons: the English, the British colonists, and the people of the United States. . . . In modern times, the peoples whose love of liberty has won it, and whose genius for self-government has preserved it, have been Anglo-Saxons. The noblest races have always been lovers of liberty. The love ran strong in early German blood, and has profoundly influenced the institutions of all the branches of the great German family; but it was left for the Anglo-Saxon branch fully to recognize the right of the individual to himself, and formally to declare it the foundation stone of government.

The other great idea of which the Anglo-Saxon is the exponent is that of a pure *spiritual* Christianity. It was no accident that the great reformation of the sixteenth century originated among a Teutonic, rather than a Latin people. . . .

There can be no reasonable doubt that North America is to be the great home of the Anglo-Saxon, the principal seat of his power, the center of his life and influence. . . .

[1] Josiah Strong, *Our Country* (New York, 1885), pp. 208–27, *passim*. The volume sold more than 175,000 copies and was extravagantly praised. On a per capita basis, a book published in 1970 would have to sell 600,000 copies to match these sales. In addition, much of the volume was reproduced serially in newspapers, and foreign-language editions were issued for the overseas market.

. . . It seems to me that God, with infinite wisdom and skill, is training the Anglo-Saxon race for an hour sure to come in the world's future. . . . The time is coming when the pressure of population on the means of subsistence will be felt here as it is now felt in Europe and Asia. Then will the world enter upon a new stage of its history—*the final competition of races, for which the Anglo-Saxon is being schooled.* Long before the thousand millions are here, the mighty *centrifugal* tendency, inherent in this stock and strengthened in the United States, will assert itself. Then this race of unequaled energy, with all the majesty of numbers and the might of wealth behind it—the representative, let us hope, of the largest liberty, the purest Christianity, the highest civilization—having developed peculiarly aggressive traits calculated to impress its institutions upon mankind, will spread itself over the earth. . . .

Whether the extinction of inferior races before the advancing Anglo-Saxon seems to the reader sad or otherwise, it certainly appears probable. . . .

(2)

VIEWS FROM THE WHITE HOUSE

Andrew Johnson, President, 1865–1869

The four presidents who occupied the White House in the years from 1865 to 1883 could hardly evade the responsibility of expressing themselves on an issue of such gravity. Less than a week after the Civil War ended, President Lincoln was dead, and the fearful burden of presiding over the country's reconstruction fell to a far less skillful and statesmanlike man. The terms on which President Andrew Johnson proposed to restore the late Confederate states to the Union, incomparably more lenient than those subsequently imposed by Congress, did not require the South to promise fair treatment to the Negro. Perhaps the plebeian President was fearful that an enfranchised black population would fall too easily under the domination of the southern landed squirearchy whom he abominated. In any case, he insisted that the Negro's admission to the franchise was a matter for individual states to regulate. Denying blacks the privileges of both suffrage and educational opportunity, the Johnson government, and the President himself, seemed to proceed from the premise that Afro-Americans should, for the foreseeable future, be held to the status of an "illiterate, unskilled, propertyless, agricultural worker," presumably because he was not fit for anything better.[1]

[1] Kenneth M. Stampp, *The Era of Reconstruction, 1865–1877* (New York, 1965), pp. 77–79.

The blacks in the South are entitled to be well and humanely governed, and to have the protection of just laws for all their rights of person and property. If it were practicable at this time to give them a Government exclusively their own, under which they might manage their own affairs in their own way, it would become a grave question whether we ought to do so, or whether common humanity would not require us to save them from themselves. But under the circumstances this is only a speculative point. It is not proposed [by Congress] merely that they shall govern themselves, but that they shall rule the white race, make and administer State laws, elect Presidents and members of Congress, and shape to a greater or less extent the future destiny of the whole country. Would such a trust and power be safe in such hands?

. . . It is the glory of white men to know that they have had these qualities in sufficient measure to build upon this continent a great political fabric and to preserve its stability for more than ninety years, while in every other part of the world all similar experiments have failed. But if anything can be proved by known facts, if all reasoning upon evidence is not abandoned, it must be acknowledged that in the progress of nations negroes have shown less capacity for government than any other race of people. No independent government of any form has ever been successful in their hands. On the contrary, wherever they have been left to their own devices they have shown a constant tendency to relapse into barbarism. In the Southern States, however, Congress has undertaken to confer upon them the privilege of the ballot. Just released from slavery, it may be doubted whether as a class they know more than their ancestors how to organize and regulate civil society. Indeed, it is admitted that the blacks of the South are . . . so utterly ignorant of public affairs that their voting can consist in nothing more than carrying a ballot to the place where they are directed to deposit it.[1]

Ulysses S. Grant, President, 1869–1877

From General Grant, who probably owed his election to the 450,000 votes cast for him by southern blacks under the temporary protection of Union armies of occupation, came this terse pronouncement.[2]

The question of suffrage is one which is likely to agitate the public so long as a portion of the citizens of the nation are excluded from its privileges in any State. It seems to me very desirable that this question should be settled now, and I entertain the hope and express the desire that it may be by the ratification of the fifteenth article of amendment to the Constitution.

Four years later, with the Fifteenth Amendment added to the Constitution, and the South now safe for the Republican party, the General told his countrymen, in his Second Inaugural:[3]

The effects of the late civil strife have been to free the slave and make him a citizen. Yet he is not possessed of the civil rights which citizenship should carry with it. This is wrong, and should be corrected. To this correction I stand committed, so far as Executive influence can avail.

[1] Richardson, *Messages and Papers of the Presidents,* VI, 564–65.

[2] *Ibid.,* VII, 8.

[3] *Ibid.,* 221.

Social equality is not a subject to be legislated upon, nor shall I ask that anything be done to advance the social status of the colored man, except to give him a fair chance to develop what there is good in him, give him access to the schools, and when he travels let him feel assured that his conduct will regulate the treatment and fare he will receive.

* * *

Rutherford B. Hayes, President, 1877–1881

In his Inaugural Address Hayes, while acknowledging the federal government's "moral obligation" to use such constitutional authority as it possessed to maintain the rights of Negroes, announced his intention to abide by the "Compromise of 1877" (see p. 26), which had promised to restore to the South control over her own political processes.[1]

With respect to the two distinct races whose peculiar relations to each other have brought upon us the deplorable complications and perplexities which exist in those States, it must be a government which submits loyally and heartily to the Constitution and the laws—the laws of the nation and the laws of the States themselves—accepting and obeying faithfully the whole Constitution as it is.

Resting upon this sure and substantial foundation, the superstructure of beneficent local governments can be built up, and not otherwise. In furtherance of such obedience to the letter and the spirit of the Constitution, and in behalf of all that its attainment implies, all so-called party interests lose their apparent importance, and party lines may well be permitted to fade into insignificance. . . .

The sweeping revolution of the entire labor system of a large portion of our country and the advance of 4,000,000 people from a condition of servitude to that of citizenship, upon an equal footing with their former masters, could not occur without presenting problems of the gravest moment, to be dealt with by the emancipated race, by their former masters, and by the General Government, the author of the act of emancipation.

The evils which afflict the Southern States can only be removed or remedied by the united and harmonious efforts of both races, actuated by motives of mutual sympathy and regard; and while in duty bound and fully determined to protect the rights of all by every constitutional means at the disposal of my Administration, I am sincerely anxious to use every legitimate influence in favor of honest and efficient local *self*-government as the true resource of those States for the promotion of the contentment and prosperity of their citizens. . . .

* * *

James A. Garfield, President, March–September, 1881

Although during his brief stay in the White House Garfield made no specific recommendations to substantiate his declarations, he affirmed

[1] *Ibid.*, 442–47, *passim.*

in his Inaugural Address some principles that pointed to a better future for black citizens.[1]

The elevation of the negro race from slavery to the full rights of citizenship is the most important political change we have known since the adoption of the Constitution of 1787. . . .

No doubt this great change has caused serious disturbance to our Southern communities. This is to be deplored, though it was perhaps unavoidable. But those who resisted the change should remember that under our institutions there was no middle ground for the negro race between slavery and equal citizenship. There can be no permanent disfranchised peasantry in the United States.

. . . The emancipated race has already made remarkable progress. With unquestioning devotion to the Union, with a patience and gentleness not born of fear, they have "followed the light as God gave them to see the light." They are rapidly laying the material foundations of self-support, widening their circle of intelligence, and beginning to enjoy the blessings that gather around the homes of the industrious poor. They deserve the generous encouragement of all good men. So far as my authority can lawfully extend, they shall enjoy the full and equal protection of the Constitution and the laws.

The free enjoyment of equal suffrage is still in question, . . . but to violate the freedom and sanctities of the suffrage is more than an evil. It is a crime which, if persisted in, will destroy the Government itself.

* * *

Chester A. Arthur, President, 1881–1885

Arthur's first Annual Message to Congress offered the hint that federal aid to education might be the means of elevating the Negro to literacy, and, by that token, entitle him to the franchise which the Constitution guaranteed but practice denied him.[2]

Although our system of government does not contemplate that the nation should provide or support a system for the education of our people . . . .

A large portion of the public domain has been from time to time devoted to the promotion of education.

There is now a special reason why, by setting apart the proceeds of its sales of public lands or by some other course, the Government should aid the work of education. Many who now exercise the right of suffrage are unable to read the ballot which they cast. Upon many who had just emerged from a condition of slavery were suddenly devolved the responsibilities of citizenship in that portion of the country most impoverished by war.

I would suggest that if any fund be dedicated to this purpose it may be wisely distributed in the different States according to the ratio of illiteracy, as by this means those localities which are most in need of such assistance will reap its special benefits.

* * *

[1] *Ibid.*, VIII, 8.
[2] *Ibid.*, 58.

(3)
THE NATIONAL PARTY PLATFORMS[1]

The excerpts that follow are taken from the official platforms of the parties participating in the Presidential elections of 1868, 1872, 1876, and 1880.

Campaign of 1868

Only two parties offered national tickets in 1868. The Democratic party, in its first contest after the Civil War, was pulled one way by the urgency of living down its wartime reputation and its identification with lost causes (leading Democrats had fought hard against the adoption of the Fourteenth and Fifteenth amendments), and hauled the other way by the need to retain its primacy in the South. Counting discretion the better part of valor, the party thought it prudent to make no mention of the "Negro problem" in its platform. The Republicans, eager to make the South safe for Republicanism, could pose as the saviors of the Union and the guarantors of human freedom, and could, one supposes, have afforded to make a more forthright statement on Negro rights than the ambiguous pronouncement they chose to write.

First—We congratulate the country on the assured success of the reconstruction policy of the Congress, as evinced by the adoption, in the majority of the States lately in rebellion, of constitutions securing equal civil and political rights to all, and regard it as the duty of the Government to sustain those constitutions, and to prevent the people of such States from being remitted to a state of anarchy or military rule.

Second—The guaranty of Congress of equal suffrage to all loyal men at the South was demanded by every consideration of public safety, of gratitude, and of justice, and must be maintained; while the question of suffrage in all the loyal States properly belongs to the people of those States.

* * *

[1] By far the most convenient compilation of these documents is that provided by Kirk H. Porter and Donald Bruce Johnson, in *National Party Platforms, 1840–1964*, rev. ed. (Urbana, Ill.: 1966). The platforms for 1868, 1872, 1876, and 1880 are on pp. 37–62.

Campaign of 1872

Now the newly launched liberal Republican party challenged the historic reliance upon two major parties. Two minor groups, the Labor Reform party and the Prohibition party, also entered the race but made no allusion to the issue. The Democrats and Liberal Republicans, determined to drive Grantism from the capital, united upon the same presidential nominee and on identical platforms, including a lofty tribute to "equal and exact justice for all," which Democrats hoped would clear them of charges of disloyalty and refusal to accept in good faith the outcome of the late war. But Republicans entered the contest with the same advantages they had enjoyed in 1868, and on the "Negro question" offered a somewhat stronger plank than that of their opponents.

From the Democratic and Liberal Republican platforms:

1. We recognize the equality of all men before the law, and hold that it is the duty of the Government in its dealings with the people to mete out equal and exact justice to all, of whatever nativity, race, color or persuasion, religion or politics.

2. We pledge ourselves to maintain the union of these States, emancipation and enfranchisement; and to oppose any reopening of the questions settled by the thirteenth, fourteenth and fifteenth amendments of the Constitution.

From the Republican platform:

. . . The recent amendments to the National Constitution should be cordially sustained because they are right, not merely tolerated because they are law, and should be carried out according to their spirit by appropriate legislation, the enforcement of which can safely be entrusted only to the party that secured those amendments.

. . . Complete liberty and exact equality in the enjoyment of all civil, political, and public rights should be established and effectually maintained throughout the Union, by efficient and appropriate State and Federal legislation. Neither the law nor its administration should admit any discrimination in respect of citizens by reason of race, creed, color, or previous condition of servitude. . . .

We hold that Congress and the President have only fulfilled an imperative duty in their measures for the suppression of violent and treasonable organizations in certain lately rebellious regions, and for the protection of the ballotbox, and therefore, they are entitled to the thanks of the nation.

* * *

Campaign of 1876

This time, three of the four parties in the field—Democrats, Independent Greenbackers, and Prohibitionists—decided to look the other way when they were confronted with the inconvenient issue of the black man's predicament, while the Republicans wrote a firmly worded paragraph to demand "complete liberty and exact justice for all Americans." Once elected, the new Republican administration indefinitely postponed the redemption of the pledge.

> The permanent pacification of the Southern section of the Union and the complete protection of all its citizens in the free enjoyment of all their rights, are duties to which the Republican party is sacredly pledged. The power to provide for the enforcement of the principles embodied in the recent constitutional amendments is vested by those amendments in the Congress of the United States; and we declare it to be the solemn obligation of the legislative and executive departments of the government to put into immediate and vigorous exercise all their constitutional powers for removing any just causes of discontent on the part of any class, and securing to every American citizen complete liberty and exact equality in the exercise of all civil, political, and public rights. To this end we imperatively demand a congress and a chief executive whose courage and fidelity to these duties shall not falter until these results are placed beyond dispute or recall.

* * *

Campaign of 1880

Once again, the lesser groups—Greenbackers and Prohibitionists—ignored the Negro, and the Democrats restricted themselves to a single-sentence generality affirming that "the right to a free ballot is the right preservative of all rights, and must and shall be maintained in every part of the United States." The Republicans, smarting under the resurgence of the Solid South, found new virtues in federal enforcement of the Civil War Amendments, although their language suggests greater misgivings over a one-party South (if the Democrats were to be that one party) than over injustices suffered by black people.

From the Republican platform:

> The equal, steady and complete enforcement of the law, and the protection of all our citizens in the enjoyment of all privileges and immunities guaranteed by the Constitution, are the first duties of the Nation. The dangers of a solid south can only be averted by a faithful performance of every promise which the Nation has made to the citizen. The execution of the laws, and the punishment of all those who violate them, are the only safe methods by which an enduring peace can be secured and genuine prosperity established through the South. Whatever promises the Nation makes the Nation must perform. A Nation cannot safely relegate this duty to the State. The solid south must be divided by the peaceful agencies of the ballot, and all honest opinions must there find free expression. To this end honest voters must be protected against terrorism, violence or fraud.

(4)
STATUS OF THE EX-SLAVE: THE BLACK CODES

During the brief period between the assassination of President Lincoln and the opening of the first session of the 38th Congress, President Andrew Johnson assumed responsibility for directing the reconstruction of the Union, pursuing a policy, first announced by Lincoln, of leniency to the South. The Radical Republicans quickly challenged the President's program. After several months of bitter controversy the congressional election of 1866 placed the Radicals firmly in control, and they proceeded to enact a Reconstruction program with far less tenderness toward the hopes and expectations of the South.

The "Johnson governments," established by the southern states before the Radicals had enacted the Civil Rights Act of 1866 and the First Reconstruction Act (1867), had quickly addressed themselves to the problem of redefining the status of the 4,000,000 newly emancipated Negroes. Although this legislation, which was largely embodied in the "Black Codes," varied from state to state, it was intended to withhold from the former slaves the real fruits of emancipation by relegating them to a state of marked legal and social inferiority.

Despite their severity, the statutes seemed to southerners a necessary and constructive accommodation to the revolutionary changes wrought by the legal ending of slavery. But millions of northerners rejected this view and were instead outraged at what seemed to them the South's brazen attempt to restore the ex-slaves to involuntary servitude. In particular those who found the freeing of the slaves at least some consolation after the four bloody years of war were now convinced that the South had not accepted her defeat in good faith.

Other developments seemed to invite the same inference. The conventions which President Johnson's provisional governors had called to reconstruct their states' governments had been required to repudiate the ordinances of secession which had taken them out of the Union; instead, several of the conventions merely repealed or declared them void, which implied that they had been legal in the first place. None of the restored states moved toward compliance with Johnson's request that the vote be granted to at least a few of the most intelligent and reputable blacks. In all of the states, the electorate defiantly chose, usually by huge majorities, congressmen and state officers at every level who had been identified with the Confederacy as military or civilian officers, and who were now triumphantly "vindicated" by election over opponents whom "unreconstructed" voters denounced as "traitors to the South."

Already angered by such evidence of the South's reluctance to acknowledge her defeat—much less her error—northerners were infuriated by the Black Codes, which effectually consigned the Negro for the present if not much longer to the level of an unpropertied farm laborer, with no political rights, a legal status markedly inferior to that of whites, and under white surveillance scarcely less severe than that from which emancipation had presumably freed him.

Actually the codes did concede to the blacks some rights and privileges which they had not hitherto possessed. Marriages were at last legalized, and the ex-slaves could now normally testify in court, and sue and be sued. But by far the greater bulk of the legislation was restrictive and strongly reminiscent of the old pre-war slave codes. Marriages of apprentices required the "master's" (the terminology is significant) approval; marriage between blacks and whites was absolutely forbidden; and some of the codes forbade Negroes to "intrude upon" meetings, including religious gatherings, of whites, or upon coaches and carriages reserved for whites. Masters were authorized to punish their laborers and apprentices with the lash for misconduct, indolence, or insolence. Some codes specifically provided that penal sections of the pre-war slave code were now re-enacted. Most prescribed severer punishments for blacks than for whites for the same offenses, and offenses by blacks against whites were considered far graver than the same injury committed by whites against blacks.

Dependent Negro children were forced by the codes into compulsory apprenticeships, often until they reached the age of twenty-one. Labor contracts were stringently defined by law, and some states went so far as to ordain that the working day was to begin at dawn and end at a specified hour in the evening. Negroes leaving their employment were subject to severe punishment as "deserters," and whites who sought to entice a "servant" into leaving his employment were also liable to heavy fines or imprisonment. In no case were blacks to be permitted to receive instruction in the same schools with whites. They were all but totally excluded from any employment except that of farm laborers and household menials, and servants were forbidden to leave their masters' premises without written permission, to possess liquor or firearms, and, in some states, to own land or live in cities.

They were required by law to furnish proof of steady employment in the form of a legally executed contract or be subject to arrest as vagrants. Even those who were employed could, if caught idling in the streets, be apprehended—and subjected to a heavy fine, which, of course, they had no means to pay. They could then be bound over to a white person, normally the highest bidder (preference to be given to the blacks' former owners) who might come forward to pay the court for the right to bind them to service. It was particularly this device and that of the compulsory apprenticeship of minors that persuaded northerners that southerners had no intention of giving the Negro his freedom. And it was this apparent intransigence of the ex-Confederates that played into the Radicals' hands, driving countless moderates into their camp, and producing the succession of enactments that began with the Civil Rights Act of 1866 and the extension of the Freedmen's Bureau Act.

A "Black Code"

The following document exhibits the principal sections of the Black Code of Mississippi.[1]

CHAPTER III

Section 9

Be it further enacted, . . . that in case a freedman is committed and either he or his employer fails for five days to pay his fine or penalty the sheriff shall hire such freedman to any person who will pay such fine and costs . . . and in case the fine and costs are paid by the employer he may retain it out of any wages then due the freedman. . . .

CHAPTER IV

AN ACT to confer Civil Rights on Freedmen, and for other purposes.

Section 1

Be it enacted by the Legislature of the State of Mississippi, That all freedmen, free negroes and mulattoes may sue and be sued, . . . in all the courts of law and equity of this State, and may acquire personal property . . . by descent or purchase, and may dispose of the same, in the same manner, . . . that white persons may: Provided that the provisions of this section shall not be so construed as to allow any freedman, free negro or mulatto, to rent or lease any lands or tenements, except in incorporated towns or cities in which places the corporate authorities shall control the same.

Section 2

Be it further enacted, That all freedmen, free negroes and mulattoes may intermarry with each other. . . .

Section 3

Be it further enacted, That all freedmen, free negroes and mulattoes, who do now and have heretofore lived and cohabited together as husband and wife shall be taken and held in law as legally married, and the issue shall be taken and held as legitimate for all purposes. That it shall not be lawful for any freedman, free negro or mulatto to intermarry with any white person;

[1] *Laws of Mississippi,* 1865 (chaps. II [sect. 9], IV–VI, XXIII, XLVIII), pp. 71, 82–93, 165–67, 194.

nor for any white person to intermarry with any freedman, free negro or mulatto; and any person who shall so intermarry shall be deemed guilty of felony, and on conviction thereof, shall be confined in the State penitentiary for life, ...

Section 4

Be it further enacted, That in addition to cases in which freedmen, free negroes and mulattoes are now by law competent witnesses, freedmen, free negroes or mulattoes shall be competent in civil cases when a party or parties to the suit, either plaintiff or plaintiffs, defendant or defendants, also in cases where freedmen, free negroes and mulattoes is or are either plaintiff or plaintiffs, defendant or defendants, and a white person or white persons is or are the opposing party or parties, plaintiff or plaintiffs, defendant or defendants. They shall also be competent witnesses in all criminal prosecutions where the crime charged is alleged to have been committed by a white person upon or against the person or property of a freedman, free negro or mulatto.

Section 5

Be it further enacted, That every freedman, free negro and mulatto, shall, on the second Monday of January, one thousand eight hundred and sixty-six, and annually thereafter, have a lawful home or employment, and shall have written evidence thereof; as follows, to wit: if living in any incorporated city, town or village, a license from the mayor thereof; and if living outside of any incorporated city, town or village, from the member of the board of police of his beat, authorizing him or her to do irregular and job work, or a written contract, . . . which licenses may be revoked for cause, at any time, by the authority granting the same.

Section 6

Be it further enacted, That all contracts for labor made with freedmen, free negroes and mulattoes, for a longer period than one month shall be in writing and in duplicate, attested and read to said freedman, free negro or mulatto, by a beat, city or county officer, or two disinterested white persons of the county in which the labor is to be performed, . . . and if the laborer shall quit the service of the employer, before expiration of his term of service, without good cause, he shall forfeit his wages for that year, up to the time of quitting.

Section 7

Be it further enacted, That every civil officer shall, and every person may arrest and carry back to his or her legal employer any freedman, free negro or mulatto, who shall have quit the service of his or her employer before the expiration of his or her term of service without good cause, and said officer and person, shall be entitled to receive for arresting and carrying back every deserting employee aforesaid, the sum of five dollars, and ten cents per mile from the place of arrest to the place of delivery, [to] be paid by the employer. . . .

Section 8

Be it further enacted, That upon affidavit made by the employer of any freedman, free negro or mulatto, or other credible person, before any justice of the peace or member of the board of police, that any freedman, free negro or mulatto, legally employed by said employer, has illegally deserted said employment, such justice of the peace or member of the board of police, shall issue his warrant or warrants, . . . directed to any sheriff, constable or special deputy, commanding him to arrest said deserter and return him or her to said employer . . . and it shall be lawful for any officer to whom such warrant shall be directed, to execute said warrant in any county of this State, . . . and the said employer shall pay the cost of said warrants and arrest and return, which shall be set off for so much against the wages of said deserter.

Section 9

Be it further enacted, That if any person shall . . . attempt to persuade, entice or cause any freedman, free negro or mulatto, to desert from the legal employment of any person, before the expiration of his or her term of service, or shall knowingly employ any such deserting freedman, free negro or mulatto, or shall knowingly give or sell to [him] any food, rayment or other thing, he or she shall be guilty of a misdemeanor, and upon conviction, shall be fined not less than twenty-five dollars and not more than two hundred dollars and the costs. . . .

CHAPTER V

AN ACT to be entitled "An act to regulate the relation of Master and Apprentice, as related to Freedmen, Free Negroes, and Mulattoes."

Section 1

Be it enacted by the Legislature of the State of Mississippi, That it shall be the duty of all sheriffs, justices of the peace, and other civil officers of the several counties in this State, to report to the probate courts of their respective counties, semi-annually, at the January and July terms of said courts, all freedmen, free negroes and mulattoes, under the age of eighteen, within their respective counties, beats or districts, who are orphans, or whose parent or parents have not the means, or who refuse to provide for and support said minors, and thereupon it shall be the duty of said probate court, to order the clerk of said court to apprentice said minors to some competent and suitable person, on such terms as the court may direct. . . . Provided, that the former owner of said minors shall have the preference. . . .

Section 2

Be it further enacted, That . . . the said court shall require the said master or mistress to execute bond and security, payable to the State of Mississippi, conditioned that he or she shall furnish said minor with sufficient food and clothing, to treat said minor humanely, furnish medical attention in case of sickness; [and to] teach or cause to be taught him or her to read and write, if under fifteen years old. . . . Provided, that said apprentice shall be bound by indenture, in case of males until they are twenty-one years old, and in case of females until they are eighteen years old.

Section 3

Be it further enacted, That in the management and control of said apprentices, said master or mistress shall have power to inflict such moderate corporeal chastisement as a father or guardian is allowed to inflict on his or her child or ward at common law. . . .

Section 4

Be it further enacted, That if any apprentice shall leave the employment of his or her master or mistress, without his or her consent, said master or mistress may pursue and recapture said apprentice, and bring him or her before any justice of the peace of the county, whose duty it shall be to remand said apprentice to the service of his or her master or mistress; and in the event of a refusal on the part of said apprentice so to return, then said justice shall commit said apprentice to the jail of said county, ...

Section 5

Be it further enacted, That if any person entice away any apprentice from his or her master or mistress, or shall knowingly employ an apprentice, or furnish him or her food or clothing, without the written consent of his or her master or mistress, or shall sell or give said apprentice ardent spirits, without such consent, said person so offending shall be deemed guilty of a high misdemeanor, and shall, on conviction thereof before the county court, be punished as provided for the punishment of persons enticing from their employer hired freedmen, free Negroes or mulattoes. . . .

CHAPTER VI

AN ACT to amend the Vagrant Laws of the State.

Section 2

Be it further enacted, That all freedmen, free negroes and mulattoes in this State, over the age of eighteen years, found on the second Monday in January, 1866, or thereafter, with no lawful employment or business, or found unlawfully assembling themselves together either in the day or night time, and all white persons so assembling with [them] on terms of equality, or living in adultery or fornication with a freedwoman, free negro, or mulatto, shall be deemed vagrants, and on conviction thereof, shall be fined in the sum of not exceeding, in the case of a freedman, free negro or mulatto, fifty dollars, and a white man two hundred dollars, and imprisoned at the discretion of the court, the free negro not exceeding ten days, and the white man not exceeding six months.

Section 3

Be it further enacted, That all justices of the peace, mayors and aldermen of incorporated towns and cities of the several counties in this State, shall have jurisdiction to try all questions of vagrancy, . . . and it is hereby made their duty, whenever they shall ascertain that any person or persons are violating any of the provisions of this act, to have said party or parties arrested and brought before them, and immediately investigate said charge, and on conviction, punish said party or parties as provided for herein. . . .

Section 5

Be it further enacted, That . . . in case any freedman, free negro or mulatto, shall fail for five days after the imposition of any fine or forfeiture upon him or her for violation of any of the provisions of this act, to pay the same, that it shall be, and is hereby made the duty of the sheriff of the proper county to hire out said freedman, free negro or mulatto, to any person who will, for the shortest period of service, pay said fine or forfeiture and all costs: Provided, a preference shall be given to the employer, if there be one, in which case the employer shall be entitled to deduct and retain the amount so paid from the wages of such freedman, free negro or mulatto, then due or to become due. . . .

CHAPTER XXIII

AN ACT to punish certain offences therein named, and for other purposes.

Section 1

Be it enacted by the Legislature of the State of Mississippi, That no freedman, free negro or mulatto . . . shall keep or carry fire-arms of any kind, or any ammunition, dirk or bowie knife, and on conviction thereof, in the county court, shall be punished by fine, not exceeding ten dollars, and pay the costs of such proceedings, and all such arms or ammunition shall be forfeited to the informer, and it shall be the duty of every civil and military officer to arrest any freedman, free negro or mulatto found with any such arms or ammunition, and cause him or her to be committed for trial in default of bail.

Section 2

Be it further enacted, That any freedman, free negro or mulatto, committing riots, routs, affrays, trespasses, malicious mischief, cruel treatment of animals, seditious speeches, insulting gestures, language or acts, or assaults on any person, disturbances of the peace, exercising the function of a minister of the Gospel, without a license from some regularly organized church, vending spirituous or intoxicating liquors, or committing any other misdemeanor . . . shall, upon conviction thereof, in the county court, be fined, not less than ten dollars, and not more than one hundred dollars, and may be imprisoned, at the discretion of the court, not exceeding thirty days.

Section 3

Be it further enacted, That if any white person shall sell, lend or give to any freedman, free negro or mulatto, any firearms, dirk or bowie-knife, or ammunition, or any spirituous or intoxicating liquors, such person or persons so offending, upon conviction thereof, in the county court of his or her county, shall be fined, not exceeding fifty dollars, and may be imprisoned, at the discretion of the court, not exceeding thirty days. . . .

Section 4

Be it further enacted, That all the penal and criminal laws now in force in this State, defining offences and prescribing the mode of punishment for crimes and misdemeanors committed by slaves [*sic*!], free negroes or mulattoes, be and the same are hereby re-enacted, and declared to be in full force and effect, against freedmen, free negroes and mulattoes, except so far as the mode and manner of trial and punishment have been changed or altered by law.

Section 5

Be it further enacted, That if any freedman, free negro or mulatto, convicted of any of the misdemeanors provided against in this act, shall fail or refuse, for the space of five days after conviction, to pay the fine and costs imposed, such person shall be hired out by the sheriff or other officer, at public outcry, to any white person who will pay said fine and all costs, and take such convict for the shortest time. . . .

Approved November 29, 1865.

(5)
THE CROP LIEN SYSTEM

Plantation owners deprived by the Thirteenth Amendment of slave labor, and pauperized ex-slaves without land or other means of livelihood, were brought together by the share-cropper system. It disappointed the expectations of both, proving to be—as crusty Senator Ben Tillman of South Carolina observed—a "lazy descent into Hell." Under the share-cropper and share-tenant plans[1] typically a third of the crop was assigned to the worker for his labor, a third was retained by the landlord as rent, and the remaining third was divided between landlord and laborer in proportion as the two furnished tools, draft animals, fertilizer, and other farming needs. Usually the landlord, because he supplied all but the work, took two-thirds of the harvest.

The system, if fairly administered, might under favorable circumstances have provided the tenants and croppers with a tolerable living, some incentive, and eventually the chance to become small landowners. But circumstances were not favorable, and all too often the croppers—who had no choice but to look to their landlords for credit during the long months between crops—were cheated out of their fair share of the crop, or grievously overcharged for provisions and supplies by the country storekeeper, who, as the system matured, was more often than not the same person as the landlord. By the time his share came due, the cropper might already owe his landlord more than the cash value of his part of the crop. The unhappy truth was that the landlord-storekeeper was himself credit-starved and cruelly squeezed by *his* creditors, and thus sorely pressed to pass the burden on to his tenants or croppers, protecting his equity meanwhile through the crop lien system under which the cropper mortgaged his share as security for the debt he was piling up in the supply merchant's account books for food and other necessaries for his family.

The landlord's rights as creditor were carefully defined by crop lien laws, which protected him against loss and made it impossible for the debt-hobbled laborer to abandon the crop before it was harvested or break out of the new bondage that so closely resembled the old. The markup on goods bought from the supply merchant often amounted, in effect, to interest charged in advance at an effective rate of 40 to 100 percent per annum, or even more; but the law was on the creditor's side. As late as 1945 only one fourth of the South's Negro farm families were full or part owners of their land, the other three-quarters being tenants and croppers. From the beginning the system was only slightly more ruinous to the ex-slave share laborer—and the poor whites who were also steadily pulled into the same predicament—than to the southern economy as a whole, for it fixed upon the section more securely than ever the one-crop agriculture that had stifled the economic development of the region so long. Following is an example of a crop lien law, enacted in 1867.[2]

[1] For the precise distinction between them and a crisp description of both, see Fred A. Shannon, *The Farmer's Last Frontier* (New York, 1945), pp. 76–100.

[2] *Laws of Mississippi,* 1867, chap. 465, pp. 569–72.

CHAPTER CCCCLXV

AN ACT for the Encouragement of Agriculture.

Section 1

Be it enacted by the Legislature of the State of Mississippi, That all debts hereafter contracted for advance of money, purchase of supplies, farming utensils, working stock, or other things necessary for the cultivation of a farm or plantation, shall constitute a prior lien upon the crop of cotton, corn and other produce of such farm or plantation, which is not by law exempt from levy and sale, by virtue of execution, and also on the animals and implements employed or used in cultivating the same, which shall have been purchased with the money so advanced, or which shall have been furnished by such person, in favor of the person or persons so advancing or furnishing as aforesaid, from the time the contract or contracts therefor, or a synopsis of the same, shall be enrolled as hereinafter provided.

Section 2

Be it further enacted, That when any owner or lessee of any plantation or farm, shall make any contract with laborers to cultivate such farm or plantation for a share of the crop, in lieu of wages, and such owner or lessee shall make advances of money, provisions of clothing, in accordance with such contract, such owners or lessees shall have a lien on the share of such laborers for the payment of the same.

Section 3

Be it further enacted, That all contracts within the provision of this act, or a copy thereof, shall be filed in the office of the Clerk of the Circuit Court of the county in which the farm or plantation is situated, and such clerk shall enroll the same in the order in which they are so filed, in a well bound book, in the following form:

Name of the Debtor.	Date of Filing.	Amount of indebtedness.	When due.	Name of Cred'r.

Section 4

Be it further enacted, That proceedings to enforce such liens shall be by bill in chancery, sworn to by complainant, or by his agent, commenced in the county where such farm or plantation is situated, to be prosecuted as other cases of mortgage or lien. . . .

Section 5

Be it further enacted, That when such bill shall be filed, the Clerk of the Court shall, without fail, for that purpose, issue a writ of sequestration, commanding the proper sheriff to seize and take into his possession the property charged to be subject to such lien, and to hold the same until the further order of the court or Judge, or until the defendant from whose possession the same is taken, shall enter into bond with good security, payable to the complainant in double the value of the property, to be assessed by the officer, conditioned to have the property forthcoming, to abide the decree to be made by the court in the cause; said bond shall be returned with the writ, and in case the property shall not be delivered or forthcoming to abide the decree, shall have the force and effect of a judgment; and execution may issue thereon against all the obligors for the amount of the decree, or the value of the property, according to the nature of the case, and if such bond be not given in twenty days after levy, the court or Judge may order the sale of the property for cash, or place the same in the hands of a receiver, and make such other disposition of the proceeds of such sale, or of the property, as shall seem to him just and equitable.

Section 6

Be it further enacted, That it shall not be lawful for any sheriff or other officer to levy on or sell, by virtue of an execution, or other process, issuing from any court in this State, any crop of cotton, corn or other agricultural product, while the same is under cultivation, and before it is matured and gathered.

(6)
THE BIRTH OF JIM CROW

The short-lived "Johnson governments" were doomed by the First Reconstruction Act (March 2, 1867), but during their brief tenure those of Florida, Mississippi, and Texas supplemented the Black Codes with statutes requiring separate accommodations for the races on railway cars. The Florida enactment decreed:[1]

> That if any negro, mulatto, or other person of color shall intrude himself into . . . any railroad car or other public vehicle set apart for the exclusive accommodation of white people he shall be deemed guilty of a misdemeanor and, upon conviction, shall be sentenced to stand pillory for one hour, or be whipped, not exceeding thirty-nine stripes, or both, at the discretion of the jury, nor shall it be lawful for any white person to intrude himself into any railroad car or other public vehicle set apart for the exclusive accommodation of persons of color, under the same penalties.

The Mississippi law ordered:[2]

> That it shall be unlawful for any officer, station agent, conductor, or employee on any railroad in this State, to allow any freedman, negro, or mulatto, to ride in any first-class passenger cars set apart, or used by, and for white persons: and any person offending against the provisions of this section shall be deemed guilty of a misdemeanor, and on conviction thereof, before the circuit court of the county in which said offense was committed, shall be fined not less than fifty dollars, nor more than five hundred dollars; and shall be imprisoned in the county jail until such fine and costs of prosecution are paid: Provided, that this section of this act shall not apply in the case of negroes or mulattoes, traveling with their mistresses, in the capacity of nurses.

Except for these transient "Jim Crow" laws, which fell into abeyance when Radical Reconstruction superseded the Johnson governments less

[1] *Laws of Florida,* 1865 (chap. 1466 [No. 3], Sec. 6), p. 24.

[2] *Laws of Mississippi,* 1865 (chap. LXXIX, Sec. 14), pp. 231–32.

than two years after their enactment, no legislation to segregate travel was passed until Tennessee did so in 1881. Thereafter, contrary to the widely accepted folklore that segregation *by statute* has been an ancient southern usage, another half dozen years intervened before other southern states followed Tennessee's example. Eight states took the still novel step in 1887–1891,[1] and then, after another pause of seven years, the process was resumed. From 1898 to 1907, five more states[2] followed, so that by the latter year Missouri was the only southern state not yet committed to separate railway facilities for Negroes.

(7) CONTROL OF RECONSTRUCTION BY CONGRESS

In the eight-month interval between Andrew Johnson's accession to the Presidency in April, 1865, and the assembling of Congress, the process of reorganizing the southern states and restoring them to the Union on the Johnson Plan was completed, only to be scuttled by Congress when it assembled at the capitol in December, 1865. The Radical Republicans, though still a minority, denounced as traitors those—including the President—who did not share their more drastic views. Greatly strengthened by a smashing victory in the congressional elections of 1866, they defied Johnson, and undertook to write their own prescription for southern Reconstruction.

Early in 1866 the Radicals proposed to extend the life of the Freedmen's Bureau Act, with new provisions giving the Bureau judicial powers to protect the civil rights of the ex-slaves, and making the Act's enforcement a function of the Army. When Johnson vetoed the bill on states-rights grounds, the Congress began framing the even stronger Civil Rights Act of 1866. Again, the President responded with a stinging veto message that the law illegally conferred upon the federal government powers reserved by the Constitution to the states, and was unwisely according citizenship to a people not yet prepared for it. This

[1] Florida, 1887; Mississippi, 1888; Texas, 1889; Louisiana, 1890; Alabama, Kentucky, Arkansas, and Georgia, 1891. Gilbert Thomas Stephenson, *Race Distinctions in American Law* (New York, 1910), p. 216.

[2] South Carolina, 1898; North Carolina, 1899; Virginia, 1900; Maryland, 1904; and Oklahoma, 1907. *Ibid.*

time Congress overrode the veto, and, for good measure, succeeded also in overriding the presidential veto of a second version of the Freedmen's Bureau Act.

Johnson's vetoes of the Civil Rights and Freedmen's Bureau Acts of 1866, and his intemperate retorts to his critics, cost him the support of many moderates already deeply offended by the Black Codes and by what seemed to them the unrepentant intransigence of southern chauvinists who were enjoying a resurgence of political control in the Johnson governments.

A. *The Beginnings of Federal Civil Rights Legislation*

The basic provisions of the first federal law to protect the civil rights of Negroes follow.[1]

THE CIVIL RIGHTS ACT OF 1866

[April 9, 1866]

Be it enacted, . . . That all persons born in the United States and not subject to any foreign power, excluding Indians not taxed, are hereby declared to be citizens of the United States; and such citizens, of every race and color, without regard to any previous condition of slavery or involuntary servitude shall have the same right, in every State and Territory in the United States, to make and enforce contracts, to sue, be parties, and give evidence, to inherit, purchase, lease, sell, hold, and convey real and personal property, and to full and equal benefit of all laws and proceedings for the security of person and property, as is enjoyed by white citizens, and shall be subject to like punishment, pains and penalties, and to none other, any law, statute, ordinance, regulation, or custom to the contrary notwithstanding.

Section 2

. . . Any person who, under color of any law, statute, ordinance, regulation, or custom, shall subject, or cause to be subjected, any inhabitant of any State or Territory to the deprivation of any right secured or protected by this act, or to different punishment, pains, or penalties on account of such person having at any time been held in a condition of slavery or involuntary servitude . . . or by reason of his color or race, than is prescribed for the punishment of white persons, shall be deemed guilty of a misdemeanor, and on conviction, shall be punished by fine not exceeding one thousand dollars, or imprisonment not exceeding one year, or both, in the discretion of the court.

Section 3

. . . The district courts of the United States shall have . . . cognizance of all crimes and offenses committed against the provisions of this act, and also, concurrently with the circuit courts of the United States, of all causes, civil and criminal, affecting persons who are denied or cannot enforce in the

[1] *U.S. Statutes at Large*, XVI, 27, April 9, 1866. A century later, the law was taken more seriously than it was at the time of its enactment. See below, p. 370, 428, 532.

courts or judicial tribunals of the State or locality where they may be any of the rights secured to them by . . . this act. . . .

Section 4

. . . The district attorneys, marshals, and deputy marshals of the United States, the commissioners appointed by the circuit and territorial courts of the United States, with powers of arresting, imprisoning or bailing offenders against the laws of the United States, the officers and agents of the Freedmen's Bureau, and every other officer who may be specially empowered by the President of the United States, shall be . . . specially authorized and required . . . to institute proceedings against all and every person who shall violate the provisions of this act, and cause him or them to be arrested and imprisoned, or bailed, as the case may be, for trial before such court of the United States or territorial court as by this act has cognizance of the offense. . . .

Section 5

. . . It shall be the duty of all marshals and deputy marshals to obey and execute all warrants and precepts issued under the provisions of this act, when to them directed; and should any marshal or deputy marshal refuse to use all proper means diligently to execute [this act] he shall, on conviction thereof, be fined in the sum of one thousand dollars, to the use of the persons upon whom the accused is alleged to have committed the offense. . . .

Section 6

. . . Any person who shall knowingly and wilfully obstruct, hinder or prevent any officer, or other person charged with the execution of any warrant or process issued under the provisions of this act, or any person or persons lawfully assisting him or them, from arresting any person for whose apprehension such warrant or process may have been issued, or shall rescue or attempt to rescue such person from the custody of the officer, other person or persons, or those lawfully assisting as aforesaid . . . , or shall aid, abet, or assist any person so arrested as aforesaid, directly or indirectly, to escape from the custody of the officer or other person legally authorized as aforesaid, or shall harbor or conceal any person for whose arrest a warrant or process shall have been issued as aforesaid so as to prevent his discovery and arrest . . . , shall for either of said offenses, be subject to a fine not exceeding one thousand dollars, and imprisonment not exceeding six months, by indictment and conviction before the district court of the United States for the district in which said offense may have been committed. . . .

Section 9

. . . It shall be lawful for the President of the United States . . . to employ such part of the land or naval forces of the United States, or of the militia, as shall be necessary to . . . enforce the due execution of this act. . . .

B. *The Reconstruction Acts*

Less than a year after the final passage of the Civil Rights Act came the first in a series of Reconstruction Acts, passed by Congress over presidential vetoes, which placed the states of the late Confederacy (with the exception of the already fully restored Tennessee) under military control. Three supplementary Reconstruction Acts extended even further the subordination of civil officers and processes to the military.[1]

FIRST RECONSTRUCTION ACT

Whereas no legal State governments or adequate protection for life or property now exist in the [former] rebel States . . . Therefore

Be it enacted, . . . That said rebel States shall be divided into military districts and made subject to the authority of the United States, as hereinafter prescribed, and for that purpose Virginia shall constitute the first district; North Carolina and South Carolina the second district; Georgia, Alabama and Florida, the third district; Mississippi and Arkansas the fourth district; and Louisiana and Texas the fifth district.

Section 2

. . . It shall be the duty of the President to assign to the command of each of said districts an officer of the army, not below the rank of brigadier general, and to detail a sufficient military force to enable such officer to perform his duties and enforce [this Act].

Section 3

. . . It shall be the duty of each officer . . . to protect all persons in their rights of person and property, to suppress insurrection, disorder, and violence, and to punish, or cause to be punished, all disturbers of the public peace and criminals, and to this end he may allow local civil tribunals to take jurisdiction of and to try offenders, or, when in his judgment it may be necessary for the trial of offenders, he shall have power to organize military commissions or tribunals for that purpose. . . .

Section 4

. . . All persons put under military arrest by virtue of this act shall be tried without unnecessary delay, and no cruel or unusual punishment shall be inflicted; and no sentence of any military commission or tribunal hereby authorized, affecting the life or liberty of any person, shall be executed until it is approved by the officer in command of the district. . . .

Section 5

. . . When the people of any one of said rebel States shall have formed a constitution of government in conformity with the Constitution of the United States in all respects, framed by a convention of delegates elected by the male citizens of said State twenty-one years old and upward, of whatever race, color, or previous condition, who have been resident in that State for one year previous to the day of such election, except such as may be disfranchised for participation in the rebellion, or for felony at common law, and when such constitution shall provide that the elective franchise shall be enjoyed by all such persons as have the qualifications herein stated for electors of delegates, and when such constitution shall be ratified by a majority of the persons voting on the question of ratification who are qualified as electors of delegates, and when such constitution shall have been submitted to Congress for examination and approval, and Congress shall have approved the same, and when said State, by a vote of its legislature elected under said constitution, shall have adopted the amendment to the Constitution of the United States, proposed by the thirty-ninth Congress, and known as Article

[1] *Acts and Resolutions,* 39th Cong., 2d sess., March 2, 1867, p. 60.

fourteen, and when said article shall have become a part of the Constitution of the United States, said State shall be declared entitled to representation in Congress, and senators and representatives shall be admitted therefrom on their taking oaths prescribed by law, and then and thereafter the preceding sections of this act shall be inoperative in said State: *Provided,* That no person excluded from the privilege of holding office by said proposed amendment to the Constitution of the United States shall be eligible to election as a member of the convention to frame a constitution for any of said rebel States, nor shall any such person vote for members of such convention.

Section 6

. . . Until the people of said rebel States shall be by law admitted to representation in the Congress of the United States, any civil governments which may exist therein shall be deemed provisional only, and in all respects subject to the paramount authority of the United States at any time to abolish, modify or control, or supersede the same. . . .

* * *

To make doubly sure of the permanence of the Civil Rights Act of 1866 by putting it beyond the reach of presidential, congressional, or Supreme Court interference, Congress drafted an amendment to the Constitution of the United States, embodying the statute's provisions along with a few other details of the congressional Reconstruction program. As events were to prove, the amendment's provisions were long to lie dormant, at least so far as their ostensible purpose to protect the freedman's status as a fully participating citizen was concerned. However, this addition to the nation's organic law—notably the first section's citizenship, due process and equal protection clauses—was in the long range to be of incalculable importance. Two years later another amendment was adopted, to ward off attacks upon the Negro's right to vote.[1]

C. *The Fourteenth and Fifteenth Amendments*

ARTICLE XIV

Section 1

All persons born or naturalized in the United States, and subject to the jurisdiction thereof, are citizens of the United States and of the State wherein they reside. No State shall make or enforce any law which shall abridge the privileges or immunities of citizens of the United States; nor shall any state deprive any person of life, liberty, or property, without due process of law; nor deny to any person within its jurisdiction the equal protection of the laws.

Section 2

Representatives shall be apportioned among the several States according to their respective numbers, counting the whole number of persons in each State, excluding Indians not taxed. But when the right to vote at any elec-

[1] *Constitution of the United States of America; Analysis and Interpretation.* 88th Cong., 1st session. Senate Document No. 39 (Washington, 1964), 63–65.

tion for the choice of electors for President and Vice-President of the United States, Representatives in Congress, the Executive and Judicial officers of a State, or the members of the Legislature thereof, is denied to any of the male inhabitants of such State, being twenty-one years of age, and citizens of the United States, or in any way abridged, except for participation in rebellion, or other crime, the basis of representation therein shall be reduced in the proportion which the number of such male citizens shall bear to the whole number of male citizens twenty-one years of age in such State.

Section 3

[Bars ex-Confederate officers, military and civil, from holding public office until Congress removes the disability.]

Section 4

[Provides for the payment of the public debt of the United States.]

Section 5

The Congress shall have power to enforce, by appropriate legislation, the provisions of this article. [Adopted in 1868.]

* * *

Angered by the South's adamant refusal to accord the vote to the Negro by her own state constitutional and statutory provisions—and startled by the narrowness of General Grant's electoral victory in the presidential election of 1868, when his popular majority of a mere 300,000 would have been a *deficit* of 400,000 had he not garnered the votes of 700,000 southern Negroes voting under the protection of federal troops—the Congress proceeded to confer the franchise upon the race by federal constitutional command.

ARTICLE XV

Section 1

The right of citizens of the United States to vote shall not be denied or abridged by the United States or by any State on account of race, color, or previous condition of servitude.

Section 2

The Congress shall have power to enforce this article by appropriate legislation. [Adopted in 1870.]

D. *The "Force Acts"*

Both the Fourteenth and Fifteenth amendments contained sections endowing the Congress with power to enforce their provisions "by appropriate legislation." Overwhelming resistance in the South to both the amendments prompted Congress to the early exercise of the authority which they conferred. Notable was a series of enactments, damned by indignant southerners as "Force Acts," the first of which was essentially a re-enactment of the Civil Rights Act of 1866 repeating much of its language *verbatim*, and a reaffirmation of the political rights guaranteed to Negroes by the recent amendments.[1]

[1] *Acts and Resolutions*, 41st Cong., 2d sess., May 31, 1870, p. 95.

FIRST ENFORCEMENT ACT

Be it enacted . . . That all citizens of the United States who are or shall be otherwise qualified by law to vote at any election by the people in any State, Territory, district, county, city, parish, township, school district, municipality, or other territorial subdivision, shall be entitled and allowed to vote at all such elections without distinction of race, color, or previous condition of servitude; any constitution, law, custom, usage, or regulation of any State or Territory . . . to the contrary notwithstanding.

Section 2

. . . If by or under the authority of the constitution or laws of any State, or the laws of any Territory, any act is or shall be required to be done as a prerequisite or qualification for voting, and by such constitution or laws persons or officers . . . shall be charged with the performance of duties in furnishing to citizens an opportunity to perform such prerequisite, or to become qualified to vote, it shall be the duty of every such person and officer to give to all citizens of the United States the same and equal opportunity to perform such prerequisite, and to become qualified to vote without distinction of race, color, or previous condition of servitude; and if any such person or officer shall refuse or knowingly omit to give full effect to this section, he shall, for every such offense, . . . pay . . . five hundred dollars to the person aggrieved thereby, and shall also, for every such offense, be deemed guilty of a misdemeanor, and shall, on conviction thereof, be fined not less than five hundred dollars, or be imprisoned not less than one month and not more than one year, or both, at the discretion of the court. . . .

Section 5

. . . If any person . . . shall attempt to prevent, hinder, control, or intimidate any person from exercising . . . the right of suffrage, to whom the right of suffrage is . . . guaranteed by the fifteenth amendment to the Constitution of the United States, by means of bribery, threats, or threats of depriving such person of employment or occupation, or of ejecting such person from rented house, lands, or other property, or by threats of refusing to renew leases or contracts for labor, or by threats of violence to himself or family, such person so offending shall be deemed guilty of misdemeanor, and shall, on conviction thereof, be fined not less than five hundred dollars, or be imprisoned not less than one month and not more than one year, or both, at the discretion of the court.

Section 6

. . . If two or more persons shall band or conspire together, or go in disguise upon the public highway, or upon the premises of another, with intent to violate any provision of this act, or to injure, oppress, threaten, or intimidate any citizen with intent to prevent or hinder his free exercise and enjoyment of any right or privilege . . . secured to him by the Constitution or laws of the United States, . . . such persons shall be held guilty of felony, and, on conviction thereof, shall be fined or imprisoned, or both, at the discretion of the court,—the fine not to exceed five thousand dollars, and the imprisonment not to exceed ten years,—and shall be ineligible to . . . any office or place of honor, profit or trust created by the Constitution or laws of the United States. . . .

Sections 8–15

[Contain enforcement provisions closely paralleling Sections 3–9 of the Civil Rights Act of 1866, above, p. 46].

Section 16
[Substantially repeats Section 1 of the Civil Rights Act of 1866.]

* * *

A second act, dated February 28, 1871, stimulated at least in part by Republican reverses in state and congressional elections of the previous year, lodged the responsibility for supervising elections in the hands of federally appointed officials. A third act, passed on April 20, 1871, was known as the "Ku Klux Act" though officially it was designated in the statute itself as "an Act to enforce the 14th Amendment." The "Ku Klux Act" was directed at secret, conspiratorial, and terroristic groups and organizations, like the Klan, which were effectually thwarting Negro registration, voting, jury service, and office-holding.[1]

THE ENFORCEMENT ("KU KLUX") ACT OF 1871

Section 1

Be it enacted . . . That any person who, under color of any law, statute, ordinance, regulation, custom, or usage of any State, shall subject, or cause to be subjected, any person within the jurisdiction of the United States to the deprivation of any rights, privileges, or immunities secured by the Constitution of the United States, shall, any such law, statute, ordinance, regulation, custom, or usage of the State to the contrary notwithstanding, be liable to the party injured in any action at law . . . such proceeding to be prosecuted in the several district or circuit courts of the United States.

Section 2

That if two or more persons within any State or territory of the United States shall conspire to . . . oppose by force the authority of the government of the United States, or by force, intimidation, or threat to prevent, hinder, or delay the execution of any law of the United States, or by force, intimidation, or threat to prevent any person from accepting or holding any office or trust or place of confidence under the United States . . . or from discharging the duties thereof, or by force, intimidation, or threat to induce any officer of the United States to leave any State, district or place where his duties as such officer might lawfully be performed, or to injure him in his person or property on account of his lawful discharge of the duties of his office . . . or by force, intimidation, or threat to deter any party of witness in any court of the United States from attending such court, or from testifying in any matter pending in such court fully, freely, and truthfully, or to injure any such party or witness in his person or property on account of his having so attended or testified, or by force, intimidation, or threat to influence the verdict, presentment, or indictment, of any juror or grand juror in any court of the United States, or to injure such juror in his person or property on account of any verdict, presentment, or indictment lawfully assented to by him, or on account of his being or having been such juror, or shall conspire together, or go in disguise upon the public highway or upon the premises of another for the purpose, either directly or indirectly, of depriving any person or any class of persons of the equal protection of the laws, or of equal privileges or im-

[1] *Acts and Resolutions*, 41st Cong., 1 sess., April 20, 1871, p. 294.

munities under the laws, or for the purpose of preventing or hindering the constituted authorities of any State from giving or securing to all persons within such State the equal protection of the laws, or shall conspire together for the purpose of in any manner impeding, hindering, obstructing, or defeating the due course of justice in any State or Territory, with the intent to deny to any citizen of the United States the due and equal protection of the laws, or to injure any person in his person or his property for lawfully enforcing the right of any person or class of persons to the equal protection of the laws, or by force, intimidation, or threat to prevent any citizen of the United States lawfully entitled to vote from giving his support or advocacy in a lawful manner towards or in favor of the election of any lawfully qualified person as an elector of President or Vice-President of the United States, or as a member of the Congress of the United States, or to injure any such citizen in his person or property on account of such support or advocacy, each and every person so offending shall be deemed guilty of a high crime, and, upon conviction thereof in any district or circuit court of the United States or district or supreme court of any Territory of the United States having jurisdiction of similar offenses shall be punished by a fine not less than five hundred nor more than five thousand dollars, or by imprisonment, with or without hard labor, as the court may determine, for a period of not less than six months nor more than six years, as the court may determine, or by both such fine and imprisonment as the court may determine. . . .

Section 3

That in all cases where insurrection, domestic violence, unlawful combinations, or conspiracies in any State shall so obstruct or hinder the execution of the laws thereof, and of the United States, as to deprive any portion or class of the people of such State of any of the rights, privileges, or immunities, or protection, named in the Constitution and secured by this act, and the constituted authorities of such State shall either be unable to protect, or shall from any cause fail in or refuse protection of the people in such rights, such facts will be deemed a denial by such State of the equal protection of the laws to which they are entitled under the Constitution of the United States; and in all such cases . . . it shall be lawful for the President, and it shall be his duty to take such measures, by the employment of the militia or the land and naval forces of the United States . . . or by other means, as he may deem necessary for the suppression of such insurrection, domestic violence, or combinations. . . .

Section 4

That whenever in any State or part of a State the unlawful combinations named in the preceding section of this act shall be organized and armed, and so numerous and powerful as to be able, by violence, to either overthrow or set at defiance the constituted authorities of such State, and of the United States within such State, or when the constituted authorities are in complicity with, or shall connive at the unlawful purposes of, such powerful and armed combinations; and whenever, by reason of either or all of the causes aforesaid, the conviction of such offender and the preservation of the public safety shall become in such district impracticable, in every such case such combinations shall be deemed a rebellion, against the government of the United States, and . . . it shall be lawful for the President of the United States, when in his judgment the public safety shall require it, to suspend the privileges of the writ of habeas corpus, to the end that such rebellion may be overthrown: *Provided further,* That the President shall first have made proclamation, as now provided by law, commanding such insurgents to disperse: *And provided also,* That the provisions of this section shall not be in force after the end of the next regular session of Congress.

Section 5

That no person shall be a grand or petit juror in any court of the United States upon any inquiry, hearing, or trial of any suit, proceeding, or prosecution based upon or arising under the provisions of this act who shall, in the judgment of the court, be in complicity with any such combination or conspiracy; and every such juror shall, before entering upon any such inquiry, hearing, or trial, take and subscribe an oath in open court that he has never, directly or indirectly, counseled, advised, or voluntarily aided any such combination or conspiracy . . . .

Section 6

That any person, having knowledge that any of the wrongs conspired to be done and mentioned in the second section of this act are about to be committed, and having power to prevent or aid in preventing the same, shall neglect or refuse to do so, and such wrongful act shall be committed, such person or persons shall be liable to the person injured, or his legal representatives, for all damages caused by any such wrongful act which such first-named person or persons by reasonable diligence could have prevented; and such damages may be recovered in an action on the case in the proper circuit court of the United States, and any number of persons guilty of such wrongful neglect or refusal may be joined as defendants in such action . . . .

Section 7

That nothing herein contained shall be construed to supersede or repeal any former act or law except so far as the same may be repugnant thereto; and any offenses heretofore committed against the tenor of any former act shall be prosecuted, and any proceeding already commenced for the prosecution thereof shall be continued and completed, the same as if this act had not been passed, except so far as the provisions of this act may go to sustain and validate such proceedings.

E. *The Civil Rights Act of 1875*

A supplementary Civil Rights Act of March 1, 1875, destined to be the last piece of federal civil rights legislation until 1957, was also denounced as a "force act" by its opponents, but it was in fact an extension of the Civil Rights Act of 1866. Framed by Republicans in Congress as a memorial tribute to Charles Sumner, the Massachusetts pre-Civil War Abolitionist and post-Civil War Radical United States senator (who had died the previous year), this law went beyond the earlier civil rights law in that it sought *social* as well as political equality for southern Negroes. It specifically guaranteed to black Americans equal accommodations in inns, public conveyances, and places of amusement; by its terms refusal by private persons to accord equal access to such facilities was defined as a misdemeanor, and the aggrieved Negro was given the right to sue the discriminator for damages.[1]

Section 1

. . . *Be it enacted*, . . . That all persons within the jurisdiction of the United States shall be entitled to the full and equal enjoyment of the accommodations, advantages, facilities, and privileges of inns, public conveyances on land or water, theatres, and other places of public amusement; subject only to the conditions and limitations established by law, and applicable alike to citizens of every race and color, regardless of any previous condition of servitude.

Section 2

That any person who shall violate the foregoing section by denying to any citizen, except for reasons by law applicable to citizens of every race and color, and regardless of any previous condition of servitude, the full enjoyment of any of the accommodations, advantages, facilities, or privileges in said section enumerated, or by aiding or inciting such denial, shall, for every such offense, forfeit and pay the sum of five hundred dollars to the person aggrieved thereby, to be recovered in an action of debt, with full costs; and shall also, for every such offense, be deemed guilty of a disdemeanor, and, upon conviction thereof, shall be fined not less than five hundred nor more than one thousand dollars, or shall be imprisoned not less than thirty days nor more than one year. . . .

Section 3

That the district and circuit courts of the United States shall have, exclusively of the courts of the several States, cognizance of all crimes and offenses against, and violations of, the provisions of this act, . . . and the district attorneys, marshals, and deputy marshals of the United States, and commissioners appointed by the circuit and territorial courts of the United States, with powers of arresting and imprisoning or bailing offenders against the laws of the United States, are hereby specially authorized and required to institute proceedings against every person who shall violate the provisions of this act, and cause him to be arrested and imprisoned or bailed, as the case may be, for trial before such court of the United States, or territorial court, as by law has cognizance of the offense . . . *Provided*, That any district attorney who shall wilfully fail to institute and prosecute the proceedings herein required, shall, for every such offense, forfeit and pay the sum of five hundred dollars to the person aggrieved thereby, on conviction thereof, be deemed guilty of a misdemeanor, and be fined not less than one thousand nor more than five thousand dollars. . . .

Section 4

That no citizen possessing all other qualifications which are or may be prescribed by law shall be disqualified for service as grand or petit juror in any court of the United States, or of any State, on account of race, color, or previous condition of servitude; and any officer or other persons charged with any duty in the selection or summoning of jurors who shall exclude or fail to summon any citizen for the cause aforesaid shall, on conviction thereof be deemed guilty of a misdemeanor, and be fined not more than five thousand dollars. . . .

[1] *U.S. Statutes at Large*, XVIII, March 1, 1875, 335.

(8)
DEFYING THE FIFTEENTH AMENDMENT

Even in the North, thanks to constitutional and statutory as well as extra-legal dodges and devices, and to local custom and social pressures, Negro voting was in 1865 as yet rare. Indeed, outside the South suggestions that the color line be erased in elections were stoutly opposed by some of the very men who clamored for the enfranchisement of the Negro ex-slave in the South. Black voting in northern and western states began to rise after the Fifteenth Amendment forbade abridgement of the privilege, but it was still very light in 1883. It was in the South, however, where nine-tenths of the nation's black population was concentrated, that the really significant history of Negro suffrage was to be recorded.

The precise motives of northern Radical Republicans in insisting upon the vote for the freedmen have been endlessly debated, but there can be little doubt that the complex of intentions included vindictive hatred of the South on the part of some, democratic idealism on the part of others, and, for yet others, a determination to maintain the Republican party's ascendancy in the nation. President Johnson, as we have seen, was persuaded that the former slaves were not yet ready for the responsibilities of full citizenship, and that according to the federal Constitution the regulation of the franchise was left to the states. Even so, he urged that the newly restored southern states extend the vote to at least a few of the most cultivated blacks; but, before the Reconstruction Acts forced them to move, none of the states made any significant gesture in that direction.

After the congressional election of 1866, however, the Radical Republicans and "Vindictives" had secured control of the reconstruction process, and they insisted upon full enfranchisement of the Negroes in the South. Negro suffrage, coupled with extensive civil disqualification of whites, resulted in rule by Radical Republicans and their allies for as much as eight years in some states, and as little as two in others; but everywhere the old white ruling class, lately toppled from power, rallied to "redeem" their states, with assistance from poor whites who were equally appalled by the spectacle (as grossly exaggerated by that generation as by later historians of the Rhodes-Dunning tradition) of Carpetbagger-Scalawag-and-Negro rule.

Negro suffrage, guaranteed on paper by state constitutions and statutes until 1870, and thereafter by the Fifteenth Amendment, was steadily undermined almost from the moment it was first proclaimed, despite the presence of Union troops and the enactment of the federal enforcement acts authorized by Section 2 of the amendment. Southern victory on this issue was achieved for all practical purposes well before the Compromise of 1877 withdrew the federal troops and restored home rule to the South.

This nullification of state and federal constitutional and statutory provisions, which took place both before the formal end of Reconstruction rule and for years thereafter, was accomplished by a wide range of pressures, subterfuges, and downright fraud. At first the methods used were mostly violence or the threat of violence, notably as exerted by the Ku Klux Klan and other terroristic groups whose heyday was in the years 1869–1871. Scarcely less devastating was the more sophisticated use of economic pressures, actual and threatened: the job withheld, credit denied at the country store, eviction by an obliging sheriff.

But these were only the first means used to prevent the Negroes from voting. Soon there were the deliberately complicated registration and election laws, which increasingly fell under the superintendence of Democratic election officials, as the Redeemers and their plebeian congeners elbowed their way back into power. Such legislation could be, and was, used as well against white trouble-makers who were considered "disloyal to the South," for the statutes made no mention of race. Voter registration scheduled months before an election, and with a minimum of publicity, coupled with the requirement that any voter (which, of course meant any *black* voter) could be challenged to show his registration certificate, struck directly at a propertyless people who were not accustomed to filing papers, and who frequently changed their place of residence.

Statutes denying the ballot to persons whose record showed previous convictions for petty larceny served a similar purpose, as did ballots printed without party designations or emblems (except perhaps a picture of General Grant on a *Democratic* ballot), particularly when the aspiring black voter (who knew better than to ask the poll officials for help) was, under many local rules, allowed a maximum of two and a half minutes in the booth. There was, moreover, the ingenious "eight-box voting" trick, in which only those ballots dropped into the correct (unlabeled) box would be counted. The baffled voter was confronted with eight boxes, one for each separate category of offices; and while this posed no problem for the acceptable white voter, who could count on the assistance of Democratic poll officials, it confronted the Negro elector with astronomical odds against the probability that his ballot would figure in the tally.

And if a wary Negro voter could pick his way through this thicket, there remained yet other hazards of an extra-legal sort: simple ballot-box stuffing; ballot boxes with false bottoms; falsified counts; doctored registration books. Even stealing the ballot box was available to the Redeemer when other means failed. Polls were located at points remote from Negro communities, or were suddenly relocated without notice to black citizens in time for elections. Or again, there were the tissue-paper ballots which a blindfolded election official could pick out from the mass of ballots when the local judge of elections solemnly ruled that the number of ballots cast had exceeded the number of voters presenting themselves at the election, and that the only solution was to remove, by "impartial lot," a sufficient number to bring the quantity of ballots into balance with the number of voters. Finally, only one more of many other ruses was the rule that whites must be allowed to vote first, which enabled the dominant race to go about the task so slowly that nightfall closed the polls before the Negro line had reached the booth.

To these discouragements was added the presence at the polls of blustering whites, some of them conspicuously armed, and emboldened by whiskey, who jeered, jostled, and threatened the would-be black voters, or, at the very least, marked them for economic reprisal and social ostracism. The results were precisely what anyone might have predicted. Long before 1883 the Negro had disappeared as a direct participant in southern politics.[1]

[1] See C. Vann Woodward, *Origins of the New South, 1877–1913* (Baton Rouge, 1951), pp. 55–57; Paul Lewinson, *Race, Class, and Party* (New York, 1932), chaps. 2–4; George Brown Tindall, *South Carolina Negroes, 1877–1900* (Columbia, S.C., 1952), pp. 68–91.

(9)
THE SUPREME COURT AND THE NEGRO, 1865–1883

A. *Devitalizing the Fourteenth and Fifteenth Amendments*

In their program to frustrate the Fourteenth and Fifteenth amendments, conservative southerners, especially after 1872, were aided by the Republican party and many northerners who had wearied of the Reconstruction fiasco, who had come to doubt that the earlier objects of Radical Reconstruction could—or even should—be realized, and who were more and more disposed to re-establish national harmony by sacrificing the Negro.

This new drift was powerfully assisted by the nation's highest tribunal. Decisions involving the amendments and legislation growing out of them steadily weakened the recently drafted guarantees of Negro rights. Moved partly by a determination to check the shift in power from the states to the nation, partly by a legalistic insistence upon the letter of the law and the clear commands of legal justice before the vaguer claims of social justice, and partly by public racial attitudes, the Court developed several principles of constitutional construction.

It decreed that the amendments applied only to measures taken by the states themselves or by their agents; that if a law was not on the face of it clearly discriminatory, the Court would not presume to determine whether it was in effect more burdensome to blacks than to whites; that the police power of the states took priority over less pressing considerations like the enjoyment of the equality promised by the nation's organic law; that while *discrimination* might in some circumstances be forbidden by the nation's fundamental law, racial *distinctions* were not.[1]

These doctrines were partially defined in a cluster of decisions beginning with the *Slaughter House Cases* of 1873 and culminating in the *Civil Rights Cases* ten years later. They were more fully elaborated in the succeeding generation, as a later chapter will show.

The first severe contraction of the scope of the Fourteenth Amendment's command that no state might "abridge the privileges and immunities of citizens of the United States; nor . . . deprive any person of life, liberty, or property without due process of law; nor deny to any person the equal protection of the laws," came in the *Slaughter House Cases*.[2] The dogma here laid down virtually nullified the "privileges and immunities" clause, and deprived Negroes of the remedy it had promised against state acts abridging their civil rights. The Court took the position that state and federal citizenship are separate and distinct; that the amendment forbade *state* impairment of the privileges and immunities that persons enjoyed as citizens of the United States; that most civil rights are attributes of *state* citizenship and therefore beyond the reach of the amendment.

The case did not in fact arise out of a dispute involving Negro rights. A Louisiana statute of 1869 had granted a private corporation a twenty-five-year monopoly of slaughtering operations in and around New Orleans. It was defended by its sponsors as a legitimate exercise of the

[1] Benjamin Quarles, *The Negro in the Making of America* (New York, 1964), pp. 142–43.
[2] *16 Wall.* 36 (1873).

state's police power to protect the public health and safety. A group of butchers challenged the statute on grounds of the Thirteenth Amendment's prohibition of involuntary servitude and the Fourteenth Amendment's privileges-and-immunities, due-process, and equal-protection clauses. By a 5 to 4 vote, the Court rejected as unreasonable the aggrieved butchers' plea that such restrictions upon the free use of property imposed a species of servitude. More fateful for the Negro's future, however, was the dictum propounded with respect to "privileges and immunities."

MILLER, J. . . . The first section of the fourteenth [amendment] . . . opens with a definition of citizenship—not only citizenship of the United States, but citizenship of the States. . . . "All persons born or naturalized in the United States, and subject to the jurisdiction thereof, are citizens of the United States and of the State wherein they reside." . . .

It is quite clear, then, that there is a citizenship of the United States, and a citizenship of a State, which are distinct from each other, and which depend upon different characteristics or circumstances in the individual. . . . The next paragraph of this same section, which is the one mainly relied on by the plaintiffs in error, speaks only of privileges and immunities of citizens of the United States, and does not speak of those of citizens of the several states. . . .

If, then, there is a difference between the privileges and immunities belonging to a citizen of the United States as such . . . and those belonging to the citizen of the State as such, the latter must rest for their security and protection where they have heretofore rested; for they are not embraced by this paragraph of the amendment. . . .

Having shown that the privileges and immunities relied on in that argument are those which belong to citizens of the States as such, and that they are left to the state governments for security and protection, and not by this article placed under the special care of the federal government, we may hold ourselves excused from defining the privileges and immunities of citizens of the United States which no State can abridge, until some case involving those privileges may make it necessary to do so. . . .

Perhaps even more fascinating to students of American constitutional law is the following passage from the opinion, in which the Court, in concluding that the butchers who had brought the suit were not entitled to relief, laid down the rule that the "rights clauses" of the Fourteenth Amendment were not available as restrictions upon state-legislated economic regulation, because the amendment was intended specifically, if not exclusively, for the protection of the Negro people. Soon the Court would move to the opposite position and would for several decades apply Section 1 of the amendment as a means of checking economic and social legislation; but almost never as a shield to protect the Negro against state aggression upon his privileges and immunities, his life, liberty and property, and his right to equal protection of the laws.

. . . We repeat then, in the light of this recapitulation of events, almost too recent to be called history, but which are familiar to us all; and on the most casual examination of the language of these amendments, no one can fail to be impressed with the one pervading purpose found in them all, lying at the foundation of each, and without which none of them would have been even suggested; we mean the freedom of the slave race, the security and firm establishment of that freedom, and the protection of the newly-made freedman and citizen from the oppressions of those who had formerly exercised unlimited dominion over him. It is true that only the fifteenth amendment mentions the negro by speaking of his color and his slavery. But it is just as true that [the thirteenth and fourteenth] were addressed to the grievances of that race, and designed to remedy them.

In *United States* v. *Reese*[1] the Supreme Court declared unconstitutional portions of the Enforcement Act of 1870[2] which, it will be recalled, imposed heavy penalties upon individuals who, by whatever means, might undertake to prevent citizens from voting. This legislation the Court now struck down, with the argument that the Fifteenth Amendment extends no positive guarantees of the franchise, and does not "confer the right of suffrage upon anyone," but merely prohibits both the federal and state governments from excluding persons from voting by reason of "race, color, or previous condition of servitude." The South's predictable reaction was, in time, the enactment of literacy tests, poll tax laws, grandfather clauses, and white primary laws.

The Fifteenth Amendment does not confer the right of suffrage upon anyone. It prevents the States, or the United States, however, from giving preference, in this particular, to one citizen of the United States over another, on account of race, color or previous condition of servitude. Before its adoption, this could be done. It was as much within the power of a State to exclude citizens of the United States from voting on account of race, etc.; as it was on account of age, property or education. Now it is not. . . . This, under the express provisions of the 2d section of the Amendment, Congress may enforce by "appropriate legislation."

This leads us to inquire whether the Act now under consideration is "appropriate legislation" for that purpose. The power of Congress to legislate at all upon the subject of voting at state elections rests upon this Amendment. . . . If, therefore, the 3d and 4th sections of the Act are beyond that limit, they are unauthorized.

The 3d section does not, in express terms, limit the offense of an inspector of elections, for which the punishment is provided, to a wrongful discrimination on account of race. . . .

[And] when we go beyond the 3d section and read the 4th, we find there no words of limitation, or reference even, that can be construed as manifesting any intention to confine its provisions to the terms of the Fifteenth Amendment. That section has for its object the punishment of all persons, who by force, bribery, etc., hinder, delay, etc., any person from qualifying for voting. In view of all these facts, we feel compelled to say that, in

[1] 92 U.S. 214 (1876).
[2] See p. 51 above.

our opinion, the language of the 3d and 4th sections does not confine their operation to unlawful discriminations on account of race, etc. . . .

Another long stride toward the restoration of white supremacy in the South during the twilight of the Reconstruction program came in the vigorous declaration by the Supreme Court, in *United States* v. *Cruikshank*,[1] that the Fourteenth Amendment did not put ordinary private rights under the protection of the nation except as against state action. The defendants in the *Cruikshank* case were among more than a hundred persons indicted together in a federal court in Louisiana for violating the Enforcement Act of May 31, 1870.[2] They had, in fact, been found guilty in the trial court of flagrant infraction of the statute by breaking up a meeting of Negroes and conspiring to prevent them by force and intimidation from voting. The Supreme Court reversed the district court's judgment on the ground that such interference by private individuals could be a federal crime only if the meeting had some objects connected with *national* citizenship, and that since the gathering had assembled to discuss Louisiana elections, it was not under the protection of the federal Constitution or statutes.

The Fourteenth Amendment prohibits a State from depriving any person of life, liberty or property, without due process of law; but this adds nothing to the rights of one citizen as against another. It simply furnishes an additional guaranty against any encroachment by the States upon the fundamental rights which belong to every citizen as a member of society.

The fourth and twelfth counts charge the intent to have been to prevent and hinder the citizens named, who were of African descent and persons of color, in "the free exercise and enjoyment of their several rights and privileges to the full and equal benefit of all laws and proceedings, then and there, before that time, enacted or ordained by the said State of Louisiana and by the United States. . . ." When stripped of its verbiage, the case as presented amounts to nothing more than that the defendants conspired to prevent certain citizens of the United States, being within the State of Louisiana, from enjoying the equal protection of the laws of the State and of the United States.

The Fourteenth Amendment prohibits a State from denying to any person within its jurisdiction the equal protection of the laws; but this provision does not . . . add anything to the rights which one citizen has under the Constitution against another. The equality of the rights of citizens is a principle of republicanism . . . The only obligation resting upon the United States is to see that the States do not deny the right. This the Amendment guarantees, but no more. The power of the National Government is limited to the enforcement of this guaranty.

Another thrust at Reconstruction legislation was administered by the Supreme Court in *Hall* v. *De Cuir*.[3] Hall, the plaintiff in this action,

[1] 92 U.S. 542 (1876).
[2] See p. 51 above.
[3] 95 U.S. 485 (1878).

operated a Mississippi steamboat between New Orleans and Vicksburg. In violation of Louisiana's Reconstruction legislature's statute guaranteeing "equal rights and privileges on all parts of the conveyance . . . without distinction or discrimination on account of race or color," he barred Mrs. DeCuir, an educated Negro woman of property, from the use of cabin space in the vessel, accommodations which he always reserved for whites only. Her plea had been sustained by the Supreme Court of Louisiana, and Hall carried his case to the United States Supreme Court, which then overruled the state tribunal, declaring the law invalid, as an unconstitutional invasion by a state of the federal government's exclusive jurisdiction over interstate commerce. Relying on the familiar device (once characterized as "the parade of the imaginary horribles") of judging a policy by its conceivable ultimate conclusion if pressed to its limits, the Court held that a state statute *forbidding* discrimination on public carriers is an undue burden on interstate commerce. Later courts, as we shall see, had no difficulty discovering that state statutes *requiring* segregation are not open to that objection.

> Commerce [said the court] cannot flourish in the midst of such embarrassments. No carrier of passengers can conduct his business with satisfaction to himself, or comfort to those employing him, if on one side of a State line his passengers, both white and colored, must be permitted to occupy the same cabin, and on the other be kept separate. Uniformity in the regulations by which he is to be governed from one end to the other of his route is a necessity in his business, and to secure it Congress, which is untrammelled by State lines, has been invested with the exclusive legislative power of determining what such regulations shall be. If this statute can be enforced against those engaged in inter-state commerce, it may be as well against those engaged in foreign; and the master of a ship clearing from New Orleans for Liverpool, heaving passengers on board, would be compelled to carry all, white and colored, in the same cabin during his passage down the river, or be subject to an action for damages, "exemplary as well as actual," by anyone who felt himself aggrieved because he had been excluded on account of his color.

B. *The Fourteenth Amendment and Jury Service*

The Fourteenth Amendment's equal protection clause might have been moribund, but it was not dead. On March 1, 1880, the Supreme Court handed down several decisions relating to jury service and equal protection of the laws. In one of them a West Virginia statute which confined jury service to white male citizens was held unconstitutional.

In a landmark case reaching the Supreme Court from West Virginia a black who had been indicted for murder in a West Virginia county court petitioned for the transfer of his trial to a federal court, basing his prayer on Section 641 of the *Revised Code of the United States,* which permitted such a shift when any person was denied "a right secured to him by any law providing for the equal civil rights of citizens of the United States." The state of West Virginia defended its law excluding Negroes from juries with the argument that federal legislation forbidding the distinction was itself contrary to the Constitution of the United States. Strauder's petition had been denied by the state courts on that premise, but the Supreme Court now interposed and overruled the courts below.[1]

The Court:

We do not say that, within the limits from which it is not excluded by the Amendment, a State may not prescribe the qualifications of its jurors, and in so doing make discriminations. It may confine the selection to males, to freeholders, to citizens, to persons within certain ages, or to persons having educational qualifications. . . . [The Amendment's] design was to protect an emancipated race, and to strike down all possible legal discriminations against those who belong to it. . . .

Concluding, therefore, that the statute of West Virginia, discriminating in the selection of jurors, as it does against negroes because of their color, amounts to a denial of the equal protection of the laws to a colored man when he is put upon trial for an alleged offense against the State, it remains only to be considered whether the power of Congress to enforce the provisions of the 14th Amendment by appropriate legislation is sufficient to justify the enactment of Section 641 of the Revised Statutes.

A right or an immunity, whether created by the Constitution or only guarantied [*sic*] by it, even without any express delegation of power, may be protected by Congress. . . . But there is express authority to protect the rights and immunities referred to in the 14th Amendment, and to enforce observance of them by appropriate congressional legislation. And one very efficient and appropriate mode of extending such protection and securing to a party the enjoyment of the right or immunity, is a law providing for the removal of his case from a State Court, in which the right is denied by a state law into a Federal Court, where it will be upheld. This is an ordinary mode of protecting rights and immunities conferred by the Federal Constitution and Laws. Section 641 is such a provision. . . .

The judgment of the Supreme Court of West Virginia is reversed and the case is remitted, with instructions to reverse the judgment of the Circuit Court of Ohio County.

On the same day, equal protection was also afforded Negroes' rights to serve on juries in *Ex parte Virginia.*[2] In this action the Supreme Court denied relief to a Virginia judge who declared that his arrest for deliberately keeping Negroes off juries in alleged violation of the Civil Rights Act of 1875 was improper, and who petitioned for release under a writ of habeas corpus on the ground that his conduct was a judicial

[1] *Strauder* v. *West Virginia,* 100 U.S. 303 (1880).
[2] 100 U.S. 339 (1880).

act and therefore not within reach of an act of Congress. The Court disagreed:

> But the [Fourteenth] Amendment was ordained for a purpose. It was to secure equal rights to all persons, and, to insure to all persons the enjoyment of such rights, power was given to Congress to enforce its provisions by appropriate legislation. Such legislation must act upon persons, not upon the abstract thing denominated a State, but upon the persons who are the agents of the State in the denial of the rights which were intended to be secured.
>
> It was insisted during the argument in behalf of the petitioner that . . . [he] was performing a judicial act. This assumption cannot be admitted. . . . The duty of selecting jurors . . . is often given to [officers other than judges]. . . . But [even] if the selection of jurors could be considered in any case a judicial act, can the act charged against the petitioner be considered such when he acted outside of his authority, and in direct violation of the spirit of the state statute? That statute gave him no authority . . . to exclude all colored men merely because they were colored. . . . It is idle, therefore, to say that the Act of Congress is unconstitutional because it inflicts penalties upon state judges for their judicial action. It does no such thing.

A few weeks later, however, the Court took the more latitudinarian view that where state statutes did not specifically exclude Negroes from juries, the mere fact that no Negroes had sat on the grand and trial juries in a murder case was not a valid obstacle to conviction.[1]

> . . . The complaint is that there were no colored men in the jury that indicted them, nor in the petit jury summoned to try them. The petition expressly admitted that by the laws of the State all male citizens twenty-one years of age and not over sixty, who are entitled to vote and hold office under the Constitution and laws thereof, are made liable to serve as jurors. And it affirms (what is undoubtedly true) that this law allows the right, as well as required the duty of the race to which the petitioners belong to serve as jurors. It does not exclude colored citizens.
>
> Now, conceding as we do, and as we endeavored to maintain in the case of *Strauder* v. *West Va.*, just decided . . . that discrimination by law against the colored race, because of their color, in the selection of jurors, is a denial of the equal protection of the laws to a negro when he is put upon trial for an alleged criminal offense against a State, the laws of Virginia make no such discrimination. . . .
>
> The assertions in the petition for removal, that the grand jury by which the petitioners were indicted, as well as the jury summoned to try them, were composed wholly of the white race, and that their race had never been allowed to serve as jurors in the County of Patrick in any case in which a colored man was interested, fall short of showing that any civil right was denied, or that there had been any discrimination against the defendants because of their color or race. The facts may have been as stated, and yet the jury which indicted them, and the panel summoned to try them, may have been impartially selected. . . .

[1] *Virginia* v. *Rives*, 100 U.S. 545 (1880).

C. *The Franchise, The Civil Rights Acts, and the Constitution*

Election officials in Maryland had been indicted for ballot-box stuffing in a congressional election, an act defined as a criminal offense by federal civil rights legislation. In *Ex parte Siebold*[1] counsels' argument that the authority of the states in such matters is equal to that of the nation brought from the Supreme Court the retort that such reasoning is "based on a strained and impracticable view of the nature and powers of the National Government. . . ."

> The doctrine laid down at the close of counsels' brief, that the State and National Governments are co-ordinate and altogether equal, on which their whole argument, indeed, is based, is only partially true.
>
> The true doctrine, as we conceive, is this, that whilst the States are really sovereign as to all matters which have not been granted to the jurisdiction and control of the United States, the Constitution and constitutional laws of the latter are, as we have already said, the supreme law of the land; and, when they conflict with the laws of the States, they are of paramount authority and obligation. This is the fundamental principle on which the authority of the Constitution is based; and unless it be conceded in practice, as well as theory, the fabric of our institutions, as it was contemplated by its founders, cannot stand. The questions involved have respect not more to the autonomy and existence of the States, than to the continued existence of the United States as a government to which every American citizen may look for security and protection in every part of the land.

D. *Unequal Punishment and the Fourteenth Amendment*

That the *Siebold* ruling did not betoken a new disposition to infuse life into the equal protection clause was more than hinted at in *Pace* v. *Alabama*.[2] Section 4189 of the *Code of Alabama* provided for severer punishment for adultery and fornication between whites and Negroes than that prescribed by Section 4184 for the same offense between members of the same race. In any particular offense, however, the prescribed punishments were the same for both parties. In 1881 Tony Pace, a Negro, and Mary J. Cox, white, were indicted, convicted, and sentenced under this statute by a state court. Pace brought his case on a writ of error to the Alabama Supreme Court, insisting that the statute, by ordaining a severer punishment to both parties when one was a Negro than to the two parties when both were of the same race, was a violation of the Fourteenth Amendment's equal protection clause. The United States Supreme Court rejected Pace's plea in this language:

[1] 100 U.S. 371 (1880).
[2] 106 U.S. 583 (1882).

The two sections of the Code are entirely consistent. The one prescribes, generally, a punishment for an offense committed between persons of different sexes; the other prescribes a punishment for an offense which can only be committed where the two sexes are of different races. There is in neither section any discrimination against either race. Section 4184 equally includes the offense when the persons of the two sexes are both white and when they are both black. Section 4189 applies the same punishment to both offenders, the white and the black. Indeed, the offense against which this latter section is aimed cannot be committed without involving the persons of both races in the same punishment. Whatever discrimination is made in the punishment prescribed in the two sections is directed against the offense designated and not against the person of any particular color or race. The punishment of each offending person, whether white or black, is the same.

E. *The Supreme Court and the "Ku Klux" Act*

In *United States* v. *Harris* the federal protection of the Afro-American's claim to equality was still further weakened. Twenty members of a lynching mob in Tennessee snatched four prisoners from a deputy sheriff's custody and beat them so severely that one of them died. They were indicted under the provisions of the Ku Klux Act of April 20, 1871 (see above), which prohibited conspiracies to deprive persons of privileges, immunities, and equal protection and to hamper state authorities in affording such protection. Again, as in *United States* v. *Cruikshank* and *Virginia* v. *Rives,* the Court reiterated in 1883 that only *state* action is controlled by the Fourteenth Amendment.[1]

The language of the [fourteenth] amendment does not leave this subject in doubt. When the State has been guilty of no violation of its provisions; when it has not made or enforced any law abridging the privileges or immunities of citizens of the United States; when no one of its departments has deprived any person of life, liberty, or property, without due process of law, nor denied to any person within its jurisdiction the equal protection of the laws . . . the Amendment imposes no duty and confers no power upon Congress. . . . As, therefore, the section of the law under consideration is directed exclusively against the action of private persons, . . . [we] are clear in the opinion that it is not warranted by any clause in the 14th Amendment to the Constitution.

In the same case the Court addressed itself to the question of whether the Thirteenth Amendment, prohibiting slavery and involuntary servitude, warranted the statute in question. It did not, said the Court, for the statute, by extending protection to *both* Negroes and whites, was broader than the Amendment, and hence not authorized by it.

[1] *U.S.* v. *Harris,* 106 U.S. 629 (1883).

F. *The Supreme Court Stops Federal Protection of Civil Rights*

In the *Civil Rights Cases* of 1883 came yet another blow, perhaps the severest to be struck at the Negro by the Supreme Court in the two decades after the Emancipation Proclamation. The proceedings related to a number of indictments charging refusal, in defiance of the Civil Rights Act of March 1, 1875, to grant accommodations to blacks in a hotel and in theaters in San Francisco and New York, as well as a civil suit brought by a black woman who had been refused admission to the ladies' car on a train in Tennessee. Rarely has the Supreme Court, as Professor Pritchett has argued,[1] shown so little regard for Congress's intent; indeed, the Court presumed to say in effect that the Congress which had framed the Fourteenth Amendment and enacted legislation for its effectuation (see p. 49ff, above) had not understood what it was doing at the time. The one dissenting Justice, in fact, rebuked his brethren for "a subtle and ingenious verbal criticism" which plainly controverted the substance and spirit of the Fourteenth Amendment. But Justice John Marshall Harlan, whose dissent is also reproduced in the following excerpt, stood alone upon Congress's clear intention; and by overruling his position in an 8 to 1 vote, the Court categorically divested Congress of any power to remedy or punish discrimination by individuals, and confined that body to correcting positive *state* action. Seventy years later the lonely heresy of Justice Harlan became orthodoxy for a unanimous Court.[2]

Mr. Justice Bradley . . .

The essence of the law is, not to declare broadly that all persons shall be entitled to the full and equal enjoyment of the accommodations, advantages, facilities, and privileges of inns, public conveyances, and theatres; but that such enjoyment shall not be subject to any conditions applicable only to citizens of a particular race or color, or who had been in a previous condition of servitude. . . .

Has Congress constitutional power to make such a law? Of course, no one will contend that the power to pass it was contained in the Constitution before the adoption of the last three amendments . . .

[The Court then refers to Section 1 of the Fourteenth Amendment.]

It is State action of a particular character that is prohibited. Individual invasion of individual rights is not the subject-matter of the amendment. It has a deeper and broader scope. It nullifies and makes void all State legislation, and State action of every kind, which impairs the privileges and immunities of citizens of the United States, or which injures them in life, liberty or property without due process of law, or which denies to any of them the equal protection of the laws. It not only does this, but, in order that the

[1] C. Herman Pritchett, *The American Constitution* (New York, 1959), pp. 597–98.

[2] *Civil Rights Cases,* 109 U.S. 3 (1883).

national will, thus declared, may not be a mere *brutum fulmen,* the last section of the amendment invests Congress with power to enforce it by appropriate legislation. To enforce what? To enforce the prohibition. To adopt appropriate legislation for correcting the effects of such prohibited State laws and State acts, and thus to render them effectually null, void, and innocuous. This is the legislative power conferred upon Congress, and this is the whole of it. It does not invest Congress with power to legislate upon subjects which are within the domain of State legislation, or State action, of the kind referred to. It does not authorize Congress to create a code of municipal law for the regulation of private rights; but to provide modes of redress against the operation of State laws, and the action of State officers executive or judicial, when these are subversive of the fundamental rights specified in the amendment. . . .

But the power of Congress to adopt direct and primary, as distinguished from corrective legislation, on the subject in hand, is sought [by the plaintiffs], in the second place, from the Thirteenth Amendment, which abolishes slavery. . . .

Conceding the major proposition to be true, that Congress has a right to enact all necessary and proper laws for the obliteration and prevention of slavery with all its badges and incidents, is the minor proposition also true, that the denial to any person of admission to the accommodations and privileges of an inn, a public conveyance, or a theatre, does subject that person to any form of servitude, or tend to fasten upon him any badge of slavery? If it does not, then power to pass the law is not found in the Thirteenth Amendment. . . .

Can the act of a mere individual, the owner of the inn, the public conveyance, or place of amusement, refusing the accommodation, be justly regarded as imposing any badge of slavery or servitude upon the applicant, or only as inflicting an ordinary civil injury, properly cognizable by the laws of the State, and presumably subject to redress by those laws until the contrary appears?

After giving to these questions all the consideration which their importance demands, we are forced to the conclusion that such an act of refusal has nothing to do with slavery or involuntary servitude. . . . It would be running the slavery argument into the ground to make it apply to every act of discrimination which a person may see fit to make as to the guests he will entertain, or as to the people he will take into his coach or cab or car, or admit to his concert or theatre, or deal with in other matters of intercourse or business. . . .

When a man has emerged from slavery, and by the aid of beneficent legislation has shaken off the inseparable concomitants of that state, there must be some stage in the progress of his elevation when he takes the rank of a mere citizen, and ceases to be the special favorite of the laws, and when his rights as a citizen, or a man, are to be protected in the ordinary modes by which other men's rights are protected. . . .

Mr. Justice Harlan dissenting.

The opinion in these cases proceeds, it seems to me, upon grounds entirely too narrow and artificial. I cannot resist the conclusion that the substance and spirit of the recent amendments of the Constitution have been sacrificed by a subtle and ingenious verbal criticism. "It is not the words of the law but the internal sense of it that makes the law: the letter of the law is the body;

the sense and reason of the law is the soul." Constitutional provisions, adopted in the interest of liberty, and for the purpose of securing, through national legislation, if need be, rights inhering in a state of freedom, and belonging to American citizenship, have been so construed as to defeat the ends the people desired to accomplish, which they attempted to accomplish, and which they supposed they had accomplished by changes in their fundamental law. . . .

. . . I do not contend that the Thirteenth Amendment invests Congress with authority, by legislation, to define and regulate the entire body of the civil rights which citizens enjoy, or may enjoy, in the several States. But I hold that since slavery, as the court has repeatedly declared, was the moving or principal cause of the adoption of that amendment, and since that institution rested wholly upon the inferiority, as a race, of those held in bondage, their freedom necessarily involved immunity from, and protection against, all discrimination against them, because of their race, in respect of such civil rights as belong to freemen of other races. Congress, therefore, under its express power to enforce that amendment, by appropriate legislation, may enact laws to protect that people against the deprivation, *because of their race,* of any civil rights granted to other freemen in the same State; and such legislation may be of a direct and primary character, operating upon States, their officers and agents, and, also, upon, at least, such individuals and corporations as exercise public functions and wield power and authority under the State. . . .

[Justice Harlan then turns to a consideration of the Fourteenth Amendment.]

The assumption that this amendment consists wholly of prohibitions upon State laws and State proceedings in hostility to its provisions, is unauthorized by its language. The first clause of the first section—"All persons born or naturalized in the United States, and subject to the jurisdiction thereof, are citizens of the United States, and of the State wherein they reside"—is of a distinctly affirmative character. . . .

The citizenship thus acquired, by that race, in virtue of an affirmative grant from the nation, may be protected, not alone by the judicial branch of the government, but by congressional legislation of a primary direct character; this, because the power of Congress is not restricted to the enforcement of prohibitions upon State laws or State action. It is, in terms distinct and positive, to enforce "the *provisions of this article*" of the amendment; not simply those of a prohibitive character, but the provisions—*all* of the provisions—affirmative and prohibitive, of the amendment. It is, therefore, a grave misconception to suppose that the fifth section of the amendment has reference exclusively to express prohibitions upon State laws or State action. If any right was created by that amendment, the grant of power, through appropriate legislation, to enforce its provisions, authorizes Congress by means of legislation, operating throughout the entire Union, to guard, secure, and protect that right. . . .

But what was secured to colored citizens of the United States—as between them and their respective States—by the national grant to them of state citizenship? . . . There is one [right] if there be no other—exemption from race discrimination in respect of any civil right belonging to citizens of the white race in the same State. That, surely, is their constitutional privilege when within the jurisdiction of other States. And such must be their constitutional right, in their own State, unless the recent amendments be splendid baubles, thrown out to delude those who deserved fair and generous treatment at the hands of the nation. . . .

It is said that any interpretation of the Fourteenth Amendment different from that adopted by the majority of the court, would imply that Congress had authority to enact a municipal code for all the States, covering every matter affecting the life, liberty, and property of the citizens of the several States. Not so. Prior to the adoption of that amendment the constitutions of the several States, without perhaps an exception, secured all *persons* against deprivation of life, liberty, or property, otherwise than by due process of law, and, in some form, recognized the right of all *persons* to the equal protection of the laws. Those rights, therefore, existed before that amendment was proposed or adopted, and were not created by it. . . . Exemption from race discrimination in respect of the civil rights which are fundamental in *citizenship* in a republican government, is, as we have seen, a new right, created by the nation, with express power in Congress, by legislation, to enforce the constitutional provision from which it is derived. If, in some sense, such race discrimination is, within the letter of the last clause of the first section, a denial of that equal protection of the laws, which is secured against State denial of all persons, whether citizens or not, it cannot be possible that a mere prohibition upon said State denial, or a prohibition upon State laws abridging the privileges and immunities of citizens of the United States, takes from the nation the power which it has uniformly exercised of protecting, by direct primary legislation, those privileges and immunities which existed under the Constitution before the adoption of the Fourteenth Amendment, or have been created by that amendment in behalf of those thereby made *citizens* of their respective States. . . .

[Mr. Justice Harlan here discusses *Ex parte Virginia,* 100 U.S. 334]

In every material sense applicable to the practical enforcement of the Fourteenth Amendment, railroad corporations, keepers of inns, and managers of places of public amusement are agents or instrumentalities of the State, because they are charged with duties to the public, and are amenable, in respect of their duties and functions, to governmental regulation. It seems to me that, within the principle settled in *Ex parte Virginia*, a denial, by these instrumentalities of the State, to the citizen, because of his race, of that equality of civil rights secured to him by law, is a denial by the State, within the meaning of the Fourteenth Amendment. If it be not, then that race is left, in respect of the civil rights in question, practically at the mercy of corporations and individuals wielding power under the States.

My brethren say, that when a man has emerged from slavery, and by the aid of beneficent legislation has shaken off the inseparable concomitants of that state, there must be some stage in the progress of his elevation when he takes the rank of a mere citizen, and ceases to be the special favorite of the laws. . . . It is, I submit, scarcely just to say that the colored race has been the special favorite of the laws. The statute of 1875, now adjudged to be unconstitutional, is for the benefit of citizens of every race and color. What the nation, through Congress, has sought to accomplish in reference to that race, is—what had already been done in every State of the Union for the white race—to secure and protect rights belonging to them as freemen and citizens; nothing more. It was not deemed enough "to help the feeble up, but to support him after." The one underlying purpose of congressional legislation has been to enable the black race to take the rank of mere citizens. . . . If the constitutional amendments be enforced, according to the intent with which, as I conceive, they were adopted, there cannot be, in this republic, any class of human beings in practical subjection to another class, with power in the latter to dole out to the former just such privileges as they may choose to grant. The supreme law of the land has decreed that no authority shall be exercised in this country upon the basis of discrimination, in respect of civil rights, against freemen and citizens because of their race, color, or previous condition of servitude. To that decree—for the due enforcement of which, by appropriate legislation, Congress has been invested with express power—every one must bow, whatever may have been, or whatever now are, his individual views as to the wisdom or policy, either of the recent changes in the fundamental law, or of the legislation which has been enacted to give them effect.

(10)
STATE LAWS TO PROTECT CIVIL RIGHTS

The ill-fated Civil Rights Act of 1875 was the last attempt by Congress to guarantee civil rights to Negroes until 1957. Meanwhile, the years 1865–1883 saw also the enactment of civil rights laws by several states, both North and South. In the latter case, these laws were, of course, framed while the states were still being governed under the Reconstruction Acts (see p. 47, above). Some representative statutes follow.

LOUISIANA[1]

Section 1

Be it enacted . . . That all persons engaged within this State in the business of common carriers of passengers shall have the rights to refuse to admit any person to their . . . cars, . . . water crafts, or . . . vehicles, or to expel any person therefrom after admission, when such person . . . shall be of infamous character, or shall be guilty . . . of gross, vulgar or disorderly conduct, . . . *provided,* [they] . . . make no discrimination on account of race or color. . . .

Section 2

Be it further enacted . . . That except in the case enumerated in section one of this act, no person shall be refused admission to or entertainment at any public inn, hotel or place of public resort within the State.

Section 3

Be it further enacted . . . That all licenses hereafter granted by this State, and by all parishes and municipalities therein, to persons engaged in business

[1] *Acts of Louisiana,* 1869, p. 57, as quoted in Pauli Murray, *States' Laws on Race and Color* (n. p., 1951), p. 171.

or keeping places of public resort shall contain the express provision that the place of business or public resort shall be open to the accommodation and patronage of all persons without distinction or discrimination on account of race or color, and any person who shall violate the condition of such license, shall, on conviction thereof, be punished by forfeiture of his license, and his place of business or of public resort shall be closed and, moreover, shall be liable at the suit of the person aggrieved to such damages as he shall sustain thereby before any court of competent jurisdiction.

FLORIDA[1]

A BILL to be entitled An act to Protect all Citizens of the State of Florida in their Civil Rights, and to Furnish the Means for their Vindication.

The people of the State of Florida, represented in Senate and Assembly, do enact as follows:

Section 1

That no citizen of this State shall, by reason of race, color, or previous condition of servitude, be excepted or excluded from the full and equal enjoyment of any accommodation, advantage, facility, or privilege furnished by inn-keepers, by common carriers, whether on land or water, by licensed owners, managers, or lessees of theaters or other places of public amusement; by trustees, commissioners, superintendents, teachers, and other officers of common schools and public institutions of learning, the same being supported by moneys derived from general taxation, or authorized by law, also of cemetery associations and benevolent associations, supported or authorized in the same way: *Provided,* That private schools, cemeteries, and institutions of learning established exclusively for white or colored persons, and maintained respectively by voluntary contributions, shall remain according to the terms of the original establishment.

Section 2

That any person violating any of the provisions of the foregoing section, or aiding in their violation or inciting thereto, shall for every such offense forfeit and pay the sum of one hundred dollars to the person aggrieved thereby, to be recovered in an action on the case, with full costs, and shall also for every such offense be deemed guilty of a misdemeanor, and upon conviction thereof shall be fined not less than one hundred nor more than one thousand dollars, or shall be imprisoned not less than thirty days nor more than one year: *Provided,* That the party aggrieved shall not recover more than one penalty; and when the offense is a refusal of burial, the penalty may be recovered by the heirs at law of the person whose body has been refused burial.

Section 3

That every discrimination against any citizen on account of color by use of the word "white" or any other term in any law, statute, ordinance, or regulation, is hereby repealed and annulled.

Section 4

That no citizen possessing all other qualifications which are or may be prescribed by law, shall be disqualified for service as juror in any court in this State by reason of race, color, or previous condition of servitude; and any officer or other person charged with any duty in the selection or summon-

[1] *Laws of Florida,* 1873 (chap. 1947 [No. 13]), p. 25.

ing of jurors, who shall exclude or fail to summon any citizen for the reason above named, shall, on conviction thereof, be guilty of a misdemeanor, and be fined not less than one hundred nor more than one thousand dollars.

That the foregoing laws should have been spread on the statute books throughout the South during Reconstruction rule is hardly surprising, and that they were immediately lost to sight when Reconstruction ended is even less so. More unusual is the passing by the legislature of North Carolina of the following resolution *after* the collapse of the Reconstruction government, when the state government had been restored to the Democratic party and Governor Zebulon Baird ("Zeb") Vance, the state's salty wartime executive.

NORTH CAROLINA[1]

Whereas, In the providence of God, the colored people have been set free, and this is their country and their home, as well as that of the white people, and there should be nothing to prevent the two races from dwelling together in the land in harmony and peace;

Whereas, We recognize the duty of the stronger race to uphold the weaker, and that upon it rests the responsibility of an honest and faithful endeavor to raise the weaker race to the level of intelligent citizenship; and

Whereas, The colored people have been erroneously taught that legislation under Democratic auspices would be inimical to their rights and interests, thereby causing a number of them to entertain honest fears in the premises,

The General Assembly of North Carolina do resolve, That, while we regard with repugnance the absurd attempts, by means of "Civil Rights" Bills, to eradicate certain race distinctions, implanted by nature and sustained by the habits of forty centuries; and while we are sure that good government demands for both races alike that the great representative and executive offices of the country should be administered by men of the highest intelligence and best experience in public affairs, we do, nevertheless, heartily accord alike to every citizen, without distinction of race or color, equality before the law.

Resolved, That we recognize the full purport and intent of that amendment to the Constitution of the United States which confers the right of suffrage and citizenship upon the people of color, and that part of the Constitution of North Carolina conferring educational privileges upon both races: that we are disposed and determined to carry out in good faith these as all other constitutional provisions.

Because they were waiting to learn what the federal government's intentions were, the states of the North, East, and West enacted so little civil rights legislation that nearly all of it is accounted for by brief statutes passed by Massachusetts, Kansas, and New York. The New York statute follows.[2]

1 *Laws and Resolutions of North Carolina,* 1876–1877 (Resolution of Jan. 31, 1877), p. 589.

2 *Laws of New York,* 1873 (chap. 186), p. 303.

AN ACT to provide for the protection of citizens in their civil and public rights.

Passed April 9, 1873. . . .

Section 1

No citizen of this state shall, by reason of race, color or previous condition of servitude, be excepted or excluded from the full and equal enjoyment of any accommodation, advantage, facility, or privilege furnished by innkeepers, by common carriers, whether on land or water, by licensed owners, managers or commissioners, superintendents, teachers and other officers of common schools and public institutions of learning, and by cemetery associations.

Section 2

The violation of any part of the first section of this act shall be deemed a misdemeanor, and the party or parties violating the same shall, upon conviction thereof, be subject to a fine of not less than fifty dollars, or more than five hundred dollars.

Section 3

Discriminations against any citizen on account of color, by the use of the word "white," or any other term in any law, statute, ordinance or regulation now existing in this state, is hereby repealed and annulled.

(11)
DISCRIMINATION BY STATE LAW

The bulk of the legislation by the states to fix the Afro-American's inferior status—despite the Civil War Amendments, the Enforcement Acts, and the Civil Rights Laws—was to come after 1883, but a beginning was made in the years here under review.

A. *Anti-Civil Rights Legislation*

Delaware, a slave-holding state until the ratification of the Thirteenth Amendment, was not subject to Radical Reconstruction, since she had not seceded. That she had no intention of giving equality to her black population, however, was made plain in a resolution passed by the legislature in 1873.[1]

Resolved by the Senate and House of Representatives of the State of Delaware . . . , That the members of this General Assembly, for the people they represent, and for themselves, jointly and individually, do hereby

[1] *Laws of Delaware,* 1871–1873 (chap. 612), p. 686.

declare uncompromising opposition to a proposed act of Congress, introduced by Hon. Charles Sumner at the last session, and now on file in the Senate of the United States, known as the "Supplemental Civil Rights Bill," and all other measures intended or calculated to equalize or amalgamate the negro race with the white race, politically or socially, and especially do they proclaim unceasing opposition to making negroes eligible to public offices, to sit on juries, and to their admission into public schools where white children attend, to their admission on terms of equality with white people in churches, public conveyances, places of amusement, or hotels, and to any and every measure designed or having the effect to promote the equality of the negro with the white man in any of the relations of life, or which may by possibility conduce to such result.

Resolved, That our Senators in Congress be instructed, and our Representative requested to vote against and use all honorable means to defeat the passage by Congress of the bill referred to in the foregoing resolution . . . to make the negro the peer of the white man.

Two years later, on March 25, 1875, the Delaware lawmakers, plainly defying the federal Civil Rights Act which had been enacted less than a month earlier, insisted that any proprietor of a public carrier or accommodation of any sort was by state law authorized to exclude or segregate those who "would be offensive to the major part of his customers."[1]

Section 1

Be it enacted . . . That no keeper of an inn, tavern, hotel, or restaurant, or other place of public entertainment or refreshment of travelers, guests, or customers, shall be obliged, by law, to furnish entertainment or refreshment to persons whose reception or entertainment by him, would be offensive to the major part of his customers, and would injure his business. . . .

Section 2

[Makes similar provision for "the proprietor of a theatre, or other public place of amusement."]

Section 3

And be it further enacted, That carriers of passengers may make such arrangements in their business, as will, if necessary, assign a particular place in their cars, carriages or boats, to such of their customers as they may choose to place there, and whose presence elsewhere would be offensive to the major part of the traveling public, where their business is conducted, *Provided,* however, that the quality of the accommodation shall be equal for all, if the same price for carriage is required from all.

B. *Marriage and Other Rights of Ex-Slaves*

Like other ex-Confederate states during the Johnson governments, and before the Reconstruction Acts of 1867, North Carolina in 1866 passed a comprehensive law which, while guaranteeing certain privi-

[1] *Laws of Delaware,* 1875 (chap. 194), p. 322.

leges and immunities, restricted Negroes in various ways with a plain purpose to deny them legal equality with whites.[1] Such statutes typically contained provisions regularizing ex-slave marriages, which prior to emancipation had had no real standing in law.

AN ACT CONCERNING NEGROES AND PERSONS OF COLOR OR OF MIXED BLOOD

Section 1

Be it enacted . . . That negroes and their issue, even where one ancestor in each succeeding generation to the fourth inclusive, is white, shall be deemed persons of color.

Section 2

Be it further enacted, That all persons of color, who are now inhabitants of this State, shall be entitled to the same privileges and subject to the same burthen and disabilities as by the laws of the State were conferred on, or were attached to, free persons of color, prior to the ordinance of emancipation, except as the same may be changed by law.

Section 3

Be it further enacted, That persons of color shall be entitled to all the privileges of white persons in the mode of prosecuting, defending, continuing, removing and transferring their suits at law, and in equity; and, likewise, to the same mode of trial by jury, and all the privileges appertaining thereto. . . .

Section 5

Be it further enacted, That in all cases where men and women, both or one of whom were lately slaves and are now emancipated, now cohabit together in the relation of husband and wife, the parties shall be deemed to have been lawfully married as man and wife at the time of the commencement of such cohabitation, although they may not have been married in due form of law. And all persons whose cohabitation is hereby ratified into a state of marriage, shall go before the clerk of the court of pleas and quarter sessions of the county in which they reside, at his office, or before some justice of the peace, and acknowledge the fact of such cohabitation, and the time of its commencement; and the clerk shall enter [or the justice of the peace shall cause to have entered] the same in the book kept for that purpose; and such entry shall be deemed *prima facie* evidence of the allegations therein contained. . . .

Section 6

Be it further enacted, That if any of such persons shall fail to go before the clerk of the county court, or some justice of the peace of the county in which they reside, and have their marriage recorded before the first of September [1866], they shall be deemed guilty of a misdemeanor, and punished at the discretion of the court. . . .

Section 7

Be it further enacted, That all contracts between any persons whatever, whereof one or more of them shall be a person of color, for the sale or purchase of any horse, mule, ass, jennet, neat cattle, hog, sheep or goat, whatever may be the value of such articles, and all contracts between such persons

[1] *North Carolina . . . Public Laws . . .* 1865–1866 (chap. 40), p. 99.

for any other article or articles of property whatever of the value of ten dollars or more; . . . shall be void as to all persons whatever, unless the same be put in writing and signed by the venders or debtors, and witnessed by a white person who can read and write.

Section 8

Be it further enacted, That marriage between white persons and persons of color shall be void; and every person authorized to solemnize the rites of matrimony, who shall knowingly solemnize the same between such persons; and every clerk of a court who shall knowingly issue license for their marriage, shall be deemed guilty of a misdemeanor, and, moreover, shall pay a penalty of five hundred dollars to any person suing for the same.

Section 9

Be it further enacted, That persons of color, not otherwise incompetent, shall be capable of bearing evidence in all controversies at law and in equity, where the rights of persons or property of persons of color, shall be put in issue, and would be concluded by the judgment or decree of court; and also in pleas of the State, where the violence, fraud or injury alleged shall be charged to have been done by or to persons of color. In all other civil and criminal cases such evidence shall be deemed inadmissible, unless by consent of the parties of record. . . .

Section 10

Be it further enacted, That whenever a person of color shall be examined as a witness, the court shall warn the witness to declare the truth.

Section 11

Be it further enacted, That any person of color, convicted by due course of law, of an assault with an intent to commit rape upon the body of a white female, shall suffer death.

Section 12

Be it further enacted, That the criminal laws of the State, embracing and affecting a white person, are hereby extended to persons of color, except where it is otherwise provided in this act, and whenever they shall be convicted of any act made criminal, if committed by a white person, they shall be punished in like manner, except in such cases when other and different punishment may be prescribed or allowed by this act.

C. *Laws Prohibiting Mixed Marriages*

Among the commonest constitutional and statutory provisions redefining the former bondmen's status were clauses prohibiting marriage of blacks and whites, a proscription that was directed equally to both races. An Alabama constitutional provision follows:[1]

ARTICLE IV

Section 31

It shall be the duty of the General Assembly at its next session, and from time to time thereafter as it may deem proper, to enact laws prohibiting the intermarriage of white persons with negroes, or with persons of mixed blood,

[1] *Constitution of Alabama,* 1865, in *Alabama Revised Code,* 1867, p. 32.

declaring such marriages null and void *ab initio,* and making the parties to any such marriage subject to criminal prosecutions, with such penalties as may be by law prescribed.

Responding to this command, the Alabama legislature enacted the following:[1]

Marriages between white persons and negroes.—If any white person and any negro, or the descendants of any negro, to the third generation inclusive, though one ancestor of each generation was a white person, intermarry or live in adultery or fornication with each other, each of them must on conviction be imprisoned in the penitentiary, or sentenced to hard labor for the county for not less than two nor more than seven years.

Any [civil officer] or minister of the gospel . . . who performs a marriage ceremony of such persons . . . must each on conviction be fined not less than one hundred nor more than one thousand dollars, and may also be imprisoned in the county jail, or sentenced to hard labor for the county, for not more than six months.

Florida law provided that:[2]

It shall not be lawful for any white male person . . . to marry any negro, mulatto or quarteroon [*sic*], or other colored female, and it shall in like manner be unlawful for any white female person to intermarry with any negro, mulatto or quarteroon, or other colored male person.

This statute was first enacted in 1832 and was still in force in 1883. Such statutes and state constitutional provisions were by no means confined to the South. Arizona, which was still in the territorial stage, made similar provision,[3] as did California.[4]

ARIZONA

All marriages of white persons with negroes, mulattoes, Indians, or mongolians are declared illegal and void.

Whoever shall contract . . . and whoever shall solemnize any such marriage, shall be punished by fine or imprisonment, or both, at the discretion of the jury . . . the fine to be not less than one hundred nor more than ten thousand dollars, and the imprisonment to be not less than three months nor more than ten years.

CALIFORNIA

All marriages of white persons with negroes or mulattoes are illegal and void. [First enacted in 1852.]

1 *Alabama Revised Code,* 1867 (Part 4, Title 1, chap. 5, 3602–3603), p. 690.
2 *Florida Digest of Laws,* 1881 (chap. 149, Sec. 8), p. 753.
3 *Acts of Territory of Arizona,* 1865 (chap. XXX, Sec. 3), p. 58.
4 *California Civil Code,* 1872, I, 30.

D. *Definitions of "Negro"*

Legislation laying disabilities upon Negroes inevitably raised the question of who precisely was a Negro, and to that query the states now addressed themselves. Georgia prescribed that:[1]

> . . . all negroes, mulattoes, mestizoes, and their descendants, having one-eighth negro, or African blood, in their veins, shall be known in this State as "persons of color."

Tennessee affords another example[2]

> . . . all negroes, mulattoes, mestizoes, and their descendants, having any African blood in their veins, shall be known in this state as "persons of color."

E. *Unequal Punishment for Blacks*

Common also in the Johnson governments (and once again after 1883) were provisions prescribing severer punishments for Negroes than for whites who committed a similar offense. They related usually to intermarriage and to interracial sexual relations. Following are examples from Kentucky and Florida.

KENTUCKY[3]

If any negro or slave be guilty of murder [or] rape committed upon a white woman of any age, or the attempt to commit such rape, or be an accessory before the fact to either of the aforesaid crimes, upon conviction, he shall suffer death. [Enacted in 1852.]

FLORIDA[4]

All persons without distinction of color are declared subject to the same penalties for offenses, except that the laws for the punishment of negroes for rape on white women are continued.

[1] *Acts of Georgia*, 1865–66, p. 235; quoted in Murray, *States' Laws*, p. 90. A later Georgia enactment was even more sweeping: "All negroes, mulattoes, mestizoes, and their descendants, having any ascertainable trace of either Negro or African, West Indian, or Asiatic Indian blood in their veins, and all descendants of any person having either Negro or African, West Indian, or Asiatic Indian blood in his or her veins, shall be known in this State as persons of color." *Georgia Laws*, 1927 (No. [illegible]), p. 272.

[2] *Tennessee Laws*, 1865–1866 (chap. 40, Sec. 1), p. 65.

[3] *Revised Statutes of Kentucky*, 1867 (chap. 93, Art. VII, Sec. IV), p. 375.

[4] *Florida General Laws*, 1866, p. 736.

KENTUCKY[1]

This Kentucky law denied to black women protections that it made available to white women.

Whoever shall unlawfully and carnally know any white woman against her will or consent, or by force, or while she is insensible, shall be guilty of rape, and shall be punished by confinement in the penitentiary for a period not less than ten nor more than twenty years, or by death, in the discretion of the jury.

F. *Exclusion from Jury Service*

Many southern States (and for that matter northern) excluded blacks from jury service in practice, but only a few took the trouble to write the discrimination into their statutes. West Virginia, one of the exceptions, chose to enact the principle into law.[2]

All white male persons who are twenty-one years of age and who are citizens of this State shall be liable to serve as jurors, except as herein provided. [The exceptions are state officials.]

G. *Separate Schools by Legislation*

Contemporary scholarship relating to the Civil War Amendments leans to the view that the Fourteenth Amendment was probably not intended by its framers to prevent the segregation of Negroes in public schools. In any case, the southern states were prompt to establish a "permanent" system of separate schools when Radical Reconstruction collapsed. Some early examples follow.

ALABAMA[3]

The General Assembly shall establish, organize, and maintain a system of public schools throughout the State, for the equal benefit of the children thereof, between the ages of seven and twenty-one years; but separate schools shall be provided for the children of African descent.

1 *Kentucky Laws,* Adj. Sess., 1869 (chap. 1659), p. 52.

2 *Acts of West Virginia,* 1872–73 (chap. XLVII), p. 102. But see p. 64, above, for *Strauder* v. *West Virginia* (1880), in which the statute was declared unconstitutional by the United States Supreme Court.

3 Constitution of Alabama, 1875, Art. XIII, in *Code of Alabama,* 1876, p. 147.

GEORGIA[1]

Paragraph I. Common Schools. There shall be a thorough system of common schools for the education of children in the elementary branches of an English education only, as nearly uniform as practicable, the expenses of which shall be provided for by taxation, or otherwise. The schools shall be free to all children of the State, but separate schools shall be provided for white and colored races.

MISSISSIPPI[2]

Sec. 35. *Be it further enacted,* That the schools in each county shall be so arranged as to afford ample free school facilities to all the educable youths in that county, but white and colored pupils shall not be taught in the same school-house, but in separate school-houses.

H. *The First "Permanent" Jim Crow Laws: Tennessee*

Curiously, the first bona fide Jim Crow law was enacted by Tennessee, the only one of the Confederate states to escape Radical Reconstruction. It alone had, before the Reconstruction Act of 1867, complied—at least to the satisfaction of Congress—with the congressional requirement that the states show their repentance, and their acceptance of a new order, by ratifying the Fourteenth Amendment. On March 23, 1875, three weeks after the passage of the United States Civil Rights Act of that year, Tennessee passed a law giving any proprietor, or his employees, wide latitude in excluding "any person, whom he shall for any reason whatever, choose not to entertain, carry, or admit, to his house, hotel, carriage, or means of transportation or place of amusement."[3]

Section 1

Be it enacted by the General Assembly of the State of Tennessee, That the rule of a common law giving a right of action to any person excluded from any hotel, or public means of transportation, or place of amusement, is hereby abrogated; and hereafter no keeper of any hotel, or public house, or carrier of passengers for hire, or conductors, drivers, or employees of such carrier or keeper, shall be bound, or under any obligation to entertain, carry, or admit, any person, whom he shall for any reason whatever, choose not to entertain, carry, or admit, to his house, hotel, carriage, or means of transportation or place of amusement; nor shall any right exist in favor of any such person so refused admission; but the right of such keepers of hotels and public houses, carriers of passengers, and keepers of places of amusement,

[1] Constitution of Georgia, 1877, Art. VIII, in *Code of Georgia*, 1882, p. 1321.
[2] *Mississippi Laws*, 1878 (chap. XIII, Sec. 35), p. 103.
[3] *Acts of Tennessee*, 1875 (chap. 130), p. 216.

and their employees, to control the access and admission or exclusion of persons to or from their public houses, means of transportation, and places of amusement, shall be as perfect and complete as that of any private person over his private house, carriage, or private theater, or places of amusement for his family.

This statute merely *authorized* the supplier of public facilities and accommodations to discriminate. Six years later came a law *requiring* segregation on railroads. Except for the very short-lived pre-Reconstruction railway segregation laws in Mississippi, Florida, and Texas[1] this was the only "permanent" Jim Crow law in the South before 1887. Such segregation by specific legal command was, with the minor exceptions noted, breaking new ground. It was destined to become almost universal in the South by 1907, and to persist for half a century—defended eventually on the false ground that laws of this sort had for generations been part of the southern way of life. Indeed, it should be noted that the merely *permissive* statute of 1875, just quoted, began with a declaration that by that law the common law was now being abrogated.

The newer statute, of 1881, specified separate cars or portions of cars only for first-class passengers. Others, of both races, could still, so far as the law was concerned, continue to share the same facilities, without regard to race. The declared purpose of the act is of special interest.[2]

AN ACT to prevent discriminations by railroad companies among passengers who are charged and paying first class passage, and fixing penalty for the violation [of] the same.

Whereas, it is the practice of railroad companies located and operated in the State of Tennessee to charge and collect from colored passengers traveling over their roads first class passage fare, and compel said passengers to occupy second class cars where smoking is allowed, and no restrictions [*sic*] enforced to prevent vulgar or obscene language; therefore,

Section 1

Be it enacted . . . that all railroad companies located and operated in this State shall furnish separate cars, or portions of cars cut off by partition walls, in which all colored passengers who pay first class passenger rates of fare, may have the privilege to enter and occupy, and such apartments shall be kept in good repair, and with the same conveniences, and subject to the same rules governing other first class cars, preventing smoking and obscene language.

Section 2

Be it further enacted [that railroads violating this law] shall forfeit and pay the sum of one hundred dollars, recoverable before any court having jurisdiction thereof, one-half to be paid to the person sueing, and the other half to go to the common school fund of the State. Passed April 7, 1881.

[1] See p. 44, above.
[2] *Acts of Tennessee*, 1881 (chap. 155), p. 211.

(12) CIVIL RIGHTS AND THE STATE COURTS, 1865–1883

Litigation in the state courts over the Afro-American's civil rights was not nearly so common before 1883 as one might suppose, but significant precedents for statutory and constitutional interpretation had begun to accumulate. Such cases as did arise were primarily concerned with intermarriage of the races, the separation of the races in schools, segregation in transportation, restrictions upon employment, and statutes providing for unequal punishments as between whites and blacks.

A. *Prohibition of Intermarriage*

Laws forbidding race-mixing, both in and out of wedlock, were not unusual before the Civil War, and were by no means confined to the South. Thereafter they became more, rather than less, common. By 1910, some twenty-six states, either by constitutional provision or by legislation, prohibited intermarriage, among them all of the eleven former states of the Confederacy, the five ex-slave-holding states of the border South (Missouri, Kentucky, Delaware, Maryland, and West Virginia), five western states (Arizona, California, Colorado, Idaho), and one mid-western state, Indiana. To these, four more western states were added not long afterward: Montana, North Dakota, South Dakota, and Wyoming.

State tribunals, except those temporarily under Radical Reconstruction, showed a universal disposition to sustain such laws, and found that they could do so without interference from the Supreme Court of the United States. In 1875 the Reconstruction Alabama Supreme Court was confronted with a challenge to Alabama's laws against intermarriage. The appellant, a white justice of the peace, had been convicted and fined by a lower court for performing a marriage ceremony for an interracial couple. His counsel argued that the state statute violated the rights clauses of the Fourteenth Amendment and the nation's Civil Rights Act of 1866, and the court upheld this view, taking the position that Negroes, having been raised to full citizenship, must be accorded all the rights and privileges of whites, and "may not be distinguished by legislation."[1]

This victory for opponents of anti-interracial marriage laws was short-lived, however. Two years later, as home rule was being restored to the South, the Alabama Supreme Court took the more familiar stand that a marriage is not an ordinary contract. Citing *State* v. *Gibson,*[2] an Indiana decision of 1871, and *West Chester and Philadelphia Railroad Co.* v. *Miles* (1867),[3] the court concluded:[4] "The amendments to the Constitution were evidently designed to secure to citizens, without distinction of race, rights of a civil or political kind only—not such as are merely social, much less those of a purely domestic nature. The regulation of these belongs to the states."

Then in its defense of state laws forbidding interracial marriage, the court delivered itself of this impassioned homily:

> . . . It is through the marriage relation that the *homes* of a people are created—those homes in which, ordinarily, all the members of all the families of the land are, during a part of every day, assembled together; where the elders of the household seek repose and cheer, and reparation of strength from the toils and cares of life; and where, in an affectionate intercourse and conversation with them, the young become imbued with the principles, and animated by the spirit and ideas, which in a great degree give shape to their characters and determine the manner of their future lives. . . . Who can estimate the evil of introducing into their most intimate relations, elements so heterogeneous that they must naturally cause discord, shame, disruption of family circles and estrangement of kindred?
>
> . . . Hence it is, that, if not in every State of the Union, in all of them in which any considerable numbers of the negro race resided, statutes have been enacted prohibiting marriages between them and persons of the white race. Said the Supreme Court of Pennsylvania, in a recent case: "Why the Creator made one white and the other black, we do not know; but the fact is apparent, and the races are distinct, each producing its own kind, and following the peculiar law of its constitution. . . . The natural law, which forbids their intermarriage and that amalgamation which leads to a corruption of races, is as clearly divine as that which imparted to them different natures."
>
> . . . It is, also, a fact not always sufficiently felt, that the more humble and helpless families are, the more they need this sort of protection. Their spirits are crushed, or become rebellious, when other ills, besides those of poverty, are heaped upon them. And there are (we presume) but few localities any where in the United States, in which the conviction has not obtained, and been approved by minds the most sedate, that the law should absolutely frustrate and prevent the growth of any desire or idea of such an alliance, and all the secret arts, practices and persuasions of servants or others upon the weak-minded or forward, to bring it about—by making marriage between the two races, legally impossible, and severely punishing those who perform,

[1] 48 Ala. 195 (1875).

[2] See below, p. 86.

[3] See below, p. 88.

[4] *Green* v. *State,* 58 Ala. 190 (1871).

and those who, with intent to be married, go through the ceremonies thereof. Manifestly, it is for the peace and happiness of the black race, as well as of the white, that such laws should exist. And surely there can not be any tyranny or injustice in requiring both alike, to form this union with those of their own race only, whom God hath joined together by indelible peculiarities, which declare that He has made the two races distinct. . . .

In 1871 the supreme court of the mid-western state of Indiana declared in an opinion which it argued at considerable length, that neither the Fourteenth Amendment nor the Civil Rights Act of 1866 reach state laws forbidding marriage between whites and blacks.[1] The court cited the Ninth and Tenth amendments of the Constitution of the United States[2] in support of the rule that the national government has no authority over marriage. In addition, the court quoted extensively from *West Chester and Philadelphia Railroad Co.* v. *Miles*,[3] in which the Supreme Court of Pennsylvania had affirmed that separation of the races had been decreed by God Himself. But the heart of the decision was the proposition that the states and not the nation must regulate marriage.

We utterly deny the power of Congress to regulate, control, or in any manner to interfere with the states in determining what shall constitute crimes against the laws of the State. . . . In this State marriage is treated as a civil contract; but it is more than a civil contract. It is a public institution established by God himself, is recognized in all Christian and civilized nations, and is essential to the peace, happiness, and well-being of society. . . . The right, in the states, to regulate and control, to guard, protect, and preserve this God-given, civilizing, and Christianizing institution is of inestimable importance, and cannot be surrendered, nor can the states suffer or permit any interference therewith. . . .

In March 1875, Charles Frasher, white, had married a black woman in Gregg County, Texas, contrary to the laws of the state. His counsel staked his case in the theory that the law in question had been superseded by the Fourteenth Amendment and the Civil Rights Act of 1875. A lower court had convicted Frasher and sentenced him to four years in prison. In the case before us,[4] the Appellate Court of Texas ordered a new trial because of errors in the lower court's conduct of the action, but sustained the law against the charge of violating the Constitution of the United States. Citing the *Slaughter House Cases*[5] as a guide to the construction of the Fourteenth Amendment, and declaring that marriage is not one of the "privileges and immunities" contemplated

[1] *State* v. *Gibson*, 36 Ind. 389 (1871).
[2] See above, p. 6.
[3] See below, p. 88.
[4] *Frasher* v. *State*, 3 Tex. App. 263 (1877).
[5] See above, p. 59.

by the amendment, the judges concluded that marriage is a civil status subject to regulation by the states and not the United States. After quoting from *Gibson* v. *State* the excerpt cited above, the court continued:

> Marriage is not a contract protected by the Constitution of the United States, or within the meaning of the Civil Rights Bill. . . . Again, the counsel for the defendant insists that, because the statute . . . affixes a penalty upon the white person alone, and none upon the Negro, it therefore violates the 14th and 15th amendments of the Constitution of the United States, and the first section of the Civil Rights Bill. [This] objection to our statute should be addressed to the legislature, and not to the judicial, branch of the government. Can it be truly said that the law is illegal because the race sought to be protected by "the amendments" and "the Civil Rights Bill" is not punished?

In *Francois* v. *State* the Texas Court of Criminal Appeals heard an appeal from a white defendant who had been sentenced to five years in prison for violating the state's anti-mixed marriage law, and marrying a Negro. At the time of the offense, the state provided that "If any white person . . . shall marry a Negro. . . . [he shall, upon conviction, be imprisoned in the] penitentiary not less than two nor more than five years." Counsel for the defendant argued that the law was an unconstitutional discrimination against whites. The court, however, affirmed the judgment of the lower court:[1]

> It is earnestly contended . . . that [the statute] is unconstitutional and void, because it discriminates against the white race in assessing the punishment. The questions raised were all before this court and settled in the case of *Frasher* v. *State,* 3 Tex. Ct. App. 263, in which it was held that the statute had not been abrogated, but was in force as part of the law of the State . . . [and it was established in *Green* v. *State,* 58 Ala. 190, that] "marriage is not a mere contract, but a social or domestic institution upon which are founded all society and order . . . and the several states of the Union, in the adoption of the recent amendments to the Constitution of the United States, designed to secure to citizens rights of a civil or political nature only, and did not part with their hitherto unquestioned power of regulating, within their own borders, matters of purely social and domestic concern. . . ."
>
> The States alone have the right to declare how their citizens may marry, whom they may marry, and the consequences of their marrying. . . . Art. 386 [forbidding intermarriage] was but a part and parcel of the law of the State upon the subject, a regulation which she had the right to make and the power to enforce. She has never intended to abrogate this wise social provision; on the contrary, she has by recent enactment so extended the prohibition as to make it doubly effective, and this latter statute is no evidence of the fact that our law-makers deemed the former void, or that it was void.

[1] 9 Tex. Crim. App. 144 (1880).

B. *Public Transportation: Segregation Affirmed*

Litigation over legally imposed discrimination in public conveyances was rare before 1883, in part because the practice of such segregation, as we have seen, had not yet become widespread. Two important cases, however, which did go through the courts are here noted: one from a northern state and one from a southern state still under Reconstruction rule.

The case of *West Chester and Philadelphia Railroad Co.* v. *Miles* (1867),[1] a judgment of the Supreme Court of Pennsylvania reflecting prevailing judicial philosophy on the question at issue, was to be cited frequently in later years when courts sustained state statutes ordaining separate accommodations for the races on railways and other carriers. In March 1867, Pennsylvania had enacted a law forbidding discrimination on the basis of race or color on railroads. One Mary E. Miles boarded a railroad car in Philadelphia and took a seat near the center of the coach. The conductor reminded her of the rule of the road which required Negroes to sit in the rear of the car, and when she refused to comply he put her off the train. In the trial court a judgment in her favor and against the road resulted, but the cause was moved on appeal to the state supreme court, which, though conceding that no one may be excluded from a car because of "color, religion, or prejudice," insisted that it was perfectly legal for a common carrier to segregate the races, and that, therefore, the lower court's judgment must be reversed.

> . . . The simple question is, whether a public carrier may, in the exercise of his private right of property, and in due performance of his public duty, separate passengers by any other well-defined characteristic than that of sex. . . .
>
> This question must be decided upon reasonable grounds. If there can be no clear and reasonable difference to base it upon, separation cannot be justified by mere prejudice. Nor is merit a test. . . .
>
> [The carrier] may use his property . . . in a reasonable manner. It is not an unreasonable regulation to seat passengers so as to preserve order and decorum, and to prevent contacts and collisions arising from natural and well-known customary repugnancies, which are likely to breed disturbance by a promiscuous sitting. This is a proper use of the right of private property, because it tends to protect the interests of the carrier as well as the interests of those he carries. . . . The right of the passenger is only that of being carried safely, and with a due regard to his personal comfort and convenience, which are promoted by a sound and well-regulated separation of passengers. . . .
>
> The public also has an interest in the proper regulation of public conveyances for the preservation of the public peace. A railroad company has the right and is bound to make reasonable regulations to preserve order in their

[1] 55 Pa. 209 (1867).

cars. . . . It is much easier to prevent difficulties among passengers by regulations for their proper separation, than it is to quell them. . . . If a negro take his seat beside a white man or his wife or daughter, the law cannot repress the anger, or conquer the aversion which some will feel. However unwise it may be to indulge the feeling, human infirmity is not always proof against it. It is much wiser to avert the consequences of this repulsion of race by separation, than to punish afterward the breach of the peace it may have caused.

The right to separate being clear in proper cases . . . the question remaining to be considered is, whether there is such a difference between the white and black races. . . , resulting from nature, law and custom, as makes it a reasonable ground of separation. The question is one of difference, not of superiority or inferiority. Why the Creator made one black and the other white, we know not; but the fact is apparent and the races distinct, each producing its own kind, and following the peculiar law of its constitution. Conceding equality, with natures as perfect and rights as sacred, yet God has made them dissimilar, with those natural feelings and instincts He always imparts to His creatures when He intends that they shall not overstep the natural boundaries He has assigned to them. The natural law which forbids their intermarriage and that social amalgamation which leads to a corruption of races, is as clearly divine as that which imparted to them different natures. . . . The natural separation of the races is . . . an undeniable fact, and all social organizations which lead to their amalgamation are repugnant to the law of nature. From social amalgamation it is but a step to illicit intercourse, and but another to intermarriage. But to assert separateness is not to declare inferiority in either. . . . It is simply to say that following the order of Divine Providence, human authority ought not to compel these widely separated races to intermix. . . .

Although the decision of the Louisiana Supreme Court in *De Cuir* v. *Benson*[1] was soon overruled by the Supreme Court of the United States,[2] the case is of peculiar interest because it anticipates, by more than half a century, the legal logic that the United States Supreme Court was itself later to accept. A Louisiana law of 1869, passed during Reconstruction days, forbade common carriers to discriminate against passengers because of race or color.

The case arose when Mrs. Josephine De Cuir, a light-skinned Negro, undertook to travel by steamboat from New Orleans to her plantation in the Parish of Pointe Coupe. She was refused a berth and dining room service because of her color, and was directed instead to a small rear compartment of the vessel. An educated woman who had lived for a time in Paris, she sued for $25,000 actual damages, and $50,000 exemplary damages, on the ground that her rights under the constitutions and laws of the United States and Louisiana had been violated, and that the refusal to accommodate her had been "an indignity to her personally, which shocked her feelings and caused her mental pain, shame, and mortification."

[1] 27 La. Ann. 1 (1875).
[2] See above, p. 62.

The court raised two questions: (1) Was the statute of 1869 an infraction of the clause in the Constitution of the United States which gives Congress exclusive jurisdiction over interstate commerce? (2) Did the statute violate the rights protected by the Fourteenth Amendment?

The act does not make any regulation of commerce. The act was passed to carry into effect the provisions of Article 13 of the State Constitution which [guarantees equal treatment for all persons in public conveyances and facilities]. . . . It was enacted solely to protect the newly enfranchised citizens of the United States, within the limits of Louisiana, from the effects of prejudice against them. It does not, in any manner, affect the commercial interest of any State or foreign nation or of the citizens thereof.

The objection that the [statute] violates Section 1 of Article 14 is utterly untenable. No one is deprived of life, liberty, or property, without due process of law by said statute. The position that because one's property cannot be taken without due process of law, therefore a common carrier can conduct his business as he chooses without reference to the rights of the public, is so illogical that it is only necessary to state it to expose its fallacy. . . . In truth the right of the plaintiff to sue the defendant for damages would be the same, whether [the 1869 statute] existed or not; but the act is in perfect accord with the Constitution of the United States. . . . It is settled, in this state at least, that colored persons now have all the civil and political rights which white persons enjoy. . . .

That the common carrier may make reasonable rules and regulations for the government of the passengers on board his boat or vessel is admitted, but it cannot be pretended that a regulation, which is founded on prejudice and which is in violation of law is reasonable. . . .

C. *Segregated Schools Sustained*

State constitutional and statutory support of segregation in the public schools—whether by failure to include black children in the general provision of schools for the children of the state, or by authorizing or requiring separate schools—were commonplace before 1865.[1] Even under Radical Reconstruction, southern states were permitted to separate the races in schools, and it is by no means certain that the framers of the Fourteenth Amendment intended the equal protection clause to forbid this form of racial distinction throughout the country.[2] Such challenges as did reach the state courts in this period came in nonsouthern states, and brought judicial approval of school segregation. No cases arose in which the United States Supreme Court ruled otherwise. An Illinois court, however, in *Chase* v. *Stephenson,* although it

1 Stephenson, *Race Distinctions*, pp. 165–69.

2 Alfred H. Kelly and Winfred A. Harbison, *The American Constitution; Its Origins and Development*, 3rd ed. (New York, 1963), p. 462.

left unanswered what its ruling might have been if a hundred children, instead of three or four, had been involved, declared that keeping a separate school for a mere three or four colored children could properly be stopped by taxpayers who might object to such extravagance. Conceding that a school district's directors did have large discretionary powers to operate the schools in the absence of statutory directives concerning the separation or mixing of the races in schools, they did not, said the court "have power to make class distinctions, nor can they discriminate . . . on account of color, race, or social position." Nor could they, if taxpayers desired otherwise, maintain a separate school for a tiny number of colored children when there was "a white school convenient to them."[1]

More typical was this ruling in California in the same year:[2]

Mary Frances Ward, a black child, was taken to be enrolled in a public school near her home in San Francisco. After her rejection by the principal, Noah F. Flood, her parents appealed to the state courts for a writ of mandamus, compelling Flood to admit her. In considering the plea, the Supreme Court of California observed that a school principal may on certain grounds decline to enroll a child, and that the privilege of attending a public school is not a privilege pertaining to or derived from *national* citizenship. Then, noting that California's constitution guaranteed to children the benefits of a common school system, the court denied the writ on the premise that separate facilities do not inherently discriminate more heavily against one race than another (since each group is excluded from the other's schools) and do not therefore constitute the sort of denial of equal protection of the laws that the Fourteenth Amendment forbids:

> In short the policy of separation of the races for educational purposes is adopted by the legislative department, and it is in this mere policy that the counsel for the petitioner professes to discern "an odious distinction of cast[e], founded on a deep-rooted prejudice in public opinion." But it is hardly necessary to remind counsel that we cannot deal here with such matters, and that our duties lie wholly within the much narrower range of determining whether this statute, in whatever mode it originated, denied to the petitioner, in a constitutional sense, the equal protection of the laws; and in the circumstances that the races are separated in the public schools, there is certainly to be found no violation of the constitutional rights of the one race more than of the other, and we see none of either, for each, though separated from the other, is to be educated upon equal terms with the other, and both at the common public expense. . . .

A decade after *Ward* v. *Flood,* the New York Court of Appeals upheld separate schools for black children on similar grounds. A statute

[1] 71 Ill. 383 (1874).
[2] *Ward* v. *Flood,* 48 Cal. 36 (1874).

of 1864 authorized such segregation if the school authorities deemed it in the best interests of education. In *People* v. *Gallagher*[1] a twelve-year-old Negro child, whose parents complained not that she was barred from an education equal to that of white children, but "she is not receiving those facilities at the precise place which would be most gratifying to her feelings," had been denied a writ of mandamus by the city court of Brooklyn. The Court of Appeals, in the case at hand, affirmed that judgment. Separate schools, declared Chief Justice Ruger, do not violate the privileges-and-immunities or equal-protection clauses of the Fourteenth Amendment so long as the privilege of securing an education at public expense is available to all children "under the same advantages."

[Chief Justice Ruger:] It would be unfortunate if it should be found that any imperative rule of law prevents those who are charged with the management of the common schools of the State, from adopting such arrangements for instruction as their experience had shown to be adapted to the highest educational interests of the people. . . . The system of authorizing the education of the two races separately has been for many years the settled policy of all departments of the State government, and it is believed obtains very generally in the States of the Union. . . .

It would seem to be a plain deduction from the rule in [the *Slaughter House Cases*] that the privilege of receiving an education at the expense of the State, being created and conferred solely by the laws of the State, and always subject to its discretionary regulation, might be granted or refused to any individual or class at the pleasure of the State. . . .

The right of the individual, as affected by the question in hand, is to secure equal advantages in obtaining an education at public expense, and where that privilege is afforded him by the school authorities, he cannot justly claim that his educational privileges have been abridged, although such privileges are not accorded him at the precise place where he most desires to receive them. . . . Equality and not identity of privileges and rights is what is guaranteed to the citizen, and this we have seen the [appellant] enjoy. . . . It is not discrimination between the two races which is prohibited by law, but discrimination against the interests of the colored race.

D. *Vocational Exclusions Approved*

Laws or other state action closing particular employments to Negroes were not extensively challenged in the state courts during these years. One rare instance is that testing a Maryland statute which in effect barred Negroes from the legal profession.[2]

Charles Taylor, a colored citizen of Maryland, applied for admission to the Maryland bar, but was prevented by a recent statute (1876) which limited such admission to "white male citizens above the age of

[1] 93 N.Y. 438 (1883).
[2] *In re Taylor*, 48 Md. 28 (1877).

twenty-one years." Claiming protection under the rights clauses of the Fourteenth Amendment, Taylor appealed to the state's supreme bench. The court denied his plea.

> [Chief Justice Bartol]: In our opinion [the *Slaughter House* decisions] are conclusive of the present case. They determine that the 14th Amendment has no application. . . . The privilege of admission to the office of an attorney cannot be said to be a right or immunity belonging to the citizen, but is governed and regulated by the Legislature, who may prescribe the qualifications required, and designate the class of persons who may be admitted. The power of regulating the admission of attorneys in the courts of a State, is one belonging to the State and not to the Federal Government. As said by Mr. Justice Bradley in *Bradwell's Case,* "In the nature of things, it is not every citizen of every age, sex and condition that is qualified for every calling and position. It is the prerogative of the Legislature to prescribe regulations founded on nature, reason and experience, for the due admission of qualified persons to professions and callings demanding special skill and confidence. This fairly belongs to the police power of the state."

E. *Definitions of the "Negro" Appraised*

As legal distinctions between the races multiplied, it became increasingly necessary to define exactly what a Negro is. Many states, as we have seen,[1] either by constitutional provisions or by statute, carefully designated as Negroes persons having, e.g., "one-fourth negro blood," or "one-eighth African blood," or "any trace of African blood whatsoever." In the absence of such precise formulas, the courts were sometimes called on to pronounce upon this baffling question. Two answers from Michigan and Ohio—more liberal, apparently, than most of the statutory definitions or public attitudes on the problem—follow:

Michigan's constitution confined the right to vote to "white male citizens." A man named Dean, presumed to be one-sixteenth black, and otherwise white except for a trace of Indian blood, was prosecuted for voting in violation of the constitutional restriction. The Michigan Superior Court took the pragmatic position that persons who are more than three-fourths white are to be considered white within the meaning of the clause. Justice Campbell spoke for the majority:[2]

> . . . persons are white within the meaning of our constitution, in whom white blood so far preponderates that they have less than one-fourth of African blood; and that no other persons of African descent can be so regarded. As the defendant came very far within this rule, I think a new trial should be granted.

But the more liberal Chief Justice, though outnumbered by his fellow judges, dissented:

[1] See above, p. 80, and below, p. 131.
[2] *People* v. *Dean,* 14 Mich. 406 (1866).

> . . . A *preponderance*[1] of blood decides the question of the right to vote, and . . . within the letter and meaning of [the constitution] Dean is white, and would have been, had he possessed much more African blood than he is shown to have.

An Ohio law of 1868 denied the vote to persons with "a visible admixture of African blood," unless they met certain additional requirements not laid upon whites. A man named Collins, admitting his part-African ancestry, brought suit because he was excluded from an election in Xenia, Ohio. The view expressed by the Ohio Supreme Court was, of course, strongly at variance with state constitutions and statutes in the South.[2]

> A colored man . . . having more white than black blood, is a *white man* within the meaning of the constitution, and the legislature have no more power to deny or intrench upon his right to vote, than they have to deny or intrench upon that of a man of pure white blood.

F. *Unequal Punishment for Blacks Upheld*

State laws prescribing severer punishment for blacks than for whites committing the same offense, and severer penalties for *both* parties to an offense when one was a Negro than for the two parties when both were members of the same race, were with few exceptions concerned with interracial marriages and interracial extramarital sexual relations. The cases that follow are representative of controversies arising under such statutes.

Thornton Ellis, descended from African ancestors, and Susan Bishop, white, were indicted in Alabama for "living together in adultery or fornication." Section 3598 of the state code fixed the standard penalties for this offense, but section 3602 provided substantially harsher punishment when the offense was committed by an interracial pair. The lower state court had refused to impose the penalty, presumably on the assumption that the discrimination violated the federal Civil Rights Act of 1866. The Alabama Supreme Court ruled, however, that the statute under scrutiny was not illegal, so long as both parties to the offense were subject to the same penalties.[3]

> We think the court erred in the conclusion that #3602 contravenes the act of Congress. That act requires that persons of "every race and color . . . shall be subject to like punishment, pains and penalities, and to none other." It prohibits a discrimination, on account of color or race, in the imposition of

[1] Emphasis added.
[2] *Monroe* v. *Collins,* 17 Ohio 665 (1867).
[3] *Ellis* v. *State,* 42 Ala. 525 (1868).

punishment. It does not prohibit the making of race and color a constituent of an offense, provided it does not lead to a discrimination in punishment. #3602 creates an offense, of which a participation by persons of different race is an element. To constitute the offense, there must be not only criminal intercourse, but it must be by persons of different race. When the constituents of the offense are ascertained, no discrimination in punishment is made between the guilty white and black parties. The white man who lives in adultery with a black woman is punished in precisely the same manner, and to the same extent, with the black woman. So also the white woman is punishable in precisely the same manner with the black man with whom she may have maintained an adulterous connexion. Adultery between persons of different races is the same crime as to white persons and negroes, and subject to the same punishment.

Seven years later the same tribunal reviewed a lower court's conviction of a white man and a black woman who had been indicted for "living together in adultery and fornication." Appellants' counsel had argued that the legislature was forbidden by the Fourteenth Amendment's equal protection clause to enact that an offense which, when committed by persons of the same race was a misdemeanor, became a felony when committed by persons of diverse races. But the court brushed this logic aside on the theory that interracial sexual transgressions are more heinous than those committed by persons of the same race: "Every state has the right to regulate its domestic affairs, and to adopt a domestic policy most conducive to the interest and welfare of the people. . . . Living in adultery is offensive to all laws human and divine, and human laws must impose punishments adequate to the enormity of the offense and its insult to public decency."[1]

In still another decision[2] later sustained by the United States Supreme Court[3] the Alabama Supreme Court again approved the proposition that interracial adultery should properly be more harshly punished than adultery committed by persons of the same race. The reasoning on which the court constructed its opinion is interesting as an example of the increasingly explicit judicial invocation of the "race-mongrelization" argument, which had captured the public mind long before it found such candid articulation on the bench.

The statute, under which this indictment is found, is not, in our opinion, obnoxious to any constitutional objection. It is not, as insisted by appellants' counsel, violative of the first section of the Fourteenth Amendment. . . . The punishment of each offending party, white and black, is precisely the same. There is obviously no difference or discrimination in the punishment. The evil tendency of the crime of living in adultery or fornication is greater when it is committed between persons of the two races, than between persons of the same race. Its result may be the amalgamation of the two races,

[1] *Ford* v. *State,* 53 Ala. 150 (1875).
[2] *Pace and Cox* v. *State,* 69 Ala. 231 (1881).
[3] See above, p. 66.

producing a mongrel population and a degraded civilization, the prevention of which is dictated by a sound public policy affecting the highest interests of society and government. To thus punish the crime denounced by the statute, by imposing the same term of imprisonment and the identical amount of fine upon each and every person guilty of it, can in no sense result in any inequality in the operation or protection of the law. . . .

PART THREE

Fading Hopes: 1883–1910

AFTER 1875, the Congress did not again until 1957 enact a single law to protect or promote the Negro's civil and legal status. The period now to be reviewed opened in the wake of the *Civil Rights Cases,* which had signalized the intention of the federal judiciary to decline the role of guarantor of the Negro's rights, privileges, and immunities; it closed with the launching of the National Association for the Advancement of Colored People, which in the succeeding era would mount a vigorous offensive in the Afro-American's behalf.

In the country at large—but especially in the South—extreme racism captured the public mind, extending even to the pulpit, the scholar's study, and the bench. Barred almost completely from any but the most menial employments, increasingly segregated both by public authority and private proscription, hustled from the polls, and excluded from juries, the harassed black man found little refuge in the courts even when constitutions and laws were on his side. Lynchings, the overwhelming majority of them in the South, reached their awesome crescendo in these years (there were 235 in 1892 alone), averaging three per week for two decades.

The shift of the Afro-American population to the city had now begun. It may be doubted that more than 15 percent of the nation's blacks lived in cities in 1883; by 1910 the figure stood at 27.4 percent and was rapidly accelerating. The massive movement to the North was not yet fairly under way, however, for the proportion living in the South had been 90 percent in 1883, and in 1910 was still 89 percent.

It was in this period also that the legal framework of compulsory segregation was constructed in the southern commonwealths, paralleled by the more casual extralegal patterns of *apartheid* in the rest of the country. And it was in these years that the accommodationist philosophy of Booker T. Washington recommended itself to whites, as well as to Negroes who had come to believe that this sacrifice would purchase for them early economic and social gains, at least for the foreseeable future, as the best *modus vivendi.* The ascendancy, in this era, of popular racist theory and of downright *fear* of the Negro, buttressed by pseudo-scientific sanctions, and religious primitivism, and exacerbated by the changing immigration flow from Europe that threatened the old Anglo-

Puritan model, lent further authority to the country's deepening determination to "keep the Negro in his place."

The prevailing conservative drift in legislative and judicial attitudes (not, after all, seriously countered even by the "Progressive Movement" of the first decade of the twentieth century) conspired further against the Negro's advance. A minority, systematically deprived of economic and social opportunity, to say nothing of a *hearing* in the nation's counsels, was peculiarly defenseless and precariously dependent for its social redemption upon an activist, welfare-oriented state—precisely at a time when the dominant laissez-faireism made that recourse unavailable.

It is hardly surprising that a leading student of this era of Afro-American history, Rayford Logan, should have called the first edition of his book, which covered the years 1877 to 1901, *The Negro in American Life and Thought: The Nadir;* and that the revised edition, which extended the study to 1912, was named, *The Betrayal of the Negro.* And yet, there were signs, occasional glimmerings on the horizon, that the deepening darkness would be followed by a hopeful dawn.

(1)

RACIAL IDEOLOGY: TURN-OF-THE-CENTURY VIEWS

Fears of the black male's presumed lust for white women, and of the "mongrelization" of the white race, combined with apprehensions that the blacks would overrun the white man's employments, his neighborhoods, churches, and schools, and even wrest from him his traditional monopoly of government, intensified the search for sanctions in religion and science to justify the sequestering of the Afro-Americans. A steadily growing body of racial ideology, some samples of which are herewith presented, supplied the need. But it began also, though on only a tiny scale as yet, to evoke some rebuttal, as the quoted excerpt from Franz Boas (p. 109) illustrates. Such formal treatises did not reach so wide an audience in the South as did the new leaders of the masses like James K. Vardaman in Mississippi, "Pitchfork Ben" Tillman in South Carolina, and Tom Watson in Georgia, who preached a curious mixture of progressive democracy and strident denunciation of the Negro—a sure-fire appeal for the common white man's vote.

C. Vann Woodward has demonstrated that the South's capitulation to extreme racism in this era was due less to conversion than to the relaxation of the opposition. Intemperate racism had always been common enough. What was new was the circumstance that the more responsible men who had held it in check in the past were now supplanted by a new breed: southern conservatives who had abandoned the older caution, and Populists who had shed much of their reformist zeal, while northern concern for the Negro's predicament had nearly vanished.

James K. Vardaman who campaigned—successfully—for the governorship of Mississippi in 1900, on an eight-wheeled lumber wagon pulled by eight yoke of oxen, excited the passions of back-country yokels by screaming that "we would be justified in slaughtering every Ethiop on earth to preserve unsullied the honor of one Caucasian home." The Negro, said he, is a "lazy, lying, lustful animal which no conceivable amount of training can transform into a tolerable citizen." And again, "Anything that causes the negro to aspire above . . . the functions of a servant, will be the worst thing for [him]." On another occasion he thundered, "I am opposed to negro voting; . . . I am just as much opposed to Booker Washington as a voter, with all his Anglo-Saxon reinforcements, as I am to the cocoanut-headed, chocolate-colored, typical little coon, Andy Dotson, who blacks my shoes every morning. Neither is fit to perform the supreme function of citizenship."

In South Carolina, Ben Tillman vowed that *"Governor as I am, I'd lead a mob to lynch a man* who had ravished a white woman. . . . I justify lynching for rape, and, before Almighty God, I'm not ashamed of it"; and Tom Watson, leader of the Agrarian malcontents in Georgia, was equally certain that the Negro had "no comprehension of virtue, honesty, truth, gratitude and principle . . . [and that the South was forced] to lynch him occasionally, and flog him, now and then, to keep him from blaspheming the Almighty, by his conduct, on account of his smell and his color."[1]

A typical example of the literature written to support such racist views is found in a volume published in 1900, in which the author passionately maintains the propositions that the Negro is not a human being but an ape, and that it was the white man's lustful association with the animal which in gross fashion resembled him that was the real original sin and has ever since been *the* cardinal transgression toward which God's wrath is directed.[2]

1 William A. Sinclair, *The Aftermath of Slavery* (Boston, 1905), p. 196; Thomas F. Gossett, *Race: The History of an Idea in America* (Dallas, 1963), p. 271; George Brown Tindall, *South Carolina Negroes, 1877–1900* (Columbia, 1952), pp. 251–52.

2 Charles Carroll, *"The Negro a Beast," or "In the Image of God"; the Reasoner of the Age, the Revelator of the Century! The Bible as it is. The Negro and his Relation to the Human Family! . . . . The Negro not the Son of Ham* (St. Louis, 1900). The paragraphs here given are from pp. 87, 88, 221, 233–34, 339–49, 367.

All scientific investigation . . . proves the Negro to be an ape, . . . stand[ing] at the head of the ape family, as the lion stands at the head of the cat family. When God's plan of creation [is] properly understood, it will be found that the teachings of scripture upon this, as upon every other subject, harmonize with those of science. . . . [I]t follows that the Negro is the only anthropoid, or man-like ape; and that the gibbon, ourang, chimpanzee and gorilla are merely negro-like apes. Hence, to recognize the Negro as a "man and a brother," they were compelled to declare man an ape. Thus the modern Christian, like the atheist, takes man, whom God created "in his own image," and takes the Negro, whom God made "after his kind"—the ape kind—and places them in the same family, as different "races" of one "species" of animal. . . .

The Bible plainly teaches that man was created a single pair, "in the image of God." And we feel assured that a careful consideration of this subject must lead any rational mind to decide that the White, with his exalted physical and mental characters, and the Negro with his ape-like physical and mental characters, are not the progeny of one primitive pair. . . . [I]f the White was created "in the image of God," then the Negro was made after some other model. And a glance at the Negro indicates the model; his very appearance suggests the ape.

. . . It seems plain that in addition to his general plan of salvation God devised a great labor plan for development of the resources of the earth. That the execution of this plan was entrusted to man, who was designed to perform the mental labor. That the beasts or apes should furnish in the negro the creature which, in the capacity of servant, should perform the manual labor.

The Bible is simply a history of the long conflict which has raged between God and man, as the result of man's criminal relations with the negro. [And] when we accept the teachings of scripture that man is a distinct creation "in the image of God;" and that the negro is an ape; and that man's criminal relations with the negro have been the prolific source of all the trouble between God and man since the Creation, the mystery with which atheism has enveloped the Bible disappears. . . .

The Negro, being an ape, entered the ark with the rest of the animals; and as the descendants of Noah spread out over the earth they carried with them their negroes and other domestic animals, domestic plants, metallic implements, etc., and developed those superb civilizations the remains of which are found on every continent of the earth. . . . These people respected the design of God in creating man, in obedience to his law, and maintained the relation of master and servant between themselves and the Negro, and were happy and prosperous. But in the course of ages they forgot God, descended to amalgamation, and this, in its turn, gave birth to idolatry. Then. . . . God in his wrath and disgust showered his curses upon them in the form of war, famine, pestilence and disease. . . , laid their civilizations in ruins, and transformed their once prosperous country into the abode of savages; or left . . . their civilization to descend to their mixed-blooded descendants, as in the case of the Mexicans, Peruvians, Malays, Hindoos, Chinese, Japanese, Koreans, etc., and these barbarous creatures possess them today.

In A.D. 1867, there appeared . . . a work entitled, "The Negro, What is His Ethnological Status?" by the Rev. B. H. Payne, who wrote under the nom de plume of "Ariel." He asserted that the Negro is . . . "not a descendant of Adam or Eve," that he is simply "a beast," and that he has "no soul."

History will yet accord to "Ariel" the proud distinction of being the first man of modern times to . . . fearlessly declare the negro "a beast," and support his declaration with scriptural proof. . . . The laurels that adorn his brow . . . will grow brighter as "the years roll on." [S]ufficient for us is the honor of being "A [fellow] worker for the Lord" and humanity in that great cause, which, sooner or later will culminate in the expulsion of the negro from his present unnatural position in the family of man, and the resumption of his proper place among the apes.

. . . The presence of the Negro and his amalgamated progeny in the family of man, and in the church, is largely due to [the] anti-scriptural and erroneous theory that mind and soul are identical. . . . Nothing is more common than to hear the defenders of the Negro exclaim. "The Negro has a mind; he reasons, forms ideas and expresses them; he can distinguish between right and wrong, and this proves that he is a man with an immortal soul and may be civilized, enlightened and Christianized!" This is absolutely no evidence at all! Mind is common to all animals; they all reason, form ideas and convey them by certain sounds and signs, though in less degree than man.

The excitement created by Carroll's book provoked a long rebuttal from the Rev. W. S. Armistead, from whose volume the following passage is taken.[1] The bulk of the book is devoted to proof that the Negro is not a beast but a thoroughly depraved man, and therefore even more dangerous than Carroll supposed him to be. Armistead concluded his volume with this warning:

It may be concluded, from the argument made in defense of the negro['s] . . . right to claim a common parentage with the White, and his descent from the Original Pair,—that I am the advocate of *negro political,* and *social, equality—followed by race intermingling or intermarriage.* Without a moment's hesitation do I declare that I am *not* an *advocate* of such *equality.* . . . Intermarriage of whites and blacks from my standpoint is interdicted of God! . . . Whatever His decision is must be absolutely right, for Infinite Wisdom cannot err. . . .

The hope of the blacks is posited on prohibition of anything that looks like, or approaches Racial Socialism. He . . . must have, the *white man,* as his exemplar—his stimulus—to high endeavor and great undertaking. He needs him as his *guide* in . . . life, and his *chaperone* to the skies.

The hope of the whites is alike *posited* on the *deadliest opposition,* the most determined *antagonism* to *Racial Equalization.* Therefore I favor *digging deeper* the *foundations* and *building higher* the *walls* that *intervene Racial Social Equality.* God has drawn the line—*a continental one.* To remove it would be the ruin of the negro race; to abolish it would be to destroy the white race morally and religiously. . . .

There is another subject of vast importance to both whites and blacks, . . . I refer to the practice of the blacks in *assaulting* white females. A more *dangerous practice* could have never been *started* by *the blacks.* Were there no other argument against *social equality* . . . I would urge the *brutality* of such *outrageous conduct* as *evidence* of the *strongest character* that the *blacks* were not *prepared* for such *social* relations with the whites. For a strong man to meet an unprotected female in some lonely place, seize her person, choke

[1] *The Negro Is a Man* (Tifton, Georgia, 1903), pp. 536–41, *passim.*

her to insensibility and rape her person, and then, in most instances, murder her to prevent detection, argues a *beastliness,* a *cold-blooded, murderous heart,* a *depth of criminality* that *demonstrates fitness for equalization with beasts, rather than with human beings.* . . . The whites have never pursued such a course towards *black* females,. . . True, white men . . . have carnal association with black women and girls, but such association is . . . conceded by the colored woman or girl, of *her own free will,* and rarely is it ever *forced.* Such a thing as a white man's meeting a colored woman or girl in some secluded place, and waylaying her, seizing her person, choking her into insensibility, ravishing her person and murdering her to prevent detection and punishment, has never been practiced by . . . even the lowest and most degraded [whites]. So . . . the blacks have no provocation, no excuse for such outrages.

In William Benjamin Smith's *The Color Line,*[1] the alarmed author begins with a reference to Theodore Roosevelt's hospitality to Booker T. Washington at the White House, and then proceeds with majestic instancy to what some wits have call "the post-prandial non sequitur." The menace he warned of was, however, no laughing matter to countless southerners, or, for that matter, to considerable numbers of northerners.

. . . In the controversy precipitated by the luncheon at the White House, . . . the attitude of the South presents an element of the pathetic. The great world is apparently hopelessly against her. Three-fourths of the virtue, culture, and intelligence of the United States seems to view her with pitying scorn; . . . England has no word of sympathy, but applauds the conduct that her daughter reprehends; . . . Europe looks on with amused perplexity . . . .

What . . . is the real point at issue, and what does the South stand for in this contention—stand alone, friendless, despised, with the head and heart, the brain and brawn, the wealth and culture of the civilized world arrayed almost solidly against her? The answer is simple: She stands for *blood,* for the *continuous germ-plasme of the Caucasian Race.* . . .

. . . Southerners are merely human; and there is, perhaps no great historical example of an inferior race or class treated with all proper consideration by the superior. . . . Tried by this standard, it is very doubtful whether the South falls even one notch below the average set everywhere by the example of the ruling class. If she does, then let her bear the blame, with neither excuse nor extenuation for her shortcomings. But in the matter of social separation we can and we will make no concessions whatever. . . . Here, then, is laid bare the nerve of the whole matter: *Is the South justified in this absolute denial of social equality to the Negro, no matter what his virtues or abilities or accomplishments?*

We affirm, then, that the South is entirely right in thus keeping open at all times, at all hazards, and at all sacrifices an impassable social chasm between Black and White. This she *must* do in behalf of her blood, her essence, of the stock of her Caucasian Race. . . . Is there any doubt whatever as to the alternative? If we sit with Negroes at our tables, if we entertain them as our guests and social equals, if we disregard the colour line in all other relations, is it possible to maintain it fixedly in the sexual relation, in the marriage of

[1] (New York, 1905), pp. 3–9.

our sons and daughters, in the propagation of our species? Unquestionably, No! It is certain as the rising of tomorrow's sun, that, once the middle wall of social partition is broken down, the mingling of the tides of life would begin instantly and proceed steadily. . . . It would make itself felt at first most strongly in the lower strata of the white population; but it would soon invade the middle and menace insidiously the very uppermost. Many bright Mulattoes would ambitiously woo, . . . and . . . win well-bred women disappointed in love or goaded by impulse. . . . *As a race, the Southern Caucasian would be irreversibly doomed.* . . . Remove the barrier between two streams flowing side by side—immediately they begin to mingle their molecules; in vain you attempt to replace it . . . The moment the bar of absolute separation is thrown down in the South, that moment the bloom of her spirit is blighted forever, the promise of her destiny is annulled, the proud fabric of her future slips into dust and ashes. No other conceivable disaster that might befall the South could, for an instant, compare with such miscegenation within her borders. Flood and fire, fever and famine and the sword—even ignorance, indolence, and carpet-baggery—she may endure and conquer while her blood remains pure; but once taint the well-spring of her life, and all is lost—even honour itself. It is this immediate jewel of her soul that the South watches with such a dragon eye, that she guards with more than vestal vigilance, with a circle of perpetual fire. . . .

Quoted here are excerpts from a monograph published under the impressive imprimatur of an immensely respected professional association of scholars.[1]

For the root of the evil lies in the fact of an immense amount of immorality, which is a race trait, and of which scrofula, syphilis, and even consumption are the inevitable consequences. So long as more than one-fourth (26.5 per cent. in 1894) of the births for the colored population of Washington are illegitimate . . . , in which at the same time only 2.6 per cent. of the births among the whites are illegitimate,—it is plain why we should meet with a mortality from scrofula and syphilis so largely in excess of that of the whites. And it is also plain now, that we have reached the underlying causes of the excessive mortality from consumption and the enormous waste of child life. It is not in the *conditions of life*, but in *the race traits and tendencies* that we find the causes of the excessive mortality. So long as immorality and vice are a habit of life of the vast majority of the colored population, the effect will be to increase the mortality by hereditary transmission of weak constitutions, and to lower still further the rate of natural increase, until the births fall below the deaths, and gradual extinction results. . . .

The two essential virtues of modern progress, self reliance and chastity, have not been the result of easy conditions of life. Self reliance in the Anglo-Saxon race is the result of the struggle of ages rather than of book education or missionary efforts. . . . Self reliance in man and chastity in woman are qualities that must be developed, and thus far they have not been developed by the aid of charity or liberal philanthropy.

A study of the race traits and tendencies of the negro in America makes plain the failure of modern education and other means in encouraging . . .

[1] Frederick L. Hoffman, *Race Traits and Tendencies of the American Negro,* in *Publications of the American Economic Association,* xi, 1–3 (New York, 1896), 95, 327, 329.

the development of these most important factors, without which no race has ever yet been able to gain a permanent civilization. Easy conditions of life, a liberal construction of the doctrine of the forgiveness of sins and an unwarranted extension of the principle of state or private interference in the conduct of individual life, have never yet raised a race or individual from a lower to a higher plane. . . .

All the facts brought together in this work prove that the colored population is gradually parting with the virtues and the moderate degree of economic efficiency developed under the regime of slavery. All the facts prove that a low standard of sexual morality is the main and underlying cause of the low and anti-social condition of the race at the present time. All the facts prove that education, philanthropy and religion have failed to develop a higher appreciation of the stern and uncompromising virtues of the Aryan race. . . . [I]t is merely a question of time when the actual downward course . . . will take place. In the meantime, however, the presence of the colored population is a serious hindrance to the economic progress of the white race.

G. Stanley Hall was holder of the nation's first Ph. D. in psychology, founder of the psychological laboratory at the Johns Hopkins University (1883) and of the *American Journal of Psychology* (1887), first president of the American Psychological Association (1891), and president of Clark University (1899–1919). He shared the views of Social Darwinists that nature had marked inferior peoples, like Negroes, for lesser roles in society and, perhaps, for eventual extinction:[1]

In history no two races . . . differ so much in their traits, both physical and psychic, as the Caucasian and the African. The color of the skin and the crookedness of the hair are only the outward signs of many far deeper differences, including cranial and thoracic capacity, proportions of body, nervous system, glands and secretions, vita sexualis, food, temperament, disposition, character, longevity, instincts, customs, emotional traits, and diseases. All these differences, as they are coming to be better understood, are seen to be so great as to qualify if not imperil every inference from one race to another, whether theoretical or practical, so that what is true and good for one is often false and bad for the other. [T]he emancipation destroyed much of the interest of slave owners in their chattels, so that intimate knowledge of the blacks by the whites in the South has in many respects steadily declined since the war. . . . On the other hand, during this period a new scientific study of the negro has arisen, and is fast developing established results which are slowly placing the problems of the future of this race upon a more solid and intelligent basis, and which seem destined sooner or later to condition philanthropy and legislation, make sentiment more intelligent, and take the problem out of the hands of politicians, sentimentalists, or theorists, and place it where it belongs,—with economists, anthropologists, and sociologists.

To select the single question of health from many of the racial differences above enumerated, we find . . . that [Negroes'] diseases are very different from ours . . . having a different prognosis and requir[ing] modifications of

[1] G. Stanley Hall, "A Few Results of Recent Scientific Study of the Negro in America," *Proceedings of the Massachusetts Historical Society,* 2d ser., 19 (1905), 95–107 *passim.* Reprinted by permission of the Massachusetts Historical Society.

treatment, so that the training of physicians for the two races needs differentiation. Immune to many conditions morbific for Caucasians, they are very susceptible to others harmless to whites. In tropical Africa men and women are extremely fond of bathing, which their very active skin needs; but this disposition decreases almost exactly as clothing increases, and as the negro goes North is often changed into exceptional aversion to the bath which is suggestive for cooks and nurses. . . . a Southern physician has said . . . that a successful experience in treating one race impaired a physician's usefulness with the other, and made two hygienes and two regimens necessary. . . .

The chief event in the history of the Southern negro is the infiltration of white blood [without which] the negro in mind and body would be so distinct from us that all our problems connected with the race would be vastly simplified. . . . The extreme minimal estimate that I have found is that one-tenth have some white blood, and one maximal estimate is that two-thirds are partly white. . . .

Whatever the biological laws may be, they are, however, here obscured and rendered ineffective by social prejudice which draws a color line and ostracizes not only quadroons and octoroons, but those with one-sixteenth, one thirty-second, and, Booker Washington says, one one-hundredth negro blood, even though it be so attenuated as to leave no sign discernible save by scrutiny of hair, nails, etc., and condemns mulattoes of whatever degree to association with those whose pure Hamitic blood has known no dash or strain of white. It is this that has intensified racial solidarity and helps to make every question in the South tend to become a race question, and often now divides Southern towns and cities by a color line so drawn that instead of the best whites seeing most of the best mulattoes, the former prefer contact with the pure blacks, and race friction is between the lower whites and the mulattoes. Whether the mulattoes are better or worse than either parent race, prejudice, not only in our own, but in every land where the races coexist, has made it impossible to tell. While there are some pure Africans born with gifts far above the average of their race, most of its leaders are those who have by heredity, association, or both, derived most from the whites. It is their aspirations, discontent, struggles, ending often in discouragement, which makes them either sink to vice or grow revengeful and desperate, that constitute the pathos of the present condition, and make it hardest for the men to preserve their hope and just ambition, and for the women to keep their virtue in the presence of the whites. A recent writer says, "Ninety-nine percent of the whites regard all with any negro blood as about alike." . . .

. . . Another racial trait of the negro is found in the sphere of sexual development. Special studies show that the negro child up to about twelve is quite as bright as the white child; but when this instinct develops it is earlier, more sudden, and far more likely permanently to retard mental and moral growth, than in the white, who shoots ahead. Thus the virtues and defects of the negro through life remain largely those of puberty. Hence his disthesis, both psychic and physical, is erethic, volatile, changeable, prone to trancoidal, intensely emotional, and even epileptoid states. W. H. Thomas, himself a negro, in his book entitled "The American Negro," says, "The chief and overpowering element in his make-up is an imperious sexual impulse, which, aroused at the slightest incentive, sweeps aside all restraint." This he deems the chief cause of the arrest of the higher development of this tropical race. During slavery regular hard work, temperance, awe of his

> white master, were potent restraints. . . . Now idleness, drink, and a new sense of equality have destroyed these restraints of imperious lust, which in some cases is reinforced by the thought of generations of abuse of his own women by white men upon whom he would turn the tables. At any rate, the number, boldness, and barbarity of the rapists, and the frequency of the murder of their victims have increased. . . . Of the 3,008 lynchings in this country during the twenty years ending with the close of 1904, a clear majority are connected with murder or with this crime so often associated with it . . . . There has also been a gradual increase in the barbarity of this punishment for rape, slightly known before the war. The brutality of these assaults is often such that the most staid communities and heads of families, who have strongly and publicly denounced lynching, find themselves swept away in a frenzy of vengeance. . . . As a preventative of crime, lynching has something to be said for it, but more to be said against it. This wild justice is brutalizing upon those who inflict it. . . . Some drastic cures have been suggested,—a drumhead court-martial with immediate execution of [rapists], emasculation, instant trial, abolishment of appeal, and even the legalization of burning at the stake. These suggestions show . . . how desperate is . . . the white South ['s resolve] that this crime must be checked. . . .
>
> [T]he negro should now address himself to the solution of his own problems, carry on the work of studying his race so well begun at Atlanta under Professor Du Bois, and make his own social life as he has made the life of his church . . . and recognize that his race has gifts that others lack,—such as an intense and large emotional life, an exquisite sensitiveness to nature, gifts in the field of music and oratory, a peculiar depth of religious life (connected in part with the sense of dependence, which is its psychic root), a strong belief in invisible powers, rare good humor, jollity, patience, etc. An African museum has been suggested in which should be gathered the folk-lore and records of tribal customs (which a parliamentary commission in Africa has just found to be very elaborate, and in many respects better for the natives than English law, and of which many traces survive here), the anthropological literature upon the race here and elsewhere, and mementoes of Hamitic culture generally. Some have suggested a special permanent commission of those most competent and interested, white and black, to be consulted both by philanthropists and legislators. One of the most hopeful facts in the situation is that there are now for the first time such experts. Their knowledge certainly ought to be utilized. This we have notoriously failed to do in the case of the Indian. . . . Let no such mistakes be made concerning the negro. He has capacities for friendship, loyalty, patriotism, piety, and industry in regions where white men cannot work, which in some respects perhaps exceed ours and which the country sorely needs. If he can only be made to accept without . . . self-pity his present situation, prejudice and all, hard as it is, take his stand squarely upon the fact of his race, respect its unique gifts, develop all its capacities, make himself the best possible black man and not desire to be a brunette imitation of the Caucasian, he will in coming generations fill a place of great importance, and of pride both to himself and to us, in the future of the republic. . . .

Destined in the longer future to be far more important than Hall's views were those of Franz Boas who, when he wrote the following, stood almost alone upon these premises, among American scholars. Still a young man, recently migrated from Germany, in the early stages of a career that was to make him the most celebrated cultural anthropologist in America, he delivered the address from which these excerpts are taken as vice president of a section of the American Association for the Advancement of Science. Here is the first serious scientific assault upon racism by a leading American scholar. He was later to develop his thesis in greater detail, but in this early effort are foreshadowed the contributions that were to win for him the reputation of having done more to combat race prejudice than perhaps any other person in history.[1]

Proud of his wonderful achievements, civilized man looks down upon the humbler members of mankind. He has conquered the forces of nature and compelled them to serve him. . . . His genius has moulded inert matter into powerful machines which wait a touch of his hand to serve his manifold demands. . . . What wonder if civilized man considers himself a being of higher order as compared to primitive man; if it is claimed that the white race represents a higher type than all others.

When we analyze this assumption, it will soon be found that the superiority of the civilization of the white race alone is not a sufficient basis for this inference. As the civilization is higher, we assume that the aptitude for civilization is also higher; and as the aptitude for civilization presumably depends upon the mechanism of body and mind, the inference is drawn that the white race represents the highest type of perfection. In this conclusion, which is reached through a comparison of the social status of civilized man and of primitive man, the achievement and the aptitude for an achievement have been confounded. Furthermore, as the white race is the civilized race, every deviation from the white type is considered a characteristic feature of a lower type. That these two errors underlie our judgments of races can be easily shown by the fact that, other considerations being equal, a race is always described as the lower the more fundamentally it differs from the white race. . . .

In judging social distinctions the same error is frequently committed. As the mental development of the white race is the highest, it is also supposed to have the highest aptitude in this direction, and therefore its mind is supposed to have the most subtle organization. As the ultimate psychical causes are not so apparent as anatomical characters, the judgment of the mental status of a people is generally guided by the difference between its social status and our own; the greater the difference between their intellectual, emotional and moral processes and those which are found in our civilization the harsher the judgment of the people. . . .

We have . . . considered the question in how far human faculty is determined by race from three points of view. We have shown that the anatomical evidence is such, that we may expect to find the races not equally gifted. While we have no right to consider one more ape-like than the other, the differences are such that some have probably greater mental vigor than others. The variations are, however, such that we may expect many individuals of all races to be equally gifted, while the number of men and women

[1] Franz Boas, "Human Faculty as Determined by Race," *Proceedings of the American Association for the Advancement of Science . . .*, 1894, pp. 301–27; see pp. 301, 302, 326–27.

of higher ability will differ. When considering the psychological evidence, we found that most of it is not a safe guide for our inquiry, because causes and effects are so closely interwoven that it is impossible to separate them in a satisfactory manner, and as we are always liable to interpret as racial character what is only an effect of social surroundings. We saw, however, that investigations based on physiological psychology and experimental psychology will allow us to treat the problem in a satisfactory manner. In these and in detailed studies of the anatomy of the central nervous system of the races we must look for a final solution of our problem.

Finally, we found that there is no satisfactory evidence that the effects of civilization are inherited beyond those which are incident to that domestication to which civilization corresponds. We know that these are hereditary to a limited degree only and that domestication requires only few generations. We did not find proof of cumulative increase of faculty caused by civilization.

Although, as I have tried to show, the distribution of faculty among the races of man is far from being known, we can say this much: the average faculty of the white race is found to the same degree in a large proportion of individuals of all other races, and although it is probable that some of these races may not produce as large a proportion of great men as our own race, there is no reason to suppose that they are unable to reach the level of civilization represented by the bulk of our own people.

Notice should be taken here of the shift, during the two decades following 1883, from the older militancy typified by the rocklike Frederick Douglass, to a conservatism that accepted racial segregation at least for the time being in return for economic opportunity. The "accommodationist" strategy was by no means universally accepted by Negroes and their well-wishers, but it was in a significant sense the dominant drift in the racial struggle (decreasingly so after 1904), especially identified with Booker T. Washington, head of Tuskegee Institute in Alabama and spokesman of the "Tuskegee Idea." In Washington's view, Negroes should for the present postpone further demands for political and social gains in favor of self-improvement and of industrial training. By making themselves economically indispensable to America at large, they would, presumably, eventually earn from their admiring and grateful white countrymen the full freedom and equality to which they aspired.

The most celebrated expression of Washington's racial stance is provided by his "Atlanta Exposition Address," sometimes called the "Atlanta Compromise," delivered in 1895, the year of Douglass's death.[1]

. . . Ignorant and inexperienced, it is not strange that in the first years of our new life we began at the top instead of at the bottom; that a seat in Congress or the state legislature was more sought than real estate or industrial skill; that the political convention or stump speaking had more attractions than starting a dairy farm or truck garden.

[1] The speech is reprinted in Booker T. Washington, *Up from Slavery* (Boston, 1901), pp. 218–25.

A ship lost at sea for many days suddenly sighted a friendly vessel. From the mast of the unfortunate vessel was seen a signal, "Water, water; we die of thirst!" The answer . . . at once came back, "Cast down your bucket where you are." A second . . . and a third and fourth signal for water was answered, "Cast down your bucket where you are." The captain of the distressed vessel, at last heeding the injunction, cast down his bucket, and it came up full of fresh, sparkling water from the mouth of the Amazon River. To those of my race who depend on bettering their condition in a foreign land or who underestimate the importance of cultivating friendly relations with the southern white man I would say: "Cast down your bucket where you are"—cast it down in making friends in every manly way of the people of all races by whom we are surrounded.

Cast it down in agriculture, mechanics, in commerce, in domestic service, and in the professions. . . . [W]hen it comes to business, pure and simple, it is in the South that the Negro is given a man's chance in the commercial world, and in nothing is this exposition more eloquent than in emphasizing this chance. Our greatest danger is that in the great leap from slavery to freedom we may overlook the fact that the masses of us are to live by the productions of our hands, that we shall prosper in proportion as we learn to glorify common labor and put brains and skill into the common occupations of life; shall prosper in proportion as we learn to draw the line between the superficial and the substantial, the ornamental . . . and the useful. No race can prosper till it learns that there is as much dignity in tilling a field as in writing a poem. It is at the bottom of life we must begin, and not at the top. Nor should we permit our grievances to overshadow our opportunities.

To those of the white race who look to immigrant labor . . . for the prosperity of the South, . . . I would repeat what I say to my own race, "Cast down your bucket among these people who have, without strikes and labor wars, tilled your fields, cleared your forests, builded your railroads and cities, . . . and helped make possible this magnificent representation of the progress of the South. Casting down your bucket among my people, helping and encouraging them as you are doing this, you can be sure in the future, as in the past, that you . . . will be surrounded by the most patient, faithful, lawabiding, and unresentful people that the world has seen. As we have proved our loyalty . . . in the past, in nursing your children, watching by the sick-bed of your mothers and fathers, and often following them with tear-dimmed eyes to their graves, so in the future, in our humble way, we shall stand by you with a devotion that no foreigner can approach, ready to lay down our lives, if need be, in defense of yours, interlacing our industrial, commercial, civil, and religious life with yours in a way that shall make the interests of both races one. In all things that are purely social we can be as separate as the fingers, yet one as the hand in all things essential to mutual progress. . . .

Nearly sixteen millions of hands will aid you in pulling the load upward, or they will pull against you . . . We shall constitute one-third and more of the ignorance and crime of the South, or one-third its intelligence and progress; we shall contribute one-third to the business and industrial prosperity of the South, or we shall prove a veritable body of death, stagnating, depressing, retarding every effort to advance the body politic.

Gentlemen of the Exposition, as we present to you our humble effort at an exhibition of our progress, you must not expect overmuch. Starting thirty years ago with ownership here and there in a few quilts and pumpkins and chickens (gathered from miscellaneous sources), remember the path that has led from these to the inventions and production of agricultural implements, buggies, steam-engines, newspapers, books, statuary, carving, paintings, the management of drugstores and banks, has not been trodden without contact with thorns and thistles. While we take pride in what we exhibit as a result of our independent efforts, we do not for a moment forget that our part in this exhibition would fall far short of your expectations but for the constant help that has come to our educational life, not only from the southern states, but especially from northern philanthropists. . . .

The wisest among my race understand that the agitation of questions of social equality is the extremest folly, and that progress in the enjoyment of all the privileges that will come to us must be the result of severe and constant struggle rather than of artificial forcing. No race that has anything to contribute to the markets of the world is long in any degree ostracized. It is important and right that all privileges of the law be ours, but it is vastly more important that we be prepared for the exercises of these privileges. The opportunity to earn a dollar in a factory just now is worth infinitely more than the opportunity to spend a dollar in an opera house.

Washington met his most formidable critic in William E. B. DuBois, a brilliant young Harvard-trained sociologist, soon to become the dominant figure in the NAACP and editor of its crusading journal, *The Crisis*. The following passage is an early statement of his conviction that his race, far from resigning itself to disfranchisement, segregation, and other forms of discrimination, should stand up to its white aggressors.[1] And, although he did not oppose industrial education for the Negro masses, DuBois insisted that the race's "Talented Tenth" must obtain the finest higher education to be had.

Among his own people . . . Mr. Washington has encountered the strongest and most lasting opposition, amounting at times to bitterness, and even today continuing strong and insistent even though largely silenced in outward expression by the public opinion of the nation. Some of this opposition is, of course, mere envy; the disappointment of displaced demagogues and the spite of narrow minds. But aside from this, there is among educated and thoughtful colored men in all parts of the land a feeling of deep regret, sorrow, and apprehension at the wide currency and ascendancy which some of Mr. Washington's theories have gained. These same men admire his sincerity of purpose, and are willing to forgive much to honest endeavor which is doing something worth the doing. . . .

. . . Booker T. Washington arose as essentially the leader not of one race but of two,—a compromiser between the South, the North, and the Negro. Naturally the Negroes resented, at first bitterly, signs of compromise which surrendered their civil and political rights, even though this was to be exchanged for larger chances of economic development. The rich and dominating North, however, was not only weary of the race problem, but was investing largely in southern enterprises, and welcomed any method of peaceful cooperation. Thus, by national opinion, the Negroes began to recognize Mr. Washington's leadership; and the voice of criticism was hushed.

[1] William E. DuBois, *The Souls of Black Folk* (Chicago, 1903), pp. 45–54, *passim.*

Mr. Washington represents in Negro thought the old attitude of adjustment and submission; but adjustment at such a peculiar time as to make his program unique. This is an age of unusual economic development, and Mr. Washington's program naturally takes an economic cast, becoming a gospel of Work and Money to such an extent as apparently almost completely to overshadow the higher aims of life. Moreover, this is an age when the more advanced races are coming in closer contact with the less developed races, and the race-feeling is therefore intensified; and Mr. Washington's program practically accepts the alleged inferiority of the Negro races. Again, in our own land, the reaction from the sentiment of wartime has given impetus to race prejudice against Negroes, and Mr. Washington withdraws many of the high demands of Negroes as men and American citizens. In other periods of intensified prejudice all the Negro's tendency to self-assertion has been called forth; at this period a policy of submission is advocated.

[I]t has been claimed that the Negro can survive only through submission. Mr. Washington distinctly asks that black people give up, at least for the present, three things,—First, political power; Second, insistence on civil rights; Third, higher education of Negro youth; and concentrate all their energies on industrial education, the accumulation of wealth, and the conciliation of the South. This policy has been courageously and insistently advocated for over fifteen years, and has been triumphant for perhaps ten years. As a result of this tender of the palmbranch, what has been the return? In these years there have occurred: (1) The disfranchisement of the Negro; (2) The legal creation of a distinct status of civil inferiority for the Negro: (3) The steady withdrawal of aid from institutions for the higher training of the Negro.

These movements are not, to be sure, direct results of Mr. Washington's teachings; but his propaganda has . . . helped their speedier accomplishment. . . . And Mr. Washington thus faces the triple paradox of his career:

1. He is striving nobly to make Negro artisans, businessmen, and property-owners; but it is utterly impossible, under modern competitive methods, for workingmen and property-owners to defend their rights and exist without the right of suffrage.

2. He insists on thrift and self-respect, but at the same time counsels a silent submission to civic inferiority such as is bound to sap the manhood of any race in the long run.

3. He advocates common-school and industrial training, and depreciates institutions of higher learning; but neither the Negro common-schools, nor Tuskegee itself, could remain open a day were it not for teachers trained in Negro colleges, or trained by their graduates.

This triple paradox in Mr. Washington's position is the object of criticism by two classes of colored Americans. One class . . . hate the white South blindly and distrust the white race generally, [and] think that the Negro's only hope lies in emigration. . . .

The other class of Negroes who cannot agree with Mr. Washington . . . deprecate the sight of scattered counsels, of internal disagreement; and especially they dislike making their just criticism of a useful and earnest man an excuse for a general discharge of venom from small-minded opponents. . . . Such men feel in conscience bound to ask of this nation three things:

1. The right to vote.
2. Civil equality.
3. The education of youth according to ability.

They acknowledge Mr. Washington's invaluable service in counseling patience and courtesy in such demands; they do not ask that ignorant black men vote when ignorant whites are debarred, or that any reasonable restrictions in the suffrage should not be applied; they know that the low social level of the mass of the race is responsible for much discrimination against it, but they also know, and the nation knows, that relentless color prejudice is more often a cause than a result of the Negro's degradation. . . . They advocate, with Mr. Washington, a broad system of Negro common schools supplemented by thorough industrial training; but they are surprised that a man of Mr. Washington's insight cannot see that no such educational system . . . can rest on any other basis than that of [a few] institutions throughout the South to train the best of the Negro youth as teachers, professional men, and leaders.

One other document that illustrates the rising militancy in the Negro rights movement during the first years of the twentieth century must be included here: the "Declaration of Principles" adopted by the "Niagara Movement," in 1905.[1] A group of young Negroes, led by Dr. DuBois, determined to combat the Tuskegee philosophy and launch a drive for full citizenship for Negroes, met at Niagara Falls in Canada, in June 1905, to draw up a platform. Although the Niagara Movement failed, it did manage to clip Booker Washington's wings, and it prepared the way for the founding, soon thereafter, of the NAACP, by a number of white liberals and Negro-rights crusaders, joined by the remnant of the Niagara group.

Progress: The members of the conference, . . . congratulate the Negro-Americans on certain undoubted evidences of progress in the last decade, particularly the increase of intelligence, the buying of property, the checking of crime, the uplift in home life, the advance in literature and art, and the demonstration of constructive and executive ability in the conduct of great religious, economic and educational institutions.

Suffrage: . . . we believe that this class of American citizens should protest emphatically . . . against the curtailment of their political rights. We believe in manhood suffrage. . . .

Civil Liberty: We believe also in protest against the curtailment of our civil rights. All American citizens have the right to equal treatment in places of public entertainment. . . .

Economic Opportunity: We especially complain against the denial of equal opportunities to us in economic life; in the rural districts of the South this amounts to peonage and virtual slavery; all over the South it tends to crush labor and small business enterprises; and everywhere American prejudice, helped often by iniquitous laws, is making it more difficult for Negro-Americans to earn a decent living.

Education: Common school education should be free to all American children and compulsory. High school training should be adequately provided for all, and college training should be the monopoly of no class or race. . . .

[1] Reprinted in Herbert Aptheker, *A Documentary History of the Negro People of the United States* (third paperback edition, 2 vols., New York, 1968), II, 901–4.

We believe that . . . the United States should aid common school education, particularly in the South. . . . We urge an increase in public high school facilities in the South, where the Negro-Americans are almost wholly without such provisions. We favor well-equipped trade and technical schools . . . and the need of adequate and liberal endowment for the few institutions of higher education must be patent to sincere well-wishers of the race.

Courts: We demand upright judges in courts, juries selected without discrimination on account of color and the same measure of punishment and the same efforts at reformation for black as for white offenders. . . .

Public Opinion: We note with alarm the evident retrogression in this land of sound public opinion on the subject of manhood rights, republican government and human brotherhood, and we pray God that this nation will not degenerate into a mob of boasters and oppressors, but rather will return to the faith of the fathers, that all men were created free and equal, with certain unalienable rights.

Health: We plead for health—for an opportunity to live in decent houses and localities, for a chance to rear our children in physical and moral cleanliness.

Employers and Labor Unions: We hold up for public execration . . . the practice among employers of importing ignorant Negro-American laborers in emergencies, and then affording them neither protection nor permanent employment; and the practice of labor unions in proscribing and boycotting and oppressing thousands of their fellow-toilers, simply because they are black. . . .

Protest: We refuse to allow the impression to remain that the Negro-American assents to inferiority, [or] is submissive under oppression. . . . [T]he voice of protest of ten million Americans must never cease to assail the ears of their fellows, so long as America is unjust.

Color-Line: . . . Differences made on account of ignorance, immorality, or disease are legitimate methods of fighting evil, and against them we have no word of protest; but discriminations based simply and solely on physical peculiarities, place of birth, color of skin, are relics of that unreasoning human savagery of which the world is and ought to be thoroughly ashamed.

"Jim Crow" Cars: We protest against the "Jim Crow" car, since its effect is and must be to make us pay first-class fare for third-class accommodations, render us open to insults and discomfort and to crucify wantonly our manhood, womanhood and self-respect.

Soldiers: We regret that this nation has never seen fit adequately to reward the black soldiers who, in its five wars, have defended their country with their blood, and yet have been systematically denied the promotions which their abilities deserve. . . .

War Amendments: We urge upon Congress the enactment of appropriate legislation for securing the proper enforcement of . . . the thirteenth, fourteenth and fifteenth amendments of the Constitution of the United States.

Oppression: We repudiate the monstrous doctrine that the oppressor should be the sole authority as to the rights of the oppressed. The Negro race in America, stolen, ravished and degraded, struggling up through difficulties and oppression, needs sympathy and receives criticism; needs help and is given hindrance, needs protection and is given mob-violence, needs justice and is given charity, needs leadership and is given cowardice and apology, needs bread and is given a stone. . . .

The Church: Especially are we surprised and astonished at the recent attitude of the church of Christ—of an increase of a desire to bow to racial prejudice, to narrow the bounds of human brotherhood, and to segregate black men to some outer sanctuary. . . .

Agitation: . . . Persistent manly agitation is the way to liberty, and toward this goal the Niagara Movement has started and asks the cooperation of all men of all races.

Help: At the same time we want to acknowledge with deep thankfulness the help of our fellowmen from the Abolitionist down to those who today still stand for equal opportunity and who have given and still give of their wealth and of their poverty for our advancement.

Duties: And while we are demanding, and ought to demand, and will continue to demand the rights enumerated above, God forbid that we should ever forget to urge corresponding duties upon our people:

The duty to vote.
The duty to respect the rights of others.
The duty to work.
The duty to obey the laws.
The duty to be clean and orderly.
The duty to send our children to school.
The duty to respect ourselves, even as we respect others.

This statement, complaint and prayer we submit to the American people, and Almighty God.

(2)

VIEWS FROM THE WHITE HOUSE

Grover Cleveland, President, 1885–1889; 1893–1897

Grover Cleveland, the first Democratic President after the Civil War, was not unaware that the return of his party to the White House after an absence of a quarter of a century had stirred fears in some quarters that slavery would be restored. To quiet these apprehensions, he took the opportunity in his first inaugural, on March 4, 1884, to speak these soothing words, and then did not again in his messages to Congress express himself on the subject of Afro-Americans except to recommend the payment of the balance to which depositors in the defunct Freedmen's Savings Bank and Trust Company were entitled.[1]

In the administration of a government pledged to do equal and exact justice to all men there should be no pretext for anxiety touching the protection of the freedmen in their rights or their security in the enjoyment of their privileges under the Constitution and its amendments. All discussion as to

[1] Richardson, *Messages and Papers of the Presidents,* VIII, p. 302.

their fitness for the place accorded to them as American citizens is idle and unprofitable except as it suggests the necessity for their improvement. The fact that they are citizens entitles them to all the rights due to that relation and charges them with all its duties, obligations, and responsibilities.

In the same year, Cleveland's enthusiastic concurrence in Booker T. Washington's "Atlanta Compromise" position was conveyed by letter to Washington by the President shortly after Washington had delivered the Cotton Exposition speech. A part of the letter is here quoted.[1]

The Exposition would be fully justified if it did not do more than furnish the opportunity for [this speech's] delivery. Your words cannot fail to delight and encourage all who wish well for your race; and if our colored fellow-citizens do not from your utterances gather new hope and form new determinations to gain every valuable advantage offered them by their citizenship, it will be strange indeed.

Benjamin Harrison, President, 1889–1893

President Harrison's first annual message to Congress, December 3, 1889, alarmed not a few southerners, even though, as Rayford Logan has written, there was so little that threatened their interests that Mississippi need hardly have felt impelled to revise her constitution in the following year and to introduce the "Mississippi Plan" of disfranchisement. A calm reading of the pertinent passage[2] should have reassured nervous southerners, by its studied ambiguity, that no immediate revolution in race relations impended.

The colored people did not intrude themselves upon us. They were brought here in chains and held in the communities where they are now chiefly found by a cruel slave code. Happily for both races, they are now free. They have . . . made remarkable advances in education and in the acquisition of property. They have as a people shown themselves to be friendly and faithful toward the white race under temptations of tremendous strength. They have their representatives in the national cemeteries, where a grateful Government has gathered the ashes of those who died in its defense. . . . In civil life they are now the toilers of their communities, making their full contribution to the widening streams of prosperity which these communities are receiving. . . . Generally they do not desire to quit their homes, and their employers resent the interference of the emigration agents who seek to stimulate such a desire.

But notwithstanding all this, in many parts of our country where the colored population is large the people of that race are by various devices deprived of any effective exercise of their political rights and of many of their civil rights. . . .

Surely no one supposes that the present can be accepted as a permanent condition. If it is said that these communities must work out this problem for themselves, we have a right to ask whether they are at work upon it. . . .

[1] Basil Mathews, *Booker T. Washington* (Cambridge, 1948), p. 91.

[2] Richardson, *Messages and Papers of the Presidents,* IX, pp. 55–56.

When and under what conditions is the black man to have a free ballot? When is he in fact to have those full civil rights which have so long been his in law? When is that equality of influence which our form of government was intended to secure to the electors to be restored? This generation should courageously face these grave questions, and not leave them as a heritage of woe to the next. The consultation should proceed with candor, calmness, and great patience, upon the lines of justice and humanity, not of prejudice and cruelty. . . .

I earnestly invoke the attention of Congress to the consideration of such measures within its well-defined constitutional powers as did secure to all our people a free exercise of the right of suffrage and every other civil right under the Constitution and laws of the United States. . . . The colored man should be protected in all of his relations to the Federal Government, whether as litigant, juror, or witness in our courts, as an elector for members of Congress, or as a peaceful traveler upon our interstate railways.

William McKinley, President, 1897–1901

In his first inaugural, President McKinley tacitly identified himself with the country's disposition to sacrifice the Negro for the sake of sectional harmony. Although he insisted that lynching should have no place in this free land, he congratulated the nation upon the growing accord between the North and South; and he vowed that he would not permit anything to disturb this precarious equipoise.[1]

. . . The great essential to our happiness and prosperity is that we adhere to the principles upon which the Government was established and insist upon their faithful observance. Equality of rights must prevail, and our laws be always and everywhere respected and obeyed. We may have failed in the discharge of our full duty as citizens of the great Republic, but it is consoling and encouraging to realize that free speech, a free press, free thought, free schools, and free and unmolested right of religious liberty and worship, and free and fair elections are dearer and more universally enjoyed to-day than ever before. These guaranties must be sacredly preserved and wisely strengthened. The constituted authorities must be cheerfully and vigorously upheld. Lynchings must not be tolerated in a great and civilized country like the United States; courts, not mobs, must execute the penalties of the law. The preservation of public order, the right of discussion, the integrity of courts, and the orderly administration of justice must continue forever the rock of safety upon which our Government securely rests. . . .

In conclusion, I congratulate the country upon the fraternal spirit of the people and the manifestations of good will everywhere so apparent. The recent election not only most fortunately demonstrated the obliteration of sectional or geographical lines, but to some extent also the prejudices which for years have distracted our councils and marred our true greatness . . . [This] will be both a gain and a blessing to our beloved country. It will be my constant aim to do nothing, and permit nothing to be done, that will arrest or disturb this growing sentiment of unity and co-operation, this revival of esteem and affiliation which now animates so many thousands in

[1] Richardson, *Messages and Papers of the Presidents,* X, pp. 14–15, 19.

both the old antagonistic sections, but I shall cheerfully do everything possible to promote and increase it.

Theodore Roosevelt, President, 1901–1909

Theodore Roosevelt, smarting under southern censure for having dined with Booker T. Washington in the White House and, like other Republicans, willing to profit by the disenchantment of conservative southerners with the radical drift of a Bryan-dominated Democratic party, made increasing efforts to woo the South for the Republicans. One line of this strategy, along which his successor, William Howard Taft, was to follow Roosevelt's lead, was that of giving increasing support to the lily-white elements of the party in the South, and urging Negroes to stay out of the white man's professions and occupations while looking upon southern whites as their best friends. Roosevelt's most widely noticed speech of conciliation to the South at the Negro's expense was his Lincoln Dinner address at the Republican Club of New York City, on February 13, 1905.[1]

The ideal of elemental justice meted out to every man is the ideal we should keep ever before us. It will be many a long day before we attain to it, and unless we show not only devotion to it, but also wisdom and self-restraint in the exhibition of that devotion, we shall defer the time for its realization still further. In striving to attain to so much of it as concerns dealing with men of different colors, we must remember two things.

In the first place, it is true of the colored man, as it is true of the white man, that in the long run his fate must depend far more upon his own effort than upon the efforts of any outside friend. . . . The colored man's self-respect entitles him to do that share in the political work of the country which is warranted by his individual ability and integrity and the position he has won for himself. But the prime requisite of the race is moral and industrial uplifting.

Laziness and shiftlessness, these, and above all, vice and criminality of every kind, are evils more potent for harm to the black race than all acts of oppression of white men put together. The colored man who fails to condemn crime in another colored man, who fails to co-operate in all lawful ways in bringing colored criminals to justice, is the worst enemy of his own people, as well as an enemy to all the people. . . .

In the next place . . . it is wise to remember that each can normally do most for the brother who is his immediate neighbor. If we are sincere friends of the negro let us each in his own locality show it by his action therein, and let us each show it also by upholding the hands of the white man, in whatever locality, who is striving to do justice to the poor and the helpless, to be a shield to those whose need for such a shield is great.

The heartiest acknowledgments are due to the ministers, the judges and law officers, the grand juries, the public men, and the great daily newspapers in the South, who have recently done such effective work in leading the

[1] The speech is in Hermann Hagedorn, ed., *The Works of Theodore Roosevelt* (Memorial Edition, 24 vols., New York, 1923–1926), XVIII, pp. 460–75, *passim.*

crusade against lynching in the South. . . . Let us uphold in every way the hands of the men who have led in this work, who are striving to do all their work in this spirit. I am about to quote from the address of the Right Reverend Robert Strange, Bishop Coadjutor of North Carolina, as given in the "Southern Churchman" of October 8, 1904.

The bishop first enters an emphatic plea against any social intermingling of the races; a question which must, of course, be left to the people of each community to settle for themselves, as in such a matter no one community . . . can dictate to any other. . . . Civil law can not regulate social practices. Society, as such, is a law unto itself, and will always regulate its own practices and habits. Full recognition of the fundamental fact that all men should stand on an equal footing, as regards civil privileges, in no way interferes with recognition of the further fact that all reflecting men of both races are united in feeling that race purity must be maintained. The bishop continues:

What should the white men of the South do for the negro? They must give him a free hand, a fair field, and a cordial Godspeed, the two races working together for their mutual benefit and for the development of our common country. He must have liberty, equal opportunity to make his living, to earn his bread, to build his home. He must have justice, equal rights, and protection before the law. He must have the same political privileges; the suffrage should be based on character and intelligence for white and black alike. He must have the same public advantages of education; the public schools are for all the people, whatever their color or condition. The white men of the South should give hearty and respectful consideration to the exceptional men of the negro race, to those who have the character, the ability and the desire to be lawyers, physicians, teachers, preachers, leaders of thought and conduct among their own men and women. . . . Finally, the best white men of the South should have frequent conferences with the best colored men, where, in frank, earnest, and sympathetic discussion they might understand each other better, smooth difficulties, and so guide and encourage the weaker race.

Surely we can all of us join in expressing our substantial agreement with the principles thus laid down by this North Carolina bishop, this representative of the Christian thought of the South. . . .

. . . Throughout our land things on the whole have grown better and not worse, and this is as true of one part of the country as it is of another. I believe in the Southerner as I believe in the Northerner. I claim the right to feel pride in his great qualities and in his great deeds exactly as I feel pride in the great qualities and deeds of every other American. For weal or for woe we are knit together, and we shall go up or go down together; and I believe that we shall go up and not down. . . .

The Southern States face difficult problems; and so do the Northern States. Some of the problems are the same for the entire country. Others exist in greater intensity in one section; and yet others exist in greater intensity in another section. . . . I admire and respect and believe in and have faith in the men and women of the South as I admire and respect and believe in and have faith in the men and women of the North. All of us alike, Northerners and Southerners, Easterners and Westerners, can best prove our fealty to the Nation's past by the way in which we do the Nation's work in the present; for only thus can we be sure that our children's children shall inherit Abraham Lincoln's single-hearted devotion to the great unchanging creed that "righteousness exalteth a nation."

William Howard Taft, President, 1909–1913

Much of the same spirit animated the following passages by President-elect Taft, taken from "An Address Delivered at the Dinner of the North Carolina Society in New York, at the Hotel Astor, December 7, 1908."[1] Here was a candid promise that there would be no reason to fear, for the next four years at least, that the national administration in Washington would take the Fifteenth Amendment seriously in those states which chose to defy it.

After reassuring his audience that "in all the southern states it is possible, by election laws prescribing proper qualifications for the suffrage, which square with the Fifteenth Amendment and which shall be equally administered as between the black and white races, to prevent entirely the possibility of a domination of southern state, county, or municipal governments by an ignorant electorate, white or black," Taft went on to say:

> The Negro should ask nothing other than an equal chance to qualify himself for the franchise, and when that is granted by law, and not denied by executive discrimination, he has nothing to complain of.
>
> We believe that the solution of the race question in the South is largely a matter of industrial and thorough education. We believe that the best friend that the Southern Negro can have is the Southern white man, and that the growing interest which the Southern white man is taking in the development of the Negro is one of the most encouraging reasons for believing the problem is capable of solution. The hope of the Southern Negro is in teaching him how to be a good farmer, how to be a good mechanic; in teaching him how to make his home attractive and how to live more comfortably and according to the rules of health and morality. . . .
>
> The Negro is essential to the Southern order that it may have proper labor. . . .

[1] Published as a pamphlet (n.p., n.d.).

(3)

THE NATIONAL PARTY PLATFORMS, 1884–1908[1]

Campaign of 1884

Preoccupied with their particular panaceas for freeing the country from the evils of drink, big business, and high interest rates, the American Prohibition, National, Prohibition, Anti-Monopoly, and Greenback

[1] The platforms for the electoral campaigns of 1884–1908 are in Porter and Johnson, *National Party Platforms,* pp. 63–167.

parties made no reference to race relations in their platforms. The two major parties, meanwhile, confined themselves to single-sentence lofty pronouncements that the electorate had by now learned need not be taken seriously.

Said the Democrats' Platform:

Asserting the equality of all men before the law, we hold that it is the duty of the Government, in its dealings with the people, to mete out equal and exact justice to all citizens of whatever nativity, race, color, or persuasion—religious or political.

The Republican platform expressed itself thus:

We extend to the Republicans of the South, regardless of their former party affiliations, our cordial sympathy; and we pledge to them our most earnest efforts to promote the passage of such legislation as will secure to every citizen, of whatever race and color, the full and complete recognition, possession and exercise of all civil and political rights.

Campaign of 1888

This time, the Republican and Prohibition parties paid their respects to the free ballot in language that aroused few apprehensions among defenders of the status quo, while several lesser parties (American, Union Labor, and United Labor) said nothing. The Democratic party, haunted by the narrowness of its victory in 1884, preferred also to make no allusion to the Negro, but chose instead to express, with unintended irony, its "cordial sympathy" with Ireland and "with the struggling people in all nations in their effort to secure for themselves the inestimable blessings of self-government and civil and religious liberty."

[This was the Republican party's pledge:] We reaffirm our unswerving devotion to the National Constitution and the indissoluble Union of the States; to the autonomy reserved to the States under the Constitution; to the personal rights and liberties of citizens in all the States and Territories of the Union, and especially to the supreme and sovereign right of every lawful citizen, rich or poor, native or foreign born, white or black, to cast one free ballot, in public elections, and to have that ballot duly counted. We hold the free and honest popular ballot and the just and equal representation of all the people to be the foundation of our Republican government and demand effective legislation to secure the integrity and purity of elections, which are the fountains of all public authority.

The Prohibition party said it in these words:

6. . . . the right of suffrage rests on no mere circumstances of race, color, sex or nationality, and . . . where, from any cause, it has been withheld from citizens who are of suitable age, and mentally and morally qualified for the exercise of an intelligent ballot, it should be restored by the people through the Legislatures of the several States, on such educational basis as they may deem wise.

Campaign of 1892

Still stinging from their defeat of 1888 by the narrowest of margins, the Democrats lashed out at federal control of elections and the "subjugation of the colored people to the control" of Republicans:

We warn the people of our common country, jealous for the preservation of their free institutions, that the policy of Federal control of elections, to which the Republican party has committed itself, is fraught with the gravest dangers, scarcely less momentous than would result from a revolution practically establishing monarchy on the ruins of the Republic. It strikes at the North as well as at the South, and injures the colored citizens even more than the white; it means a horde of deputy marshals at every polling place, armed with Federal power; returning boards appointed and controlled by Federal authority, the outrage of the electoral rights of the people in the several States, the subjugation of the colored people to the control of the party in power, and the reviving of race antagonisms, now happily abated, of the utmost peril to the safety and happiness of all; a measure deliberately and justly described by a leading Republican Senator as "the most infamous bill that ever crossed the threshold of the Senate."

The minor groups (People's, Prohibition, and Socialist Labor parties) decided to pass over the problem, while the Republicans thought it best to reaffirm their dedication to "a free ballot for all."

From the Republican platform:

We demand that every citizen of the United States shall be allowed to cast one free and unrestricted ballot in all public elections, and that such ballot shall be counted and returned as cast; that such laws shall be enacted and enforced as will secure to every citizen, be he rich or poor, native or foreign-born, white or black, this sovereign right, guaranteed by the Constitution. The free and honest popular ballot, the just and equal representation of all the people, as well as their just and equal protection under the laws, are the foundation of our Republican institutions, and the party will never relax its efforts until the integrity of the ballot and the purity of elections shall be fully guaranteed and protected in every state.

Southern Outrages

We denounce the continued inhuman outrages perpetrated upon American citizens for political reasons in certain Southern States of the Union.

Campaign of 1896

Above the pentecostal fervors of the Battle of the Standards, the Negro's claims upon the country's consideration were only faintly heard. The National, National Democratic, and National Silver parties ignored them altogether, while the two major parties and the Socialist Laborites made brief declarations of fidelity to universal male suffrage. The Republicans, in addition, condemned the growing practice of lynching. It is noteworthy, however, that less than four years after this indignant rebuke to lynchers, Republicans and Democrats in Congress combined to smother the first attempt (by the last Negro to serve in Congress until 1929) to introduce a federal antilynching bill. Thus:

[Democrats:] We, the Democrats of the United States in National Convention assembled, do affirm our allegiance to those great essential principles of justice and liberty, upon which our institutions are founded, and which the Democratic Party has advocated from Jefferson's time to our own—freedom of speech, freedom of the press, freedom of conscience, the preservation of personal rights, the faithful observance of constitutional limitations.

[Republicans:] We demand that every citizen of the United States shall be allowed to cast one free and unrestricted ballot, and that such ballot shall be counted and returned as cast.

We proclaim our unqualified condemnation of the uncivilized and preposterous [barbarous] practice well known as lynching, and the killing of human beings suspected or charged with crime without process of law.

[Socialist Labor party:] Direct vote and secret ballots in all elections. Universal and equal right of suffrage without regard to color, creed, or sex. Election days to be legal holidays. The principle of proportional representative [*sic*] to be introduced.

Campaign of 1900

Once more the Democratic platform had no word in behalf of the Negro American, although it expended two paragraphs regretting that "liberty is being stifled in Africa." The People's, Prohibition, Silver Republican, Social Democratic, and Socialist Labor parties also maintained a discreet quiet. Only the Republicans looked in the black Americans' direction, and then only to deplore the frustration of the Fifteenth Amendment, without promising remedial action:

It was the plain purpose of the fifteenth amendment to the Constitution, to prevent discrimination on account of race or color in regulating the elective franchise. Devices of State governments, whether by statutory or constitutional enactment, to avoid the purpose of this amendment are revolutionary, and should be condemned.

Campaign of 1904

This time, while the People's, Prohibition, and Socialist Labor parties preserved their traditional aloofness from the Negro's predicament, the Democrats took the occasion to rebuke the Republican platform for seeking to "kindle anew the embers of racial and sectional strife" by its demand that the disfranchising states be penalized with a reduction in their representation in Congress and in the electoral college.

[Democrats:] The race question has brought countless woes to this country. The calm wisdom of the American people should see to it that it brings no more.

To revive the dead and hateful race and sectional animosities in any part of our common country means confusion, distraction of business, and the reopening of wounds now happily healed. North, South, East and West have but recently stood together in line of battle from the walls of Pekin to the hills of Santiago, and as sharers of a common glory and a common destiny, we should share fraternally the common burdens.

We therefore deprecate and condemn the Bourbon-like selfish, and narrow spirit of the recent Republican Convention at Chicago which sought to kindle anew the embers of racial and sectional strife, and we appeal from it to the sober common sense and patriotic spirit of the American people.

[Republicans:] We favor such Congressional action as shall determine whether by special discrimination the elective franchise in any State has been unconstitutionally limited, and, if such is the case, we demand that representation in Congress and in the electoral college shall be proportionately reduced as directed by the Constitution of the United States.

. . . He [Theodore Roosevelt] has held firmly to the fundamental American doctrine that all men must obey the law; that there must be no distinction between rich and poor, between strong and weak, but that justice and equal protection under the law must be secured to every citizen without regard to race, creed, or condition.

Campaign of 1908

Again, as in 1904, the Republican party alone, of seven parties in the field (Democratic, Independence, People's, Prohibition, Socialist, and Socialist Labor parties) took notice of the "Negro question," primarily to deplore the devices by which the southern Negroes were being denied the privilege of rolling up Republican majorities in the southern states:

Rights of the Negro

The Republican party has been for more than fifty years the consistent friend of the American Negro. It gave him freedom and citizenship. It wrote into the organic law the declarations that proclaim his civil and political rights, and it believes to-day that his noteworthy progress in intelligence, industry and good citizenship has earned the respect and encouragement of the nation. We demand equal justice for all men, without regard to race or color; we declare once more, and without reservation, for the enforcement in letter and spirit of the Thirteenth, Fourteenth and Fifteenth amendments to the Constitution which were designed for the protection and advancement of the negro, and we condemn all devices that have for their real aim his disfranchisement for reasons of color alone, as unfair, un-American and repugnant to the Supreme law of the land.

(4)
STATE LAWS TO PROTECT CIVIL RIGHTS

When the Supreme Court invalidated the Civil Rights Act of 1875 in the *Civil Rights Cases* of 1883, it in effect shifted responsibility for the Negro's protection from the federal government back to the states. To no one's surprise, the southern states, with a single exception, declined to assume this duty, but so, for that matter, did the fifteen that lay to the north and west of the former Confederacy. Curiously the only southern state to enact a civil rights law was Tennessee—the first of the states to pass a bona fide Jim Crow law.

THE TENNESSEE CIVIL RIGHTS ACT OF 1885[1]

Section 1

Be it enacted by the General Assembly of the State of Tennessee, that it shall be unlawful for owners, proprietors, lessees, keepers, agents, employees or servants of any theaters, shows, parks, places of public resort for observation of scenery or amusement of any kind whatever, where a fee or toll is charged for entrance or admission into such places or premises, to refuse admission to any person or persons on account of the fact that such person or persons travel to and from such parks or places over a particular route, turnpike or railway, or in the vehicles, carriages or other means of conveyance of any person, firm or corporation rather than another. And it shall be the duty of all such owners, proprietors, lessees or keepers of such public places, to admit all well behaved persons thereto upon equal terms, without regard to the particular route, turnpike or railway traveled over, or the particular carriages or vehicles of any person, firm or corporation used in going to and from such places.

Section 2

Be it further enacted, That all places kept open for the public, and at which a fee or toll is charged, either at such place or for travelling over any route, turnpike or railway where the place is the inducement to such travel, shall be conclusively taken to fall within the provisions of this Act.

Section 3

[Provides penalties up to $50 for each violation, and makes violators liable for damage, and subjects them to injunctive remedies to restrain further discriminations.]

Section 4

Be it further enacted, That nothing herein contained shall be construed as interfering with the existing rights to provide separate accommodations and seats for colored and white persons at such places.

[1] *Acts of Tennessee,* 1885 (chap. 68), 124–25; see above, p. 82.

Section 5
Be it further enacted, That the provisions of this Act shall be liberally construed and enforced, so as to prevent evasions and subterfuges, and to secure to the public the benefit of free and fair competition in the business of carrying passengers, and to prevent discrimination and monopoly.

Some states of the South did, however, legislate against the Ku Klux Klan and its tactics for terrorizing Negroes. Arkansas was an example.[1]

Section 1
—If two or more persons shall unite, confederate or band themselves together for the purpose of doing any unlawful act in the night time, or for the purpose of doing any unlawful act while wearing any mask, white caps or robes, or being otherwise disguised, or for the purpose of going forth armed or disguised for the purpose of intimidating or alarming any person, or to do any felonious act, or if any person shall knowingly meet or act clandestinely with any such band or order, be such organization known as night riders, black hand, white caps, or by any other name, they shall each be guilty of a felony, and upon conviction shall be punished by imprisonment in the penitentiary for a term not to exceed five years.
Section 2
—If two or more persons belonging to or acting with any such band or organization as defined in section one of this Act shall go forth at night, or shall go forth at any time disguised, and shall alarm or intimidate . . . any other person [they] shall be deemed guilty of a felony and upon conviction shall be punished by imprisonment in the penitentiary for a term not to exceed ten years nor to be less than two years, and by a fine of not more than $5,000.00.
Section 3
—If any person shall by means of any writing, drawing or printed matter, or by any sign or token, such as the delivery of matches or bundles of switches or other things, seek to intimidate, threaten or alarm any person, or shall knowingly be connected either in the preparation or delivery of any such message or token, by saying or intimidating [or by other specific means], which in its substance or nature is intended to intimidate or threaten any person, [he] shall be deemed guilty of a felony and upon conviction shall be confined in the penitentiary for a term of not less than one or more than seven years.
Section 4
—If any such secretly organized band . . . shall assault or frighten any person . . . and such person shall die as a result of such injury or alarm, they . . . and any person who shall be present aiding, advising, abetting or encouraging any such unlawful act which shall result in the death of any person, as above set out, shall be deemed guilty of murder in the first degree and punished as by law provided.

Kentucky outlawed at least one form of race-baiting.[2]

Section 1
It shall be unlawful for any person to present, or to participate in the presentation of, or to permit to be presented in any opera house, theater, hall

[1] *Acts of Arkansas,* 1909 (chap. 68), 316.
[2] *Acts of Kentucky,* 1906 (chap. 59), 315.

or other building under his control, any play that is based upon antagonism alleged formerly to exist between master and slave, or that excites race prejudice.

Section 2

Any person violating the provisions of the act shall be subject to a fine of not less than one hundred dollars, nor more than five hundred dollars, or to imprisonment in the county jail of not less than one or more than three months, or both such fine and imprisonment.

The Kansas Civil Rights Law of 1874 has already been cited.[1] Thereafter, in the years from 1883 to 1910 seventeen other states of the North and West passed such laws, ranging from relatively comprehensive legislation, like that of Illinois and Minnesota, to more modest laws like those of Connecticut and Rhode Island, which specified non-discrimination only in public conveyances and places of public accommodation and amusement. The more liberal laws of Illinois, for example, by 1910 had extended the protection to Negroes seeking accommodation at inns, restaurants, eating houses, cafes, hotels, soda fountains, ice cream parlors, bath houses, barber shops, theaters, skating rinks, bicycle rinks, elevators, public conveyances, places of public accommodation, and places of public amusement. An example of such laws, this one enacted in Michigan in 1885, follows.[2]

AN ACT to protect all citizens in their civil rights.

Section 1

The people of the State of Michigan enact, That all persons within the jurisdiction of said State shall be entitled to the full and equal accommodations, advantages, facilities, and privileges of inns, restaurants, eating-houses, barber shops, public conveyances on land and water, theatres, and all other places of public accommodation and amusement, subject only to the conditions and limitation established by law and applicable alike to all citizens.

Section 2

[Provides penalties for those making such discrimination or helping or inciting others to do so: fines up to $100; imprisonment up to 30 days; or both.]

Section 3

That no citizen of the State of Michigan, possessing all other qualifications which are or may be prescribed by law, shall be disqualified to serve as grand or petit juror in any court of said State on account of race or color, and any officer or other person . . . who shall exclude or fail to summon any citizen for the cause aforesaid, shall on conviction thereof, be deemed guilty of a misdemeanor, and be fined not more than one hundred dollars, or imprisoned more than thirty days, or both.

Connecticut in 1887 forbade discrimination against Negroes by life insurance companies and a similar law was passed by New York State in 1891. New Jersey outlawed discrimination in cemeteries.[3]

[1] See above, p. 74.

[2] *Public Acts of Michigan,* 1885 (chap. 130), 131–32.

[3] *Laws of New Jersey,* 1898 (chap. 235, sec. 213), 853.

No cemetery corporation, association or company organized under any law of this state, owning or having control of any cemetery or place for the burial of the dead, shall refuse to permit the burial of any deceased person therein because of the color of such deceased person, and any cemetery corporation, association or company offending against this section shall be guilty of a misdemeanor.

It is of course not to be assumed that laws like those cited above did in fact banish Jim Crow practices in the North, for discrimination was effectually maintained by private action, and by social and economic pressures of many sorts. It appears that no cases of race discrimination in hotels reached the higher courts of Massachusetts during the years here under review, but it may be worth noting that in 1896 the state's legislature passed the following resolution.[1]

Whereas, On the twenty-ninth day of January, eighteen ninety-six, the Reverend Benjamin W. Arnett, D.C., of Wilberforce, Ohio, senior bishop of the African Methodist Episcopal Church, president of the board of trustees of Wilberforce University, and member of many learned societies, was refused entertainment at certain reputable hotels in the city of Boston, because he was a colored man, in spite of the state law against discrimination on account of color; therefore,

Resolved, That the senate and house of representatives of the Commonwealth of Massachusetts, in general court assembled, successors of those bodies which repeatedly elected Charles Sumner to the senate of the United States, and for four years received messages from John A. Andrew, hereby express their severest reprobation of such discrimination and their firm conviction of the truth of the clause of the declaration of independence wherein all men are declared to be created equal; and it is further

Resolved, That still more to be reprobated is the sentiment of any part of the public against any class of our fellow citizens whereby such discrimination is rendered possible, and that a vigorous campaign for statute rights by the persons most aggrieved will meet the hearty approval and cooperation of the two branches of the General Court.

Indiana provided an early fair-employment law:[2]

Proprietors, agents or managers of any manufacturing or mercantile establishment, mine or quarry, laundry, renovating works, bakery or printing office, are prohibited from discriminating against any person or persons, or class of labor seeking work, by posting notices or otherwise.

1 *Acts and Resolves of Massachusetts,* 1896, 659–60.
2 *Laws of Indiana,* 1899 (chap. 142, sec. 16), 231–40.

(5)
DISCRIMINATION BY STATE LAW

It was in this period that the legally prescribed patterns of discrimination were written into the statutes. It must, however, again be emphasized that in many cases social pressures and privately imposed restraints, backed up by the threat of (and the actual resort to) violence or economic reprisal, preceded such enacted distinctions and proved so effectual that the laws were hardly necessary.

A. *Reinforcing the Ban on Racial Intermarriage*

Of all the discriminatory laws none were more universally insisted upon than those against intermarriage and race mixing. By 1910 six states forbade the practice, in *both* constitution and statutes; and twenty more (soon to be followed by another four)[1] enacted laws against miscegenation. Five others had such laws but had repealed them between 1863 and 1887. Thus, by 1910 (and, in the case of four states, very soon thereafter) thirty-five of all of the states had anti-miscegenation laws, and in thirty of them they were still in force. Such provisions had, in fact, as we have noted, been widely established even before 1883, and it is not necessary now to multiply examples in succeeding decades. It may, however, be useful to offer a sample of two of the newer laws to indicate the firmer tone as well as the inflexible attitude toward the issue.

Substantially re-enacting a law that had first been passed in 1832 and which had been in force during the intervening half century, Florida's Constitution of 1885 embodied the following clause:

ARTICLE XVI

Section 24

All marriages between a white person and a negro, or between a white person and a person of negro descent to the fourth generation, inclusive, are hereby forever prohibited.

[1] The only states *not* included in these numbers were the following: Connecticut, Illinois, Iowa, Kansas, Massachusetts, Minnesota, New Hampshire, New Jersey, New York, Pennsylvania, Vermont, Washington, and Wisconsin.

The 1901 Constitution of Alabama was equally adamant.[1]

> The legislature shall never pass any law to authorize or legalize any marriage between any white person and a negro, or descendant of a negro.

Montana's law was typical of those on the statute books across the nation.[2]

> *Section 1*
> Every marriage hereafter Contracted or Solemnized between a White Person and a Negro or a person of Negro blood or in part Negro, shall be utterly Null and Void.
> [Sections 2 and 3 forbade intermarriage between whites and Chinese or Japanese; section 4 declared null and void marriages contracted in other states, between Montanans and persons of African or Asian descent.]
> *Section 5*
> Any Person or Officer who shall solemnize any such marriage within the State of Montana, shall be guilty of a misdemeanor and upon conviction thereof be punished by a fine of Five Hundred Dollars or imprisonment in the county jail for one month, or both. . . .

B. *Defining the Negro*

Southern states continued to write legal definitions of the Negro.

> . . . the word or words "colored" or "colored race," "negro," or "negro race" . . . shall be construed to mean or apply to all persons of African descent. The term "white race" shall include all other persons.[3]

The Arkansas separate coach law stipulated that:[4]

> Persons in whom there is visible any distinct admixture of African blood shall, for purposes of this act, be deemed to belong to the African race; all others shall be deemed to belong to the white race.

In the same state a later enactment provided that:[5]

> The words "person of negro race" . . . shall be held to apply and include [*sic*] any person who has in his veins any negro blood whatever.

C. *Prescribing Segregation in Public Conveyances*

Laws requiring the separation of races in common carriers—trains, street cars, and boats—attracted more attention and provoked more

[1] Art. IV, Sec. 102. See *Code of Alabama,* 1903, III, 82.
[2] *Laws of Montana,* 1909 (chap. 49) 57.
[3] Constitution of Oklahoma (1907), Art. XXIII, Sec. 11. See *Compiled Laws of Oklahoma,* 1909, 136.
[4] *Acts of Arkansas,* 1891 (No. XVII, Sec. 4), 17.
[5] *Acts of Arkansas,* Ex. Sess., 1911 (No. 320, Sec. 3), I, 295–99.

discussion than did any other form of legalized discrimination. Separate school laws applied only to children; antimiscegenation statutes affected those of marriageable age; suffrage laws applied only to adult males. But Jim Crow laws for public conveyances extended to every person of color who had occasion to travel, if only across town, in a common carrier. Separate accommodations for blacks, moreover, affected the *entire* colored traveling public, not merely those who lived in the state enacting the law, and they seemed therefore more explicitly to pronounce a judgment on an entire race than did other legal distinctions.

It has been noted that Tennessee alone had passed a Jim Crow law before the years here under study, and that the next laws of this kind came in the period from 1887 to 1907, when all the other southern states except Missouri followed Tennessee's example. The requirement that the races be separated in trains was in most instances supplemented by additional discriminatory laws relating to sleeping cars and waiting rooms, and in all cases the laws specified that separate accommodations required for blacks be substantially equal to those supplied for whites. From the outset, however, almost no one seriously maintained that the accommodations were in fact anything but separate and unequal.

Separation of the races in street cars came somewhat later. Only Georgia (in 1891) had made such a law before 1900; and then in the first decade of the twentieth century most of the other southern states did likewise, though in some cases applying the rule only to specified cities.

The Louisiana law requiring separate accommodations on trains may be taken as fairly typical.[1]

> *Section 1*
>
> *Be it enacted by the General Assembly of the State of Louisiana,* That all railway companies carrying passengers in their coaches in this State, shall provide equal but separate accommodations for the white, and colored races, by providing two or more passenger coaches for each passenger train, or by dividing the passenger coaches by a partition so as to secure separate accommodations; *provided* that this section shall not be construed to apply to street railroads. No person or persons, shall be permitted to occupy seats in coaches, other than the ones assigned to them on account of the race they belong to.
>
> *Section 2*
>
> *Be it further enacted etc.,* That the officers of such passenger trains shall have power and are hereby required to assign each passenger to the coach or compartment used for the race to which such passenger belongs; any passenger insisting on going into a coach or compartment to which by race he does not belong, shall be liable to a fine of twenty-five dollars or in lieu thereof to imprisonment for a period of not more than twenty days in the parish prison and any officer of any railroad insisting on assigning a passenger to a coach or compartment other than the one set aside for the race to which

[1] *Acts of Louisiana,* 1890 (No. 111), 152–54.

said passenger belongs shall be liable to a fine of twenty-five dollars or in lieu thereof to imprisonment for a period of not more than twenty days in the parish prison; and should any passenger refuse to occupy the coach or compartment to which he or she is assigned by the officer of such railway, said officer shall have power to refuse to carry such passenger on his train, and for such refusal neither he nor the railway company which he represents shall be liable for damages in any of the courts of this State.

Section 3

Be it further enacted etc., That all officers and directors of railway companies that shall refuse or neglect to comply with the provisions and requirements of this act shall be deemed guilty of a misdemeanor and shall upon conviction before any court of competent jurisdiction be fined not less than one hundred dollars nor more than five hundred dollars; any conductor or other employees of such passenger train, having charge of the same, who shall refuse or neglect to carry out the provisions of this act shall on conviction be fined not less than twenty-five dollars nor more than fifty dollars for each offense; all railroad corporations carrying passengers in this State other than street railroads shall keep this law posted up in a conspicuous place in each passenger coach and ticket office, provided that nothing in this act shall be construed as applying to nurses attending children of the other race. . . .

The same state, like southern states generally, made similar provision for separate waiting rooms.[1]

Section 1

Be it enacted by the General Assembly of the State of Louisiana, That all railway companies carrying passengers in this State shall upon the construction or renewal of depots at regular stations provide equal but separate waiting rooms in their depots for the white and colored races by providing two waiting rooms in each depot, provided that the requirements of this Act shall be fully complied with by the first day of January A.D. 1896. No person or persons shall be permitted to occupy seats or remain in a waiting room other than the one assigned to them on account of the race to which they belong.

Section 2

[Like the last mentioned statute, above, this section provides for enforcement and penalties for violations, except that fines were set at $25 instead of $50.]

The following Georgia law respecting sleeping cars was much like that of other southern states.[2]

Section 1

Be it enacted [that] sleeping-car companies and railroad companies operating sleeping-cars in this State shall have the right to assign all passengers to seats and berths under their charge, and shall separate the white and colored races in making said assignments, and the conductor and other employees on the train of cars to which said sleeping-car or cars may be attached, shall not permit white and colored passengers to occupy the same compartment.

[1] *Acts of Louisiana,* 1894 (No. 98), 132–34.
[2] *Statutes of Georgia,* 1899 (No. 369), 66–67.

And any passenger remaining in any compartment other than that to which he may be assigned shall be guilty of and punished as for a misdemeanor; *provided*, that nothing in this Act shall be construed to compel sleeping-car companies or railroads operating sleeping-cars to carry persons of color in sleeping or parlor-cars; *provided*, that this Act shall not apply to colored nurses or servants traveling with their employers.

Section 2

Be it further enacted by the General Assembly, That any conductor or other employee of any sleeping-car, as well as any conductor or other employee of the train to which any sleeping-car may be attached, are hereby empowered with full police power to enforce the preceding section, and any [one of them] who fails or refuses to assist in ejecting any passenger violating the provisions of this Act, shall be guilty of a misdemeanor and punished as for a misdemeanor. . . .

The North Carolina Jim Crow street car law which follows had its counterpart in most of the southern states.[1]

Section 1

That all street, inter-urban railway companies, engaged as common carriers, . . . shall . . . set apart so much of the front portion of each car operated by them as shall be necessary, for occupation by the white passengers therein, and shall likewise provide and set apart so much of the rear part of said car as shall be necessary, for occupation by the colored passengers therein, and shall require as far as practicable the white and colored passengers to each occupy the respective parts of such car so set apart for them. . . .

Section 2

That any white person entering a street car for the purpose of becoming a passenger thereon shall, if necessary to carry out the purposes of this act, occupy the first vacant seat or unoccupied space in the aisle nearest the front of said car, and any colored person entering said car for a like purpose shall occupy the first vacant seat or unoccupied space in the aisle nearest the rear end of said car. . . .

Section 5

That any officer, . . . or . . . employee of any street railway . . . who shall wilfully violate . . . this act shall be guilty of a misdemeanor, and upon conviction fined or imprisoned. . . .

Section 6

Any person wilfully violating . . . this act shall be guilty of a misdemeanor, and fined not more than fifty dollars or imprisoned not exceeding thirty days, and may also be ejected from said car by the conductor and other agent or agents charged with the operation of said car. . . .

Section 7

The provisions of this act shall not apply to colored nurses of white children, while in attendance upon such children then in their charge, or a colored attendant in charge of a sick or infirm white person.

[1] *Public Laws and Resolutions of North Carolina,* 1907 (chap. 850), 1238–1239.

D. *Miscellaneous Provisions for Separate Facilities*

By 1910 the separation of the races in public schools was required both by constitution and statute in twelve states: Alabama, Florida, Georgia, Kentucky, Louisiana, Mississippi, North Carolina, South Carolina, Tennessee, Texas, Virginia, West Virginia; and by statute alone in three others: Arkansas, Maryland, and Delaware. In addition, school boards were *authorized* to establish, if they chose, separate schools for the races in Arizona and Indiana; in Kansas, in cities with a population of more than 150,000; and in Wyoming in districts having not less than sixteen colored pupils. Several states (Illinois, Massachusetts, Nevada, New Jersey, New York, Ohio, and Pennsylvania), in which separate schools had been either permitted or required, had, by 1910, enacted laws to prohibit such segregation, while others (Colorado, Idaho, Iowa, Michigan, Minnesota, New Mexico, and Rhode Island), which had never authorized separate schools, had by 1910 enacted laws to prohibit them.

Here follow sections from three southern state constitutions and the text of one state law requiring separate schools for white and black children.

FLORIDA[1]

ARTICLE XII

Section 12

White and colored children shall not be taught in the same school, but impartial provision shall be made for both.

KENTUCKY[2]

ARTICLE VI

Section 187

In distributing the school fund no distinction shall be made on account of race or color, and separate schools for white and colored children shall be maintained.

ALABAMA[3]

ARTICLE XIV

Section 256

The legislature shall establish, organize, and maintain a liberal system of

[1] Florida Constitution of 1885, in *Revised Statutes of Florida,* 1892, 65.
[2] Kentucky Constitution of 1891, in *Kentucky Statutes,* 1894, 137.
[3] Alabama Constitution of 1901, in *Code of Alabama,* 1903, III, 187.

public schools throughout the state for the benefit of children thereof between the ages of seven and twenty-one years. Separate schools shall be provided for white and colored children, and no child of either race shall be permitted to attend schools of the other race.

KENTUCKY[1]

AN ACT to prohibit white and colored persons from attending the same school.

Be it enacted by the General Assembly of the Commonwealth of Kentucky:

Section 1

That it shall be unlawful for any person, corporation or association of persons to maintain or operate any college, school or institution where persons of the white and negro races are both received as pupils for instruction; and any person or corporation who shall operate any such college, school or institution shall be fined one thousand dollars, and any person or corporation who may be convicted of violating . . . this act, shall be fined one hundred dollars for each day they may operate said school, college or institution, after such conviction.

Section 2

That any instructor who shall teach in any school, college or institution where members of said two races are received as pupils for instruction shall be guilty of operating and maintaining same and fined as provided in the first section hereof.

Section 3

That . . . any person [of either race, attending a school for the other race] shall be fined fifty dollars for each day he attends such institution or school.

Section 4

Nothing in this act shall be construed to prevent any private school, college or institution of learning from maintaining a separate and distinct branch thereof, in a different locality, not less than twenty-five miles distant, for the education exclusively of one race or color.

Kentucky, like Mississippi and Alabama, even went so far as to declare that taxes paid by whites should be used only for white schools and taxes paid by Negroes only for Negro schools. The following is an excerpt from a law concerning the management and control of schools in "cities of the fourth class."[2]

No tax raised from the property or poll of any white person or corporation in said city shall be used for the support of said graded free colored common schools of said city, nor shall any tax raised from the property or poll of any colored person be used for the support of said graded free white schools of said city.

There were, in addition to the more conspicuous kinds of legally established racial discrimination, other miscellaneous distinctions. The Florida Militia Law, for example, decreed that "in no case shall any

[1] *Acts of Kentucky*, 1904 (chap. 85), 181.
[2] *Laws of Kentucky*, 1904 (chap. 53), 129–31.

colored officer command white troops."[1] And Arkansas, like most southern states, insisted upon keeping white and Negro convicts segregated.[2]

ARKANSAS

Be it enacted by the General Assembly of the State of Arkansas:

Section 1

That in the State penitentiary and in all county jails, stockades, convict camps, and all other places where State or county prisoners may at any time be kept confined, separate apartments shall be provided and maintained for white and negro prisoners.

Section 2

That separate bunks, beds, bedding, separate dining tables and all other furnishings, shall be provided and kept by the State and counties, respectively, for the use of white and negro prisoners, [and such items] after having been assigned to the use of, or after having been used by white or negro prisoners [shall never] be changed the one for the use of the other [*sic*].

Section 3

That it shall be unlawful for any white prisoner to be handcuffed or otherwise chained or tied to a negro prisoner.

E. *Restricting the Franchise*

Attention has already been given the devices by which the southern states undertook to set at naught the Fifteenth Amendment's categorical command that the right to vote shall not be abridged on account of race. Beginning in 1890, however, when Mississippi in its new Constitution introduced what came to be called the "Mississippi Plan," the older stratagems gave way increasingly, in one southern state after another, to more forthright "legal" disfranchisement. The basic strategy was (1) to direct the disabilities ostensibly not against blacks—all racial designations were in fact scrupulously avoided—but against *conditions* to which they were peculiarly susceptible; and (2) to enforce the restrictions "selectively," so that "deserving" white voters who fell short of the qualifications were either not challenged at all, or (especially after 1898) were specifically exempted from the restrictions under the protection of "grandfather clauses."

The pertinent provisions of the 1890 Mississippi Constitution will serve to illustrate the new reliance upon "legal disfranchisement."[3] The Mississippi Plan, it will be noted, laid down five basic tests: (a)

1 *Laws of Florida,* 1903 (chap. 5202, No. 97, sec. 22), 158.

2 *Acts of Arkansas,* 1903 (No. 95), 161.

3 Art. 12, *Constitution of Mississippi,* of 1890, in *Annotated Code of Mississippi,* 1892, 80.

residence requirements; (b) complete absence of previous convictions for any of a specified list of common offenses; (c) tax payment (including poll tax); (d) a reading-and-understanding test; (e) a registration requirement, to be complied with at least four months before an election. Closely patterned upon this formula were the suffrage provisions of other state constitutions (among them, those of Alabama, Louisiana, Georgia, and North Carolina).

Section 241

Every male inhabitant of this state, except idiots, insane persons, and Indians not taxed, who is a citizen of the United States, twenty-one years old and upwards, who has resided in this state two years, and one year in the election district, or in the incorporated city or town in which he offers to vote, and who is duly registered, and who has never been convicted of bribery, burglary, theft, arson, obtaining money or goods under false pretenses, perjury, forgery, embezzlement, or bigamy, and who has paid, on or before the first day of February on the year in which he shall offer to vote, all taxes which may have been legally required of him, and which he has had an opportunity of paying according to law, for the two preceding years, and who shall produce to the officers holding the election satisfactory evidence that he has paid said taxes, is declared to be a qualified elector. . . .

Section 243

A uniform poll-tax of two dollars, to be used in aid of the common schools . . . is hereby imposed on every male inhabitant of this state between the ages of twenty-one and sixty years, except certain physically handicapped persons . . . said tax to be a lien only upon taxable property. . . .

Section 244

On and after the first day of January, A.D. 1892, every elector shall, in addition to the foregoing qualifications, be able to read any section of the constitution of this state; or he shall be able to understand the same when read to him, or give a reasonable interpretation thereof. . . .

Section 249

No one shall be allowed to vote for members of the legislature or other officers who has not been duly registered under the constitution and laws of this state, by an officer of this state, legally authorized to register the voters thereof. . . .

Section 251

Electors shall not be registered within four months next before any election at which they may offer to vote. . . .

A Grandfather Clause

Louisiana's grandfather clause, enacted in 1898, was typical of similar provisions thereafter prescribed by other southern states until the Supreme Court of the United States declared such artifices unconstitutional in *Guinn* v. *United States*.[1] Their admitted purpose was to exempt whites from voting qualifications, which ostensibly were

[1] See below, p. 211.

directed at all who could not meet them, but which by this contrivance would now reach only Negroes, presumably without offending the federal constitution's guarantee that the franchise was not to be abridged on account of race.[1]

[Section 5.] No male person who was on January 1st, 1867, or any date prior thereto, entitled to vote under the Constitution or statutes of any State of the United States, wherein he then resided, and no son or grandson of any such person not less than twenty-one years of age at the date of the adoption of this Constitution, and no male person of foreign birth, who was naturalized prior to the first day of January, 1898, shall be denied the right to register and vote in this State by reason of his failure to possess the educational or property qualification prescribed by this Constitution. . . .

Disfranchisement and the Virginia Constitutional Convention of 1901–1902

Embarrassed by the frauds attending subterfuges by which Negroes were denied the ballot, the Democratic leadership in Virginia persuaded the state's voters to authorize a convention to draft a new constitution in 1901. Its proceedings, published in more than 3,000 closely printed pages, established beyond argument that the object of the convention was to find more satisfactory modes of disfranchising the Negro than those heretofore employed.

Among the devices used for "counting out" the Negro voter in the 1880's and 1890's were disqualification by reason of change in residence; slowing down the line of Negro voters by making protracted challenges; ruling semiliterate Negroes ineligible because of errors, however inconsequential, in their answers to questions concerning their places of residence; discarding of entire bundles of ballots because they had been improperly tied up with string; discarding ballots on the ground that a candidate's initials had been improperly given, or because the voter had marked his ballot for presidential and vice-presidential candidates rather than for *electors;* and (after the secret, uniform ballot had been introduced about 1890) failure to provide enough booths to accommodate Negro voters.

Some election officials exchanged ballots handed to them for deposit, for others already marked. In some cases unlettered Negroes were coached about the position of the names on the ballot, but when they entered the booth to vote, the names were in fact in a wholly different order. Election laws permitted the citizen only two and a half minutes in the booth, during which time he was required to indicate a vote *against* a candidate by drawing a line three-fourths of the way through

[1] *Constitution of Louisiana,* of 1898; bound with *Acts of Louisiana,* 1898; see Part II.

his name. If the line was too long, too short, or not straight, election judges had the right to throw the ballot out.

"It is more courageous," said the *Richmond Times*, on January 27, 1901, "and honorable and better for public morals and good government to come out boldly and disfranchise the negro than to make a pretense of letting him vote and then cheating him at the polls."

It was in that spirit that the Virginia Constitutional Convention of 1901 met. The task of the special committee to frame the constitution's suffrage article was an egregiously difficult one. They were charged with the responsibility of disfranchising approximately 150,000 Negro voters by measures which would at the same time leave undisturbed some 300,000 white voters, and this without violating the Fifteenth Amendment of the Constitution of the United States.

The sharpest debate, when the article reached the convention floor, centered upon the reading-and-understanding clause, because delegates from areas with especially dense Negro population feared not only that whites would sooner or later be disfranchised by these proposals, but that the rising literacy rate among Negroes (while that of poor whites remained constant) would in the end render the clause ineffective as a bar to Negro voting and as a guarantee of white supremacy.

The leading student of the convention, writing in or about 1928, concluded that the suffrage clause as it was finally enacted not only promptly eliminated the Negro from Virginia politics, but also drastically reduced white participation in elections because "the elimination of the Negro has brought a feeling of security and an attitude of indifference among the whites. . . . As a result the state lacks a real party of opposition, is still solidly Democratic, and has delivered itself into the hands of less than 10 percent of its citizens."[1]

The following is from the official proceedings of the Convention.[2] Particular attention is drawn to the candid admission of the then young Carter Glass.[3]

[Mr. McDaniel]: Gentlemen. . . . we are not here as enemies of the colored man. On the contrary the good people of Virginia look upon him with interest, and with pity and compassion and friendship for the condition in which he is. We must not forget that he has been the plaything of the politicians of this country. We must not forget that considering his untutored condition he has borne himself well during the civil war, and as well as the mean white men would permit him since the war. (Applause).

[1] Ralph Clipman McDanel, *The Virginia Constitutional Convention of 1901–1902* (Baltimore, 1928), p. 58.

[2] *The Debates of the Constitutional Convention of Virginia, . . . June 12, 1901, to June 26, 1902* (Richmond, 1906), p. 58.

[3] See below, p. 143.

The evils that have come out of him in these later days were not evils generated in him, but it came first from his projection into a theatre of action in which he was not prepared to officiate, and it came from the inspiration of devious and designing men who desired [to use] him for their purposes. . . . There is no greater enemy of the colored man upon this earth than the white man who goes to him and misleads him to opposition of the white race in their triumphal march of progress. (Applause).

. . . The mocking cries that reach my ears from political opponents and from some of my own party, neither disconcert nor discourage me in this great effort. I do not forget that there were even those who mocked at Christ as he carried the heavy cross upon Calvary where he died for the sins of mankind, and the burden which you are to bear in this campaign, and in getting this better Constitution for the people of Virginia, is a burden which you should be encouraged to bear by the memory of the Master and those who taunted and perplexed him in His noble Work. (Applause). . . .

[Mr. Thom]: It is the high province of this Convention to make a solution of this problem and to set our people free. . . . [T]o do it we must remove [the Negro] as a disturbing factor in our public affairs. And it is for this, Mr. Chairman, that . . . I plead for a new emancipation, not now of the black man, but of the white man, whom the black man has enslaved in turn. . . . You think that the only thing you are called upon to do is to give us a white majority. Gentlemen, that is not what we want. We want freedom and independence. . . .

I have argued, Mr. Chairman, that the plan of the minority overlooked what we were after; that it was framed in disregard of the problem; that it at one fell swoop laid open the registration books to one half of the negro population; and that by the ratio of decrease of illiteracy, which had already been established[,] in ten years there would be as little illiteracy among the colored population of this State as there is among the white population to-day.

. . . With [our present] Herculean efforts to destroy illiteracy, and, if that be the obstruction to suffrage, to destroy the obstruction that would exist between the negro and the ballot-box, can we as sane, as thoughtful, as patriotic men, be content with basing the whole of our future upon such a fleeting and disappearing factor?

Now, Mr. Chairman, inasmuch as we stand here face to face with the fifteenth amendment to the Constitution of the United States, when what we want to do is to write the one word "white," in the Constitution, and when we are prevented from doing that by this Constitution of the United States, it must be realized by every one that what we do in this direction must be at least an expedient; it cannot reach the dignity of the ideal; it must be simply the best thing that we can do under the adverse conditions. . . .

[After arguing at some length that a carefully drafted reading-and-explaining clause would achieve the goal of Negro disfranchisement without disfranchising "illiterate but worthy" whites, Mr. Thom continued:]

But it would not be frank in me, Mr. Chairman, if I did not say that I do not expect an understanding clause to be administered with any degree of friendship by the white man to the suffrage of the black man. I expect the examination with which the black man will be confronted, to be inspired by the same spirit that inspires every man upon this floor and in this convention. I would not expect an impartial administration of the clause.

I would not expect for the white man a rigid examination. The people of Virginia do not stand impartially between the suffrage of the white man and the suffrage of the black man. If they did, this Convention would not be assembled upon this floor. If they did, the uppermost thoughts in the hearts of every man within the sound of my voice would not be to find a way of disfranchising the black man and enfranchising the white man. We do not come here prompted by an impartial purpose in reference to negro suffrage. We come here to sweep the field of expedients for the purpose of finding some constitutional method of ridding ourselves of [Negro suffrage] forever; and we have the approval of the Supreme Court of the United States in making that effort. [He was referring to *Williams* v. *Mississippi* (1897)[1]] What did the United States Supreme Court [say]?

It . . . said that, within the limitations of the Federal Constitution, it is permissible for this people to search for expedients to exclude the negro race. If, then, a rigid examination permitted by the Constitution excluded the negro; then, in law, he is excluded by virtue of his failure to attain a certain standard, and not for the reason that he is a negro; and, therefore, the law itself is constitutional. But, again, I expect this clause to be efficient, because it will act "in terrorem" upon the negro race. They believe that they will have a hostile examination put upon them by the white man . . . and they will not apply for registration. They will know that they first have to pass an examination; that they then have to make out their application for registration in their own handwriting; that they then have to make out their ballot without assistance; and that they then have to pay a capitation tax. These impediments will be too great for the negro, and he will find himself, as a practical question, excluded from the suffrage. . . .

And again, we think, Mr. Chairman, that this clause will not exclude any worthy white citizen of this Commonwealth from the suffrage; for the white man is friendly to the white man's suffrage; and the white man will find a friendly examiner when he goes to stand this examination. . . .

But, gentlemen, this understanding clause is not the horrible thing that it is painted to be. . . . By purging your electorate and making it, to all intents and purposes, an Anglo-Saxon electorate, you liberate the honest people of Virginia to demand honesty in elections.

Heretofore they had to listen . . . to the suggestion that fraud was necessary in order to preserve their civilization; but, when you have taken the black man off the registration book . . . there is no reason any longer why this people cannot rise up in its majesty and in its glory, and demand absolute purity in elections; and it will do it. Not only will the people demand it, but in this very article of the Constitution there is a guarantee that elections be honest . . . that hereafter the ballot-box shall, during elections, be kept in public view, that the ballots shall not be either canvassed or counted in secret, and that the Legislature must supplement this article by everything that is necessary to insure the freedom and purity [of the ballot]. . . .

Mr. R. L. Gordon: Wouldn't it be a very easy matter for a sharp negro lawyer, who felt a great interest in the question . . . to hold schools, and go around . . . teach them enough to go and stand this examination; while the illiterate and ignorant white class would not have the same benefit, because there would not be the same amount of interest felt by the white people

[1] See below, p. 147.

who might be willing to instruct them. . . . The Negro is quick at that kind of thing, and would feel a very lively interest in it. . . .

Mr. Thom: We must run whatever risk is involved in that suggestion. We think that when the negro understands that that provision is to be administered by people hostile to his vote; that in addition to that he has to make out his own application for registration; that in addition to that he has to make out his own ballot, without assistance, and in addition to that he has to pay the poll-tax, we think that that will keep him from the ballot-box. . . .

[Mr. Pedigo, a Republican from Henry County, though agreeing that the Negro was incapable of intelligent voting, objected to his disfranchisement:] In order that I may not be misunderstood I will here state that I do not consider the negro as being equal or anything near equal to the white man in intelligence, or learning, or capacity for self-government. I do not believe that they, if left to themselves, could carry on a free republican government.

. . . I am well aware that if Virginia is to have even a decent government, it must be, in the main, a government by the white people. But, the negro is here, he is a part of us; we cannot do him a wrong without, at the same time, doing ourselves a wrong. We must hold him up; we must help him along; and, above all things, we must do him justice. We are in the same ship with him. If that ship sinks we will all be drowned together. . . .

[Mr. Carter Glass:] Mr. President, the assaults upon this plan of suffrage have been of a varied nature. . . . We are thus between the cross-fire of those who protest that the scheme is too drastic in the elimination of the negro and those who think it is not drastic enough. But, Mr. President, in the midst of differing contentions and suggested perplexities, there stands out the uncontroverted fact that the article of suffrage which the Convention will to-day adopt does not necessarily deprive a single white man of the ballot, but will inevitably cut from the existing electorate four-fifths of the negro voters. (Applause.) That was the purpose of this Convention; that will be the achievement.

Mr. Pedigo: Will it not be done by fraud and discrimination?

Mr. Glass: . . . Discrimination! Why, that is precisely what we propose; that, exactly, is what this Convention was elected for—to discriminate to the very extremity of permissible action under the limitations of the Federal Constitution, with a view to the elimination of every negro voter who can be gotten rid of, legally, without materially impairing the numerical strength of the white electorate. As has been said, we have accomplished our purpose strictly within the limitations of the Federal Constitution by legislating against the characteristics of the black race, and not against the "race, color or previous condition" of the people themselves. It is a fine discrimination, indeed, that we have practiced in the fabrication of this plan; and now, Mr. President, we ask the Convention to Confirm our work and emancipate Virginia. I ask you for a vote on the article of suffrage. . . .

(6)

THE SUPREME COURT AND THE BLACK AMERICAN, 1883–1910

The reluctance of the Supreme Court of the United States to advance minority rights, clearly apparent for a century preceding the *Civil Rights Cases* in 1883, persisted throughout the years now being reviewed. In the previous chapter, notice was taken of the Court's whittling away of the protections which Congressional legislation of Reconstruction days and the Fourteenth and Fifteenth amendments seemed to guarantee to Negroes. The Fourteenth's privileges and immunities clause, neutralized by the *Slaughter House* and *Cruikshank* Cases,[1] remained a dead letter, so far as the Negro was concerned, for the rest of the nineteenth century and far beyond. The amendment's due process clause, meanwhile, was employed to protect property rather than disadvantaged and defenseless minorities; and the equal protection clause—virtually unused as a shield for black rights before 1896—was in that year rendered all but meaningless as a guarantee against discrimination when the Court in *Plessy* v. *Ferguson*[2] gave its approval to the separate-but-equal doctrine. Thereafter that tribunal did not, until very much later, seriously examine the equality of the separate facilities that the states could provide under the protection of the *Plessy* principle.

The black man fared no better in reaping the harvest promised by the Fifteenth than he did in garnering the fruits of the Fourteenth Amendment, for it was in these years that the structure of Negro disfranchisement was effectually completed, not to be disturbed, with minor exceptions, until well into the twentieth century.

That the volume of cases concerning Negro rights reaching the Supreme Court between 1883 and 1910 was very small was perhaps not surprising, in view of the racial conservatism of the courts and of the public generally. It should be recalled too that the NAACP and its Legal and Educational Defense Fund had not yet begun its fateful mission as the race's champion at the bar until five years after the close of this era, when it won its first major triumph, in *Guinn* v. *United States* (1915), which struck down the grandfather clauses.[3]

[1] See above, pp. 59, 62.
[2] See below, p. 149.
[3] See below, p. 211.

The following selection of cases represents the leading court decisions of the period. They deal with the franchise, jury service, segregation in public conveyances, separate schools for the races, and peonage.

A. *Preserving the Restricted Franchise*

In *Ex parte Yarbrough* (1884) the Court found adequate constitutional sanction for congressional power to deal with *private* interference with Negro voting, not only in Article I, Section 4 (which empowers Congress to regulate congressional elections);[1] but also in the federal government's implied power to safeguard its own elections by protecting the voter in his enjoyment of the right to vote for congressmen, a privilege of United States citizenship.[2]

Yarbrough and other members of the Ku Klux Klan were indicted in a federal court in Georgia for conspiring to intimidate Barry Saunders, a Negro who proposed to vote in a congressional election. The Klansmen were found guilty, in violation of the Enforcement Act of 1870, of going out upon the highways, in disguise, and using violence to dissuade Saunders from voting. Yarbrough appealed to the Supreme Court, pleading that Congress had no delegated authority to police elections, but the Court ruled otherwise.

. . . That a government whose essential character is republican, whose executive head and legislative body are both elective, whose most numerous and powerful branch of the legislative is elected by the people directly, has no power by appropriate laws to secure this election from the influence of violence, of corruption, and of fraud, is a proposition so startling as to arrest attention and demand the gravest consideration. . . . [T]he general government, . . . must have the power to protect the elections on which its existence depends from violence and corruption. . . .

. . . The proposition that it has no such power is supported by the old argument often heard, often repeated, and in this court never assented to, that when a question of the power of Congress arises the advocate of the power must be able to place his finger on words which expressly grant it. The brief of counsel before us . . . uses the same language [that] [b]ecause there is no *express* power to provide for preventing violence exercised on the voter as a means of controlling his vote, no such law can be enacted. It destroys at one blow . . . the doctrine universally applied to all instruments of writing, that what is implied is as much a part of the instrument as what is expressed. This principle, in its application to the Constitution of the United States, more than to almost any other writing, is a necessity, by reason of the inherent inability to put into words all derivative powers,—a difficulty which the instrument itself recognizes by conferring on Congress the

[1] See below, p. 5.
[2] *Ex parte Yarbrough*, 110 U.S. 651 (1884).

authority to pass all laws necessary and proper to carry into execution the powers expressly granted. . . .

We know of no express authority to pass laws to punish theft or burglary of the treasury of the United States. Is there therefore no power in the Congress to protect the treasury by punishing such theft and burglary? Are the mails of the United States, and the money carried in them, to be left at the mercy of robbers and of thieves who may handle the mail, because the Constitution contains no express words of power in Congress to enact laws for the punishment of those offenses? The principle, if sound, would abolish the entire criminal jurisdiction of the courts of the United States, and the laws which confer that jurisdiction. . . .

. . . [T]he Congress has been slow to invoke the fourth section of the first article of the Constitution. This section declares that: "The times, places, and manner of holding elections for Senators and Representatives shall be prescribed in each State by the legislature thereof; but the Congress may at any time make or alter such regulations, except as to the place of choosing Senators." . . .

. . . Can it be doubted that Congress can, by law, protect the act of voting, the place where it is done, and the man who votes from personal violence or intimidation, and the election itself from corruption or fraud? If this be so, and it is not doubted, are such powers annulled because an election for state officers is held at the same time and place? Is it any less important that the election of members of Congress should be the free choice of all the electors, because state officers are to be elected at the same time? . . . These questions answer themselves; and it is only because the Congress of the United States, through long habit and long years of forbearance, has, in deference and respect to the states, refrained from the exercise of these powers, that they are now doubted. . . .

. . . In a republican government, like ours, where political power is reposed in representatives of the entire body of the people, chosen at short intervals by popular elections, the temptations to control these elections by violence and by corruption is a constant source of danger. . . . If the recurrence of such acts as these prisoners stand convicted of are too common in one quarter of the country, and give omen of danger from lawless violence, the free use of money in elections, arising from the vast growth of recent wealth in other quarters, presents equal cause for anxiety. If the government of the United States has within its constitutional domain no authority to provide against these evils,—if the very sources of power may be poisoned by corruption or controlled by violence and outrage, without legal restraint,—then, indeed, is the country in danger. . . .

The Yarbrough principle was unused for two years; it was then weakened, when the Supreme Court in *James* v. *Bowman* decided that an act of Congress (*Revised Statutes* 5507), which presumed to reach *all* elections—was unauthorized, whether by the Fifteenth Amendment or by Article I, Section 4.[1] The Fifteenth, said the Court, applied only to interference by *states*, not by individuals; and Article I, Section 4 extended federal authority only to elections of *federal* officers.

Two persons indicted for bribery and otherwise preventing a Negro

[1] 190 U.S. 127 (1903).

from voting in a congressional election in Kentucky had been convicted of violating the federal law which forbade the intimidating or hindering of any person from voting, by various enumerated devices. The Supreme Court reversed the conviction upon appeal.

The single question presented for our consideration is whether [sec. 5507 of the US Rev. Stat.] can be upheld as a valid enactment, for, if not, the indictment must also fall, and the defendant was rightfully discharged [by the court below]. On its face the section purports to be an exercise of the power granted to Congress by the 15th Amendment, for it declares a punishment upon anyone who, by means of bribery, prevents another to whom the right of suffrage is guaranteed by such amendment from exercising that right. But that amendment relates solely to action "by the United States or by any state," and does not contemplate wrongful individual acts. It is in this respect similar to the [civil rights clauses] of the 14th Amendment. [The court then cited *Virginia* v. *Rives; Ex parte Virginia; U.S.* v. *Cruikshank;* the *Civil Rights Cases; U.S.* v. *Harris;* the *Slaughter House Cases;* and *U.S.* v. *Reese* in support of its position on the Fourteenth Amendment.[1]]

In *Williams* v. *Mississippi* the Supreme Court was, curiously, compelled to rule on the constitutionality of the Mississippi Plan of Negro disfranchisement because the plaintiff had been indicted for murder by an all-white grand jury and convicted by an all-white trial jury. Mississippi law required that only duly qualified *voters* might serve as jurors; and Williams' attorney argued that because the state's constitution and laws in effect denied the franchise to Negroes, the latter were by the same token denied the right of trial by juries of their peers. The Court, however, came to the remarkable conclusion that the constitution and statutes of Mississippi did not "on their face discriminate between the races," and that while evil was possible under them, it had not been shown in this case that their administration had in fact been evil, nor had it been proved that the mode of selecting the jurors had been improper. The Court, in a word, upheld both the Mississippi disfranchising plan (specifically the literacy test and the poll tax) and the exclusion of Negroes from jury service. Granting that the administrative officers in judging the eligibility of applicants for the franchise *might* rule unfairly against the applicant, the Court went on to say:[2]

To make the possible dereliction of the officers the dereliction of the Constitution and laws, the remarks of the supreme court of the state are quoted by plaintiff in error as to their intent. . . . But nothing tangible can be deduced from this. If weakness were to be taken advantage of, it was to be done "within the field of permissible action under the limitations imposed by the Federal Constitution," and the means of it were the alleged characteristics of the negro race, not the administration of the law by the officers of the state. Besides, the operation of the Constitution and laws is not limited by their language or effects to one race. They reach weak and vicious white

[1] See above, pp. 59–72.
[2] *Williams* v. *Mississippi,* 170 U.S. 213 (1897).

men as well as weak and vicious black men, and whatever is sinister in their intention, if anything, can be prevented by both races by the exertion of that duty which voluntarily pays taxes and refrains from crime.

It cannot be said, therefore, that the denial of the equal protection of the laws arises primarily from the Constitution and laws of Mississippi, nor is there any sufficient allegation of an evil and discriminating administration of them. . . .

B. *Separate-but-Equal Upheld: Public Conveyances*

A Mississippi statute required separate accommodations for the races on "all railroads carrying passengers in this State," but made no distinction between inter- and intrastate traffic. In *Louisville, New Orleans, and Texas Railway* v. *Mississippi* the United States Supreme Court affirmed the Mississippi Supreme Court's findings that such regulation by a state does not burden interstate commerce, and does not, therefore, trespass upon Congress' exclusive power over such traffic.[1] (It will be remembered that in *Hall* v. *De Cuir*[2] the Court had earlier concluded that state laws *forbidding* segregation on trains *do* burden interstate commerce and are therefore unconstitutional infringement upon federal prerogative.) Following are excerpts from the majority's view and from Justice Harlan's dissent.

The question is whether the Act is a regulator of interstate commerce and therefore beyond the power of the State. [Because no individual claims to have been injured in this case] the question is limited to the power of the State to compel railroad companies to provide within the State separate accommodations for the two races. . . .

In this case, the Supreme Court of Mississippi held that the Statute applied solely to commerce within the State; and that construction, being the construction of the Statute of the State by its highest court, must be accepted as conclusive here: if it be a matter respecting wholly commerce within a State, and not interfering with commerce between the States, then obviously there is no violation of the commerce clause of the Federal Constitution. Counsel for plaintiff in error strenuously insists that it does affect and regulate interstate commerce, but this contention cannot be sustained. . . .

All that we can consider is, whether the State has the power to require that railroad trains within her limits shall have separate accommodations for the two races. That affecting only commerce within the State is no invasion of the powers given to Congress by the commerce clause. . . .

It has often been held in this court, and there can be no doubt about it, that there is a commerce wholly within the State, which is not subject to the constitutional provision, and the distinction between commerce among the States and the other class of commerce between the citizens of a single State, and conducted within its limits exclusively, is one which has been fully

[1] 133 U.S. 587 (1890).

[2] See above, p. 63.

recognized in this court, although it may not always be easy . . . to distinguish between the one and the other. . . . The Statute in this case, as settled by the Supreme Court of the State of Mississippi, affects only such commerce within the state, and comes therefore within the principles laid down. . . . We see no error in the ruling of the Supreme Court of the State of Mississippi, and *its judgment* is therefore affirmed.

* * *

(Justice Harlan, *dissenting*) While [the Act] purports only to control the carrier when engaged within the State, it must necessarily influence his conduct to some extent in the management of his business throughout his entire voyage. . . . It is difficult to understand how a state enactment, requiring the separation of the white and black races in interstate carriers of passengers (as in *Hall* v. *De Cuir*) is a regulation of commerce among the States, while a similar enactment forbidding such separation is not a regulation of that character. . . . I dissent . . . upon the ground that the Statute of Mississippi is . . . a regulation of commerce among the States, and is therefore void.

The *Civil Rights Cases* had ended for the present any genuine check by the federal government upon segregation and discrimination when imposed by *private* action. In the historic case of *Plessy* v. *Ferguson*,[1] however, *state* action was at issue: a Louisiana law of 1890, which required all railway companies to provide separate accommodations—either by separate cars or separate compartments—for Negroes and whites. Plessy, who was believed to be seven-eighths white, refused to vacate a seat in a white compartment, and was arrested. When the case was appealed from the Supreme Court of Louisiana to the United States Supreme Court, the latter gave its approval to the doctrine that state laws requiring separate accommodations do not offend against the equal protection clause if the separated facilities are "substantially equal." The doctrine was destined to stand as constitutional orthodoxy until 1954. Justice Harlan alone dissented.

Portions of both the majority and minority opinions are here reproduced. It is not without interest that the majority opinion was written by Justice Brown, a Yale man from Michigan, while the vigorous and prophetic dissent was written by a Kentuckian.

. . . The object of the [Fourteenth] Amendment was undoubtedly to enforce the absolute equality of the two races before the law, but in the nature of things it could not have been intended to abolish distinctions based upon color, or to enforce social, as distinguished from political, equality, or a commingling of the two races upon terms unsatisfactory to either. Laws permitting, and even requiring, their separation in places where they are liable to be brought into contact do not necessarily imply the inferiority of either race to the other, and have been generally, if not universally, recognized as within the competency of the state legislatures in the exercise of their police power. The most common instance of this is connected with the establishment of separate schools for white and colored children, which has

[1] 163 U.S. 537 (1896).

been held to be a valid exercise of the legislative power even by courts of States where the political rights of the colored race have been longest and most earnestly enforced. . . .

Laws forbidding the intermarriage of the two races may be said in a technical sense to interfere with the freedom of contract, and yet have been universally recognized as within the police power of the State. . . .

The distinction between laws interfering with the political equality of the negro and those requiring the separation of the two races in schools, theatres, and railway carriages has been frequently drawn by this court. . . .

. . . Every exercise of the police power must be reasonable, and extend only to such laws as are enacted in good faith for the promotion of the public good, and not for the annoyance or oppression of a particular class. . . .

So far, then, as a conflict with the Fourteenth Amendment is concerned, the case reduces itself to the question of whether the statute of Louisiana is a reasonable regulation, and with respect to this there must necessarily be a large discretion on the part of the legislature. In determining the question of reasonableness it is at liberty to act with reference to the established usages, customs and traditions of the people, and with a view to the promotion of their comfort, and the preservation of the public peace and good order. Gauged by this standard, we cannot say that a law which authorizes or even requires the separation of the two races in public conveyances is unreasonable, or more obnoxious to the Fourteenth Amendment than the acts of Congress requiring separate schools for colored children in the District of Columbia, the constitutionality of which does not seem to have been questioned, or the corresponding acts of State legislatures.

We consider the underlying fallacy of the plaintiff's argument to consist in the assumption that the enforced separation of the two races stamps the colored race with a badge of inferiority. If this be so, it is not by reason of anything found in the act, but solely because the colored race chooses to put that construction upon it. . . . The argument also assumes that social prejudices may be overcome by legislation, and that equal rights cannot be secured to the negro except by an enforced commingling of the two races. We cannot accept this proposition. If the two races are to meet on terms of social equality, it must be the result of natural affinities, a mutual appreciation of each other's merits and a voluntary consent of individuals. . . . Legislation is powerless to eradicate racial instincts or to abolish distinctions based upon physical differences, and the attempt to do so can only result in accentuating the difficulties of the present situation. If the civil and political rights of both races be equal, one cannot be inferior to the other civilly or politically. If one race be inferior to the other socially, the Constitution of the United States cannot put them upon the same plane. . . .

Mr. Justice Harlan wrote a dissenting opinion, saying in part:

In respect of civil rights, common to all citizens, the Constitution of the United States does not, I think, permit any public authority to know the race of those entitled to be protected in the enjoyment of such rights. Every true man has pride of race and under appropriate circumstances when the rights of others, his equals before the law, are not to be affected, it is his privilege to express such pride and to take such action based upon it as to him seems proper. But I deny that any legislative body or judicial tribunal may have regard to the race of citizens when the civil rights of those citizens are involved.

The white race deems itself to be the dominant race in this country. And so it is, in prestige, in achievements, in education, in wealth and in power. So, I doubt not, it will continue to be for all time, if it remains true to its great heritage and holds fast to the principles of constitutional liberty. But in view of the Constitution, in the eye of the law, there is in this country no superior, dominant, ruling class of citizens. There is no caste here. Our Constitution is color-blind, and neither knows nor tolerates classes among citizens. In respect of civil rights, all citizens are equal before the law. The humblest is the peer of the most powerful. The law regards man as man, and takes no account of his surroundings or of his color when his civil rights as guaranteed by the supreme law of the land are involved.

In my opinion, the judgment this day rendered will, in time, prove to be quite as pernicious as the decision made by this tribunal in the Dred Scott Case. . . . The recent amendments to the Constitution, it was supposed, had eradicated these principles from our institutions. But it seems that we have yet, in some of the States, a dominant race, a superior class of citizens, which assumes to regulate the enjoyment of civil rights, common to all citizens, upon the basis of race. The present decision, it may well be apprehended, will not only stimulate aggressions, more or less brutal and irritating, upon the admitted rights of colored citizens, but will encourage the belief that it is possible, by means of state enactments, to defeat the beneficent purposes which the people of the United States had in view when they adopted the recent amendments of the Constitution, by one of which the blacks of this country were made citizens of the United States and of the States in which they respectively reside and whose privileges and immunities, as citizens, the States are forbidden to abridge. Sixty millions of whites are in no danger from the presence here of eight millions of blacks. [T]he interests of both require that the common government of all shall not permit the seeds of race hate to be planted under the sanction of law. What can more certainly arouse race hate, what more certainly create and perpetuate a feeling of distrust between these races, than State enactments which in fact proceed on the ground that colored citizens are so inferior and degraded that they cannot be allowed to sit in public coaches occupied by white citizens? That, as all will admit, is the real meaning of such legislation as was enacted in Louisiana. . . .

This question is not met by the suggestion that social equality cannot exist between the white and black races in this country. That argument, if it can be properly regarded as one, is scarcely worthy of consideration, for social equality no more exists between two races when travelling in a passenger coach on a public highway than when members of the same races sit by each other in a street car or in the jury box, or stand or sit with each other in a political assembly, or when they use in common the streets of a city or town, or when they are in the same room for the purpose of having their names placed on the registry of voters, or when they approach the ballot-box in order to exercise the high privilege of voting. . . .

The arbitrary separation of citizens, on the basis of race, while they are on a public highway, is a badge of servitude wholly inconsistent with the civil freedom and the equality before the law established by the Constitution. It cannot be justified upon any legal grounds.

If evils will result from the commingling of the two races upon public highways established for the benefit of all, they will be infinitely less than those that will surely come from State legislation regulating the enjoyment of civil rights upon the basis of race. We boast of the freedom enjoyed by our people above all other peoples. But it is difficult to reconcile that boast with a state of the law which, practically, puts the brand of servitude and degradation upon a large class of our fellow-citizens, our equals before the law. The thin disguise of "equal" accommodations for passengers in railroad coaches will not mislead any one, or atone for the wrong this day done. . . .

C. *Separate Schools Approved*

Even though *Plessy* v. *Ferguson* related only to segregation on railroads, it could hardly have come as a surprise when the Court in the *Berea College*[1] case held that the state could, under the separate-but-equal doctrine, forbid even a *private* college to instruct whites and blacks together. Thereafter, it was clear—clear enough to render a test case unnecessary—that separate facilities in tax-supported, public school sytems would suffer no censure from the Supreme Court.

There is no dispute as to the facts. That the act does not violate the Constitution of Kentucky is settled by the decision of its highest court, and the single question for our consideration is whether it conflicts with the Federal Constitution. . . .

Again, the decision by a state court of the extent and limitation of the powers conferred by the state upon one of its own corporations is of a purely local nature. In creating a corporation a state may withhold powers which may be exercised by and cannot be denied to an individual. It is under no obligation to treat both alike. In granting corporate powers the legislature may deem that the best interests of the state would be subserved by some restriction, and the corporation may not plead that, in spite of the restrictions, it has more or greater powers because the citizen has. . . .

It may be said that the court of appeals sustained the validity of this section of the statute, both against individuals and corporations. It ruled that the legislation was within the power of the state, and that the state might rightfully restrain all individuals, corporations, and associations.

. . . We need concern ourselves only with the inquiry whether the 1st section can be upheld as coming within the power of a state over its own corporate creatures.

We are of opinion, for reasons stated, that it does come within that power, and, on this ground, the judgment of the Court of Appeals of Kentucky is affirmed.

A decade earlier the Court, demonstrating the latitude it would permit itself in construing the term "separate but equal," had ruled that there was no denial of equal protection in the failure of a Georgia county to provide a high school for sixty black children. Satisfied with the county's defense that it could not without hardship afford

[1] *Berea College* v. *Kentucky,* 211 U.S. 26 (1908).

to maintain two high schools, the Court concluded that the alternative of providing *no* high school for either race was not an appropriate remedy, because Negro children would not be benefited by the closing of the high school for whites.[1]

> [W]hile all admit that the benefits and burdens of public taxation must be shared by citizens without discrimination against any class on account of their race, the education of the people in schools maintained by state taxation is a matter belonging to the respective states, and any interference on the part of Federal authority with the management of such schools cannot be justified except in the case of a clear and unmistakable disregard of rights secured by the supreme law of the land. We have here no such case to be determined; and as this view disposes of the only question which this court has jurisdiction to review and decide, the judgment is *affirmed*.

D. *Jury Service and Equal Protection*

One of the leading cases relating to juries in the period between the *Civil Rights Cases* of 1883 and the launching of the NAACP in 1910 was *Williams* v. *Mississippi* (1897), already mentioned as a test of the legality of the Mississippi disfranchising clauses.[2] Two other cases deserve brief mention. In *Murray* v. *Louisiana* (1896) the Supreme Court held that a criminal prosecution is not removable from a state to a federal court (as prescribed by *U.S. Revised Statutes* 641), merely because jury commissioners or other inferior officers had excluded Negro citizens from juries on account of their race, unless it was done by authority derived from the constitution and laws of the state.[3] Three years later, in *Carter* v. *Texas* (1899), when the Court had before it a plea from a Negro who had been indicted for murder by a grand jury from which all Negroes were shown to have been systematically excluded, because of their race, it took a more liberal view. The decision did not, however, materially improve the southern Negro's position as a prospective juror, or as a defendant, for the old abuses continued unabated. Said the Court in the *Carter* case:[4]

> Whenever by an action of a state, whether through its legislature, through its courts, or through its executive or administrative officers, all persons of the African race are excluded, solely because of their race or color, from serving as grand jurors in the criminal prosecution of a person of the African race, the equal protection of the laws is denied to him, contrary to the Four-

[1] *Cumming* v. *County Board of Education,* 175 U.S. 528 (1899).
[2] See above, p. 147.
[3] 163 U.S. 101 (1896).
[4] 177 U.S. 443 (1899).

teenth Amendment of the Constitution of the United States. . . . [The Court here invoked the decisions in *Strauder* v. *West Virginia, Neal* v. *Delaware,* and *Gibson* v. *Mississippi.*[1]]

E. *Peonage Outlawed*

The semiservile condition imposed on Negroes after the Civil War in the rural South by the share-cropper system, buttressed by crop lien laws, easily degenerated, in specific cases, into peonage. The practice of imposing penalties for petty crimes and then permitting employers to pay the fines for impecunious Negroes in exchange for their labor until they had worked off the debt was another easy road to peonage. A "Peonage Abolition Act," passed by Congress on March 2, 1867, was subsequently upheld as constitutional by the United States Supreme Court in *Clyatt* v. *United States*[2]; but peonage—"the condition of compulsory service, based upon the indebtedness to the master" (to use the language employed by the Court in the *Clyatt* case)—did not in fact lose its legal sanction until 1910, when, in *Bailey* v. *Alabama,*[3] the Court, on Thirteenth and Fourteenth Amendment grounds, declared unconstitutional state laws which authorized the prosecution of defaulting or "deserting" share-croppers for "obtaining credit under false pretenses." Even then, peonage did not wholly disappear.

. . . There is no more important concern than to safeguard the freedom of labor upon which alone can enduring prosperity be based. The provision designed to secure it would soon become a barren form if it were possible to establish a statutory presumption of this sort, and to hold over the heads of laborers the threat of punishment for crime, under the name of fraud, but merely upon evidence of failure to work out their debts. The [Abolition of Peonage] Act of Congress deprives of effect all legislative measures of any state through which, directly or indirectly, the prohibited thing, to wit, compulsory service to secure the payment of a debt, may be established or maintained; and we conclude that . . . the Code of Alabama, in so far as it makes the refusal or failure to perform the act or service, without refunding the money or paying for the property, prima facie evidence of the commission . . . of the crime which the section defines, is in conflict with the 13th Amendment, and the legislation authorized by that Amendment, and is therefore invalid.

In this view it is unnecessary to consider the contentions which have been made under the 14th Amendment.

[1] See above, p. 95.
[2] 197 U.S. 207 (1905).
[3] 219 U.S. 191 (1911).

(7)
THE STATE COURTS AND CIVIL RIGHTS

The multiplying laws defining the relationships between the races—whether designed, as in the case of northern and western state civil rights laws, to guarantee the Negroes' claim upon society for the privileges, immunities, and equal protection that the federal Constitution underwrites, or, as in the case of separate-facilities laws in the South, to sequester the Negro from the larger community—were conspicuous targets for suits to challenge their authority. But the hostility of the white community, to say nothing of the black American's meager access to funds and legal counsel to plead his cause in unfriendly courtrooms, held litigation of this sort to a modest volume.

The enumeration of some typical cases should not mislead the reader to the conclusion that strong pressure was being steadily exerted against the color line. The fact is that white America in this era either acquiesced in, or was apathetic to, the black American's deteriorating status, and that Negroes, if they were not unacquainted with the rights promised them by constitutions, statutes, and the common law, for the most part accepted their disabilities with hopeless resignation.

The cases now to be cited produced, after all, little difference in the condition of the black masses, but they are significant nevertheless as expressions of contemporary legal doctrine and as auguries of change. The growing friendliness of northern state courts to state civil rights laws is also noteworthy.

A. *Separate Schools Sustained*

The leading state court cases dealing with segregation in education did not address themselves to the principle of segregation—which the whole country all but universally accepted—but rather to peripheral considerations relating to the degree of equality which the separate facilities afforded.

A Kentucky act of 1904,[1] for example, prohibited the instruction of whites and Negroes in the same school, but permitted any particular school to establish separate branches for Negroes and whites on con-

[1] See above, p. 136.

dition that the two facilities be at least twenty-five miles apart. In the *Berea College* case[1]—involving a private college, be it noted, where, therefore, the association of the races would be purely voluntary—the state supreme court established the rule (subsequently sustained by the United States Supreme Court; see p. 152 above) that the section forbidding "mixing" in schools was not a denial of equal protection or of due process, but that the twenty-five-mile clause was "unreasonable and oppressive." The opinion of the Kentucky court read, in part, as follows:

> No jurist has dared to attempt to state the limit in law of that quality of government which is exercised through what is termed the "police power." All agree that it would be inadvisable to attempt it. Yet very broadly and indefinitely speaking, it is the power and obligation of government to secure and promote the general welfare, comfort, and convenience of the citizens, as well as the public peace, the public health, the public morals, and the public safety. . . . It inheres in every state, is fundamental in the existence of every independent government, enabling it to conserve the well-being of society, and prohibit all things hurtful to its comfort or inimical to its existence. . . . Yet this power itself fortunately has its limitations. . . . The duty is upon the courts upon a proper application, to declare void an attempted exercise of such power, which is not fairly and reasonably related to a proper end. Thus balanced, there is little danger that oppression can result from its arbitrary employment. . . . For each age must judge—and will judge—of what is hurtful to its welfare, of what endangers the existence of society, of what threatens to destroy the race of people who are applying this primal law of self-protection to their own case.
>
> The question is, is it a fair exercise of the police power to prohibit the teaching of the white and negro races together . . . in a private school? . . . The mingling of the blood of the white and negro races by interbreeding is deemed by the political department of our state government as being hurtful to the welfare of society. Marriage by members of one race with those of the other is prohibited by statute. . . . No one questions the validity of such statutes, enacted . . . under the police power. . . .
>
> [Laws requiring] the separation of the two races [by] requiring them to use separate coaches . . . have been upheld wherever their validity has been questioned . . . and by many of the states, a separation of the races is enforced by requiring separate schools to be provided for each. . . . In every instance in which the question has arisen as to the validity of such legislation, it has been upheld as a valid exercise of its police power by the state.
>
> . . . A teaching in different rooms of the same building, or in different buildings so near to each other as to be practically one, would violate the statute, as it was such intimate personal association of the pupils that was being prohibited. It was attempted by the fourth section to make this impossible, by prohibiting such teaching in branches of the same school if done within 25 miles of each other. This last section we think violates the limitations upon the police power. . . . It is unreasonable and oppressive. The state itself teaches both races, but in separate schools. They are both taught within 25 miles of each other, and within very short distances of each other.

[1] *Berea College* v. *Commonwealth*, 123 Ky. App. Ct. 209; 94 S.W. 623 (1906).

The remaining question is whether the act as construed by this court violates the fourteenth amendment to the Constitution of the United States. That amendment guarantees the equal protection of the laws to all citizens of the United States, and prohibits any state from depriving any citizen of the United States of his property, life, or liberty without due process of law. The act involved applies equally to all citizens. It makes no discrimination against those of either race. The right to teach white and negro children in a private school at the same time and place is not a property right. Besides, appellant, as a corporation created by this state, has no natural right to teach at all. Its right to teach is such as the state sees fit to give to it. The state may withhold it altogether, or qualify it. . . . We do not think the act is in conflict with the federal Constitution.

The state and federal courts steadily reiterated in these years that the police power—a state's inherent authority to legislate for the protection and promotion of the health, safety, morals, welfare, and convenience of its inhabitants—was sufficient warrant for separate-school laws. However, the Kansas Supreme Court took the position that considerations of public health, safety, and convenience could also compel the courts to set aside the segregation principle on equal protection grounds. In the case quoted below the judges held that the assignment of a black child to a particular colored school could not be legally required when it increased hazard to life and limb.[1] In the future this principle could be extended to protect black children from assignment to schools inconveniently distant from their homes.

The question is whether the perils that must be encountered are so obvious and so great that, in the exercise of reasonable prudence, their parents should not permit them to incur the hazard necessarily and unavoidably involved in attending the school. The schoolhouse was located after the tracks referred to had been laid, and, it is fair to suppose, were being used. The extent of the area included in the school grounds thus surrounded by these tracks, or the number of pupils attending the school does not appear. . . . The plaintiff is called upon to choose between the violation of a law and the risk of fine and imprisonment by refusing to send his children to school, as provided in the act compelling such attendance. . . . and the peril to their lives in passing twice a day 16 railroad tracks upon which cars are constantly being switched, and trains made up and operated, with the incidental sounds of whistles and bells and all the noise and excitement incident to such a situation. It would seem that ordinary prudence, as well as just parental anxiety, would impel the father and mother to refrain from exposing their children to such hazards. . . .

Having power to maintain separate schools . . . the duty rests upon boards of education . . . to give equal educational facilities to both white and colored children in such schools. This requirement must have a practical interpretation, so that it is such as to substantially deprive a part of the children of the district of any educational facilities, it is manifest that this equality is not maintained. . . .

[1] *Williams* v. *Board of Education of City of Parsons,* 79 Kan. 202, 99 P. 216 (1908).

In the *Puitt* case,[1] the North Carolina Supreme Court was confronted with the interesting question of whether a law which earmarked taxes paid by Negroes to be used for Negro schools only and taxes paid by whites for white schools only, was contrary to the state constitution's command that the public school system may not discriminate "in favor of or to the prejudice of either race." The court—which was careful to point out that it was not questioning the constitutionality of separate schools and of laws forbidding intermarriage—concluded that the law could not stand.

The principle of uniformity pervades the fundamental law. . . . If the separating line can be thus run, why may it not be between children of different sexes, or between natives and naturalized persons of foreign birth, or even between the former and citizens of other states, removing and settling in this state?

. . . [We cannot] shut our eyes to the fact, that the vast bulk of property, yielding the fruits of taxation, belongs to the white people of the State, and very little is held by the emancipated race; and yet needs of the latter for free tuition, in proportion to its numbers, are as great or greater than the needs of the former. The act, then, in directing an appropriation of what taxes are collected from each class, to the improved education of the children of that class, does necessarily discriminate "in favor of the one and to the prejudice" of the other race. . . . In the opinion we have expressed of the operation of our own [state] Constitution upon such discriminating legislation, it is unnecessary to inquire into its consistency with the recent amendments made to the Constitution of the United States.

B. *Public Conveyances: Jim Crow Defended*

Suits brought in southern state courts to set aside Jim Crow railway and street car laws were unavailing. In *Ex parte Plessy*[2], an action later to become famous as *Plessy* v. *Ferguson,* when it reached the United States Supreme Court, the Louisiana Supreme Court held that the state's railway segregation law of 1890 did not violate the Thirteenth Amendment because such segregation was not a "badge of slavery or involuntary servitude," nor the Fourteenth Amendment's equal protection clause, because "equality and not identity is the test of conformity to the amendment."

We thus reach the sole question involved in this case, which is whether a statute requiring railroads to furnish separate, but equal, accommodations for the two races, and requiring domestic passengers to confine themselves to the accommodations provided for the race to which they belong, violates

[1] *Puitt v. Gaston County,* 94 N.C. 709 (1886).
[2] 45 La. Ann. 80, 11 So. 948 (1892).

the fourteenth amendment. The first branch of the above question, as to the binding effect of the statute on railways, has been definitely decided by the Supreme Court of the United States, on a statute almost identical, holding that the provision requiring the railroads to furnish separate, but equal, accommodations was valid. *Louisville, N.O. & T. Ry Co.* vs. *Mississippi,* 133 U.S. 587, 10 Sup. Ct. Rep. 348. . . . The validity of such statutes, in so far as they require passengers, under penalties, to confine themselves to the separate and equal accommodations. . . . has not, as yet, been directly presented to . . . the Supreme Court of the United States. But the validity of similar regulations of statutes, as applied to public schools, has arisen in very many cases before the highest courts of the several states, and before inferior federal courts, resulting in almost uniform course of decision to the effect that, statutes or regulations enforcing the separation of the races in public conveyances or in public schools, so long, at least, as the facilities or accommodations provided are substantially equal, do not abridge any privilege or immunity of citizens, or otherwise contravene the fourteenth amendment. . . . They all accord in the general principle that, in such matters, equality, and not identity or community of accommodations, is the extreme test of conformity to the requirements of the fourteenth amendment.

Ten years after the United States Supreme Court had sustained *Ex parte Plessy,* Florida's highest court found it easy to rule that a Jacksonville city ordinance requiring Negroes to sit in the rear portion of street cars did not constitute denial of equal protection of the laws. The ordinance had been passed late in 1905 and was promptly attacked when a Negro who refused to accept a rear seat was convicted, fined, and then in default of payment was sentenced to fourteen days' confinement at hard labor. He sued for a writ of habeas corpus, but the court refused, invoking *Plessy* v. *Ferguson* in support of its judgment.[1]

It is . . . contended that said ordinance . . . is a denial of the equal protection of the laws . . . and that [the] rear end of the car . . . does not afford equal facility of ease and comfort, and deprives petitioner and all other colored persons of the benefit of pure fresh air when riding on said cars. . . . and brands petitioner and his race as an inferior race, and this discrimination against petitioner and his race is on account of race, color, and previous condition of servitude.

There is no merit in this contention. A passenger on a street car has no right to any particular seat in such car, nor to a seat in any particular end of the car, but when he becomes a passenger thereon he does so subject alike to its comforts and discomforts. As we have seen the questioned ordinance makes lawful provision for the separation of the two races on street cars. . . . In order to accomplish such separation in the same car one or the other of the two races would necessarily be required to occupy the front end of the car and the other race the other end, and when so placed neither race would have any more just cause for complaint . . . than he would have to the same locality in a separate car occupied by and devoted exclusively to the use of members of that race to which he belongs.

1 *Patterson* v. *Taylor,* 51 Fla. 275, 40 So. 493 (1906).

C. *Public Accommodations: Inequality Overruled*

Cases probing the applicability of state civil rights laws now and then reached the courts in states where such laws obtained, and the verdicts were usually on the Negro's side. Some examples are here listed.

In one vigorously expressed opinion, the Chief Justice of Michigan sharply rebuked the conscience-easing presumption that God had fixed the Negro's color as a badge of inferiority. Indeed, he argued, if it be a misfortune to be born a Negro, the law should "lessen, rather than increase, the burden of the black man's life." The case arose when Gies, a Detroit restaurant manager who served Negroes only in a separate portion of his premises, refused to serve Ferguson, a Negro, in the main section of his establishment. The lower court, citing *West Chester and Philadelphia R.R.* v. *Miles,*[1] had sustained Gies with the argument that the "full and equal accommodations" required by the Michigan Civil Rights Act of 1885[2] contemplated not identical, but only substantially equal, facilities. The Chief Justice's eloquent reply follows:[3]

> . . . This reasoning does not commend itself either to the heart or judgment. The negro is here, and [was] brought here by the white man. He must be treated as a freeman or a slave; as a man or a brute. The humane and enlightened judgment of our people has decided—although it cost blood and treasure so to determine—that the negro is a man; a freeman; a citizen; and entitled to equal rights before the law with the white man. This decision was a just one. Because it was divinely ordered that the skin of one man should not be as white as that of another furnishes no more reason that he should have less rights and privileges under the law than if he had been born white, but cross-eyed, or otherwise deformed. The law, as I understand it, will never permit a color or misfortune, that God has fastened upon a man from his birth, to be punished by the law unless the misfortune leads to some contagion or criminal act. . . . The law is tender, rather than harsh, towards all infirmity; and, if to be born black is a misfortune, then the laws should lessen, rather than increase, the burden of the black man's life.
>
> The prejudice against association in public places with the negro which does exist, to some extent, in all communities, less now than formerly, is unworthy of our race; and it is not for the courts to cater to or temporize with a prejudice which is not only not humane, but unreasonable. . . . And I should have but little respect or love for Deity if I could for one moment admit that . . . color was designed by Him to be forever a badge of inferiority, which would authorize human law to drive the colored man from public places. . . . The man who goes either by himself or with his family to a public place must expect to meet and mingle with all classes of people.

[1] See above, p. 88.
[2] See above, p. 128.
[3] *Ferguson* v. *Gies,* 82 Mich. 358, 46 N.W. 718 (1890).

. . . He may draw his social lines as closely as he chooses at home, or in other private places, but he cannot in a public place carry the privacy of his home with him, or ask that people not as good or great as he is shall step aside when he appears. . . .

The only question to have been properly submitted to the jury was the amount of the plaintiff's damages. The judgment is reversed, and a new trial granted. . . .

Through a third party, Josephine M. Curry had purchased a ticket for the first balcony in a Chicago theater. On the night of the performance she was ordered to a special row "reserved for colored," seats which the plaintiff contended were as good as any others of the same price. His attorney argued also that no racial prejudice was expressed or implied by the separation of the races, and that it had been established for the sole purpose of preserving peace and order. Going farther, he maintained that the statute under which the suit was brought was itself unconstitutional because it deprived the theater proprietor of liberty and property without due process of law. After a brief analysis of the statute, the Illinois Supreme Court made short shrift of the plaintiff's brief.[1]

It would be difficult to employ more comprehensive and sweeping language to abolish all distinctions in accommodations, facilities, privileges or advantages in theaters on account of race or color than this [law] employed. But it is enough for the present that it includes denial of access to the theater, and denial to the first balcony of the theater, and that it is not contended, nor, in our opinion, can it reasonably be contended, that these sections are inoperative by reason of repugnance to provisions of the constitution of this State or of the United States.

The courts were careful, however, not to read into state civil rights laws more than their framers intended. The Minnesota statute of 1885, for example, equaled in its liberality only by that of Illinois, specified seventeen varieties of public accommodations, and included the words "and other places of refreshment," from which it was declared unlawful to exclude persons on account of race. In the present case, a Negro who was refused a glass of beer in a saloon contended that, although saloons were not explicitly mentioned in the law, they were clearly implied by the phrase "and other places of refreshment." The lower court had rendered a judgment in the Negro's favor, but the Supreme Court of Minnesota now reversed it.[2]

Lord Tenterden's rule . . . [holds] that where a statute . . . specifically enumerates several classes or persons or things, and immediately following, and classed with such enumeration, the clause embraces "other" persons or things, the word "other" will generally be read as "other such like". . . . Reasons can be readily conceived of why the legislature might have seen fit

[1] *Baylies* v. *Curry,* 128 Ill. 286 (1899).
[2] *Rhone* v. *Loomis,* 74 Minn. 200, 77 N.W. 31 (1898).

to exclude saloons from the operation of the act. It being a "civil rights" act, the object of which was to secure to all citizens equal accommodation . . . in certain places of entertainment, amusement, etc., the legislature might have thought that the right to be furnished intoxicating drink would be of doubtful benefit to any class of people, and for that reason excluded saloons from the operation of the act. It is a well-known fact that, owing to an unreasonable race prejudice which still exists to some extent, the promiscuous entertainment of persons of different races in places where intoxicating drinks are sold not infrequently results in personal conflicts, especially when the passions of men are inflamed by liquor. . . .

Cases challenging the constitutionality of laws forbidding intermarriage continued occasionally to reach state courts in these years, without damage to the laws, for the courts continued to apply the logic (and to quote the language) of the 1871 case of *Indiana* v. *Gibson*.[1] The growing liberality of northern courts on other issues, however, is illustrated by the following passage from *In re Russ's Application* (1898). Russ, a Negro, had sought a license to open a restaurant in Pennsylvania. The court granted it and used the occasion to deliver a rebuke to racial prejudice and discrimination:[2]

A sober, respectable, and well behaved colored man or woman is entitled under the law of Pennsylvania to be received in any house of entertainment and be treated in the same manner as any other guest. It is time that race discrimination ceased in this State. . . . No one objects any longer to [the Negro's] presence in a public conveyance or place of entertainment; thus far the prejudice of race has been overcome; it is quite certain that the objection to his presence in a hotel or restaurant will also pass away as soon as his right under the law to be there is recognized in fact as it now is by the letter of the statute. . . . It would be vain to deny that some race prejudice still exists among us, but the law does not countenance it, and good citizens should strive to rise above it. We trust the effort will be made and that toleration and moderation will mark the conduct of both races.

D. *Jury Service: Equal Protection in Doubt*

The Supreme Court of Florida reviewed a case in which a Negro convicted of murder contended that the indictment should have been quashed because Negroes had been systematically excluded from the grand jury. But the court refused relief, insisting that even though there were more than 500 Negroes qualified for jury service in the county, their total absence from the grand jury was not conclusive evidence that they had been excluded solely because of race.[3]

[1] See above, p. 88.
[2] 20 *Pa. Co. Ct. Rep.* 510 (1898).
[3] *Tarrance* v. *Florida*, 43 Fla. 446, 30 So. 685 (1901).

Defendants entered their challenges . . . , each challenge being substantially to the effect that the sheriff of Escambia county in selecting the names of persons to serve on the trial of this cause discriminated against all colored men . . . on account of their race, color, and previous condition of servitude, and knowingly refused and failed to select or summon any colored persons to so serve, although he well knew there were more than 500 colored men of African descent in said county fully qualified for jury duty, who were well known to said sheriff, by which discrimination defendants . . . were deprived of the equal protection of the law as guarantied [*sic*] by the fourteenth amendment of the Constitution of the United States. Each of these challenges was submitted to the court, and the court on consideration overruled each of them, to each of which rulings defendants excepted. No evidence in support of either of said challenges was introduced or offered to be introduced by defendants. . . . The presumption is that those charged with administering the laws have properly discharged their duty, and against any misconduct on their past, until the contrary is made to appear.

The North Carolina Supreme Court took a more liberal view than that entertained by the Florida court just cited. A Negro named Peoples, who had been convicted of "gaming," appealed to the state supreme court on the plea that he had been indicted by a grand jury from which all Negroes had, solely because of their race, been excluded. Said the court:[1]

[The defendant's] complaint is that, notwithstanding it is required by our laws that such of its citizens as possess the proper qualifications shall be placed on the jury lists, the colored race, of which he is a member, although many of them possess the requisite qualifications, are excluded by the officers who are charged by the law with the duty of selecting jurors, solely because they are of that race. . . .

We know of common knowledge that prejudices sometimes exist in communities against certain classes which . . . operate to deny such privileges as others enjoy; and race antipathy is as old as historic time. . . . It is difficult to understand how the conduct of the officers, whose duty it is to select jurors in Mecklenberg County, if it is such as it is declared to be in the motion and affidavit of the defendant, can be considered as fair and undiscriminating against colored persons . . . who may be tried. . . . It is incomprehensible that while all white perrsons entitled to jury trials have only white jurors selected by the authorities to pass upon their conduct and their rights, and the negro has no such privilege; the negro can be said to have equal protection with the white man. . . . There can be but one answer, and that is that it is an unlawful discrimination. A wrong, then, has been done against the defendant if the facts set forth in the motion and affidavit be true. . . . There was error in the judgment of the Court, and error in the refusal of His Honor to grant the motion and have the matter set out in the motion and affidavit properly considered and tried. The case is remanded to that end.

[1] *State* v. *Peoples,* 131 N.C. 784 (1902).

PART FOUR

Hopes Deferred: The Color Line Holds 1910–1938

IN the quarter century now to be examined, both the fiftieth and the seventy-fifth anniversaries of President Lincoln's Emancipation Proclamation were commemorated. The occasions moved not a few white Americans to take stock of their black countrymen's predicament; and on both anniversaries they felt compelled to conclude that gains were so modest that the daybreak for the Negro's social redemption could, as yet, be discerned only with the eye of faith. Few would dispute that the period ended with only small promise and even less fulfillment.

The previous generation's Atlanta Compromise of 1895 had arranged an unofficial truce by whose terms Afro-Americans were to purchase racial peace and modest job opportunities in the nation's general economy in exchange for the deferment of their social and political aspirations. By 1910 it was clear that the bargain had broken down. The first decade of the new century had seen nearly a thousand lynchings. Police brutality showed little sign of abating. Denial of economic and educational opportunity was in some respects even more unyielding in 1910 than it had been a quarter of a century earlier, and exclusion from the voting booth and the jury box was more stubborn than ever.

The deepening suspicion that the white community's good intentions could not be relied upon evoked from a growing number of the more intelligent and industrious, the prouder spirits in the black enclave, a revolt which renounced Booker Washington's program of confidence in the southern whites' benevolence, and heralded a more positive drive for civil, political, economic, and educational opportunity: a program bold enough to frighten away timid Negroes, as well as white conservatives who had been tolerantly disposed to improve the Negro's lot so long as he was mindful of his "place."

Of the several Negro rights groups who now increased the pressure upon the color line, three were more conspicuous than the others: the National Association for the Advancement of Colored People, the National Urban League, and the Universal Negro Improvement Association.

The latter, under the leadership of Marcus Garvey, was essentially a "Black Zionist" or back-to-Africa movement, which, though it had for a time a very strong appeal among the black masses, came to little in the end.[1] Far different was the story of the NAACP, launched in 1910 to press for an end of lynching, police brutality, disfranchisement, and public discrimination. The new organization's goals were pursued especially in the courts, but also in protest meetings, and by exposure through published reports and its militant organ, the *Crisis*. One compilation by the NAACP's Legal Defense and Educational Fund of cases argued before the Supreme Court of the United States in the years from 1915 to 1958 reveals that the association successfully pleaded the Negro's cause in more than fifty major cases affecting the franchise, residential segregation, restrictive covenants, public education, interstate and local transportation, recreation, due process and equal protection controversies, and the like. It is hardly an exaggeration to say that nearly every major courtroom triumph for the race as a whole in these years was accomplished through the NAACP.

The more conciliatory National Urban League, which like the NAACP was founded in 1910, was sometimes characterized as the Negro rights movement's State Department, paralleling the NAACP as the race's War Department. It relied particularly on negotiation and parley, supplemented by publicity and exhortation—through countless pamphlets and tracts, advertising in the public press, and by way of its national periodical, *Opportunity*. Under the motto "Not alms, but opportunity," it labored to win for the city Negroes a better chance for jobs, for education, and an improved standard of living. It was also active in carrying on welfare services like day nurseries, cooperating with law enforcement agencies to reduce juvenile delinquency, and pushing for neighborhood playgrounds, public housing, and better schools and public facilities for the black urban poor. It assumed the role of conciliator and mediator, dedicated to the promotion of good will between the races as a means of opening up more opportunities for the disadvantaged Negro in a white man's world.

By 1937 the Negro population of America had increased to 12,400,000. Of these, nearly a fourth were now in the North, nine-tenths of them massed in large urban centers. Even in the South, a third of the black population had moved to the cities. The relocation from the land to the cities, and especially from the South to the North, was a bid for better employment opportunities first, and for freedom from Jim Crow second—a revolution in expectations which could, if the expectations were too long deferred, produce menacing social pressures. As the black migrations flooded northern urban centers faster than the region could assimilate them, there followed a mounting white resistance to their absorption, not infrequently expressed in the form of

[1] The standard account is Edmund David Cronon, *Black Moses; the Story of Marcus Garvey and the Universal Negro Improvement Association* (Madison, 1955).

discrimination and segregation far more conspicuous than formerly in the Harlems and Bronzevilles of the North.

Meanwhile, the cityward tide raised the Negro's self-respect and increased his consciousness of race, a development nourished by the maturing of the Negro church and press, by the widening of educational opportunity, by the emergence of a Negro middle class, and by the general decline of illiteracy in the Afro-American community—from roughly 40 percent in 1910 to 20 percent in 1936, most of it confined to the rural South, and middle-aged and elderly Negroes in the North.

Although the first World War brought new forms of discrimination in war industries and the armed forces, some of the older inequities were moderated in response to rising Negro protest and to the race's loyal support of a war that promised it few rewards. The postwar Red Scare, resurgent Ku-Kluxism, the almost paranoid anti-foreignism (extending, ironically, to tenth-generation Americans of African blood) had largely spent itself by the early 1930's when the Great Depression gave Americans other things to worry about. The economic collapse engulfed blacks and whites alike with lordly disregard of race or creed. The Negro to be sure was, as usual, hit first and hardest; but it was a common ruin, a general leveling which left the gap between races and between other groups significantly narrowed. Thereafter, the New Deal program of economic and social meliorism had the effect of preventing the old disparities from recurring in quite their old degree; and this, in turn, shifted the Negro's historic allegiance from the Republicans to the Democrats. In becoming an important bloc in the majority coalition, they could, at least after 1936, expect their political leverage in the North to win benefits for the race even in the South where they did not vote.

But despite the very real changes that were recasting the black community in the quarter century after 1910, the relationships between the races had shown little change by 1938. While a few prophets of the scientific assault upon racism were beginning to be heard, the national mind had hardly begun by that year to divest itself of the old creeds upon which the structure of discrimination was grounded. The Negro's status as a second-class citizen, as hewer of wood and drawer of water, was still deeply embedded in law and custom. Black Americans were still tightly trapped in urban and rural slums. The black worker's income in 1938 still fell short of being half that of white workers. Jim Crow trains, buses, and street cars were still the common lot of millions of Negroes; and even in New York and Boston most hotel and restaurant facilities were segregated.

In the churches and the Christian associations no significant crack in the color line could yet be discerned, and eleven o'clock Sunday morning was still the most segregated hour of the week. In hospitals and medical services the line was just as rigorously insisted upon. In 1937 the appearance of the first Negro in major-league baseball was still a decade in the future, and only the most incorrigible visionary expected, unless he was very young, to see the desegregation of the armed forces in his lifetime. Voting and jury service by blacks was still brazenly thwarted by legal connivance if not by legal dictum, and he would have been a rash Negro, indeed, who would have offered himself as a candidate for public office in the deep South.

In the middle 1930's not a single known Negro was as yet enrolled in a state graduate or professional school in the South, where three-fourths of the Afro-American population resided; and the prospect of elementary and secondary schools being opened to all comers irrespective of race could hardly have seemed more remote.

The black man's plight was not the creation of laws. It was primarily rooted in private prejudice, old habits, and misinformation, and it was, at bottom, enforced by private sanctions, even though it was also buttressed at many points by public authority. The laws of the land, and the temper of the courts, whether federal, state or local, as we shall now see, had not yet by 1938 seriously weakened—indeed, they had in many respects strengthened—the system of separate schools, separate neighborhoods, separate public facilities, and the rest of the whole segregation complex. In those commonwealths in which various forms of segregation were either required or authorized, the state courts, with the indulgence of the nation's supreme tribunal, steadily defended the arrangement against the allegation that it was unwarranted discrimination.

Reduced to layman's language, the argument ran something like this: it has always been a principle of law, no less after the ratification of the Fourteenth Amendment and its equal protection clause than before, that reasonable "classification" is wholly consistent with fair treatment. Laws levying higher tax rates upon the rich than upon the poor; laws extending special protections to women and children in industry, to the aged, to the weak and the handicapped, without showing the same indulgence to others more favorably situated; laws exacting higher tuition fees in state universities, or higher fishing license fees, from out-of-state residents than from residents of a state; laws requiring doctors to pass certain examinations and to be licensed while no similar constraints were laid upon bakers or plumbers; these and countless other "discriminations" were based upon reasonable distinctions, and so long as all persons *within* such a classification were treated equally, the law not only did not violate the concept of equal protection; it promoted it. That is, *equal* taxes on rich and poor, equal tuition fees for resident taxpayers and nonresidents who paid no taxes, etc., would in practical effect be unequal and unfair.

Similarly, so ran the popular argument, concurred in by the courts, separation of the races in many of the aspects of the community's life, so long as all individuals in the separate categories are treated fairly and equally, constitutes a reasonable classification, calculated to benefit the whole community, and to promote the public peace and happiness by reducing social strains and preventing racial collisions—a benefit shared alike by both races.

(1)
RACIAL IDEOLOGY: SOME EARLY TWENTIETH-CENTURY ATTITUDES

Perhaps because of the rising protests from liberal groups—particularly from the NAACP—and because of the nation's preoccupation with American ideals in the World War I era, anti-Negro thought at the popular level, already feeling itself increasingly on the defensive, became more aggressively assertive in the two decades after 1910. Then in the twenties the postwar disillusionment, the panicky fear of radicals of every stripe, an almost psychotic hostility against all strangers, all exotic influences, spawned a new outburst of loyalty oaths, the frenetic Red Scare, a new wave of lynchings, the Scottsboro case, and a resurgent Ku-Kluxery—this time as strong in the Middle West as in the South, and directed against a whole catalogue of "undesirables," of whom the Negro was only one.

The myths and superstitions, the old wives' tales and half-truths, upon which rested much of the anti-Negro feeling of the masses of the undereducated and unsophisticated Americans, were familiar enough by now, and the increasing influence of such ideas, endlessly reiterated, upon the racial attitudes of a growing portion of the population was perhaps not surprising. More remarkable was the steady growth of a body of sophisticated racist thought, an expanding literature, increasingly bold in its affirmations and produced by respected intellectuals—scholars, publicists, jurists, journalists, and even religious leaders—embodying a quasi-scientific corpus of racial theory.

The way had been prepared by the vogue of Social Darwinism and imperialist fervor late in the nineteenth century and early in the twentieth, but much of the inspiration for the augmented propaganda is to be found also in the immensely popular writings of two European prophets of racism: the French Count Arthur de Gobineau, and Houston Stewart Chamberlain, an Englishman by birth and education whose obsession with the myth of a Teutonic super-race prompted him to transfer his allegiance to Germany. Among the chief American contributors to this literary vogue of racism which Gobineau and Chamberlain did so much to inspire were Henry Fairfield Osborn, Madison Grant, Henry Pratt Fairchild, and Theodore Lothrop Stoddard.

On the other side of the argument a literature of shattering rebuttal by American scholars now began to emerge in significant quantity. The effect of their studies was as yet scarcely felt in 1938, but they initiated a revolution in social thought. In a few years the new scientific study of race, and the deepening knowledge of human nature which this scholarship presaged, would begin to reach where such things count: first the universities and the scholarly journals, then the textbooks, and through them to the people whom these agencies instruct—the teachers and editors, writers, lawyers, jurists, religious leaders, and in time even entertainers and makers of movies. Indeed, they would affect, in some measure at least, everyone who reads books or magazines or newspapers, or went to church or to the movies or to school. The materials were being assembled that would supply the lever for a silent but portentous shift in the public philosophy.

The racists—Osborn, Grant, Fairchild, Stoddard, and lesser preachers of the same gospel—actually gave very little specific attention to Negroes, but their ideas are important for our purposes because of their wide and enthusiastic, if worried, acceptance, and their heavy emphasis upon the vast distance that they felt separated "Nordics," the blond, blue-eyed, long-headed races of northern Europe, from all others in intelligence, enterprise, mechanical and social inventiveness, character, vitality, industry, emotional and aesthetic development: in all the qualities, in short, that mark the civilized man. The implication was plain. The distance must be maintained at all hazards if civilization was to continue its forward and upward march.

Henry Fairfield Osborn, a highly respected paleontologist and biologist, who was for a quarter of a century (1908–1933) president of the American Museum of Natural History, derived from a socially prominent and well-to-do family. His extensive writings on scientific subjects (some 12,000 pages) included relatively little in the way of formal treatises on race, but his views were widely known and respected. Proceeding from the assumptions (which he considered too plainly obvious to require defense) that enormous differences in intelligence and temperament set off the races from each other, and that the very survival of civilization depended upon the frank recognition of such differences, he was a vehement advocate of rigorously selective and restrictive immigration laws.

A characteristic expression of his favorite thesis that Nordics have accounted for most of man's civilized achievements is embodied in this passage taken from a letter published by the *New York Times.*[1]

The Northern races, as is well known to anthropologists, include all those peoples which originally occupied the western plateau of Asia and traversed Northern Europe, certainly as early as 12,000 B.C. In the country which they occupied the conditions of life were hard, the struggle for existence severe, and this gave rise to their principal virtues, as well as to their faults, to their fighting qualities and to their love of strong drink. Increasing beyond the power of their own country to support them, they invaded the countries to the South, not only as conquerors but as contributors of strong moral and intellectual elements to more or less decadent civilizations. Through the Nordic tide which flowed into Italy came the ancestors of Raphael, Leonardo da Vinci, Galileo, Titian; also according to Gunther . . . of Giotto, Donatello, Botticelli, Andrea del Sarto, Petrarch and Tasso. . . . Columbus from his portraits and from busts, authentic or not, was clearly of Nordic ancestry. . . . Kossuth was a Calvinist and of noble family, and there is a presumption in favor of his being a Nordic. . . . In France, Coligny, Colbert, Richelieu, and Rochambeau, beyond all question, were of French (Norman) Nordic nobility . . . France includes among her great artists Rodin, of Nordic origin; among her leading lettermen, Lamartine, Racine, Anatole France, all Nordics. The intellectual influence of the Northern race is also apparent in Spain, where it appears in her greatest man of letters, Cervantes; also in Portugal in the poet-hero Camoens, whose ancestors were Gothic. Of the fighting stock of Italy, Napoleon, although born in Corsica, was descended from the old Lombard nobility, of Nordic origin, and it is probable that Garibaldi, with his Teutonic name, was largely of Northern stock.

Madison Grant's *The Passing of the Great Race* became at once a model for a flood of racist books and articles which poured from American presses in the next two decades, and was immensely influential in moving countless Americans from an indifference respecting racial distinctions to an impassioned belief in their crucial importance. Like Osborn, Grant was fearful that hordes of inferior immigrants crowding America's shores were polluting the country's superior Nordic racial stock, and would, if unchecked, doom American civilization. It was to stem this tide that he wrote his famous volume.[2]

There exists today a widespread and fatuous belief in the power of environment, as well as of education and opportunity to alter heredity, which arises from the dogma of the brotherhood of man, derived in its turn from the loose thinkers of the French Revolution and their American mimics. Such beliefs have done much damage in the past and if allowed to go uncontradicted, may do even more serious damage in the future. . . . The cross between a white man and an Indian is an Indian; the cross between a white man and a Negro is a Negro; the cross between a white man and a

[1] April 8, 1924.

[2] (New York: Charles Scribner's Sons, 1916), pp. 16, 18, 48, 60. Reprinted by permission of Dr. D. G. Brinton Thompson, executor of the will of DeForest Grant.

Hindu is a Hindu; and the cross between any of the three European races and a Jew is a Jew. . . . Where altruism, philanthropy or sentimentalism interfere with the noblest purpose and forbid nature to penalize the unfortunate victims of reckless breeding, the multiplication of inferior types is encouraged and fostered. . . . When it becomes thoroughly understood that the children of mixed marriages between contrasted races belong to the lower type, . . . to bring halfbreeds into the world will be regarded as a social and racial crime of the first magnitude. The laws against miscegenation must be greatly extended if the higher races are to be maintained. . . . Negroes have demonstrated throughout recorded time that they are a stationary species and that they do not possess the potentiality of progress or initiative from within. . . .

Nearly two decades later, when he had had time to reflect still further upon this theme, Grant published his *The Conquest of a Continent* for which Osborn wrote the introduction, hailing Grant's volume as "the first racial history of America," a study "giving an entirely indisputable historic, patriotic, and governmental basis to the fact that in its origin and evolution our country is fundamentally Nordic."[1]

The differentiation of the human species into types so distinctly contrasted as Whites and Blacks and the problems of the evolution of higher types of man from original stocks bring us to a new classification of the genus Homo. Some anthropologists still maintain that all human beings are included in the species *Homo sapiens;* but this is an old-fashioned grouping. Sooner or later a new system must be formulated based on the same fundamental rules that are applied to the classification of other mammals. For instance, the physical differences between the Nordics and the Negroes, the Australoids and Mongols, if found among the lower mammals, would be much more than sufficient to constitute not only separate species, but even subgenera, and they are now so regarded by some anthropologists. . . .

The Southerners understand how to treat the Negro—with firmness and with kindness—and the Negroes are liked below the Mason and Dixon line so long as they keep to their proper relation to the Whites, but in the North the blocks of Negroes in the large cities, migrating from the South, have introduced new complications, which are certain to produce trouble in the future, especially if Communist propaganda makes headway among them. . . .

Whatever be the final outcome, the Negro problem must be taken vigorously in hand by the Whites, without delay. States which have no laws preventing the intermarriage of white and black should adopt them. During the last quarter-century, many such bills, introduced in Northern legislatures, have been defeated by an organized pro-Negro lobby. The Christian churches in some parts of the North have also taken an unwise stand, in trying to break down the social barriers between Negro and White.

Senator Roscoe Conkling hit this attitude off neatly when some one asked him what had happened in the Senate that day. He replied: "We have been discussing Senator Sumner's annual bill entitled 'An act to amend the act of God whereby there is a difference between white and black.' "

[1] (New York: Charles Scribner's Sons, 1933), pp. 20–21, 282–83, 288–89. Reprinted by permission of Dr. D. G. Brinton Thompson, executor of the will of DeForest Grant.

More necessary than legislation is a more vigorous and alert public opinion among the Whites, which will put a stop to social mixing of the two races. Social separation is the key to minimizing the evils of race mixture at the present time. Negroes should be encouraged to respect their own racial integrity. Finally, knowledge of methods of Birth Control now widespread among the Whites, should be made universally available to the Blacks.

Henry Pratt Fairchild, a famous social scientist whose eminence among his professional colleagues was attested by his elevation to the presidency of the American Eugenic Society, the Population Association of America, and the American Sociological Society, was somewhat less certain of the inherent and ineradicable inferiority of darker peoples than were others of the scholarly and scientific community who, like him, called fervently for immigration restriction. But he was no less convinced than they that "America . . . must continue a white man's country for an indefinite period to come."[1]

The principle has been propounded and urged by certain broad-minded and sympathetic persons that there should be no racial discrimination in any American legislation. Nothing could be more unsound, unscientific, or dangerous. Racial discrimination is inherent in biological fact and in human nature. It is unsafe and fallacious to deny in legislation forces which exist in fact.

Lothrop Stoddard (his father was John Stoddard, famous for the popular *Stoddard Lectures*) was a Harvard Ph.D. and self-styled "scientific humanist," who, to use his own words, was "convinced that the key-note of the twentieth-century world-politics would be the relations between the primary races of mankind." He expounded his social philosophy in twenty-two books and countless articles, many of them in popular magazines like *The Saturday Evening Post* and *Collier's*. Their dominant theme was that the Nordic is by nature and almost exclusively the carrier of the power for progress and civilization, and that this superman is in danger of being overwhelmed by baser races which have a higher birth rate. This sample of his writing is from his most celebrated work, *The Rising Tide of Color* (New York, 1923), pp. 90–91.

From the first glance we see that, in the negro, we are in the presence of a being differing profoundly not merely from the white man but also from those human types which we discovered in our surveys of the brown and yellow worlds. The black man is, indeed, sharply differentiated from the other branches of mankind. His outstanding quality is superabundant animal vitality. In this he easily surpasses all other races. To it he owes his intense emotionalism. To it, again, is due his extreme fecundity, the negro being the quickest of breeders. This abounding vitality shows in many other ways,

[1] See Henry Pratt Fairchild, *The Melting-Pot Mistake* (Boston: Little, Brown and Company, 1926), pp. 239–40.

such as the negro's ability to survive harsh conditions of slavery under which other races have soon succumbed. Lastly, prepotency, for black blood, once entering a human stock, seems never really bred out again. . . .

. . . [T]he black peoples have no historic pasts. Never having evolved civilizations of their own, they are practically devoid of that accumulated mass of beliefs, thoughts, and experiences which render Asiatics so impenetrable and so hostile to white influences. Although the white race displays sustained constructive power to an unrivalled degree, particularly in its Nordic branches, the brown and yellow peoples have contributed greatly to the civilization of the world and have profoundly influenced human progress. The negro, on the contrary, has contributed virtually nothing. Left to himself, he remained a savage, and in the past his only quickening has been where brown men have imposed their ideas and altered his blood. The originating powers of the European and the Asiatic are not in him.

A landmark in the scientific study of race was the publication in 1911 of Franz Boas' *The Mind of Primitive Man.* Boas, the cultural anthropologist whom we have already encountered[1] as a pioneer in the scientific assault upon racism, was increasingly persuaded, as his career advanced, that not race but cultural influences and environment account for the principal differences that divide men. An illustration of his stance at the opening of this period is afforded by this brief passage from *The Mind of Primitive Man.*[2]

. . . [T]he essential point that anthropology can contribute to the practical discussion of the adaptability of the negro is a decision of the question how far the undesirable traits that are at present undoubtedly found in our negro population are due to racial traits, and how far they are due to social surroundings for which we are responsible. To this question anthropology can give the decided answer that the traits of African culture as observed in the aboriginal home of the negro are those of a healthy primitive people, with a considerable degree of personal initiative, with a talent for organization, and with imaginative power, with technical skill and thrift. . . . There is nothing to prove that licentiousness, shiftless laziness, lack of initiative, are fundamental characteristics of the race. Everything points out that these qualities are the result of social conditions rather than of hereditary traits.

. . . There is . . . no evidence whatever that would stigmatize the negro as of weaker build, or as subject to inclinations and powers that are opposed to our social organization. An unbiased estimate of the anthropological evidence so far brought forward does not permit us to countenance the belief in a racial inferiority which would unfit an individual of the negro race to take his part in modern civilization. We do not know of any demand made on the human body or mind in modern life that anatomical or ethnological evidence would prove to be beyond the powers of the negro.

The traits of the American negro are adequately explained on the basis of his history and social status. The tearing-away from the African soil and the

[1] See above, p. 108.

[2] Franz Boas, *The Mind of Primitive Man* (New York: The Macmillan Company, 1911), pp. 271–73 *passim.* Copyright 1911 The Macmillan Company, renewed 1938 Franz Boas, renewed © 1966 by Franziska Boas Nicholson. Reprinted with permission of The Macmillan Company.

consequent complete loss of the old standards of life, which were replaced by the dependency of slavery and by all it entailed, followed by a period of disorganization and by a severe economic struggle against heavy odds, are sufficient to explain the inferiority of the status of the race, without falling back upon the theory of hereditary inferiority.

In short, there is every reason to believe that the negro when given facility and opportunity, will be perfectly able to fulfill the duties of citizenship as well as his white neighbor. . . . There will be endless numbers who will be able to outrun their white competitors, and who will do better than the defectives whom we permit to drag down and to retard the healthy children of our public schools.

Important also was the testimony that psychologists in the 1920's and early 1930's were beginning to bring to the argument over racial differences. In 1931, for example, Thomas Russel Garth, a professor of experimental psychology at the University of Denver, published a volume which carefully examined the very considerable quantity of literature which had by then accumulated on the question of mental differences among the races. He found that the data compelled the conclusion that "there are no sure evidences of real racial differences in mental traits." The passage that follows is from his *Race Psychology: A Study of Racial Mental Differences.*[1]

Differences so far found in the intelligence of races can be easily explained by the influence of nurture and of selection. . . . The low I.Q.'s of such racial groups as the Negroes and the Indians are undoubtedly due to these factors. Rarely has a society endeavored to breed up the Negro or the Indian. Nor has their education ever been properly undertaken and generously supported. Recalcitrancy on their part toward the well-meant but inadequate Caucasian efforts at uplift are not to be taken as a sign of inferiority. This may indicate the opposite.

Any disposition upon our part to withhold from these, or similar, races, because we deem them inferior, the right to a free and full development to which they are entitled must be taken as an indication of rationalization on account of race prejudice; and such an attitude is inexcusable in any intelligent populace.

Of special interest was the work of Otto Klineberg, a social psychologist at Columbia University, whose *Race Differences* (New York, 1935) promptly took rank as a minor classic of social science. Its method and mood is suggested by this passage:[2]

Although it is true, as was mentioned in the preceding chapter, that Negroes rank below Whites in most intelligence test studies, it must also be kept in mind that Negro groups may differ markedly from one another, and that they are by no means invariably inferior. It is well known, for example, that during the war the Army testers found Negro recruits from the North far superior to Negroes from the South, and, in the case of certain of the

[1] New York, 1931, pp. 84–85.

[2] Otto Klineberg, *Race Differences* (New York: Harper & Row, 1935), pp. 182, 188–89. Reprinted by permission of the publisher.

northern states, superior also to southern Whites (24). This is shown in [the following table].

Southern Whites and Northern Negroes, by States, Army Recruits

WHITES		NEGROES	
State	Median Score	State	Median Score
Mississippi	41.25	Pennsylvania	42.00
Kentucky	41.50	New York	45.02
Arkansas	41.55	Illinois	47.35
Georgia	42.12	Ohio	49.50

. . . The real test of Negro-White equality as far as intelligence tests are concerned can be met only by a study in a region in which Negroes suffer no discrimination whatsoever and enjoy exactly the same educational and economic opportunities. Such a region is difficult to find, although there may be an approximation to it in Martinique or Brazil. Davenport and Steggerda . . . describe their Negro group in Jamaica as living on substantially the same plane as the Whites. From that point of view it is interesting to note that the differences between the two groups in Army Alpha were much smaller than in most other countries. There are eight sub-tests in Army Alpha; in four of these the Whites are superior, and in four they were surpassed by the Blacks. The total score for the Whites was 10.23, and for the Blacks, 9.64, a difference which is not statistically significant. It is safe to say that as the environment of the Negro approximates more and more closely that of the White, his inferiority tends to disappear.

It is the writer's opinion that this is where the problem of Negro intelligence now stands. The direct comparison between Negroes and Whites will always remain a doubtful procedure because of the impossibility of controlling the various factors which may influence the results. Intelligence tests may therefore not be used as measures of group differences in native ability, though they may be used profitably as measures of accomplishment. When comparisons are made within the same race or group, it can be demonstrated that there are very marked differences depending upon variations in background. These differences may be satisfactorily explained, therefore, without recourse to the hypothesis on innate racial differences in mental ability.

The National Urban League

Twelve years after its establishment, the National Urban League began publication of its monthly organ, *Opportunity, a Journal of Negro Life*. In its first number[1] it carried the following editorial by its Executive Secretary, Eugene Kinckle Jones, setting forth the League's mood and strategy.

[1] Eugene Kinckle Jones, "Editorial," *Opportunity, A Journal of Negro American Life,* 1 (January, 1923), 3–4 *passim.* Reprinted by permission of The National Urban League.

"Co-operation" and "Opportunity"

The National Urban League for nearly twelve years has sought to merit a reputation as a doer of things worth while in the interest of the relations between the Negro and the white races in America. Its field work has in the main consisted of efforts to raise the standards of living among Negroes. Its slogan has been "Not Alms, but Opportunity." It has sought to make its contribution towards elevating the Negro in the social scale, the motive being to make it easier for the Negro to assimilate the cultural advantages of American civilization and to aid more Negroes of capacity and talent to emerge from the mass of their fellows of less promise.

The League has also attempted to make available to white people information on the Negro that would tend to clear up many of the mooted questions about the Negro. . . .

Cooperation or good fellowship between the racial elements in America presupposes the existence of an inclination on the part of members of each race to meet the members of other races on a platform of good will. It assumes the existence of an intelligence and a standard of living common to both races, members of which observe in each other similar interests and ideals. The whites sooner or later, no matter what their present status or environment, are vouchsafed in time a chance to rise above their present level. Such is not the case with the Negro in anything like the same degree that it obtains for the whites. His case calls for drastic and special attention, not only to secure for him the operation of improvement programs, educational in character involving the whole race, but to promote the establishment of agencies dealing with fundamentals, agencies which more or less are common among the whites but among Negroes practically non-existent, such as day nurseries, settlement houses and health clinics.

The Urban League feels that the Negro, as a group, must be brought up to a higher social plane so that he can accept his rightful place in society as his opportunities come. His leaders must be trained and given a chance to gain wider experience with his fellows. The League furnishes a field of labor for these leaders. In many cases such potential leaders as executives of the League are men short of forty, and many just turning thirty. They see life from a new angle and are preparing new fields for their fellow-race members. They attempt programs which require great faith and energy. They have helped to revolutionize social work among Negroes, which has changed from the street-corner missionary type of work to the up-to-date scientific social service.

In the past this service has been promoted and publicity on achievements has been secured in a desultory, hit-or-miss fashion. Experiences have been exchanged between communities through correspondence and an occasional conference where representatives of various organizations have met to exchange ideas. The first method—that of correspondence—is a slow process. The second—that of occasional conferences—is inadequate because only a very few representatives from each organization get the direct benefit. The League feels that the very generous space which has been given to it by the newspapers and magazines has been of great help. But the League should not and could not command as much space to express its ideals as the importance of its mission justifies. The reports on its investigations and research work alone call for considerable space if only the practical parts of its findings are presented. The League therefore has launched on a new venture which should have the wholehearted support and encouragement of all white and colored people who are interested in the scientific treatment of "the problem" and who wish to see more "cooperation" between the races.

The National Association for the Advancement of Colored People

Formally organized in 1910 by Negro and white liberals, the NAACP was vigorously led by the brilliant William E. B. Dubois, who was one of the founders of the Association and at first its only Negro officer, and also served for many years as editor of its crusading periodical, *The Crisis*. The group announced as its goals: (1) the abolition of enforced segregation; (2) equal educational opportunities for Negroes and whites; (3) enfranchisement of the Negro; (4) enforcement of the Fourteenth and Fifteenth amendments.

The organization's earliest efforts were especially concentrated upon ending lynching and securing to the Negro his right to vote. The campaign against lynching included relentless exposure of that evil by persistent investigation of every rumored or reported instance of it, by protest meetings, by publicity through the press, and by tireless efforts in behalf of a federal antilynching law (the Dyer Bill). The law never materialized, but lynchings did in fact dwindle rapidly in number as local governments and private groups—moved in part at least by the fear of federal intervention as well as by humanitarian impulses—worked to eradicate the practice.

The annual statistics compiled by Tuskegee Institute and by the *Chicago Tribune* reveal that nearly two thousand Negroes were lynched in the two decades from 1890 to 1909. Then the number for 1910–1929 fell to 845, and for 1930–1947 to 146. Not long thereafter the annual reports began to record years in which no lynchings occurred at all.

One piece of ammunition used by the NAACP was a 105-page pamphlet it published in 1919, called *Thirty Years of Lynching in the United States, 1889–1918*. In addition to assembling a mass of statistical data, including the names of the victims and the place and the pretext for each of the murders, the booklet had a section called "The Story of One Hundred Lynchings," in which the blood-chilling details of these gruesome murders were spread before the country.

No less important were the association's epic courtroom battles. Beginning with their stunning triumph in *Guinn* v. *United States* in 1915, the NAACP legal strategists returned again and again to win additional beachheads in the war for first-class citizenship. Their first equal-education victory in the Supreme Court still lay in the future (*Gaines* v. *Canada*, 1938),[1] but in other areas they made steady headway against

[1] See below, p. 271.

discrimination and prepared the way for the impressive breakthrough which in the next two decades was to culminate in the historic desegregation decisions of 1954.

Perhaps no document will more appropriately illustrate the NAACP's contribution to the race's struggles from 1910 to 1938 than a simple listing of the cases in which the Association's battery of lawyers hammered away at the color line, using only the weapons which were placed in their hands by the very Constitution which the white man had written. For to list these cases is in fact to list virtually all the major constitutional controversies relating to Negro rights upon which the United States Supreme Court was asked to pronounce during this period.[1]

Guinn v. *United States,* 238 U.S. 347 (1915). Voting and registration.

Buchanan v. *Warley,* 245 U.S. 60 (1917). Residential segregation ordinances.

Moore v. *Dempsey,* 261 U.S. 86 (1923). Due process and equal protection in criminal cases.

Corrigan v. *Buckley,* 271 U.S. 323 (1926). Restrictive covenants.

Harmon v. *Tyler,* 273 U.S. 668 (1927). Residential segregation ordinances.

Nixon v. *Herndon,* 273 U.S. 536 (1927). White primaries.

Richmond v. *Deans,* 281 U.S. 704 (1930). Residential segregation ordinances.

Nixon v. *Condon,* 286 U.S. 73 (1932). White primaries.

Hill v. *Oklahoma,* 295 U.S. 394 (1935). Due process and equal protection in criminal cases.

University of Maryland v. *Murray,* 165 Md. 478 (1935). A state supreme court case relating to equal education.

Brown v. *Mississippi,* 297 U.S. 278 (1936). Due process and equal protection in criminal cases.

The Association suffered a major disappointment in its failure to secure passage of a federal law against lynching. Near the close of 1919, Executive Secretary James Weldon Johnson first lined up a number of congressmen and senators who pledged their support, and then persuaded Congressman L. C. Dyer, of Missouri, to introduce what came to be known as the Dyer Anti-Lynching Bill. Despite vigorous and carefully organized opposition from southern representatives, the House passed the measure by a two-to-one vote. It failed in the Senate, however, even though the proposal had impressive support—from the country at large, from state and local public officials, from college and university presidents and professors, from religious leaders, from lawyers and judges and editors. Thereafter, repeated efforts to secure passage of similar bills met with no better success.[2]

[1] The compilation is taken from Jack Greenberg, *Race Relations and American Law* (New York, 1959), p. 401.

[2] The full text is in *The Crisis,* XXVII (February, 1924), 164–65.

(2)
VIEWS FROM THE WHITE HOUSE

Woodrow Wilson, President, 1913–1921

One searches in vain for positive public utterances in the Negro's behalf from the White House in the quarter-century following 1910. Woodrow Wilson, for all his dedication to the "New Freedom" which he so eloquently proclaimed, not only gave no encouragement to the race's struggles, he strengthened the practice of segregation in the great federal agencies in Washington. Both his southern origins and the urging of his wife have often been blamed for his taking a course that even his admiring biographer, Ray Stannard Baker, found it impossible to condone.

Shortly after his inauguration Wilson was waited upon by delegations of Negroes apprehensive over the prospects for the race under a southern-born Democratic President, and when crusading editor Oswald Garrison Villard, a grandson of William Lloyd Garrison, complained that federal employees were being increasingly segregated, the president lamely replied:[1]

> It is true that the segregation of the colored employees in the several departments was begun upon the initiative and at the suggestion of several of the heads of departments, but as much in the interest of the negroes as for any other reason, with the approval of some of the most influential negroes I know, and with the idea that the friction, or rather the discontent and uneasiness, which had prevailed in many of the departments would thereby be removed. It is as far as possible from being a movement *against* negroes. I sincerely believe it to be in their interest. And what distresses me about your letter is to find that you look at it in so different a light. . . . My own feeling is, by putting certain bureaus and sections of the service in the charge of negroes we are rendering them more safe in their possession of office and less likely to be discriminated against.

On other occasions the President wrote:

> It would be hard to make any one understand the delicacy and difficulty of the situation I find existing here with regard to the colored people. You know my own disposition in the matter, I am sure, but I find myself absolutely blocked by the sentiment of Senators; not alone Senators from the South, by any means, but Senators from various parts of the country.

[1] Ray Stannard Baker, *Woodrow Wilson: Life and Letters*, 6 vols. (New York: Doubleday and Company, 1927–37), 4:221–24. Reprinted by permission of Rachel Baker Napier in behalf of the heirs of Ray Stannard Baker.

I want to handle the matter with the greatest possible patience and tact, and am not without hope that I may succeed in certain directions. But just because the situation is extremely delicate and because I know the feeling of irritation that comes with every effort at systematic inquiry into conditions—because of the feeling that there is some sort of indictment involved in the very inquiry itself—I think that it would be a blunder on my part to consent to name the commission you speak of and which we discussed at our conference in Trenton. I never realized before the complexity and difficulty of this matter in respect of every step taken here. . . .

In reply to your kind letter of September fourth, I would say that I do approve of a segregation that is being attempted in several of the departments. . . . I think if you were here on the ground you would see, as I seem to see, that it is distinctly to the advantage of the colored people themselves that they should be organized, so far as possible and convenient, in distinct bureaus where they will center their work. Some of the most thoughtful colored men I have conversed with have themselves approved of this policy.

I hope that you will try to see the real situation down here with regard to the treatment of the colored people. What I would do if I could act alone you already know, but what I am trying to do must be done, if done at all, through the cooperation of those with whom I am associated here in the Government. . . . I believe that by the slow pressure of argument and persuasion the situation may be changed and a great many things done eventually which now seem impossible. But they can not be done . . . if a bitter agitation is inaugurated and carried to its natural ends. . . .

Warren G. Harding, President, 1921–1923

From Warren Harding, whose thought processes were once described as "an army of clichés moving uncertainly over the landscape in search of an idea," came these bland words in a speech at Birmingham, Alabama, on October 26, 1921.[1]

Politically and economically there need be no occasion for great and permanent differentiation, provided on both sides there shall be recognition of the absolute divergence in things social and racial. . . . I would say let the black man vote when he is fit to vote; prohibit the white man's voting when he is unfit to vote. . . . I would insist upon equal educational opportunity for both.

Men of both races may well stand uncompromisingly against every suggestion of social equality. This is not a question of social equality, but a question of recognizing a fundamental, eternal, inescapable difference.

Racial amalgamation there cannot be. Partnership of the races in developing the highest aims of all humanity there must be if humanity is to achieve the ends which we have set for it. The black man should seek to be, and he should be encouraged to be, the best possible black man and not the best possible imitation of a white man. . . .

One must urge the people of the South to take advantage of their superior understanding of this problem and assume an attitude toward it that will deserve the confidence of the colored people. . . .

[1] As reported in the *New York Times,* October 27, 1921.

Calvin Coolidge, President, 1923–1929

Calvin Coolidge, scarcely one to stir things up, reassured the country that he was soundly conservative on ethnic questions, in an article written while he was still vice-president entitled "Whose Country Is This?" for *Good Housekeeping*.[1] This passage suggests his views on race:

> There are racial considerations too grave to be brushed aside by any sentimental reasons. Biological laws tell us that certain divergent people will not mix or blend. The Nordics propagate themselves successfully. With other races, the outcome shows deterioration on both sides. Quality of mind and body suggests that observance of ethnic law is as great a necessity to a nation as immigration law.

Herbert Hoover, President, 1929–1933

Mr. Hoover, like the majority of his countrymen, thought it prudent to leave racial matters alone. Perhaps the strongest statement on the subject to be read into the record during his presidency are these words, in a brief address to the "Republican Joint National Planning Committee to Get Out the Negro Vote" he delivered during the closing weeks of his futile campaign for reelection:[2]

> The friendship and consideration of the [Republican] party for the American Negro has borne fruit . . . in the advancement of the race. That . . . is evident in business, in the arts and sciences, in the professions—and recently we have seen great achievement of two splendid youths, Tolan and Metcalfe, in world supremacy in the Olympiad.
>
> It has been gratifying to me to have participated in many measures for advancement of education and welfare amongst the Negroes of our Nation. I have received the cooperation and counsel of a distinguished leadership of the Negroes themselves in these institutions and movements. . . . You may be assured that our Party will not abandon or depart from its traditional duty toward the American Negro. I shall sustain this pledge given in the first instance by the immortal Lincoln and transmitted by him to those who followed as a sacred trust. The right of liberty, justice and equal opportunity is yours. The President of the United States is ever obligated to the maintenance of those sacred trusts to the full extent of his authority.

Franklin D. Roosevelt, President, 1933–1945

A drive for minority rights and opportunities was not a high priority on Franklin Roosevelt's agenda during his first term in the White

[1] XXII (February, 1931), 13–14, 106, 108.

[2] Herbert Hoover, *The State Papers and Other Public Writings of Herbert Hoover*, ed. William Starr Myers, 2 vols. (New York: Doubleday and Company, Inc., 1934), II, p. 293, *passim*. Reprinted by permission of the Herbert Hoover Foundation.

House. One finds, in fact, no reference at all to the Negro's plight in the volumes of *Public Papers* which cover the first term of his presidency. Mrs. Roosevelt, to be sure, was quickly recognized as a sincere friend of the race, but in the case of the President, it was his efforts in behalf of all the poor and downtrodden, rather than any exertions specifically for the advancement of black Americans, that endeared him to the latter and produced the massive shift of Negro voters from their historic Republican allegiance to Roosevelt's party. He was, in a sense, for the present at least, under no immediate political necessity to court black voters because they were overwhelmingly on his side anyhow. Even in his later terms, as we shall see in the next chapter, his policy was still one of cautious conservatism on this issue, and he acted only when hard pressed by mounting demands from restive leaders of the race.

(3)
THE NATIONAL PARTY PLATFORMS[1]

Campaigns of 1912, 1916, and 1920

That the Progressive movement of the early twentieth century had little or no interest in a better day for the Afro-American is strikingly attested to by the fact that in 1912, the high-water year of Progressivism, not one of the six parties in the field (Democratic, Republican, Prohibition, Progressive, Socialist, and Socialist-Labor parties) made any reference whatsoever to Negroes in their national platforms, while the nation was on the crest of a wave of reformism. Four years later the same lineup of parties, diminished now by the absence of the Prohibition and Progressive parties, again passed over the issue without a word.

In 1920, Democrats, Farmer Laborites, and Prohibitionists, seeing and hearing no evil, again kept mute, while Republicans confined themselves to a brief sentence, "We urge Congress to consider the most effective means to end lynching in this country which continues to be a terrible blot on our American civilization." The Socialists made a forthright, if brief, demand for their black countrymen: "Congress should enforce the provisions of the Thirteenth, Fourteenth and Fifteenth Amendments with reference to the Negroes, and effective federal legislation should

[1] The platforms for the electoral campaigns of 1912–1936 are in Porter and Johnson, *National Party Platforms*, pp. 168–375.

be enacted to secure to the Negroes full civil, political, industrial and educational rights."

Campaign of 1924

This time the silence maintained by the Democrats, Progressives, Prohibitionists, Socialist Laborites, and Communists was broken only by this paragraph offered by the Republicans:

> We urge the Congress to enact at the earliest possible date a federal antilynching law so that the full influence of the federal government may be wielded to exterminate this hideous crime. We believe that much of the misunderstanding which now exists can be eliminated by humane and sympathetic study of its causes. The president has recommended the creation of a commission for the investigation of social and economic conditions and the promotion of mutual understanding and confidence.

Campaign of 1928

Now while the Democratic, Farmer Labor, Prohibition, and Socialist Labor parties held their peace, the Republicans and Socialists made short, single-sentence appeals for a federal antilynching law. The Communists, however, seizing upon the race issue with startling energy, devoted more than a thousand words to demand that the Negro be emancipated from white capitalist-imperialism. After a hard-hitting indictment of the country's oppression of the blacks, they offered a list of twelve specific demands. (It is not without interest that forty years later virtually all of the demands had become the law of the land.)

1. Abolition of the whole system of race discrimination. Full racial, political, and social equality for the Negro race.
2. Abolition of all laws which result in segregation of Negroes. Abolition of all Jim Crow laws. The law shall forbid all discrimination against Negroes in selling or renting houses.
3. Abolition of all laws which disfranchise the Negroes.
4. Abolition of laws forbidding intermarriage of persons of different races.
5. Abolition of all laws and public administration measures which prohibit, or in practice prevent, Negro children or youth from attending general public schools or universities.
6. Full and equal admittance of Negroes to all railway station waiting rooms, restaurants, hotels, and theatres.
7. Federal law against lynching and the protection of the Negro masses in their right of self-defense.
8. Abolition of discriminatory practices in courts against Negroes. No discrimination in jury service.
9. Abolition of the convict lease system and of the chain gang.
10. Abolition of all Jim Crow distinctions in the army, navy, and civil service.

11. Immediate removal of all restrictions in all trade unions against the membership of Negro workers.

12. Equal opportunity for employment, wages, hours, and working conditions for Negro and white workers. Equal pay for equal work for Negro and white workers.

Campaign of 1932

Once more, no word was forthcoming from the conventions of the Democratic, Farmer Labor, Socialist Labor, and Prohibition parties. This time the Communists offered no platform at all, and the Socialists made a laconic declaration for Negro rights (demanding "the enforcement of constitutional guarantees of economic, political, and legal equality for the Negro and the enactment and enforcement of drastic anti-lynching laws"), while the Republican party promised solemnly to continue a long tradition:

For seventy years the Republican Party has been the friend of the American Negro. Vindication of the rights of the Negro citizen to enjoy the full benefits of life, liberty and the pursuit of happiness is traditional in the Republican Party, and our party stands pledged to maintain equal opportunity and rights for Negro citizens. We do not propose to depart from that tradition nor to alter the spirit or letter of that pledge.

Campaign of 1936

In this year of the referendum on the New Deal, there were six parties in the field. Of these, the Democrats, Prohibitionists, and Socialist-Laborites fell silent when confronted by the Negro issue. The Republicans, Communists, and Socialists chose to speak. Said the first of these:

. . . We favor equal opportunity for our colored citizens. We pledge our protection of their economic status and personal safety. We will do our best to further their employment in the gainfully occupied life of America, particularly in private industry, agriculture, emergency agencies and the Civil Service.

We condemn the present New Deal policies which would regiment and ultimately eliminate the colored citizen from the country's productive life, and make him solely a ward of the federal government.

From the Socialists came this pledge:

We urge the abolition of all laws that interfere with the right of free speech, free press, free assembly, and the peaceful activities of labor in its struggle for organization and power; the enforcement of constitutional guarantees of economic, political, legal, and social equality for the Negro and all other oppressed minorities; and the enactment and enforcement of a Federal anti-lynching law.

The Communists boiled their 1,100-word manifesto of 1928 down to less than a hundred in 1936:

> We demand that the Negro people be guaranteed complete equality, equal rights to jobs, equal pay for equal work, the full right to organize, vote, serve on juries, and hold public office. Segregation and discrimination against Negroes must be declared a crime. Heavy penalties must be established against mob rule, floggers, and kidnappers, with the *death penalty for lynchers.* We demand the enforcement of the Thirteenth, Fourteenth and Fifteenth Amendments to the Constitution.

(4)
STATE LAWS TO PROTECT CIVIL RIGHTS

For the years 1910 to 1938, there is nothing to report in the way of federal legislation to protect Negroes from injury and outrage, and to accelerate their progress toward full enjoyment of their civil rights. Even repeated efforts to secure congressional action against lynching invariably met with defeat, thanks to massive resistance from the South. The opposition sprang, however, not from an indulgent attitude toward the crime but from the fear that with an act of Congress directed against the practice, the nation would be entering once more upon a process, as it had in 1866–1875, that could end with the federal government supplanting the states in the policing of race relations—a consummation which the South was anxious to prevent. Indeed, it may be assumed that increasing state and local efforts to stamp out lynching near the end of this era were at least in part prompted by the fear that if murder-by-mob were not stopped by state and county authorities, federal authority would inevitably step in.

These years, however, did see the enactment of some new state legislation for the protection of the life, liberty, and property of Negroes, and for the reinforcement of the privileges and immunities to which, as citizens, they were entitled. But these statutes, examples of which are given below, were only indifferently enforced. To judge by the rarity in the record of civil and criminal cases arising under the laws, they were all but dead letters; still, it cannot be denied that they were taken seriously in some jurisdictions, as some of the cases to be cited later on will illustrate; and there was at least some importance, if only for the more distant future, in the fact that the law was now clearly shifting to the black man's side.

A. *Antidefamation Laws*

One hopeful sign of change was the emergence of occasional laws forbidding both the open defamation and disparagement of black Americans and the publication of inflammatory materials calculated to stir up hatred for minorities.

CALIFORNIA[1]

No textbook, chart or other means of instruction hereafter adopted by the state, county, city, or city and county boards of education for use in the public schools of this state shall contain any matter reflecting upon citizens of the United States because of their race, color, or creed; and no teacher in giving instruction as herein provided, nor any amusements nor entertainments permitted in or about any school shall reflect in any way upon citizens of the United States because of their race, color, or creed.

ILLINOIS[2]

It shall be unlawful for any person, firm or corporation to manufacture, sell or offer for sale, advertise or publish, present or exhibit in any public place in this state any lithograph, moving picture, play, drama or sketch, which publication or exhibition portrays depravity, criminality, unchastity, or lack of virtue of a class of citizens, of any race, color, creed or religion which said publication or exhibition exposes the citizens of any race, color, creed or religion to contempt, derision, or obloquy or which is productive of breach of the peace or riots. Any person, firm, or corporation violating any of the provisions of this section, shall be guilty of a misdemeanor, and upon conviction thereof, shall be punished by a fine of not less than fifty dollars ($50.00), nor more than two hundred dollars ($200.00).

It shall be unlawful for any person, firm, or corporation to manufacture, sell, or offer for sale, or advertise or present or exhibit in any public place in the State any publication or representation by lithograph, moving picture, play, drama or sketch representing or purporting to represent any hanging, lynching or burning of any human being. Any person, firm or corporation violating any of the provisions of this section, shall be guilty of a misdemeanor, and upon conviction thereof, shall be punished by a fine of not less than fifty dollars ($50.00) nor more than two hundred dollars ($200.00).

B. *Laws Against Violence and Lynching*

Southern as well as northern states also began passing laws against lynching, and strengthened older laws against terrorism of the Ku Klux Klan variety.[3]

[1] *Statutes of California*, 1925 (chap. 276, sec. 1666), 460.

[2] *Laws of Illinois*, 1917 (Act of June 29, 1917), 362; *ibid.*, 1919 (Act of June 28, 1919), 433–35.

[3] *Acts of Kentucky*, 1920 (chap. 41), 187–88.

KENTUCKY

AN ACT to suppress mob violence and prevent lynching; . . . .

Be it enacted by the General Assembly of the Commonwealth of Kentucky:

#1. [After defining "mobs" and lynching," this section provides:]

The penalty for lynching shall be death or life imprisonment.

The penalty for attempted lynching shall be confinement in the penitentiary for not less than two years nor more than twenty-one years.

#2. Accessories.—Any person not standing in the relationship of husband or wife, parent or grandparent, child or grandchild, brother or sister, by consanguinity or affinity, who, after the crime of lynching or attempted lynching, shall harbor or conceal, or aid any member of the mob who participated in the offense with the intent that such member of such mob shall escape arrest or punishment, shall be deemed accessory after the fact, and may be indicted, tried and convicted and punished, and on conviction shall be punished by imprisonment in the penitentiary for not less than two nor more than twenty-one years.

#3. Officers.—If any person, being a prisoner, or lawfully in custody, shall be taken from the the hands of any sheriff, deputy sheriff, constable or any other peace officer, or from the hands or custody of any jailer, and shall be lynched, killed, maimed or injured, it shall be *prima facie* evidence of failure of the officer to perform his duty, and . . . the Governor shall at once publish a proclamation declaring the office or offices of the officer or officers vacant. . . .

LOUISIANA[1]

If any person using a hood . . . or a mask . . . or anything in the nature thereof . . . as a disguise calculated to conceal his identity, . . . shall enter upon the premises . . . of another, or demand admission into the house . . . of another with intent to inflict bodily injury or injury to property or to intimidate or threaten any one therein, . . . he shall be deemed guilty of a felony and upon conviction thereof shall be imprisoned at hard labor for not less than one nor more than ten years.

C. *A Law to Prohibit Segregated Schools*

A few of the northern states forbade the establishment of separate schools for the races. Pennsylvania, for example, incorporated the following words in its basic public school law:[2]

. . . [H]ereafter it shall be unlawful for any school director, superintendent, or teacher to make any distinction whatever, on account of, or by reason of, the race or color of any pupil or scholar who may be in attendance upon, or seeking admission to, any public school maintained wholly or in part under the school laws of the Commonwealth.

[1] *Acts of Louisiana*, 1924 (No. 4, Sec. 2), 9.

[2] *Laws of Pennsylvania*, 1911 (Art. XIV, Sec. 1405), 381.

D. *Fair Employment Laws*

A modest beginning was also made in the outlawing of discrimination in employment, but there is no evidence that such provisions were in fact enforced.[1]

NEW YORK

[Amending a statute originally passed in 1909; the italicized words indicate the new material in the 1918 version.]

A person who:

1. Excludes a citizen of this state, by reason of race, color, *creed* or previous condition of servitude, *from any public employment or* from the equal enjoyment of any accommodation, facility, or privilege furnished by innkeepers or common carriers, or by owners, managers, or lessees of theatres or other places of amusement or by teachers and officers of common schools and public institutions of learning, or by cemetery associations; or

2. [Aids or incites others to do this] is guilty of a misdemeanor, punishable by fine of not less than fifty dollars nor more than five hundred dollars.

ILLINOIS[2]

AN ACT to prohibit discrimination and intimidation on account of race or color in employment under contracts for public buildings or public works.

Be it enacted by the People of the State of Illinois, represented in the General Assembly:

Section 1

No person shall be refused or denied employment in any capacity on the ground of race or color, nor be discriminated against in any manner by reason thereof, in connection with the contracting for or the performance of any work or service of any kind, by, for, on behalf of, or for the benefit of this State, or of any department, bureau, commission, board, or other political subdivision or agency, officer or agent thereof, providing for or relating to the performance of any of the said work or services or of any part thereof.

. . . . .

Section 3

The provisions of this Act also shall apply to all contracts entered into by or on behalf of all independent contractors, subcontractors, and any and all other persons, associations or corporations, providing for or relating to the doing of any of the said work or the performance of any of the said services, or any part thereof.

Section 4

No contractor, subcontractor, nor any person on his behalf shall, in any manner, discriminate against or intimidate any employee hired for the performance of work for the benefit of the State or for any department, bureau, commission, board, other political subdivision or agency, officer or agent thereof, on account of race or color; and there may be deducted from the

[1] *Laws of New York,* 1913 (chap. 380), II, 1201.

[2] *Laws of Illinois,* 1933 (Act of July 8, 1933), 296–97.

amount payable to the contractor by the State of Illinois or by any municipal corporation thereof, under this contract, a penalty of five dollars for each person for each calendar day during which such person was discriminated against or intimidated in violation of the provisions of this Act.

Section 5

[Provides for penalties of $100 for each separate offense, to be recovered by the aggrieved.]

Section 6

[Provides that violators shall be punished, for each separate conviction, by fines up to $500 and/or imprisonment up to thirty days.]

E. *A Comprehensive Civil Rights Law*

Finally, general civil rights laws, already common, were further refined in these years. One of the most advanced, at least on paper, was that of the state of New York.[1]

The People of the State of New York, represented in Senate and Assembly, do enact as follows:

Section 1

. . . #40. Equal rights in places of public accommodation, resort or amusement. All persons within the jurisdiction of this state shall be entitled to the full and equal accommodations, advantages and privileges of any place of public accommodation, resort or amusement, subject only to the conditions and limitations established by law and applicable alike to all persons. No person, being the owner, lessee, proprietor, manager, superintendent, agent or employee of any such place, shall directly or indirectly refuse, withhold from or deny to any person any of the accommodations, advantages or privileges thereof, or directly or indirectly publish, circulate, issue, display, post or mail any written or printed communication, notice or advertisement, to the effect that any of the accommodations, advantages and privileges of any such place shall be refused, withheld from or denied to any person on account of race, creed or color, or that the patronage or custom thereat, of any person belonging to or purporting to be of any particular race, creed or color is unwelcome, objectionable or not acceptable, desired or solicited. The production of any such written or printed communication, notice or advertisement, purporting to relate to any such place and to be made by any person being the owner, lessee, proprietor, superintendent or manager thereof, shall be presumptive evidence in any civil or criminal action that the same was authorized by such person. A place of public accommodation, resort or amusement within the meaning of this article, shall be deemed to include any inn, tavern or hotel, whether conducted for the entertainment of transient guests, or for the accommodation of those seeking health, recreation or rest, any restaurant, eating-house, public conveyance on land or water, bath-house, barber-shop, theater and music hall. Nothing herein contained shall be construed to prohibit the mailing of a private communication in writing sent in response to a specific written inquiry. . . .

[1] *Laws of New York*, 1913 (chap. 265), I, 481–82.

#41. Penalty for violation. Any person who shall violate any of the provisions of the foregoing section, or who shall aid or incite the violation of any of said provisions shall for each and every violation thereof be liable to a penalty of not less than one hundred dollars nor more than five hundred dollars, to be recovered by the person aggrieved thereby . . . in any court of competent jurisdiction in the county in which the plaintiff or the defendant shall reside; and shall, also, for every such offense be deemed guilty of a misdemeanor, and upon conviction thereof shall be fined not less than one hundred dollars nor more than five hundred dollars, or shall be imprisoned not less than thirty days nor more than ninety days, or both such fine and imprisonment.

(5)
DISCRIMINATION BY STATE LAW

The elaboration of the rules that consigned Negroes to their separate and inferior status was in this generation, as in the past, less a matter of explicit legislation than of private proscription backed by social and economic sanctions outside the written law. But legislation continued to be important, nevertheless. Especially when the victims of discrimination (emboldened, in some instances, by the knowledge that agencies for Negro advancement stood ready to plead their cause) showed a rising determination to challenge the unofficial color line, did the champions of white supremacy look to the strengthening of the legal foundations of the segregation system.

A. *Restricting the Franchise: The White Primary*

Many white southerners, although believing in disfranchisement of Negroes in principle, were embarrassed and chagrined by the frauds, intimidations and subterfuges by which Negroes were kept from the polls. Because of their feelings, and also because the Supreme Court's 1915 "grandfather clause" ruling, in *Guinn* v. *United States,* seemed to portend a more literal judicial reading of the Fifteenth Amendment, the search was pressed for judge-proof ways of evading the intent of constitutional protections for the Negro.

The white primary offered what seemed to be a happy solution. On the grounds that the constitutional power of Congress to regulate elections (Article 1, Section 4) did not extend to party primaries (because the latter were not in fact general elections, but only decisions by private individuals associating together for the purpose of nominating candidates), and on the additional grounds that the Fifteenth Amendment forbade only the "United States or . . . any State" to abridge the right to vote on account of race or color, and that the Fourteenth Amendment forbade only "any State" to "deny to any person within its jurisdiction the equal protection of the laws," it followed, so reasoned the authors of this device, that the Constitution did not bar political parties themselves from excluding whomever they chose from party counsels. In the South, where only Democratic candidates could hope to win elections, the Democratic white primaries would, for all real purposes, eliminate the Negro as a factor in elections, even though he voted in the November general elections.

The Texas legislature led the way with an enactment of May 10, 1922, and other southern states moved to follow its example.[1]

Be it enacted by the Legislature of the State of Texas:
Section 1

. . . All qualified voters under the laws and constitution of the State of Texas who are bona fide members of the Democratic party, shall be eligible to participate in any Democratic party primary election, provided such voter complies with all laws and rules governing party primary elections; however, in no event shall a negro be eligible to participate in a Democratic party primary election held in the State of Texas, and should a negro vote in a Democratic primary election, such ballot shall be void and election officials are herein directed to throw out such ballot and not count the same. . . .

When the United States Supreme Court in *Nixon* v. *Herndon,* (1927) struck the Texas law down as an "obvious infringement" of the equal protection clause, the legislature promptly repealed the law and substituted as a less obvious infringement a measure which also failed to survive a court challenge,[2] authorizing any political party to "prescribe the qualifications of its own members."[3]

Be it enacted by the Legislature of the State of Texas:
Section 1

. . . Every political party in this State through its State Executive Committee shall have the power to prescribe the qualifications of its own members and shall in its own way determine who shall be qualified to vote or otherwise participate in such political party; provided that no person shall ever be denied the right to participate in a primary in this State because of former political views or affiliations or because of membership or non-membership in organizations other than the political party.

[1] *General Laws of Texas,* called sessions, 1923 (chap. 32), 74–75.
[2] See below, p. 212.
[3] *General Laws of Texas,* first called session, 1927 (chap. 67), 193–94.

B. *School Segregation Laws*

The creation of separate school systems in the states electing to take that step was virtually completed before the opening of this era. One refinement on the older laws is illustrated by an act of Arizona permitting a "local option plan" for segregated high schools.[1]

Sec. 54–918. Racial Segregation.—Whenever there shall be registered in any high school, union high school, or county high school in the State of Arizona, twenty-five or more pupils of the African race, the board of trustees of any such school shall, upon petition of 15 percent of the school electors, as shown by the poll list at the last preceding annual election, residing in the district, call an election to determine whether or not such pupils of the African race shall be segregated from pupils of the Caucasian race. The question to be submitted, including the . . . estimated cost to the district of such segregation, shall be substantially in the following form: Are you in favor of segregating the pupils of the African race from the pupils of the Caucasian race on condition that the board of trustees shall provide equal accommodations and facilities for pupils of the African race as are now or may be hereafter provided for pupils of the Caucasian race; it being understood that the estimated cost of segregation will be $_______ over and above the cost of maintaining the school without such segregation?

If a majority of the electors voting at such election vote in favor of such segregation, then the school trustees . . . shall segregate the pupils of the African race from the pupils of the Caucasian race and shall provide equal accommodations and facilities for such pupils of the African race as are now or may be hereafter provided for the pupils of the Caucasian race in any such high schools.

C. *Miscellaneous Jim Crow Laws*

Custom and local usage defined the segregation system with increasing particularity in the second and third decades of the twentieth century, sometimes—when custom did not crystallize fast enough to suit segregationists—with assistance from legislatures. A not unusual example of such assistance was a Kentucky law prescribing separate (and presumably equal) textbooks for white and black school children.[2]

No textbook issued or distributed under this act to a white school child shall ever be reissued or redistributed to a colored school child, and no textbook issued or distributed to a colored school child shall ever be reissued or redistributed to a white school child.

[1] *Acts of Arizona, Reg. Sess.,* 1927 (chap. 88, Sec. 1), 234.
[2] *Acts of Kentucky,* 1928 (chap. 48, Sec. 11), 188.

Arkansas, like several other southern states, was at some pains to keep white and black coal miners and convicts separated.[1]

The superintendent shall use as guards such convicts as may, in his judgment, be trusted with such service; provided, that none but white men be used to guard white convicts.

. . . White convicts shall not be required to eat at the same table or sleep with any persons of the negro race, and female convicts shall not be required to work on the roads.

. . . All coal mines operating in this State shall by partition, or other means, in the discretion of the state mine inspector, maintain separate wash houses for whites and blacks.

Southern states, including Georgia and Alabama, also thought it necessary to legislate against mingling of the races in poolrooms, jails, and hospitals.

GEORGIA[2]

No license to operate a billiard room shall be issued to any person who is not 21 years of age and a citizen of the United States, or who has been convicted of a felony; nor to any person of the white or Caucasian race to operate a billiard room to be used, frequented, or patronized by persons of the Negro race; nor to any person of the Negro race to operate a billiard room to be used, frequented or patronized by persons of the white or Caucasian race. . . .

ALABAMA[3]

It shall be unlawful for any sheriff, or jailer, or other keeper of the jail or the town or city prison, to confine in the same room or apartment of any jail or prison white and negro prisoners . . .

. . . It shall be unlawful for any person or corporation to require any white female nurse to nurse in wards or rooms in hospitals, either public or private, in which negro men are placed for treatment, or to be nursed.

It shall be unlawful for any white female nurse to nurse in wards or rooms in hospitals, either public or private, in which negro men are placed for treatment, or to be nursed.

Oklahoma wanted less mixing of the races in telephone booths, Louisiana insisted upon separate entrances in circus tents, and Mississippi defined even "suggestions in favor of social equality" of the races as a criminal offense.

[1] *Acts of Arkansas*, 1909 (No. 398, Sec. 11), 1133; *ibid.*, 1913 (No. 306, Sec. 20), 1248; *ibid.*, 1919 (No. 134, Sec. 5), 107.

[2] *Laws of Georgia*, 1925 (No. 407, Sec. 3), 286.

[3] *General Laws of Alabama*, 1911 (No. 303, Sec. 9), 359; *ibid.*, 1915 (No. 667, Sec. 1), 727.

OKLAHOMA[1]

The Corporation Commission is hereby vested with power and authority to require telephone companies in the state of Oklahoma to maintain separate booths for white and colored patrons when there is a demand for such separate booths. . . .

LOUISIANA[2]

All circuses, shows and tent exhibitions, to which the attendance of the public of more than one race is invited or expected to attend shall provide for the convenience of its patrons not less than two ticket offices with individual ticket sellers, and not less than two entrances to the said performance, with individual ticket takers and receivers, and in the case of outside or tent performances, the said ticket offices shall not be less than twenty-five feet apart; that one of the said entrances shall be exclusively for the white race, and another exclusively for persons of the colored race. . . .

MISSISSIPPI[3]

Races—social equality, marriages between—advocacy of punished.—Any person, firm or corporation who shall be guilty of printing, publishing or circulating printed, typewritten or written matter urging or presenting for public acceptance or general information, arguments or suggestions in favor of social equality or of intermarriage between whites and negroes, shall be guilty of a misdemeanor and subject to a fine not exceeding five hundred dollars or imprisonment not exceeding six months or both fine and imprisonment in the discretion of the court.

D. *Residential Segregation Prescribed*

Another important addition to state-prescribed separation after 1910 was statutes like the following act of the state of Virginia requiring residential segregation in cities and towns:[4]

Whereas, the preservation of the public morals, public health and public order, in the cities and towns of this commonwealth, is endangered by the residence of white and colored people in close proximity to one another; therefore,

1. Be it enacted by the general assembly of Virginia, That in the cities and towns of this commonwealth where this act shall be adopted in accordance with the provisions of section eleven hereof, the entire area within the respective corporate limits thereof shall, by ordinance adopted by the council of

[1] *Laws of Oklahoma,* 1915 (chap. 26), 513.
[2] *Acts of Louisiana,* 1914 (No. 235, Sec. 1), 465.
[3] *Laws of Mississippi,* 1920 (chap. 214), 307.
[4] *Acts of Virginia,* 1912 (chap. 157), 330–32.

each such city or town, be divided into districts, the boundaries whereof shall be plainly designated in such ordinance and which shall be known as "segregation districts."

2. That no such district shall comprise less than the entire property fronting on any street or alley, and lying between any two adjacent streets or alleys, or between any street and an alley next adjacent thereto.

3. That the council of each such city or town shall provide for, and have prepared, within six months after such council shall have adopted the provisions of this act, a map showing the boundaries of all such segregation districts, and showing the number of white persons and colored persons residing within such segregation district, on a date to be designated in such ordinance of adoption, but which shall be within sixty days of the passage of such ordinance; and such map shall designate as a white district each district where there are, on the date so designated, more residents of the white race than there are residents of the colored race, and shall designate as a colored district each district so defined, in which there are on the said date as many or more residents of the colored race, as there are residents of the white race.

4. That after twelve months from the passage of the ordinances adopting the provisions of this act, it shall be unlawful for any colored person, not then residing in a district so defined and designated as a white district, or who is not a member of a family then therein residing to move into and occupy as a residence any building or portion thereof in such white district, and it shall be unlawful, after the expiration of said period of twelve months from the passage of the ordinance adopting the provisions of this act, for any white person not then residing in a district so defined and designated as a colored district, or who is not a member of a family then therein residing, to move into and occupy as a residence any building, or portion thereof, in such colored district. . . .

6. That the said map shall be certified by the clerk of the council of such city or town, and shall be at all times kept open to inspection by the public in the office of such clerk. . . .

8. That any person who, after the expiration of twelve months from the passage of the ordinance of adoption, shall reside in any such district, contrary to the provisions of this act, shall be guilty of a misdemeanor, and upon conviction thereof, shall be fined for the first week of such prohibited residence not less than five nor more than fifty dollars, and for each succeeding day of such residence the sum of two dollars. . . .

11. This act shall apply only to the cities or towns which by a recorded vote of a majority of the members selected to the council thereof, or if there be two branches of such council by a recorded vote of a majority of the members elected to each branch thereof, shall adopt the provisions of this act, and in all respects comply with the requirements hereof.

(6)
THE FEDERAL COURTS AND THE BLACK AMERICAN, 1910–1938

It has been suggested in preceding chapters that the Supreme Court steadily weakened the Thirteenth, Fourteenth, and Fifteenth amendments, whose avowed purpose was to advance the ex-slave quickly to the freedom and equality that accompany American citizenship. The Thirteenth Amendment prohibiting slavery and involuntary servitude was, as we have seen, read only literally, and the Court declined to accept the view that various forms of discrimination are in fact "badges of slavery" which the amendment empowers Congress and the states to forbid. The Fifteenth was so narrowly construed as to permit a wide variety of devices to keep the Negro from voting. And, particularly important, the Fourteenth Amendment, whose three great "rights clauses" seemed to promise so much for the Negro's political and social redemption, was until 1938 relatively meaningless so far as the Negro was concerned. Indeed, as Professor Berger has demonstrated, the Court was in fact "buttressing the caste order" from 1868 to 1937.[1]

As most students of the amendment point out, it was employed to protect property rights, corporations, and various economic interests, and not the Afro-American. From 1868 to 1911, for example, the United States Supreme Court handed down 604 decisions in which the Fourteenth Amendment was involved. Only twenty-eight of these were concerned with black interests, and of these twenty-two were decided against the blacks for whose protection the amendment had been invoked. From 1920 to the beginning of 1937, the Court on 132 occasions declared state laws unconstitutional on Fourteenth Amendment grounds; but only a tiny fraction of these decisions related to Afro-Americans, while at least two-thirds of them invalidated state statutes related to property rights or to the regulation of economic interests of one sort or another.

Particular interest attaches to the equal protection clause. The doctrine, laid down as long ago as 1883, that only *specific discrimination* by *state* action was restrained by the clause; the principle that state laws forbidding segregation in public carriers are not only not required by the equal protection clause, but are by inference prohibited by the

[1] Morroe Berger, *Equality by Statute: Legal Controls over Group Discrimination* (New York, 1952), pp. 37–71.

interstate commerce clause, which gives exclusive power to regulate interstate commerce to Congress; and the Court's judgment that separate facilities, when substantially equal, do not offend the clause—all these were still judicial orthodoxy in 1938, the end of the era now being surveyed.

A. *Separate-But-Equal Reaffirmed*

The separate-but-equal formula was so loosely applied that the words "but equal" were virtually without force. In some phases of Negro-white relationships the Court even tolerated the entire absence of a particular facility for blacks while public provision was being made for whites. But there were areas to which the Court would not extend so lax an application of the rule. Oklahoma's Jim Crow railway law of 1907, for example, although requiring separate but equal coaches and waiting rooms for the races, authorized the roads to run sleeping, dining, and observation cars for the exclusive use of either race. The intention, as everyone understood, was to spare the road the expense of providing facilities which Negroes would not use in sufficient numbers to make the separate cars profitable. A unanimous Supreme Court, speaking through Justice Hughes, came squarely to the point in the *McCabe* case.[1]

> This argument with respect to volume of traffic seems to us to be without merit. It makes the constitutional right depend upon the number of persons who may be discriminated against, whereas the essence of the constitutional right is that it is a personal one. Whether or not particular facilities shall be provided may doubtless be conditioned upon there being a reasonable demand therefor; but, if facilities are provided, substantial equality of treatment of persons traveling under like conditions cannot be refused. It is the *individual*[2] who is entitled to the equal protection of the laws, and if he is denied by a common carrier, acting in the matter under the authority of a state law, a facility or convenience in the course of his journey which, under substantially the same circumstances is furnished to another traveler, he may properly complain that his constitutional privilege has been invaded.

B. *Residential Segregation: Cracking the Ghetto's Walls*

Another highly significant application of the equal protection clause in the Negro's behalf began with a residential segregation case in 1917. Federal law had, indeed, long been clear on this point. Section 1978 of the *Revised Statutes of the United States,* which derived from the Civil

[1] *McCabe* v. *Atchison, Topeka and Santa Fe Ry. Co.,* 235 U.S. 181 (1914).
[2] Emphasis added.

Rights Act of 1866, provides that "All citizens of the United States shall have the same right in every state and territory, as is enjoyed by white citizens thereof to inherit, purchase, lease, sell, hold, and convey real and personal property." At issue before the Supreme Court in 1917 was a Louisville, Kentucky, city ordinance which forbade Negroes the right to move into neighborhoods in which the majority of houses were occupied by whites, and also forbade whites to occupy houses in neighborhoods, where the greater number of residences were inhabited by blacks.[1]

This drastic measure is sought to be justified under the authority of the state in the exercise of the police power. It is said such legislation tends to promote the public peace by preventing racial conflicts; that it tends to maintain racial purity; that it prevents the deterioration of property owned and occupied by white people. . . .

The authority of the state to pass laws in the exercise of the police power, having for their object the promotion of the public health, safety, and welfare, is very broad, as has been affirmed in numerous and recent decisions of this court. . . . But it is equally well established that the police power, broad as it is, cannot justify the passage of a law or ordinance which runs counter to the limitations of the Federal Constitution; that principle has been so frequently affirmed in this court that we need not stop to cite the cases. . . .

The 14th Amendment protects life, liberty, and property from invasion by the states without due process of law. Property is more than the mere thing which a person owns. . . . Property consists of the free use, enjoyment, and disposal of a person's acquisitions without control or diminution save by the law of the land. . . .

It is the purpose of such enactments [as the ordinance which is challenged here today], and it is frankly avowed it will be their ultimate effect, to require by law, at least in residential districts, the compulsory separation of the races on account of color. Such action is said to be essential to the maintenance of the purity of the races, although it is to be noted in the ordinance under consideration that the employment of colored servants in white families is permitted, and nearby residences of colored persons not coming within the blocks, as defined in the ordinance, are not prohibited.

The case presented does not deal with an attempt to prohibit the amalgamation of the races. The right which the ordinance annulled was the civil right of a white man to dispose of his property if he saw fit to do so to a person of color, and of a colored person to make such disposition to a white person.

It is urged that this proposed segregation will promote the public peace by preventing race conflicts. Desirable as this is, and important as is the preservation of the public peace, this aim cannot be accomplished by laws or ordinances which deny rights created or protected by the Federal Constitution.

It is said that such acquisitions by colored persons depreciate property owned in the neighborhood by white persons. But property may be acquired by undesirable white neighbors, or put to disagreeable though lawful uses with like results.

[1] *Buchanan* v. *Warley,* 245 U.S. 60 (1917).

We think this attempt to prevent the alienation of the property in question to a person of color was not a legitimate exercise of the police power of the state, and is in direct violation of the fundamental law enacted in the 14th Amendment of the Constitution preventing state interference with property rights except by due process of law. That being the case, the ordinance cannot stand.

Buchanan v. *Warley* quickly elicited a substitute for legislatively imposed residential segregation: private agreements, commonly known as "restrictive covenants," by which persons seeking to keep Negroes (and in some cases Jews) from acquiring real estate in certain communities undertook to do so by private contracts in which they mutually pledged themselves not to sell or lease property to any but their own ethnic group. The expectation that such contracts would meet with judicial approval, since they were not state-imposed restraints, was realized when the Supreme Court in 1926 took the position, in a unanimous opinion, that such action did not transgress the Fourteenth Amendment, because it did not involve "state action" in the sense contemplated by the amendment. Counsel for the plaintiff had argued that the *enforcement* of such covenants by means of suits brought into state courts did, in fact, constitute state action, but the Court rejected this view.[1]

Under the pleadings in the present case the only constitutional question involved was that arising under the assertions in the motions to dismiss that the indenture or covenant which is the basis of the bill, is "void" in that it is contrary to and forbidden by the 5th, 13th, and 14th Amendments. The contention is entirely lacking in substance or color of merit. The 5th Amendment "is a limitation only upon the powers of the general government" and is not directed against the action of individuals. The 13th Amendment denouncing slavery and involuntary servitude, that is, a condition of enforced compulsory service of one to another, does not in other matters protect the individual rights of persons of the negro race. And the prohibitions of the 14th Amendment "have reference to state action exclusively, and not to any action of private individuals. It is state action of a particular character that is prohibited. Individual invasion of individual rights is not the subject-matter of the Amendment." It is obvious that none of these Amendments prohibited private individuals from entering into contracts respecting the control and disposition of their own property; and there is no color whatever for the contention that they rendered the indenture void. . . .

In the following year, however, a unanimous Court, in *Harmon* v. *Tyler*,[2] extending the rule laid down in *Buchanan* v. *Warley*, struck down an ordinance which barred Negroes from establishing residences in white communities, "except on the written consent of a majority of the persons of the opposite race inhabiting such community or portion of the City to be affected." Both the *Buchanan* and *Harmon* decisions

[1] *Corrigan* v. *Buckley*, 271 U.S. 323 (1926).
[2] 273 U.S. 668 (1927).

were based on the premise that *white sellers* were being deprived by such restrictions of liberty and property without due process of law. Three years after *Harmon* v. *Tyler,* the Court granted injunctive relief to a Negro who claimed injury and denial of due process and equal protection, when he was prevented from acquiring a building for occupancy by a zoning ordinance prohibiting persons from using as a residence any building in a neighborhood where the majority of residences were occupied by those with whom such persons were forbidden to intermarry. Defenders of the ordinance staked their case on the plea that the *Buchanan* and *Harmon* cases did not apply, because in this instance zoning ordinances based on the police power and laws against intermarriage were the foundation of the ordinance, and both of these types of legislation had long been accepted by the Supreme Court as legitimate exercise of the police power. The Supreme Court, however, affirmed the ruling of the Court of Appeals, which had read, in part:[1]

> We agree with the learned judge below that this case is controlled by the decision of the Supreme Court in *Buchanan* v. *Warley* . . . and *Harmon* v. *Tyler*. . . . Attempt is made to distinguish the case at bar from these cases on the ground that the zoning ordinance here under consideration bases its interdiction on the legal prohibition of intermarriage and not on race or color; but, as the legal prohibition of intermarriage is itself based on race, the question here, in final analysis, is identical with that which the Supreme Court has twice decided in the cases cited.
>
> We have carefully considered the cases . . . upon which the defendant relies; but we do not think that they are in point. They deal with the right of a city to forbid the erection of buildings of a particular kind or for a particular use within certain sections of the city, which manifestly is a very different question from that involved here.

C. *Fair Trials: New Gains*

One other aspect of Afro-American life to which the Supreme Court showed its willingness to extend the influence of the equal protection clause was that of the administration of justice—particularly in the matter of fair trials.

The case of *Moore* v. *Dempsey* concerned a man named Moore and others, all Negroes, charged in Arkansas with murder, who were gravely menaced by a mob which had marched upon the jail where the accused were confined. The mob was prevented from lynching Moore and his co-petitioners only by the promise of a "Committee of Seven" (appointed by the governor) that the accused would be speedily and fully punished. Witnesses were whipped, according to evidence read into the

[1] *Richmond* v. *Deans,* 37 F. 2d 712 (4th Cir. 1930).

record, and an indictment was quickly returned by a grand jury from which Negroes had been excluded, and of which one of the Committee of Seven was himself a member. Blacks had, in fact, long been systematically excluded from grand and petit juries, and in this case the accused were defended only by a court-appointed attorney, who—in a courtroom thronged with a hotly hostile crowd—made only perfunctory use of legal recourses available to him, called no defense witnesses, and had not even consulted with the defendants before the trial. The trial itself consumed less than 45 minutes, and the jury took only five minutes to return a verdict of guilty of murder in the first degree. Defendants had sought a writ of habeas corpus in the United States district court, and appealed to the United States Supreme Court from the district court's order denying the writ. The defendants entered into the record several affidavits affirming that no juror who voted to exonerate the defendants could have continued to live in that county. The district court had taken the position that the state's own laws and courts afforded sufficient remedies in cases of this sort to render unnecessary a writ of habeas corpus issued by a federal court, and added that defendants had not first exhausted those remedies before turning to the federal judiciary. The following excerpt is from the majority opinion (which ordered a new trial), written by Mr. Justice Holmes:[1]

> . . . The corrective processes supplied by the state may be so adequate that interference by habeas corpus ought not to be allowed. It certainly is true that mere mistakes of law in the course of a trial are not to be corrected in that way. But if the case is that the whole proceeding is a mask,—that counsel, jury, and judge were swept to the fatal end by an irresistible wave of public passion, and that the state courts failed to correct the wrong—neither perfection in the machinery for correction nor the possibility that the trial court and counsel saw no other way of avoiding an immediate outbreak of the mob can prevent this court from securing to the petitioners their constitutional rights.

In *Aldridge* v. *United States,* which reached the Court from the court of appeals in the District of Columbia, the trial judge in the district court had overruled the request of a Negro defendant, accused of murder, that every prospective juror be questioned concerning racial prejudice. The court of appeals sustained the district court on the novel doctrine that such questions, proper enough in some jurisdictions, were not appropriate in the District of Columbia. The Supreme Court, speaking through Chief Justice Hughes, ruled otherwise, and reversed the judgment of the court of appeals.[2]

> The practice of permitting questions as to racial prejudice is not confined to any section of the country, and this fact attests the widespread sentiment

[1] *Moore* v. *Dempsey,* 261 U.S. 86 (1923).
[2] 283 U.S. 308 (1931).

that fairness demands that such inquiries be allowed. Thus, in New York, on the trial of a negro for the murder of his wife, who was white, a talesman, who had testified to a disqualifying prejudice, was excluded by the court on its own motion, and the Court of Appeals held that the exclusion was no error, although in the absence of a challenge to the talesman by either party.

The right to examine jurors on the *voir dire* as to the existence of a disqualifying state of mind, has been upheld with respect to other races than the black race, and in relation to religious and other prejudices of a serious character. . . . The question is not as to the civil privileges of the negro, or as to the dominant sentiment of the community and the general absence of any disqualifying prejudice, but as to the bias of the particular jurors who are to try the accused. If in fact, sharing the general sentiment, they were found to be impartial, no harm would be done in permitting the question, but if any one of them was shown to entertain a prejudice which would preclude his rendering a fair verdict, a gross injustice would be perpetrated in allowing him to sit. Despite the privileges accorded to the negro, we do not think that it can be said that the possibility of such prejudice is so remote as to justify the risk in forbidding the inquiry. And this risk becomes most grave when the issue is of life or death. . . . Judgment reversed.

The federal judiciary's position in cases of this sort was not always predictable, however. In *Downer* v. *Dunaway*,[1] a Georgia Negro, convicted of rape and sentenced to death in circumstances similar to those under which Moore had been tried and convicted in Arkansas, turned to the federal courts. Here again the Supreme Court pointed out that the trial had been conducted in a spirit of mob violence, which had attended the whole case from the day of the crime to the moment of sentencing. If acquitted, the accused could not have left the courtroom without certain death. A trial conducted under mob domination must be considered void, said the Court. But a few years later, in *Curruthers* v. *Reed*,[2] two Arkansas Negroes, sentenced to death for rape in a trial dominated by a mob, applied to the federal courts for relief on the ground that they had been deprived of life and liberty without due process of law. This time, however, the circuit court held that once the jury had been accepted by defendants' counsel, they could not, after conviction, claim denial of due process because of the absence of Negroes from the grand and petit juries, nor was the presence of an angry crowd sufficient reason to conclude that the trial had not been reasonably fair.

The most famous of all criminal cases raising the issue of fair trial for Negroes was that involving the "Scottsboro Boys" in the 1930's. *Powell* v. *Alabama* (1932) and *Norris* v. *Alabama* (1935), known as the First and Second Scottsboro Cases, arose when nine Negro youths, aged 13 to 19, were arrested in circumstances described below in the

[1] 53 F. 2d 586 (5th Cir. 1931).
[2] 102 F. 2d 933 (8th Cir. 1939).

Supreme Court's own language. The NAACP's legal division undertook vigorous defense of the accused, and, in the end—after death sentences had been imposed and appealed, reversed, reimposed and again appealed—none of the prisoners was executed and all except one (who had died in jail) were released.

In the first of the two Scottsboro cases, the Court ruled that the Fourteenth Amendment's due process clause is violated when a state fails to provide a defendant in a criminal case with adequate legal counsel.[1]

The petitioners, hereinafter referred to as defendants, are negroes charged with the crime of rape, committed upon the persons of two white girls. The crime is said to have been committed on March 25, 1931. The indictment was returned in a state court of first instance on March 31, and the record recites that on the same day the defendants were arraigned and entered pleas of not guilty. . . . [N]o counsel had been employed, and aside from a statement made by the trial judge several days later during a colloquy immediately preceding the trial, the record does not disclose when, or who was appointed. . . .

The record shows that on the day when the offense is said to have been committed, these defendants, together with a number of other negroes, were upon a freight train on its way through Alabama. On the same train were seven white boys and two white girls. A fight took place between the negroes and the white boys, in the course of which the white boys, with the exception of one named Gilley, were thrown off the train. A message was sent ahead, reporting the fight and asking that every negro be gotten off the train. The participants in the fight, and the two girls, were in an open gondola car. The two girls testified that each of them was assaulted by six different negroes in turn, and they identified the seven defendants as having been among the number. None of the white boys was called to testify, with the exception of Gilley, who was called in rebuttal.

Before the train reached Scottsboro, Alabama, a sheriff's posse seized the defendants and two other negroes. Both girls and the negroes then were taken to Scottsboro, the county seat. Word of their coming and of the alleged assault had preceded them, and they were met at Scottsboro by a large crowd . . . [and the] attitude of the community was one of great hostility. The sheriff thought it necessary to call for the militia to assist in safeguarding the prisoners. . . . Soldiers took the defendants to Gadsden for safe-keeping while awaiting trial, escorted them to Scottsboro for trial a few days later, and guarded the courthouse and grounds at every stage of the proceedings. It is perfectly apparent that the proceedings, from beginning to end, took place in an atmosphere of tense, hostile, and excited public sentiment. During the entire time, the defendants were closely confined or were under military guard. The record does not disclose their ages, except that one of them was nineteen; but the record clearly indicates that most, if not all, of them were youthful, and they are constantly referred to as "the boys." They were ignorant and illiterate. All of them were residents of other states, where alone members of their families or friends resided.

However guilty defendants, upon due inquiry, might prove to have been,

[1] *Powell* v. *Alabama*, 287 U.S. 45 (1932).

they were, until convicted, presumed to be innocent. It was the duty of the court having their cases in charge to see that they were denied no necessary incident of a fair trial. . . . The sole inquiry which we are permitted to make is whether the federal Constitution was contravened . . . and as to that, we confine ourselves, as already suggested, to the inquiry whether the defendants were in substance denied the right of counsel, and if so, whether such denial infringes the due process clause of the Fourteenth Amendment. . . .

. . . In any event, the circumstance lends emphasis to the conclusion that during perhaps the most critical period of the proceedings against these defendants, that is to say, from the time of their arraignment until the beginning of their trial, when consultation, thorough-going investigation and preparation were vitally important, the defendants did not have the aid of counsel in any real sense, although they were as much entitled to such aid during that period as at the trial itself. . . .

In the light of the facts outlined in the forepart of this opinion—the ignorance and illiteracy of the defendants, their youth, the circumstances of public hostility, the imprisonment and the close surveillance of the defendants by the military forces, the fact that their friends and families were all in other states and communication with them necessarily difficult, and above all that they stood in deadly peril of their lives—we think the failure of the trial court to give them reasonable time and opportunity to secure counsel was a clear denial of due process. . . .

[W]e are of opinion that, under the circumstances just stated, the necessity of counsel was so vital and imperative that the failure of the trial court to make an effective appointment of counsel was likewise a denial of due process within the meaning of the Fourteenth Amendment. . . . In a capital case, where the defendant is unable to employ counsel, and is incapable adequately of making his own defense because of ignorance, feeblemindedness, illiteracy, or the like, it is the duty of the court, whether requested or not, to assign counsel for him as a necessary requisite of due process of law; and that duty is not discharged by an assignment at such a time or under such circumstances as to preclude the giving of effective aid in the preparation and trial of the case. . . .

The judgments must be reversed, and the causes remanded for further proceedings not inconsistent with this opinion.

In the Second Scottsboro case, defects in the retrial of the accused were explored, and the Court now determined that systematic exclusion of Negroes from the trial jury had occurred.[1]

Petitioner, Clarence Norris, is one of nine negro boys who were indicted in March, 1931, in Jackson County, Alabama, for the crime of rape. On being brought to trial in that county eight were convicted. This Court reversed the judgments of conviction upon the ground that the defendants had been denied due process of law in that the trial court had failed in the light of the circumstances disclosed, and of the inability of the defendants at that time to obtain counsel, to make an effective appointment of counsel to aid them in preparing and presenting their defense. *Powell* v. *Alabama,* 287 U.S. 45. . . .

After the remand, . . . Norris was brought to trial in November, 1933. At the outset, a motion was made on his behalf to quash the indictment upon the ground of the exclusion of negroes from juries in Jackson County where the

[1] *Norris* v. *Alabama,* 294 U.S. 587 (1935).

indictment was found. A motion was also made to quash the trial venire in Morgan County [where the new trial was held] upon the ground of the exclusion of Negroes from juries in that county. In relation to each county, the charge was of long continued, systematic and arbitrary exclusion of qualified negro citizens from service on juries, solely because of their race and color, in violation of the Constitution of the United States. . . . The trial then proceeded and resulted in the conviction of Norris who was sentenced to death. On appeal, the Supreme Court of the State considered and decided the Federal question which Norris had raised and affirmed the judgment. . . . We granted a writ of certiorari.

First. There is no controversy as to the constitutional principle involved. . . . this Court thus stated the principle in *Carter* v. *Texas*, 117 U.S. 442, in relation to exclusion from service on grand juries: "Whenever by any action of a State . . . all persons of the African races are excluded, solely because of their race or color, from serving as jurors in the criminal prosecution of a person of the African race, the equal protection of the laws is denied to him, contrary to the Fourteenth Amendment. . . ."

Second. In 1930, the total population of Jackson County, where the indictment was found, was 36,881, of whom 2688 were negroes. The male population over twenty-one years of age numbered 8801, and of these 666 were negroes. . . .

The clerk of the jury commission and the clerk of the circuit court had never known of a negro serving on a grand jury in Jackson County. The court reporter, who had not missed a session in that county in twenty-four years, and two jury commissioners testified to the same effect. One of the latter, who was a member of the commission which made up the jury roll for the grand jury which found the indictment, testified that he had "never known of a single instance where any negro sat on any grand or petit jury in the entire history of that county."

. . . The case thus made was supplemented by direct testimony that specified negroes, thirty or more in number, were qualified for jury service. Among these were negroes who were members of school boards, or trustees, of colored schools, and property owners and householders. It also appeared that negroes from that county had been called for jury service in the federal court. Several of those who were thus described as qualified were witnesses. . . .

We think that the evidence that for a generation or longer no negro had been called for service on any jury in Jackson County, that there were negroes qualified for jury service, that according to the practice of the jury commission their names would normally appear on the preliminary list of male citizens of the requisite age but that no names of negroes were placed on the jury roll, and the testimony with respect to the lack of appropriate consideration of the qualifications of negroes, established the discrimination which the Constitution forbids. The motion to quash the indictment upon that ground should have been granted.

Third. The population of Morgan County, where the trial was had, was larger than that of Jackson County, and the proportion of negroes was much greater. The total population of Morgan County in 1930 was 46,176, and of this number 8311 were negroes.

Within the memory of witnesses, long resident there, no negro had ever served on a jury in that county or had been called for such service. Some of these witnesses were over fifty years of age and had always lived in Morgan

County. Their testimony was not contradicted. A clerk of the circuit court, who had resided in the county for thirty years, and who had been in office for over four years, testified that during his official term approximately 2500 persons had been called for jury service and that not one of them was a negro; that he did not recall "ever seeing any single person of the colored race serve on any jury in Morgan County."

There was abundant evidence that there were a large number of negroes in the county who were qualified for jury service. Men of intelligence, some of whom were college graduates, testified to long lists (said to contain nearly 200 names) of such qualified negroes, including many business men, owners of real property and householders. . . .

For this long-continued, unvarying, and wholesale exclusion of negroes from jury service we find no justification consistent with the constitutional mandate. . . .

We are concerned only with the federal question which we have discussed, and in view of the denial of the federal right suitably asserted, the judgment must be reversed and the cause remanded for further proceedings not inconsistent with this opinion.

Reversed.

Finally, the United States Supreme Court in 1936 held that the use of a confession extorted from the accused by brutality and violence is a denial of due process, even though coercion was not established until after the confession had been admitted in evidence and counsel for the accused had not thereafter moved for its exclusion. The evidence in a Mississippi action convinced the Supreme Court that the plaintiff had, in the effort to force a confession from him, been subjected to overwhelming agony—that he had in fact been twice hanged and cut down, and then whipped. After being allowed to return to his home he was once more apprehended, taken outside the state, severely whipped again, and told that the whipping would go on until he confessed. He had then agreed to a statement which a sheriff's deputy had dictated. When asked at the trial how severely the defendant had been beaten, the deputy testified "not too much for a Negro; not as much as I would have done if it were left to me."[1]

. . . Because a State may dispense with a jury trial, it does not follow that it may substitute trial by ordeal. The rack and torture chamber may not be substituted for the witness stand. The State may not permit an accused to be hurried to conviction under mob domination—where the whole proceeding is but a mask—without supplying corrective process. . . . It would be difficult to conceive of methods more revolting to the sense of justice than those taken to procure the confessions of these petitioners, and the use of the confessions thus obtained as the basis for conviction and sentence was a clear denial of due process.

In the instant case, the trial court was fully advised . . . of the way in which the confessions had been procured. The trial court knew that there was no other evidence upon which conviction and sentence could be based.

[1] *Brown* v. *Mississippi,* 297 U.S. 278 (1936).

Yet it proceeded to permit conviction and to pronounce sentence. . . . It was challenged before the Supreme Court of the State by the express invocation of the Fourteenth Amendment . . . but that court declined to enforce petitioners' constitutional right. The court thus denied a federal right fully established and specially set up and claimed and the judgment must be reversed.

D. *Separate Schools Sustained*

The growing disposition of the federal courts to invoke the Fourteenth Amendment's equal protection clause against state-imposed residential segregation was, in effect, neutralized (at least until 1948) by the Supreme Court's willingness to condone restrictive covenants, which, incidentally, came to be more common in northern cities than in southern, and which, after all, accomplished the same thing. The Court's insistence upon fair trials for Negroes accused of crime was, to be sure, a real gain for the cause of minority rights. But the number of persons directly affected by such judicial liberalization was statistically unimportant compared with the numbers involved in two other areas where little or no gains were achieved under the shield of the equal protection clause.

One of these was the field of public education. In 1938 nearly half the states still either required (as did all the southern states) or expressly permitted segregation in the schools. In 1935–1936, when the gap had in fact narrowed, current expenditures per pupil in daily attendance in ten southern states were $17.04 for Negroes, compared with nearly three times that amount for whites, $49.30. In Mississippi and Georgia the difference was in the ratio of one to five. These figures reflected lower salaries for teachers in Negro schools, substantially larger classes than those in white schools, less transportation, shorter school terms, and inferior physical facilities.

The fact is that almost no one seriously doubted that black children were being denied educational opportunity equal to that of whites—many people insisted that such provision would either be wasted on Negroes or would "spoil" them—and yet the record of federal cases in these years (reflecting, one suspects, dominant popular preferences) shows no serious breach in the color line so far as decisions of the federal courts are concerned until the *Gaines* case[1] in 1938, after the close of this era.

[1] See below, p. 271.

E. *The Franchise: The Struggle Continues*

The other area in which Negroes, with powerful assistance from the NAACP's lawyers, won significant concessions was that of the franchise, but even here the victories were, for the present at least, more apparent than real. The grandfather clause[1] was thrown out by the Supreme Court in 1915, but the clause's purpose of exempting whites from disfranchising statutes which on their face extended to all citizens who could not measure up to the qualifications they prescribed, was thereafter accomplished just as effectively by the simple expedient of discriminatory *enforcement* of the same statutes.

The next discriminatory practice to be successfully attacked was the white primary,[2] but here too the victory was short-lived, for the ultimate effect of the *Nixon* decisions, by which the Court threw out that ingenious disfranchising device on the ground that it had been established by state action, and hence violated the Fourteenth Amendment, was only to intensify the search—pronounced successful by a unanimous Supreme Court in 1935 in the *Grovey* case—for a more "legal" way to achieve the same purpose. The solution was an arrangement by which the Democratic party *itself,* without positive action by the state, excluded Negroes from membership and participation.

In *Guinn* v. *United States* the grandfather clause finally met its legal end when the Oklahoma Constitution's version of the stratagem was challenged.[3]

. . . . . The [Oklahoma Constitution's] provision is this:

"But no person who was, on January 1, 1866, or at any time prior thereto, entitled to vote under any form of government, or who at that time resided in some foreign nation, and no lineal descendant of such person, shall be denied the right to register and vote because of his inability to so read and write sections of such constitution."

We have difficulty in finding words to more clearly demonstrate the conviction we entertain that this standard has the characteristics which the [United States] government [as defendant] attributes to it than does the mere statement of the text. It is true it contains no express words of an exclusion from the standard which it establishes of any person on account of race, color, or previous condition of servitude, prohibited by the Fifteenth Amendment, but the standard itself inherently brings that result into existence since it is based purely upon a period of time before the enactment of the Fifteenth Amendment, and makes that period the controlling and dominant test of the right of suffrage. In other words, we seek in vain for any ground which would sustain any other interpretation but that the provision . . . was adopted in direct and positive disregard of the Fifteenth Amend-

[1] See above, p. 138, for example.

[2] See above, p. 193.

[3] 238 U.S. 347 (1915).

ment. . . . We say this because we are unable to discover how, unless the prohibitions of the Fifteenth Amendment were considered, the slightest reason was afforded for basing the classification upon a period of time prior to the Fifteenth Amendment. Certainly it cannot be said that there was any peculiar necromancy in the time named which engendered attributes affecting the qualification to vote which would not exist at another and different period unless the Fifteenth Amendment was in view.

. . . These considerations established that the standard fixed on the basis of the 1866 test . . . was void from the beginning because of the operation upon it of the prohibitions of the Fifteenth Amendment. . . .

The Supreme Court, in *Nixon* v. *Herndon* struck its first blow at the white primary, the particular statute at issue being the law enacted by the state of Texas in 1922.[1] The statute was so obvious a violation of the Fourteenth Amendment that it may well be doubted that its framers expected it to serve for more than one election before an aggrieved Negro would successfully challenge it in the federal courts. The objection came from a Negro dentist from Houston named Nixon. When the case reached the Supreme Court, that tribunal disposed of it in a crisp one-page opinion read by Mr. Justice Holmes:[2]

The important question is whether the statute can be sustained. But although we state it as a question the answer does not seem to us open to a doubt. We find it unnecessary to consider the 15th Amendment, because it seems to us hard to imagine a more direct and obvious infringement of the 14th. That Amendment, while it applies to all, was passed, as we know, with a special intent to protect the blacks from discrimination against them. . . . [I]t denied to any state the power to withold the equal protection of the laws . . . What is this but declaring that the law in the states shall be the same for the black as for the white; that all persons, whether colored or white, shall stand equal before the laws of the states. . . ? . . . The statute of Texas, in the teeth of the prohibitions referred to, assumes to forbid negroes to take part in a primary election . . . discriminating against them by the distinction of color alone. States may do a good deal of classifying that it is difficult to believe rational, but there are limits, and it is too clear for extended argument that color cannot be made the basis of a statutory classification affecting the right set up in this case.

The legislature immediately repealed the stricken statute and replaced it with another,[3] by which each political party was authorized to "prescribe the qualifications of its own members." The Democratic party then adopted its own primary rule, and Nixon, after being barred at a subsequent primary election, sued again. This time, still evading the question of whether a political party, as a private association, could legally confine its membership to whites, the Supreme Court once more found in Nixon's favor, in this instance on the principle that

[1] See above, p. 194.
[2] 273 U.S. 536 (1927).
[3] See above, p. 194.

the party's executive committee had acted under the prompting of state law, and that this, in effect, made the committee an agent of the state. The state, in short, was attempting to achieve by indirection what it had been unable to achieve by direct action.[1]

The second *Nixon* case moved the Democratic party's officials in Texas to try yet another scheme, this time by adopting its own party rule, in 1932, not in response to any legislative or executive committee action, but upon motion of the party's own state convention. Now the issue turned upon the question of whether the reincarnated white primary had been brought into being, *bona fide,* by the action of a voluntary and private association. A unanimous court held that it had.

The Court was here following the logic expressed more than a decade earlier by a United States district court in Texas, when, in *Chandler* v. *Neff*,[2] that court had affirmed categorically that a primary is not an election, and therefore not protected by the Fourteenth and Fifteenth amendments. On that occasion the district court went so far as to say that even *state* action restraining Negroes from voting in primaries was not in conflict with the Fourteenth Amendment's privileges and immunities clause, because the privileges and immunities contemplated by that clause are those which depend immediately upon the Constitution of the United States, not those rights which accrue from *state* citizenship. Moreover, said the court, state law excluding Negroes from primaries lies legitimately within the *police* power of the state, "to regulate its internal and political affairs, and to enact statutes covering elections within its borders."

"While it is true," said the Supreme Court in *Grovey* v. *Townsend*,[3]

> that Texas has by its laws elaborately provided for the expression of party preference as to nominees, has required that preference to be expressed in a certain form of voting, and has attempted in minute detail to protect the suffrage of the members of the organization against fraud, it is equally true that the primary is a party primary; the expenses of it are not borne by the state, but by members of the party seeking nomination; the ballots are furnished not by the state, but by the agencies of the party; the votes are counted and the returns made by instrumentalities created by the party; and the state recognizes the state convention as the organ of the party for the declaration of principles and the formulation of policies.

At a later point in the decision the Supreme Court paraphrased with approval the finding of the Supreme Court of Texas:

> After a full consideration of the nature of political parties in the United States, the court concluded that such parties in the state of Texas arise from the exercise of free will and liberty of the citizens composing them; that they are voluntary associations for political action, and are not the creatures of the

[1] *Nixon* v. *Condon,* 286 U.S. 73 (1932).
[2] 298 F. 515 (W.D. Tex. 1924).
[3] 295 U.S. 45 (1935).

state. The Democratic party in [Texas] is a voluntary political association and, by its representatives assembled in convention, has the power to determine who shall be eligible for membership and, as such, eligible to participate in the party's primaries. . . . We find no ground for holding that the respondent has . . . discriminated against the petitioner or denied him any right guaranteed by the Fourteenth and Fifteenth Amendments.

Two years before the United States Supreme Court reinstated the white primary as a legitimate obstacle to Negro voting, in *Grovey* v. *Townsend* (1935), the federal judiciary had reiterated its approval—expressed on several occasions in the past—of the reading-and-understanding clauses which since 1890 had become common in southern state constitutions and laws as a stratagem for disfranchising persons of color. In *Trudeau* v. *Barnes,* the Fifth United States Court of Appeals sustained the finding of a district court that such provisions do not violate the Fourteenth or Fifteenth Amendment. Brushing aside the plaintiff's insinuation that these literacy tests were framed and enforced for the overriding purpose of keeping Negroes from the polls, the Court confined itself to determining the legality of the provision per se, without reference to its unstated purpose or its practical effect.[1]

It is at once apparent that the clause of the [Louisiana] State Constitution which is under attack applies to all voters alike, denies to none of them the equal protection of the laws, does not undertake to deny or abridge the right of citizens of the United States to vote on account of race, color, or previous condition of servitude. . . . It lays down but one test, that of intelligence, which applies uniformly and without discrimination to voters of every race and color. It is essentially different from the Grandfather Clause of the Oklahoma Constitution which was held void in *Guinn* v. *United States*. . . . It is idle to say that the defendant as registrar had the arbitrary power to deny plaintiff the right to vote. We cannot say, and refuse to assume, that, if the plaintiff had pursued the administrative remedy that was open to him [i.e., the right, guaranteed by the Louisiana Constituton, to apply without delay and without expense to the trial court for relief, and to submit his qualifications of vote to a jury], he would not have received any relief to which he was entitled. At any rate, before going into court to sue for damages he was bound to exhaust the remedy afforded him by the Louisiana Constitution.

[1] 65 F. 2d 563 (5th Cir. 1933).

(7)

CIVIL RIGHTS AND THE STATE COURTS, 1910–1938

Patterns of segregation were upheld in state courts, usually on police power grounds, as necessary devices for preserving public peace and tranquillity, in a world whose Creator, for His own inscrutable reasons, had chosen to set the various branches of the human family apart from each other. Efforts to preserve those distinctions through law were, so ran the argument, not prompted by presumptions of the inferiority or superiority of either of the races, nor was their *effect* a disparagement of the Negro people. It was only the latter, according to the defenders of segregation, who chose to put that construction upon it. Not identity, but equality, of facilities was required by the canons of justice and equity, and if the facilities allotted to Negroes were somewhat less than equal, it was to that defect, rather than to any supposed fault in the principle of segregation itself, that the remedies should be applied.

In the matter of fair trial, state courts were disposed to agree that the law's safeguards must be equally available to all, though this was not to be understood as meaning that only Negroes may try Negroes, or even that there must be any Negroes at all on a jury which tried a Negro. All-white juries, courts were inclined to hold, often meant only that there were no qualified Negroes available for jury service; or, perhaps, it meant only that the citizens *best* qualified for jury service were whites, and those charged with the responsibility of selecting jurors were simply selecting the best-qualified jurors.

In the case of the franchise, state courts continued to sustain virtual disfranchisement either on police power grounds, or on the principle that the United States Constitution leaves the regulation of elections and the franchise to the states, or, more particularly, on the premise that the white primary is a purely private arrangement managed by private organizations.

A modest volume of litigation arose out of violations of state civil rights laws, and here too the issue usually centered around the inherent tension between the equal protection concept and the state authority to pass laws for the public health, safety, morality, and welfare. It is noteworthy that, while the police power was offered as the justification for a loose reading of the Fourteenth Amendment and for Jim Crow laws, it was also used for the *opposite* purpose of justifying rules that forbade discrimination. In such cases it was asserted that discrimination itself produced friction and disturbed the public peace, and must therefore be outlawed by the state under its police power.

A. *Segregated Education: Increasing Ambivalence*

Segregation in education was especially resistant to attack. According to one tabulation, in the seven decades from 1865 to January 1, 1935, cases challenging the validity of school segregation reached state courts of last resort thirty-seven times, and in each instance the courts upheld the separate school. There were, in addition, some twenty-nine cases in which Negro plaintiffs managed to prevent segregation in states where there were no laws on the subject; but nowhere was the legal principle of school segregation successfully opposed. In twenty-eight suits, blacks initiated court action to compel the provision of more genuinely equal facilities in the separate schools, and in only nine of these instances were they wholly or in part successful. In all the other cases, the courts, while conceding that substantial equality must be provided, ruled that unreasonable inequality had not been conclusively proved.

At the end of this period, there occurred a case involving higher education which is of special interest because it closed off an avenue by which some states hoped they could legally preserve separation and yet escape the inconvenience of building separate facilities for Negroes. (Three years later, the United States Supreme Court, in the *Gaines* case[1] made a similar ruling with respect to a like statute of the state of Missouri.) The University of Maryland, while excluding Negroes from its law school, offered them, instead of a school of their own, scholarships to enable them to study outside Maryland. A twenty-year-old Baltimore black graduate of Amherst College declined one of the out-of-state tuition grants and applied for admission to the University Law School. When the trial court to which he turned issued a writ of mandamus, compelling the University to admit him, the University appealed to the state's court of appeals, but that tribunal also sustained him. The student was represented by distinguished NAACP lawyers: Thurgood Marshall, Charles Houston, and William I. Gosnell.[2]

Equality of treatment does not require that privileges be provided members of the two races in the same place. The State may choose the method

[1] See above, p. 271.
[2] *University of Maryland* v. *Murray*, 165 Md. 478 (1935).

by which equality is maintained. [Here the court cited, in support of this view, *Ward* v. *Flood, People* v. *Gallagher,* and *Roberts* v. *Boston*[1] etc.]

Separation of the races must nevertheless furnish equal treatment. The constitutional requirement cannot be dispensed with in order to maintain a school or schools for whites exclusively. That requirement comes first. . . . and as no separate law school is provided by this State for colored students, the main question in the case is whether the separation can be maintained, and negroes [be] excluded from the present school, by reason of equality of treatment furnished the latter in scholarships for studying outside the state, where law schools are open to negroes.

After arguing that the number of fellowships offered was limited, so that a particular applicant could not rely upon receiving one if any considerable number applied, and after demonstrating that the recipient of a scholarship still had to carry serious financial burdens in excess of the grant, the court went on to say:

The method of furnishing the equal facilities required is at the choice of the State, now or at any future time. At present it is maintaining only the one law school. . . . No separate school for colored students has been decided upon and only an inadequate substitute has been provided. Compliance with the Constitution cannot be deferred at the will of the State. Whatever system it adopts for legal education now must furnish equality of treatment now. . . . And as in Maryland now the equal treatment can be furnished only in the one existing law school, the petitioner, in our opinion, must be admitted there. . . . And as the officers and regents are the agents of the State entrusted with the conduct of that one school, it follows that they must admit. . . .

A cluster of cases reaching the highest courts of North and South Carolina illustrate other aspects of separate-school laws. The Constitution of North Carolina, for example, required a segregated school system but forbade inequality of treatment on the basis of color. A private law of 1911 authorized a county to increase its tax rate and to issue bonds for the erecting of a school for whites, if the voters of the district should approve. A lower court had held the statute unconstitutional, and the North Carolina Supreme Court here sustained the court below.[2]

We must declare it void, as being in direct conflict with the plain requirements of the fundamental law. The law provides for only one thing, the levying of a tax for the purpose of erecting a school building "for the whites," and only for that purpose. . . . The proceeds of such tax . . . are to be applied entirely to the purpose thus clearly indicated and to no other. There is no room whatever for the exercise of any judgment or discretion by the local authorities themselves in the application or appropriation of the tax fund, according to the mandate of the Constitution; that is, without racial discrimination. . . .

This decision has nothing to do with the requirements of the Constitution that the two races shall be taught in separate schools. We will maintain that

[1] See above, pp. 16, 91, 92.

[2] *Williams* v. *Bradford,* 158 N.C. 36, 73 S.E. 154 (1911).

provision inviolate and in its full integrity. It is not a question in this case whether there shall be such a separation, but whether the Constitution [of North Carolina] shall be obeyed when it commands that there shall be no discrimination.

In *Tucker* v. *Blease* the South Carolina Supreme Court confronted a delicate issue. The state's laws provided that persons having one-eighth or more of Negro blood were Negroes for purposes of the state's separate-school laws. In this litigation, suit had been brought in behalf of the children of one John Kirby, who were at least fifteen-sixteenths white. They were the grandchildren of a pensioned Confederate veteran, seven-eighths white, who had been severely wounded in the Civil War. The Kirby family associated almost exclusively with whites, and the children had been admitted to a white school. The school officials were subjected to pressures from all-white parents, however, and the Board of Education, fearing that retention of the Kirby children (who were in fact not identifiable as Negroes) might encourage a movement of other near-white children into white schools, offered to open a separate school for the fair-skinned Negro children of the community, even though they were very few in number. The state's Supreme Court, relying on the provision of the school laws which permitted school trustees to "suspend or dismiss pupils when the best interest of the schools make it necessary," ruled against the Kirbys.[1]

While the testimony shows that the children are entitled to be classed as white, nevertheless the action of the board of trustees was neither capricious nor arbitrary, as they are willing to provide equal accommodations for the Kirby children and those in the same class [ification] with them. The testimony also shows that the decided majority of the patrons would refuse to send their children to the Dalcho school if the Kirby children were allowed to continue in attendance. Tested by the maxim, "The greatest good to the largest number," it would seem to be far better that the children in question should be segregated than that the large majority of the children attending that school should be denied educational advantages.

Subdivision 3 of section 1761, Code of Laws, 1912, which provides "that the board of trustees shall also have authority, and it shall be their duty to suspend or dismiss pupils when the best interests of the schools make it necessary," shows that the action of the trustees in dismissing the said children was justified by the law of the land, and that the petition should be dismissed.

Two decades later, in *State* v. *Board of School Commissioners*[2] (1933), some Alabama parents who declared that their children were white were refused permission to enroll them in white schools because they were in the ambiguous category of "Creoles." The court rested its refusal on the premise that it had not been established beyond a reasonable doubt that the children were white, and that persons having "any appreciable Negro blood" must be presumed to be black.

[1] 97 S.C. 303, 81 S.E. 668 (1914).
[2] 226 Ala. 62, 145 So. 575 (1933).

A Kansas case was a typical response of state courts faced with cases in which Negro plaintiffs objected to separate Negro schools when there were white schools much nearer their homes. In this instance suit was brought by George Wright in behalf of his daughter Wilhelmina, who had been ordered transferred from the (white) Randolph school in Topeka to one of the city's black schools. The trial court had denied the injunction Wright sought, and the Kansas Supreme Court affirmed the lower court's judgment because the transfer was not sufficiently unreasonable to require injunctive relief by the courts.[1]

Our statute (R.S. 72–1724) authorizes boards of education . . . to organize and maintain separate schools for . . . white and colored children. This statute is valid. . . . Plaintiff lives within a few blocks of Randolph school, and it is convenient for her to attend school there. Buchanan school is some 20 blocks from plaintiff's residence, and to attend school there would require her to cross numerous intersections where there is much automobile traffic in going to and from school. No contention is made that the Buchanan school is not as good a school and as well equipped in every way as is the Randolph school. The sole contention made by the appellant here is that defendant's order that plaintiff attend school at the Buchanan school is unreasonable, in view of the distance she would have to go and the street intersections she would be compelled to cross. . . . This contention is taken out of the case when we examine the pleadings, for plaintiff alleged that defendant [Board of Education] furnishes transportation by automobile bus for plaintiff to and from the Buchanan school without expense to her or to her parents, and the answer of defendant admitted that it does so. There is no contention that this transportation is not adequate, appropriate, or sufficient. The trial court properly held that the order of the board of education was not so unreasonable that it should be enjoined.

B. *Residential Segregation: Affirmed and Denied*

The United States Supreme Court's landmark decision of 1917, *Buchanan* v. *Warley*,[2] invalidating *legislated* segregation of the races by neighborhoods, was the final chapter in an action commenced under the same name in the state courts of Kentucky, where it had had a conclusion far different from that later reached by the nation's highest tribunal. The Kentucky Court of Appeals, upon reviewing a lower court's decision in a case challenging Louisville's segregation ordinance, accepted the enactment as a valid exercise of the police power. The Louisville ordinance was simultaneously involved in two cases in which the Kentucky court analyzed the ordinance in detail and then addressed itself to the contention of the appellant that it was not a

[1] *Wright* v. *Board of Education of Topeka*, 129 Kan. 852, 284 P. 363 (1929).
[2] See above, p. 201.

valid exercise of the police power. After observing that the Fourteenth Amendment's rights clauses "are not absolute guaranties, but are subordinate to the paramount right of government to impose reasonable restraints thereupon when the public welfare renders such legislation expedient," the court proceeded:[1]

It is contended that the ordinance is violative of the Fourteenth Amendment because it will prevent the residence of negroes in the more desirable portions of the city.

If such should chance to be its practical effect . . . we do not understand how this could be construed to be a denial of the equal protection of the law. The enforced separation of the races alone is not a discrimination or denial of the constitutional guaranty; and if such separation should result in the members of the colored race being restricted to residence in the less desirable portions of the city, they may render those portions more desirable through their own efforts, as the white race has done. Economic equality is not created by statutory declaration or guaranteed by the Fourteenth Amendment.

Nor are we disposed to concede that the ordinance here involved transcends the authority of the municipal legislature, or to doubt that it constitutes a valid exercise of the police power and a reasonable and expedient measure for the public welfare.

The public policy of this State in respect of the separation of the races has long been exhibited in legislation. By legislative mandate, the races have been separated upon public conveyances where by virtue of necessity they must otherwise have been associated; by legislative mandate, they have been separated in the public schools; and, notwithstanding the fact that attendance upon private schools is purely a matter of individual volition, by legislative mandate, the races have been separated therein; and the use of private property for the maintenance of a school wherein students of both races are taught together, is, by legislative mandate, prohibited. . . .

In view of the fact that this legislation is upheld partly in recognition of the peril to race integrity induced by mere propinquity, we see but little difference in the prevention by law of the association of white and colored pupils in the schools of the State and in the prevention of their living side by side in their homes. It is said by appellant that "in a man's house no such association and contact is necessary" as in the schools or on public conveyances. But the court will not close its eyes to the fact that under the congested conditions of modern municipal life, there is practically as much, if not a greater degree of association among the children of white and colored inhabitants when living side by side than there would be in mixed schools under the direct observation of teachers. . . .

An Atlanta city ordinance forbade Negroes to move into houses in a block where the greater number of dwellings were already occupied by whites. In a case testing its legality, the Supreme Court of Georgia was unable to find in the enactment a violation of the Georgia Constitution's bill of rights, or of the due process and equal protection clauses of the

[1] *Buchanan* v. *Warley*, and *Harris* v. *City of Louisville*, 165 Kentucky 559, 117 S.W. 472 (1915).

Fourteenth Amendment. The court, after pointing out that zoning laws, confining glue factories, for example, to designated parts of the city, were universally accepted as good law, went on to say[1]

> But it may be contended that such restrictions are permissible as a protection for the public safety and the public health, and that these considerations do not apply to a race segregation ordinance. Courts are not blind to the fact that by nature there are several races of people, and that the conditions of civilization compel certain regulations relating to the contact of the races. A public policy long in existence in this state, firmly entrenched in our statutes and decisions, upholds racial integrity. The white and black races have been forbidden intermarriage, and have been separated in public conveyances, inns, hotels, theatres, and public schools. If it be justifiable to separate the races in the public schools in recognition of the peril to race integrity, then we cannot see why the same policy cannot be invoked to prohibit the black and white races from living side by side. Segregation is not imposed as a stigma upon either race, but in order to uphold the integrity of each race and to prevent conflicts between them resulting from close association. . . . The principle is well rooted in our jurisprudence that reasonable restraints upon the use of private property and upon the liberty to contract do not constitute a deprivation of life, liberty, or property without due process of law. . . . After careful consideration we do not think the ordinance either unreasonable or opposed to the Constitution of this state or of the United States upon the grounds stated.

Although the United States Supreme Court's decision in *Buchanan* v. *Warley* categorically struck down legally imposed residential segregation, the ruling was not thereafter uniformly followed by state courts. For example, in the year following the historic *Buchanan* ruling, the Maryland Court of Appeals was called upon to determine the legality of a Baltimore City ordinance forbidding occupancy by a member of one race of a house in a block where members of the other race were the only residents.[2]

> The decision of . . . the Supreme Court of the United States in *Buchanan* v. *Warley,* 245 U.S. 60 38 . . . , has declared regulations of this character to be in contravention of the Fourteenth Amendment to the Federal Constitution. This conclusion was announced with particular reference to an ordinance of the city of Louisville, but the principle . . . applies with equal force to the ordinance under consideration. The two enactments are essentially alike in theory and purpose. . . . The Louisville ordinance provided in effect that no member of either race should occupy as a residence any house in a city block in which the majority of the houses were inhabited by members of one of the races of a house in a block in which members of the other race were the only residents. In each instance an exception was made in favor of property rights already vested. . . .
>
> It is thus definitely settled, upon the highest authority, that the right of the individual citizen to acquire or use property cannot be validly restricted by state or municipality on the ground of his color. . . . The principle is broad

[1] *Harden* v. *City of Atlanta,* 147 Ga. 248, 93 S.E. 401 (1917).
[2] *Jackson* v. *State,* 132 Md. Ct. App. 311, 103 A. 910 (1918).

enough to invalidate any ordinance or statute which seeks to make the ownership or occupancy of property, in particular localities, depend upon the color of the persons by whom the right may be asserted. . . .

Much like the opinion in *Jackson* v. *State* was that in *Allen* v. *Oklahoma City*.[1] In *Tyler* v. *Harmon*,[2] however, the highest court of Louisiana took a wholly different view. Here the court was unmoved by the *Buchanan* ruling and approved a state law authorizing cities with populations in excess of 25,000 to forbid persons of either race to build or move into houses in neighborhoods in which the other race was preponderant, except with the written consent of the majority of the persons of the latter. The court held this statute, and an ordinance of New Orleans made pursuant to it, a valid use of the police power. City ordinances of this kind, the court maintained, were mere zoning laws, clearly justified by the municipality's power to preserve the public peace and general welfare. In the concurring opinion, which is also reproduced below, one of the justices even went so far as to rebuke the United States Supreme Court for its disposition of the *Buchanan* case.

What the Fourteenth Amendment did for the colored people in the United States was to give them citizenship and its privileges, to forbid the states to withold from them the equal protection of the laws, and thus to prevent any discrimination against them, with regard to their political and civil rights, because of their color. . . .

There is nothing in either the Fourteenth Amendment or the [Civil Rights] Acts of Congress suggestive of social equality between the white race and the colored race, or forbidding the states to discourage amalgamation or social intercourse between the white and colored race.

Even in the strong and passionate appeal of Justice Harlan, in defense of the negroes' constitutional rights, in his dissenting opinion in *Plessy* v. *Ferguson* . . . it was not denied that the Fourteenth Amendment and the Acts of 1866 and 1870 dealt only with civil and political rights, and had nothing to do with the matter of social equality. . . .

The decision in *Plessy* v. *Ferguson* . . . could not be reconciled with a ruling that the statutes and ordinance in this case are unconstitutional. There is more substantial reason for the public sentiment and policy against allowing white persons and negroes to live in the same neighborhood than there is for the public sentiment and policy against allowing them to ride in the same railroad coach. . . . The statutes and ordinances in this case are as free from discrimination as was the statute that was held valid in the case of *Plessy* v. *Ferguson*. There is no discrimination whatsoever against either race in the statutes or in the ordinances in contest. . . . Each race is, under precisely the same conditions, denied the right to live among the people of the other race. . . . The only question, therefore, is whether it is within the police power of the states to enact laws to discourage social intercourse between the white and colored race. And that question has been answered by the de-

[1] 175 Okla. 421, 52 P. 2d 1054 (1935).
[2] 158 La. 441, 104 So. 200 (1925).

cisions of the Supreme Court of the United States upholding laws requiring separate seats for colored people in street cars, or separate coaches for them on railroad trains, laws forbidding the attendance of white and colored children in the same schools, laws forbidding miscegenation, or intermarriage between white and colored people. [Here the court again invoked *Plessy* v. *Ferguson*, and went on to cite *West Chester & Philadelphia Railroad Co.* v. *Miles*, and a dozen other cases.]

Although we cannot quite reconcile our judgment in the present case with all that is said in *Buchanan* v. *Warley*, the two cases may be distinguished in this, that in *Buchanan* v. *Warley* the court found, as a fact, that the ordinance of Louisville, which the court declared violative of the Fourteenth Amendment, forbade a white person to sell property in a neighborhood of white persons to a colored person, and forbade a colored person to sell property in a colored neighborhood to a white person. . . . [whereas] there is nothing in the statute or in the ordinance [involved in the present case] forbidding a white man to sell his property to a colored man, or forbidding a colored man to sell to a white man in any community or neighborhood.

In a concurring opinion, Justice St. Paul added:

A man is none the less free because restrained in his personal conduct by wholesome laws; nor is his property any less valuable because restricted to such use as will best promote the general welfare. . . .

If the doctrine in *Buchanan* v. *Warley* conflicts with these views, and that doctrine be adhered to, then that case marks a long step backwards in the march of civilization; not so much because it interferes with the segregation of the races (which will take care of itself) but more especially because it will serve in future as a precedent against still *other* restrictions on the use of property, which, in time, may become necessary in the public interest; and it ought therefore to be *overruled* before the rolling pebble becomes an avalanche. At any rate, this court should add nothing to the growing mass.

In *Tyler* v. *Harmon*[1] the Supreme Court of Louisiana, standing upon its 1925 ruling, declined to rehear the case; but in the following year the Supreme Court of the United States sharply rejected what it considered the specious reasoning of the Lousiana high court, and in a few stinging sentences reversed the judgment. The racial-restrictive covenant, meanwhile, remained unscathed, in the courts of northern as well as southern states. When blacks bought a lot in a subdivision which was blanketed by restrictive covenants shutting out Negroes and retailers of liquor, whites in the neighborhood sought to exclude them. The Michigan Supreme Court, siding with the whites, cited a number of cases in support of the principle that the Thirteenth and Fourteenth amendments were directed at the states and not at private individuals.[2]

The plat of land containing the restriction was of record. It was also a part of defendant's deed. He knew or should have known all about it. He did not have to buy the land and he should not have bought it unless willing to observe the restrictions it contained.

[1] 160 La. 946, 107 So. 704 (1926). And see above, p. 202.

[2] *Parmalee* v. *Morris*, 218 Mich. 625, 188 N.W. 330 (1922).

The issue involved . . . is a simple one, *i.e.*, shall the law applicable to restrictions as to occupancy contained in deeds to real estate be enforced or shall one be absolved from the provision of the law simply because he is a negro? The question is a purely legal one and we think it was rightly solved by the chancellor under the decisions found in his opinion.

The decree is affirmed, with costs to the appellees [i.e., the Negroes].

In 1927 the Supreme Court of Alabama held, in *Wyatt* v. *Adair*, that a white tenant who voluntarily left a building, part of which had been leased to a black tenant "contrary to established custom," could sue to recover for "constructive eviction and mental anguish"—that in short, to rent to a Negro tenant was in effect to evict the whites from the dwelling, because joint use by whites and blacks of the same toilet facilities was "unthinkable." The court held further that the white plaintiff was wholly justified in assuming that his lease implied that Negroes would never be permitted to occupy the portion of the house he had rented, because the sharing of a toilet by two lessees was here involved, whereas the common use of a toilet by persons of different races was contrary to local usage.[1]

We consider the decision in *Corrigan* v. *Buckley* . . . ample authority that the landlord and white tenant may make a valid contract to the effect that negroes shall not be rented an apartment in the same building.

Matters which may be expressly agreed may be implied, if the circumstances in evidence warrant the conclusion that such was the intention of the parties.

A well-known general custom vitally affecting the peaceful and quiet enjoyment of the premises may well be considered an implied element of the contract between landlord and tenant. . . .

While common knowledge of a custom excluding negroes from the same building or neighborhood may be limited to white residence districts, it is certainly competent to aver and prove a known and well-established custom in what may be termed a negro district to the effect that, if premises are leased to white persons, negroes shall not be put in connected premises with a common toilet for both tenants and their families. 'twould be strange and deplorable if such custom did not exist, however humble the habitation.

C. *Public Facilities: Limited Progress Toward Equality*

In view of the United States Supreme Court's hospitality to separate public facilities in this era, it is hardly surprising that state courts found no defect in them either. When, for example, a Louisville Negro challenged in the Kentucky Court of Appeals a ruling of his city's Board of Park Commissioners which assigned Negroes to parks, swimming pools, and playgrounds set aside for their exclusive use, while whites were

[1] 215 Ala. 363, 110 So. 801 (1927).

restricted to others intended solely for that group, the court held that the provisions did not transgress the federal due process and equal protection clauses.[1] Plaintiffs "cite the Fourteenth Amendment," said the court, "because of which they say the rules and regulations complained of are invalid. To go into this would be but a rethrashing of old straw." And with that, the tribunal, in support of its judgment, simply listed by name such United States Supreme Court cases as *Hall* v. *De Cuir*, and *Plessy* v. *Ferguson*.[2]

Better success attended cases brought by Negroes complaining of infractions of state civil rights laws. California, for example, had a law forbidding discrimination based entirely on race in theaters. When a Negro patron was refused a seat in a section he preferred, the California District Court of Appeals, in *Jones* v. *Kehrlein*, held that tickets admitting persons only to particular sections reserved for persons of a specified race violated the statutory prohibition against discrimination. The fact, moreover, that the purchaser knew of the restriction when he bought the ticket did not debar him from suing for damages.[3]

Again, in a case reviewed by an Ohio appellate court, blacks found judicial support in their claim that assignment to particular seats, however desirable they were, fell under the ban imposed by the state's civil rights law, which forbade the denial of full "privileges" in public accommodations. On August 1, 1916, Melinda Guy, a black, went with a Wilberforce University student to a motion picture theater, and sat down in the center tier. Asked to move to another tier reserved for Negro patrons, they declined and left. When they brought suit, the trial court sided with the theater-owners, but the appellate court reversed the judgment.[4]

> If the section of the General Code is rightly understood, all patrons are entitled to enjoy alike all the privileges accorded to patrons within the theater.
>
> It might be contended here that these persons had just as good an opportunity to see the pictures or vaudeville performance . . . seated on the right-hand side, as if they were seated in the center section. However, if these colored people were required to be so seated they would only be allowed partial enjoyment of the privileges of that theater, because white persons were permitted to occupy the center section [while] colored people . . . were certainly denied some of the privileges that were given to persons of the white race. . . .
>
> To hold otherwise, would be to render these sections [of the statute] as sounding brass. Said sections were passed by our legislature not for an imaginary, but a real purpose. A little more consideration, a little more

[1] *Warley* v. *Board of Park Commissioners*, 233 Ky. Ct. App. 699, 26 S.W. 2d 554 (1930).

[2] See above, pp. 63 and 149.

[3] 194 P. 55 (1920).

[4] *Guy* v. *Tri-State Amusement Co.*, 7 Ohio App. 509 (1918).

willing obedience to these laws, on the part of the people of the white race might render some of the problems which have arisen a little less perplexing. . . . The case must be . . . remanded for a new trial. . . .

Holden v. *Grand Rapids Operating Co.*[1] is of particular interest because the bench—in this instance the Supreme Court of Michigan—instead of taking the more familiar position that *segregation* statutes and ordinances are a valid exercise of the police power because they are necessary to the preservation of public safety and the general welfare, took the then still novel view that *antidiscrimination* laws and ordinances are a valid exercise of the police power because *they* promote public safety and the general welfare.

The [Civil Rights] Act in question . . . was enacted with special reference to those of African descent. It clearly provides against discrimination . . . by withholding from or denying to colored people the accommodations, advantages, facilities or privileges accorded to others. The power of the Legislature to so provide rests upon its so-called police power. The existence of this power and the enactment of laws pursuant to it are necessary to the well-being of the people of all civilized communities. . . .

Our state Legislature has enacted many such laws. Among [those which] affect theaters are provisions for fire escapes, for ample means of egress, and that the doors in the halls thereof shall be made to open outward. These serve to illustrate by examples those by which it is sought to regulate and control the conduct of a private business based on the claim that it is of such a character that it is clothed with a public interest. . . .

The intent and purpose of the Legislature in [the] enactment [of the statute in question] . . . clearly indicates a belief on their part that the public safety and general welfare of our people demand that, when the public are invited to attend places of public accommodation, amusement, and recreation, there shall be no discrimination among those permitted to enter because of race, creed, or color. It is bottomed upon the broad ground of the equality of all men before the law. . . . In our opinion, the act is a valid regulation imposed by the state in its exercise of the police power.

D. *Segregated Transportation on the Defensive*

Jim Crow laws had as yet little to fear from state courts, least of all in the South, but even there the judges often required at least some deference to the principle of equal facilities. At issue in *Illinois Central Railway Co.* v. *Redmond*, for example, was the Mississippi law of 1906 which required separate but equal accommodations on trains. A male black passenger on a train in Mississippi was compelled to travel in the coach's Negro section which afforded no access to a smoking area, and provided only a single toilet marked "Women." The defendant

[1] 239 Mich. 318, 214 N.W. 241 (1927).

was told by the conductor that the toilet facility was intended for males also, but he declined to use it and brought suit. The Supreme Court of Mississippi took his part.[1]

The separate coach laws here under consideration do not require that the accommodations furnished to passengers of the one race be identical with those furnished to passengers of the other, but they do require in plain and unambiguous language that the accommodations (which, of course, include not only those things which are necessary for, but also such as add to comfort and convenience) provided for passengers of the one race shall be equal to those provided for passengers of the other race, from which it necessarily follows that, if separate toilets are provided for the sexes of the one race, separate toilets must also be provided for the sexes of the other, and if a place in which to smoke is provided for the one race, such a place must also be provided for the other.

It may be that . . . the appellant was under no duty to equip its cars with smoking compartments and separate toilets for the sexes, as to which we express no opinion, but, be that as it may, when it so equipped its cars set apart for its white passengers, and thereby added to their comfort and convenience, it became its duty under these statutes to so equip its cars set apart for colored passengers. . . .

E. *Juries and Fair Trial: Increasing Surveillance*

Southern supreme courts and intermediate courts of appeal showed in these years an increasing disposition to rule that trial courts were in error if they declined to hear evidence in support of Negro defendants' contentions that their rights under the Fourteenth Amendment were infringed when Negroes were excluded, by reason of their color, from grand and petit juries. (See e.g., an Arkansas case, *Ware v. State*[2], and *Bruster* v. *State*[3] [of Oklahoma].) Although they continued also to maintain that the mere absence of blacks from juries is not per se a denial of equal protection, they often took the position that deliberate and systematic exclusion of Negro jurors, on the basis of color alone, was a violation of the equal protection clause. Fairly typical was the following opinion.[4]

. . . [T]he constitutional guarantees of equal protection of the laws does not give to any person a right to a jury composed in whole or in part of his own or of any particular race; but every person being tried in a court of justice is entitled to have a jury selected and summoned without illegal discrimination of any character. A large discretion is necessarily allowed the officers charged with the responsibility of selecting jurors. This discretion

[1] 119 Miss. 765, 81 So. 115 (1919).
[2] 146 Ark. 321, 225 S.W. 626 (1920).
[3] 266 P. 486 (Okla., 1920).
[4] *Washington* v. *State,* 95 Fla. 289, 116 So. 470 (1928).

should be carefully exercised so as to aid in the proper administration of the law by securing the best juries possible without illegal discrimination against any citizen of the state qualified for jury duty under the law. . . . The mere fact that the sheriff, in executing a venire for petit jurors to try the defendant, who was a colored man, . . . refused to select any colored men . . . is not of itself evidence of discrimination against persons of color solely on account of their color; neither is it a denial of the equal protection of the laws as contemplated by the Fourteenth Amendment. . . .

In another case, the Oklahoma Court of Criminal Appeals held in *Carrick* v. *State* that the lower court had erred in refusing to quash a panel of jurors in the face of evidence that Negroes were clearly being excluded because of their color. At one point in the transcript the following colloquy appeared in the record, when a jury commissioner had been asked why he had not placed any blacks on the list from which jurors would be drawn.[1]

"Because I never saw a member of the colored race qualified as a juror in this state, and I don't believe, taking them as a whole, that Negroes are competent to serve as jurors.

(Question) Then you are prejudiced against the Negro race?

(Answer) No, sir. I don't believe they would be competent to try one of their own race or any one else."

The court's opinion read in part:

It has been repeatedly held by the Supreme Court of the United States that, when a person of African descent, charged with crime, challenges the array or panel of jurors on the ground of the exclusion of citizens of the African race therefrom, he must affirmatively prove that such citizens were excluded solely because of their race or color. . . . Upon a careful consideration of all the evidence offered in support of appellant's challenge to the panel, we cannot resist the conclusion that the trial committed reversible error in overruling the motion to quash the panel of jurors, because it was shown and admitted that the aforesaid jury commissioners had purposely excluded from the jury list because of their color citizens of the African race, qualified to perform jury duty.

F. *The Franchise: The White Primary Approved*

Two years before the United States Supreme Court rendered its judgment in *Nixon* v. *Herndon*,[2] the Texas Court of Civil Appeals at Galveston reviewed a case centering about the state's white primary law of 1926, and found the statute unobjectionable.[3]

[1] 41 Okla. Crim. 336, 274 P. 896 (1929).

[2] See above, p. 212.

[3] *White* v. *Lubbock*, 30 S.W. 2d 722 (Tex. Civ. App., 1930).

In a state like Texas, where the political parties have not by law been made either to perform any governmental function or to constitute any governmental agency by the payment by the State of their expenses of operation, or otherwise, but have only been regulated—however elaborately—as to how they shall elect their nominees . . . they are not state instrumentalities, but merely bodies of individuals banded together for the propagation of the political principles or beliefs that they desire to have incorporated into the public policies of the government, and as such have the power, beyond statutory control, to prescribe what persons shall participate as voters in their conventions or primaries; in no event, therefore, did the inveighed-against course of party officials constitute action by the state of Texas itself . . . but only the valid exercise through its proper officers of such party's inherent power . . . to determine who should make up the membership of its own private household.

PART FIVE

Reviving Hopes: 1938–1954

In the sixteen years now to be surveyed, the pace of change in Afro-American life was notably accelerated. Income levels of the race rose faster during these years than did those for whites, so that instead of a third, as in 1936, the black wage-earner was paid, by the end of 1954, substantially more than half as much as his white counterpart, and there were reasons to suppose that it would soon reach two-thirds.

The diminishing black farm population was climbing increasingly into the small landowner group. Health standards crept steadily upward so that the race's lag in life expectancy was cut from twelve to six years in the two decades after 1935, and in the Negro's education the improvement in opportunity and achievement was equally promising. The literacy rate among those under forty years of age now approached parity with the figures for whites, and there were in the 1950's as many blacks in American colleges and universities (conceding a substantial difference in quality of education) as there were white students in Britain's institutions of higher learning.

New employment opportunities began to open up for black workers in industry, in skilled and quasi-professional vocations, as well as in the professions; a few labor unions were lowering their racial bars; and the substantial progress, registered by 1954, toward the equalization of educational opportunity in graduate and professional schools promised a gathering momentum for the years immediately ahead. This era saw also the racial integration of the armed forces at a spectacular rate by presidential order; the end of lynching; the leveling of barriers in professional sports; a sharp increase in the number of appointed and elected federal, state, city, county, and local governmental officials; the outlawing of segregation and discrimination in public places in the national capital; the judicial invalidation of racial restrictive covenants; and, above all, the Supreme Court's decisions of 1954, decreeing the end of segregation in the public schools and other public facilities.

The changing attitudes of a growing number of whites promised an abatement of old hostilities. Opinion surveys (like a carefully conducted poll reported in the *Scientific American* in December 1956) revealed that a mere seventh of northerners and two-fifths of southerners still believed that Negroes are inherently less intelligent than whites. Related to this change, both as cause and effect, was the growing disposition of the communications media to shelve the old stereotypes, while churches and schools educated countless white Americans in the amenities and civilities—and the very *vocabulary*—of racial tolerance.

It is easier to recount examples than account for causes of the race's hastening drift toward the mainstream of American life. The long-term momentum of America's spiritual and ideological history was a real, if unmeasurable factor, and certainly the reforming mood of the country in the New Deal years was important here, as were the enthusiasms, the loyalties, and the preoccupation with the nation's destinies and purposes aroused by World War II. The national emergency that began in 1938 increased both the economic and the political bargaining power of the Negro community, and the long postwar boom sustained for another decade a highly favorable employment level. The country's identification with the cause of democracy, its position as the leader of the free world, focused its own and its friends' (and for quite different reasons, its very enemies') concerns upon the plight of its largest minority, so that considerations of both conscience and policy came vigorously to the race's rescue.

Growing economic and social security, improved living standards, increasing political power, expanding educational attainments, and rising "acceptance" in the nation at large—all of these reciprocally stimulated each other, fostering all the while a new self-confidence and militancy in a growing black middle class, doubly confirmed now (as "exaggerated Americans," as one shrewd observer has said) in their traditional allegiance to American values and goals.

The stultifying Social Darwinism of an earlier generation had given way now to a melioristic social philosophy; religious, humanitarian, and civil agencies were enlisted in the cause of racial democracy with persuasive appeals to the national conscience. By the middle 1950's every major church body in America had condemned racial discrimination and intolerance in principle. Hundreds of tax-supported municipal and semi-official agencies were working to promote racial peace and friendship. An accumulating body of literature by scholars and publicists, white and black, brought to an expanding audience scientific data on race overwhelmingly on the side of equality, and went virtually unchallenged by any really considerable literature of rebuttal. By 1954, in short, racism was fast losing its intellectual respectability.

The continued northward and city-ward migration of Negro masses, and the social and economic diversification they brought in their train, added further to the influence of the changes we have listed. By the 1950's nearly 40 percent of Afro-Americans lived outside the South, and of these nearly 95 percent were urbanites, two-thirds of them concentrated in greater metropolitan New York, Chicago, Detroit, and Philadelphia alone. Southern Negroes, also, were leaving the land in such numbers that half the black population of the old slave states had moved to cities and towns by 1955.

And still, it must be set down in candor that this fateful mutation was as yet, in 1954, rich in promise only, and not in performance. It still left relatively untouched the daily lives of millions in the South's rural slums and the northern ghettoes. Millions of black Americans still encountered the rejections and brutalities, the privations and insults that their fathers had known. The penalty for being black was still enormous. Discrimination, with its stigmata of inferiority, was still the overarching fact of Afro-American life. There was still the galling necessity of "climbing a mountain of yessirs," as one of the race's poets expressed it; there was still the decayed, shabby, and rat-infested housing in congested ghettoes; there were still the bitter social rebuffs, the paralyzing differential in job opportunities and economic well-being, in the quality of education, and in the prospects for getting on in the world.

In some instances, doors were opening for which there were not enough qualified Negroes, precisely because the openings came sooner than the race had been enabled or permitted to prepare for them. One massive gain emerged from the period now before us. It was during these sixteen years that it became clear that the law was now unequivocally on the Negro's side, and that a shift in the public philosophy and sentiment in his favor was timorously but unmistakably under way. The ground was being cleared for a social transformation of epic proportions. But if, as the chapter to follow this one attests, the battle had not been won by 1954 (and, in fact, in some respects prospects were *worse* in the middle 1960's than in the early 1950's), it could at least be said that America's best energies were beginning to be committed and engaged. Few dared venture to predict the date of the Afro-American's victory, but as 1955 opened, few doubted the final outcome of the struggle. It would, in the perspective of history, be a triumph whose legal foundations were laid in the years 1938–1954, on groundwork first begun in 1863–1870.

(1)
RACIAL IDEOLOGY: EQUALITARIANISM AND DISSENT

With these years came some decline in anti-Negro thought. Scientific evidence impressively piled up by scholarly investigators persuaded not a few educated Americans (including lawmakers and judges) to modify if not abandon older notions of inherent white superiority. The movement was further accelerated by World War II; for the nation's supreme struggle against totalitarian aggressors aroused a new national dedication to the historic American credo of liberty and equality. Confirmation for the more liberal views came also with the comprehensive study made by Gunnar Myrdal and his associates under the auspices of the Carnegie Foundation.

The steadily growing volume of scientific literature on race, adumbrated in the early works of Franz Boas, now became orthodoxy in the universities, and thence affected the whole range of the country's opinion molders, so that well before 1954 anti-Negro thought was being repudiated in educated circles, and was fast becoming unpopular in less learned precincts as well. Once scientists abandoned the older racial clichés, it is hardly remarkable that a people so peculiarly deferential as Americans are to the authority of science should have begun to reconsider.

A few brief passages will illustrate the changed attitude toward racial differences and the assumption of superior and inferior races. The first is taken from the Myrdal study.[1]

> Even as long ago as 1930 . . . a questionnaire circulated among "competent scholars in the field of racial differences" revealed that only 4 percent of the respondents believed in race superiority and inferiority. It is doubtful whether the proportion would be as large today. . . .
>
> But while they seem to be negative, these conclusions of psychological research have probably been more revolutionary and practically important, with respect to the Negro problem, than the conclusions from any other sphere of science. It is true that science's last word has not been said even on the Negro's innate intelligence and still less on his other psychic traits. But the undermining of the basis of certitude for popular beliefs has been accomplished. . . . [E]ven if future research should be able to establish . . .

[1] Gunnar Myrdal, *An American Dilemma; The Negro Problem and Modern Democracy*, 2 vols. (New York: Harper & Row, 1944), p. 148. Reprinted by permission of the publisher.

certain innate psychic differences between American Negroes and whites, on the average, *it is highly improbable that such differences would be so large, that—particularly when the overlapping is considered—they could justify a differential treatment in matters of public policy, such as in education, suffrage and entrance to various sections of the labor market.* This is a practical conclusion of immense importance.

For the theoretical study of the Negro problem in all its other branches —from breadwinning and crime to institutions and cultural accomplishments—the negative results in regard to heredity and the positive findings in regard . . . to *milieu* are also of paramount importance. It means that when *we approach those problems on the hypothesis that differences in behavior are to be explained largely in terms of social and cultural factors, we are on scientifically safe ground. If we should, however, approach them on the hypothesis that they are to be explained primarily in terms of heredity, we do not have any scientific basis for our assumption.*

Now follows an excerpt from a standard college textbook in introductory anthropology:[1]

The present position. In view of all these facts, the only reasonable conclusion is that there is no scientific evidence to show either racial inferiority or superiority on the part of any of the major races of mankind. . . . In short, in the present state of our knowledge, the concept of biologically determined psychological differences between hereditary varieties of mankind is scientifically useless. We achieve the best results in interpreting and predicting culture by proceeding, for the present, on the assumption that all normal hereditary varieties and subgroups of the species . . . are fundamentally equal in cultural ability. In other words, the ability factor may be considered to be relatively constant, and we may proceed to the consideration of more significant variables in our consideration of cultural phenomena.

Still another sample is taken from Wilton Marion Krogman, "The Concept of Race," in Ralph Linton, editor, *The Science of Man in the World Crisis,*[2] published during World War II.

Races react to one another, especially in a majority-minority situation, in two interrelated ways: in the first place they may be . . . set apart by visible markers of morphological difference—skin color, hair form, and so on. This tends to enhance a feeling of group solidarity, of the we-versus-you attitude. All things being equal the more marked the visible differences the more manifest will be the feeling of group consciousness or of group attitude (in the present conflict, for example, the average American soldier reacts much more vigorously against the Japanese than against the Nazi). In the second place it is assumed . . . using the majority physical type and cultural level as a standard, that the presumed cultural inadequacies of the minority group are related to the fact that they differ physically from the dominant group. The logic may run something like this: the Negro's skin is black, and . . . because he is set apart in this fashion it must follow that he is likewise set

[1] John Gillin, *The Ways of Men* (New York, 1948), p. 143.

[2] Wilton Marion Krogman, "The Concept of Race," *The Science of Man in the World Crisis,* ed. Ralph Linton (New York: Columbia University Press, 1945), pp. 60–62, *passim.* Copyright 1945 by Columbia University Press. Reprinted by permission of the publisher.

apart, in some mysterious fashion, in social and cultural aptitude; his cultural level is not inadequate because his skin is black, but because the whites behave toward a darker skin as though it were a major bio-social difference. The difference in skin color gets the blame, but it is the social attitude that is at fault.

. . . All too often, and most unfortunately, it is society, operating via prejudice and socio-economic pressure, that brands the mark of disapproval and nonacceptance. . . .

If we accept that there *are* stocks and races, we accept also that such a classification is not a rigorous one, not even a clearly circumscribed one, and certainly *not* a hierarchical one. The physical anthropologist sorts out mankind, he does not evaluate—he, alas, too often leaves that to the harsh judgment of society. But he can and does place this evaluation: that biologically there are no fundamental physical differences in all stocks and in all races; that bio-genetic potentials are shared equally by all stocks and by all races. The physical anthropologist, we repeat, can and does place an evaluation upon his fellow men: biological equality! . . . .

Knowledge is slow of foot and wisdom trails far behind knowledge. The important fact emerges, however, that the march to equality is on, and that the tempo is being accelerated by the facts and hypotheses of the biological and the social sciences, working together toward the common goal of a new world of peace and understanding, national and international.

Views like the foregoing reached the general public indirectly, through the intellectuals who read such books, or studied them in college, and then transmitted the ideas from the pulpit, from magazines and daily newspapers, and even through the entertainment media. More directly accessible to the larger public, however, was the ten-cent pamphlet prepared under the supervision of a committee of the American Association of Scientific Workers, and written during World War II as a contribution to the war effort, by two eminent Columbia University anthropologists, trained in the Boas tradition: Ruth Benedict and Gene Weltfish. Issued in the *Public Affairs Pamphlets* series, it was frequently reprinted and widely circulated (and bitterly attacked by the dwindling number of racists, who were now on the defensive).[1]

WHAT ABOUT INTELLIGENCE?

The most careful investigations of intelligence have been made in America among Negroes and whites. The scientist realizes that every time he measures intelligence in any man, black or white, his results show the intelligence that man was born with plus what happened to him since he was born. The scientist has a lot of proof of this. For instance, in the First World War, intelligence tests were given to the American Expeditionary Forces; they showed that Negroes made a lower score on intelligence tests than whites. But the tests also showed that Northerners, black and white, had higher scores than Southerners, black and white. Everyone knows that Southerners are inborn equals of Northerners, but in 1917 many southern states' per capita expenditures for schools were only fractions of those in northern

[1] No. 85 (October, 1943). The portion that follows is from pp. 17–21, *passim.*

states, and housing and diet and income were far below average too. Since the vast majority of Negroes lived in the South, their score on the intelligence test was a score they got not only as Negroes, but as Americans who had grown up under poor conditions in the South. Scientists therefore compared the scores of Southern whites and Northern Negroes.

Median Scores on A.E.F. Intelligence Tests

Southern Whites:	
Mississippi	41.25
Kentucky	41.50
Arkansas	41.55
Northern Negroes:	
New York	45.02
Illinois	47.35
Ohio	49.50

Negroes with better luck after they were born got higher scores than whites with less luck. The white race did badly where economic conditions were bad and schooling was not provided, and Negroes living under better conditions surpassed them. *The differences did not arise because they were white or black, but because of differences in income, education, cultural advantages, and other opportunities.*

Scientists then studied gifted children. They found that children with top scores turn up among Negroes, Mexicans, and Orientals. Then they went to European countries to study the intelligence of children in homelands from which our immigrants come. Children from some of these countries got poor scores in America, but in their homeland children got good scores. Evidently the poor scores here were due to being uprooted, speaking a foreign language, and living in tenements; the children were not unintelligent *by heredity.*

CHARACTER NOT INBORN

The second superiority which a man claims when he says, "I was born a member of a superior race," is that his race has better *character.* The Nazis boast of their racial soul. But when they wanted to make a whole new generation into Nazis they didn't trust to "racial soul"; they made certain kinds of teaching compulsory in the schools, they broke up homes where the parents were anti-Nazi, they required boys to join certain Nazi youth organizations. By these means they got the kind of national character they wanted. But it was a planned and deliberately trained character, not an inborn "racial soul." . . .

It can go the other way, too. In 1520 the ancient Mexicans were like the Germans. They talked like Nazis, thought like them, in many ways felt like them. They, too, believed war to be man's highest mission. They, too, trained their children for it, placing their boys in great state schools where they learned little else but the glories of battle and the rituals of their caste. They, too, believed themselves invincible, and against small, defenseless villages, they were. But they were defeated in battle by the Spaniards with the help of the peoples whom the Aztecs had oppressed; their leaders were killed, their temples destroyed, their wealth pillaged, and their power broken. The Mexican peasant, who still speaks the Aztec language and in whose veins still runs the blood of Aztec conquerors, no longer dreams of glorious death in battle and eternal life in an Indian Valhalla. He no longer goes on the warpath, no longer provokes war with peaceful villages. He is a humble peon, wishing only to be left in peace to cultivate his little field, go to church, dance, sing, and make love. These simple things endure.

Americans deny that the Nazis have produced a national character superior to that of Goethe's and Schiller's day, and that the ruthless Japanese of today are finer human beings than in those generations when they preferred to write poetry and paint pictures. Race prejudice is, after all, a determination to keep a people down, and it misuses the label "inferior" to justify unfairness and injustice. Race prejudice makes people ruthless; it invites violence. It is the opposite of "good character" as it is defined in the Christian religion—or in the Confucian religion, or in the Buddhist religion, or the Hindu religion, for that matter. . . .

It is not to be assumed that the older racism was about to disappear; it survived among millions of Americans, North and South. Especially after 1940 racist writers realized that they were a beleaguered minority, but they did not fall silent. The Nordic-supremacy literature offered little that was new, however, and it was clearly handicapped by the difficulty of squaring discrimination and segregation with American ideals, in the face of mounting scientific evidence of the essential equality of men.

One of the more strident voices of racism in the 1930's and 1940's was Theodore G. Bilbo, Mississippi's United States senator and former governor. An impassioned advocate of transporting blacks to Africa, and given to such public utterances as "the nigger is only 150 years from the jungles of Africa [where he cut up] fried nigger steak for breakfast,"[1] he bluntly told blacks that Mississippi had no intention of permitting them to vote, no matter what the Supreme Court and the Constitution had to say on the matter.

The following item is from a book written by the Senator. The book was based, he said, on his study of race relationships, "covering a period of close on to thirty thousand years," which led him to believe that it would be better to see civilization "blotted out with the atomic bomb than to see it slowly but surely destroyed in the maelstrom of miscegenation, interbreeding, intermarriage, and mongrelization."[2]

If we sit with Negroes at our tables, if we attend social functions with them as our social equals, if we disregard segregation in all other relations, is it then possible that we maintain it fixedly in the marriage of the South's Saxon sons and daughters? The answer must be "No." By the absolute denial of social equality to the Negro, the barriers between the races are firm and strong. But if the middle wall of the social partition should be broken down, then the mingling of the tides of life would surely begin. . . . The Southern white race, the Southern Caucasian, would be irretrievably doomed.

[1] As quoted in *Time*, July 1, 1945.

[2] Theodore G. Bilbo, *Take Your Choice: Separation or Mongrelization* (Poplarville, Miss., 1947), p. 55.

Some of this bombast must be discounted as demagogic electioneering, but there was also an occasional serious volume on racial theory in the old idiom, like Iran Calvin's *The Lost White Race* (1945). Master race philosophy was preached even by so respected an American hero as Colonel Charles A. Lindbergh, who, at the outbreak of World War II, thought it better for the United States to make common cause with Germany, as well as France and Britain, to preserve the supremacy and purity of "that most priceless possession, our . . . European blood . . . against dilution by foreign races," than to "commit racial suicide" by dissipating her strength in a losing war against Germany.[1]

[1] Charles A. Lindbergh, "Aviation, Geography, and Race," *Reader's Digest,* XXXV (November, 1939), 64–67.

(2)
VIEWS FROM THE WHITE HOUSE

Franklin D. Roosevelt, President, 1933–1945

The first significant public utterance on the subject of the Negro's struggle that one encounters in a search through the huge compilation of *The Public Papers and Addresses of Franklin D. Roosevelt*—he had already begun his third term—is a memorandum addressed to William S. Knudsen and Sidney Hillman, of the Office of Production Management, dated June 2, 1941, in which the President called for an end to discrimination in defense industries. The idea did not originate with Mr. Roosevelt. It was the acute manpower shortage and a threatened march on Washington (to be led by A. Philip Randolph, president of the Sleeping Car Porters) that prompted the Chief Executive to act. Two weeks after he wrote the Knudsen-Hillman note, he employed a more formal means for achieving its object when he issued Executive Order No. 8802, establishing a Committee on Fair Employment Practice (FEPC).[2] The memorandum noted:

> Complaints have repeatedly been brought to my attention that available and much-needed workers are being barred from defense production solely

[2] Samuel I. Rosenmann, comp., *The Public Papers and Addresses of Franklin D. Roosevelt,* 13 vols. (New York: Random House, Inc., 1938; The Macmillan Company, 1941; Harper & Brothers, 1950; Russell & Russell, 1969), 10:214–15. Reprinted by permission of Harper & Row, and Russell & Russell.

because of race, religion, or national origin. . . . This situation is a matter of grave national importance, and immediate steps must be taken to deal with it effectively. . . .

No nation combating the increasing threat of totalitarianisms can afford arbitrarily to exclude large segments of its population from its defense industries. Even more important is it for us to strengthen our unity and morale by refuting at home the very theories which we are fighting abroad.

Our Government cannot countenance continued discrimination against American citizens in defense production. Industry must take the initiative in opening the doors of employment to all loyal and qualified workers regardless of race, national origin, religion, or color. . . . In the present emergency, it is imperative that we deal effectively and speedily with this problem. I shall expect the Office of Production Management to take immediate steps to facilitate the full utilization of our productive manpower.

Three years later, in a radio speech from the White House, the President discussed the citizen's obligation to make full use of the franchise. In the course of the address he made a brief allusion to the Negro and the vote.[1]

It is true that there are many undemocratic defects in voting laws in the various states, almost forty-eight different kinds of defects, and some of these produce injustices which prevent a full and free expression of public opinion.

The right to vote must be open to our citizens irrespective of race, color, or creed—without tax or artificial restriction of any kind. The sooner we get to that basis of political equality, the better it will be for the country as a whole.

Harry S. Truman, President, 1945–1953

President Truman was notably more outspoken on the subject than was his predecessor. He too issued a far-reaching executive order, abolishing segregation in the armed forces,[2] and on several occasions expressed himself vigorously on the Negro's behalf. Following are a few paragraphs from his address to the 38th Annual Conference of the NAACP, delivered at the Lincoln Memorial in Washington on June 29, 1947.[3]

Our immediate task is to remove the last remnants of the barriers which stand between millions of our citizens and their birthright. There is no justifiable reason for discrimination because of ancestry, or religion, or race, or color.

We must not tolerate such limitations on the freedom of any of our people and on their enjoyment of basic rights which every citizen in a truly democratic society must possess.

Every man should have the right to a decent home, the right to an educa-

[1] *Ibid.*, XII, 318.

[2] See below, p. 306.

[3] *Public Papers of the Presidents of the United States: Harry S. Truman, 1945–1953* (8 vols., Washington, 1961–1966). See vol. for 1947, pp. 311–13. Reprinted by permission of Harry S. Truman.

tion, the right to adequate medical care, the right to a worthwhile job, the right to an equal share in making the public decisions through the ballot, and the right to a fair trial in a fair court.

We must insure that these rights—on equal terms—are enjoyed by every citizen.

To these principles I pledge my full and continued support.

Many of our people still suffer the indignity of insult, the harrowing fear of intimidation, and, I regret to say, the threat of physical injury and mob violence. Prejudice and intolerance in which these evils are rooted still exist. The conscience of our Nation, and the legal machinery which enforces it, have not yet secured to each citizen full freedom from fear.

We cannot wait another decade or another generation to remedy these evils. We must work, as never before, to cure them now. The aftermath of war and the desire to keep faith with our Nation's historic principles make the need a pressing one.

. . . . .

Our National Government must show the way.

This is a difficult and complex undertaking. Federal laws and administrative machineries must be improved and expanded. We must provide the Government with better tools to do the job. As a first step, I appointed an Advisory Committee on Civil Rights last December. Its members, fifteen distinguished private citizens, have been surveying our civil rights difficulties and needs for several months. I am confident that the product of their work will be a sensible and vigorous program for action by all of us.

. . . . .

The way ahead is not easy. We shall need all the wisdom, imagination and courage we can muster. We must and shall guarantee the civil rights of all our citizens. Never before has the need been so urgent for skillful and vigorous action to bring us closer to our ideal.

. . . . .

(3)

THE NATIONAL PARTY PLATFORMS[1]

Campaign of 1940

The progressive spirit of the New Deal at home and the aggressions of totalitarian-racists abroad now came to the aid of the Afro-American's cause, and the party platforms began—although timidly as yet—to reflect the country's rising misgivings over his predicament. In addition to the two major parties, four minor parties offered national candidates and platforms. The Prohibition and Socialist Labor parties preserved

[1] The platforms for the presidential campaigns of 1940–1952 are in Porter and Johnson, *National Party Platforms*, pp. 376–522.

their customary silence, but the other four groups spoke out with varying degrees of force and, one suspects, with varying degrees of sincerity.

Democratic: Our Negro citizens have participated actively in the economic and social advances launched by this Administration, including fair labor standards, social security benefits, health protection, work relief projects, decent housing, aid to education, and the rehabilitation of low-income farm families. We have aided more than half a million Negro youths in vocational training, education and employment. We shall continue to strive for complete legislative safeguards against discrimination in government service and benefits, and in the national defense forces. We pledge to uphold due process and the equal protection of the laws for every citizen, regardless of race, creed or color.

Republican: We pledge that our American citizens of Negro descent shall be given a square deal in the economic and political life of this nation. Discrimination in the civil service, the army, navy, and all other branches of the Government must cease. To enjoy the full benefits of life, liberty and pursuit of happiness universal suffrage must be made effective for the Negro citizen. Mob violence shocks the conscience of the nation and legislation to curb this evil should be enacted.

Communist: Pass the Geyer Anti-Poll Tax Bill to give the vote to the Negro and white masses in the South. For full civil rights and the right to vote for all men in the armed services, migratory workers and seafaring men. . . . Guarantee the Negro people complete equality, equal rights to jobs, equal pay for equal work, the full right to organize, serve on juries and hold public office. Pass the Anti-Lynching Bill. Demand the death penalty for lynchers. Enforce the 13th, 14th and 15th Amendments to the United States Constitution.

Socialist: We renew our pledge for the maintenance and increase of civil liberty for all groups, regardless of race, color or creed. We support everywhere the fight against poll taxes, undemocratic laws, and all limitations of suffrage. . . . Discrimination against Negroes must be abolished.

Campaign of 1944

That the momentum that had carried the parties into the racial struggle in 1940 had not spent itself four years later is evident from the platforms of 1944. The Communist party had dissolved itself in the spring of that year, so that the civil rights movement's loudest voice was stilled, at least for the present. Of the parties actually in the field, only the Socialist Laborites still chose to stand off from the issue. The Democratic platform affirmed simply: "We believe that racial and religious minorities have the right to live, develop and vote equally with all citizens and share the rights that are guaranteed by our Constitution.

Congress should exert its full constitutional powers to protect those rights."

From the Republican platform:

Racial and Religious Intolerance

We unreservedly condemn the injection into American life of appeals to racial or religious prejudice. We pledge an immediate Congressional inquiry to ascertain the extent to which mistreatment, segregation and discrimination against Negroes who are in our armed forces are impairing morale and efficiency, and the adoption of corrective legislation. We pledge the establishment by Federal legislation of a permanent Fair Employment Practice Commission.

Anti-Poll Tax

The payment of any poll tax should not be a condition of voting in federal elections and we favor immediate submission of a Constitutional amendment for its abolition.

Anti-Lynching

We favor legislation against lynching and pledge our sincere efforts in behalf of its early enactment.

From the Prohibition platform:

Recognizing that God created of one blood all nations to dwell upon the face of the earth, we declare in favor of full justice and equal opportunity for all people, whatever their religion, racial or national origin.

The Socialist platform was more specific:

Equality and Fraternity of Races

Democracy requires the application of the principle that each person is to be accorded social, political and economic equality, and judged solely on the basis of his own deeds, rather than by his race, religion, or national origin.

Specifically, we pledge ourselves to work for American hospitality to war refugees and the end of the exclusion of certain Asiatic peoples. The law applying to the Chinese the general provisions concerning immigration and admitting them to citizenship, should be extended to all Asiatic countries.

We demand the complete restoration of their rights as citizens to the 70,000 Americans of Japanese origin on the West Coast who were evacuated en masse, without trial or even hearing, and confined in centers which, however humanely run, are concentration camps.

We condemn anti-Semitism, Jim-Crowism, and every form of race discrimination and segregation in the armed forces as well as civil life. We urge the passage of anti-lynching and anti-poll tax laws and the prompt enactment of legislation to set up a permanent federal Fair Employment Practice Committee.

We reaffirm our historic opposition to any doctrine or practice of a master or favored race, not only in the realm of law, but in such labor unions—fortunately a minority—churches, political parties, and other basic social organizations as today countenance it. One of the conditions that will help make permanent the end of racial prejudice is the maintenance of full employment.

Campaign of 1948

Once again the party platforms demonstrated that the black man's claim upon the country could no longer be ignored. Indeed, the gradually appreciating fortunes of the race now evoked a reaction from rightist proto-fascists in the Christian Nationalist party and from conservative, white-supremacy foes of federal efforts in the Negro's behalf, who bolted the Democrats to form the States Rights party as an angry rebuke to President Truman's civil rights efforts and to the Democratic platform's civil rights plank. The Democratic convention had shown little disposition to placate Dixie fire-eaters. After the latter faction had rejected the platform committee's compromise plank on civil rights and demanded the adoption of the southern position, the convention went on to adopt an even more advanced platform than the one at first proposed. No fewer than ten parties offered platforms in the 1948 election, and of these all except the Socialist Labor party had something to say on the question. Seven (four of which are quoted here) endorsed at least some measure of civil rights advance, while two took strong stands against the movement.

From the Democratic platform:

The Democratic Party commits itself to continuing its efforts to eradicate all racial, religious and economic discrimination.

We again state our belief that racial and religious minorities must have the right to live, the right to work, the right to vote, the full and equal protection of the laws, on a basis of equality with all citizens as guaranteed by the Constitution.

We highly commend President Harry S. Truman for his courageous stand on the issue of civil rights.

We call upon the Congress to support our President in guaranteeing these basic and fundamental American principles: (1) the right of full and equal political participation; (2) the right to equal opportunity of employment; (3) the right of security of person; (4) and the right of equal treatment in the service and defense of our nation. . . .

From the Republican platform:

Lynching or any other form of mob violence anywhere is a disgrace to any civilized state, and we favor the prompt enactment of legislation to end this infamy.

One of the basic principles of this Republic is the equality of all individuals in their right to life, liberty, and the pursuit of happiness. This principle is enunciated in the Declaration of Independence and embodied in the Constitution of the United States; it was vindicated on the field of battle and became the cornerstone of this Republic. This right of equal opportunity to work and to advance in life should never be limited in any individual because of race, religion, color, or country of origin. We favor the enactment and just enforcement of such Federal legislation as may be necessary to maintain this right at all times in every part of this Republic.

We favor the abolition of the poll tax as a requisite to voting.

We are opposed to the idea of racial segregation in the armed services of the United States.

From the Communist platform:

We call upon all progressives, especially white progressives, to carry on an unceasing day-to-day struggle to outlaw the poll tax, lynchings, segregation, job discrimination and all other forms of Jim-Crowism, official and unofficial, and to give their full support to the rising national liberation movement of the Negro people. This is vital to the Negro people, to the white workers, and to the whole fight for democracy in America.

We demand a national F.E.P.C. law, to be vigorously and fully enforced.

We demand that the Ingram family be freed and adequately compensated for the ordeals to which they have been subjected.

We demand that the Ku Klux Klan and all other hate-and-terror organizations be outlawed.

We condemn President Truman's cynical evasion of the issue of segregation in the armed forces. We demand that he immediately issue an Executive Order ending every form of segregation and discrimination in the armed forces and the government services.

We defend the right of the Negro people to full representation in government, and demand Federal enforcement of the thirteenth, fourteenth, and fifteenth Amendments, so that the Negro people, North and South, may participate freely and fully in the 1948 elections and all elections thereafter.

We call for a democratic agricultural program which will give land and other forms of assistance to millions of Negro and white tenants and sharecroppers in the South, and thereby help put an end to the semi-feudal plantation system.

From the Progressive platform:

End Discrimination

The Progressive Party condemns segregation and discrimination in all its forms and in all places.

We demand full equality for the Negro people, the Jewish people, Spanish-speaking Americans, Italian Americans, Japanese Americans, and all other nationality groups.

We call for a Presidential proclamation ending segregation and all forms of discrimination in the armed services and Federal employment.

We demand Federal anti-lynch, anti-discrimination, and fair-employment-practices legislation, and legislation abolishing segregation in interstate travel.

We call for immediate passage of anti-poll tax legislation, enactment of a universal suffrage law to permit all citizens to vote in Federal elections, and the full use of Federal enforcement powers to assure free exercise of the right to franchise.

We call for a Civil Rights Act for the District of Columbia to eliminate racial segregation and discrimination in the nation's capital.

We demand the ending of segregation and discrimination in the Panama Canal Zone and all territories, possessions and trusteeships. . . .

We will develop special programs to raise the low standards of health, housing, and educational facilities for Negroes, Indians and nationality groups, and will deny Federal funds to any state or local authority which withholds opportunities or benefits for reasons of race, creed, color, sex or national origin.

We will initiate a Federal program of education, in cooperation with state, local, and private agencies to combat racial and religious prejudice.

We support the enactment of legislation making it a Federal Crime to disseminate anti-Semitic, anti-Negro, and all racist propaganda by mail, radio, motion picture or other means of communication.

From the Christian Nationalist party platform:

The enemies of America are missing no opportunity to organize and exploit the American Negro. This exploitation takes on three forms of abuse. The Communists would make the Negro a revolutionary backlog for an era of bloodshed and slaughter. The organized Jew is attempting to use the American Negro to break down the influence and power of the white man's leadership. Numerous Jewish pressure groups encourage intermarriage, mongrelization and social intermixture. The political demagogue is using the Negro vote in doubtful states as a pawn in his greed for power. . . .

Therefore, the Christian Nationalist Party supports the Abraham Lincoln Plan for the Negro—a homeland in Africa. We believe that this homeland should be opened to all American Negroes and that $5,000 per family should be set aside for Negroes willing to migrate to this homeland where all public officials shall be Negroes and where only Negroes shall be eligible for office. . . .

Segregation

In the light of the historic fact that the intermarriage of the black and white races invariably spells the destruction of a civilization, we Christian Nationals shall support an amendment to the Constitution of the United States which would require the segregation of the black and white races and which would outlaw intermarriage and make of same a Federal crime. . . .

From the States' Rights platform:

We stand for the segregation of the races and the racial integrity of each race; the constitutional right to choose one's associates; to accept private employment without governmental interference, and to earn one's living in any lawful way. We oppose the elimination of segregated employment by Federal bureaucrats called for by the misnamed civil rights program. We favor home rule, local self-government and a minimum interference with individual rights.

We oppose and condemn the action of the Democratic convention in sponsoring a civil rights program calling for the elimination of segregation, social equality by Federal fiat, regulation of private employment practices, voting and local law enforcement.

We affirm that the effective enforcement of such a program would be utterly destructive of the social, economic and political life of the Southern people, and of other localities in which there may be differences in race, creed or national origin in appreciable numbers. . . .

Campaign of 1952

The issue was now squarely joined, and it was clear that the day when party strategists could ignore the aspirations of the country's largest and most visible majority had passed. This time there were eight platforms (the Communists and States' Righters having withdrawn), two of which (Christian Nationalists and Socialist Laborites) made no mention of the Negro and his plight. Here follow quotations from the platforms of the Democratic, Republican, and Progressive parties:

From the Democratic platform:

Civil Rights

The Democratic Party is committed to support and advance the individual rights and liberties of all Americans.

Our country is founded on the proposition that all men are created equal. This means that all citizens are equal before the law and should enjoy equal political rights. They should have equal opportunities for education, for economic advancement, and for decent living conditions.

We will continue our efforts to eradicate discrimination based on race, religion, or national origin.

We know this task requires action, not just in one section of the Nation, but in all sections. It requires the cooperative efforts of individual citizens and action by State and local governments. It also requires Federal action. The Federal Government must live up to the ideals of the Declaration of Independence and must exercise the powers vested in it by the Constitution. . . .

[W]e favor Federal legislation effectively to secure these rights to everyone: (1) the right to equal opportunity for employment; (2) the right to security of persons; (3) the right to full and equal participation in the Nation's political life, free from arbitrary restraints. We also favor legislation to perfect existing Federal civil rights statutes and to strengthen the administrative machinery for the protection of civil rights.

From the Republican platform:

Civil Rights . . .

The Republican Party will not mislead, exploit, or attempt to confuse minority groups for political purposes. All American citizens are entitled to full, impartial enforcement of Federal laws relating to their civil rights.

We believe that it is the primary responsibility of each State to order and control its own domestic institutions, and this power, reserved to the states, is essential to the maintenance of our Federal Republic. However, we believe that the Federal Government should take supplemental action within its constitutional jurisdiction to oppose discrimination against race, religion or national origin.

We will prove our good faith by:

Appointing qualified persons, without distinction of race, religion or national origin, to responsible positions in the Government.

Federal action toward the elimination of lynching.

Federal action toward the elimination of poll taxes as a prerequisite to voting.

Appropriate action to end segregation in the District of Columbia.

Enacting Federal legislation to further just and equitable treatment in the area of discriminatory employment practices. Federal action should not duplicate state efforts to end such practices; should not set up another huge bureaucracy.

From the Progressive platform:

III. End America's Shame: Guarantee Full Civil Rights for the Negro People and Other Minorities: End Segregation

In vigorous and uncompromising support of these aims and steps toward stamping out every form of discrimination against the Negro people, the Mexican-American people, the Puerto Rican people, the Jewish people and other minority groups, the Progressive Party calls for:

1. A Federal Fair Employment Practices Law with effective enforcement powers to guarantee equality in job opportunities and training for the Negro people, Puerto Ricans, Mexican-Americans and all other minorities.

2. A Federal anti-poll tax law together with Federal legislation to guarantee to the Negro people, Puerto Ricans, Mexican-Americans and other minorities the right to register and to vote in primary and general elections for Federal office. Revise Senate cloture rules to make filibusters impossible.

3. A Federal anti-lynch law to direct the full power of the Federal government against lynchers.

4. The immediate issuance of an Executive Order by the President to prohibit discrimination in employment, under any contract entered into by the Federal government or any of its agencies.

5. The immediate issuance of an Executive Order by the President for effective prosecution under the Federal civil rights statutes of the violation of the civil rights of Negro citizens and other minorities.

6. End segregation and discrimination in housing; replace Jim Crow ghettos with low-rent, unsegregated housing.

7. The immediate issuance of an Executive Order to end segregation and discrimination in the armed forces, in all Federal departments and agencies, and in the Panama Canal Zone.

8. Real Home Rule for the District of Columbia and Congressional legislation to prohibit every form of segregation and discrimination in the nation's capital.

9. Full representation of the Negro and Puerto Rican and Mexican-American people in Congress, in State legislatures and all levels of public office, elective and appointive.

10. Provide that all Federal laws appropriating Federal monies for any public purpose contain a specific provision prohibiting the use of any such funds in a manner which discriminates against the Negro people, Puerto Ricans, Mexican-Americans or any other minorities. . . .

(4)

STATE CIVIL RIGHTS LEGISLATION

State civil rights laws and other statutes protecting blacks from various kinds of discrimination were still relatively unusual in this era. Pauli Murray's compilation of laws directed against discrimination in places of public accommodation and amusement lists only 18 states having at least some such legislation in effect in September 1949:[1]

California	Indiana	Michigan	New York	Washington
Colorado	Iowa	Minnesota	Ohio	Wisconsin
Connecticut	Kansas	Nebraska	Pennsylvania	
Illinois	Massachusetts	New Jersey	Rhode Island	

The same study discloses 47 categories of accommodations in which one or more states had outlawed racial discrimination, and notes that in twelve of the eighteen states with antidiscrimination laws only ten or fewer (the average was under five) of these types of accommodations were placed under regulation by these laws. The following tabulation indicates the number of states forbidding discrimination in the accommodations listed:

Air Travel	5	Houses of Entertainment	3
Auditoriums	3	Motion Picture Theaters	5
Barber Shops	12	Museums	1
Bar Rooms, Saloons	5	Music, Concert Halls	7
Bath Houses	6	Other Amusement Places	18
Bath Rooms	1	Parks, Amusement	4
Beauty Parlors	1	Public Conveyances	17
Bicycle Rinks	1	Public Conveyances (water)	11
Billiard and Pool Rooms	4	Public Halls	1
Boarding Houses	1	Public Libraries	3
Boardwalks, Seashore Accommodations	1	Race Courses	3
Bowling Alleys	3	Refreshment Places	3
Cemeteries	3	Restaurants, Eating Places	15
Confectioneries	2	Rest Rooms	2
Drug Stores	1	Road Houses	5
Elevators	1	Roof Gardens	3
Fairs, Circuses	4	Shooting Galleries	3
Funeral Hearses	1	Skating Rinks	7
Garages	3	Soda Fountains	3
Golf Courses	1	Soft Drink and Ice Cream Parlors	5
Gymnasiums	3	Stores, Retail	4
Hospitals and Clinics	3	Taxicabs	1
Hotels	9	Theaters	15
Inns and Taverns	16		

In fields other than public accommodations, the tabulation of antidiscrimination laws affecting Negroes, which were on the statute books in September 1949, shows that of the forty-eight states and the District

[1] Murray, *States' Laws on Race and Color, passim.*

of Columbia only the District and nine states (Georgia, Mississippi, Montana, Nevada, South Dakota, Utah, Vermont, Virginia, and Wyoming) had no such rules at all. It may be assumed that in four of these the lawmakers felt that discrimination was not so widespread that enactments of this kind were needed to cope with it. Several states, notably in the South, had antidiscrimination laws extending to only one or two or three categories primarily affecting Negroes. Kentucky, for example, had only an antilynching law; Arkansas, Alabama, Louisiana, Oklahoma, and Tennessee had only "antimask" laws aimed at the Klan and other terrorists; and Delaware, Maryland, Missouri, and West Virginia had only laws prohibiting discrimination in teachers' salaries on the basis of race. Florida had only a law against libel and hate literature, Maine only a law forbidding discriminatory advertising; and North Carolina's only antibias law forbade discrimination in the administration of the Firemen's Relief Fund. South Carolina and Texas each had a mere pair of laws: an antimask law and an antilynching law.

The statutes of which a significant number of the forty-eight states (but, still, in only one case exceeding a third of the states) afforded examples are listed below, together with the number of states having each law:

EDUCATION

Forbidding racial discrimination in public schools	16
Forbidding racial discrimination in private schools	5
Forbidding racial discrimination in state universities	1

EMPLOYMENT

Forbidding discrimination in civil service employment	9
Requiring fair employment practices	8
Forbidding discrimination in union membership	12
Forbidding discrimination in public works	11

KU KLUX KLAN

Antimask laws	19

MILITARY

Forbidding discrimination in militia and National Guard	11

MISCELLANEOUS

Forbidding discrimination in advertising	9
Forbidding group libel and hate literature	9

These account for the great bulk—small though it is—of state statutes on the books in September 1949. In addition a very small number of states (typically two to four) had laws barring race discrimination in employment for defense and war contracts; in housing construction; in public utilities employment; in restrictive covenants; in residential zoning; in public and veterans' housing; in redevelopment housing; in school textbooks; in the sale of insurance; in public welfare and relief. Only three states had antilynching laws, despite the fact that southern congressmen justified their overwhelming opposition to federal antilynching bills on the grounds of states' rights.

Examples of some of the most important or characteristic laws passed by states during these years to promote or protect civil rights follow:

A. *Outlawing School Segregation*

AN ACT[1] establishing a public policy in public education and abolishing and prohibiting separate schools organized on the basis of race, color or creed, and prohibiting racial or creed segregation, separation or discrimination in public schools, colleges and universities in the state of Indiana and prohibiting discrimination in the transportation of public school pupils and students.

Section 1

It is hereby declared to be the public policy of the state of Indiana to provide, furnish, and make available equal, non-segregated, non-discriminatory educational opportunities and facilities for all regardless of race, creed, national origin, color or sex; to provide and furnish public schools equally open to all and prohibited and denied to none because of race, creed, color or national origin; to reaffirm the principles of our Bill of Rights, Civil Rights and our Constitution and to provide for the State of Indiana and its citizens a uniform democratic system of common and public school education; and to abolish, eliminate and prohibit segregated and separate schools or school districts on the basis of race, creed or color; and to eliminate and prohibit segregation, separation and discrimination on the basis of race, color or creed in the public kindergartens, common schools, public schools, colleges and universities of the state.

Section 2

The school commissioners, superintendents, trustee or trustees of any township, city or school city or county or state or any other public school, college or university official or officials, shall not build or erect, establish, maintain, continue or permit any segregated or separate public kindergartens, public schools or districts or public school departments or divisions on the basis of the race, color, creed or national origin of the attending pupil or pupils.

Section 3

[Provides that in existing separate schools enrollment on the basis of race shall cease on September 1, 1949.]

[1] *Laws of Indiana,* 1949 (chap. 186), 603.

B. *Forbidding the Spread of Racial Hatred*

Section 1[1]

It is hereby declared to be the public policy of the State of Indiana and of this Act to protect the economic welfare, health, peace, domestic tranquility, morals, property rights and interests of the state of Indiana and the people thereof, to protect the civil rights and liberties of the people, to effectuate the Bill of Rights, to prevent racketeering in hatred and to prohibit persons from agreeing, combining, uniting, confederating, conspiring, organizing, associating or assembling for the purpose of creating, advocating, spreading or disseminating hatred by reason of race, color or religion.

Section 2

(A) It shall be unlawful for any person or persons to combine, unite, confederate, conspire, organize, or associate with any other person or persons for the purpose of creating, advocating, spreading or disseminating malicious hatred by reason of race, color, or religion not prohibited by law, for or against any person, persons, or group of persons, individually or collectively, not alien enemies of the United States.

(B) It shall be unlawful for any person or persons acting with malice to create, advocate, spread, or disseminate hatred for or against any person, persons or group of persons, individually or collectively, by reason of race, color or religion which threatens to, tends to, or causes riot, disorder, interference with traffic upon the streets or public highways, destruction of property, breach of peace, violence, or denial of civil or constitutional rights.

Section 3

[Provides punishments for violations, including disfranchisement for ten years and fines up to $10,000 and imprisonment for two years.]

C. *A Fair Employment Practices Law*

A number of states also began passing fair employment practices laws. The statute enacted by the state of Connecticut may be cited as an example.[2]

Section 7400

Inter-racial commission. Appointment. Duties.—The inter-racial commission shall continue to consist of ten persons appointed by the governor. . . . Said commission shall investigate the possibilities of affording equal opportunity of profitable employment to all persons, with particular reference to job training and placement. The commission shall compile facts concerning discrimination in employment, violations of civil liberties and other related matters. Said commission shall report to the governor biennially the result of its investigations, with its recommendations for the removal of such injustices as it may find to exist.

[1] *Laws of Indiana,* 1947 (chap. 56), 157.

[2] *Connecticut General Statutes,* Revision of 1949, III, 2704.

Section 7401
[Definitions.]
Section 7402
Additional duties of inter-racial commission.—The interracial commission shall investigate and proceed in all cases of discrimination in employment because of race, color, religion, national origin or ancestry.
Section 7403
[Provides for the appointment of ten hearing examiners with powers of subpoena.]
Section 7404
Powers of the inter-racial commission.—The commission shall have the following powers and duties: (a) To establish and maintain an office in the city of Hartford; (b) to appoint such investigators and other employees and agents as it may deem necessary, fix their compensation within the limitations provided by law and prescribe their duties; (c) to adopt, publish, amend and rescind regulations consistent with and to effectuate the provisions of sections 7401 to 7404, inclusive; (d) to recommend policies and make recommendations to agencies and officers of state and local subdivisions of government to effectuate the policies of said sections; (e) to receive, initiate, investigate and mediate complaints of unfair employment practices; (f) by itself or with or by hearing examiners, to hold hearings, subpoena witnesses and compel their attendance, administer oaths, take the testimony of any person under oath and require the production for examination of any books and papers relating to any matter under investigation or in question. The commission may make rules as to the procedure for the issuance of subpoenas by individual commissioners and hearing examiners. Contumacy or refusal to obey a subpoena issued pursuant to this section shall constitute contempt punishable, upon the application of the authority issuing such subpoena, by the superior court in the county in which the hearing is held or in which the witness resides or transacts business. No person shall be excused from attending or testifying or from producing records, correspondence, documents or other evidence in obedience to subpoena, on the ground that the testimony or evidence required of him may tend to incriminate him, or subjected to any penalty or forfeiture for or on account of any transaction, matter or thing concerning which he is compelled, after having claimed his privilege against self-incrimination, to testify or produce evidence, except that such person so testifying shall not be exempt from prosecution and punishment for perjury committed in so testifying. The immunity herein provided shall extend only to natural persons so compelled to testify; (g) to utilize such voluntary and uncompensated services of private individuals, agencies and organizations as may from time to time be offered and needed; (h) with the cooperation of such agencies, (1) to study the problems of discrimination in all or specific fields of human relationships, and (2) to foster through education and community effort or otherwise good will among the groups and elements of the population of the state. From time to time, but not less than once a year, the commission shall report to the governor, making such recommendations as it deems advisable and describing the investigations, proceedings and hearings it has conducted and their outcome, the decisions it has rendered and the other work performed by it.
Section 7405
Unfair employment practices.—It shall be an unfair employment practice (a) for an employer, by himself or his agent, except in the case of a bona

fide occupational qualification or need, because of the race, color, religious creed, national origin or ancestry of any individual, to refuse to hire or employ or to bar or to discharge from employment such individual or to discriminate against him in compensation or in terms, conditions or privileges of employment; (b) for any employment agency, except in the case of bona fide occupational qualification or need, to fail or refuse to classify properly or refer for employment, or otherwise to discriminate against, any individual because of his race, color, religious creed, national origin or ancestry; (c) for a labor organization, because of the race, color, religious creed, national origin or ancestry of any individual to exclude from full membership rights or to expel from its membership such individual or to discriminate in any way against any of its members or against any employer or any individual employed by an employer, unless such action is based upon a bona fide occupational qualification; (d) for any person, employer, labor organization or employment agency to discharge, expel or otherwise discriminate against any person because he has opposed any unfair employment practice or because he has filed a complaint or testified or assisted in any proceeding under section 7406; (e) for any person, whether an employer or an employee or not, to aid, abet, incite, compel or coerce the doing of any of the acts herein declared to be unfair employment practices or to attempt to do so.

Section 7406

[After prescribing the procedures for the bringing and hearing of complaints, the section provides:] If, upon all the evidence, the tribunal finds that a respondent has engaged in any unfair employment practice as defined in section 7405, it shall state its findings of fact and shall issue and file with the commission and cause to be served on such respondent an order requiring such respondent to cease and desist from such unfair employment practice. If, upon all the evidence, the tribunal finds that the respondent has not engaged in any alleged unfair employment practice, it shall state its findings of fact and shall similarly issue and file an order dismissing the complaint. . . .

D. *A Fair Educational Practices Law*

One of the pioneer statutes of this kind was that of the state of New York. The law became effective July 1, 1948.[1]

[Discrimination in admission of applicants to educational institutions.] (1) *Declaration of policy.*—It is hereby declared to be the policy of the state that the American ideal of equality of opportunity requires that students, otherwise qualified, be admitted to educational institutions without regard to race, color, religion, creed or national origin, except that, with regard to religious or denominational educational institutions, students, otherwise qualified, shall have the equal opportunity to attend therein without discrimination because of race, color or national origin. It is a fundamental American right for members of various religious faiths to establish and maintain educational institutions exclusively or primarily for students of their own religious faith or to effectuate the religious principles in furtherance of which they were maintained. Nothing herein contained shall impair or abridge that right.

[1] *Laws of New York,* 1948 (chap. 753), 1380.

(2) [Definitions]

(3) *Unfair educational practices.*—It shall be an unfair educational practice for an educational institution after September fifteenth, nineteen hundred forty-eight:

(a) To exclude or limit or otherwise discriminate against any person or persons seeking admission as students to such institution because of race, religion, creed, color, or national origin; except that nothing in this section shall be deemed to affect, in any way, the right of a religious or denominational educational institution to select its students exclusively or primarily from members of such religion or denomination or from giving preference in such selection to such members or to make such selection of its students as is calculated by such institution to promote the religious principles for which it is established or maintained.

(b) To penalize any individual because he has initiated, testified, participated or assisted in any proceedings under this section.

(c) It shall be an unfair educational practice for any educational institution to use criteria [such as] race, religion, creed, color or national origin in the admission of students.

(4) *Certification of religious and denominational institutions.*—An educational institution operated, supervised or controlled by a religious or denominational organization may, through its chief executive officer, certify in writing to the commissioner that it is so operated, controlled or supervised, and that it elects to be considered a religious or denominational educational institution, and it thereupon shall be deemed such an institution for the purposes of this section.

(f) *Procedure*. . . .

E. *Discrimination Outlawed in Public Housing*

The new wave of protective legislation also extended to public housing in a few states. Here follows the legislation of Massachusetts, enacted in 1946–1948.[1]

There shall be no discrimination; provided, that if the number of qualified applicants for dwelling accommodations exceeds the dwelling units available, preference shall be given to inhabitants of the city or town in which the project is located, and to the families who occupied the dwellings eliminated by demolition, condemnation and effective closing as part of the project as far as is reasonably practicable without discrimination against persons living in other sub-standard areas within the same city or town. For all purposes of this chapter, no person shall, because of race, color, creed or religion, be subjected to any discrimination. . . .

F. *A General Civil Rights Law*

The older civil rights laws, as in the following legislation in New York, were also strengthened and clarified.[2]

[1] *Acts and Resolves of Massachusetts*, 1948 (chap. 51), 48–49.

[2] *Laws of New York*, 1945 (chap. 292, secs. 13 and 40), 672, 673.

#13—Right to serve on juries—No citizen of the state possessing all other qualifications which are or may be required or prescribed by law, shall be disqualified to serve as a grand or petit juror in any court of this state on account of race, creed, color, national origin or sex. . . . [The section then provides penalties for violations of $100 to $500 in fines, and 30 to 90 days in jail, or both.]

#40. Equal rights in places of public accommodation, resort or amusement. —All persons within the jurisdiction of this state shall be entitled to the full and equal accommodations, advantages, facilities and privileges of any places of public accommodations, resort or amusement, subject only to the conditions and limitations established by law and applicable alike to all persons. No person, being the owner, lessee, proprietor, manager, superintendent, agent or employee of any such place shall directly or indirectly refuse, withhold from or deny to any person any of the accommodations, advantages, facilities or privileges thereof, or directly or indirectly publish, circulate, issue, display, post or mail any written or printed communication, notice or advertisement, to the effect that any of the accommodations, advantages, facilities and privileges of any such place shall be refused, withheld from or denied to any person on account of race, creed, color or national origin, or that the patronage or custom thereat, of any person belonging to or purporting to be of any particular race, creed, color or national origin is unwelcome, objectionable or not acceptable, desired or solicited. The production of any such written or printed communication, notice or advertisement, purporting to relate to any such place and to be made by any person being the owner, lessee, proprietor, superintendent or manager thereof, shall be presumptive evidence of any civil or criminal action that the same was authorized by such person . . . or restaurants, or eating houses, or any place where food is sold for consumption on the premises; buffets, saloons, barrooms, or any store, part or enclosure where spirituous or malt liquors are sold; ice cream parlors, confectioneries, soda fountains, and all stores where beverages of any kind are retailed for consumption on the premises; retail stores and establishments, dispensaries, clinics, hospitals, bathhouses, barber-shops, beauty parlors, theatres, motion picture houses, air-domes, roof gardens, music halls, race courses, skating rinks, amusement and recreation parks, fairs, bowling alleys, golf courses, gymnasiums, shooting galleries, billiard and pool parlors, public libraries, kindergartens, primary and secondary schools, high schools, academies, colleges and universities, extension courses, and all educational institutions under the supervision of the regents of the state of New York; and any such public library, kindergarten, primary and secondary school, academy, college, university, professional school, extension course, or other educational facility, supported in whole or in part by public funds or by contributions solicited from the general public; garages, all public conveyances, operated on land or water, as well as the stations and terminals thereof; public halls and public elevators of buildings and structures occupied by two or more tenants, or by the owner and one or more tenants. . . .

#41. Penalty for violation. [Violators] shall for each and every violation thereof be liable to a penalty of not less than one hundred dollars nor more than five hundred dollars, to be recovered by the person aggrieved thereby . . . in any court of competent jurisdiction in the county in which the plaintiff or the defendant shall reside; and such person and the manager or owner of or each officer of such agency, bureau, corporation or association, and such officer or member of a labor organization or person acting in his behalf, as the case may be shall, also, for every such offense be deemed guilty of a misdemeanor, and upon conviction thereof shall be fined not less than one hundred dollars nor more than five hundred dollars, or shall be imprisoned not less than thirty days nor more than ninety days, or both such fine and imprisonment.

G. *An Antidefamation Statute in the South*

Southern states in some instances went further than some northern states in legislating against public defaming of Negroes and against the use of racial designations. For example, according to Florida law:[1]

Section 1
It shall be unlawful to print, publish, distribute or cause to be [so done] by any means, or in any manner whatsoever, any publications, handbill, dodger, circular, booklet, pamphlet, leaflet, card, sticker, periodical, literature, paper, or other printed material which tends to expose any individual or any religious group to hatred, contempt, ridicule, or obloquy unless [the name and address of those so doing] is clearly printed or written thereon. . . .

[1] *Laws of Florida,* 1945 (chap. 22749, No. 230, Sec. 1), 417.

(5)
DISCRIMINATION BY STATE LAW

In Pauli Murray's survey of state laws which, as of September 1949, either authorized or required various forms of discrimination, she demonstrates that only fifteen states (Connecticut, Illinois, Iowa, Maine, Massachusetts, Michigan, Minnesota, New Hampshire, New Jersey, Ohio, Pennsylvania, Rhode Island, Vermont, Washington, and Wisconsin) had no such provisions. Of the remainder, thirty states forbade mixed marriages and "race mixing." The next most frequent were laws—in twenty states—authorizing or prescribing separate schools for Negroes and whites, followed by statutes—in fourteen states—permitting or commanding separate railroad accommodations.

A. *The Reach of Discriminatory Legislation*

The various services and functions for which the laws of nine or more states required separate provision for the races were these:

EDUCATION

Separate public schools	20	Separate colleges and universities	17
Separate schools for the deaf	9	Separate teacher training schools	18
Separate schools for the blind	11	Separate reform schools	18
Separate trade schools	14		

HOSPITALS

Separate mental hospitals	13

PENAL INSTITUTIONS

Racial separation of convicts	10

TRANSPORTATION

Separate bus accommodations	10	Separate streetcar accommodations	10
Separate accommodations on trains	14	Separate bus and railway waiting rooms	10

K. MISCEGENATION

Prohibitions of racially mixed marriages	30

In addition, a small number of states had laws requiring separate textbooks for blacks and whites; requiring separate libraries; requiring separate workrooms, toilets, and washrooms for the races in factories and mines; requiring separate homes for the aged, for orphans, and for paupers; requiring separate steamboats, ferries, and sleeping compartments on trains; prohibiting cohabitation of whites and Negroes; forbidding interracial boxing or wrestling contests; forbidding the chartering of fraternal orders with mixed membership; requiring separate voting booths and separate voters' and poll tax-payers' lists; requiring separate telephone booths; prohibiting advocacy of racial equality.

In addition to the foregoing, a comprehensive sampling of state laws on the books at the close of the 1940's reveals the following: laws to restrict the franchise by literacy tests, residence requirements, poll-tax payment, publication of voting lists, frequency-of-voting tests, complicated registration procedures and "private club laws" giving political parties the status of nonpublic organizations; laws requiring separate seating at race tracks, separate entrances, drinking cups, and pay windows in factories and mines; laws forbidding white nurses to serve

Negro patients in hospitals; laws to prohibit whites from patronizing Negro poolrooms and blacks from patronizing white poolrooms; laws to prohibit whites and Negroes from living in the same structure; laws to forbid blacks to have custody of or to adopt white children; laws to forbid Pullman porters to sleep in berths in Pullman cars or to use bedding intended for white passengers; laws defining as Negroes persons possessing "any trace of African blood whatsoever"; laws prescribing separate seating in public halls, theaters, concert halls; laws permitting railroads to exclude Afro-Americans from dining and sleeping accommodations; laws requiring separation of the races on beaches and in public parks.

Following are a few representative enactments made during these years. The first attracted considerable attention and raised the expectations of whites who hoped by its enforcement to eliminate the black man from the electorate, but the provision, as we shall see, was struck down in *Davis* v. *Schnell.*[1]

B. *The Franchise: New Constraints*

The "Boswell Amendment" was submitted to the voters of Alabama, and ratified in 1945 as a revision of Section 181 of the Constitution of Alabama.[2]

> . . . [t]he following persons and no others who, if their place of residence shall remain unchanged, will have, at the date of the next general election, the qualifications as to residence prescribed in Section 178 of this article, shall be qualified to register as electors provided they shall not be disqualified under Section 182 of this constitution: those who can read and write, understand and explain any article of the Constitution of the United States in the English language and who have worked or been regularly engaged in some lawful employment, business, or occupation, trade, or calling for the greater part of the twelve months next preceding the time they offer to register, including those who are unable to read and write if such inability is due solely to physical disability; provided, however, no persons shall be entitled to register as electors except those who are of good character and who understand the duties and obligations of good citizenship under a republican form of government. . . .

Georgia also sought to strengthen its measures for Negro disfranchisement.[3]

(Approved February 25, 1949)

Section 1

[Provides that from the effective date of the approval of this Act, no person shall be permitted to vote in any election in Georgia for federal, state,

[1] see below, p. 268.

[2] *General Laws of Alabama,* 1945 (No. 236), 551.

[3] *Acts of Georgia,* 1949 (No. 287), 1204.

or local officers "unless such person shall have been registered and qualified as hereinafter provided."]

Section 2

[Provides that except with reference to any special election occurring before the first general election list shall have been prepared, "all registrations heretofore effected are hereby declared null and void."]

Section 3

[Provides that the first registration list under the provisions of this Act be prepared in 1950, and stipulates that "all persons seeking to register and qualify as voters shall be registered and qualified as herein provided."]

Section 4

[Requires electors to vote at least once every two years to maintain their standing as qualified voters.]

Section 21

[Requires all applicants for registration as voters to submit to oral examinations to be administered by local registrars. Provides further:] In order to ascertain whether an applicant is eligible for qualification as a voter in this classification, the registrars shall orally propound to him the thirty questions on the standardized list set forth in the following section. If the applicant can give factually correct answers to ten of the thirty questions as they are propounded to him, then the registrars shall enter an order declaring him to be prima facie qualified. If he cannot correctly answer the ten out of the thirty questions propounded to him, then an order shall be entered rejecting his application. [Section 22 set forth the questions to be propounded. They ranged from simple queries ("Who is President of the United States?") to questions calculated to give unwanted applicants some difficulty ("Who is Lieutenant Governor of Georgia?" "Who is Chief Justice of the Supreme Court of Georgia?" "Who is Chief Judge of the Court of Appeals of Georgia?" "In what Congressional District do you live?" "In what State Senatorial District do you live?" "Who represents your County in the House of Representatives of Georgia? If there are [sic] more than one representative, name them." "Who is the Ordinary of your County?" "Who is the Solicitor General of your circuit?")]

C. *Segregated Transportation Reaffirmed*

The same legislature which passed the Boswell Amendment in Alabama reinvigorated the older laws for the segregation of bus travel.[1]

All passenger stations in this State operated by any motor transportation company shall have separate waiting rooms or space and separate ticket windows for the white and colored races, but such accommodations for the races shall be equal. All motor transportation companies or operators of vehicles carrying passengers for hire in this State, whether intrastate or interstate passengers, shall at all times provide equal but separate accommodations on each vehicle for the white and colored races. The conductor or agent of the motor transportation company in charge of any vehicle is authorized

[1] *General Laws of Alabama,* 1945 (No. 508, Sec. 1), 731.

and required to assign each passenger to the division of the vehicle designated for the race to which the passenger belongs; and, if the passenger refuses to occupy the division to which he is assigned, the conductor or agent may refuse to carry the passenger on the vehicle; and, for such refusal, neither the conductor or agent of the motor transportation company nor the motor transportation company shall be liable in damages. Any motor transportation company or person violating the provisions of this act shall be guilty of a misdemeanor and, upon conviction, shall be fined not more than five hundred dollars for each offense; and each day's violation of this act shall constitute a separate offense.

D. *Segregated Cemeteries Preserved*

Southern states continued their efforts (as did some states in the North by the more indirect method of conniving at private discrimination by passing no laws on the subject, thus preserving the fiction that the discrimination was wholly private) to segregate the dead as well as the living, by enacting laws requiring separate cemeteries for the races. The following was enacted by North Carolina in 1947:[1]

Racial restrictions as to use of cemeteries for burial of dead. In the event said property [municipal cemeteries] has been heretofore used exclusively for the burial of members of the Negro race, then said cemetery or burial ground so established shall remain and be established as a burial ground for the Negro race. In the event said property has been heretofore used exclusively for the burial of members of the White race, then said cemetery ground so established shall remain and be established as a burial ground for the White race.

E. *The Southern Regional Education Program*

On February 8, 1948, fourteen southern states, acting through their governors, concluded an interstate compact for regional education, the agreement to be submitted to their state legislatures for ratification. The several states ratified the plan, but it failed, as we shall see, to achieve its objective of forestalling the enrollment of Negroes in state university graduate and professional schools. The following are opening paragraphs of the compact.[2]

1 *North Carolina Session Laws*, 1947 (chap. 821, sec. 2), 1115.

2 *Acts of Louisiana*, 1948 (No. 367), 982. Substantially the same document was also spread upon the statute books of the other states who were parties to the covenant.

AN ACT

Providing that the State of Louisiana may enter into a compact with any of the United States for co-operative regional education purposes and providing for the ratification thereof.

Section 1

Be it enacted by the Legislature of Louisiana, That the action of the Governor of this State in entering into a compact on behalf of the State of Louisiana with the states joining therein for co-operative regional education purposes is hereby authorized and ratified subject to the approval of said compact by the Congress of the United States, which compact is substantially as follows:

A COMPACT

Whereas, the States who are parties hereto have during the past several years conducted careful investigation looking towards the establishment and maintenance of jointly owned and operated regional educational institutions in the Southern states in the professional, technological, scientific, literary and other fields, so as to provide greater educational advantages and facilities for the citizens of the several States who reside within such region, and

Whereas, Meharry Medical College of Nashville, Tennesee, has proposed that its lands, building, equipment, and the net income from its endowment, be turned over to the Southern States, or to an agency acting in their behalf, to be operated as a regional institution for medical, dental and nursing education upon terms and conditions to be hereafter agreed upon between the Southern states and Meharry Medical College, which proposal, because of the present financial condition of the institution, has been approved by the said States who are parties hereto, and

Whereas, the said States desire to enter into a compact with each other providing for the planning and establishment of regional educational facilities;

Now therefore, in consideration of the mutual agreements, covenants and obligations assumed by the respective states who are parties hereto (hereinafter referred to as "States"), the said several States do hereby form a geographical district or region consisting of the areas lying within the boundaries of the contracting States which, for the purposes of this compact, shall constitute an area for regional education supported by public funds derived from taxation by the constituent States for the establishment, acquisition, operation and maintenance of regional education schools and institutions for the benefit of citizens of the respective States residing within the region so established as may be determined from time to time in accordance with the terms and provisions of this compact.

(6)

THE FEDERAL COURTS AND THE BLACK AMERICAN, 1938–1954

The most dramatic victories for formal civil rights in these years were won in the federal courts, typically by the NAACP. The association now had the satisfaction of seeing the achievement of both the objectives it had, in the beginning, set as its primary goals. Lynching had virtually disappeared by 1954, and *legal* artifices for denying the Afro-American the vote were eliminated. Hereafter the obstacles to voting would be private and extralegal and more difficult to dislodge. It was by means of the Fourteenth Amendment's equal protection clause, the Fifteenth Amendment, and Congress's constitutional powers (Article 1, Sec. 4) to regulate federal elections, that the transformation in the suffrage was accomplished.

Other forms of discrimination also began to fall before the equal protection clause. School segregation, restrictive covenants, discrimination in transportation, separate public facilities, unequal justice were now at last beginning to feel the force of the clause which had so long lain dormant.

A. *The Franchise: Toward Compliance with the Constitution*

Grovey v. *Townsend* (1935)[1] had resurrected the white primary. That contrivance, especially when supplemented by "reading-and-understanding" requirements, new versions of the grandfather clause, and private, extralegal pressures, social and economic, proved almost perfectly effective in states and counties determined to keep blacks from voting, but they were now clearly on the defensive. The reincarnated grandfather clause and the white primary were dealt deadly blows, and the effectiveness of literacy tests was sharply contracted in the cases now to be noted.

When Oklahoma's grandfather clause was struck down in 1915[2] the state's legislature quickly passed another ingenious law, this time providing that all those who had voted in 1914 automatically retained their

[1] See above, p. 213.
[2] See above, p. 211.

status as voters, while all others must apply for registration between April 30 and May 11, 1916, or permanently lose the right to register. This tricky law had survived the scrutiny of the United States Court of Appeals, but the Supreme Court, before which it was assailed by James M. Nabrit for the NAACP, declared:[1]

> The Fifteenth Amendment secures freedom from discrimination on account of race in matters affecting the franchise. . . . The theory of the plaintiff's action is that the defendants, acting under color of [law], did discriminate against him because that [law] inherently operates discriminatorily. . . . The . . . Fifteenth Amendment against contrivances by a state to thwart equality in the enjoyment of the right to vote by citizens of the United States regardless of race or color . . . , nullifies sophisticated as well as simple-minded modes of discrimination. It hits onerous procedural requirements which effectively handicap exercise of the franchise by the colored race although the abstract right to vote may remain unrestricted as to race. . . . The [Oklahoma] legislation of 1916 partakes too much of the infirmity of the "grandfather clause" to be able to survive. . . . Unfair discrimination was . . . retained by automatically granting voting privileges for life to the white citizens whom the constitutional "grandfather clause" had sheltered while subjecting colored citizens to a new burden. . . . We believe that the opportunity thus given Negro voters to free themselves from the effects of discrimination to which they should never have been subjected was too cabined and confined.

Grovey v. *Townsend* seemed to put the white primary under the protection of the Constitution. But six years later *U.S.* v. *Classic,*[2] (which had no relation to Negro voting, but turned instead upon the question of the applicability of federal election laws to corrupt practices in a primary in Louisiana) announced the new doctrine that primaries had in fact become so much a part of the whole election machinery that the fiction that they were merely private matters could no longer be countenanced. Legal strategists for the NAACP soon had on the way through the courts a case challenging the presumption that primaries, because they were not "elections," were not affected by the Fourteenth Amendment's equal protection clause. The new decision outlawed the white primary.[3]

> . . . Classic bears upon *Grovey* v. *Townsend* not because exclusion of Negroes from primaries is any more or less state action by reason of the unitary character of the electoral process but because the recognition of the place of the primary in the electoral scheme makes clear that state delegation to a party of the power to fix the qualifications of primary elections is delegation of a state function that may make the party's action the action of the state. When *Grovey* v. *Townsend* was written, the Court looked upon the denial of a vote in a primary as a mere refusal by a party membership. . . . [But now] our ruling in Classic as to the unitary character of the

[1] *Lane* v. *Wilson,* 307 U.S. 266 (1939).
[2] 313 U.S. 299 (1941).
[3] *Smith* v. *Allwright,* 321 U.S. 649 (1944).

electoral process calls for a reexamination as to whether or not the exclusion of Negroes from a Texas party primary was state action. . . .

It may now be taken as a postulate that the right to vote in such a primary for the nomination of candidates without discrimination by the State, like the right to vote in a general election, is a right secured by the Constitution. . . . By the terms of the Fifteenth Amendment that right may not be abridged by any state on account of race. . . .

The party takes its character as a state agency from the duties imposed upon it by state statutes; the duties do not become matters of private law because they are performed by a political party. . . . When primaries become a part of the machinery for choosing officials, state and national, as they have here, the same texts to determine the character of discrimination or abridgement should be applied to the primary as are applied to the general election. If the state requires a certain electoral procedure, prescribes a general election ballot made up of party nominees so chosen and limits the choice of the electorate in general elections for state offices, practically speaking, to those whose names appear on such a ballot, it endorses, adopts and enforces the discrimination against Negroes, practiced by a party entrusted by Texas law with the determination of the qualifications of participants in the primary. This is state action within the meaning of the Fifteenth Amendment. . . .

[T]he opportunity for choice is not to be nullified by a state through casting its electoral process in a form which permits a private organization to practice racial discrimination in the election. Constitutional rights would be of little value if they could be thus indirectly denied. . . . *Grovey* v. *Townsend* is overruled.

Immediately after the *Allwright* decision, the governor of South Carolina convened his state's legislators to cope with the crisis, asking them to repeal all laws relating to primaries, and thus leave the conduct of primaries wholly to rules prescribed by the party itself. This would presumably give parties the status of associations or private clubs, immune to restrictions laid by the federal Constitution upon states. The legislature followed the governor's recommendations, and the Democratic party thereupon enacted rules essentially identical to those which the lawmakers had repealed. Suit was then brought against officials of the party, to restrain them from denying blacks the right to vote in the primaries. An injunction was issued by Judge J. Waties Waring in the United States district court and sustained by the court of appeals in *Rice* v. *Elmore*.[1] Subsequently the United States Supreme Court declined to reopen the case. In the language of the circuit court:

. . . Elections in South Carolina remain a two step process, whether the party primary be accounted a preliminary of the general election, or the general election be regarded as giving effect to what is done in the primary; and those who control the Democratic primary as well as the state government cannot by placing the first of the steps under officials of the party rather than of the state, absolve such officials from the limitations of the Constitution. . . .

[1] 165 F. 2d 387 (4th Cir. 1947).

An essential feature of our form of government is the right of the citizen to participate in the governmental process. . . . The Fourteenth and Fifteenth Amendments . . . have had the effect of creating a federal basis of citizenship and of protecting the rights of individuals and minorities from many abuses of governmental power which were not contemplated at that time. Their primary purposes must not be lost sight of, however; and no election machinery can be upheld if its purpose or effect is to deny to the Negro, on account of his race or color, any effective voice in the government of his country or the state or community wherein he lives.

Still refusing to acknowledge defeat, the Democratic party of South Carolina now made certain changes in the rules governing party organization and primary elections. The party was organized into clubs, open only to white Democrats. All properly enrolled members were entitled to vote in the primaries. Black electors were also admitted to the primaries "if they present their general election certificates." No person, white or black, could vote in the primary unless he took an oath that he supported the principles of the South Carolina Democratic party; that he supported the social and educational separation of the races; that he believed in "States' Rights" and was opposed to the Federal "so-called F.E.P.C. law." In *Brown* v. *Baskin* (1948),[1] Judge J. Waties Waring issued an injunction, on the ground that different requirements for Negroes and whites were a "clear and flagrant evasion of the law" as they had been declared in *Rice* v. *Elmore:*

It is important that once and for all, the members of this Party be made to understand . . . that they will be required to obey and carry out the orders of this court . . . in the true spirit and meaning of the same. This court is convinced that they are fully aware of what is the law, and it will not excuse further evasions, subterfuges or attempts to get around the same. It is time that either the present officials of the Party, or such as may be in the future chosen, realize that the people of the United States expect them to follow the American way of elections. It is believed that the great body of people in this state as well as in this Nation, truly believe in the American ideals and methods, and it is hoped that the actions of the Party officials do not represent the true view of the people of South Carolina. But irrespective of whether that be true or not, it becomes the duty of this court to say to the Party officials that they will have to obey the true intent of the law, which is so clear and apparent that even they must know what it is, and that no excuse or evasion in the future will be tolerated. [Judge Waring's ruling was subsequently affirmed by the Court of Appeals.]

A United States district court in Alabama held in *Davis* v. *Schnell* that states may prescribe qualifications for the franchise, including literacy tests, not inconsistent with the Fifteenth Amendment, but that state action denying Negroes equal protection of the laws in elections violates both the Fourteenth Amendment's equal protection clause and the Fifteenth Amendment's prohibition against abridging the right to

[1] 78 F. Supp. 933 (E.D. S.C. 1948).

vote on account of race.[1] The court ruled not only that Alabama's Boswell Amendment[2] violated the equal protection clause but also that the state Democratic Executive Committee is an official arm of the state of Alabama and thus also subject to the federal Constitution. Moreover, said the court, the evidence was clear that the intent of the Boswell Amendment was to bar Negroes from voting, and that it had been arbitrarily administered to achieve that end:

> [The record in this case, and the history of the enactment and administration of the Boswell Amendment] demonstrates that this restrictive Amendment, coming on the heels of the decision of the Supreme Court of the United States in the *Smith* v. *Allwright* case, was intended as a grant of arbitrary power in an attempt to obviate the consequences of that decision.
>
> [The court here considered the state's argument that the amendment was not "racist in its origin, purpose or effect," and noted that the *Alabama Democrat*, a campaign document, in the form of a newspaper, carried the headline " 'WARNING' IS SOUNDED: BLACKS WILL TAKE OVER IF AMENDMENT LOSES. VOTE WHITE—VOTE RIGHT—VOTE FOR AMENDMENT NO. 4."—The same document reproduced from the *Talladega Home* an editorial which asked the question "What is the Boswell Amendment?" and answered the question with these words: "It is a measure designed simply and solely to enable registrars legally to hold down the number of Negro registrants."]
>
> Furthermore, the administration of the Boswell Amendment by the defendant board demonstrates that the ambiguous standard prescribed has, in fact, been arbitrarily used for the purpose of excluding Negro applicants for the franchise, while white applicants with comparable qualifications were being accepted. . . .
>
> It, thus, clearly appears that this Amendment was intended to be, and is being used for the purpose of discriminating against applicants for the franchise on the basis of race or color. Therefore we are necessarily brought to the conclusion that this Amendment to the Constitution of Alabama, both in its object and the manner of its administration, is unconstitutional, because it violates the Fifteenth Amendment. . . . The Fifteenth Amendment "nullifies sophisticated as well as simple-minded modes of discrimination." . . .
>
> We cannot ignore the impact of the Boswell Amendment upon Negro citizens [merely] because it avoids mention of race or color; "To do this would be to shut our eyes to what all others than we can see and understand."

Some Texans felt reasonably sure that they had found, in the "Jaybird Primary," a dependable means for evading *Smith* v. *Allwright*. Since 1889 the Jaybird Democratic Association of Fort Bend County had conducted a preliminary poll of its own, preceding the official primary. The nominees of the Jaybird primary then entered the regular contest, virtually certain of winning the party's formal nomination, often without opposition. Negroes were, of course, barred from the Jaybird

[1] 81 F. Supp. 872 (S.D. Ala. 1949); *aff'd* by U.S. Sup. Ct., 336 U.S. 933 (1949).

[2] See above, p. 261.

Association, but were permitted to vote in the official primary, where their participation was meaningless since the outcome there was a foregone conclusion. The hopes of the party regulars that such indirection was not "state action" were dashed by the Supreme Court's ruling in *Terry* v. *Adams*.[1] Speaking through Justice Black, the highest tribunal concluded that:

> . . . For a state to permit such a duplication of its election processes is to permit a flagrant abuse of those processes to defeat the purposes of the Fifteenth Amendment. . . . The only election that has counted in this Texas county for more than fifty years has been that held by the Jaybirds from which Negroes have been excluded. It is immaterial that the state does not control that part of this elective process which it leaves for the Jaybirds to manage. The Jaybird primary has become an integral part, indeed the only effective part, of the elective process that determines who shall rule and govern in the county. The effect of the whole procedure, Jaybird primary plus Democratic primary plus general election, is to do precisely that which the Fifteenth Amendment forbids—strip Negroes of every vestige of influence in selecting the officials who control the local county matters that intimately touch the daily lives of citizens. . . . Reversed and remanded.

Justice Frankfurter's concurring opinion rested primarily on the fact that the county election officials had participated in and condoned the device for excluding Negroes from voting. Justices Clark, Vinson, and Reed, while also concurring with the majority, on the other hand, took the position that the Jaybird organization was in fact a political party subject to the restrictions laid down in the Fifteenth Amendment.

B. *Segregated Education: The Beginning of the End*

The exclusion of blacks from state universities—especially at the graduate and professional school levels—offered an inviting target for champions of racial equality. The immediate object, admission of Negroes to these institutions, was overshadowed in such lawsuits by the much larger purpose of establishing the principle that the requirements of due process and equal protection imposed upon the states the obligation to supply opportunities that were bona fide equal. The enormous expense of maintaining two sets of genuinely equal facilities, it was hoped, would perhaps force the abandonment of the segregation system in higher education, and then, by degrees, in other areas of society as well.

Beyond that, the more optimistic among the engineers of these judicial challenges hoped that the courts would eventually find separate facilities *inherently* unequal, not only because of intangible privations

[1] 345 U.S. 461 (1953).

and disabilities that might accrue to the disadvantaged race when they were sequestered in their own institutions, but also because the act of segregation carried with it implications of inferiority and disparagement of the minority race that produced emotional distress, psychic shock, and spiritual anguish. It was precisely that position which the highest court did, in the end, adopt. From that moment forward, legal segregation by state action was doomed.

In short, by pressing for an increasingly literal interpretation of equality, the race's spokesmen—again primarily in the NAACP—gradually succeeded in establishing the doctrine that separate-but-equal could not fully satisfy the demands of equal protection; that only actual *identity* of facilities, the shared use of the *same* public institutions, would suffice.

The first important victory in this concerted strategy came in 1938, when the Supreme Court of the United States sharpened the definition of the term "equal" in the separate-but-equal formula by voiding a Missouri law by which the state, determined not to admit black applicants to the state university's law school, offered them the opportunity to attend schools in nonsegregated states with the aid of cash grants from Missouri.[1] The defendant in the case was one Canada, the university's registrar. The plaintiff, Lloyd Gaines, disappeared mysteriously soon after his legal triumph, and was never again located. Soon thereafter the state erected a separate law school for Negroes. Here follows a portion of the court's conclusion as to the legality of the tuition-grant plan.

> The state court stresses the advantages that are afforded by the law schools of the adjacent States,—Kansas, Nebraska, Iowa and Illinois,—which admit non-resident negroes. . . . [T]he state court found that the difference in distances to be traveled afforded no substantial ground of complaint and that there was an adequate appropriation to meet the full tuition fees which petitioner would have to pay.
>
> We think that these matters are beside the point. The basic consideration is not as to what opportunities other States provide, or whether they are as good as those in Missouri, but as to what opportunities Missouri itself furnishes to white students and denies to negroes solely upon the ground of color. . . . The question here is not of a duty of the State to supply legal training, or the quality of the training which it does supply, but of its duty when it provides such training to furnish it to the residents of the State upon the basis of an equality of right. By the operation of the laws of Missouri . . . the white resident is afforded legal education within the State: the negro resident having the same qualifications is refused it there and must go outside the State to obtain it. That is a denial of the equality of legal right . . . and the provision for the payment of tuition fees in another State does not remove the discrimination.
>
> Manifestly, the obligation of the State to give the protection of equal laws

[1] *Missouri ex rel. Gaines* v. *Canada,* 305 U.S. 337 (1938).

can be performed only where its laws operate, that is, within its own jurisdiction. It is there that the equality of legal right must be maintained. . . . [Petitioner's] right was a personal one. It was as an individual that he was entitled to the equal protection of the laws, and the State was bound to furnish him within its borders facilities for legal education substantially equal to those which the State there afforded for persons of the white race, whether or not other negroes sought the same opportunity.

The *principle* of separate-but-*equal* was left unimpaired by the *Gaines* case. Two years later, in *Bluford* v. *Canada*,[1] when Lucille Bluford, a Negro, sued the university's registrar for admission to the school of journalism, the United States District Court of Missouri (Western District) emphatically reaffirmed that a state's right, under the Constitution of the United States, to furnish separate but equal schools for the races had not been in any way disparaged by the *Gaines* decision. In *Sipuel* v. *Board of Regents of the University of Oklahoma*, the screw was given another turn. Ada Sipuel applied for admission to the University of Oklahoma Law School, but was refused because of her color. When she was advised to seek entry to a separate law school for Negroes, soon to be established, she declined. The case was argued before the United States Supreme Court by Thurgood Marshall for the NAACP, and elicited from the Court the ruling that the demands of the equal protection clause were not met by mere future availability of equal facilities; they must be available at once. And since the only law school which the state maintained at the moment was that in the state university, Miss Sipuel must be admitted there. The Court made its point in a one-paragraph opinion:[2]

The petitioner is entitled to secure legal education afforded by a state institution. To this time, it has been denied her although during the same period many white applicants have been afforded legal education by the State. The State must provide it for her in conformity with the equal protection clause of the Fourteenth Amendment and provide it as soon as it does for applicants of any other group (*Missouri ex rel. Gaines* v. *Canada*). The judgment of the Supreme Court of Oklahoma is reversed and the cause is remanded to that court for proceedings not inconsistent with this opinion. The mandate shall issue forthwith. Reversed.

Two years later, in *Parker* v. *University of Delaware*,[3] a federal court again gave its approval to the abstract *principle* of separate schools. Although ordering the admission of a Negro to a white state college when it found the Negro college inferior, the justices refused to hold that the latter was inferior merely *because* it was a segregated school.

The next landmarks on the road to desegregation were erected on June 5, 1950, a fateful day in American constitutional history, when the

[1] 32 F. Supp. 707 (W.D. Mo., 1940).
[2] 332 U.S. 631 (1948).
[3] 31 Del. Ch. 381, 75 A. 2d 225 (1950).

United States Supreme Court handed down three simultaneous opinions which further undermined the whole structure of segregation: *McLaurin* v. *Oklahoma State Regents,* and *Sweatt* v. *Painter,* both involving higher education; and *Henderson* v. *the United States Interstate Commerce Commission,*[1] which concerned interstate railway transportation.

While the *Sipuel* ruling preserved unscathed the *Plessy* doctrine that separate facilities do not inherently offend the equal protection clause, it indicated a more rigorous definition of equality of facilities than had prevailed in the past. In the *McLaurin* case two years later, the lines were drawn still more precisely when the Court ruled that even token disabilities laid upon the Negro when he was admitted to the *same* facility with whites could not be permitted. In the companion case of *Sweatt* v. *Painter* the Court took the position that—whatever may be said to excuse separate institutions and services for Negroes in other kinds of public agencies—in the matter of state-supported schools blacks are being denied the equal protection of the laws even if the separate accommodations provided them are substantially equal in the fullest sense of the term. The NAACP lawyers had hoped that in these cases the Court would unequivocally repudiate the *Plessy* doctrine. Said they, in the *Sweatt* brief: "It is clear not only that the *Plessy* doctrine . . . has not produced equality, but [it] can never provide the equality required by the Fourteenth Amendment." Paralleling this plea was another from a Committee of Law Teachers against Segregation in Law Education, which filed a brief as "friend of the court," arguing that it was time to overrule *Plessy* v. *Ferguson.*

Preferring to follow the rule that the Court should not, except in extraordinary circumstances, answer a broader question than the issue necessarily raised by the case at bar, the justices in the *McLaurin* and *Sweatt* actions declined to address themselves to the constitutionality of separate-but-equal. And yet, while the Court confined itself to the further tightening of the definition of "equal" in *McLaurin,* and to ruling in *Sweatt* that separate law schools cannot be equal, the way was now opened to challenges to other forms of legally imposed segregation.

The details of the *Sweatt* case follow. Heman Sweatt, a Houston mail carrier, applied for admission to the University of Texas Law School. The University refused, on the ground that Texas law required instruction of blacks and whites in separate but equal institutions. Texas had no law school for Negroes when the suit was instituted, but while the case was awaiting trial, the state took rapid steps to establish such a school at Houston. In the meantime, the state also prepared to set up a temporary law school in the basement of a building near the Capitol in

[1] Because *Henderson* was a case involving public transportation, discussion of it is reserved to a later point. See below, p. 287.

Austin. Sweatt declined this counteroffer as a clear denial of equal protection. Here follows a portion of Chief Justice Vinson's opinion, delivered for a unanimous Court:[1]

The University of Texas Law School, from which petitioner was excluded, was staffed by a faculty of sixteen full-time and three part-time professors, some of whom are nationally recognized authorities in their field. Its student body numbered 850. The library contained over 65,000 volumes. Among the other facilities available to the students were a law review, moot court facilities, scholarship funds, and Order of the Coif affiliation. The school's alumni occupy the most distinguished positions in the private practice of the law and in the public life of the State. It may properly be considered one of the nation's ranking law schools. . . . Since the trial of this case, respondents report the opening of a law school at the Texas State University for Negroes. It is apparently on the road to full accreditation. It has a faculty of five full-time professors; a student body of 23; a library of some 16,500 volumes serviced by a full-time staff; a practice court and legal aid association; and one alumnus who has become a member of the Texas Bar.

Whether the University of Texas Law School is compared with the original or the new law school for Negroes, we cannot find substantial equality in the educational opportunities offered white and Negro law students by the State. In terms of number of the faculty, variety of courses and opportunity for specialization, size of the student body, scope of the library, availability of law review and similar activities, the University of Texas Law School possesses to a far greater degree those qualities which are incapable of objective measurement but which make for greatness in a law school. Such qualities, to name but a few, include reputation of the faculty, experience of the administration, position and influence of the alumni, standing in the community, traditions and prestige. It is difficult to believe that one who had a free choice between these law schools would consider the question close.

Moreover, although the law is a highly learned profession, we are well aware that it is an intensely practical one. The law school, the proving ground for legal learning and practice, cannot be effective in isolation from the individuals and institutions with which the law interacts. Few students and no one who has practiced law would choose to study in an academic vacuum, removed from the interplay of ideas and the exchange of views with which the law is concerned. The law school to which Texas is willing to admit petitioner excludes from its student body members of the racial groups which number 85 percent of the population of the State and include most of the lawyers, witnesses, jurors, judges and other officials with whom petitioner will inevitably be dealing when he becomes a member of the Texas Bar. With such a substantial and significant segment of society excluded, we cannot conclude that the education offered petitioner is substantially equal to that which he would receive if admitted to the University of Texas Law School. . . .

In accordance with the *Gaines* and *Sipuel* cases, petitioner may claim his full constitutional right: legal education equivalent to that offered by the State to students of other races. Such education is not offered to him in a separate law school as offered by the State. . . .

We hold that the Equal Protection Clause of the Fourteenth Amendment

[1] *Sweatt* v. *Painter*, 339 U.S. 629 (1950).

requires that petitioner be admitted to the University of Texas Law School. The judgment is reversed and the cause is remanded for proceedings not inconsistent with this opinion.

The *McLaurin* decision was no less damaging than the *Sweatt* opinion to the foundations of segregated higher education and, in the long run, to the *Plessy* doctrine itself. In this action, McLaurin, an Oklahoma Negro, had been admitted to the University of Oklahoma's Graduate School as a candidate for the degree of Doctor of Education. Such a curriculum was not available at a state school for blacks, so McLaurin was admitted to the state university with certain restrictions, which were, in fact, deliberately softened by the time the case reached the Supreme Court, to lend color to the state's contention that the plaintiff was enjoying a reasonable and substantial degree of equality. The following passage is taken from the Court's unanimous opinion, prepared by Chief Justice Vinson:[1]

Following the *Sipuel* decision, the Oklahoma legislature amended these statutes to permit the admission of Negroes to [white] institutions of higher learning . . . in cases where [they] offered courses not available in the Negro schools. The amendment provided, however, that in such cases the program of instruction "shall be given at such colleges or institutions of higher education upon a segregated basis." Appellant was thereupon admitted to the University of Oklahoma Graduate School [and] . . . his admission was made subject to "such rules and regulations as to segregation as the President of the University shall consider to afford to Mr. G. W. McLaurin substantially equal educational opportunities as are afforded to other persons seeking the same education in the Graduate College," a condition which does not appear to have been withdrawn. Thus he was required to sit apart at a designated desk in an anteroom adjoining the classroom; to sit at a designated desk on the mezzanine floor of the library, but not to use the desks in the regular reading room; and to sit at a designated table and to eat at a different time from the other students in the school cafeteria.

In the interval between the decision of the court below and the hearing in this Court, the treatment afforded appellant was altered. For some time, the section of the classroom in which appellant sat was surrounded by a rail on which there was a sign stating, "Reserved for Colored," but these have been removed. He is now assigned to a seat in the classroom in a row specified for colored students; he is assigned to a table in the library on the main floor; and he is permitted to eat at the same time in the cafeteria as other students, although here again he is assigned to a special table.

It is said that the separations imposed by the State in this case are in form merely nominal. McLaurin uses the same classroom, library and cafeteria as students of other races; there is no indication that the seats to which he is assigned in these rooms have any disadvantage of location. He may wait in line in the cafeteria and there stand and talk with his fellow students, but while he eats he must remain apart.

These restrictions signify that the State, in administering the facilities it affords for professional and graduate study, sets McLaurin apart from the

[1] *McLaurin* v. *Oklahoma State Regents,* 339 U.S. 737 (1950).

other students. . . . Such restrictions impair his ability to study, to engage in discussions and exchange views with other students, and, . . . to learn his profession.

Our society grows increasingly complex, and our need for trained leaders increases correspondingly. Appellant's case represents, perhaps, the epitome of that need, for he is attempting . . . to become . . . a leader and trainer of others. Those who will come under his guidance . . . must be directly affected by the education he receives. Their own education and development will necessarily suffer to the extent that his training is unequal to that of his classmates. State-imposed restrictions which produce such inequalities cannot be sustained.

It may be argued that appellant will be in no better position when these restrictions are removed, for he may still be set apart by his fellow students. This we think irrelevant. There is a vast difference—a Constitutional difference—between restrictions imposed by the state which prohibit the intellectual commingling of students, and the refusal of individuals to commingle where the state presents no such bar. . . .

We conclude that the conditions under which this appellant is required to receive his education deprive him of his personal and present right to the equal protection of the laws. We hold that under these circumstances the Fourteenth Amendment precludes differences in treatment by the state based upon race. Appellant . . . must receive the same treatment at the hands of the state as students of other races. . . .

Finally, in *Brown* v. *Board of Education of Topeka,* the Court extended the *Sweatt* and *McLaurin* principle (that there are circumstances in which segregation per se necessarily means inequality of treatment) to the much broader field of public schools—and, by implication, to other forms of separate facilities as well. Here again was another NAACP triumph, won by a corps of lawyers, historians, and social scientists, who perfected the brief, and particularly by Thurgood Marshall, the association's chief legal voice, and later Associate Justice of the United States Supreme Court.

As early as the fall of 1952, cases from four states—Kansas, South Carolina, Virginia, and Delaware—and the District of Columbia were awaiting review by the Supreme Court, all of them challenging the constitutionality of segregated public schools. In each, the facts showed that in all tangible respects equality had in fact (or nearly so) been attained. The issue at last confronting the Court was, in short, no longer a mere question of the *degree* to which Negro schools approached equality with white schools; before the Court now was the deeper issue: Is separate-but-equal really "equal protection of the laws"? Could *Plessy* v. *Ferguson* still be maintained?

The cases were first argued in December, 1952, and then restored to the docket for later argument while further data were assembled for the Court's information. Finally, on May 17, 1954, the tribunal handed down the decision which promised a social transformation of the first magnitude. The Court rendered a unanimous judgment, expressed in a single opinion. The gravity of the judgment was further acknowledged by the Court's announcement that it was allowing a breathing spell by prescribing that in the autumn of 1954 the Court would hear arguments on the nature of the decree by which the decision might best be carried into effect.

The five cases were treated as a unit, and are commonly cited collectively as *Brown* v. *Board of Education.* In strict point of fact, the decision was binding only upon the school boards who were parties to the suits. Thereafter, stubborn school boards were able to further forestall desegregation until they themselves had been successfully sued. This resulted in slow and uneven progress in desegregation until other pressures, notably those generated by the Civil Rights Act of 1964, accelerated the processes of compliance with the Court's dictum.

The opinion itself was written for the Court by Chief Justice Earl Warren, only lately appointed to his high post by President Eisenhower. After pointing out that in the recent *McLaurin* and *Sweatt* cases it had not been necessary to confront the specific question of the constitutionality of separate-but-equal, the written opinion explained that this time the issue could not be avoided, because it had been established in the lower court that:[1]

> the Negro and white schools involved had been equalized or are being equalized, with respect to buildings, curricula, qualifications and salaries of teachers, and other "tangible" factors. Our decision, therefore, cannot turn on merely a comparison of these tangible factors in Negro and white schools involved in each of the cases. We must look instead to the effect of segregation itself in public education.

In temperate language the Court went on to apply to the question of equality the test of the practical effects of segregation upon the segregated, and then moved resolutely to a conclusion which the country in general, and the outside world, applauded. Some, however, ranging from angry racists to sincere and kindly-disposed believers in legal literalism and local self-government, deplored the decision as "sociological jurisprudence," "judge-made law," "federal dictation," and "subversion of the Constitution," for which the Chief Justice should be impeached. What the loudest critics of the *Brown* decision overlooked, incidentally, when they attacked the Court for supplanting *Plessy* v. *Ferguson,* was that the *Plessy* doctrine, certainly no less than the *Brown* opinion, was open to the charge that it too was "judge-made law," imposed by the federal judiciary, and derived ultimately from psychological, historical, and sociological rather than purely legal sanctions.

> In approaching this problem, we cannot turn the clock back to 1868 when the Amendment was adopted, or even to 1896 when *Plessy* v. *Ferguson* was

[1] *Brown* v. *Board of Education of Topeka,* 347 U.S. 483 (1954).

written. We must consider public education in the light of its full development and its present place in American life throughout the Nation. Only in this way can it be determined if segregation in public schools deprives these plaintiffs of the equal protection of the laws.

Today, education is perhaps the most important function of state and local governments. Compulsory school attendance laws and the great expenditures for education both demonstrate our recognition of the importance of education to our democratic society. It is required in the performance of our most basic public responsibilities, even service in the armed forces. It is the very foundation of good citizenship. Today it is a principal instrument in awakening the child to cultural values, in preparing him for later professional training, and in helping him to adjust normally to his environment. . . .

We come then to the question presented: Does segregation of children in public schools solely on the basis of race, even though the physical facilities and other "tangible" factors may be equal, deprive the children of the minority group of equal educational opportunities? We believe that it does. . . .

To separate them from others of similar age and qualifications solely because of their race generates a feeling of inferiority as to their status in the community that may affect their hearts and minds in a way unlikely ever to be undone. The effect of this separation on their educational opportunities was well stated by a finding in the Kansas case by a court which nevertheless felt compelled to rule against the Negro plaintiffs:

"Segregation of white and colored children in public schools has a detrimental effect upon the colored children. The impact is greater when it has the sanction of the law; for the policy of separating the races is usually interpreted as denoting the inferiority of the Negro group. A sense of inferiority affects the motivation of a child to learn. Segregation with the sanction of law, therefore, has a tendency to retard the education and mental development of Negro children and to deprive them of some of the benefits they would receive in a racially integrated school system." Whatever may have been the extent of psychological knowledge at the time of *Plessy* v. *Ferguson,* this finding is amply supported by modern authority. Any language in *Plessy* v. *Ferguson* contrary to this finding is rejected.

We conclude that in the field of public education the doctrine of "separate but equal" has no place. Separate educational facilities are inherently unequal. Therefore, we hold that the plaintiffs and others similarly situated for whom the actions have been brought are, by reason of the segregation complained of, deprived of the equal protection of the laws guaranteed by the Fourteenth Amendment. This disposition makes unnecessary any discussion whether such segregation also violates the Due Process Clause of the Fourteenth Amendment. . . .

We have now announced that such segregation is a denial of the equal protection of the laws. In order that we may have the full assistance of the parties in formulating decrees, the cases will be restored to the docket, and the parties are requested to present further argument on Questions 4 and 5 previously propounded by the Court for the reargument this Term. The Attorney General of the United States is again invited to participate. The Attorneys General of the states requiring or permitting segregation in public education will also be permitted to appear as amici curiae upon request to do so by September 15, 1954, and submission of briefs by October 1, 1954.

A special form of discrimination in the field of public education which deserves notice here is the payment of lower salaries to black teachers than to white teachers in the same county or city school system. Here, too—well before the *Sipuel, McLaurin, Sweatt,* and *Brown* decisions—the federal courts insisted upon more literal compliance with the spirit and letter of the Fourteenth Amendment guaranties than state and local school laws and administrators were, on their own motion, prepared to render.

In *Mills* v. *Board of Education of Anne Arundel County* a United States district court in Maryland ruled that the poor financial condition of a county offers no defense of a salary differential between teachers of the two races. At issue was a statute which, while it stipulated no maximum salary for either race, did prescribe a lower minimum salary for Negro teachers than for whites. Conceding the right of school boards to exercise discretion in fixing salaries on nonracial grounds, the court pointedly rejected differentials based on race, including those for which other, presumably nonracial, justifications were offered in extenuation.[1]

> The controlling question in the case . . . is not whether the statutes are unconstitutional on their face but whether in their practical application they constitute an unconstitutional discrimination on account of race and color prejudicial to the plaintiff. . . . I . . . find . . . that in Anne Arundel County . . . *not one* colored teacher receives so much salary as *any* white teacher of similar qualifications and experience.
>
> The crucial question in the case is whether the very substantial differential between the salaries of white and colored teachers in Anne Arundel County is due to discrimination on account of race or color. I find it a fact from the testimony that it is. Some effort has been made by counsel for the defendants to justify the difference in salaries on other grounds. Thus it is said that until recently the school term was somewhat longer in the white schools than in the colored schools; and it is also said that the colored teachers are less efficient than the white teachers because the results of examinations in the white and colored schools in Anne Arundel County show a substantially lower average for colored pupils than for white pupils. But . . . it is to be noted that the school term has now been made equal for white and colored schools; and the lower grade in examinations attained by colored pupils is readily explained by other grounds than the alleged inefficiency of colored teachers. . . .
>
> [The plaintiff] is entitled to an injunction against the continuation of such discrimination to the extent that it is based solely on the grounds of race and color, and he is also entitled to a declaratory decree to the effect that such unlawful discrimination exists. . . .

Shortly thereafter, in *Alston* v. *School Board of Norfolk,*[2] the United States Fourth Circuit Court of Appeals (in a decision which the Supreme Court later declared it unnecessary to review) emphasized that

[1] 30 F. Supp. 245 (D. Md., 1939).
[2] 112 F. 2d 992 (4th Cir. 1940).

the fixing of salary scales by local boards is a form of state action and thus subject to Fourteenth Amendment constraints. Again, in *McDaniel* v. *Board of Public Instruction of Escambia, Florida,*[1] the federal judiciary emphasized that local school administrative officers and agencies are agents of the state, and that their assignment of lower salaries to Negroes than to whites with similar credentials constitutes denial by the state of equal protection of the laws. The same principles were reiterated in *Thomas* v. *Hibbitts,* 46 Fed. Supp. 368 (1942), by a United States district court in Tennessee, a case involving the Nashville public school system. In that instance, the defendant objected that the difference was justified by the consideration that it was based on the differences between the types of schools that were being compared, and not upon differences, racial or otherwise, between the teachers of the schools. Moreover, the city argued, if the school board should assign a Negro to a white school he would receive the higher salary scale prevailing in the white schools. The court dismissed this as puerile sophistry, because the fact was that no Negro had ever been appointed to teach in a white school in Nashville.

C. *Segregated Housing and Restrictive Covenants*

Residential segregation suffered some major legal defeats during these years which in effect rendered the racially restrictive covenant unenforceable as a device for preserving the racial exclusivity of neighborhoods. Discrimination in *public* housing, however, still found support in the federal courts. In *Favors* v. *Randall*[2] a federal district court in Pennsylvania held that "proper segregation" as prescribed by the Philadelphia Housing Authority under the Federal Housing Act was not a violation of equal protection. The court was moved to this conclusion by the facts that (1) there was a larger number of blacks in the housing development here in litigation than their numbers in the city or their needs, on a proportional basis, would entitle them to; and that (2) the Philadelphia Housing Authority was basing its procedures of selecting tenants upon a policy of preserving "the existing neighborhood pattern . . . as far as possible." Plaintiff had argued, however, that racial considerations should not enter the selection process at all.

. . . [T]he only question . . . for decision is whether or not the action of the Philadelphia Housing Authority in certifying tenants in conformity with the neighborhood pattern is a reasonable regulation or a discrimination, arbitrary, illegal and unjust.

[1] 39 F. Supp. 638 (N.D. Fla., 1941).
[2] 40 F. Supp. 743 (E.D. Pa., 1941).

A thorough examination of the testimony . . . shows that the action of the defendants is neither arbitrary, discriminatory nor illegal. In view of the scope of the problem which confronted the Philadelphia Housing Authority . . . it is felt that far from being discriminatory or arbitrary the Authority in the performance of the duties incumbent upon them . . . is meeting the problem with forbearance and tolerance as is evidenced by the fact that when the program is completed, although the need is much greater among white people for low "economic rent," nevertheless there will be a much greater preponderance of negroes in occupancy of the various units than their need entitles them to. . . .

In determining the question of reasonableness, the Philadelphia Housing Authority was at liberty to act with reference to the established usages, customs and traditions of the people, and with a view to the preservation of public peace and good order as well as a promotion of their comfort, which was the purpose for the creation of the Authority. This it is felt the Philadelphia Housing Authority has carefully done.

The application for the preliminary injunction is denied.

Buchanan v. *Warley*, 1917 had branded state-and-city-imposed residential segregation as a violation of the Fourteenth Amendment.[1] Thereafter, increasing reliance was placed upon privately arranged restrictive covenants, which for a time continued to withstand judicial challenge.[2] In 1948, however, in *Shelley* v. *Kraemer*, these too were rendered unenforceable, when the Supreme Court took the position that their judicial enforcement by state courts makes the state government an accomplice in the denial of equal protection.[3]

The first of the two excerpts from the *Shelley* decision reproduced below is the covenant—typical of hundreds of thousands that burdened property deeds across the country—which gave rise to this case. The second is from the opinion itself. Events leading up to the suit began when J. D. Shelley and his wife purchased and moved into a home in St. Louis in 1945. The property was located on a tract comprising some fifty-seven parcels. Its owner had signed the agreement quoted here in 1911, but the Shelleys were unaware of the restriction at the time they bought the land. Action was brought against them by owners of neighboring lots, who asked the city court to void the sale and order the Shelleys out of their new home. Four of the plots were in fact occupied by Negroes, and had been so for periods ranging from twenty-three to sixty-three years. These other Negroes had moved into the neighborhood *before* the covenant was made and could, therefore, not be reached by the restriction.

The St. Louis city circuit court denied Kraemer and his associates the remedy they sought, but the Supreme Court of Missouri reversed and directed the trial court to grant the respondents' plea.[4] The case

[1] See above, p. 201.
[2] See above, p. 202.
[3] 334 U.S. 1 (1948).
[4] See below, p. 298.

came to the United States Supreme Court in 1948 on writ of certiorari. It is interesting to note that the Attorney General of the United States filed a brief for the United States as amicus curiae, and that the Solicitor General argued the cause for the government, pleading the unconstitutionality of restrictive covenants. Part of the covenant as it was quoted in the decision read as follows:

> . . . the said property is hereby restricted to the use and occupancy for the term of fifty (50) years from this date, so that it shall be a condition all the time and whether recited and referred to or not in subsequent conveyances and shall attach to the land as a condition precedent to the sale of the same, and hereafter no part of said property or any portion thereof shall be, for said term of fifty years, occupied by any person not of the Caucasian race, it being intended hereby to restrict the use of said property for said period of time against the occupancy as owners or tenants of any portion of said property for resident or other purposes by people of the Negro or Mongolian Race.

The gist of the opinion delivered by Chief Justice Vinson follows:

> The short of the matter is that from the time of the adoption of the Fourteenth Amendment until the present, it has been the consistent ruling of this Court that the action of the States to which the Amendment has reference, includes action of state courts and state judicial officials. . . . It has never been suggested that state court action is immunized from the operation of those provisions simply because the act is that of the judicial branch of the state government.
>
> Against this background of judicial construction, extending over . . . three-quarters of a century, we are called upon to consider whether enforcement by state courts of the restrictive agreements in these cases may be deemed to be the acts of those States [and a denial of the] equal protection of the laws which the Amendment was intended to insure.
>
> We have no doubt that there has been state action in these cases in the full and complete sense of the phrase. . . . It is clear that but for the active intervention of the state courts, supported by the full panoply of state power, petitioners would have been free to occupy the properties in question without restraint.
>
> These are not cases, as has been suggested, in which the States have merely abstained from action, leaving private individuals free to impose such discriminations as they see fit. Rather, these are cases in which the States have made available to such individuals the full coercive power of government to deny to petitioners, on the grounds of race or color, the enjoyment of property rights in premises which petitioners are willing and financially able to acquire and which the grantors are willing to sell. . . .
>
> We hold that in granting judicial enforcement of the restrictive agreements in these cases, the States have denied petitioners the equal protection of the laws and that, therefore, the action of the state courts cannot stand. . . . Because of the race or color of these petitioners they have been denied rights of ownership or occupancy enjoyed as a matter of course by other citizens of different race or color. . . .
>
> The historical context in which the Fourteenth Amendment became a part of the Constitution should not be forgotten. Whatever else the framers

sought to achieve, it is clear that the matter of primary concern was the establishment of equality in the enjoyment of basic civil and political rights and the preservation of those rights from discriminatory action on the part of the States based on considerations of race or color. Seventy-five years ago this Court announced that the provisions of the Amendment are to be construed with this fundamental purpose in mind. . . .

Finally, in *Barrows* v. *Jackson*,[1] the NAACP pressed for, and won, further clarification of the status of efforts by white citizens to exclude Negroes from their neighborhoods by concerted private action. In this instance, one of the white cosigners of a restrictive covenant was sued by the other parties to the contract because he had repented of his action and, in breach of the agreement, had sold his property to a person of color. The Court now laid down the somewhat novel doctrine that the defendant could properly offer in defense of his breach of the covenant the argument that the constitutional rights of *others* (in this case prospective black purchasers) were impaired by the covenant that he had signed. In these circumstances, the Court reasoned, "it would be difficult if not impossible for the persons whose rights are asserted to present their [own] grievance before any court," and hence another may properly bring the complaint in their behalf.

Not only is *Barrows* v. *Jackson* of special interest because it testifies to the Court's growing disinclination to countenance racial discrimination in its many guises; it was also notable for its findings that a state's refusal to enforce restrictive covenants is not the sort of impairment of contractual obligations that the contract clause forbids, and that the federal Constitution confers on no one the right to demand state action which in effect would result in denial of equal protection. For good measure, the Court made the further declaration that the Constitution's clause forbidding states to impair obligations of contracts restrains legislatures, not courts.

D. *Segregated Transportation: the Collapse of Legal Jim Crow*

Enforced segregation of the races in interstate travel—whether by law or by the transportation company's own rules—was now also clearly doomed by the federal judiciary's growing adherence to the letter and spirit of the Fourteenth Amendment, and by its broadened application of the interstate commerce clause.

In a remarkable controversy in 1941, Arthur W. Mitchell, of Chicago, a Negro member of the United States House of Representatives, argued his own case, with some assistance from another lawyer, before the

[1] 346 U.S. 249 (1953).

Supreme Court. He had purchased a first-class ticket for a railway trip from Chicago to Hot Springs, Arkansas. After the train left Memphis and crossed the Mississippi into Arkansas, the conductor took up the Memphis-to-Hot Springs portion of Mitchell's ticket, and, refusing the Congressman's payment for Pullman accommodations, ordered him into the coach reserved for Negroes, to comply with Arkansas laws. The conductor subsequently informed Mitchell that he was entitled to apply for refund of the amount representing the difference in the first-class and coach fares from Memphis to Hot Springs.

It was established in the court of original jurisdiction that unused Pullman space was in fact available in the portion of the sleeping car reserved for whites, but in the space normally allotted to Negroes (in compartments and drawing rooms) all the accommodations were already occupied by black passengers, leaving only coach space for Mitchell. The question for adjudication therefore was whether the rules of the road did in fact, in violation of the Interstate Commerce Act, subject Mitchell to "undue or unreasonable prejudice or disadvantage."

At an earlier stage of the dispute the Interstate Commerce Commission had dismissed Mitchell's complaint on the ground that the extremely small demand for Pullman accommodations for Negroes justified the railroad in making only limited Pullman space available to the race. This factor, the Commission had ruled, plus the fact that Arkansas law required separate facilities for the races, warranted the Commission's finding that such disadvantage and prejudice as the road laid upon Mitchell in this instance was "plainly not unjust or undue." Mitchell's complaint was also dismissed by the United States District Court of Northern Illinois. Later, when the case was brought to the Supreme Court on appeal, the government of the United States, rejecting the judgment of the lower court, itself came into the case, standing with Mr. Mitchell as a co-appellant, and argued in his support.[1]

> It does not appear that colored passengers who have bought first-class tickets for transportation by the carrier are given accommodations which are substantially equal to those afforded to white passengers. The Government puts the matter succinctly: "When a drawing room is available, the carrier practice of allowing colored passengers to use one at Pullman seat rates avoids inequality as between the accommodations specifically assigned to the passenger. But when none is available, the discrimination and inequality of accommodation become self-evident. It is no answer to say that the colored passengers can make their reservations so far in advance as to be assured of first-class accommodations. So long as white passengers can secure first-class reservations on the day of travel and the colored passengers cannot, the latter are subjected to inequality and discrimination because of their race." . . .

[1] *Mitchell* v. *United States,* 313 U.S. 80 (1941).

We take it that the chief reason for the Commission's action was the "comparatively little colored traffic." But the comparative volume of traffic cannot justify the denial of a fundamental right of equality of treatment, a right specifically safeguarded by the provisions of the Interstate Commerce Act. . . . While the supply of particular facilities may be conditioned upon there being a reasonable demand therefore, if facilities are provided, substantial equality of treatment of persons traveling under like conditions cannot be refused. It is the individual . . . who is entitled to the equal protection of the laws,—not merely a group of individuals, or a body of persons according to their numbers. . . .

On the facts here presented, there is no room, as the Government properly says, for administrative or expert judgment with respect to particular difficulties. It is enough that the discrimination shown was palpably unjust and forbidden by the Act.

The decree of the District Court is reversed and the cause is remanded with directions to set aside the order of the Commission and to remand the case to the Commission for further proceedings in conformity with this opinion.

Morgan v. *Virginia* was another NAACP case, argued by Thurgood Marshall and William Hastie. The appellant, traveling in a Greyhound bus from Hayes' Store, Virginia, to Baltimore, was ordered by the driver, when the bus stopped at Saluda, Virginia, to move to the rear in order to make room for a white passenger. (Virginia law authorized such reassignment of seats to preserve segregation.) When she refused, the driver called in a sheriff, but she remained adamant, and a brief scuffle ensued. In the litigation that followed, the lower court sustained the state of Virginia's contention that this state-prescribed segregation of races on the bus was a valid exercise of the police power to regulate highways and common carriers for the preservation of the public peace and safety. The Supreme Court, however, reversed the decision of the court below, basing its judgment on interstate commerce clause grounds. This decision, it will be noted, was sharply at variance with the Court's 1878 ruling in *Hall* v. *DeCuir*.[1] The gist of the *Morgan* decision was expressed in these words:[2]

In weighing the factors that entered into our conclusion as to whether this statute so burdens interstate commerce or so infringes the requirements of national uniformity as to be invalid, we are mindful of the fact that conditions vary between northern or western states such as Maine or Montana, with practically no colored population; industrial states such as Illinois, Ohio, New Jersey and Pennsylvania with a small, although appreciable, percentage of colored citizens; and the states of the deep South. . . . Local efforts to promote amicable relations in difficult areas by legislative segregation in interstate transportation emerge from the latter racial distribution. As no state law can reach beyond its own border nor bar transportation of passengers across its boundaries, diverse seating requirements for the races

[1] See above, p. 63.

[2] 328 U.S. 373 (1945).

in interstate journeys result. As there is no federal act dealing with the separation of races in interstate transportation, we must decide the validity of the Virginia statute on the challenge that it interferes with commerce, as a matter of balance between the exercise of the local police power and the need for national uniformity in the regulation of interstate travel. It seems clear to us that seating arrangements for the different races in interstate motor travel require a single, uniform rule to promote and protect national travel. Consequently, we hold the Virginia statute in controversy invalid. Reversed.

A significant extension of the *Morgan* principle came three years later in *Whiteside* v. *Southern Bus Lines,* when a federal court of appeals handed down the opinion that in a state having no bus segregation law, segregation by rule of the bus company itself is as truly a violation of the interstate commerce clause as if it were imposed by statute. (In the same year, in *Lee* v. *Commonwealth of Virginia,* the Morgan doctrine was held to apply as much to railroads as to buses.[1])

Elizabeth Whiteside, after boarding a bus in Missouri, had been ejected at a station in Kentucky when she declined to find a seat in the rear of the bus. She sued for damages. When the United States district court ruled in the bus company's favor, the plaintiff appealed to a federal court of appeals, which, in the case before us, reversed the judgment of the trial court. Kentucky law at the time authorized carriers to make their own rules regarding segregation of the races, subject only to the requirement that equal accommodations be afforded. The court's reasoning follows:[2]

We are aware that a number of district court decisions . . . have undertaken to distinguish such situations as are here involved from the facts of the Morgan case by drawing a line between the action of a state in attempting to regulate the business of a carrier and the right of a carrier to operate its own business. . . . conceding that the fact that Congress has refrained from acting in a field exclusively entrusted to it, gives no right to a state to enter this field, and that a regulation or custom deemed reasonable a generation ago may not necessarily be so at the present time. [Judge Paul, for example, in the *Simmons* case] sustains a regulation made by a motor carrier in Virginia on the ground that it has a reasonable basis, viewed in the light of the responsibility resting on such carriers, to assure that travel upon their conveyances shall, so far as possible, be free from disorder, disturbance or unpleasant incident. He points out, however, that in the *Simmons* case the plaintiff would not have been subjected to different rules or customs in the different states through which he traveled for he would have been confronted with the same rule in North Carolina which he met with in Virginia, and there was therefore no burden or inconvenience arising from meeting the varying customs of different states. . . . [In the case before us, however] that requirement that [the plaintiff] change her seat with all her accompanying impedimenta the moment she crossed the Kentucky line, was a breach of

[1] 189 Va. 890, 54 S.E. 2d 888 (1949).
[2] 177 F. 2d 949 (6th Cir. 1949).

that uniformity which, under the Morgan case, is a test of the burden placed upon interstate commerce.

It must also be observed that acts burdening interstate commerce are not, like those inhibited in the Fourteenth Amendment, limited to state action. Burdens may result from the activities of private persons as the great mass of federal criminal legislation, validated under the authority of the Commerce Clause, discloses. . . . We indicate no view as to the reasonableness or necessity of the challenged regulation under conditions which exist in Kentucky, nor as to its validity under state law when applied to local traffic. We hold that as here applied to a passenger traveling on an interstate journey upon interstate conveyance, it constitutes a burden upon interstate commerce and furnishes no immunity to the appellee for damages which may flow from its enforcement.

Finally, in the *Henderson* case handed down at the same time with the *McLaurin* and *Sweatt* opinions, the Supreme Court considered the question of whether the segregation of Negro passengers in dining cars violated the Interstate Commerce Act. Here, curiously, even though the United States government was itself a defendant (as required by statute when a ruling of the I.C.C. is challenged), it argued on the side of the aggrieved Negro plaintiff against itself and its own agency's ruling, in order to throw its weight on the side of civil rights.

The case arose under Section 3 (1) of the Interstate Commerce Commission Act of 1887, which forbade railroads in interstate commerce to "subject any particular person . . . to any undue or unreasonable prejudice or disadvantage in any respect whatsoever"—the same clause that Congressman Mitchell had invoked. Henderson was traveling from Washington to Atlanta and had been refused service in the diner, despite the fact that vacant places were available. The I.C.C. had earlier determined that the reservation for blacks of one table of the eleven in a dining car was "proportionately fair." Henderson brought suit, and the Supreme Court of the United States supported his demand for equal treatment.[1]

The similarity between the Mitchell case[2] and this is inescapable. The appellant here was denied a seat in the dining car although at least one seat was vacant and would have been available to him, under the existing rules, if he had been white. The issue before us, as in the Mitchell case, is whether the railroad's current rules and practices cause passengers to be subjected to undue or unreasonable prejudice or disadvantage in violation of section 3 (1). We find that they do.

The right to be free from unreasonable discriminations belongs, under Section 3 (1), to each particular person. Where a dining car is available to passengers holding tickets entitling them to use it, each such passenger is equally entitled to its facilities in accordance with reasonable regulations. . . . Under the rules, only four Negro passengers may be served at one time and

[1] *Henderson* v. *United States Interstate Commerce Commission and Southern Ry.*, 339 U.S. 816, 843 (1950).

[2] See above, p. 283.

then only at the table reserved for Negroes. Other Negroes who present themselves are compelled to await a vacancy at that table, although there may be many vacancies elsewhere in the diner. . . . The rules impose a like deprivation on white passengers whenever more than 40 of them seek to be served at the same time and the table reserved for Negroes is vacant.

We need not multiply instances in which these rules sanction unreasonable discriminations. The curtains, partitions and signs emphasize the artificiality of a difference in treatment which serves only to call attention to a racial classification of passengers holding identical tickets and using the same public dining facility.

The judgment of the District Court is reversed and the cause is remanded to that court . . . for further proceedings in conformity with this opinion.

E. *Fair Trials: Qualified Gains*

The unequal administration of justice, especially in the southern states, continued during these years to be a preoccupation of the federal courts. Biased all-white juries, coerced confessions, and police brutality were the most common complaints, as they had been in preceding decades. In one not unusual case, for example, a Negro convicted of a capital offense (in this case it was rape) by an all-white jury asked the United States Supreme Court to review a judgment by a Texas court which had denied a motion to quash an indictment by a grand jury from which Negroes had been excluded. The record established that Negroes made up 20 percent of the population and 10 percent of the poll-tax-payers; and that at least 3,000, and perhaps as many as 6,000, Negroes in the county possessed the legally prescribed qualifications for jury service. Yet in the preceding seven years, only five of 384 grand jurors had been blacks. The state replied that no systematic racial exclusion had been practiced, and that the only test applied had been that of competence. The Supreme Court, speaking through Justice Black, said:[1]

One [Commissioner] said that their failure to select negroes was because they did not know the names of any who were qualified and the other said that he was not personally acquainted with any member of the negro race. This is, at best, the testimony of [only] two individuals who participated in drawing 1 out of 32 jury panels discussed in the record. But even if their testimony were . . . considered typical of that of the 94 commissioners who did not testify, we would still feel compelled to reverse the decision below. What the Fourteenth Amendment prohibits is racial discrimination in the selection of grand juries. Where jury commissioners limit those from whom grand juries are selected to their own personal acquaintance, discrimination can arise from commissioners who know but eliminate them. If there has been discrimination, whether accomplished ingeniously or ingenuously, the conviction cannot stand.

[1] *Smith* v. *Texas*, 311 U.S. 127 (1940).

Chambers v. *Florida* was still another case, among many of its kind, involving four Negroes who, after endlessly protracted questioning over a period of several days, "broke down" and confessed to a murder. The decision brought out no new principles, nor even a new formulation of old ones, but the lofty peroration of Justice Black, then one of the most advanced civil libertarians on the Court (his appointment to the bench by Franklin D. Roosevelt, it will be recalled, was loudly, if speciously, deplored in some quarters on the ground that he had once held a Klan membership card!) is worthy of quotation.[1]

For five days petitioners were subjected to interrogations culminating in Saturday's all night examination. Over a period of five days they steadily refused to confess and disclaimed guilt. The very circumstances surrounding their confinement and the questioning without any formal charges having been brought, were such as to fill petitioners with terror and frightful misgivings. Some were practical strangers in the community; three were arrested in a one-room farm tenant house which was their home; the haunting fear of mob violence was around them in an atmosphere charged with excitement and public indignation. From virtually the moment of their arrest until their eventual confessions, they never knew just when anyone would be called back to the fourth floor room, and there, surrounded by his accusers and others, interrogated by men who held their very lives—so far as these ignorant petitioners could know—in the balance. The rejection of petitioner Woodward's first "confession," given in the early hours of Sunday morning, because it was found wanting, demonstrates the relentless tenacity which "broke" petitioners' will and rendered them helpless to resist their accusers further. To permit human lives to be forfeited upon confessions thus obtained would make the constitutional requirement of due process of law a meaningless symbol.

We are not impressed by the argument that law enforcement methods such as those under review are necessary to uphold our laws. . . . Due process of law, preserved for all by our Constitution, commands that no such practice . . . shall send any accused to his death. No . . . more solemn responsibility, rests upon this Court, than that of translating into living law and maintaining this constitutional shield deliberately planned and inscribed for the benefit of every human being subject to our Constitution—of whatever race, creed or persuasion.

The Supreme Court of Florida was in error and its judgment is reversed.

Section 242 of Title 18 of the United States Code provides that

Whoever, under color of any law, statute, ordinance, regulation, or custom, willfully subjects any inhabitant of any State, Territory, or district to the deprivation of any rights, privileges, or immunities secured or protected by the Constitution or laws of the United States, or to different punishments, pains, or penalties, on account of such inhabitant being an alien, or by reason of his color, or race, than are prescribed for the punishment of citizens, shall be fined not more than $1,000 or imprisoned not more than one year, or both.

[1] 309 U.S. 227 (1940).

In 1945 the recently created (1939) Civil Rights Section in the Department of Justice invoked this paragraph in a case that seemed to many Americans to manifest a surprising aberration on the part of a Court otherwise inclined to increasingly liberal judgments on racial issues. The Court's majority opinion indeed began with the words "This case involves a shocking and revolting episode in law enforcement," and yet Claude Screws, who committed the act complained of, wholly escaped punishment.

Screws was the sheriff of Baker County, Georgia. In January 1943, assisted by a local policeman, he arrested a Negro, Robert Hall, on a warrant charging that Hall had stolen a tire. Hall was handcuffed and taken by car to the county court house, but as he alighted from the vehicle he was beaten by the two men with their fists and with a "solid-bar blackjack about eight inches long and weighing two pounds." In the language of Justice Black, "They claimed Hall had reached for a gun and had used insulting language as he alighted from the car. But after Hall, still handcuffed, had been knocked to the ground they continued to beat him from fifteen to thirty minutes until he was unconscious. Hall was then dragged feet first through the courthouse yard into the jail and thrown upon the floor dying. An ambulance was called and Hall was removed to a hospital where he died within the hour and without regaining consciousness. There is evidence that Screws held a grudge against Hall and had threatened to 'get him.'"

Screws was indicted for violating Section 242 (formerly known as Section 20 of the Criminal Code, 18 U.S.C. Section 52). He was tried by a jury in a district court and found guilty. The circuit court of appeals sustained the verdict, and the case then moved to the Supreme Court of the United States on writ of certiorari. And although six of the justices agreed that the federal statute could properly be applied to the kind of conduct that had been proved against Screws, five justices ruled that Screws was entitled to a new trial because the trial court had not properly charged the jury that only if Screws's violation was shown to have been "willful" could he be convicted. In the second trial Screws was acquitted, and the people of Georgia, far from rebuking him, elected him to the state senate.

The decision in the Supreme Court promoted equal rights, nevertheless, because the Court had now made clear that the federal government could punish state officers (if properly convicted) for violation of federally guaranteed civil rights. This was a matter of no small significance in view of the delinquency of southern state and local governments and their agents in the matter of punishing and preventing police brutality against Negroes accused of crime. The Court's reasons for requiring a new trial appear in this passage from the majority opinion.[1]

[1] *Screws* v. *United States,* 325 U.S. 91 (1945).

. . . An analysis of the cases in which "willfully" has been held to connote more than an act which is voluntary or intentional would not prove helpful as each turns on its own peculiar facts . . . The Court, indeed, has recognized that the requirement of a specific intent to do a prohibited act may avoid those consequences to the accused which may otherwise render a vague or indefinite statute invalid. The constitutional vice in such a statute is the essential injustice to the accused of placing him on trial for an offense, the nature of which the statute does not define and hence of which it gives no warning. But where the punishment imposed is only for an act knowingly done with the purpose of doing that which the statute prohibits, the accused cannot be said to suffer from lack of warning or knowledge that the act which he does is a violation of law. . . .

It is said, however, that this construction of the Act will not save it from the infirmity of vagueness since neither a law enforcement official nor a trial judge can know with sufficient definiteness the range of rights that are constitutional. But that criticism is wide of the mark. For the specific intent required by the Act is an intent to deprive a person of a right which has been made specific either by the express terms of the Constitution or laws of the United States or by decisions interpreting them. . . . He who defies a decision interpreting the Constitution knows precisely what he is doing. If sane, he hardly may be heard to say that he knew not what he did. Of course, willful conduct cannot make definite that which is undefined. But willful violators of constitutional requirements, which have been defined, certainly are in no position to say that they had no adequate advance notice that they would be visited with punishment. . . .

The difficulty here is that this question of intent was not submitted to the jury with the proper instructions. The court charged that petitioners acted illegally if they applied more force than was necessary to make the arrest effectual or to protect themselves from the prisoner's alleged assault. But in view of our construction of the word "willfully" the jury should have been further instructed that it was not sufficient that petitioners had a generally bad purpose. To convict it was necessary for them to find that petitioners had the purpose to deprive the prisoner of a constitutional right, e.g. the right to be tried by a court rather than by ordeal. . . .

We agree that when this statute is applied to the action of state officials, it should be construed so as to respect the proper balance between the States and the federal government in law enforcement. Violation of local law does not necessarily mean that federal rights have been invaded. The fact that a prisoner is assaulted, injured, or even murdered by state officials does not necessarily mean that he is deprived of any right protected or secured by the Constitution or laws of the United States. . . . Our national government is one of delegated powers alone. . . . It is only state action of a "particular character" that is prohibited by the Fourteenth Amendment and against which the Amendment authorizes Congress to afford relief. Thus Congress in Section 20 of the Criminal Code did not undertake to make all torts of state officials federal crimes. It brought within Section 20 only specified acts done "under color" of law and then only those acts which deprived a person of some right secured by the Constitution or laws of the United States. . . .

Since there must be a new trial, the judgment below is

Reversed.

Despite the ambiguities of the *Screws* decision, Justice Douglas's opinion in that action, that "willful" as used in Section 242 means with "the purpose to deprive the prisoner of a constitutional right, e.g. the right to be tried by a court rather than by ordeal," had a more salutary outcome in *Williams* v. *United States*[1], which held that even a private detective with quasi-police status acts "under color of law" and is subject to federal constraints and punishment.

F. *Public Accommodations: Approaching Equal Treatment*

Circuitous exclusions of blacks from public facilities were, as yet, able to escape judicial censure, but few constitutional lawyers doubted that the days of these expedients too were numbered. One trick which still continued to survive was that of leasing city-owned facilities to private operators, with a view to placing the exclusion of Negroes beyond the reach of the Fourteenth Amendment's reproof.

In *Sweeney* v. *City of Louisville* for example, a federal district court in Kentucky held that such exclusions did not constitute a forbidden discrimination unless it could be proved that blacks had unsuccessfully sought to secure possession of the facility on the same terms on which it had been leased to whites.[2] In short, if a city allows various groups, including Negroes, to rent its auditorium temporarily, for private operation, there is no violation of the Fourteenth Amendment if the group renting the facility excludes certain persons or groups from the entertainment it sponsors. The court insisted, however, that if a city park system provides separate parks for the races and fails to provide equal facilities in them, the Fourteenth Amendment is breached. More specifically, the court held that although there were seventeen parks for whites and four for blacks, there were golf courses in three of the white parks and none in the parks for Negroes. Consequently the latter must be permitted to use the golf courses in the white parks, at least on certain days, unless a separate course was constructed for their use.

Again, in *Muir* v. *Louisville Park Theatrical Association*[3] a United States court of appeals, in a *per curiam* ruling, sustained a lower court's finding that where a private association leased from the city an amphitheater in a park, and the city did not participate, directly or indirectly, in the operation of the public performance, the association was guilty of no discrimination offensive to the Fourteenth Amendment when it refused to admit Negroes.

As long ago as 1872 and 1873, the legislative assembly of the District of Columbia passed laws which forbade proprietors of ice cream par-

[1] 345 U.S. 91 (1951).
[2] 102 F. Supp. 525 (W.D. Ky. 1951).
[3] 202 F. 2d 275 (6th Cir. 1953).

lors, soft drink counters, barber shops, bath houses, restaurants, and bar-rooms to refuse sales or service to "any respectable, well-behaved person [because of] race, color or previous condition of servitude." By 1950 these enactments had long gone unenforced, and Washington was still a tightly segregated community.

In 1951, the aged Mary Church Terrell (she was nearing her ninetieth birthday), an Oberlin graduate, widow of Washington's first Negro judge, and daughter of Robert R. Church, a near-white wealthy real estate operator and influential Republican politician in Memphis in the 1880's and 1890's, determined to defy the city's unwritten rules against "mixed eating" in restaurants. When Mrs. Terrell, with two white friends and a black clergyman, was refused service in one of the establishments of the Thompson's Restaurant chain, suit was brought in their behalf. The case was argued by Charles H. Houston, a Howard University law professor and counsel for the NAACP, who resurrected the forgotten laws of the 1870's. The legal action in Mrs. Terrell's behalf was in fact initiated for her by the District's corporation counsel, and a vigorous friend-of-the-court brief was filed for her by the United States Department of Justice.

The Supreme Court rejected defense attorneys' pleas that the drastic change in the District's form of government (particularly as it affected the law-making power) in the intervening years rendered the rules obsolete; that Congress had unconstitutionally delegated to the District the power under which the antidiscrimination laws had been passed; and that the forgotten laws had, by decades of disuse, become dead letters. The Supreme Court's firm declaration that "well-behaved persons of color" could not be denied service was unanimous, and very shortly thereafter Washington's restaurants, hotels, motion picture theaters, swimming pools, and bowling alleys began to open their doors to Negroes. Though the legal collapse of segregation in the nation's capital was important enough to attract national and international attention, it was destined to enjoy only brief notice. Soon thereafter, the far more dramatic and pervasive ruling in *Brown* v. *Board of Education* and the companion case of *Bolling* v. *Sharpe* (affecting the District's schools, which on a constitutional technicality were not reached by the *Brown* decision itself) demolished the officially sanctioned foundations of segregated education—and, by implication, all other forms of publicly ordained segregation, as well—throughout the nation.

Following are some passages from the Thompson Restaurant decision:[1]

This is a criminal proceeding prosecuted by information against respondent for refusal to serve certain members of the Negro race at one of its restaurants

[1] *District of Columbia* v. *John R. Thompson Co.*, 346 U.S. 100 (1953).

in the District of Columbia solely on account of the race and color of those persons. The information is in four counts, . . . charging . . . violation[s] of . . . Act[s] of the Legislative Assembly of the District of Columbia, each [of which] makes it a crime to discriminate against a person on account of race or color or to refuse service to him on that ground. . . .

[6,7] We conclude that Congress had the authority under Art. I, #8, cl. 17 of the Constitution to delegate its lawmaking authority to the Legislative Assembly of the municipal corporation which was created by the Organic Act of 1871 and that the "rightful subjects of legislation" within the meaning of #18 of that Act was as broad as the police power of a state. . . .

It is our view that these anti-discrimination laws governing restaurants in the District are "police regulations" and acts "relatng to municipal affairs." . . . The laws which require equal service to all who eat in restaurants in the District are as local in character as laws regulating public health, schools, streets, and parks. Regulation of public eating and drinking establishments in the District has been delegated by Congress to the municipal government from the very beginning. In terms of the history of the District of Columbia there is indeed no subject of legislation more firmly identified with local affairs than the regulation of restaurants.

[13–15] There remains for consideration only whether the Acts of 1872 and 1873 were abandoned or repealed as a result of non-use and administrative practice. There was one view in the Court of Appeals that these laws are presently unenforceable for that reason. We do not agree. The failure of the executive branch to enforce a law does not result in its modification or repeal. . . . The Acts of 1872 and 1873 survived the intervening changes in the government of the District of Columbia and are presently enforceable. . . .

(7) THE STATE COURTS AND CIVIL RIGHTS, 1938–1954

While the federal courts moved with accelerating pace to make a reality of equal protection of the laws, state tribunals declined in influence as shapers of American social history. Compelled by the new judicial drift either to concurrence with the federal bench or to futile reaffirmation of legal principles now in eclipse, their role was steadily diminished, for the initiative had passed to the national judiciary. On some issues the differences that distinguished developments in constitutional doctrines in state courts were accounted for by geography and regional history, southern courts choosing the path of obstruction or delay, and northern courts following the national judiciary's lead. Upon a closer view, however, it appears that there were so many instances in which northern judges took "unprogressive" views and southern courts handed down "progressive" judgments, that the generalization was attenuated to the point of meaninglessness.

A. *Higher Education: Gains for Equal Protection*

In the realm of higher education many state courts did what they could to forestall the inevitable, but it made, in the end, little difference. A case in point was the Regional Compact[1] by which fourteen southern states had, without the consent of Congress (which is required by Article I, Section 10 of the United States Constitution for such interstate arrangements), entered into an agreement to acquire or create, and operate, special regional schools for Negroes, to be jointly owned by the states, to provide students with training in "professional, technological, scientific, literary and other fields."

In 1949 one Esther McCready, who met all the published requirements for admission to the University of Maryland's School of Nursing, was denied entrance because of her color, and was invited, instead, to enter Meharry Medical School in Nashville, one of the participating institutions in the Regional Compact, assisted by a state subsidy to make up the difference in cost to her between this expedient and the cost of attending the University of Maryland. She declined and the Maryland Court of Appeals, citing the *Gaines* case,[2] sustained her position. The court went so far as to concede that the facilities at Meharry were actually superior to those at Maryland, but concluded that the requirements of equal protection compelled the state to give her professional training in her own state.

Four months later came another ruling that helped to hasten the end of legal segregation in higher education, this time from Delaware's Court of Chancery. Brooks M. Parker and others had asked for an injunction to restrain the state from requiring applicants for admission to the University of Delaware to supply data concerning their race. The state was then referring black candidates to Delaware State College [for Negroes]. The court in a carefully formulated opinion, supported by statistical data, held that Delaware State was vastly inferior to the university, and that (on the basis of the *Sipuel, Sweatt,* and *McLaurin* cases cited on p. 272ff) the exclusion of blacks from the latter constituted a denial of equal protection of the laws.[3]

1 See above, p. 263.
2 See above, p. 271.
3 195 Md. 131, 73 A. 2d 8 (1950); and 31 Del. Ch. 381, 75 A. 2d 225 (1950).

I now consider whether . . . the College is equal to the University within the constitutional requirement that segregated facilities must be equal. [There follows a detailed comparison of such factors as per capita capital assets; curricula and richness and variety of courses; competence, experience and training of faculty; library resources; special services; maintenance; athletic facilities. The judge, who visited the two campuses and made the comparative study himself, then concludes:]

The College is woefully inferior to the University in the physical facilities available to and in the educational opportunities offered its undergraduates in the School of Arts and Sciences. In consequence, the State of Delaware is not providing these plaintiffs and others similarly situated with educational opportunities at the College which are equal to those provided at the University [and] the Trustees of the University by refusing to consider plaintiffs' applications because they are Negroes have violated the guarantee contained in the Equal Protection Clause of the United States Constitution. The plaintiffs are therefore entitled to a permanent injunction in accordance with the prayers of their complaint.

B. *Miscegenation: Challenging the Ban*

On the issue of interracial marriage and sexual relations between blacks and whites, southern state courts showed no disposition to relent, nor was there any pressure from the federal judiciary upon state courts to abandon traditional views on this point. But outside the South the newer jurisprudence was beginning to assert itself. In *Jackson* v. *State,* for example, the Alabama Court of Appeals had occasion to examine the constitutionality of Alabama constitutional and legal prohibitions against intermarriage and miscegenation. When a lower court had found a defendant guilty, he made petition for a rehearing on the plea that the laws in question violated the Fifth and Fourteenth amendments of the Constitution of the United States. In a very brief opinion, however, the Alabama Court of Appeals overruled the petition,[1] citing *Green* v. *State, Hoover* v. *State,* and *Pace and Cox* v. *State,*[2] as its authority for the established principle that antimiscegenation laws, so long as identical punishments were prescribed for both white and Negro offenders, were in harmony with the nation's Constitution. When a petition for certiorari was sent to the United States Supreme Court, that tribunal declined to question the state court's ruling.

Six years before the *Jackson* decision, however, the Supreme Court of California held, in these words, that the state's anti-interracial-marriage law violated the Constitution of the United States:[3]

[1] 72 So. 2d 114 (Ala. App. 1954).
[2] See above, pp. 85 and 95.
[3] *Perez* v. *Lippold,* 32 Cal. 2d 711, 198 P. 2d 17 (1948).

The regulation of marriage is considered a proper function of the state. . . . If the miscegenation law . . . employs a reasonable means to prevent [a social] evil, it is valid regardless of its incidental effect upon the conduct of particular religious groups. If, on the other hand, the law is discriminatory and irrational, its unconstitutionality restricts not only religious liberty but the liberty to marry as well. . . .

The right to marry is as fundamental as the right to send one's child to a particular school or the right to have offspring. . . . Legislation infringing such rights must be based upon more than prejudice . . . to comply with the constitutional requirements of due process and equal protection. . . . A state law prohibiting members of one race from marrying members of another race is not designed to meet a clear and present peril arising out of an emergency. . . . There are now so many persons in the United States of mixed ancestry that the tensions upon them are already diminishing. . . . For many years progress was slow in the dissipation of the insecurity that haunts racial minorities, for there are many who believe that their own security depends on its maintenance. Out of earnest belief, or out of irrational fears, they reason in a circle that such minorities are inferior in health, intelligence, and culture, and that this inferiority proves the need of the barriers of race prejudice. . . .

[In] the legislation in question . . . "there is absent the compelling justification which would be needed to sustain discrimination of that nature."

C. *Segregated Transportation Sustained*

The separation of the races in interstate travel on common carriers was still safe from judicial reprimand in some state courts. In *New* v. *Atlantic Greyhound Corporation*,[1] for example, Virginia's Supreme Court of Appeals decided that the lower trial court was correct in denying damages to a passenger who had been forcibly ejected from a bus after she had refused to move to the rear to give place to a white traveler. The court took the long-familiar position that so long as facilities were reasonably equal (as the record in this case showed they were), state statutes requiring segregation, and the carrier's own action in carrying them into execution, if accomplished without undue force or violence, were permissible. The court pointed out also that the *Morgan* case[2] did not apply to the present action, because that controversy had involved *interstate* commerce, whereas Mrs. New was traveling only between two points in Virginia. She had, however, contended that the rear seats in the bus were not equal to those up front; but the detailed record on this question satisfied the court that the two were equal enough because, after all, "it is impossible for the accommodations on a bus to be absolutely identical in all respects."

1 186 Va. 726, 43 S.E. 2d 872 (1947).
2 See above, p. 285.

Again, in *Commonwealth* v. *Carolina Coach Co. of Va.*, the same court made a similar ruling in these words:[1]

> By this legislation, no paramount rights or privileges are given to one race over the other. . . . It is not due to any discrimination, but to circumstances, applying alike to all . . . that a member of one race or the . . . other may under some conditions find no seating accommodation available.
>
> We find no discrimination against the enjoyment of fundamental rights and thus denial of the "equal protection of the law" when seating accommodations have been *bona fide* and fairly allotted alike to each race, if, because a greater number of one race seeks transportation upon the carrier than may be then fully accommodated in the space allotted their race, one has to stand and thus to undergo a minor inconvenience not then incurred by others.

D. *Residential Segregation Approved*

That state courts, North and South, saw no impediment to restrictive covenants in the federal Constitution is illustrated in these two cases: the first was the earlier stage of the case which later reached the United States Supreme Court as *Shelley* v. *Kraemer*[2]; the second was an opinion of the Supreme Court of Michigan. Said the Supreme Court of Missouri in examining the constitutional aspects of a restrictive covenant case:[3]

> Agreements restricting property from being transferred to or occupied by negroes have been consistently upheld by the courts of this state as one which the parties have the right to make and which is not contrary to public policy. . . . The restriction does not contravene the guaranties of civil rights of the Constitution of the United States. . . . Nor can it be claimed that the enforcement of such a restriction by court process amounts to action by the state itself in violation of the Fourteenth Amendment which relates to state action exclusively. To sustain such a claim would be to deny the parties to such an agreement one of the fundamental privileges of citizenship, access to the courts.

A few days after the Missouri Supreme Court handed down the *Kraemer* ruling, the Supreme Court of Michigan took a similar position in *Sipes* v. *McGhee*:[4]

> We have never hesitated to set aside a law which was repugnant to the equal protection clause of the amendment, but, on the other hand, we have never applied the constitutional prohibition to private relations and private contracts. . . .

[1] 192 Va. 745, 66 S.E. 2d 572 (1951).
[2] See above, p. 281.
[3] *Shelley* v. *Kraemer*, 355 Mo. 814, 198 S.W. 2d 679 (1946).
[4] 316 Mich. 614, 25 N.W. 2d 638 (1946).

> In this appeal we are obliged to differentiate between public rights and private or contractual rights. The former is unquestionably the responsibility of the State, but the action of the State court in requiring or refusing enforcement of private contractual rights is, in our opinion, not within the prohibitions of the 14th Amendment.

The United States Supreme Court's ruling in 1917 in *Buchanan* v. *Warley* had invalidated city ordinances prescribing residential segregation, but the practice continued, and state courts in the South sometimes struck it down in particular instances. The city of Winston-Salem, North Carolina, for example, passed an ordinance in 1930 which divided the city into zones and applied certain restrictions to them. For some of the zones the following rule was established: "No building or part thereof shall be occupied by persons of the Negro race"; and for the other zones the ordinance stipulated that "No building or part thereof shall be occupied or used by a person of the white race."

Plaintiffs were whites who had leased their houses to Negroes. City authorities had thereupon directed the Negro tenants of the houses to vacate, and the white owners sought a court order to restrain the city from enforcing the ordinance. The Supreme Court of North Carolina conceded that the areas assigned to the different races "are fairly located and equitably apportioned according to the respective percentage of each race as compared with the total population of the city," but still found the ordinance invalid.[1]

> The question for decision is whether reciprocal inhibitions of occupancy of residential districts by members of the white and Negro races, fairly apportioned, but admittedly invalid if they stood alone, may be inserted in a general zoning ordinance. . . . We think not. The law will not permit the indirect accomplishment of that which it directly forbids. . . .
>
> We are [also] presently concerned, as was the Court in the *Buchanan* case, with municipal restrictions upon the use and occupancy of property as affected solely by the racial status of the proposed occupant. The matter is regarded as beyond the reach of the police power. . . . "The reserved police power of the state must stop when it encroaches on the protection accorded the citizen by the Federal Constitution."

E. *Fair Trials*

Increasingly after 1935, but as yet not often, southern state courts protected the right to a fair trial for Negroes accused of crime. In *Rounds* v. *State*,[2] to take one example, the Supreme Court of Tennessee came to the rescue of a Negro sentenced to death for murder. He had

[1] *Clinard* v. *City of Winston-Salem*, 217 N.C. 119, 6 S.E. 2d 867 (1940).

[2] 171 Tenn. 511, 106 S.W. 2d 212 (1937).

appealed on the ground that his conviction stemmed from a confession extorted from him after he had been painfully mutilated and then questioned almost continuously from a Monday night until the following Friday morning, when he had become hysterical and made a "confession." The court held the confession inadmissible as evidence and reversed the judgment, and remanded the case for a new trial.

In *State* v. *Logan* a Negro convicted of murder by a jury from which Negroes had obviously been excluded, appealed to the Supreme Court of Missouri. The practice of selecting only white jurors had been the rule in the county for many years. At the time of Logan's trial in 1937 there were 8,311 blacks among the county's 46,178 inhabitants. The county's deputy sheriff had sworn that he had "gone out to get thirty good men" for the panel but knew no Negroes whom he thought qualified. He went on to say that he doubted that he would have selected Negro jurors even if he did know some "good" Negro men. The court remanded the case for a new trial.[1]

> It is not the law that the appellant was absolutely entitled to have negroes on the jury that tried him, or even on the panel from which that jury was drawn. It may happen that no negroes (or members of any other particular class of our citizens) will be on the regular panel for a given term of court, or on the special venire for a particular case. If that occurs in due course and good faith because of the ratio of white to negro population, or because of actual disqualifications, pure chance or the like, it is within the law; but if the defendant be deprived by design of the *chance* of having negroes on the jury which is to try him, the Federal Constitution may be invoked.

[1] 341 Mo. 1164, 111 S.W. 2d 110 (1937).

(8)

FEDERAL EXECUTIVE ACTION PROMOTING CIVIL RIGHTS, 1938–1954

The national judiciary was in this era the principal federal agent for promoting the Afro American's cause, but the executive branch also made a notable contribution. The Department of Justice, with its newly created Civil Rights Section, intensified the enforcement of existing statutes, pressed for additional legislation, and lent its skills and prestige, as "friend of the court," to Negro plaintiffs in cases before the Supreme Court. Even more important, the President, by means of executive orders and by his pressure upon legislative and administrative bodies, added impetus to the revolution in race relations now going forward.

The record of the legislative branch meanwhile was disappointing to black hopes. Repeated efforts were made, to be sure, to pass antilynching and anti-poll-tax bills, only to founder on Senate filibusters conducted by southern Democratic senators with the connivance of conservative northern Republicans.

At the close of the period five states (Alabama, Arkansas, Mississippi, Texas, and Virginia) still maintained the poll tax, but Florida (1941), Georgia (1945), South Carolina (1951), and Tennessee (1953) repealed their poll tax provisions, moved at least in part by the fear that congressional action might prove to be a prelude to still further federal policing of race relations. In 1942, for example, the House of Representatives passed anti-poll-tax laws four times by 2-to-1 majorities, only to see the measures stopped by Senate filibusters. Antilynching laws also failed of passage, but here too the prospect of their future enactment may presumably have been a major factor in the successful state and private efforts in the South which all but eliminated the evil.

Chief among the presidential executive orders which enlarged the Negro's freedom, security and opportunity were those relating to fair employment practices, to the establishment of a Civil Rights Commission, and to the desegregation of the armed forces.

Early in 1941, almost a year before Pearl Harbor, when the booming American defense industries were bringing full employment and high wages to the economy as a whole, blacks found themselves still waiting outside the factory gates. Their grievances and demands were eloquently articulated by A. Philip Randolph, president of the Brotherhood of Sleeping Car Porters, who undertook to organize a "March upon Washington," to take place on July 1, 1941. To avert the proposed pilgrimage, President Roosevelt issued his celebrated Executive Order 8802.[1]

EXECUTIVE ORDER 8802 (June 25, 1941)

REAFFIRMING POLICY OF FULL PARTICIPATION IN THE DEFENSE PROGRAM BY ALL PERSONS, REGARDLESS OF RACE, CREED, COLOR, OR NATIONAL ORIGIN, AND DIRECTING CERTAIN ACTION IN FURTHERANCE OF SAID POLICY

Whereas it is the policy of the United States to encourage full participation in the national defense program by all citizens of the United States,

[1] 6 *Federal Register,* 3109.

regardless of race, creed, color, or national origin, in the firm belief that the democratic way of life within the Nation can be defended successfully only with the help and support of all groups within its borders; and

Whereas there is evidence that available and needed workers have been barred from employment in industries engaged in defense production solely because of considerations of race, creed, color, or national origin, to the detriment of workers' morale and of national unity: Now, therefore, by virtue of the authority vested in me by the Constitution and the statutes, and as a prerequisite to the successful conduct of our national defense production effort, I do hereby reaffirm the policy of the United States that there shall be no discrimination in the employment of workers in defense industries or government because of race, creed, color, or national origin. . . .

And it is hereby ordered as follows:

1. All departments and agencies of the Government of the United States concerned with vocational and training programs for defense production shall take special measures appropriate to assure that such programs are administered without discrimination because of race, creed, color, or national origin;

2. All contracting agencies of the Government of the United States shall include in all defense contracts hereafter negotiated by them a provision obligating the contractor not to discriminate against any worker because of race, creed, color, or national origin;

3. There is established in the Office of Production Management a Committee on Fair Employment Practices, which shall consist of a chairman and four other members to be appointed by the President. The Committee shall receive and investigate complaints of discrimination in violation of the provisions of this order and shall take appropriate steps to redress grievances which it finds to be valid.

The wartime FEPC suffered from several crippling disabilities. Other government agencies largely ignored it; the committee was given no powers of enforcement and only the most miserly appropriations. And yet, while it was forced to rely upon moral suasion and public opinion for its authority, it managed, in its brief five-year existence, to deal with more than 10,000 complaints, with no small success. A number of northern plants completely erased the employment color line, and some southern plants eased their hiring practices rather than face charges by the FEPC. More important perhaps was its practical demonstration that government regulations could substantially reduce employment bias.

In 1951 President Truman created, by Executive Order No. 10308,[1] a Committee on Government Contract Compliance to handle complaints of alleged violations of nondiscrimination provisions in government contracts. Two years later President Eisenhower established a new Government Contracts Committee, which succeeded the 1951 agency and carried on its work on an expanded scale.

[1] 16 *Federal Register*, 12303.

Harry Truman used presidential authority in behalf of civil rights more vigorously than did any of his predecessors. In 1946 he established a Commission on Higher Education which included in its comprehensive report the warning that "there will be no fundamental correction of the total condition [of inadequacy in American higher education] until segregation legislation is repealed." More important was his establishment in the same year[1] of a Committee on Civil Rights, to which he assigned the task of publishing their findings and recommendations in a formal report. The resulting document, *To Secure These Rights,* supplied the nation with a searching 178-page appraisal of national shortcomings, called upon the federal government to take bold initiative in ending racial discrimination, and to realize this purpose urged the enactment of no less than twenty-seven measures.

The committee and its report made civil rights a paramount national issue. In February 1948, the President laid before Congress a comprehensive program of federal civil rights legislation, and the Democratic party, urged on especially by Senator Hubert H. Humphrey, incorporated a strong civil rights plank in its 1948 national platform.[2] Once again, however, the United States Senate proved to be the graveyard of the hopes of the reformers. The harvest was by no means inconsiderable, though, for a number of states began in earnest to enact very substantial civil rights statutes, and the American conscience had been aroused.

THE COMMITTEE'S RECOMMENDATIONS[3]

I. To Strengthen the Machinery for the Protection of Civil Rights, the President's Committee Recommends:

1. The reorganization of the Civil Rights Section of the Department of Justice to provide for: The establishment of regional offices; A substantial increase in its appropriation and staff to enable it to engage in more extensive research and to act more effectively to prevent civil rights violations; An increase in investigative action in the absence of complaints; The greater use of civil sanctions; Its elevation to the status of a full division in the Department of Justice.
2. The establishment within the FBI of a special unit of investigators trained in civil rights work.
3. The establishment by the state governments of law enforcement agencies comparable to the federal Civil Rights Section.

[1] Executive Order 9809, 11 *Federal Register,* 14153.

[2] See above, p. 246.

[3] A few minor or technical provisions, and some sections not directly related to Negro rights, are here omitted from this summary, which appears in *To Secure These Rights: The Report of the President's Committee on Civil Rights* (Washington: U.S. Government Printing Office, 1947), pp. 151–73.

4. The establishment of a permanent Commission on Civil Rights in the Executive Office of the President, preferably by Act of Congress; And the simultaneous creation of a Joint Standing Committee on Civil Rights in Congress.
5. The establishment by the states of permanent commissions on civil rights to parallel the work of the Federal Commission at the state level.
6. The increased professionalization of state and local police forces.

II. To Strengthen the Right to Safety and Security of the Person, the President's Committee Recommends:

1. The enactment by Congress of new legislation . . . which would impose the same liability on one person as is now imposed on two or more [anti-civil rights] conspirators. . . .
4. The enactment by Congress of a new statute, specifically directed against police brutality and related crimes.
5. The enactment by Congress of an antilynching act.
6. The enactment by Congress of a new criminal statute on involuntary servitude. . . .

III. To Strengthen the Right to Citizenship and Its Privileges, the President's Committee Recommends:

1. Action by the states or Congress to end poll taxes as a voting prerequisite.
2. The enactment by Congress of a statute protecting the right of qualified persons to participate in federal primaries and elections against interference by public officers and private persons.
3. The enactment by Congress of a statute protecting the right to qualify for, or participate in, federal or state primaries or elections against discriminatory action by state officers based on race or color, or depending on any other unreasonable classification of persons for voting purposes.
4. The enactment by Congress of legislation establishing local self-government for the District of Columbia; and the amendment of the Constitution to extend suffrage in presidential elections, and representation in Congress to District residents. . . .
6. The modification of the federal naturalization laws to permit the granting of citizenship without regard to the race, color, or national origin of applicants. . . .
9. The enactment by Congress of legislation, followed by appropriate administrative action, to end immediately all discrimination and segregation based on race, color, creed, or national origin, in the organization and activities of all branches of the Armed Services.
10. The enactment by Congress of legislation providing that no member of the armed forces shall be subject to discrimination of any kind by any public authority or place of public accommodation, recreation, transportation, or other service or business.

IV. To Strengthen the Right to Freedom of Conscience and Expression, the President's Committee Recommends:

1. The enactment by Congress and the state legislatures of legislation requiring all groups, which attempt to influence public opinion, to disclose the pertinent facts about themselves through systematic registration procedures.

V. To Strengthen the Right to Equality of Opportunity, the President's Committee Recommends:

1. In general:
   The elimination of segregation, based on race, color, creed, or national origin, from American life. The conditioning by Congress of all federal grants-in-aid and other forms of federal assistance to public or private agencies for any purpose on the absence of discrimination and segregation based on race, color, creed, or national origin.
2. For employment:
   The enactment of a federal Fair Employment Practice Act prohibiting all forms of discrimination in private employment, based on race, color, creed, or national origin; The enactment by the states of similar laws; The issuance by the President of a mandate against discrimination in government employment and the creation of adequate machinery to enforce this mandate.
3. For education:
   Enactment by the state legislatures of fair educational practice laws for public and private educational institutions, prohibiting discrimination in the admission and treatment of students based on race, color, creed, or national origin.
4. For housing:
   The enactment by the states of laws outlawing restrictive covenants; Renewed court attack, with intervention by the Department of Justice, upon restrictive covenants.
5. For health services:
   The enactment by the states of fair health practice statutes forbidding discrimination and segregation based on race, creed, color, or national origin, in the operation of public or private health facilities.
6. For public services:
   The enactment by Congress of a law stating that discrimination and segregation, based on race, color, creed, or national origin, in the rendering of all public services by the national government is contrary to public policy; The enactment by the states of similar laws; The establishment by act of Congress or executive order of a unit in the federal Bureau of the Budget to review the execution of all governmental programs, and the expenditures of all government funds, for compliance with the policy of nondiscrimination; The enactment by Congress of a law prohibiting discrimination or segregation, based on race, color, creed, or national origin, in interstate transportation and all the facilities thereof, to apply against both public officers and the employees of private transportation companies: The enactment by the states of laws guaranteeing equal access to places of public accommodation, broadly defined, for persons of all races, colors, creeds, and national origins.

7. For the District of Columbia:
   The enactment by Congress of legislation to accomplish the following purposes in the District; Prohibition of discrimination and segregation, based on race, color, creed, or national origin, in all public or publicly supported hospitals, parks, recreational facilities, housing projects, welfare agencies, penal institutions, and concessions on public property; The prohibition of segregation in the public school system of the District of Columbia; The establishment of a fair educational practice program directed against discrimination and segregation by public or private agencies, based on race, color, creed, or national origin, with respect to the training of doctors and nurses, the admission of patients to hospitals, clinics, and similar institutions, and the right of doctors and nurses to practice in hospitals; The outlawing of restrictive covenants; Guaranteeing equal access to places of public accommodation, broadly defined, to persons of all races, colors, creeds, and national origins.
8. The enactment by Congress of legislation ending the system of segregation in the Panama Canal Zone.

VI. TO RALLY THE AMERICAN PEOPLE TO THE SUPPORT OF A CONTINUING PROGRAM TO STRENGTHEN CIVIL RIGHTS, THE PRESIDENT'S COMMITTEE RECOMMENDS:

A long-term campaign of public education to inform the people of the civil rights to which they are entitled and which they owe to one another. . . .

On a single day in July 1948, President Truman issued two more unprecedented executive orders. One was a sweeping mandate that fair employment practices be universally instituted and scrupulously practiced in the United States government's civilian agencies; another sent out the word that discrimination in the armed forces was to cease forthwith.

At the end of World War II the wall of racial separation stood high and impenetrable in the military. The President hurled his bomb at the barriers on July 26, 1948. Although the full effectuation of the decree was to require seven years (and, therefore, the cooperation of Mr. Truman's successor), it was quickly apparent that the abrupt changeover would be an astonishing success, beyond the expectations of many of the most optimistic students of race relations.

It wrought, in fact, one of the most profound changes in American racial patterns since the Emancipation. As late as 1949, Negro servicemen were still rigorously segregated in 220 all-Negro units. In 1951 these outfits had been reduced to a mere fifteen, and in another four years there were none, for the whole military establishment had by then been fully integrated. Opportunities for earning officer commissions were thrown open to black soldiers, seamen, and airmen, and in a short time thousands of white enlisted men were commanded by Negroes who had surpassed them in the competition for commissions. Seven years after President Truman's startling directive, the Defense Department furnished this writer with a list of some fifty Negro colonels and lieutenant colonels assigned to virtually the entire range of staff and field commands. One Negro officer, Benjamin O. Davis, Jr., had by that time attained the rank of Brigadier General and served as Chief of Staff of the Twelfth United States Air Force.

The effect of this spectacular social transformation was not limited to the military community. The men who saw it work in their own units returned to civilian life with changed perspectives, wondering whether, if integration could be so quickly and smoothly achieved in the military, it would not also be easier to attain in civilian life than the nation had been prepared to expect.

EXECUTIVE ORDER 9981[1]

ESTABLISHING THE PRESIDENT'S COMMITTEE ON EQUALITY OF TREATMENT AND OPPORTUNITY IN THE ARMED FORCES

Whereas it is essential that there be maintained in the armed services of the United States the highest standards of democracy, with equality of treatment and opportunity for all those who serve in our country's defense:

Now, therefore, by virtue of the authority vested in me as President of the United States, by the Constitution and the statutes of the United States, and as Commander-in-Chief of the armed services, it is hereby ordered as follows:

1. It is hereby declared to be the policy of the President that there shall be equality of treatment and opportunity for all persons in the armed forces without regard to race, color, religion, or national origin. This policy shall be put into effect as rapidly as possible. . . . without impairing efficiency or morale.

2. There shall be created in the National Military Establishment an advisory committee to be known as the President's Committee on Equality of Treatment and Opportunity in the Armed Services, which shall be composed of seven members to be designated by the President.

3. The Committee is authorized on behalf of the President to examine the rules, procedures, and practices of the armed services in order to determine in what respect [these] may be altered or improved with a view to carrying out the policy of this order. The Committee shall confer and advise with the Secretary of Defense, the Secretary of the Army, the Secretary of the Navy, and the Secretary of the Air Force, and shall make such recommendations to the President . . . as in the judgment of the Committee will effectuate the policy hereof.

4. All executive departments and agencies of the Federal Government are authorized and directed to cooperate with the Committee in its work, and to furnish the Committee such information or the services of such persons as the Committee may require in the performance of its duties.

5. When requested by the Committee to do so, persons in the armed

[1] 13 *Federal Register* 4313.

services or in any of the executive departments and agencies of the Federal Government shall testify before the Committee and shall make available for the use of the Committee such documents and other information as the Committee may require.

6. The Committee shall continue to exist until such time as the President shall terminate its existence by Executive order.

Harry S. Truman

THE WHITE HOUSE
July 26, 1948

PART SIX

Progress, Stalemate, or Reaction? 1954–1970

THE *School Segregation* cases, far from producing a detente in the civil rights movement, were soon followed by startling escalation. The devices to frustrate or postpone the effectuation of the *Brown* decree, which are described in the following pages, brought a fateful shift as the 1950's waned. The struggle moved from its early principal reliance upon the familiar pattern of litigation and appeals to the country's conscience, to more insistent modes of entreaty edged with firmer resolution. On February 1, 1960, when four Negro college students began a sit-in demonstration at a ten-cent-store lunch counter in Greensboro, North Carolina, the civil rights drive turned a corner. Demonstrations, boycotts, sit-ins, though still peaceful and relatively unmarred by rages and rancors, replaced the lawsuits and petitions for legislation. They were replaced in turn by steadily rising clamors, in 1964–1965, from marching crusaders (whose clapping, chanting, and hymn-singing reassured apprehensive whites that this was still comfortably short of revolution) and by ever bolder ingressions into places of public resort from which they had lately been barred.

Mounting belligerence brought mounting resistance. A string of isolated and as yet, in 1970, unpunished murders of Negro activists stiffened the mood of aggrieved blacks and were soon paralleled by still angrier demonstrations, followed, in the "long hot summers" from 1965 forward, by rioting, arson, looting, and gunfire in the great inner-city ghettoes.

As tempers rose, the feebler Civil Rights Acts of 1957 and 1960 were succeeded by the more intensive acts of 1964 and 1965, which paradoxically, because they outlawed Jim Crow's most overt forms, had much the same effect upon the movement as did the disappointing pace of school desegregation and the growing sense of futility in the slums: another significant shift in battle lines. As rising expectations collided sharply with disappointed hopes, the younger leadership and its angry young followers pushed the crusade leftward, widening its agenda from regional to national objectives, particularly in the swarming ghettoes. The older directorate of the moderate majority found itself challenged by young hotspurs who rejected the traditional tactics of nonviolence about 1966 and took up the chant of "Black Power."

That electrifying slogan, all the more attractive for its ambiguities, won over recruits in sufficient numbers to force the old-line civil rights organizations to reinvigorate and, in some measure, to redesign their programs. Not the least astonishing element of the new radicalism was the impassioned cry of such firebrands as Stokely Carmichael, H. Rap Brown, Eldridge Cleaver, and James Forman, who urged blacks to mount "total revolution" *now,* with whatever violence was required to destroy "racism, capitalism, and imperialism" once and for all. Rejecting integration as a fraud, the insurgents preached varying degrees of separatism, some going even so far as to call for a separate Negro nation, on territory exclusively their own—a proposal which their foes quickly branded as racism-in-reverse. Whites were indignantly read out of the movement, and blacks were prodded toward implacable hostility to their oppressors.

With important exceptions, long-time champions of civil rights repudiated the tactics of the separatists, but many sympathetically conceded the reasonableness—from the frustrated black man's view—of salient elements in their position: blacks must find their identity without compromising themselves with white allies; black political power and self-confidence must be achieved by the organization and training of blacks, by blacks; their associations, their community power structure, their economic enterprises, their schools must be staffed and financed by blacks for blacks, and dedicated to black values instead of furthering the discredited white middle class standards. Only when this solidarity and tightly massed strength was attained could blacks, at last in a position to bargain from strength, reenter coalitions and resume cooperation with whites. But until that day, said a SNCC position paper, "the broad masses of black people [must] react to American society in the same manner as colonial people react to the West . . . that of the colonized toward the colonizer."

Meanwhile the more moderate (and still by an impressive margin the majority) elements in the struggle for full identity and self-realization still resisted joining in the angry, blanket indictment of American society. Still buoyed by faith in the country's professed ideals, still relying on the will and ability of whites to cooperate with blacks and, through private and government enterprise, to enable the black man to enter upon his full American inheritance, they deplored extremists who "alienated whites, divided Negroes, and confused everybody."

But rhetoric would not still the rising wind. The sharp confrontation of contending forces had at least the merit of clarifying the issues and educating both blacks and whites to the urgency of the crisis. The battle was joined. Yield a little or lose the whole thing, urged the moderates; justice for all or justice for nobody, shouted the militants, weary of unfulfilled promises.

By 1967, it was clear that the nation had found in the racial crisis (now so indissolubly fused with the crisis of poverty and decay in the cities that the two had become a single awesome problem) one of the thorniest dilemmas it had ever encountered. It was still, in 1970, a desperate choice between majority moderates and minority militants; and few doubted that if despair and futility continued to deepen in the cities, the hopeful majority could shrink to a minority, and the despairing minority would swell to a majority, with consequences that no one could contemplate with tranquillity.

The right to sit in the front of the bus, uninhibited access to restaurants and hotels, a choice of schools—these were no longer enough. Indeed, many blacks were even ready to admit that all the laws and court decisions and administrative rulings necessary to complete the revolution in race relations were already on the books. Now it remained for individuals, private groups, and communities to comply fully, honestly, without condescension, with their letter and spirit; to forswear racism and prejudice, and to make America at last "one nation, indivisible, with liberty and justice for all."

Whites, including not a few liberals, were hurt and angered when blacks continued to raise their demands after a decade and a half of civil rights victories in courts and legislatures had made concession after concession. They failed to understand that the concessions should not have been necessary in the first place, and that they had not, after all was said, made very much difference. The ultimate reason for seeking admission to unsegregated schools and buses and theaters had been the imputation of racial inferiority which segregation so clearly proclaimed. But after the courts decreed an end to segregation the implication was still there, even if it was somewhat less bluntly expressed. It was still echoed, all too plainly, in private and personal ostracisms and condescensions; in shabby employment opportunities; in inferior schools; in ghetto stores where shoddy merchandise was sold at inflated prices to a trapped black clientele; in the drab life of decaying tenements and filthy streets (half the housing in Harlem was built before 1900); in the "adversary relationship" between the police and slum residents; in the unavenged murder of civil rights workers, to say nothing of children at worship; in the cashiering of Congressman Powell as a congressional committee chairman: this and much more reminded the Negro, whatever the government might do to console him, of the low esteem in which he was still held by his white countrymen.

It was, moreover, precisely because there were notable improvements in some of the external conditions of their lives that many blacks, encouraged also by what scientists and writers and reformers were saying about the myth of race, felt their drooping spirits revive, and were drawn by the hope, and then the expectation, and finally to impatient demand that things could and must be much better still. As that mood deepened, disappointments and vexations were less cheerfully borne.

The grounds for exasperation were everywhere in evidence. Black Americans were still, sixteen years after *Brown*, massed in the ghettoes, or, if they were more fortunate, on hardscrabble little farms or in the poorer sections of lesser cities and towns. When at long last the public authorities assisted them in finding homes in the greener neighborhoods, whites fled before their advance, leaving them once again with predominantly Negro schools staffed by second-rate teachers. On the tenth anniversary of the *School Segregation* decisions only one percent of the South's black children were in schools that could show any degree of integration at all; and indeed, in the North in 1970 racial isolation in the schools was more extreme than it had been before 1954.

Unions were still blocking Negro membership, keeping closed the doors of employment in markets already all but closed to them by biased employers and their white workers. Wages were still only half those paid to whites for comparable work, and in some localities a great deal less than that; in fact, in some large segments of the black labor force, pay rates relative to those for whites were somewhat lower in 1965 than they had been in 1955. Unemployment rates for blacks were usually two or three times above the figures for the country as a whole, and in some ghetto communities reached as high as fifty percent of all employables. In 1960 the black infant mortality rate was two-thirds again as high as that for white babies; the maternal death rate for blacks was six times as high as that for whites; and the average Negro's life expectancy was six years less than his white countryman's. Though comprising 11 percent of the nation's population, the black race had only 4.6 percent of its college students, many of them concentrated in substandard all-Negro, or nearly all-Negro, southern institutions; and from 1960 to 1965 the average family income for blacks dropped 8 percent in the nation's larger cities while the national average for whites increased 14 percent.

The indictment could be endlessly extended. But because the theme of this volume is the progress of the civil rights movement, more particular notice is directed toward advances in special areas of black American life, conceding always that these were only hopeful auguries that the inequities we have just recited might be ameliorated in the future; they are in no sense intended to suggest that the Afro-American's struggle was nearly over.

The general outlines of the geographical setting were not encouraging. The years 1955–1970 saw a continuation and intensification of demographic trends that the previous decades had witnessed, and as in the past they brought for the Negro both perils and opportunity. In 1940 the nation's black population was three-fourths southern and still chiefly rural. In 1970 half of all Afro-Americans were in the North and two-thirds of all blacks were clustered in and around the nation's cities, where squalor and painfully narrow economic opportunity eroded the spirit.

Between 1960 and 1967, 3.7 million Negroes moved North and in 1968 they were still coming at the rate of 200,000 a year. Three cities already had black majorities: Washington, D.C. (66 percent), Gary, Indiana (55 percent), and Newark (51 percent), and demographers were predicting that eight more cities would join them by 1982: Baltimore, Chicago, Cleveland, Detroit, Oakland, Philadelphia, St. Louis, and Trenton. One in nine Americans was a Negro, and the proportion was rising, for a sixth of the babies born each year were black. Every week, two or three Chicago city blocks crossed the line from predominantly white to predominantly black, as residents spilled over the ghetto boundaries, as the birth rate soared, and as whites fled to the city's perimeter or the suburbs.

High unemployment in the inner cities; the domination by whites of enterprise in the slums, from grocery stores to savings banks and from brothels to numbers banks; restrictive membership policies of unions, and the preference in industry given to white workers tempted a distressing number of black youths to find solace in liquor or drugs, or to prove their manhood by sex or violence (chiefly against other Negroes) which others, more fortunate, could demonstrate by holding good jobs and supporting wives and children.

Indeed, while income levels for the race as a whole were rising, the economic plight of the Negro in the slums grew worse. In the middle 1960's a Department of Labor survey found that one in three ghetto blacks was either unemployed or submarginally employed, and that Negroes the country over possessed only a tiny fraction of the nation's professional, managerial, and skilled-trade jobs. Median family income was only 58 percent of that for white families, and much lower in the ghetto. A third of the country's blacks in 1970 were living in substandard homes, and more than a fifth of them had no home access to tubs or showers. More than a third of the country's 22 million Afro-Americans were in 1968 officially classed as poor, and only a third of these received public assistance, which was supplied with grudging parsimony by a nation spending 75 billions a year for defense and less than a tenth as much for welfare.

But there were glimmerings of a better future. For one thing, the *proportion* of Negro Americans living in ghettoes had stopped rising by 1967 and had begun a small decline. A report released by the Bureau of Labor Statistics and the Bureau of the Census in November 1968 disclosed also that 23 percent of the country's nonwhite families had incomes of $8,000 or more in 1966—up from a mere 13 percent in

1960—and in 1967 the proportion jumped to 27 percent. (These figures are expressed in 1967 constant dollars. It must be pointed out, however, that whites in the $8,000-and-over bracket were meanwhile increasing even faster.) The percentage in the group who lived below the government's official poverty line continued to shrink: from 55 percent in 1960 to 40 percent in 1966, and to 35 percent in 1967. Only 3 percent of married Negro men over twenty years of age were unemployed, and fewer blacks were dropping out of high school. Between 1960 and 1966 the median income of nonwhites rose about a third, while that of whites rose only a fifth.

In the central cities, where much of America's non-farm black labor is concentrated, the wage figures for the year 1967 show that among male workers in the professional and managerial class, blacks earned 65 percent as much as whites; in clerical and sales jobs they received 80 percent as much as whites; black factory operatives were paid 84 percent as much as whites; in crafts and foremen's jobs the figure was 79 percent; and for service workers, excluding household work, it was 75 percent. Though not equal to the average white wage of ten years earlier, the average pay of black Americans in the later 1960's was rising proportionately faster than the average white wage; the gap, in short, was slowly closing.

The educational gap was also narrowing; it was, in fact, down (from a full two years in 1960) to a scant half year in 1967, though the quality gap was still very large. In the late 1960's job recruiters for the nation's major corporations were scouting the Negro-dominated campuses for employees, and there was also an impressive movement of blacks from blue-collar to white-collar jobs. Between 1950 and 1960 blacks moved into professional and managerial jobs at twice the rate of whites (56 percent, compared with 27 percent); sales and clerical employees multiplied 38 percent while among whites they declined 2.7 percent. Not all of this was pure felicity, for increased opportunities created higher aspirations and expectations, only to produce new frustration in some quarters. In addition, it engendered growing alienation between the poor and the successful Afro-Americans, adding to the race problem a class problem as well.

At the end of 1966, 39 percent of black Americans lived in substandard housing (compared with 10 percent of whites); the percentage had been 44 percent in 1960. Another hopeful sign was the increasing interest of the business community, for reasons of enlightened self-interest, in improving the black man's condition. An aircraft factory built a plant near Watts, for example, hiring and training principally "unemployables"; and the life insurance industry in the middle sixties was pouring hundreds of millions into real estate in hard-core slums, where mortgage money was scarce.

The Civil Rights Acts of 1957, 1960, 1964, 1965, and 1968 made the right to vote essentially secure to the Negro for the first time, effectually doomed exclusion of blacks from public accommodations, and at least foreshadowed some decline in segregated housing. This was, of course, no small social transformation, contributing immensely to black morale and giving new impetus to the blacks' determination to persevere until full victory was achieved. The effect upon national and local political behavior was stunning. The "backlash" vote in 1966 and 1967, which swept some of the Negro's friends out of office and put Lester Maddox and the wife of George Wallace into governorships, and the defeat of Vice-President Humphrey in the presidential election of 1968 (while George Wallace carried five southern states, came close to carrying several more, and won a surprising number of ballots in the North) were keen disappointments to friends of civil rights. But against these defeats could be set an impressive score of triumphs.

Huge increases in Negro voter registration (as much as ten-fold or more in portions of some southern states, from 1964–1969) were matched by equally significant increase in actual voting. Immediately following the 1968 elections, a Bureau of the Census survey disclosed that 51.4 percent of the nonwhite population of voting age in the South cast ballots in the 1968 national election, compared with 44 percent in 1964, while the national average dropped from 69.3 percent to 67 percent. Enlarged office-holding by Negroes was a predictable consequence of these changes. In 1969 Massachusetts had a black United States senator, and nine blacks had seats in the United States House of Representatives. Recently *appointed* public officials included a justice of the United States Supreme Court, a member of the President's cabinet (who retired in January 1969), several high-level subcabinet officers and agency officials, and the chief executive for the city of Washington, D.C.

Early in 1969 there were 385 blacks holding elective public office in the eleven states of the old Confederacy alone. Curiously, Alabama stood first, with seventy-two, closely followed by four other traditionally hard-core segregationist states: Arkansas, Louisiana, Mississippi, and Georgia; while traditionally moderate North Carolina (where the 1968 election sent the first Negro to the General Assembly in a century) showed the smallest number. The new black legislator in North Carolina, Henry Frye, was an exception to the rule that nearly all of the black elected officeholders in the South were chosen in political units with black majorities.

At the close of 1969 *The New York Times* reported[1] that there were then more than 1,200 black elected officials in the nation. This figure

[1] *The New York Times,* Dec. 30, 1969, p. 18.

loses some of its force when it is accompanied by the observation that this number accounted for a mere fifth of one percent of all the officeholders in the country; but it should also be noted that the black membership in the United States House of Representatives was expected to rise from nine in 1969 to at least twenty-one in the early 1970's, bringing the black delegation in that chamber to five percent.

Of the 385 elected southern black public officials in 1969, 107 had been chosen in the November 1968 general election; of these twenty-seven were incumbents, while the other eighty either replaced whites or were elected to newly established posts. Typically the 107 were chosen at county or city levels, the largest single group being state legislators, chosen by county-wide constituencies. Georgia had fourteen black members in its 1969 state legislature. There were in 1969 some 126 black city councillors in southern cities. Of Alabama's seventy-two black officeholders in 1969, thirty were members of city councils, twenty-one were justices of the peace, six were school board members.

By 1969 several American cities had black mayors, among them Cleveland (Ohio), Gary (Indiana), and Compton (California). The latter is a suburb of Los Angeles, with a population of 80,000, more than 60 percent of whom are black. Washington, D.C., had a black chief executive, appointed by the President, and Los Angeles in the spring of 1969 came very close to electing a Negro mayor. Recent southern cities electing black mayors were Chapel Hill, North Carolina (a predominantly white, university town), and Fayette, Mississippi, whose black majority elected Charles Evers, the local head of the NAACP.[1]

Another measure of the black voters' growing authority in public decision-making was the rejection by the United States Senate of President Nixon's second nominee for a seat on the United States Supreme Court. His choice of Warren Burger as Chief Justice, although regretted by blacks and civil rights advocates, was confirmed. But the nomination of Clement F. Haynesworth as Associate Justice was so stoutly resisted by a combination of spokesmen for civil rights and labor that he failed to be confirmed. The ostensible grounds for his defeat was his alleged imprudence in failing to divest himself of financial holdings that could have impaired his objectivity on the bench. It was widely understood, however, that his past decisions affecting the aspirations of blacks and of organized labor were unacceptable to those powerful constituencies, and counted heavily against him.

Negroes were also becoming more visible in the entertainment world, in public relations, in advertising illustrations in magazines and on television, as newscasters, and as high church administrators. While such

[1] *Christian Science Monitor,* November 23, December 6, 1968; *The New York Times,* November 12, 1968, and January 1, 1969.

progress owed little to the new civil rights legislation, less conspicuous gains in these fields and others were appreciably helped by the laws. That the acts were being taken seriously by the government was attested by the fact that the Justice Department of the United States filed more than a hundred civil rights suits in fiscal 1967, and in 1968, 125 suits were instituted by the Department in behalf of school desegregation alone.

The effort to end discrimination in the schools continued to excite more public comment than did any other phase of civil rights endeavor. Ironically, just as the effort to end dual school systems began at last to register measurable successes, many blacks—and not a few whites—had begun to doubt that integrated schools were as important to disadvantaged blacks as *better* schools, regardless of the racial constituency. Militants as well as some moderates were in fact now talking of black schools for blacks, under black control.

Desegregation continued, however, to represent the goal of most civil libertarians and of the government itself. Statistics on the slow pace of integration in the South from 1954 to 1966 are all too familiar, as are figures on the intensification of racial isolation in the de facto segregation of the North. Less widely noticed was the strong upturn that began after the spring of 1967. A landmark decision of a United States court of appeals (Fifth Circuit) in *United States* v. *Jefferson County*[1] (March 29, 1967) and a half dozen cases consolidated with it, laid down clear standards for desegregation and bluntly decreed that the era of tokenism was over, that *"the only school desegregation plan that meets constitutional standards is one that works."* The ruling was followed, within a matter of weeks, by forty desegregation suits and greatly increased active negotiation between school districts and the Department of Health, Education, and Welfare. When the new fall school term began six months later, the proportion of Negro children in the South who were enrolled in desegregated schools (which HEW now defined as schools in which at least half the students were white) had risen to fourteen percent.

Another cluster of Supreme Court decisions, notably *Green* v. *New Kent County*[2] (Virginia), in June 1968, gave the movement still further impetus by striking yet another blow at the waning tokenism. Spurred by *Jefferson* and *New Kent County,* HEW abandoned the policy of accepting as adequate compliance a mere showing of measurable progress from year to year. The new formula required districts, if they were to remain eligible for federal funds, to submit plans which would produce complete desegregation by the fall of 1969 (in some cases 1970).

The 1968–69 school year opened with 20.3 percent of the Negro

[1] See below, p. 452.
[2] See below, p. 456.

school children in the eleven southern states in "fully integrated" schools, and the proportion continued to rise. In some of the states the figure was very much higher, but the slower change in Virginia, Alabama, and Mississippi pulled down the section's average. In HEW's "region 4," for example, comprising the states of South Carolina, Alabama, Mississippi, Florida, Georgia, and Tennessee, the Department entered negotiations with 560 school districts (which did not include districts desegregating under court-ordered plans precipitated by lawsuits). In the autumn of 1968, 118 of the 560 had already, by HEW standards, been "completely desegregated" for more than a year, and twenty-two others for something under a year. Plans had been submitted by 112 others, which if carried out in good faith would result in complete desegregation. Some 169 other districts were "in trouble" with HEW, eighty-three of which had already been cut off from federal funds, and eighty-nine more of which were soon to be if they did not promptly capitulate. The remaining 139 districts were still involved in HEW investigations and negotiations.

The Department reported that some 124 districts, all of them in the South, and most of them small, had elected to forego federal funds rather than desegregate, preferring to take their chances with later litigation and court-ordered desegregation. The progress of compliance was notably faster in areas working with HEW than in those which were under court-ordained programs. Among the devices most used by schools moving into complete compliance were those of eliminating a dual bus transportation system, assigning all pupils to schools nearest their homes, using formerly all-Negro schools for all pupils of both races for a particular grade (or grades), creating new geographical attendance zones, and closing small and substandard schools.

The surge of desegregation in the South owed much to the *Jefferson* and *New Kent County* rulings, and to HEW's increased vigor and tightened guidelines, but another important element was the initiative of local school officials, who took their courage in their hands and hired the best legal talent they could afford to help them submit plans to HEW that would accomplish the purpose. They worked, in some areas, against sharp public resistance. Indeed, so resentful was much of the general public, including many northerners, at guidelines and HEW that both major political parties in the 1968 general elections avoided the school desegregation issue, while George Wallace, the third party candidate, railed at it before cheering thousands.

In the North the more complex dilemma of de facto segregation was so resistant to resolution that local gains there were more than offset by local losses, and there was no net progress at all. Wedded to the neighborhood school principle, and unable, of course, to arrange mass transfers of population, not a few school authorities felt that the only "practical" plan was the cumbersome one of bussing children to schools remote from their own neighborhoods. Several urban centers turned to precisely that resort, only to confront a storm of criticism: from white parents who complained that the quality of education would suffer; from black *and* white parents who deplored the inconvenient, time-consuming, and costly transportation; from militant blacks because they had come to prefer their own schools, under their own control and dedicated to their own values, rather than yield to the suggestion that a good education was obtainable only in the company of whites.

There were other difficulties. Some cities, or major sections of cities, simply did not have a sufficient number of children of one or the other color to achieve real racial balance. In St. Louis, for instance, 70 percent of the city's public school children were black (in Washington, D.C., the figure was at least 95 percent), and racial balance was all but impossible to attain, no matter how, and how far, the minority of white children were deployed. St. Louis reportedly called upon the suburbs to lend them some white children, but none came forward.

Some northeastern states—New York, Massachusetts, and Connecticut in particular—enacted programs to promote racial balance and to outlaw de facto segregation, with results which at least one wry observer considered "about as effective as nailing Jello to a brick wall with a ten-inch spike." Such programs provided for the withholding of state funds from cities and towns with schools in which more than 50 percent of the pupils were nonwhites. In some instances they offered to help finance the closing of existing schools and the construction of others in new locations, where the effect would be to produce balance.

Berkeley, California, became in 1968 the first city in the nation with a considerable Negro population to achieve full desegregation by two-way, crosstown bussing. It was, in fact, a carefully designed scheme, involving widespread participation by local communities, and intensive, imaginative training of teachers and parents as well as children. Boldly committed to an ambitious and "conscious attempt to create within each classroom a microcosm of the community as a whole, a social organism integrated heterogeneously on the basis of race, sex, academic achievement, and economic status," the plan embraced sixteen schools enrolling 9,000 children, 3500 of whom were transported at a yearly cost of $200,000 (less than 1 percent of the school system's annual budget). Initial successes of the experiment promptly led several other cities—Galveston, Texas, Oklahoma City, and Pontiac, Michigan, among them—to begin moving toward a similar undertaking.[1]

The bussing of public school children or some equivalent of it is, of course, as old as segregated education itself. Whether by vehicles or on

[1] Ray Halpern, "Tactics for Integration," *Saturday Review,* 51 (December 21, 1968), 47–49, 66.

foot, Negro children especially, but also white children in a smaller measure, have been transported across town to *preserve* segregation for more than a century. Particularly when Negroes made up a small part of a city population, as was often the case, and when they were not confined to a single area, the maintenance of a separate school for black children necessitated their transportation for considerable distances. Not uncommonly, they passed by one or more white schools in the course of the twice-daily trip. Not surprisingly, the same urban whites who once insisted most loudly upon bussing to *maintain* segregation are now loudest, when it is proposed as a means of *ending* segregation, in condemning it on the ground of expense and because it causes serious inconvenience and a calamitous waste of time for children. There is a further argument, which is less frequently heard because of the past inequities that it implies, but is more passionately felt by white critics of bussing. Some people feel that the infusion of black pupils and teachers into "white" schools will lower the quality of the school's instructional program over the immediate future, as well as unsettle the social climate in the classroom, the playground, and the neighborhood.

Litigation and HEW pressure were not attempted until 1967 as means of breaking up northern de facto segregation; but that pattern, hitherto seemingly immune from the law, also began to dissolve when the Justice Department launched its first northern lawsuit against some suburbs south of Chicago in 1967, and when HEW, in October 1968, ordered Union Township, New Jersey (soon followed by Middletown, Ohio) to abandon its lily-white policies and to bring itself into full faith compliance with the Civil Rights Act of 1964 by December 14, 1968, or suffer the cutoff of federal funds.

The shifting of what was after all a small minority of the country's Negro children from formerly all black to formerly all white schools brought, of course, no startling improvement in the education of blacks; indeed, the transfer did not even begin in the North until 1968, and it was against discrimination in the North that the main thrust of the Negro's struggle was directed after 1965. There very little had been changed by court decisions and the Civil Rights Acts of 1957–1965, not only because de facto residential segregation had produced a dual school system even more difficult to break up than that in the South, but also because Negroes in the North had been voting and riding in the front of the bus and had had some access to public accommodations long before the liberating decisions and laws of the 1950's and 1960's.

As the year 1970 opened, the Department of Health, Education, and Welfare published the results of a survey of racial isolation in the country's public schools as it existed at the end of the 1968–1969 school year. By at least one criterion it found segregation to be almost as extensive in the North as in the South, and still very extensive in both, despite recent courtroom victories for desegregation. The survey provided, said Leon E. Panetta, director of HEW's civil rights division, "a stark portrayal of ethnic isolation in the schools."

In 32 northern and western states, 27.6 percent of Negro pupils attended desegregated, but predominantly white, schools in 1968–1969. In 11 southern states the figure was 18.4 percent, and for the nation it was 23.4 percent. But in the percentage of black children attending all-black schools, the regions showed a notable difference: 12.3 percent in the 32 northern and western states; 68 percent in the eleven southern states; 81.9 percent in the five states of the deep South: Alabama, Georgia, Louisiana, Mississippi, and South Carolina.[1]

Precisely at the time when this published report found its way into the public's hands, the news from the deep South made plain that if a similar survey were to be published a year later, covering the 1969–1970 school year, the statistics would be radically different. The Supreme Court's decision in *Alexander* v. *Holmes County* (October 29, 1969),[2] and the judgments of lower federal courts that immediately succeeded it, made that clear enough to prompt the Governor of Mississippi to acknowledge "We have been defeated. . . . We must accept the situation." Not only was the dismantling of the dual school system proceeding, at last, in the deep South with startling speed and thoroughness; but the process was also beginning at long last to make a significant beginning outside the South as a preliminary to a full-scale attack upon de facto segregation everywhere.

In America as a whole, the gains to which the preceding pages have alluded reached only a fraction of blacks, confined largely to the upper stratum, perhaps 20 percent, of the Afro-American population—those who had the means to move out of the congested inner cities, or who had a background of comparative affluence, family antecedents, education, or other social advantages that enabled them to merge by barely perceptible degrees into the fringes of the majority community. This one-sided distribution of benefits only depressed further the mood of the blighted or deteriorating sections of the cities, which contained another and larger minority of the race, perhaps 35 or 40 percent of the whole black population.

It was in the minority thus located that the combustibles of rebellion were accumulating, and to which the appeal of black nationalists and separatists was addressed, by none so effectively as Malcolm X, who understood perhaps better than anyone else the revolutionary potential of the black man who had given up hope. After his assassination it was Stokely Carmichael, Rap Brown, and Eldridge Cleaver whose Black

[1] *Christian Science Monitor*, January 7, 1970.

[2] *Alexander* v. *Holmes County Board of Education*, United States Supreme Court, No. 632, October Term, 1969; 38 LW 3161.

Power crusade most successfully stimulated the mounting rage of the ghetto. Their leadership caused more and more of its residents to feel that, with nothing to lose, their best response to oppression was a desperate lunge for freedom even if defeat could mean laying waste the society which denied them their birthright.

Perhaps nothing made the shallow penetration of recent progress more apparent, to those who were willing to see it, than the habit of the popular press of reporting Negro "firsts": the first Negro "regulars" on television shows; the first members of boards of trustees and directors of foundations or corporations; the first faculty members of leading universities; the first holders of major governmental posts; the first Negro sheriffs; the first editors on leading magazine and newspaper staffs; the first business executives, hospital directors, and public relations officers. Conservatives cited these instances as proof that Afro-American life was now truly entering the mainstream; others pointed out that even where such promotions were not mere gestures of tokenism, the bare fact that such stories were still prime news was itself the strongest proof that all of this was, as yet, only a matter of tiny junctures, at widely separated points, which gradually fed a miniscule fraction of blacks, largely from the middle class, into tributaries flowing toward the mainstream. But, of course, they *were* beginnings and seemed at least to promise broader, deeper, and swifter streams on which social change would later be borne.

The growing big-city Negro response to Black Power and cultural separatism compelled the older civil rights organizations like the NAACP and the Urban League to revise their programs with a view to holding their following—in 1970 they still had the majority on their side—for the less revolutionary goals of integration and an open society. There was less emphasis, at least for the time being, on the more familiar program of salvation by laws and by parley, in favor of pushing for greater black self-determination in all the aspects of ghetto life and a greater pride in the race and its achievements, both here and now and in the remote African past. This development was further prospered by the steady withdrawal of white support, financial and moral, that resulted in part from the assumption on the part of old friends of Negro advance that all the necessary legal remedies to cure black grievances were now in hand, and in part as a reaction, or "backlash," to growing violence, intensified demands, and the insistent cry of Black Power.

In some sense the burgeoning militance was in itself evidence that blacks were moving upward, for it was the gains of the previous fifteen years that had generated rising expectations. Moreover, these gains, buttressed by changes in the attitudes of both blacks and whites, added to the Negro's power, leverage, and self-trust. The Negro had, in short, more pride and confidence in his group and its cause; and whites in growing numbers, especially among the educated class where the public philosophy is formulated—whatever its distortions when it has filtered down to the millions—had a growing respect for their black countrymen and their goals, and a livelier sympathy for their distresses. This evolution was slowed somewhat, perhaps, by the disposition of both sides to take stronger stands; but in this process of polarization, while the adamant became more adamant, the sympathetic more sympathetic, the issues were more clearly drawn and were in growing measure, at least in some important quarters, debated on their merits rather than *ad hominem* in a conflict of passions.

The debate was not, admittedly, an unmixed boon to the black man's cause, for it divided the leaders and split the masses into factions, hopelessly divided over questions of strategy, ultimate goals, and timetables. A case in point was the ill-starred Poor People's Campaign in the summer of 1967, which evoked strong reactions among both blacks and whites, ranging from perfervid support to derision, and which disintegrated in the mud of Resurrection City.

The deepened pride of race, engendered after 1966 by the Black Power and "think-black" vogues (with their "Afro" clothing and hair styles, and their "soul" music and food) helped, however, to draw blacks closer together around a shared heritage, and to undermine the old theory, dear to the hearts of white supremacy spokesmen, that the Negro was less the victim of white exploitation than of his own "self-hatred." Indeed, some whites even hoped that the think-black cult, the upsurge of pride in things African and Afro-American, would replace the presumed self-hatred with a new creative self-love, which might render blacks content to live in self-imposed sequestration and thus hold off the social, cultural, and biological miscegenation that white (to say nothing of black) conservatives had so long feared.

The conclusions of the Kerner Commission Report seemed to a number of blacks to place the blame for their woes upon whites, and to demonstrate that majority white opinion was still incorrigibly committed to white supremacy and a racist society, destined for the long future to continue as "two Americas." From that premise it was an easy step to the inference that it was futile to look for truly significant voluntary concessions from whites, or to hope for a genuinely successful open society in which Negroes could rise in fair competition with whites. Such a conclusion counseled continued and increasing pressure on the oppressors and colossal public expenditure (which the Report in fact urged) to end poverty and squalor in the cities. Worried whites, on the other hand, saw all too clearly that what blacks wanted and the Commission recommended would cost far more in taxpayers' dollars than did the more traditional civil rights gains of the 1950's and 1960's. When to such considerations were added the recollections of three summers of violence and the awesome turbulence following Martin Luther King's murder in April 1968, an understandable shift in the thinking of many whites in the direction of stability, and a truce in racial contentions resulted.

Perhaps in the future, if and when the agonizing American dilemma is solved, the record will show that the changing laws and the exertions of government from 1863 to 1970 which this book records will have brought the country to the end of the first stage of the dilemma's resolution. The next may well be, as some have suggested, the bringing of private conduct abreast of conscience, the Constitution, and the laws. Revolutions are first made in men's minds; and then the laborious and often painful task of adjusting objective conditions to the new insights and values supplies the more readily observable materials, the external changes, out of which historians compound their narratives.

Perhaps it was still too optimistic to say in 1970 that deep, subterranean shifts in white opinion were at work that would finish the task. Certainly there was evidence that there were steady recruits, especially among those who mold the opinions of the millions, to the more scientific and humanitarian conceptions of race. There was beyond question a vastly increased number of Americans with a firmer understanding of the plight of their beleaguered black countrymen. One could point, for example, to the contribution to the public enlightenment by the enormous sales of such books as the *Autobiography of Malcolm X;* Claude Brown's *Manchild in the Promised Land; Black Rage,* by William H. Grier and Price M. Cobb; and Eldridge Cleaver's *Soul on Ice.* Where the degradation of the black man had so long been accounted for in terms of his inner deficiencies, it was now being explained by his psychological emasculation and the brutalizing rebuffs that had for three centuries of life in America fettered his mind and spirit.

(1)

RACIAL IDEOLOGY: CONSERVATIVES, MODERATES, AND MILITANTS

It soon became clear that the *Brown* decision, and its growing acceptance by judges and policy makers, was immense with promise for black Americans—but promise whose redemption would be long de-

In the modern West, certain physiological characteristics have been selected as diagnostic and people who bear sufficient of these characteristics are set aside as a special group, called a "race". . . .

. . . "Race" is or has recently been a concept used by some societies in the modern world to create and maintain pariah situations. Scientific men of good will have spent many hours and many words trying to determine whether racial differences are in fact accompanied by differences in intellect, cultural capacity, and the like. They might have saved much of that effort had they mustered the courage to face squarely the fact that "race" is not scientifically definable. They could have saved it all if they had refused to care whether it is so or not. . . .

Race is a folk concept, not an analytical concept. Like most folk concepts, its scientific validity is beside the point of its power to move people. Science can be used and misused to "prove" anything at all about the matter—yet science stands aloof because the only thing it has proved is that "race" is not a useable scientific category or concept.

Races, however, exist. Races are social categories based on observable physical differences. The differences are observable anywhere, by all normal people—even though "race" as a concept is not widespread.

"Race" in modern Europe—right down to the Nazi era—has had to do with class. During the Nazi era, it was perverted to create or prolong a pariah situation. Race in North America has been used to create a pariah situation out of a particular form of institutionalized servility, the Southern plantation system. . . .

Pariahs are persons who are not admitted to the rank systems or even the servile institutions of a society. Rather they exist outside that system and may even, within their own group, maintain rank organizations that reflect those of the major society. Pariah groups may be outcastes as in India, economically underprivileged kinship groups as on the Northwest Coast, or races in the modern United States. "Race" is the modern Western idiom for pariah groups.

The concept of race, interestingly and alarmingly enough, has never, so far as I know, been the subject matter of ethnographic surveys or cross-cultural analysis. Our own ideas of race have been so firm that we have not been able to question them in the light of someone else's ideas about physical differences. . . .

Nearly all of the major, and most of the minor (including some of the most evangelical and fundamentalist), church bodies in the country had by 1965 gone on record as endorsing full justice to the Negro, as a religious duty. And, again, here as in the civil community, the rank and file membership lagged behind the leadership in living up to these exhortations, but the shift of attitude on the part of millions of church members was readily apparent. The General Assembly of the National Council of Churches, for example, in a position paper in 1963—well in advance of the membership of its constituent bodies—opened its statement with this declaration:[1]

[1] General Assembly of the National Council of Churches, "Positive Paper," *Christian Century* (Chicago: Christian Century Foundation, December 18, 1963), p. 153. Copyright © 1963 by the Christian Century Foundation. Reprinted by permission of the publisher.

THIS GENERAL ASSEMBLY of the National Council of Churches is thankful for the increasing evidences that a new pattern of race relations is being established in our nation and that its constituent communions, their pastors, congregations and members all over the land, have been stirred as never before to act for justice, freedom and equality for Negroes and all other racial minorities.

We would be the first to admit that both the actions and their results have been insufficient either fully to reflect the imperatives of the Gospel or to meet the racial crisis as it develops in the nation. Recognizing that the National Council of Churches has not yet achieved in its own life and organization full implementation of its often reiterated pronouncements for racial justice and equality, this Assembly nevertheless dares once more to address an appeal to all Churches and Christians. For we believe that the Church of Jesus Christ is commanded by its Lord to rid itself of all those forms of racial injustice which have been perpetuated through the years by us all in our Churches, church organizations, agencies and institutions. With full realization that the speed of accomplishment will vary from place to place, and with thanksgiving to God for all that has already been done, we call upon national church bodies and local congregations throughout the United States to initiate specific actions now, where such actions have not already been initiated, to achieve the following objectives:

This call to action was followed by ten specific proposals, calling upon "all Christian Churches" to (1) open all churches to members from every race; (2) foster fellowship and interchange of membership between persons of all races; (3) recruit pastors, congregational secretaries, teachers, and musicians, without regard to race; (4) select, for their schools, textbooks and other instructional materials which promote racial equality and amity; (5) accelerate the integration of their hospitals and other social welfare agencies; (6) withdraw all investments from enterprises which permit racial discrimination; (7) let contracts for construction only with contractors committed to merit employment; (8) press for enactment and full enforcement of civil rights legislation at all levels of government; (9) support the civil rights organizations; (10) "remember always to act in love and without hate or bitterness, seeking always reconciliation in the church, community and nation as our new pattern of justice is being established."

The television networks made an incalculable contribution to public enlightenment on the racial issue simply by supplying extensive spot-news coverage of racial strife. The spectacle of "Bull" Connor, for example, setting his dogs upon voting registration workers, or of an enraged Lester Maddox driving young theological students from the Pickrick Restaurant with ax handles, could hardly fail to bring in converts to the cause. Television also devoted a great deal of prime time to documentaries and other presentations (like the 1963 March on Washington, and the Martin Luther King funeral in 1968) concerning the Negro's plight and the crusade to resolve it. In 1968, to take an impressive instance, the Columbia Broadcasting System offered a seven-part series, "Of Black America," over a period of months. The last in the series, "A Portrait in Black and White," aired on September 2, dealt with racial attitudes across America and suggested the conclusion that racial animosity was declining.

Basing its judgments on a carefully conducted poll of May and June, 1968, the film reported that while half of the whites surveyed still opposed social equality and integration, only a third professed hostility to blacks; and a majority of both whites and blacks opposed formal separation of the races. Both races agreed that full racial equality would eventually be achieved in the United States, and a majority of the Negroes expressed the belief that it would come in less than fifty years.

But to say that the prevailing American creed rejected racism is one thing; to assume that all but a handful of Americans conducted themselves accordingly would be another. Although there was widespread dissent from the findings of the Kerner Commission Report, on the appalling racial violence in the summer of 1967, that massive document was a sober reminder that the new racial attitudes had not cast out old fears and antipathies.[1]

SUMMARY OF REPORT

INTRODUCTION

The summer of 1967 again brought racial disorders to American cities, and with them shock, fear and bewilderment to the nation.

The worst came during a 2-week period in July, first in Newark and then in Detroit. Each set off a chain reaction in neighboring communities.

On July 28, 1967, the President of the United States established this Commission and directed us to answer three basic questions:

What happened?

Why did it happen?

What can be done to prevent it from happening again?

To respond to these questions, we have undertaken a broad range of studies and investigations. We have visited the riot cities; we have heard many witnesses; we have sought the counsel of experts across the country.

This is our basic conclusion: Our nation is moving toward two societies, one black, one white—separate and unequal.

Reaction to last summer's disorders has quickened the movement and deepened the division. Discrimination and segregation have long permeated much of American life; they now threaten the future of every American.

This deepening racial division is not inevitable. The movement apart can be reversed. Choice is still possible. Our principal task is to define that choice and to press for a national resolution.

[1] *Report of National Advisory Commission on Civil Disorders* (Washington, 1968). This volume is popularly known as the "Kerner Commission Report." The passage quoted is from pages 1 and 2 of the official edition, published on March 1, 1968.

To pursue our present course will involve the continuing polarization of the American community and, ultimately, the destruction of basic democratic values.

The alternative is not blind repression or capitulation to lawlessness. It is the realization of common opportunities for all within a single society.

This alternative will require a commitment to national action—compassionate, massive, and sustained, backed by the resources of the most powerful and the richest nation on this earth. From every American it will require new attitudes, new understanding, and, above all, new will.

The vital needs of the nation must be met; hard choices must be made, and, if necessary, new taxes enacted.

Violence cannot build a better society. Disruption and disorder nourish repression, not justice. They strike at the freedom of every citizen. The community cannot—it will not—tolerate coercion and mob rule.

Violence and destruction must be ended—in the streets of the ghetto and in the lives of people.

Segregation and poverty have created in the racial ghetto a destructive environment totally unknown to most white Americans.

What white Americans have never fully understood—but what the Negro can never forget—is that white society is deeply implicated in the ghetto. White institutions created it, white institutions maintain it, and white society condones it.

It is time now to turn with all the purpose at our command to the major unfinished business of this nation. It is time to adopt strategies for action that will produce quick and visible progress. It is time to make good the promises of American democracy to all citizens—urban and rural, white and black, Spanish-surname, American Indian, and every minority group.

Our recommendations embrace three basic principles:

- To mount programs on a scale equal to the dimension of the problems;
- To aim these programs for high impact in the immediate future in order to close the gap between promise and performance;
- To undertake new initiatives and experiments that can change the system of failure and frustration that now dominates the ghetto and weakens our society.

These programs will require unprecedented levels of funding and performance, but they neither probe deeper nor demand more than the problems which called them forth. There can be no higher priority for national action and no higher claim on the nation's conscience.

We issue this Report now, four months before the date called for by the President. Much remains that can be learned. Continued study is essential.

As Commissioners we have worked together with a sense of the greatest urgency and have sought to compose whatever differences exist among us. Some differences remain. But the gravity of the problem and the pressing need for action are too clear to allow further delay in the issuance of this Report.

Even humor was enlisted in the cause. One of the most widely noticed examples was Harry Golden's straight-faced jest, first published in 1956, that the Golden Vertical Plan would at last solve the problem. The South, he argued, had long ago grown accustomed to the vertical Negro. The race's twenty-billion-dollar buying power had seen to that, since it brought blacks into supermarkets and banks, into ten-cent-stores and department stores, where, on foot, they mingled freely with whites. It was only when blacks sit down with whites, said Golden, that "the fur begins to fly." The solution was easy:[1]

Instead of all those complicated proposals [for dealing with the *Brown* Decision], all the next session [of the legislature] needs to do is pass one small amendment which would provide only desks in all the public schools of our state—no seats.

The desks should be those standing-up jobs, like the old-fashioned book-keeping desk. Since no one in the South pays the slightest attention to a VERTICAL NEGRO, this will completely solve our problem. And it is not such a terrible inconvenience for young people to stand up during their class-room studies. In fact, this may be a blessing in disguise. They are not learning to read sitting down, anyway; maybe standing up will help. This will save more millions of dollars in the cost of our remedial English course when the kids enter college. In whatever direction you look with the GOLDEN VERTICAL NEGRO PLAN, you save millions of dollars, to say nothing of eliminating for-ever any danger to our public education system upon which rests the destiny, hopes, and happiness of this society.

The most eloquent—and to millions of Americans, black and white, the most beloved—voice for nonviolence as the way to the Negro's social redemption was Dr. Martin Luther King, Jr., a young Baptist pastor, leader of the Southern Christian Leadership Conference, and recipient of the Nobel Peace Prize in 1964. As the militancy of the younger generation of blacks steadily rose, and his own influence for moderation dwindled in the year or two before his assassination in April 1968, he began to move toward a heavier reliance upon economic pressure through boycotts and strikes than his program had earlier contemplated. But the dominant note of his appeal during most of his remarkable career was "strength through love." One characteristic statement of this emphasis is the following:[2]

The Negro, once a helpless child, has now grown up politically, culturally, and economically. Many white men fear retaliation. The job of the Negro is to show them that they have nothing to fear, that the Negro understands and forgives and is ready to forget the past. He must convince the white man that all he seeks is justice, *for both himself and the white man.* A mass movement exercising nonviolence is an object lesson in power under discipline, a demonstration to the white community that if such a movement attained a degree of strength, it would use its power creatively and not vengefully.

Nonviolence can touch men where the law cannot reach them. When the law regulates behavior it plays an indirect part in molding public sentiment. The enforcement of the law is itself a form of peaceful persuasion. But the law needs help. The courts can order desegregation of the public schools.

[1] Harry Golden, *The Best of Harry Golden* (Cleveland: World Publishing Compan, 1967), p. 220. Reprinted by permission of the publisher and the author.

[2] Martin Luther King, Jr., *Stride Toward Freedom* (New York: Harper & Row, 1958) pp. 215–16. Copyright © 1958 by Martin Luther King, Jr. Reprinted by permission of the publishers.

But what can be done to mitigate the fears, to disperse the hatred, violence, and irrationality gathered around school integration, to take the initiative out of the hands of racial demagogues, to release respect for the law? In the end, for laws to be obeyed, men must believe they are right.

Here nonviolence comes in as the ultimate form of persuasion. It is the method which seeks to implement the just law by appealing to the conscience of the great decent majority who through blindness, fear, pride, or irrationality have allowed their consciences to sleep.

The nonviolent resisters can summarize their message in the following simple terms: We will take direct action against injustice without waiting for other agencies to act. We will not obey unjust laws or submit to unjust practices. We do this peacefully, openly, cheerfully because our aim is to persuade. We adopt the means of nonviolence because our end is a community at peace with itself. We will try to persuade with our words, but if our words fail, we will try to persuade with our acts. We will always be willing to talk and seek fair compromise, but we are ready to suffer when necessary and even risk our lives to become witnesses to the truth as we see it.

The way of nonviolence means a willingness to suffer and sacrifice. It may mean going to jail. If such is the case the resister must be willing to fill the jail houses of the South. It may even mean physical death. But if physical death is the price that a man must pay to free his children and his white brethren from a permanent death of the spirit, then nothing could be more redemptive.

Seldom was the country so deeply moved by an expression of the Negro's protest and aspiration as it was on the occasion of the huge March on Washington, August 28, 1963, when 200,000 Americans, including many whites, met in the nation's capital, on the mall before the Lincoln Memorial to mark the centennial of the Emancipation with "a living petition." Dr. King was among the speakers heard by the earnest and orderly throng—and by millions more on radio and television—thousands of whom wept at his words:[1]

. . . I say to you today, my friends, even though we face the difficulties of today and tomorrow, I still have a dream. It is a dream deeply rooted in the American dream. I have a dream that one day this nation will rise up and live out the true meaning of its creed: "We hold these truths to be self-evident that all men are created equal."

I have a dream that one day on the red hills of Georgia the sons of former slaves and the sons of former slaveowners will be able to sit down together at the table of brotherhood.

I have a dream that one day even the State of Mississippi, a state sweltering with the heat of injustice, sweltering with the heat of oppression will be transformed into an oasis of freedom and justice. I have a dream that my four little children will one day live in a nation where they will not be judged by the color of their skin but by the content of their character. I have a dream today.

[1] A copy of the speech appears in *Speeches of the Leaders; The March on Washington for Jobs and Freedom, August 28, 1963* (New York: NAACP, n.p.). Copyright © 1963 Martin Luther King, Jr. Reprinted by permission of Mrs. Martin Luther King, Jr. and Joan Daves.

I have a dream that one day down in Alabama with its vicious racists, with its Governor having his lips drip with the words of interposition and nullification—one day right there in Alabama, little black boys and black girls will be able to join hands with little white boys and girls as sisters and brothers.
I have a dream today.
I have a dream that one day every valley shall be exalted, every hill and mountain shall be made low, the rough places will be made plain and the crooked places will be made straight, and the glory of the Lord shall be revealed, and all flesh shall see it together.
This is our hope. This is the faith that I go back to the South with. With this faith we will be able to hew out of the mountain of despair a stone of hope. With this faith we will be able to transform the jangling discords of our nation into a beautiful symphony of brotherhood. With this faith we will be able to work together, to pray together, to struggle together, to go to jail together, to stand up for freedom together, knowing that we will be free one day.

The oldest, and in 1970 still the largest, of the civil rights organizations was the half-million-member NAACP. In achieving for blacks the protection of the laws, it was also still the most successful of the civil rights groups; but this was no longer sufficient to win for it the degree of support it had once enjoyed. It lost ground especially among the new generation of angry young blacks. Still led in the 1960's by its soft-spoken, cultivated, and keenly intelligent executive secretary, Roy Wilkins, the organization was worried by thunder from the left, while it held to its time-tested tactics of insisting, particularly in the courts, that the Constitution and the laws be both faithfully enforced and, when they proved inadequate, amended and amplified. Harassed from the outside by critics in the more militant organizations, the association was also bedeviled by the Young Turks within its own ranks, insurgents who leaned to the Black Power concept and loudly insisted that the traditional NAACP recourse to legislation, litigation, and interracial cooperation was no longer adequate for the new day. Once again, in its 1968 annual convention, the "revolt" was beaten back by the moderate majority, but the group was clearly, if cautiously, moving to a wider and more aggressive agenda.

The split in the association's ranks was again vividly dramatized in October, 1968, when its Board of Directors fired Lewis M. Steel, a (white) member of the NAACP's legal staff, who had publicly castigated the United States Supreme Court for its "racist" philosophy and its allegedly perfunctory effectuation of the 1954 *Brown* decree in the litigation that came before the Court in the succeeding decade and a half.[1] Steel's dismissal was promptly followed by the unanimous protest of the rest of the legal staff, who resigned *en masse*.

Prompted by the demands of some of the organization's young fire eaters that the group should fight hard on many fronts, including a mas-

[1] See below, p. 429.

sive assault upon President Johnson's Viet Nam policy, the following resolution by the NAACP's Board of Directors illustrated the group's orientation on the eve of the "long, hot summer" of 1967:[1]

. . . The NAACP knows that civil rights battles will have to be fought and won on their own merits, irrespective of the state of war or peace in the world. For nearly 60 years, under nine national administrations, in periods of depression and of prosperity, through two World Wars, the Korean War and now the War in Viet Nam, the NAACP has consistently and uncompromisingly stuck to the job for which it was organized.

We are not a peace organization nor a foreign policy association. We are a civil rights organization. The NAACP remains committed to its primary goal of eliminating all forms of racial discrimination and achieving equal rights and equal opportunities for all Americans.

Therefore, we shall continue to concentrate on efforts to secure enactment of the 1967 civil rights bill, including fair housing legislation and Federal protection of civil rights workers; to combat the defiance against Federal school desegregation decrees; to obtain new job opportunities for Negro workers; to protect Negro consumers from exploitative ghetto merchants; to eliminate slum conditions; to correct inequities in the Selective Service; and to dismantle the whole sinister structure of Jim Crow.

In the following editorial in its official organ, in November 1968, the association's leadership set forth its position with respect to the new and militant separatists of the Black Power, Black Panther, and similar groups who urged blacks to revolution.[2]

The deepening schism within the Negro community over tactics and goals, gleefully fostered and distorted by insensitive and irresponsible news media, is headed toward a major internal crisis requiring each of us to stand up and be counted. Differences among black folk in this country are not new, but a new ingredient has been added—the attempt by a small minority of black extremists to force compliance with its views and tactics. This nihilistic minority professes disdain for all "white" values while at the same time invoking and utilizing, as instruments of controversy, the worst practices of the most benighted stratum of white society, to wit, obscene namecalling, threats, intimidation, suppression of opposing views and violence.

The emergence of this swaggering band of black extremists demanding abandonment of democratic methods and goals and a reversal of the trend toward integration must be met head-on by the vast majority of Negroes who reject the minority's tactics and goals. To be sure, the new mood has been generated by white America's historic racism. In turn, the new black mood nurtures further white racism.

On our part, as on the part of white folk, there is urgent need for strong and unequivocal re-affirmation of our commitment to the democratic processes as a means of attaining, here in our homeland, full equal and unfettered rights for America's 22,000,000 black folk. This means a repudiation of the nihilism of the extremists who are shrilly and insistently espousing apartheid; racism, including anti-Semitism; intimidation and violence.

Most fatuous of the extremists' exhortations is the call for "black revolu-

[1] *Crisis*, 74 (April, 1967), 126–27. Reprinted by permission of the publisher.
[2] *Ibid.*, 75 (November, 1968), 310–12.

tion"—the seizure of power by the Negro minority. Any revolution remotely possible in this country at this time would not be one that advances the position and cause of Negroes. Rather it would be a revolution of the Right suppressing not only the black community but also curtailing the basic liberties of the total society.

Repeated surveys and polls by reputable and impartial opinion testers show that this minority misrepresents the true views and aspirations of the majority of the nation's Negro population. A September, 1968, survey by the Columbia Broadcasting System found that the "great majority of Negroes still want integration and want to achieve equality through legal means. Only a very small minority of Negroes approve of violent tactics, nine out of ten in the survey expressing disapproval of violence to achieve equality."

Notwithstanding the evidence that the Negro masses remain committed to the program and tactics which have brought substantial gains in the struggle for equality, the voices within the Negro community which publicly express this majority view have been few and, often, lonely. Partly this has been because of a tendency on the part of the news media to by-pass spokesmen for the majority and to project the minority spokesmen as the authentic voices of the Negro community. There is the additional factor that responsible leaders who speak out against the extremists have been subjected to threats of violence. Moreover, Negro leaders have traditionally been reluctant to speak out publicly in opposition to other black spokesmen.

But the time has come for speaking out loud and clear lest the entire race be branded as hate-mongers, segregationists, advocates of violence, and worse. The silent majority must let its views be known not merely in polls but also in print, on the rostrum, and via radio and television. The time for silence or muted voices is past. The extremists must be answered promptly and forthrightly in the name of the majority. Their racism and anti-Semitism condemned and repudiated. The infantilism of their "governments-in-exile" exposed and scorned. Their advocacy of Jim Crowism rejected as retrogressive. Their suicidal call for violence disavowed.

In a message to the founding conference of the National Association for the Advancement of Colored People in 1909, William Lloyd Garrison expressed the hope "that the Conference will utter no uncertain sound on any point affecting the vital subject. No part of it is too delicate for plain speech."

So it is today. Let there be "no uncertain sound" on the issue confronting us. To make the record clear, let us repeat again and again so that none need be unaware of the Truth: Black America rejects and condemns separation, racism, intimidation, suppression of free speech, and violence. Let it be known that the preachers of hate, the defeatists afraid to compete in the open market, the name callers who substitute epithets and slogans for reason, the exhorters who summon Negro youth to death in futile shoot-outs with the police and the military—let it be known that these media-created "leaders" are not our spokesmen.

Dissent, protest and militancy, yes. Intimidation, disruption, suppression of free speech, extremism and violence, no!

The time to speak up in no uncertain terms, to rally the silent black majority to a constructive program of responsible militancy and resistance to extremism, is now. Tomorrow may be too late.

Whitney Young, who came to the leadership of the National Urban League in 1961, moved that organization to a firmer line than it had earlier taken, but he still preferred negotiation to demonstration and combative action, and pursued his objectives for Negro Americans in quiet parley in government offices and corporation board rooms. But his emphasis shifted, in growing degree, to preventive and compensatory measures: the dispersion of the ghetto, the rapid enlargment of job opportunities for Negroes, even at some sacrifice from the white business community, to make up to them the deprivations of centuries. And it was still an integrated society for which he contended, not a separate Negro economy.

A summary of his position may be gleaned from a passage from his book.[1]

1. Our basic definition of equal opportunity must include recognition of the need for special effort to overcome serious disabilities resulting from historic handicaps. . . .

2. America must recognize and assess at a higher value than ever before the human potential of its Negro citizens, and then our society must move positively to develop that potential. . . .

3. The best schools and the best teachers are needed. . . .

4. A conscious, planned effort must be made to bring qualified Negroes into "entrance jobs" in *all* types of employment, to upgrade them and aid them to qualify for advancement, and to place them in positions of responsibility, including the full range of management positions. . . . For employers the special effort, domestic Marshall Plan approach means exercising the same creative zeal and imagination to include Negro workers at all levels that management has used throughout the years in excluding them.

5. Effective, positive action must be taken to destroy the racial ghetto and to open housing opportunities of all types on the basis of need and ability to buy or rent.

6. Health and welfare agencies, both public and private, must bring to the ghettoized population their best services and most competent personnel. . . .

7. Qualified Negroes should be sought and named to all public and private boards and commissions, particularly those that shape policy in the areas of employment, housing, education, and health and welfare services. . . .

8. Every opportunity to acquire education and technical skills must be utilized to the fullest. . . .

9. It is vital that government at all levels, philanthropic foundations, labor, business, and industry reassess their financial support of, and cooperation with, established organizations committed to securing equal opportunity for Negro citizens to share in the fundamental privileges and rights of American democracy. . . .

10. Negro citizens must exert themselves energetically in constructive efforts to carry their full share of responsibilities and to participate in a meaningful way in every phase of community life. It is not enough to man the machinery of protest. . . .

[1] Whitney Young, Jr., *To Be Equal* (New York: McGraw-Hill Book Company, 1964), p. 28. Copyright © 1964 by Whitney Young, Jr. Reprinted by permission of the publisher.

Even as early as 1963 it was clear to some observers[1] that both the pace and the direction of the Negro Revolution were being profoundly altered. Traditional goals and leadership were under sharp challenge from a fast-growing minority who were more articulate, more aggressive, more impetuous and younger than the shrinking (but still large) majority who still adhered to the more moderate leaders and programs which had, in fact, only recently been considered radical by most white Americans who gave thought to such matters and had brought so much of the improvement in the legal status of the Negro which previous pages have recorded.

By 1968 the revolution had acquired a new mood and orientation under a new generation of leaders. As a result, the more familiar leadership, who still enjoyed a larger following than did the younger militants, broadened their agenda and they themselves took a more aggressive line. It is by no means inconceivable that they would have done so in any case, even without the prodding from the Left, in response to the growing pressures of history. But it was the newer leadership that gave the movement its particular flavor as the 1960's drew to a close.

The old goal of integration, the assimilation of blacks into the mainstream—stigmatized by some as a kind of "painless genocide"—was now increasingly rejected, at least temporarily. In its place was a new affirmation of racial pride, of cultural separatism, a vigorous thrust for political and economic self-sufficiency. The very words "Negro" and "colored people" were giving place, especially among the young, to "black" or "Afro-American," appellations which, incidentally, their elders would have found offensive to their pride twenty years ago.

As late as 1964 or 1965 the civil rights movement was still characteristically a middle-class phenomenon, and the South was its battleground. Civil rights laws enacted by Congress to outlaw discrimination in voting, in education, in criminal prosecutions, in public accommodations, in housing and in employment had been prime objectives, and blacks rejoiced at the active participation of whites in the cause. But by 1968 the newer leadership and their followers were primarily preoccupied with the problems of the ghetto in the large "inner cities" of the North, the Northeast, the Middle West, and the Far West. Civil rights legislation and courtroom victories were in growing measure shrugged off as irrelevant to the ghetto blacks and beneficial only to the upper- and middle-class Negroes whom the militants were disposed to write off as allies of whites, who had drawn away from the brothers and

[1] While composing this brief section, the writer benefited from reading a syndicated article entitled "An Acceleration Toward Black Pride," by Richard L. Worsnop for Editorial Research Reports. It appeared in newspapers in the late summer of 1968, and came to his attention in the *Greensboro* (N.C.) *Record*, September 18, 1968.

sisters. White financial support of the newer efforts was still accepted (and, indeed, as we shall see, vehemently demanded), but whites were increasingly closed out of decision-making and, not uncommonly, were denied membership in the action groups.

The establishment of a distinctive black cultural identity—geographically inside but spiritually outside white society—came to be regarded as a principal means of attaining power for blacks. The cultural self-assertion expressed itself in external symbols like African garments and "Afro" hair styles, and a corresponding contempt for "square" clothing, "processed" hair, conventional cosmetics, and, at a deeper level, "white middle class values" in general. Much was made of "soul"—an ineffable something that is presumed to separate black from white Americans, and which found expression in a predilection for "soul music" (Ray Charles and Aretha Franklin come to mind) and "soul food" (like chitlings and greens). It implied also a contempt for indirection, pretense, and sham, and a notable preference for candor and "telling it like it is."

These new currents created a powerful drift toward the replacement of integration with the opposite goal of attaining black control of the black ghetto and intensifying its insularity. Older (and not a few younger) moderates insisted that *they*, and not the excited radicals, were the genuine realists, that it was the militants who were the starry-eyed and self-deluded dreamers. The Negro's future, the moderates declared, lay in full assimilation in American society. A separate black economy would, moreover, impoverish the black man, for the aspiring black businessman or industrialist still lacked the necessary skills, admittedly because of past discriminations and deprivations. Capital, besides, had always been lacking in the ghetto, and was now even more rare—thanks to the radicals—because investors were being scared off by riots and disorder, both actual and apprehended. The problem was further complicated by the fact that the large established businesses in the country were draining off the ghetto's best minds by recruiting bright young Negro college graduates, a species of competition with which the smaller ghetto business enterprise could as yet hardly hope to cope.

The militants were not put off by this logic. They preached instead that white society only exploited the black community for its own purposes, and that blacks must emancipate themselves from their age-old paralyzing dependence upon their oppressors which the ending of slavery a century ago had done little to change.

One of the more temperate voices for the new directions for the revolution in race relations is heard in the following language of James Farmer, from 1961 to 1966 National Director of the Congress of Racial Equality (CORE), an interracial movement, largely made up of students, and, under Farmer's leadership, devoted to nonviolent, direct action. It was under his leadership especially active in training student leaders in "sit-in," "freedom ride," and voter registration techniques.[1]

> . . . Until [the 1963 March on Washington] we understood the race problem as a problem of discrimination and segregation. If only the nation would lift the unnatural barriers to economic, social, and political opportunity for Negroes, we thought; if only Negroes had full protection and equal privileges and immunities, in law and social fact, our task would be complete.
>
> Today, when much, though by no means all, of the civil rights legislation we have worked for is on the books, we are beginning to realize that civil rights alone may not be enough. Freedom is an art demanding practice, and too many of us are unpracticed. Some of the programs we now project—mobilizing local and national political action, voter registration and education, local community-development and self-help programs, cultural enrichment—are designed to encourage such practice. The fact that Negroes *can* vote, to put the matter most simply, does not mean that they will or that they will do justice to themselves and their interests when they do.
>
> Then, too, we have come to understand that a blind, broken horse will not move smartly out of an open gate. Perhaps being deprived of civil rights is the explanation for the pervasive impoverishment of Negroes, and certainly the Negro will not rise from poverty until his rights are secure, but the simple fact is that he *is* poor and does suffer all the impoverishment of soul and spirit that chronic poverty implies in America. Offering him equal rights, even equal opportunity, at this late date, without giving him a special boost, is the kind of cruel joke American individualism has played on the poor throughout American history. And so CORE and the movement of which we are part plan compensatory and remedial programs to provide the necessary boost.

Perhaps the most exotic, and one of the most implacably separatistic of all the groups in the Negro's struggle was the cult led by Elijah Muhammad (born Poole), the Black Muslims, dedicated to a set of teachings which included elements of the Islamic religion, based on the Koran and the Bible, together with rigid discipline through thrift, industry, cleanliness, modesty in dress, purity in morals, and abstinence from certain foods, alcohol, tobacco, and drugs. Coupled with these views was impassioned hostility to whites whom the leader charged with demonism and brutal suppression of blacks. A threat to his supremacy in the cult by Malcolm X ended with the latter's assassination in 1965.

The following is a brief catalog of Black Muslim demands, taken from their newspaper:[2]

> 1. We want freedom. We want a full and complete freedom.
> 2. We want justice. Equal justice under the law. . . .

[1] *Freedom—When?* (New York, 1965), pp. 169–70. Copyright © 1965 by the Congress of Racial Equality. Reprinted by permission of Random House, Inc.

[2] *Muhammad Speaks,* July 2, 1965. Reprinted by permission of the publisher.

3. We want equality of opportunity. . . .

4. We want our people in America whose parents or grandparents were descendants from slaves, to be allowed to establish a separate state or territory of their own. . . . We believe that our former slave masters are obliged to provide such land and that the area must be fertile and minerally rich. We believe that our former slave masters are obligated to maintain and supply our needs in this separate territory for the next 20 to 25 years—until we are able to produce and supply our own needs.

Since we cannot get along with them in peace and equality, after giving them 400 years of our sweat and blood and receiving in return some of the worst treatment human beings have ever experienced, we believe our contributions to this land and the suffering forced upon us by white America, justifies our demand for complete separation in a state or territory of our own.

5. We want freedom for all Believers of Islam now held in federal prisons. . . .

6. We want an immediate end to the police brutality and mob attacks against the so-called Negro throughout the United States. . . .

7. As long as we are not allowed to establish a state or territory of our own, we demand not only equal justice under the laws of the United States, but equal employment opportunities—NOW! . . .

8. We want the government of the United States to exempt our people from ALL taxation as long as we are deprived of equal justice under the laws of the land.

9. We want equal education—but separate schools up to 16 for boys and 18 for girls on the condition that the girls be sent to women's colleges and universities. . . .

10. We believe that intermarriage or race mixing should be prohibited. We want the religion of Islam taught without hindrance or suppression.

Vastly underrated and misunderstood by both black and white America, Malcolm X, after his break with Elijah Muhammad and the Black Muslims, and the spiritual transformation that followed his visit to Mecca (1964), abandoned his earlier rigorous separatism, and his preachments of violence and racial hatred, in favor of a gospel of the oneness of races under the universal fatherhood of God but without giving up resort to force if other appeals failed. The following passage is from one of the concluding chapters, dealing with the post-Mecca period, of his autobiography.[1]

They called me "the angriest Negro in America." I wouldn't deny that charge. I spoke exactly as I felt. I *believe* in anger. The Bible says there is a *time* for anger. . . . [But] I'm not for wanton violence, I'm for justice. . . . And I feel that when the law fails to protect Negroes from whites' attack, then those Negroes should use arms, if necessary to defend themselves.

"Malcolm X Advocates Armed Negroes!"

What was wrong with that? I'll tell you what was wrong. I was a black man

[1] Malcolm X with the assistance of Alex Haley, *Autobiography of Malcolm X* (New York: Grove Press, 1966), pp. 366–67, 374–75. Copyright © 1964 by Alex Haley and Malcolm X; copyright © 1965 Alex Haley and Betty Shabazz. Reprinted by permission of the publisher.

talking about physical defense against the white man. The white man can lynch and burn and bomb and beat Negroes—that's all right. "Have patience" . . . "The customs are entrenched" . . . "Things are getting better."

Well, I believe it's a crime for anyone who is being brutalized to continue to accept that brutality without doing something to defend himself. If that's how "Christian" philosophy is interpreted, if that's what Gandhian philosophy teaches, well, then, I will call them criminal philosophies.

I tried in every speech I made to clarify my new position regarding white people—I don't speak against the sincere, well-meaning good white people. I have learned that there *are* some. I have learned that not all white people are racists. I am speaking against and my fight is against the white *racists*. I firmly believe that Negroes have the right to fight against these racists, by any means that are necessary.

I *am* for violence if non-violence means we continue postponing a solution to the American black man's problem—just to *avoid* violence. I don't go for non-violence if it also means a delayed solution. To me a delayed solution is a non-solution. Or I'll say it another way. If it must take violence to get the black man his human rights in this country, I'm *for* violence exactly as you know the Irish, the Poles, or Jews would be if they were flagrantly discriminated against. . . .

I kept having all kinds of troubles trying to build the kind of Black Nationalist organization I wanted to build for the American Negro. Then why Black Nationalism? Well, in the competitive American society, how can there ever be any white-black solidarity before there is first some black solidarity? If you will remember, in my childhood I had been exposed to the Black Nationalist teachings of Marcus Garvey—which, in fact, I had been told had led to my father's murder. Even when I was a follower of Elijah Muhammad, I had been strongly aware of how the Black Nationalist political, economic and social philosophies had the ability to instill within the black man the racial dignity, the incentive, and the confidence that the Black race needs today to get up off its knees, and to get on its feet, and get rid of its scars, and to take a stand for itself.

One of the major troubles that I was having in building the organization that I wanted—an all-Black organization whose ultimate object was to help create a society in which there could exist honest white-black brotherhood—was that my earlier public image, my old so-called "Black Muslim" image, kept blocking me. I was trying to gradually reshape that image. I was trying to turn a corner, into a new regard by the public, especially Negroes; I was no less angry than I had been, but at the same time the true brotherhood I had seen in the Holy World had influenced me to recognize that anger can blind human vision. . . .

True Islam taught me that it takes *all* of the religious, political, economic, psychological, and racial ingredients, or characteristics, to make the Human Family and the Human Society complete.

Since I learned the *truth* in Mecca, my dearest friends have come to include *all* kinds—some Christians, Jews, Buddhists, Hindus, agnostics, and even atheists! I have friends who are called capitalists, Socialists, and Communists! Some of my friends are moderates, conservatives, extremists—some are even Uncle Toms! My friends they are black, brown, red, yellow, and *white!*

I said to Harlem street audiences that only when mankind would submit to the "'One God who created all"—only then would mankind even approach the "peace" of which so much *talk* could be heard . . . but toward which so little *action* was seen.

The harder line which increasingly won the ear of disenchanted black intellectuals, especially among the young, was expressed with devastating force by such gifted poet-playwright-novelist-essayists as James Baldwin and LeRoi Jones, whose searing works made many a white American understand for the first time what it meant to be a Negro in America. The following is from an essay, "black hope." It was originally delivered as an address in Harlem, in front of the Hotel Theresa, where Jones was speaking as Director of The Black Arts Repertory Theatre.[1]

In a time of chaos, in a time of trouble, we're asking for unity, black unity as defense against these mad white people who continue to run the world.

These same mad white people who are killing black unity and black people all over the world, in Africa, Asia, Latin America, these same mad white people who every day of our lives demonstrate that they are not fit to live on the same planet with soulful human beings, these are the enemies of our world, these are the friends against whom we black people had better protect ourselves. And we must begin to protect ourselves against every aspect of the white man's thinking. Because his thinking is aimed at destroying us, or reducing us to pitiful objects known as "Negroes." And everybody knows what "Negroes" are: straight-jacketed lazy clowns, whose only job is carrying out the white man's will.

But there are some of us who will not be Negroes, who know that indeed we are something else, something stronger . . . there are some of us who know we are black people, and that we have been forced for the last few centuries to live enslaved for maniacs in the worst insane asylum in man's history. Knowing all this, we black people should be *at least* suspicious of everything coming out of a white man's mouth . . . I am telling you it is very dangerous to believe anything the white man tells you . . . you know his record . . . especially if he wants you to believe it.

And also because black people have, and must realize that we have, our own standards and references for judging the world. And we must begin to make use of them, and regard what the white man says as dealing with another reality, because we know, we black people know, what our own reality is . . . You know what you feel. You know what you have to do!!!! And let no white man or imitation white man tell you different. . . .

Black people do not be fooled by these devils. Do not let them destroy . . . any . . . project designed to help black people. Do not be fooled into letting the white man kill you and your children by letting him destroy those agencies that would save you. Do not let them tear out your hearts with their lies and contempt. Do not let them smear our leaders, do not let them enter into this community with their . . . integration fairy tales. Remember, you are at war with the devil himself . . . So now we are asking for unity, a black unity in every place where there are black people. We are asking for a massive unity. A coming together of Brothers and Sisters to enter into

[1] LeRoi Jones, *Home: Social Essays* (New York: William Morrow and Company, Inc., 1966), pp. 234–37. Copyright © 1965, 1966 by LeRoi Jones. Reprinted by permission of the publisher.

service against the devil. Black people we must at last come together to protect ourselves and what we love. In each block, in each house, in each black heart. All these groups, organizations, view-points, religions, had better come together, agreed on one term, that they are black people, and that they are tired of being weak slaves. We are asking for a unity so strong that it will shake up the world. We are asking for all black people to come on in now, and lock arms against these beasts. We must unify. We *must* have unity. We must use our strength and minds against our enemies not against each other. . . . And once we have done this, you know for yourself, there is no force on earth that can harm or twist us. No devil left in creation to mess up the world.

No less disturbing to apprehensive whites—who recognized in his blazing impeachments the accents of a man who had hold of some unpleasant truths and was determined to turn them to their victims' profit—were the impassioned philippics of Stokely Carmichael, the fiery young leader (until 1967, when he was succeeded by H. Rap Brown, who with equal belligerence preached implacable hatred for whites and urged blacks to put their trust in the torch and in guns) of the Students Nonviolent Coordinating Committee. Under Carmichael's leadership, SNCC[1], originally formed in 1960, abandoned nonviolence and moved to the angrier position that whites and blacks are irreconcilable, and that the Negro should seize "Black Power" by fiercely militant "total revolutionary action." The nation would have to choose, shouted the race's new radical tribunes, between giving the Negro full justice now, or seeing its cities burned to the ground and its whole civilization dismantled, like Samson avenging himself upon the Philistines.

Repudiating interracial cooperation and the civil rights movement as fraudulent schemes for preserving white supremacy, Carmichael and his following adopted a strong antiwhite position and rejected white participation in the Negro's struggle. Writing off some of America's most cherished heroes, including Jefferson and Lincoln, as "dumb honkies," whipping up his audiences' passions against American action in Viet Nam with the loudly defiant chant, "Hell no; we won't go!" and shouting "To hell with the laws of the United States!" he was always more incendiary before live audiences of young Negroes—especially on college campuses—than on paper.

He unequivocally scolded them for their meekness and urged them to shoot their oppressors and to burn down their cities because that was the only language their tormentors would understand. In December 1968, the local press reported that he replied, when asked how he had voted in the late presidential election, that he had stayed home and cleaned his gun. And when questioned about his attitude toward

[1] The name was eventually changed to Student National Coordinating Committee.

violence and "law and order," he drove home the devastating point that the forcible exclusion of blacks from their rightful place in American life was no less "violent" than "shooting Whitey"; that white "honkies" who hold the Negro in subjection are far more reprehensible offenders against law and order than are blacks who resort to burning and looting to advance their just cause.[1]

Another disquieting voice for black separatism was a Conference on Black Power, held in the summer of 1967, in Newark, New Jersey. Drafting a strong indictment of America's mistreatment of the black minority—which not a few moderate whites, who rejected the conference's proposed remedies, were willing to concede was a not unfair statement of the black man's grievances—the meeting called for separate American nations for blacks and whites:[2]

Resolutions, Conference on Black Power, Newark, New Jersey

Whereas the black people in America have been systematically oppressed by their white fellow countrymen

Whereas there is little prospect that this oppression can be terminated, peacefully or otherwise, within the foreseeable future

Whereas the black people do not wish to be absorbed into the larger white community

Whereas the black people in America find that their interests are in contradiction with those of white America

Whereas the black people in America are psychologically handicapped by virtue of their having no national homeland

Whereas the physical, moral, and aesthetic standards of white American society are not those of black society and indeed do violence to the self-image of the black man

Whereas black people were among the earliest immigrants to America, having been ruthlessly separated from their fatherland, and have made a major contribution to America's development, most of this contribution having been uncompensated, and

Recognizing that efforts are already well advanced for the convening of a Constitutional Convention for the purpose of revising the Constitution of the United States for the first time since America's inception, then

Be it resolved that the Black Power Conference initiate a national dialogue on the desirability of partitioning the United States into two separate and independent nations, one to be a homeland for white and the other to be a homeland for black Americans.

No less unyielding was the Black Panther Party for Self-Defense, with which Eldridge Cleaver, who acknowledged a debt to Malcolm X, was identified. The choice before the country, said Cleaver, was "Total liberty for black people or total destruction for America."[3]

[1] An example of one of Carmichael's more moderately phrased but compelling attacks on "integration" appears in the *New York Review of Books* for September 22, 1966.

[2] A copy of the resolutions is reprinted in *Ramparts, VI* (December, 1967), 46.

[3] Eldridge Cleaver, *Post-Prison Writings and Speeches* (New York: Random House, 1969). Copyright © 1967, 1968, 1969 by Eldridge Cleaver. Reprinted by permission.

For the revolutionary black youth of today, time starts moving with the coming of Malcolm X. Before Malcolm, time stands still, going down in frozen steps into the depths of the stagnation of slavery. . . . Malcolm mastered the language and used it as a sword to slash his way through the veil of lies that for 400 years gave the white man the power of the word. Through the breach in the veil, Malcolm saw all the way to national liberation, and he showed us the rainbow and the golden pot at its end. Inside the golden pot, Malcolm told us, was the tool of liberation. Huey P. Newton ["Minister of Defense" of the Black Panther Party of Self-Defense], one of the millions of black people who listened to Malcolm, lifted the golden lid off the pot and blindly, trusting Malcolm, stuck his hand inside and grasped the tool. When he withdrew his hand and looked to see what he held, he saw the gun cold in its metal and implacable in its message: Death-Life, Liberty or Death, mastered by a black hand at last! Huey P. Newton is the ideological descendant, heir and successor of Malcolm X. Malcolm prophesied the coming of the gun to the black liberation struggle. Huey picked up the gun and pulled the trigger, freeing the genie of black revolutionary violence in Babylon.

The genie of black revolutionary violence is here, and it says that the oppressor has no rights which the oppressed are bound to respect. The genie also has a question for white Americans: which side do you choose? Do you side with the oppressor or with the oppressed? The time for decision is upon you. The cities of America have tested the first flames of revolution. But a hotter fire rages in the hearts of black people today: total liberty for black people or total destruction for America.

The prospects, I confess, do not look promising. Besides being a dumb nation, America is mad with white racism. Whom the gods would destroy, they first make mad. Perhaps America has been mad for too long to make any talk of sanity relevant now. But there is a choice and it will be made, by decision or indecision, by action or inaction, by commission or omission. Black people have made their choice; a revolutionary generation that has the temerity to say to America that Huey P. Newton must be set free, also invested with the courage to kill, pins its hopes on the revolutionary's faith and says, with Che: *Wherever death may surprise us, it will be welcome, provided that this, our battlecry, reach some receptive ear, that another hand reach out to pick up weapons, and that other fighting men come forward to intone our funeral dirge with the staccato of machine guns and new cries of battle and victory.*

The most startling of the new militant strategies was the breathtaking manifesto hurled at the churches, when a vigorously led action group in dead seriousness commanded the nation's leading religious bodies to hand over the sum of half a billion dollars (this figure was later raised to three billion dollars) in "reparations" as partial atonement for the injuries that blacks had suffered at the hands of American Christians and Jews for three centuries.

The project was launched in late April 1969, when a three-day session in Detroit sponsored by the Interreligious Foundation for Community Organization (IFCO) created the National Black Economic Development Conference (NBEDC), which, during the stormy meeting, came under the control of a determined minority passionately dedicated to revolution to end racism, imperialism, and the capitalist system. The author of the plan was James Forman, International Director of the Student Nonviolent Coordinating Committee.[1] The Conference adopted a "Black Manifesto" peremptorily calling upon "the White Christian Churches and the Jewish Synagogues in the United States of America and all Other Racist Institutions," not only to pay over the sum of $500,000,000 but also to surrender to the NBEDC "a list of all church assets, unrelated business income, stock and real estate investments, pension and retirement funds," of which 60 percent of all the proceeds were hereafter to be diverted to the Conference.

These sentences are gleaned from the Manifesto's 1500-word Introduction, drafted by Forman:[2]

> Brothers and Sisters: We have come from all over the country, burning with anger and despair not only with the miserable economic plight of our people, but fully aware that the racism on which the Western World was built dominates our lives . . . [A]ny black man or Negro who is advocating a perpetuation of capitalism inside the United States is in fact seeking not only his ultimate destruction and death, but is contributing to the continuous exploitation of black people all around the world. For it is the power of the United States Government, this racist, imperialist government, that is choking the life of all people around the world. . . . [T]he day will come when we can return to our homeland. . . . But we should not think of going back to Africa today, for we are located in a strategic position. We live inside the U.S. which is the most barbaric country in the world and we have a chance to help bring this government down. . . . No oppressed people ever gained their liberation until they were ready to fight, to use whatever means necessary, including the use . . . of the gun to bring down the colonizer. . . . We shall liberate all the people in the U.S. and we will be instrumental in the liberation of colored people the world around. . . . All the parties on the left who consider themselves revolutionary will say that blacks are the Vanguard, but we are saying that not only are we the Vanguard, but we

[1] The IFCO is, incidentally, a joint Jewish-Protestant-Catholic agency, with an overwhelmingly white constituency. It is committed to the ecumenical funding of mass-based, indigenous community organizations to assist the poor and underprivileged. The Detroit meeting was evidently "captured" by a militant minority, headed by Forman, who, in the ringing speech with which he introduced his manifesto, declared: "The conference is now the property of the people who are assembled here. . . . We maintain we have the revolutionary right to do this. Our seizure of power at this conference is based on a program and our program is contained in the . . . MANIFESTO." Press reports indicated that the Detroit Conference, which originally registered more than 500 delegates, adopted the Manifesto by a vote of 187–80. Many abstained from voting; others had withdrawn. For accounts of the Conference and of the responses of some church bodies, see *New Republic*, 160 (June 21, 1969), 19–21; and a series of articles appearing in several issues of the *Christian Science Monitor*, in June, July, and August, 1969.

[2] Copies of the Manifesto were evidently widely distributed. The version in the possession of the author is a photo-duplicate of a mimographed copy apparently sent to the national office (in New York) of the Lutheran Church in America. I have taken the liberty of emending what appear to be typographical errors.

must assume leadership, total control. . . . We are the most humane people within the U.S. We have suffered and we understand suffering.

We must commit ourselves to a society where the total means of production are taken from the rich and placed into the hands of the state for the welfare of all the people. . . . [The movement] must be led by black people. . . . [W]hite people must be willing to accept black leadership. We maintain we have the revolutionary right to do this. . . . We have the same rights . . . as the Christians had in going into Africa and raping our Motherland and bringing us away from our continent of peace and into this hostile and alien environment where we have been living in perpetual warfare since 1619.

The main thrust of the Manifesto is delivered in the following preamble and ten formal demands:

We, the black people assembled in Detroit, Michigan, for the National Black Economic Development Conference, are fully aware that we have been forced to come together because racist white America has exploited our resources, our minds, our bodies, our labor. For centuries we have been forced to live as colonized people inside the United States, victimized by the most vicious, racist system in the world. We have helped to build the most industrial country in the world.

We are therefore demanding of the white Christian churches and Jewish synagogues which are part and parcel of the system of capitalism, that they begin to pay reparations to black people in this country. We are demanding $500,000,000 from the Christian white churches and the Jewish synagogues. This total comes to fifteen dollars per [Negro American] . . . not a large sum of money, and we know that the churches and synagogues have a tremendous wealth, and its membership, white America, has profited [from], and still exploits, black people. . . . [T]he exploitation of colored peoples around the world is aided and abetted by the white . . . churches and synagogues. This demand for $500,000,000 is not an idle resolution or empty words.

We are demanding $500,000,000 to be spent in the following way:

1. We call for the establishment of a Southern land bank to help our brothers and sisters. . . . We need money for land. . . . We call for $200,000,000 to implement this program.

2. We call for the establishment of four major publishing and printing industries in the United States to be funded with ten million dollars each . . . .

3. We call for the establishment of four of the most advanced scientific and futuristic audio-visual networks to provide an alternative to the racist propaganda that fills the current television networks [and to be] funded by ten million dollars each.

4. We call for a research skills center which will provide research on the problems of black people, [to] be funded with no less than 30 million dollars.

5. We call for the establishment of a training center for the teaching of skills in community organization, photography, movie making, television making and repair, radio building and repair and all other skills needed in communication . . . [to] . . . be funded with no less than ten million dollars.

6. . . . We call for ten million dollars to assist in the organization of welfare recipients. . . . so that they may demand more money from the government and better administration of the welfare system of this country.

7. We call for $20,000,000 to establish a National Black Labor Strike and Defense Fund.

8. We call for the establishment of the International Black Appeal [to] . . . be funded with no less than $20,000,000 [and to be] . . . charged with producing more capital for the establishment of cooperative businesses in the United States and Africa, our Motherland . . . [and to be] charged with three functions . . . headed by James Forman: (a) Raising money for the program of the National Black Economic Development Conference; (b) The development of cooperatives in African countries and support of African Liberation movements; (c) Establishment of a Black Anti-Defamation League which will protect our African image.

9. We call for the establishment of a Black University to be funded with $130,000,000 to be located in the South.

10. We demand that IFCO allocate all unused funds in the planning budget to implement the demands of this conference.

The balance of the document outlines a twelve-point program for mobilizing blacks "to help force the racist white Christian churches and Jewish synagogues to implement these demands." The campaign calls for "pressure by whatever means . . . applied to the white power structure"; for press conferences to "heighten the tension"; for "total disruption of selected church sponsored agencies operating anywhere in the United States and the world . . . [b]lack workers, black women, black students and the black unemployed are encouraged to seize the offices, telephones, and printing apparatus of all church sponsored agencies and to hold them in trusteeship until our demands are met"; for "the disruption of racist churches and synagogues"; for the preparation and distribution of mass literature; for concerted action with white revolutionaries, under black leadership; for the acquisition of technical skills to enable blacks to direct "the total integration of political, economic, and military components" for revolutionary ends; and for the designation of a 24-member steering committee to supply "fearless leadership" who understand that "we will have to declare war on the white Christian churches and synagogues and this means we may have to fight the total government structure of this country."

The document concludes ominously:

We must boldly go out and attack the white Western World at its power centers. The white Christian churches are another form of government in this country and they are used by the government . . . to exploit the people of Latin America, Asia and Africa. . . . [W]e know deep within our hearts that we must be prepared to use force to get our demands. . . . Our objective in issuing this Manifesto is to force the racist white Christian Church to begin the payment of reparations which are due to all black people, not only by the Church but also by private business and the United States government. . . . Our demands are negotiable, but they cannot be minimized; they can only be increased and the Church is asked to come up with larger sums of money than we are asking.

Our slogans are:

ALL ROADS MUST LEAD TO REVOLUTION
UNITE WITH WHOMEVER YOU CAN UNITE

NEUTRALIZE WHEREVER POSSIBLE
FIGHT OUR ENEMIES RELENTLESSLY
VICTORY TO THE PEOPLE
LIFE AND GOOD HEALTH TO MANKIND
RESISTANCE TO DOMINATION BY THE WHITE CHRISTIAN CHURCHES AND THE JEWISH SYNAGOGUES
WE SHALL WIN WITHOUT A DOUBT

The Manifesto was promptly transmitted—in several instances personally delivered by Forman and his aides—to particular church bodies, with firmly worded requisitions for specifically named sums. The Episcopal Church, for example, was confronted with a demand for $60,000,000; the Roman Catholic Church received a bill for $200,000,000; the Lutheran Church in America was instructed to remit $50,000,000. In addition to a demand that they supply a full list of income-yielding properties and, hereafter, 60 percent of their revenues, there were other stipulations. In some cases severely short time limits accompanied the demands. The famous Riverside Church in New York was given only a week in which to act; and in addition it was commanded to supply the NBEDC with rent-free office space, unrestricted telephone use, classrooms for Harlem residents, and unlimited use of the church's radio station for 12 hours a day.

The formal transmission of the ultimatum was in several instances accompanied by the appearance, at regular Sunday services, of Forman and his associates, who interrupted the ritual of worship, strode up to the chancel or altar, and read off the Manifesto while the startled congregations looked on in open-mouthed disbelief. The first of these episodes occurred on May 4 at Riverside Church when Forman and a half-dozen colleagues (after having given polite advance notice to the church's office of their intention) intruded upon a Communion service to make their demands.

In the months immediately following the issuance of the Manifesto, there was little evidence that the churches and synagogues would comply. Not a few church spokesmen characterized the tactic as blackmail; some, like the Roman Catholic Archdiocese of New York, flatly rejected it; some, like denominational and multidenominational bodies, were stimulated to reassess their social action programs and promised further study of their responsibilities. Some responded by citing their greatly increased expenditures in recent years to promote racial justice and related causes, and hinted that while they took the Conference's indictment with utter seriousness, they could not condone its methods. Some, like the Protestant Episcopal Church, voted substantial sums for objects like those proposed by the Manifesto, but entrusted ultimate responsibility for the disbursement of the money to some of their own agencies, working more or less closely with the NBEDC. The United

Presbyterians voted to consider the establishment of a $50,000,000 fund for the poor, to be administered by agencies other than the NBEDC.

It is difficult to escape the conclusion that the net effect of the Black Manifesto was to increase the growing alienation of whites from blacks, rather than to move whites toward the repentance and expiation that the revolutionary instrument called for.

(2)

VIEWS FROM THE WHITE HOUSE

Dwight D. Eisenhower, President 1953–1961

The bland comments elicited from President Eisenhower at his first regular news conference after the *Brown* decision prefigured his future course. Months passed, and then years, and while the country waited for a more explicit commitment from the President, or even an acknowledgment that the Supreme Court had been right in its judgment, he remained to the end of his presidency serenely aloof from the civil rights cause. From the White House came little more than his characteristic remark, "I have consistently tried . . . to show my belief that mere law will never solve this problem. . . . We have got to have reason and sense and education."

There were, to be sure, occasional executive orders or less formal statements giving his avuncular blessing to equality of public employment opportunity, and continued desegregation of the armed force; and he did dispatch troops to Little Rock when state authorities used armed force against the execution of a federal court order. And he did approve, reluctantly, the weak Civil Rights Acts of 1957 and 1960.[1] But it was not until 1959, when he was nearing the end of his presidency and after he had repeatedly declared that "you can't solve this problem with laws," that he gave visible support to civil rights reforms in his message to Congress, of February 5, 1959.[2]

Two principles basic to our system of government are that the rule of law is supreme, and that every individual regardless of his race, religion, or

[1] Anthony Lewis, *Portrait of a Decade* (New York, 1964), pp. 105–10, 112–13, and *passim.*

[2] *Congressional Record,* 86th Cong., 1st Sess., Feb. 5, 1959, 1922–23.

national origin, is entitled to the equal protection of the laws. We must continue to seek every practicable means for reinforcing these principles and making them a reality for all.

He then outlined seven recommendations, the substance of which was thereafter incorporated in the Civil Rights Act of 1960, to repair some of the more conspicuous deficiencies of the Act of 1957.

John F. Kennedy, President, 1961–1963

In President Kennedy's brief term of office, the White House adopted a more energetic policy for the advancement of civil rights, the principal fruits of which were the Civil Rights Act of 1964, enacted after his death; an increasingly resolute program for the enforcement of the Acts of 1957 and 1960; and a growing insistence upon compliance with the *Brown* decision, especially with respect to public schools, universities, and other public facilities. A characteristic statement may be excerpted from his message to Congress of February 28, 1963, in which he urged effective federal legislation to end discrimination in voting, education, employment, and public accommodations, as well as the extension and expansion of the United States Commission on Civil Rights.

The specific proposals were prefaced by these words:[1]

The Negro baby born in America today—regardless of the section or state in which he is born—has about one half as much chance of completing high school as a white baby born in the same place on the same day—one third as much chance of completing college—one third as much chance of becoming a professional man—twice as much chance of becoming unemployed—about one seventh as much chance of earning ten thousand dollars per year—a life expectancy which is seven years less—and the prospects of earning only half as much.

No American who believes in the basic truth that "all men are created equal" . . . can fully excuse . . . the picture these statistics portray. Race discrimination hampers our economic growth by preventing the maximum development and utilization of our manpower. It hampers our world leadership by contradicting at home the message we preach abroad. It mars the atmosphere of a united and classless society in which this Nation rose to greatness. It increases the costs of public welfare, crime, delinquency, and disorder. Above all, it is wrong.

Therefore, let it be clear, in our hearts and minds, that it is not merely because of the Cold War, and not merely because of the economic waste of discrimination, that we are committed to achieving true equality of opportunity. The basic reason is because it is right.

* * *

In the last two years, more progress has been made in securing the civil rights of all Americans than in any comparable period in our history.

[1] *Congressional Record,* 88th Cong., 1st Sess., February 28, 1963, 3245–46.

Progress has been made—through executive action, litigation, persuasion, and private initiative—in achieving and protecting equality of opportunity in education, voting, transportation, employment, housing, government, and the enjoyment of public accommodations.

But pride in our progress must not give way to relaxation of our effort. Nor does progress in the Executive Branch enable the Legislative Branch to escape its own obligations. On the contrary, it is in the light of this nationwide progress, . . . that I stress . . . the following . . . important legislative as well as administrative measures [still to be taken].

Lyndon B. Johnson, President, 1963–1969

It was President Johnson, however, a Texan and a late-comer to the civil rights movement, who was to give the cause the most vigorous and successful White House leadership it had ever had. He spoke often and with surprising passion on the subject. A representative quotation is taken here from his Howard University commencement address of June 4, 1965.[1]

Our earth is the home of revolution. In every corner of every continent men charged with hope contend with ancient ways in the pursuit of justice. . . . And our own future is linked to this process of swift and turbulent change in many lands in the world. But nothing in any country touches us more profoundly, and nothing is more freighted with meaning for our own destiny than the revolution of the Negro American.

In far too many ways American Negroes have been another nation: deprived of freedom, crippled by hatred, the doors of opportunity closed to hope.

In our time change has come to this Nation, too. The American Negro, acting with impressive restraint, has peacefully protested and marched, entered the courtrooms and the seats of government, demanding a justice that has long been denied. The voice of the Negro was the call to action. But it is a tribute to America that, once aroused, the courts and the Congress, the President and most of the people, have been the allies of progress.

Thus we have seen the high court of the country declare that discrimination based on race was repugnant to the Constitution, and therefore void. We have seen in 1957 and 1960, and again in 1964, the first civil rights legislation in this Nation in almost an entire century.

As majority leader of the United States Senate, I helped to guide two of these bills through the Senate. And, as your President, I was proud to sign the third. And now very soon we will have the fourth—a new law guaranteeing every American the right to vote.

No act of my entire administration will give me greater satisfaction than the day when my signature makes this bill, too, the law of the land.

The voting rights bill will be the latest, and among the most important, in a long series of victories. But this victory—as Winston Churchill said of another triumph for freedom—"is not the end. It is not even the beginning of the end. But, it is, perhaps, the end of the beginning."

[1] *The New York Times,* June 5, 1965.

That beginning is freedom; and the barriers to that freedom are tumbling down. Freedom is the right to share, share fully and equally, in American society—to vote, to hold a job, to enter a public place, to go to school. It is the right to be treated in every part of our national life as a person equal in dignity and promise to all others.

But freedom is not enough. You do not wipe away the scars of centuries by saying: Now you are free to go where you want, and do as you desire, and choose the leaders you please.

You do not take a person who, for years, has been hobbled by chains and liberate him, bring him up to the starting line of a race and then say, "You are free to compete with all the others," and still justly believe that you have been completely fair.

Thus it is not enough just to open the gates of opportunity. All our citizens must have the ability to walk through those gates.

This is the next and the more profound stage of the battle for civil rights. We seek not just freedom but opportunity. We seek not just legal equity but human ability, not just equality as a right and a theory but equality as a fact and equality as a result.

For the task is to give 20 million Negroes the same chance as every other American to learn and grow, to work and share in society, to develop their abilities—physical, mental, and spiritual, and to pursue their individual happiness.

Richard M. Nixon, President, 1969–

The Negro vote went overwhelmingly to Hubert Humphrey in the 1968 presidential contest, and Mr. Nixon's victory was greeted with no little apprehension by black America. He had hinted during the campaign that he would slow the HEW-Justice Departments' drive for accelerated school desegregation and would not "use federal funds as a club" over recalcitrant school authorities; that he would take a "hard" line against civil disorders in the cities; that he would encourage a shift from federal initiative to local community action and private investment, to renew and restore the nation's decaying cities.

Blacks and their friends were further disappointed when the President-elect announced the makeup of his cabinet, which, unlike that of his predecessor, did not include a Negro. Taking alarm, some of the President-elect's spokesmen assured Negro leaders that Mr. Nixon's administration would exceed all others in promoting Negro gains, but the black community remained skeptical as they listened in vain for any direct reference to civil rights in his inaugural address. The closest approach in the speech to reassurance for Black America was a passage which many construed as little more than yet another plea for patience, forbearance, and greater self-reliance.[1]

[1] *Ibid.,* January 21, 1969.

In these difficult years, America has suffered from a fever of words; from inflated rhetoric that promises more than it can deliver; from angry rhetoric that fans discontents into hatreds; from bombastic rhetoric that postures instead of persuading.

We cannot learn from one another until we stop shouting at one another—until we speak quietly enough so that our words can be heard as well as our voices.

For its part, government will listen. We will strive to listen in new ways—to the voices of quiet anguish, the voices that speak without words, the voices of the heart—to the injured voices, the anxious voices, the voices that have despaired of being heard.

Those who have been left out we will try to bring in. Those left behind, we will help to catch up.

For all our people, we will set as our goal the decent order that makes progress possible and our lives secure.

As we reach toward our hopes, our task is to build on what has gone before—not turning away from the old, but turning toward the new.

In this past third of a century, government has passed more laws, spent more money, initiated more programs, than in all our previous history.

In pursuing our goals of full employment, better housing, excellence in education; in rebuilding our cities and improving our rural areas; in protecting our environment, enhancing the quality of life—in all these and more, we will and must press urgently forward . . . .

But we are approaching the limits of what government alone can do.

Our greatest need now is to reach beyond government, to enlist the legions of the concerned and the committed. What has to be done has to be done by government and people together or it will not be done at all. The lesson of past agony is that without the people we can do nothing; with the people we can do everything. . . . This means black and white together, as one nation, not two. The laws have caught up with our conscience. What remains is to give life to what is the law: to insure at last that as all are born equal in dignity before God, all are born equal in dignity before man.

To this end equal opportunity is essential, but not enough, not enough. Men and women of all races are born with the same range of abilities. But ability is not just the product of birth. Ability is stretched or stunted by the family that you live with, and the neighborhood you live in—by the school you go to and the poverty or the richness of your surroundings. It is the product of a hundred unseen forces playing upon the little infant, the child, and finally the man. . . .

So, it is the glorious opportunity of this generation to end the one huge wrong of the American Nation and, in so doing, to find America for ourselves, with the same immense thrill of discovery which gripped those who first began to realize that here, at last, was a home for freedom.

All it will take is for all of us to understand what this country is and what this country must become.

(3)
THE NATIONAL PARTY PLATFORMS, 1956–1968[1]

Campaign of 1956

In 1956, besides the two major parties, only the Prohibitionists and three Socialist groups offered national tickets that attracted visible support. In this first national campaign after the *Brown* decision, it was impossible to evade an issue now so conspicuously before the public. The Prohibition party, standing on the Bible, confined itself to a lofty pronouncement. "Recognizing that 'God hath created of one blood all nations . . . ,' we declare in favor of full justice and equal opportunity for all people, regardless of race, creed or national origins." The Socialist party, pledging itself to a new order that "will eliminate war, racial antagonism, hunger, disease, poverty and oppression," concentrated upon the replacement of monopoly capitalism with the cooperative commonwealth, but professed an interest also in "other immediate problems":

> The first of these is the achievement of full equality for all Americans, regardless of race, sex, creed, color or national origin. We applaud the Supreme Court decisions that separate but equal facilities do not provide the same opportunity for all citizens, whether in regard to education, or elsewhere. We call for the protection of the law for all citizens in [*sic*] exercise of their constitutional liberties, particularly the right to vote.

The Socialist Labor platform made no specific pledge beyond the affirmation that socialism "is the cure for race prejudice because it cleanses society of the sordid material interests that profit from fomenting racism and create the cooperative climate for human brotherhood." The Socialist Workers party, after an extended homily applauding the Negro's struggle for equality, and denouncing the White Citizens' Councils' subservience to "the bankers, industrialists and big planters," and excoriating the WCC's policy of "deliberately intensifying racial antagonisms in order to split the white and Negro workers to block unionization of the South," nailed this plank into their platform:

> Full economic, political and social equality to the Negro people and to all other minority peoples. Solidarity with all mass actions of the embattled

[1] The platforms for the presidential electoral campaigns of 1956–1968 are in Porter and Johnson, *National Party Platforms,* pp. 523–698.

Negro freedom fighters. For the immediate enforcement and implementation of the Supreme Court decision against segregation.

Enact and enforce legislation to abolish lynching, the poll tax and all forms of segregation. Create an FEPC with full powers of enforcement. Put a stop to police brutality.

Chastened by the defeat of 1952 and skeptical over the prospect of unseating the unassailably popular General Eisenhower, the Democrats hoped in 1956 to increase their majority in Congress by strengthening their appeal in the populous states of the North, East and West, without alienating their traditional southern support. Their plank on civil rights discreetly acknowledged that the *Brown* decision had "brought consequences of vast importance," but an effort to amend this cautious profession by adding a pledge to help carry out the decision was overwhelmingly smothered on the convention floor. The party's dilemma produced a temperate statement on civil rights, not remarkably different in tone from that of the Republicans. It was now clear that neither party could any longer avoid confrontation with the issue; both were under a growing necessity to court the Negro vote in the North and East. Beginning with a reaffirmation of the "proposition that all men are created equal," and a declaration that the effort to "eradicate discrimination based on race . . . requires action" in all sections of the country, and the cooperation of individual citizens and federal, state, and local government, the platform announced:

The Democratic Party pledges itself to continue its efforts to eliminate illegal discriminations of all kinds, in relation to (1) full rights to vote, (2) full rights to engage in gainful occupations, (3) full rights to enjoy security of the person, and (4) full rights to education in all publicly supported institutions.

Recent decisions of the Supreme Court of the United States relating to segregation in publicly supported schools and elsewhere have brought consequences of vast importance to our Nation as a whole and especially to communities directly affected. We reject all proposals for the use of force to interfere with the orderly determination of these matters by the courts.

The Republicans, no more eager than the Democrats to embrace the *School Segregation* cases, went little further than to say that it "accepts the decision." Their platform allotted nearly five hundred words to a civil rights plank, half of them devoted to a recital of recent civil rights gains which, the convention boasted, added up to "more progress . . . in this field under the present Republican Administration than in any similar period in the last eighty years." The claim was based principally upon the increased number of Negroes appointed to high federal posts; upon the elimination of segregation in schools and public facilities in the District of Columbia, and in "all federal employment"; upon "great progress" in fair employment practices by private employers working on government contracts; upon progress by the regulatory agencies in ending discrimination in interstate commerce; and upon the termination of discrimination in the armed forces, in veterans' hospitals, and among civilians on naval bases. Professing its dedication to the Constitution and its "guarantees to all people [of] the blessings of liberty, due process and equal protection of the laws" as "an unqualified right, regardless of race, creed, or color," it offered the following guardedly specific program, limited to a promise of cautious advance in school desegregation:

> The Republican Party accepts the decision of the U.S. Supreme Court that racial discrimination in publicly supported schools must be progressively eliminated. We concur in the conclusion of the Supreme Court that its decision directing school desegregation should be accomplished with "all deliberate speed" locally through Federal District Courts. The implementation order of the Supreme Court recognizes the complex and acutely emotional problems created by its decision in certain sections of our country where racial patterns have been developed in accordance with prior and longstanding decisions of the same tribunal.
>
> We believe that true progress can be attained through intelligent study, understanding, education and good will. Use of force or violence by any group or agency will tend only to worsen the many problems inherent in the situation. This progress must be encouraged and the work of the courts supported in every legal manner by all branches of the Federal Government to the end that the constitutional ideal of equality before the law, regardless of race, creed or color, will be steadily achieved.

Campaign of 1960

As in 1956, the only measurable voter support outside the two-party system went to the Prohibition party and the various Socialist bodies; but because the aggregate vote for these parties came to less than 134,000—less than a fifth of one percent of the 69 million votes cast—notice is taken here only of the Democratic and Republican parties. Four years earlier the two big parties had walked gingerly around the issue, fearful of losing more support from some sectors of the population than they gained from others. But by 1960—so far had public attitudes changed—both resolutely picked it up and competed for the net gains that a moderately progressive stand seemed to promise. Both platforms came out for legislation that would facilitate Justice Department school desegregation suits; for federal aid for school districts in which a substantial start toward segregation was made; for advances beyond the weak Civil Rights Act of 1957 to eliminate barriers to Negro voting; for executive orders to end bias in the rental of federally assisted housing. The Democrats even went so far as to give their official blessing (which the Republicans chose still to withhold) to a permanent Fair Employment Practices Commission.

The Democratic platform's civil rights pronouncement ran to nearly 800 words. The following excerpts will serve to convey their spirit:

> . . . The Constitution of the United States rejects the notion that the Rights of Man means the rights of some men only. We reject it too. . . . It is the duty of the Congress to enact the laws necessary and proper to protect and promote [constitutional guarantees of the right to vote and equal protection of the laws]. The Supreme Court has the power to interpret these rights and the laws thus enacted. It is the duty of the President to see that these rights are respected and that the Constitution and laws as interpreted by the Supreme Court are faithfully executed. . . .
>
> If discrimination in voting, education, the administration of justice or segregated lunch counters are the issues in one area, discrimination in housing and employment may be pressing questions elsewhere. The peaceful demonstrations for first-class citizenship which have recently taken place in many parts of this country are a signal to all of us to make good at long last the guarantees of our Constitution. The time has come to assure equal access for all Americans to all areas of community life, including voting booths, schoolrooms, jobs, housing, and public facilities. The Democratic administration which takes office next January will therefore use the full powers provided in the Civil Rights Acts of 1957 and 1960 to secure for all Americans the right to vote. If these powers . . . prove inadequate, further powers will be sought. We will support whatever action is necessary to eliminate literacy tests and the payment of poll taxes as requirements for voting.
>
> A new Democratic Administration will also use its full powers—legal and moral—to insure the beginning of good-faith compliance with the Constitutional requirement that racial discrimination be ended in public education. We believe that every school district affected by the Supreme Court's school desegregation decision should submit a plan providing for at least first-step compliance by 1963, the 100th anniversary of the Emancipation Proclamation. To facilitate compliance, technical and financial assistance should be given to school districts facing special problems of transition.

The Republicans had this to say:

> Nevertheless, we recognize that much remains to be done. Each of the following pledges is practical—pledges made to result in maximum progress.
>
> 1. *Voting.* We pledge: Continued vigorous enforcement of the civil rights laws to guarantee the right to vote to all citizens in all areas of the country. Legislation to provide that the completion of six primary grades in a state accredited school is conclusive evidence of literacy for voting purposes.
>
> 2. *Public Schools.* We pledge: The Department of Justice will continue its vigorous support of court orders for school desegregation. Desegregation suits now pending involve at least 39 school districts. Those suits and others already concluded will affect most major cities in which school segregation is being practiced. It will use the new authority provided by the Civil Rights Act of 1960 to prevent obstruction of court orders. We will propose legislation to authorize the Attorney General to bring actions for school desegregation in the name of the United States in appropriate cases, as when economic coercion or threat of physical harm is used to deter persons from going to court to establish their rights. Our continuing support of the President's proposal, to extend federal aid and technical assistance to schools which in good faith attempted to desegregate. We oppose the pre-

tense of fixing a target date 3 years from now for the mere submission of plans for school desegregation . . . postponing until 1963 the legal process to enforce compliance. . . .

3. *Employment.* We pledge: Continued support for legislation to establish a Commission on Equal Job Opportunity to make permanent and to expand with legislative backing the excellent work being performed by the President's Committee on Government contracts. Appropriate legislation to end the discriminatory membership practices of . . . labor unions. . . . Special consideration of training programs aimed at developing the skills of those now working in marginal agricultural employment so that they can obtain employment in industry, notably in the new industries moving into the South.

4. *Housing.* We pledge: Action to prohibit discrimination in housing constructed with the aid of federal subsidies.

5. *Public Facilities and Services.* We pledge: Removal of any vestige of discrimination in the operation of federal facilities or procedures which may at any time be found. Opposition to the use of federal funds for the construction of segregated community facilities. Action to insure that public transportation and other government authorized services shall be free from segregation.

6. *Legislative Procedure.* We pledge: Our best efforts to change the present Rule 22 of the Senate and other appropriate congressional procedures that often make unattainable proper legislative implementation of constitutional guarantees. We reaffirm the constitutional right to peaceable assembly to protest discrimination in private business establishments. We applaud the action of the businessmen who have abandoned discriminatory practices in retail establishments, and we urge others to follow their example. . . . In summary, we pledge the full use of the power, resources and leadership of the federal government to eliminate discrimination based on race, color, religion or national origin and to encourage understanding and good will among all races and creeds.

Campaign of 1964

Again, the Republicans and Democrats polled all but a tiny fraction (150,000) of the total vote cast (68,000,000) in the national election, and it is to their 1964 platforms that we now turn.

Democrats: Reflecting the rising temper of black militants and their allies, one section of the platform, on "Democracy of Opportunity," called for full observance of the Civil Rights Act of 1964, but cautiously rebuked "lawless disregard for the rights of others . . . whether used to deny equal rights or to obtain [them]." The section also promised that the party would, in the next four years, "carry the War on Poverty forward." Another section, headed "One Nation, One People," condemned extremism, and "firmly pledged to continue the nation's march towards the goals of equal opportunity and equal treatment for all Americans regardless of race, creed, color or national origin."

A long concluding section, entitled "An Accounting of Stewardship,

1961–1964," summarized progress under the Kennedy-Johnson leadership and promised four more years of the same, without spelling out a specific program of action. It called particular attention, in a subsection on "Discrimination in Employment," to the Civil Rights Act of 1964, and to an executive order of President Kennedy establishing a Committee on Equal Employment Opportunity "to combat racial discrimination in the employment policies of the government agencies and private firms holding government contracts." Finally, a subsection of the "Accounting," specifically devoted to civil rights, recounted the party's redemption of its 1960 pledges, and concluded with these words:

> From the establishment of the President's Committee on Equal Employment Opportunity, under the chairmanship of the then Vice President Lyndon B. Johnson, on March 6, 1961 to this moment, the efforts of the Administration to provide full and equal civil rights for all Americans have never relaxed. The high point of achievement in this effort was reached with the passage of the Civil Rights Act of 1964, the greatest civil rights measure in the history of the American people.
>
> This landmark of our Democracy bars discrimination in the use of public accommodations, in employment, and in the administering of Federally-assisted programs. It makes available effective procedures for assuring the right to vote in Federal elections, directs Federal technical and financial assistance to local public school systems in desegregation, and strengthens the Civil Rights Commission. This comprehensive legislation resolves many of the festering conflicts which had been a source of irritation and uncertainty, and smooths the way for favorable resolutions of these problems.
>
> We have also insisted upon non-discrimination in apprenticeship, and have made free, unsegregated access a condition for Federal financial assistance to public libraries, programs for training of teachers of the handicapped, counseling, guidance and foreign language institutes, adult civil defense classes, and manpower development and training programs. In supporting construction of Hill-Burton hospitals, mental retardation and community health facilities, we have required non-discrimination in admission and provision of services and granting of staff privileges. . . .
>
> The 1960 platform was not directed to any one sector or group of Americans with particular interests. It proclaimed, rather, the Rights of Man. . . . The years since have been times of towering achievement. . . . In the 1,000 days of John F. Kennedy, in the eventful and culminating months of Lyndon B. Johnson, there has been born a new American greatness.
>
> Let us continue.

Republicans: The Republican National Convention, in drafting its platform, rebuked the Democrats for having "exploited interracial tension by extravagant campaign promises, without fulfillment . . . encouraging disorderly and lawless elements, and inefficiently administering the laws," permitted itself only a brief reference to civil rights, and then nominated Barry Goldwater, who had voted in the Senate against the Civil Rights Act of 1964. Hoping to build a resurgent Republican party in the South, the party did in fact carry five southern states (plus the candidate's home state, Arizona) and no others, while the Democratic ticket, capturing more than 61 percent of the total vote, reaped the largest plurality of votes in the nation's history. Here follows the 1964 platform's short section on civil rights:

> [We pledge:]
> —full implementation and faithful execution of the Civil Rights Act of 1964, and all other civil rights statutes, to assure equal rights and opportunities guaranteed by the Constitution to every citizen;
> —improvements of civil rights statutes adequate to changing needs of our times;
> —such additional administrative or legislative actions as may be required to end the denial, for whatever unlawful reason, of the right to vote. . . .
> —continued opposition to discrimination based on race, creed, national origin or sex. We recognize that the elimination of any such discrimination is a matter of heart, conscience, and education, as well as of equal rights under law.

Campaign of 1968

The national election of 1968 was a three-cornered contest between Republicans, Democrats, and the American Independent party of George C. Wallace, the uncompromising segregationist ex-governor of Alabama, who had stood in the schoolhouse door.

Neither of the parties had an explicit plank on civil rights in its platform. The Independents, seeking the broadest base upon which states' rightists and ultraconservatives could unite (and confident that they could count on the segregationist vote in any case), avoided intemperate language that might offend those who were moderate on racial issues but rightist in their general economic, social, and political philosophy. The Republican and Democratic parties, with an apprehensive eye on the passions which racial strife had stirred in the preceding four years, trod warily, hoping to win support on both ends and in the middle of the national electorate that had become increasingly polarized in its attitudes toward the civil rights movement. Pro-civil rights elements were now more militant than ever. On the other end of the spectrum, millions of Americans, distressed by riots and by steeply increased demands of the militants, felt that the crusade had gone too far too fast. Millions in between were uneasy about the future and seemed to favor a breathing spell.

The Republican Convention was the first to meet, in August. Party leaders were eager to retain and strengthen the party's base in the South, and were as doubtful that it could win over from its Democratic allegiance any very large sector of the black vote as they were persuaded that the country was not, for the present, interested in new civil rights legislation. The issue could not, of course, be wholly ignored, for it was, more than any other domestic question, very much on the people's mind. The result was a number of sidelong allusions, in widely separated parts of the platform.[1]

The preamble, in language that could be variously interpreted, insisted that "*We must* assure every individual an opportunity for satisfying and rewarding employment.—*We must* attack the root causes of poverty and eradicate racism, hatred and violence." A section on "Crisis of the Cities" deplored the "continuing decay of urban centers —the deepening misery and limited opportunity of citizens living there," but also warned that "Fire and looting . . . have brought great suffering in black communities," and that the party "strongly advocates measures to alleviate and remove the frustrations that contribute to riots. We simultaneously support decisive action to quell civil disorder, relying primarily on state and local governments to deal with these conditions . . . *We will not tolerate violence!*"

A section dealing with "Human Development . . . The Poor," pledged an attack upon poverty which would rely particularly on "state and community development corporations" and private investment. Farther than that the party chose not to express itself on what had become, by a wide margin, the liveliest and most agonizing domestic issue of the day.

The Democratic party went little further.[2] Although, like the Republicans, they did not explicitly propose any new social welfare programs, they did promise to "implement" the recommendations which the Kerner Commission on Civil Disorders[3] suggested. And, without proposing new legislation on civil rights, the platform promised laws to strengthen the Equal Employment Opportunity Commission's enforcement powers, and (as did the Republicans) endorsed the objectives of the 1968 (Open Housing) Civil Rights Act. The platform avoided the Republican party's emphasis on "law and order," because the phrase seemed to connote overzealous police repression in black ghettoes.

Passages calling attention to the party's achievement in enacting the Civil Rights Acts of 1964, 1965, and 1968 were not matched with pledges to accelerate desegregation of schools, but a lengthy statement on "Opportunity for All" contained some moving language, especially in a subsection entitled "Toward a Single Society":

> We acknowledge with concern the findings of the report of the bi-partisan National Advisory Commission on Civil Disorders and we commit ourselves to implement its recommendations and to wipe out, once and for all, the stain of racial and other discrimination from our national life.

[1] The complete text is in *Congressional Quarterly. Weekly Report,* August 9, 1968, 2126–34.

[2] The full text of the 1968 Democratic platform is in *Congressional Quarterly: Weekly Report,* August 30, 1968, pp. 2296–2308.

[3] See above, p. 331.

"The major goal," the Commission wrote, "is the creation of a true union—a single society and a single American identity." A single society, however, does not mean social or cultural uniformity. We are a nation of many social, ethnic and national groups. Each has brought richness and strength to America.

The Civil Rights Acts of 1964 and 1968 and the Voting Rights Act of 1965, all adopted under the vigorous leadership of President Johnson, are basic to America's long march toward full equality under the law.

We will not permit these great gains to be chipped away by opponents or eroded by administrative neglect. We pledge effective and impartial enforcement of these laws. If they prove inadequate, or if their compliance provisions fail to serve their purposes, we will propose new laws. In particular, the enforcement provisions of the legislation prohibiting discrimination in employment should be strengthened. This will be done as a matter of first priority.

We have also come to recognize that freedom and equality require more than the ending of repression and prejudice. The victims of past discrimination must be encouraged and assisted to take full advantage of opportunities that are now opening to them.

Mr. Wallace's platform (there had in fact been no national convention of his *ad hoc* party) predictably placed its emphasis on "law and order", local sovereignty, and the iniquities of the Supreme Court of the United States, as the following sampling of the document indicates:[1]

Clearly, our citizens are deeply concerned over the domestic plight of this nation. Its cities are in decay and turmoil; its local schools and other institutions stand stripped of their rightful authority; law enforcement agencies and officers are hampered by arbitrary and unreasonable restrictions imposed by a beguiled judiciary; crime runs rampant through the nation. . . . The Federal Government has adopted so-called "Civil Rights Acts," particularly one adopted in 1964, which have set race against race and class against class, all of which we condemn. It shall be our purpose . . . to restore to the states the powers and authority which rightfully belong to the state and local governments, so that each state shall govern and control its internal affairs without interference or domination of the Federal Government. We feel that the people of a given state are in better positions to operate its internal affairs, such as its public schools, than is the Federal Government in Washington. . . . In the period of the past three decades, we have seen the Federal judiciary, primarily the Supreme Court, transgress repeatedly upon the prerogatives of the Congress and exceed its authority by enacting judicial legislation, in the form of decisions based upon political and sociological considerations. . . . We repudiate and condemn any federal action regulating or controlling the sale or rental of private property as a socialistic assault upon not only the system of private ownership or property, but upon the right of each American citizen to manage his private affairs without regulation from an all-powerful central government. . . . The urban areas of our nation are in a state of social and economic unrest, largely brought about through unfilled promises hastily and carelessly made and the failure of ill-conceived programs enacted under duress and compulsion. . . . Those totally unfitted by training, background and environment for urban living who have been lured to the metropolitan

[1] The complete text is in *Congressional Quarterly: Weekly Report,* October 25, 1968, pp. 2962–70.

areas by the wholly false promises and commitments of self-seeking political leaders must be afforded an opportunity for training or, in the alternative, an opportunity to return to gainful employment in the less urbanized areas from whence they came. . . . Many of our primary and secondary school systems have become centers for social experimentation rather than centers of learning. . . . Sociological experiments must cease. The people of the several states, counties, cities and communities must be given the right to administer the affairs of their schools as they see fit without fear or threat of reprisal, economic or punitive, from the federal government.

(4)
STATE LAWS TO PROTECT CIVIL RIGHTS

Even though the more typical response of southern states and cities to the accelerating assault upon the segregation system was that of holding the line by various stratagems, ranging from bold re-enactment of Jim Crow statutes and ordinances to casual (and sometimes elaborate) inattention to federal court orders, a few legislatures in the South did in fact take steps to speed the demise of separate-but-equal.

Prodded by lawsuits, actual or threatened, some cities submitted plans for the gradual abandonment of at least *absolute* segregation in the public schools—some of them so slow, as we shall see, that they proved unacceptable to the courts. Others were accepted only upon the most lenient interpretation of "all deliberate speed."

A. *Anti-Segregation Statutes and Ordinances*

Northern states in a few instances made provision for positive steps to end de facto segregation in the schools. Massachusetts affords an example:[1]

AN ACT Providing for the Elimination of Racial Imbalance in the Public Schools. *Be it enacted* . . .

Section 37C

It is hereby declared to be the policy of the commonwealth to encourage all school committees to adopt as educational objectives the promotion of racial balance and the correction of existing racial imbalance in the public

[1] *Acts and Resolves of Massachusetts*, 1965 (chap. 641), 414.

schools. The prevention or elimination of racial imbalance shall be an objective in all decisions involving the drawing or altering of school attendance lines and the selection of new school sites.

Section 37D

The school committee of each city, town, and district shall, annually, at such time and in such form as the commissioner shall determine, submit statistics sufficient to enable a determination to be made of the percent of non-white pupils in all public schools and in each school under the jurisdiction of each such committee. . . . The school committee shall thereupon prepare a plan to eliminate such racial imbalance and file a copy of such plan with the [state] board . . . For purposes of this section, racial imbalance shall be deemed to exist when the percent of non-white students in any public school is in excess of fifty percent of the total number of students in such school.

[Subsequent provisions enact that (the quotation is from Race Relations Law Reporter's summary) the plan is to detail changes in existing districts, location of proposed school sites, additions to buildings, and other procedures. The board is empowered to provide technical assistance in planning and execution of corrective measures. The Commissioner of Education is authorized to withhold state funds from committees which fail to show progress after notification of imbalance. Provision is also made for judicial review of board action.][1]

Progress toward school integration, modest as it was, was in a few instances paralleled by similar changes of policy in other aspects of southern life. The city of San Antonio, Texas, for example, in March 1956, enacted an ordinance abolishing previously required segregation in the city's swimming pools and other recreational facilities. In the same spirit, Albany, Georgia, in March 1963, repealed the ordinances which had hitherto required segregation in transportation, ticket sales places and lines, and restaurants, while Asheville, North Carolina, in June 1963, repealed a thirty-year-old ordinance which had barred persons of different races from residing in the same neighborhood; and Raleigh, North Carolina, a few days earlier repealed a portion of the city code which required racial segregation in the public cemeteries. Atlanta, in December of the same year, repealed all city ordinances "which require the separation of persons because of race, color or creed in public transportation, recreation, entertainment and other facilities."[2]

Farther south, Bessemer, Alabama, in April 1962, and Birmingham, Alabama, in July 1963, ended legally required segregation in certain facilities. In the case of Birmingham the repealer struck down portions of the city code which had forbidden interracial recreation and had required separation of the races in restaurants and places of entertainment, and separate toilet facilities for Negro and white employees.[3]

[1] RRLR X, 1365.
[2] RRLR I, 589; VIII, 589.
[3] RRLR VIII, 1657, 1677.

Such measures in the first decade after the *School Segregation* cases were, however, extremely uncommon. Meanwhile, in the North, state laws and city ordinances banning discrimination in housing, in employment, and in public accommodations and recreation facilities became more and more common, even if they were often not, in all candor, very much more effective than they had been in the preceding decade. Even so, some of the older statutes were now improved, if not better enforced, and more states were added to the list of those which had comprehensive antidiscrimination laws of the sort described in Part V above.[1]

B. *Fair Employment Laws*

Fair employment practices statutes, like the Connecticut law previously cited,[2] also multiplied. In some cases they went beyond the older laws, though, again, they were not genuinely enforced, and job discrimination was only very slightly diminished except in the public service.[3] Sections of the Illinois law are here reproduced to illustrate the spirit of the new legislation:[4]

Section 1

. . . it is declared to be the public policy of this State that without in any way precluding any employer from selecting between persons of equal merit, ability, and capabilities, equal employment opportunity or apprenticeship opportunity without discrimination because of race, color, religion, national origin or ancestry should be protected by State law.

Section 2

[Definitions]

Section 3

Unfair Employment Practices. It is an unfair employment practice:

(a) For any employer, because of the race, color, religion, national origin or ancestry of an individual to refuse to hire, to segregate, or otherwise to discriminate against such individual with respect to hiring, selection and

[1] For some of the newer statutes, the reader may consult, for example, those of Michigan (RRLR I, 946); Washington (RRLR II, 461); Missouri (RRLR II, 468; Wyoming (RRLR II, 468; Kansas (RRLR VIII, 1682); Maryland (RRLR IX, 994); Oklahoma City (RRLR IX, 998); Tulsa, Oklahoma (RRLR IX, 1001); Minnesota (RRLR IX, 1481).

[2] See above, p. 254.

[3] To mention but a few examples, Baltimore passed an advanced measure of this sort in April 1956 (RRLR I, 1113), as did Des Moines, Iowa, in the same month (RRLR II, 725), and St. Louis, Missouri, in July 1956 (RRLR II, 468). California and Ohio notably strengthened their fair employment laws (RRLR IV, 441, 446; V, 242) in 1959, and Illinois and Missouri overhauled their statutes in 1961 (RRLR VI, 868, 874), to take a stronger stand against discriminatory employment practices and to prohibit discrimination in the membership rules of labor organizations.

[4] *Acts of Illinois*, 1961 (Senate Bill 609), 1845, as reprinted in RRLR VI, 868.

training for apprenticeship in any trade or craft, tenure, terms or conditions of employment; or

(b) For any employment agency to fail or refuse to classify properly, refer for employment, refer for apprenticeship, or accept applications for any apprenticeship, or otherwise to discriminate against any individual because of his race, color, religion, national origin or ancestry; or

(c) For any labor organization because of the race, color, religion, national origin or ancestry of any person to discriminate against such person, or to limit, segregate or classify its membership with respect to such person, or to limit such person's employment opportunities, such person's selection and training for apprenticeship in any trade or craft, or otherwise to take, or fail to take, any action which affects adversely such person's status as an employee or as an applicant for employment or as an apprentice, or as an applicant for apprenticeships, or such person's wages, tenure, hours or employment or apprenticeship conditions; or

(d) For any employer, employment agency or labor organization to discriminate against any person because he or she, reasonably and in good faith, has opposed any practice forbidden in this Act, or because he or she, reasonably and in good faith, has made a charge, testified or assisted in any investigation, proceeding or hearing under this Act; or

(e) For any person to compel or coerce any person to engage in any of the acts declared by this Act to be unfair employment practices.

Nothing in this Act shall preclude an employer from firing or selecting between persons for (1) any reason except for the unfair employment practices specifically prohibited by this Act, or (2) a bona fide occupational qualification.

Section 4

[Prohibits discrimination in employment by contractors and subcontractors supplying goods or services to the state or its agents.]

Section 5

[Creates an Illinois Fair Employment Commission.]

Section 6

Powers and Duties of the Commission: . . . .

(d) To adopt, promulgate, amend and rescind rules and regulations not inconsistent with the provisions of this Act.

(e) To receive, investigate and determine charges filed by complainants with it in conformity with this Act.

Section 7

[Creates a statewide, public educational program to promote fair employment.]

Sections 8–10

[Outlines procedures to be followed by complainants and by the Commission; grants the Commission power to issue cease and desist orders, subject to judicial review.]

Section 11

Judicial Enforcement. Whenever it appears that any person has violated a valid order of the Commission. . . , the Commission shall commence an action in the name of the People of the State of Illinois by petition . . . and praying for the issuance of an order directing such person . . . to comply with the order of the Commission. Upon the commencement of such action the Court shall have jurisdiction of the proceedings and power to grant or refuse . . . the relief sought. . . . The Court may punish for any violation of its order as in cases of civil contempt. . . .

In March 1966 the United States Commission on Civil Rights reported that thirty states and the District of Columbia had Fair Employment Practices Laws.

C. *Fair Housing Enactments*

In the early 1960's many states and cities in the North enacted fair housing statutes or ordinances, but their effect was so slight as to render them hardly worthy of serious consideration. Chicago, for example, passed in 1963 an impressively worded ordinance that defined as unfair a long list of usages, tactics, and ruses relating to the sale, leasing, or financing of housing; and empowered a Commission on Human Relations to cope with them (including the power to recommend to the mayor the suspension of the license of any broker who persisted in them).[1] Five years later the city's enormous Negro population was still tightly confined in some of the most congested and noisome ghettoes in America. In any case, state and local housing laws were, it would appear, for all practical purposes superseded by the Federal Civil Rights Act of 1968 and by the Supreme Court's ruling in *Jones* v. *Mayer*[2] which, ironically, found extensive federal authority to combat housing bias in the Civil Rights Act of 1866.

D. *Public Accommodations Statutes*

Northern and western states were also strengthening the guarantees of free access for all to public accommodations, without regard to race or color. Here follows a New England state's simple declaration:[3]

> *Section 1*
> *Public Accommodations; discrimination prohibited.* An owner or operator of a place of public accommodation or an agent or employee of said owner or operator shall not, because of race, creed, color or national origin of any person, refuse, withhold from or deny to such person any of the accommodations, advantages, facilities and privileges of such place of public accommodation. A place of public accommodation within the meaning of this act means any establishment which caters or offers its service or facilities or goods to the general public.
> *Section 2*
> *Penalty.* A person who violates a provision of Section 1 of this act shall be fined not more than $500.00 or imprisoned not more than thirty days, or both.

1 Chicago City Council, chap. 198. 7–B, Sept. 11, 1963; quoted in RRLR VIII, 1208.

2 See below, pp. 425, and 532.

3 *Acts and Resolves of Vermont*, 1957 (No. 109), 73.

E. *General Civil Rights Laws*

By 1966 states of the southern border were enacting comprehensive civil rights statutes. The Kentucky law[1] enacted in that year, in terms very much like those employed in the most advanced legislation of this kind in northern states, forbade racial discrimination both in employment and in the use of public accommodations. A Commission on Human Relations was established to enforce the act, with powers to receive and investigate complaints, to hold hearings and subpoena witnesses, and to undertake the elimination of unfair practices by conciliation and persuasion, and to make determinations as to the validity of charges. The Commission was authorized to issue cease and desist orders, subject to judicial review, and stiff criminal penalties were provided for persons who retaliate against those who seek the protection of the Act.

The law's opening paragraph suggests its tone:

(a) The general purposes of this Act are:

(1) To provide for execution within the State of the policies embodied in the Federal Civil Rights Act of 1964;

(2) To safeguard all individuals within the State from discrimination because of race, color, religion, and national origin in connection with employment and public accommodations; thereby to protect their interest in personal dignity and freedom from humiliation in places of public accommodation, to make available to the State their full productive capacities in employment, to secure the State against domestic strife and unrest which would menace its democratic institutions, to preserve the public safety, health and general welfare, and to further the interests, rights and privileges of individuals within the State; . . .

F. *Miscellaneous Rights Statutes*

Miscegenation and Intermarriage

At one time as many as thirty states had antimiscegenation laws on the books. Some states had never had such statutes; others had long since repealed them. In the wake of the *School Segregation* cases came several more repeals: in Nevada in 1959, Arizona in 1962, Utah in 1963. The movement reached the South in 1967 when the Supreme Court in *Loving* v. *Virginia*[2] categorically invalidated laws against intermarriage, as a violation of the Fourteenth Amendment. In the Border South, Maryland repealed its anti-mixed marriage law in 1967, some

[1] *Acts of Kentucky*, 1966 (chap. 2), 43.

[2] See below, p. 518.

months before the final decree in the *Loving* case, and in August the Attorney General of Virginia expressed an official opinion that the *Loving* ruling had the effect of invalidating that state's statute.

Hospitals

Another example of continuing legislative pressure upon the color line is illustrated by Chicago's ordinance forbidding discrimination in any hospital, public or private:[1]

> No hospital . . . nor any person connected with or rendering service in any hospital in any capacity whatsoever . . . shall deny to any person admission for care or treatment, equality of care or treatment in a hospital, or the use of any of the hospital facilities and services . . . on account of race, color, creed, national origin or ancestry. . . .

Instruction in Negro History

One imaginative enactment to combat racial bias was California's law requiring the teaching of Negro history in the schools.[2]

> *Section 1*
> Section 7604 of the Education Code is amended to read:
> . . . The course of study in the elementary schools shall include instruction in the following prescribed branches in the several grades. . . . The study of the role and contributions of American Negroes and other ethnic groups in the history of this country and this state shall be an integrated part of the required course in the history of the United States and California. . . . When adopting the textbook and teachers' manuals for use in elementary schools for the teaching of courses in civics and the history of the United States and California, the State Board of Education shall include only such textbooks which conform with the required courses and correctly portray the role and contribution of the American Negro and members of other ethnic groups in the total development of the United States and of the State of California. . . . The publisher will pay the costs in a sum not to exceed five hundred dollars ($500) of any investigation of the merits of any textbook offered and sold by him for use as a textbook in any public school in the state if a commission of impartial experts finds, after public hearing, that such textbook contained . . . material that does not correctly portray the role and contribution of the American Negro and members of other ethnic groups in the total development of the United States and of the State of California. [And in case a book fails to meet these requirements] the [State] Board of Education may order that the publisher shall cease to offer and sell such textbooks for use as a textbook in any public high school in the state. . . . [and] it shall be illegal for any district to purchase copies of such textbook . . . or to continue the use of the book as a textbook. . . .

[1] *Chicago Municipal Code,* Section B7–13.1 (March 14, 1956); quoted in RRLR II, 697.

[2] *Statutes of California,* 1964–1965 (chap. 895), II, 2499.

(5) STATE DISCRIMINATORY LAWS: REACTION TO THE *BROWN* DECISION

A. *Miscellaneous Discriminatory Statutes*

Although it was widely assumed that the *School Segregation* cases foreshadowed the end of *legally required* separate public facilities, southern legislatures continued to buttress the wall of segregation. A 1956 Louisiana statute, for example, revising older laws, required that common carriers provide separate waiting rooms for white intrastate passengers and for Negro intrastate *and* interstate passengers. Birmingham, Alabama, acted to "reaffirm, reenact and continue in full force and effect" ordinances which prescribed segregated seating on city buses, for the declared purpose of preventing "incidents, tensions, and disorder." Arkansas, early in 1959, passed a law requiring the assignment of passengers to seats on all intrastate buses and providing penalties for refusal to take such seats.

New details were added to familiar patterns of segregation, and older rules were tightened. Louisiana was one of the states in which even blood banks were required to observe strict racial isolation:[1]

> *Section 1*
> All human blood . . . to be used in the State of Louisiana for transfusions . . . shall be labeled with the word "Caucasian," "Negroid," or "Mongoloid" . . . so as to clearly indicate the race of the donor. . . . No human blood not [so] labeled . . . shall be used. . . .
> *Section 2*
> Any person about to receive a blood transfusion . . . or the next of kin of said person shall be informed of the race of the donor . . . if it is proposed to use blood from a person of a different racial classification.
> *Section 3*
> . . . a transfusion may be given without regard to the provisions of this Act, provided that [a] doctor shall certify to the fact that there was . . . an emergency.

The city of Sarasota, Florida, in 1956, "for the immediate protection . . . of the peace, safety, health, and property of the City and the inhabitants," enacted that:[2]

[1] Acts of Louisiana, Reg. Sess., 1958 (No. 519); as quoted in RRLR III, 1065.
[2] Sarasota, Florida, Ordinance No. 913 (September 4, 1967), as quoted in RRLR I, 945.

Section 1
Whenever members of . . . two or more . . . races shall . . . be upon any public . . . bathing beach within the corporate limits of the City of Sarasota, it shall be the duty of the Chief of police or other officer . . . in charge of the police forces of the City . . . with the assistance of such police forces, forthwith to clear the area involved of all members of all races present. . . .

Louisiana, by an act of July, 1956 enacted:[1]

Section 1
That all persons, firms or corporations . . . shall provide separate sanitary facilities for members of the white and negro races employed by them or permitted to come upon their premises.
Section 2
That [they] . . . shall provide separate eating places in separate rooms and separate eating and drinking utensils for members of the white and negro races.
Section 3
All such sanitary facilities, eating places and drinking facilities shall be designated "FOR WHITES ONLY" and "FOR COLORED ONLY" respectively.

The same state, a few days later ordered:[2]

Section 1
That all persons, [and] firms . . . are prohibited from . . . permitting on premises under their control any dancing, social functions, entertainments, athletic training, games, sports or contests . . . in which the participants . . . are members of the white and negro races.
Section 2
That at any entertainment or athletic contest, where the public . . . may attend, the sponsors . . . shall provide separate seating arrangements, and separate sanitary, drinking water and other facilities for members of the white and negro races, and to mark such separate accommodations . . . with signs printed in bold letters.

Virginia lawmakers proposed to enjoin racially mixed interscholastic athletic contests.[3]

. . . no athletic team of any school [shall] engage in any athletic contest of any nature within the State of Virginia with another team on which persons of any other race are members, nor [shall] any such school . . . permit any member of its student body to engage in any athletic contest within the State of Virginia with a person of another race. . . .

Montgomery, Alabama, took pains to prevent interracial games of dominoes and checkers, while Huntsville, Alabama, set aside one day a week on which Negroes might use the Municipal Golf Course:[4]

[1] *Acts of Louisiana*, Reg. Sess., 1956 (No. 395), 773.
[2] *Acts of Louisiana*, Reg. Sess., 1956 (No. 579), 578.
[3] *Acts of Virginia*, 1956 (House Joint Resolution No. 97, March 2, 1956); quoted in RRLR I, 589.
[4] *Montgomery, Alabama*, Ordinance 15-57, March 19, 1957; quoted in RRLR II, 774. Resolution of City Council, Huntsville, Ala., Feb. 23, 1956; quoted in RRLR I, 589.

a) It shall be unlawful for white and colored persons to play together . . . in any game of cards, dice, dominoes, checkers, pool, billiards, softball, basketball, baseball, football, golf, track, and at swimming pools, beaches, lakes, or ponds or any other . . . games or athletic . . . contests, either indoors or outdoors.

. . . it was unanimously voted to set aside each Monday as the day on which negroes could play on the Municipal Golf Course and that season tickets be sold to them, for this one day per week only, for $10.00 each.

Georgia was one of many southern states which proposed to sell public facilities in case integration could not be otherwise forestalled.[1]

Section 1

. . . the State or any municipal corporation, county or other political subdivision thereof, shall have authority to sell, lease, grant, exchange or otherwise dispose of any property which has been dedicated to a public use for recreational or park purposes . . . without regard to whether . . . said property has become unsuitable or inadequate for the purpose for which originally dedicated. . . .

Other states, as did Louisiana, coolly reaffirmed their intention to continue, under the police power, to segregate all recreational facilities.[2]

Section 1

All public parks, recreation centers, play grounds, community centers and other such facilities at which swimming, dancing, golfing, skating or other recreational activities are conducted shall be operated separately for members of the white and colored races. . . . This provision is made . . . for the purpose of protecting the public health, morals and the peace and good order in the state and not because of race.

The state of Mississippi expressly empowered businesses to select their clientele:[3]

Section 1

Every person, firm or corporation . . . is hereby authorized . . . to choose . . . the . . . persons he or it desires to do business with, and . . . to refuse . . . to . . . serve any person that [he or it] does not desire to . . . serve. . . .

South Carolina joined other states in preserving segregation in state parks:[4]

. . . . The State Commission of Forestry is vested with the authority to operate and supervise only racially separate parks and to admit to the facilities of the State Parks only persons having the express permission of the State. . . .

California, normally considered an "advanced civil rights state," submitted to popular referendum a proposed addition ("Proposition

[1] *Acts of Georgia,* 1956 (No. 20); quoted in RRLR I, 427.
[2] *Louisiana Acts,* Reg. Sess., 1956 (No. 14), 41.
[3] *Laws of Mississippi,* 1956 (chap. 257), 307.
[4] *Acts of South Carolina,* 1956 (No. 813, Part II, sec. 14), 1955.

14") to the state constitution, whose effect would be to permit sellers or lessors of real estate to refuse to sell or rent to Negroes, and to supersede older legislation which had banned racial discrimination in the renting of apartments and in the sale or rental of private dwellings containing more than four units.

The clause (which was later struck down by the United States Supreme Court in *Reitman* v. *Mulkey*[1]) read, in part, as follows:[2]

> Neither the State nor any subdivision or agency thereof shall deny, limit or abridge, directly or indirectly, the right of any person, who is willing or desires to sell, lease or rent any part or all of his real property, to decline to sell, lease, or rent such property to such person or persons as he, in his absolute discretion, chooses.

B. *The Franchise and Elections: Renewed Discrimination*

Beginning with the Civil Rights Act of 1957, increased pressure from the federal government upon the states to obey the Fifteenth Amendment called forth increasing resistance from southern states. It did not evoke much new legislation, for the champions of Negro disfranchisement preferred to rely, as in the past, on cumbersome registration procedures and other, extralegal, constraints to keep Negroes from voting and holding office. Some states did, nevertheless, legislate new barriers.

Louisiana required that the race of all candidates named on ballots be designated:[3]

> *Section 1-C*
> On the ballots to be used in any state or local primary, general or special election the Secretary of State shall cause to be printed within parentheses ( ) beside the name of each candidate, the race of the candidate . . . in print of the same size as the print in the names of the candidates on the ballots.

Some states, like Georgia, Louisiana, and Mississippi, placed more confidence than formerly upon elaborate forms to be filled out by those who sought to register, including questions which overtaxed a candidate's knowledge, or even exposed him, if he made a slip, to the charge of supplying false and misleading information, and thus rendering himself permanently ineligible. In some instances, reading-and-explaining clauses were reworded for greater effectiveness, or older detailed statutes of the pre-*Brown* era were carefully reinforced. Here again the principal reliance was upon the qualifications and registra-

[1] See below, p. 531.
[2] California Constitution, sec. 24, added to Article 1. See RRLR IX, 1894.
[3] *Louisiana Acts,* Reg. Sess., 1960 (No. 538), 539.

tion of voters. Georgia, for example, in 1958, passed a law full of sinuosities that common folk could scarcely trace out, and with which they would find it tedious, if not hazardous, to comply. It was designated as "AN ACT *To effect a complete revision of the laws of this State relating to the qualification and registration of voters . . .*"

Much of the law was devoted to the qualifications, selection, and powers of local registrars. In addition, persons seeking to register were asked to fill out a registration card and swear to the accuracy of the detailed information it called upon them to supply. One slippery question asked: "Under what constitutional classification do you desire to make application for registration?" Another clause provided for the suspension of the registration process for six months preceding a general election.

Section 19 propounded thirty questions of which the applicant, to be eligible for registration, must answer correctly at least twenty. Examples of the questions follow.[1]

Section 19

The standard list of questions which shall be propounded to each applicant is as follows: 1. What is a republican form of government? . . . 3. In what State Senatorial District do you live and what are the names of county or counties in such District? 4. What is the name of the State Judicial Circuit in which you live and what are the names of the counties or county in such Circuit? 5. What is the definition of a felony in Georgia? . . . . 7. What does the Constitution of Georgia prescribe as the qualifications of Representatives in the Georgia House of Representatives? 8. How does the Constitution of the United States provide that it may be amended? 9. Who is the Chief Justice of the Supreme Court of Georgia and who is the Presiding Justice of that court? . . . 11. Who is the solicitor general of the State Judicial Circuit in which you live and who is the Judge of such Circuit? (If such Circuit has more than one Judge, name them all.) 12. If the Governor of Georgia dies, who exercises the executive power, and if both the governor and the person who succeeds him die, who exercises the executive power? 13. (a) What does the Constitution of the United States provide regarding the suspension of the privilege of the writ of Habeas Corpus? (b) What does the Constitution of Georgia provide regarding the suspension of the writ of Habeas Corpus? 14. What are the names of the persons who occupy the following State offices in Georgia? (1) Governor (2) Lieutenant Governor (3) Secretary of State (4) Attorney General (5) Comptroller General (6) State Treasurer (7) Commissioner of Agriculture (8) State School Superintendent (9) Commissioner of Labor. . . . 21. What are the names of the persons who occupy the following offices in your county? (1) Clerk of the Superior Court (2) Ordinary (3) Sheriff. 22. How may a new state be admitted into the Union? . . . 25. In what Federal Court District do you live? 26. What are the names of the Federal District Judges of Georgia? . . . . .

The law further ordained that a complete list of registrants was to be kept available for public inspection, a provision that gave Negroes

[1] *Acts of Georgia,* 1958 (No. 321), I, 269.

pause, lest they antagonize whites upon whose continued good will their livelihood and well-being and felicity were contingent. It was, in fact, not uncommon in states of the Lower South for local newspapers to publish voters' lists, complete with racial designations, a hazard to which Negroes did not lightly subject themselves.

The statute also provided that any person who was registered to vote in the 1956 general election would not be required to reregister under the terms of this law. Few Negroes had dared to register in 1956, and whites who were in the habit of voting were of course not reached by the new statute.

C. *State Legislation to Thwart School Desegregation*

On the tenth anniversary of *Brown,* only one in eleven Negroes in the elementary and secondary schools of the nation was attending classes with whites. Even that statistic grossly understates the vigor of southern resistance; for the overwhelming majority of newly desegregated schools in 1964 were concentrated in the District of Columbia and the six states of the border South. In the eleven states of the Middle and Lower South, which had comprised the Confederacy, only one Negro schoolchild in eighty-five was in an "integrated situation"; indeed, in some states it was only in the early 1960's that the very first solitary breaches had been made in the wall, and in Mississippi the record could not yet show a single Negro in school with whites.

For a year after *Brown* the South marked time until the Court's decree of implementation was handed down in *Brown II.* Once the court rendered its second judgment and called for compliance with all deliberate speed, the Border states, and particularly some of their largest cities, began moving toward obedience to the newly clarified law of the land. In some school districts of the Border and Upper South, admission of a few—in some, very few indeed—Negroes to previously all-white schools was offered as a token of intention to make a reasonable beginning. One interesting example of this gradualism proposed to complete the process of integrating the elementary and high schools in twelve years, by desegregating one grade per year. This scheme, initiated in Nashville in 1957, was subsequently approved in the federal courts for some cities and counties, but considered too slow in other areas where circumstances were favorable for more rapid integration.

Elsewhere, especially in the Middle and Lower South, recalcitrance was more marked, ranging from "massive resistance" (as in Virginia, Alabama, South Carolina, Mississippi, and Louisiana) to the more moderate, though still by no means compliant, stance of Tennessee and North Carolina.

Social and economic pressures continued, after 1954, to be more effective than official public acts in restraining Negroes from availing themselves of the rights and privileges that the Court's reading of the Constitution now theoretically guaranteed them. There were still the hard realities which ensured that for several years little would be changed in the lives of millions of Negroes. Social rebuke and ostracism, devastating economic reprisal, and the threat (though not often the actuality—perhaps because the dare was not frequently taken) of bodily harm still, as of old, usually persuaded even the most intrepid black that discretion was the better part of valor, Court or no Court.

The number and diversity of laws to prevent or impede school integration was far too great to permit more here than a summary of the major forms. By Professor C. Vann Woodward's count, 106 new measures to sequester the races were added to southern statute books by the end of 1956.[1] By May 1964, a decade of response to *Brown*, according to the *Southern School Reporter*,[2] had produced in the Middle and Lower South almost 450 laws and resolutions to frustrate the Supreme Court's decree, and some 300 lawsuits relating to school desegregation.

Nullification and Interposition

One startling sequel of the *School Segregation* cases was the reiteration by southern states of the old Nullification doctrine of the late 1820's. While some, like North Carolina, confined themselves to resolutions of protest, at least eight others went the greater length of excoriating the Court's judgment as an unconstitutional usurpation of state sovereignty and declaring that they had no intention to comply.

Alabama led the procession with an ominous measure enacted on February 2, 1956:[3]

HOUSE JOINT RESOLUTION

WHEREAS the Constitution of the United States was formed by the sanction of the several states, given by each in its sovereign capacity; and

WHEREAS the states, being the parties to the constitutional compact, it follows of necessity that . . . they must decide themselves, in the last resort,

[1] *The Strange Career of Jim Crow* (second revised edition, New York, 1966), p. 162.

[2] *Southern School News: Ten Years in Review,* May 17, 1964.

[3] *Laws of Alabama,* Special Session, 1956 (No. 42), I, 70.

such questions as may be of sufficient magnitude to require their interposition, and

WHEREAS . . . : The Supreme Court of the United States asserts, for its part, that the states did . . . upon the adoption of the Fourteenth Amendment, prohibit unto themselves the power to maintain racially separate public institutions; the State of Alabama . . . asserts that it and its sister states have never surrendered such rights; and

WHEREAS this assertion upon the part of the Supreme Court of the United States, . . . constitutes a deliberate, palpable, and dangerous attempt by the court to prohibit to the states certain rights and powers never surrendered by them; and

WHEREAS the question of contested power asserted in this resolution is not within the province of the court to determine, but . . . the judgment of all other equal parties to the compact must be sought to resolve the question; be it

RESOLVED *By The Legislature of Alabama, Both Houses Thereto Concurring;*

That until the issue between the State of Alabama and the General Government is decided by the submission to the States . . . of a suitable constitutional amendment that would declare, in plain and unequivocal language, that the states do surrender their power to maintain public school and other public facilities on a basis of separation as to race, the Legislature of Alabama declares the decisions and orders of the Supreme Court of the United States relating to separation of races in the public schools are, as a matter of right, null, void, and of no effect; and the Legislature of Alabama declares to all men as a matter of right, this State is not bound to abide thereby; we declare, further, our firm intention to take all appropriate measures honorably and constitutionally available to us, to avoid this illegal encroachment upon our rights, and to urge upon our sister states their prompt and deliberate efforts to check further encroachment by the General Government, through judicial legislation, upon the reserved powers of all the states.

That the Governor is requested to transmit a copy of this resolution to . . . the Congress, and to the Supreme Court of the United States for its information.

Georgia's resolution of interposition and nullification,[1] three times as long as Alabama's, expressed the same fiery spirit, and also declared her "firm intention . . . to avoid this illegal encroachment of the rights of her people," and that the *School Segregation* decisions were "null, void and of no force or effect."

Mississippi's philippic, after lecturing the Supreme Court and the nation on the nature of the federal compact, also pronounced the disputed decisions "in violation of the Constitution of the United States and the State of Mississippi, and therefore . . . unconstitutional, invalid and of no lawful effect within the confines of the State of Mississippi."[2]

South Carolina entitled its remonstrance with these words:[3]

[1] *Acts of Georgia*, 1956 (No. 130), I, 642.
[2] *Laws of Mississippi*, 1956 (chap. 466), 741.
[3] *Acts of South Carolina*, 1956 (No. 914), 2172.

A JOINT RESOLUTION

Condemning And Protesting The Usurpation And Encroachment On The Reserved Powers Of The States By The Supreme Court Of The United States, Calling Upon The States And Congress To Prevent This And Other Encroachments By The Central Government And Declaring The Intention Of South Carolina To Exercise All Powers Reserved To It, To Protect Its Sovereignty And The Rights Of Its People.

Virginia's legislature sharply reminded the Court and its supporters of "the resolution it adopted on December 21, 1798," and went on to say:[1]

THEREFORE, the General Assembly of Virginia, appealing to our Creator as Virginia appealed to Him for Divine Guidance when on June 29, 1776, our people established a Free and Independent State, now appeals to her sister States for that decision which only they are qualified under our mutual compact to make, . . . by which an amendment, designed to settle the issue of contested power here asserted, may be proposed to all the states,

And be it finally resolved, that [we] . . . urge upon our sister States, whose authority over their own most cherished powers may next be imperiled, their prompt and deliberate efforts to check this and further encroachment by the Supreme Court, through judicial legislation, upon the reserved powers of the States.

Louisiana, Florida, and Arkansas were no less emphatic. In the latter state a constitutional amendment was adopted by initiative petition. Its major sections read as follows:[2]

Section 1

From and after the Adoption of the Amendment, the General Assembly of the State of Arkansas shall take appropriate action and pass laws opposing in every Constitutional manner the Un-Constitutional desegregation decisions of May 17, 1954 and May 31, 1955 of the United States Supreme Court, including interposing the sovereignty of the State of Arkansas to the end of nullification of these and all deliberate, palpable and dangerous invasions of or encroachment upon rights and powers not delegated to the United States nor prohibited to the States by the Constitution of the United States and Amendments thereto, and those rights and powers reserved to the states and to the People thereof by any department or commission of the Government of the United States. . . . Said opposition shall continue steadfast until such time as such Un-Constitutional invasions or encroachments shall have abated or shall have been rectified. . . .

Section 3

The General Assembly shall enact such laws under the Police Powers reserved to the States as may be necessary to regulate health, morals, education, marriage, good order and to insure the domestic tranquillity of the citizens of the State of Arkansas.

Much the same spirit pervaded the "Southern Manifesto," to which nineteen senators and seventy-seven representatives defiantly sub-

[1] *Acts of Virginia,* Ex. Sess., 1956 (Joint Resolution No. 3), 1213.

[2] Constitution of Arkansas, Amendment No. 47; reprinted in RRLR 1, 1117.

scribed their names. It prompted a young lawyer in Clinton, Tennessee, to say, "What the hell do you expect these people to do when they have ninety some odd congressmen from the South signing a piece of paper that says you're a southern hero if you defy the Supreme Court?"[1] A few lonely southern congressmen refused to sign. North Carolina's House delegation included three nonsigners, two of whom failed of renomination in the next primary, while the third, a veteran of many years' seniority and Chairman of the House Agriculture Committee, managed to retain his seat.

"THE SOUTHERN MANIFESTO": DECLARATION OF CONSTITUTIONAL PRINCIPLES[2]

The unwarranted decision of the Supreme Court in the public school cases is now bearing the fruit always produced when men substitute naked power for established law. . . .

We regard the decision of the Supreme Court in the school cases as a clear abuse of judicial power. It climaxes a trend in the Federal Judiciary undertaking to legislate, in derogation of the authority of Congress, and to encroach upon the reserved rights of the States and the people.

The original Constitution does not mention education. Neither does the 14th amendment nor any other amendment. The debates preceding the submission of the 14th amendment clearly show that there was no intent that it should affect the system of education maintained by the States.

The very Congress which proposed the amendment subsequently provided for segregated schools in the District of Columbia.

In the case of Plessy v. Ferguson in 1896 the Supreme Court expressly declared that under the 14th amendment no person was denied any of his rights if the States provided separate but equal public facilities. This decision has been followed in many other cases. It is notable that the Supreme Court, speaking through Chief Justice Taft, a former President of the United States, unanimously declared in 1927 in Lunt v. Rice that the "separate but equal" principle is "within the discretion of the State in regulating its public schools and does not conflict with the 14th amendment."

This interpretation, restated time and again, became a part of the life of the people of many of the States and confirmed their habits, customs, traditions, and way of life. It is founded on elemental humanity and common sense, for parents should not be deprived by Government of the right to direct the lives and education of their own children.

This unwarranted exercise of power by the Court, contrary to the Constitution, is creating chaos and confusion in the States principally affected. It is destroying the amicable relations between the white and Negro races that have been created through 90 years of patient effort by the good people of both races. It has planted hatred and suspicion where there has been heretofore friendship and understanding.

We reaffirm our reliance on the Constitution as the fundamental law of the land.

[1] Don Shoemaker, ed., *With All Deliberate Speed* (New York, 1957), p. 38.

[2] 102 *Congressional Record,* No. 43, 3948, 4004, March 12, 1956.

We decry the Supreme Court's encroachments on rights reserved to the States and to the people, contrary to established law, and to the Constitution.

We commend the motives of those States which have declared the intention to resist forced integration by any lawful means.

We appeal to the States and people who are not directly affected by these decisions to consider the constitutional principles involved against the time when they too, on issues vital to them, may be the victims of judicial encroachment.

We pledge ourselves to use all lawful means to bring about a reversal of this decision which is contrary to the Constitution and to prevent the use of force in its implementation.

In this trying period, as we all seek to right this wrong, we appeal to our people not to be provoked by the agitators and troublemakers invading our States and to scrupulously refrain from disorder and lawless acts.

Signed by: [Here follow the signatures of nineteen senators and seventy-nine representatives.]

Anti-Barratry Laws

One of the responses of southern state legislatures to the *School Segregation* cases was the enactment of laws to restrain those—both individuals and organized groups—who "incited" or "maintained" litigation which sought through the courts to force compliance with the historic *Brown* decision, or to defeat discrimination. Typically, these laws undertook to restate the old English common law offense of "barratry" which Blackstone had long ago described as "frequently exciting and stirring up suits and quarrels between his majesty's subjects, at law or otherwise."

The redefinitions were clearly directed against the National Association for the Advancement of Colored People; indeed, some of them frankly singled out the association by name. Other laws, with much the same intent, required applicants for public employment (and especially in the public schools) to disclose the names of all associations of which they were members or to which they made contributions; or required various associations to register with public authorities and to supply them with their membership lists and a full accounting of their financial affairs and of the objects they were seeking to achieve; or forbade the employment by the state and by county and city agencies of any person who was a member of the NAACP.

In March 1956, for example, the General Assembly of South Carolina by joint resolution created a committee, clothed with power to subpoena witnesses and records and to take testimony under oath, to conduct a searching investigation into the activities of the NAACP. The prefatory "whereases" afford a convenient summary of the assumptions that underlay such laws:[1]

[1] *Acts of South Carolina,* 1956 (No. 920), 2182.

Whereas, the . . . [NAACP] has as its major objective the fomenting and nurturing of a bitter feeling of unrest, unhappiness and resentment among the members of the Negro race with their status in . . . the South; and

Whereas, the result of this concentrated, organized and well-financed effort is to increase the tension between the two races to the extent that amicable and friendly relations, so common in the past, have deteriorated and have become extremely difficult . . .

The state's anti-barratry law typifies those enacted by other southern states:[1]

AN ACT to Define The Crime of Barratry And To Provide Penalties For The Commission Thereof.

Be it enacted by the General Assembly of the State of South Carolina:

Section 1

Any person who shall willfully solicit or incite another to bring, prosecute or maintain an action, at law or in equity, in any court having jurisdiction within this state, and who:

(a) thereby seeks to obtain employment for himself or for another to prosecute or defend such action, or (b) has no direct and substantial interest in the relief thereby sought, or (c) does so with intent to distress or harass any party to such action, or (d) directly or indirectly pays . . . any party to such an action, or any person who shall willfully bring, prosecute or maintain an action, at law or in equity, in any court having jurisdiction within this State and who: (1) has no direct or substantial interest in the relief thereby sought, or (2) thereby seeks to defraud or mislead the court, or (3) brings such action with intent to distress or harass any party thereto, or (4) directly or indirectly receives any money or other thing of value to induce the bringing of such action, shall be guilty of the crime of barratry.

Section 2

Any persons convicted of barratry shall be forever barred from practicing law in this State.

Section 3

As used in Section 1 of this act, the term "person" shall include corporations and unincorporated associations. . . .

Section 4

Any corporation or unincorporated association found guilty of the crime of barratry shall be forever barred from doing business or carrying on any activity within the State. . . .

Section 5

The crime of barratry shall be punishable by a fine of not more than $5,000.00 or by imprisonment of not more than two (2) years, or both. . . .

Another category of laws, like this one enacted by Arkansas, prescribed heavy punishments for persons who failed to register and give a detailed account of their efforts to influence public policy with respect to race relations:[2]

[1] *Acts of South Carolina,* 1957 (No. 25), 23.

[2] *Acts of Arkansas,* 1957 (No. 85), 281.

Section 5

The provisions of this Act shall apply only to such person who, . . . in any manner whatsoever, . . . solicits, collects, or receives contributions to be used . . . to aid in the accomplishment of any of the following purposes:

(a) The passage by the Congress of the United States of any . . . legislation . . . designed to limit . . . in any manner the . . . control of school districts in Arkansas by the elected and qualified officers . . . and employees of such school districts. (b) The defeat by the General Assembly of Arkansas of any . . . legislation . . . designed to . . . preserve inviolate the rights of the State of Arkansas to control . . . its own domestic institutions according to its own judgment. (c) Soliciting and recruiting plaintiffs in prospective litigation involving the operation, management and control of the domestic institutions of the State and particularly the public schools of the State. (d) The promotion of integration of races in the public schools of the State of Arkansas . . . and the rendition of legal aid . . . to such negroes as may be involved . . . in prospective . . . litigation involving their admission into any public school in the State of Arkansas.

Section 6

Any person who shall engage in [such] purposes . . . shall, before doing [so], . . . register with the State Sovereignty Commission of Arkansas and shall give the Commission in writing and under oath his name and business address, the name and address of the person by whom he is employed and for whose interest he works for such objects, the duration of such employment, how much [and] by whom he is paid, . . . , how much he is to be paid for expenses and what expenses are to be included. . . .

Anti-NAACP Laws

On September 12, 1958, the Arkansas legislature joined those states requiring applicants for public employment to disclose their affiliations; and six months later it decided to be more explicit:[1]

WHEREAS, the National Association for the Advancement of Colored People has, through its program and leaders in the state of Arkansas, disturbed the peace and tranquillity which has long existed between the White and Negro races, and has threatened the progress and increased understanding between Negroes and Whites; and

WHEREAS, the National Association for the Advancement of Colored People has encouraged and agitated the members of the Negro race in the belief that their children were not receiving educational opportunities equal to those accorded white children, and has urged [them] to exert every effort to break down all racial barriers existing between the two races in schools, public transportation facilities and society in general; and

. . . WHEREAS, . . . the Arkansas Legislative Council has found that the [NAACP] is a captive of the international communist conspiracy;

Now therefore, be it enacted by the General Assembly of the State of Arkansas:

Section 1

It shall be unlawful for any member of the [NAACP] to be employed by

[1] *Acts of Arkansas*, 1959 (No. 115), 327.

the State, school district, county or any municipality thereof, . . . so long as [such] membership . . . is maintained.

Section 2

The board of trustees of any public school or state supported college shall be authorized to demand of any teacher or other employee of the school, who is suspected of being a member of the [NAACP] that he submit to the board a written statement under oath setting forth whether or not he is a member . . . and the immediate employer of any employee of the State or of any county or municipality thereof is similarly authorized in the case any employee is suspected of being a member of the [NAACP]. . . . Any person refusing to submit a statement as provided herein, shall be summarily dismissed.

School Closing Laws

The stouter enemies of integration preferred to see public schools closed rather than open them to racially mixed constituencies. This extreme remedy was rarely applied—most conspicuously in the case of Prince Edward County, Virginia—but legislation to authorize it was enacted by several states, to be available if other means failed. A North Carolina statute, for example, provided:[1]

Section 5

Any board of education may at any time . . . call for an election of the question of closing the public schools within . . . [its] jurisdiction; provided, that an election shall be called by the board when a petition signed by at least fifteen percent . . . of the registered voters residing within the local option unit is presented to the board requesting such an election. . . . Any child living within a [district] who could attend a public school in such [district] except for the fact that operation of such school has been suspended under provisions of this Article shall not be entitled as a matter of right to attend any other public school, but in lieu thereof shall be entitled to an education expense grant. . . .

Several states empowered their governors to shut down the schools to prevent integration. A Louisiana law, for instance, enacted that:[2]

Section 1

The governor, in order to secure justice to all, preserve the peace, and promote the interest, safety, and happiness of all the people, is authorized and empowered to close any racially mixed public school or any public school which is subject to a court order requiring it to admit students of both the negro and white races. . . .

Diverting Funds to Private Schools

Where school closings were authorized, and in some cases where state laws did not explicitly authorize so extreme a measure, legisla-

[1] *Laws of North Carolina,* Ex. Sess., 1956 (chap. 4), 9.

[2] *Acts of Louisiana,* Reg. Sess., 1958 (No. 256); quoted in RRLR III, 778.

tion provided for the support of private schools through scholarships or tuition grants for pupils. Virginia thus authorized local school boards to transfer public funds for this purpose.[1]

> 1. The local school board of every county, city or town is hereby authorized when it is deemed to be for the public benefit, to transfer school funds, . . . and to expend same in furtherance of the elementary and secondary education of the children of such county, city or town in nonsectarian private schools. . . .

Laws to End Compulsory School Attendance

Another stratagem for setting the Supreme Court's decision at nought was that of amending or repealing compulsory school-attendance laws. Virginia, in a two-sentence enactment, decreed:[2]

> 1. That [all laws relating to compulsory school attendance] are repealed.
> 2. An emergency exists and this act is in force from [the day of] its passage.

North Carolina was content with an amendment to its compulsory education law:[3]

> *Section 1*
> [The] requirement shall not apply with respect to any child when the board of education of the administrative unit in which the child resides finds that . . . such child is now assigned against the wishes of his parent or guardian, or person standing in loco parentis to such child, to a public school attended by a child of another race and it is not reasonable and practicable to reassign such child to a public school not attended by a child of another race. . . .

Encouraging Teachers to Shift to Private Schools

Georgia undertook to facilitate mass migration to private schools by encouraging teachers to shift from public to private faculties:[4]

> *Section 1*
> . . . any teacher or school employee employed in any public school and coming under the provisions of . . . any retirement fund or pension system maintained by any county, city or independent school district in this State . . . who shall accept employment in any nonsectarian private school in this State in which students . . . are eligible for grants from the State under other laws of this State, shall continue subject to all provision of such laws and entitled to all the benefits provided thereby or thereunder. . . .

[1] *Acts of Virginia,* Special Session, 1956 (chap. 62), 62.
[2] *Acts of Virginia,* Special Session, 1959 (chap. 2), 4.
[3] *Laws of North Carolina,* Ex. Sess., 1956 (chap. 6), 13.
[4] *Acts of Georgia,* 1957 (No. 7), I, 8.

Scholarships for Private School Students

Some states looked to cash scholarships to enable children to transfer to schools remote from their homes. If a school was under federal duress to desegregate, the white children could promptly be shifted to a still-all-white public or private school.[1]

. . . to afford each individual freedom in choosing public or private schooling, the General Assembly finds that it is . . . in the public interest that scholarships should be provided from the public funds of the State for the education of the children in nonsectarian private schools in or outside, and in public schools located outside, the locality where the children reside; and that counties, cities and towns, if the town be a separate school district approved for operation, should be authorized to levy taxes and appropriate public funds to provide such scholarships.

2. Every child in this Commonwealth between the ages of six and twenty who has not finished . . . high school, and who desires to attend a nonsectarian private school located in or outside, or a public school located outside, the locality in which such child resides, shall be eligible and entitled to receive a State scholarship in the amount of one hundred and twenty-five dollars per school year, if attending an elementary school, and one hundred fifty dollars if attending a high school.

Cutoff of State Funds from Integrated Schools

Some states authorized school boards to provide separate schools for the two sexes as a partial remedy for the social consequences which they apprehended in racially mixed schoolhouses. Others expressly forbade the use of state funds for racially mixed schools, and prescribed penalties for state officers who did not use their full authority to preserve the separation of the races. South Carolina, for example, ordered by constitutional amendment, that:[2]

Appropriations of State aid for teachers' salaries, and all other school district, county and State appropriations for the operation of the school system, shall cease . . . for any school from which, and for any school to which any pupil may transfer pursuant to, or in consequence of, an order of any court, for the time that the pupil shall attend a school other than the school to which he was assigned before the issuance of such court order.

A Virginia county sought to stave off impending integration by threatening to cut off public funds:[3]

NOW, THEREFORE, be it resolved that in the event [that a federal] integration edict is imposed upon the public school system of Loudon County, Virginia, thereafter there will not be forthcoming as a result of the action of

[1] *Acts of Virginia*, Reg. Sess., 1960 (chap. 48), 70.

[2] *Acts of South Carolina*, Reg. Sess., 1955 (No. 49), I, 433.

[3] Resolution of Board of Supervisors of London County, Virginia, August 6, 1956; quoted in RRLR I, 940.

this board any funds for the maintenance and operation of any school ordered to be integrated in the County of Loudon.

Re-enacting Segregation Provisions

Promptly after the *Brown* decision, Louisiana, among other states, boldly re-enacted segregated-school laws and constitutional provisions. Section 1, Article XII of the Constitution of Louisiana, for example, was amended to read:[1]

> All public elementary and secondary schools in the State of Louisiana shall be operated separately for white and colored children. This provision is made in the exercise of the state police power to promote and protect public health, morals, better education and the peace and good order in the State, and not because of race. The Legislature shall enact laws to enforce the state police power.

The state legislature thereupon explicitly reaffirmed the state's policy of segregated education, and prescribed penalties of fines (from $500 to $1,000) and imprisonment (from three to six months) for anyone convicted of obstructing the provisions of the statute.[2] Not only were public officials who failed to enforce segregation statutes and ordinances subject to summary dismissal and prosecution; they were further penalized by the loss of benefits that would otherwise have accrued to them under state retirement and pension systems:[3]

> Any peace officer, . . . who knowingly refuses or fails to attempt to enforce any law of this State requiring segregation or separation of the White and colored races in any manner or activity, or . . . who knowingly fails to take any necessary or appropriate action for such enforcement thereof shall forfeit all retirement benefits, all disability payments, and all death benefits, to which such peace officer or his beneficiaries would have been otherwise entitled. . . .

Denying Funds to "Inefficient" Schools

Virginia used financial leverage to forestall integration by the novel device of restricting public school funds to "efficient schools," and then declaring that segregation was essential to efficient education:[4]

> An efficient system of . . . public schools means and shall be only that system . . . in which no . . . school consists of a student body in which white and colored children are taught.
>
> The General Assembly, for the purpose of protecting the health and welfare of the people and in order to preserve and maintain an efficient system of public . . . schools, hereby . . . establishes it to be the policy of this

[1] *Acts of Louisiana,* 1954 (No. 752), 1338.
[2] *Acts of Louisiana,* 1954 (No. 555), 1034.
[3] *Acts of Georgia,* 1956 (No. 197), I, 314.
[4] *Acts of Virginia,* Ex. Sess., 1956 (chap. 71), 78.

Commonwealth that no public . . . schools in which white and colored children are mixed and taught shall . . . receive any funds from the State Treasury for their operation, and, to that end, forbids . . . the expenditure of any part of the funds [by state law] for the establishment and maintenance of any system of public elementary or secondary schools, which is not efficient.

Pupil Assignment Laws

Several states resorted to "pupil assignment" laws to hold back segregation. Eminently reasonable on their face, they were in fact devastatingly effective as deterrents to integration, so much so that a state like North Carolina, for all its reputation for moderation, managed, by placing its reliance upon pupil assignment, to hold the line at least as successfully as did Virginia with its massive resistance. In 1960–1961, for example, Virginia with a total school enrollment of 880,000 had 208 Negro children in desegregated schools; North Carolina, with an enrollment of 1,140,000, had 82.[1]

The heart of such laws was the listing of factors—all of them ostensibly unrelated to race—which school authorities were to consider in assigning a child to a school: such elements as the familiar police-power formula of health, safety, morals, and general welfare; the psychological and scholastic qualifications of the pupil; effect on established social relationships in the community; the probability of economic reprisals or other expressions of ill will in the neighborhood; the consciousness of class and socioeconomic distinctions among pupils; and the adequacy of existing facilities.

Under these laws pupils were typically free to apply for enrollment in any school within their local administrative unit. By lodging complete and final responsibility for assigning and transferring pupils in local boards, such legislation made it necessary for litigants to sue each local authority individually, thus slowing down the pace of litigation, greatly narrowing the reach of any particular court ruling, and snarling the legal actions in complicated administrative obstacles. The 1955 North Carolina Statute, as rewritten by the Extra Session of the General Assembly in 1956 (which everybody knew was called to preserve segregation in the schools), made no mention of race, and—more cautiously than did laws passed by sister states—laid down in innocuous and presumably judge-proof language the considerations (see especially the concluding lines in Sections 1 and 2) upon which boards would base their decisions concerning enrollment and transfers. The act, as revised, reads in part as follows:[2]

[1] United States Commission on Civil Rights, 1961 *Report*, Vol. II: *Education*, 238.

[2] *Laws of North Carolina*, Ex. Sess., 1956 (chap. 7), 14.

Section 1

Each county and city board of education is hereby authorized and directed to provide for the assignment to a public school of each child residing within the administrative unit . . . . The authority of each board of education in the matter of assignment of children to the public schools shall be full and complete, and its decision . . . shall be final. . . . No child shall be enrolled in or permitted to attend any public school other than the public school to which the child has been assigned by the appropriate board of education. In exercising the authority conferred by this Section, each county and city board of education shall make assignments of pupils . . . so as to provide for the orderly and efficient administration of the public schools, and provide for the effective instruction, health, safety, and general welfare of the pupils. . . .

Section 2

[Affords a complicated procedure by which dissatisfied parents may secure a hearing on a request for reassignment, from the school board, before the original assignment is made final, provided always that any reassignment must in the opinion of the board "be for the best interests of the child, and will not interfere with the proper administration of the school, or with the proper instruction of the pupils therein enrolled."]

Section 4

[of the 1955 Act: Provides for appeals from a local board to a superior court, and thence to the state supreme court.]

Soon after the *Brown* decision, every one of the eleven southern states had enacted such placement laws, some of which listed as many as twenty or more detailed considerations upon which the board might base its judgments when considering individual requests. In none of the laws was race mentioned, but it was clear that the intent was to slow the pace of integration, if not, indeed, to forestall it altogether. Because they were not, in the opinion of the federal courts, "unconstitutional on their face" they proved highly successful for more than a decade, both because of the resourcefulness of school boards (and their lawyers) who were intent upon delay, and because of the inherent ineffectuality of any procedures that placed upon Negroes the burden of initiative, for which, in turn, they could be subjected to private and public harassment and reprisal, ranging all the way from social ostracism to physical violence and grievous economic chastisement.

Pupil Assignment and Freedom-of-Choice

In some cases less successful than the basic pupil-assignment laws, but similar in intent, were freedom-of-choice plans, enacted by every southern state except Tennessee. Their special object was to prevent or reduce the possibility that children of one race be forced to attend schools with children of another race. These varied widely from state to state, many of them contemplating the maintenance of both biracial and uniracial schools. Still another variation of freedom-of-choice was the tuition-grant plan adopted in eight states.

Freedom-of-choice became, in fact, the chief reliance of all of the southern states, especially after the other two major strategies—the rezoning of attendance areas, and pupil assignment plans—encountered increasing resistance at the bench, on the ground that they were administered in ways calculated to perpetuate dual school systems (the rock upon which, incidentally, freedom-of-choice was also to founder). Free-choice plans usually specified that a pupil upon reaching a particular grade had a choice of attending any school in the system or within a named geographical attendance area, unless limitations of space made the transfer impossible or seriously inconvenient.

Here follow the essential paragraphs in the freedom-of-choice plan for Indian River County, Florida:[1]

1. Every child eligible to enter and intending to enter the first, second, third, eleventh and twelfth grades in the public schools for [this] county at the beginning of the 1966–67 school year will have the option to attend either (a) the school nearest his or her residence for which they are otherwise eligible, or (b) the school of his or her choice for which they are otherwise eligible. . . .

2. The first paragraph of this Plan becomes effective September, 1966, and thereafter will be expanded to the next grades according to the following schedule:

School Year Beginning	Grades
1966–67	1, 2, 3, 4, 9, 10, 11 and 12
1967–68	5, 6, 7 and 8

Laws to Obstruct Title VI "Guidelines"

After the enactment of Title VI of the Civil Rights Act of 1964, and the promulgation of the Department of Health, Education, and Welfare's 1965 and 1966 Guidelines, the pattern of litigation changed significantly. States in the South continued to resist integration, nevertheless; Alabama lawmakers, in fact, went so far as to forbid the state's school authorities to file the assurances of compliances which the Guidelines prescribed:[2]

Section 1

The Legislature finds and declares that the Revised Statement of Policies for School Desegregation Plans . . . (herein called the "guidelines") purporting to have been issued by the United States Department of Health, Education and Welfare under Title VI of the Civil Rights Act of 1964, exceed

[1] Reprinted in RRLR XI, 704, from *Sharpton* v. *Board of Public Instruction of Indian River County, Florida,* U.S. District Court, S.D. Florida, April 19, November 12, and December 30, 1965.

[2] *Acts of Alabama,* 1966 (No. 446), September 2, 1966; quoted in RRLR XI, 2142. For Title VI of the Civil Rights Act of 1964, and the Guidelines, see below, pp. 408 and 412.

the authority granted by [that] Act, are unreasonable, arbitrary, capricious, and unconstitutional. . . . No local county or city Board of Education shall have the authority to give any assurance of compliance or to enter into any other agreement with any agency of the government of the United States which would obligate such local city or county Board . . . to adopt any plan for desegregation which requires the assignment of students to public schools in order to overcome racial imbalance. . . .

City Ordinance to Forestall Public Library Desegregation

Schools were not the only educational agencies in which local governments fought to preserve the color line. Public libraries also felt the constraints of racist legislation. The most widely noticed example, which sent an amused titter through the country, was that of Danville, Virginia.

The city had long maintained two separate libraries when Negro citizens filed suit in federal district court protesting their exclusion from the main library, which was substantially larger and in most respects notably superior to the branch assigned to their race. Anticipating an adverse decision, the City Manager ordered the main library closed, a measure which the city voters approved by a 2 to 1 margin in a popular referendum. The inconvenience of having no library at all for whites, however, soon moved the City Council to order the library reopened, on the terms indicated in the following ordinance, passed on April 4, 1960. Its effect would be to return to a white-only policy, since there had heretofore been no Negro card holders.[1]

WHEREAS, the facilities of the Danville Public Library are overtaxed by the demand of its patrons,

NOW THEREFORE, BE IT ORDAINED by the Council of the City of Danville as follows:

That the Central Library building located in the Memorial Mansion be used only by the present holders of library cards issued from the central library; and that no further membership cards be issued until further order of the Council.

That the City Manager be charged with responsibility of carrying out this pronounced policy with the full power to close all Library facilities should it appear that its administration has become unpracticable and to report the same to the Council.

Plaintiffs again sought service and were refused. Since no cards had ever been issued to Negroes by the Central Library, the court subsequently held that the Council's action constituted an unjust discrimination in violation of the plaintiffs' rights under the Constitution of the United States.[2] An injunction was issued directing the city to allow

[1] Danville, Virginia, Ordinance of April 4, 1960; as quoted in RRLR V, 528.

[2] *Giles* v. *Library Advisory Committee of Danville,* Civil Action No. 452, May 11 and September 14, 1960 (W.D. Va.); quoted in RRLR V, 1140.

persons holding cards to the Negro branch to use the facilities of the white library on the same basis as white persons. Shortly thereafter the city secured the dismissal of the suit, because the library had been reopened on a nondiscriminatory basis.

It was opened on a restricted basis, however. For a ninety-day trial period the terms imposed on the library's users without partiality as to race proved so onerous that the city (moved also apparently by the loss, during the period, of a prospective industrial plant, and by the discovery that the removal of the racial bar had not resulted in a rush of Negroes into the facility) decided to abandon the experiment. During the period of the restrictions the libraries were opened on a stand-up pick-up-your-books-and-go basis only—a literal adoption of the "Vertical Plan" which Harry Golden had facetiously advocated. Patrons were not to be seated; indeed, the tables and chairs were removed. There was to be no browsing in the stacks, at least at first. The new rules fixed the cost of a library card at $2.50, and applicants for cards were required to furnish two character witnesses and two credit references.

When the ninety-day trial period ended the library did not at once return to normal operation. For several more months there was a timorous return only to single tables and chairs, "well spread out" in the reading room. Six months later the remaining constraints were gradually abandoned, but the library for some time thereafter had only two-thirds of its former patronage. All the while very few Negroes had applied for cards at Central Library.

(6) EXECUTIVE AND LEGISLATIVE ACTION: THE FEDERAL GOVERNMENT RESUMES THE INITIATIVE

A. *Executive Orders*

With the enactment of the Civil Rights Act of 1957, the first federal legislation of its kind in nearly a century, the initiative for breaking down the still very formidable bulwarks of segregation once more passed to the national government. Although greatly overshadowed by the acts hammered out in 1957–1968, a number of executive and administrative measures made their contribution, with relatively little public notice. An important example of administrative procedures to be noted later was the Department of Health, Education, and Welfare's directive to school authorities for compliance with Title VI of the Civil Rights Act of 1964, which came to be known as the school desegregation "Guidelines."[1]

The first two of the recent Civil Rights Acts, those of 1957 and 1960, were largely confined to protection of the Negro's right to vote; and only in the third of the series, the Act of 1964, did the legislation begin to move to other critical areas in which blacks had long suffered their most painful exclusions. Before 1964, however, came three executive orders from President John F. Kennedy, affecting discrimination in employment and housing. Following are the summaries by which the full texts of the orders are introduced in the *Race Relations Law Reporter:*

EXECUTIVE ORDER 10925: COMMITTEE ON EQUAL EMPLOYMENT OPPORTUNITY[2]

On March 6, 1961, the President of the United States issued Executive Order No. 10925, combining the President's Committee on Government Contracts and the President's Committee on Government Employment Policy into a single committee with increased powers, to be called the President's Committee on Equal Employment Opportunity. The order also directs the Secretary of Labor to supervise the implementation of equal employment practices, sets out the obligations of government contractors in regard to nondiscrimination in employment, and requires a complete study to be made of current government employment practices.

EXECUTIVE ORDER 11063: COMMITTEE ON EQUAL OPPORTUNITY IN HOUSING[3]

The President's Executive Order No. 11063, issued November 20, 1962, directs departments and agencies of the federal government to take all necessary action to prevent discrimination because of race, color, creed or national origin in the sale or leasing of housing owned or operated by the federal government, built in whole or in part with federal loans or grants, built with federally-insured loans, or constructed on real property handled under public agencies receiving federal assistance. Discriminatory practices

[1] It has seemed appropriate to introduce this document at a later point in this volume (see below, pp. 412–19).

[2] The summary is from RRLR VI, 9. The full text of the order is in 3 *Code of Federal Regulations*, 1959–1963 Compilation, 448–54.

[3] The summary is from RRLR VII, 1019. The full text of the order is in 3 *Code of Federal Regulations*, 1959–1963 Compilation, 652–56.

in federally-insured lending are prohibited. Provision is made for enforcement of the order, including legal action and cancellation of loans, grants, etc. A President's Committee on Equal Opportunity in Housing is created, and charged with the responsibility of coordinating department activities to implement the program.

EXECUTIVE ORDER 11114: EQUAL EMPLOYMENT OPPORTUNITY[1]

The President's Executive Order No. 11114, promulgated on June 22, 1963, requires that applicants for federal financial assistance shall agree, as a condition to the approval of any grant, contract, loan, insurance or guarantee which may involve a construction contract, to comply with the terms of previously issued directives prohibiting racial discrimination in employment. Executive Order No. 10925 is amended slightly in regard to the specific provisions which are required to be included in government contracts.

B. *"Great Society" Measures*

At least passing notice should be taken here of measures enacted by the Congress or authorized by presidential order, not as civil rights projects, per se, but as part of a far-ranging program initiated on a modest scale by President John F. Kennedy, and then vigorously promoted and enormously expanded by President Lyndon B. Johnson, as his "Great Society" prospectus.[2] Much of this extraordinary harvest of social legislation was specifically intended for the poor, the deprived, and the disadvantaged, and for that reason had particular meaning for black America.

Frequently criticized by conservatives, and often producing results that fell short of the President's intentions and of the hopes of blacks and white liberals and humanitarians, they gave, nevertheless, significant impetus to racial equality, and exceeded even the New Deal legislation of the 1930's in the audacity and breadth of their attack upon human suffering, failure, and privation. Many of these measures of which blacks were often the chief beneficiaries looked to the improvement of educational opportunity as the road to lifting the plight and prospects of the underprivileged. Among them were the Adult Education Act, the College Work Study Program, the Educational Professions Development Act, the Educational Opportunity Act, the Elementary and Secondary Education Act, the Federal Fellowships

[1] The summary is from RRLR VIII, 793. The full text of the order is in 3 *Code of Federal Regulations*, 1959–1963 Compilation, 774–78.

[2] See James McGregor Burns, editor, *To Heal and to Build: The Programs of President Lyndon B. Johnson* (New York, 1968).

Program, the Head Start Program, the Higher Education Facilities Act, the National Defense Education Act, the National Vocational Student Loan Insurance Act, the Vocational Education Act, and the Upward Bound project.

Other innovations were directed to the broadening of economic and social opportunity and the cure of distressed conditions especially afflicting the Negro poor: the Child and Parent Centers Program, the Job Corps, the Demonstration Cities Program, the Neighborhood Youth Corps, the Urban Renewal Program, the Manpower Development and Training Program, Medicare, Medicaid, the Equal Employment Opportunities Commission, the National Health Centers Program, the School Lunch Program.

C. *Administrative Action*

An example of Great Society measures explicitly directed against racial discrimination was the creation of the Equal Employment Opportunity Commission, to give effect to Title VI of the Civil Rights Act of 1964. The great federal agencies, including the Civil Service Commission, thereafter established procedures of swift and thorough overhauling of hiring policies, consistent with the commands of the far-reaching 1964 Act. The latter, for example, sets forth at great length "the regulations under which an agency shall establish a program for equal opportunity in employment and personnel operations without regard to race, creed, color, or national origin and under which the Commission will review an agency's program and entertain an appeal from a person dissatisfied with an agency's processing of his complaint of discrimination on grounds of race, creed, color, or national origin."[1]

Representative of another highly important category of measures by federal agencies to combat bias and discrimination was a step taken by the Federal Communications Commission in July 1968, when it bluntly announced that radio and television broadcasters who engage in racial discrimination will be denied renewal of their licenses. The order, significantly, was drafted in response to a petition from the Committee for Racial Justice Now, of the United Church of Christ, the

[1] RRLR X, 1012. Examples of directives for the achievement of fair employment practices in government services and all work by private firms on government contracts may be found in Department of Commerce Order No. 8, July 1, 1965, 31 *Federal Register,* 580; and orders of the Department of Labor, January 17, 1966, 31 *Federal Register,* 863; the Equal Employment Opportunity Commission, November 23, 1965, and February 11, 1966, 30 *Federal Register* 14658; and 31 *Federal Register* 2832; and the Civil Service Commission, Regulations, Part 713, February 24 and March 11, 1966, 31 *Federal Register* 3069 and 4271.

full text of whose resolution, incidentally, was incorporated in the FCC regulation. The new rule required licensees to file with their applications for renewal a statement to exhibit what they were doing to promote minority employment and to provide programs for, and in the interests of, minority groups. Included also in the directive was a regulation that all broadcasters must post notices in their stations to explain their antibias policy; and one section put broadcasters under orders actively to seek out minority-group employees and to train them for high positions:[1]

Federal Communications Commission: Nondiscrimination in Employment Practices of Broadcast Licensees

. . . Thus we stress that simply to comply with the requirements of the national policy—to say, "We can't find qualified Negroes"—is not enough. What is called for is a commitment going beyond the letter of the policy and attuned to its spirit and the demands of the times. That, we believe, is the most important and urgent message of this document. . . .

The same considerations are applicable in the case of the Negro in specific programming.

. . . [Quoting from the Kerner Commission's Report on Civil Disorders, the FCC went on to say:] "Television should develop programming which integrates Negroes in all aspects of televised presentations. Television is such a visible medium that some constructive steps are easy and obvious. While some of these steps are being taken, they are still largely neglected. For example, Negro reporters and performers should appear more frequently —and at prime time—in news broadcasts, on weather shows, in documentaries, and in advertisements. . . .

"In addition to news-related programming, we think that Negroes should appear more frequently in dramatic and comedy series. Moreover, networks and local stations should present plays and other programs whose subjects are rooted in the ghetto and its problems."

. . . We stress that we are not condemning the broadcast media for past actions or neglect. It is fruitless to focus on the past. Nor are we implying that broadcasters and others are not presently engaged in meeting the challenge set out in the report. . . . The thrust of our message is that the nation requires a maximum effort in this vital undertaking and to call upon all broadcasters to make as great a contribution as they can. We stand ready fully to cooperate, as appropriate, in industry endeavors to achieve this important goal.

D. *Federal Civil Rights Laws, 1957–1968*

New public attitudes and hopes, as well as the pressures from the Negro community and from white liberals, prompted the Congress in 1957 to enact the first federal civil rights law since 1875. What emerged

[1] 33 *Federal Register*, 9964, July 11, 1968.

after protracted debate and maneuver was a compromise, reflecting the country's ambivalence. Partisan considerations also played their part. Republicans, hitherto lukewarm to the cause, saw that Negro votes would be needed to bring their party further successes at the polls, for the resounding reelection of President Eisenhower in 1956 was in fact a personal triumph, not a Republican party victory. Democrats—with feeble support and not a little opposition from their southern membership—cooperated with Republicans in Congress to overcome the adamant resistance of opponents of advanced civil rights laws.

Brazen sabotage of the *Brown* decision, especially at Little Rock, Arkansas, where the President found it necessary to send troops to enforce a federal court's school desegregation order, and the crude stratagems by which Negroes were being disfranchised in defiance of Supreme Court decisions, helped to create public opinion that made the 1957 act possible. It centered largely upon the franchise, but other titles created a special Civil Rights Division within the Department of Justice; established a United States Civil Rights Commission to make a sweeping study of the condition of civil rights in the country, and to recommend legislation; and gave authority to the Department of Justice to intervene in behalf of individuals whose general civil rights (including, presumably, the right to attend desegregated schools, but—more specifically—the right to vote) were denied or threatened.

That such solicitude over the franchise was justified was well known. A survey of the 1954 and 1956 elections conducted by the Southern Regional Council had yielded an enlightening report, the conclusions of which were published in pamphlet form in the summer of 1957.[1] It disclosed, for example, that in 13 Mississippi counties with more than 50 percent Negro population, a total of 14 Negro votes had been cast in the 1954 elections; and in five counties not a single black had been permitted to cast his ballot. Alabama, Louisiana, and Georgia were also among the most serious offenders, and sections of Virginia and North Carolina produced similar statistics.

The violent deterrents of post-Reconstruction days had, to be sure, given way to subtler pressures. The white primary was gone; the poll tax was fading. Increasing reliance was placed on literacy and "constitutional understanding" tests and other obstacles which local white registrars, sometimes themselves scarcely literate, threw in the path of aspirants for the ballot. Negroes were told, for example, that the registration books had been lost or misplaced. Lines of would-be registrants were passed into a registrar's office so slowly that only one or two Negroes per hour were served. Some jurisdictions required that an

[1] Margaret Price, *The Negro Voter in the South* (Atlanta, 1957); see also *Time,* July 29, 1957, 12.

applicant be vouched for by "some good white man." There were such tricks as asking a Negro to give, under oath, his age in years, months and days without telling him that examiners were counting or not counting the current day, whichever was necessary to declare the answer incorrect by one day; or a request that he name all the minor public officials in his county. In North Carolina there were instances of Negroes being disqualified when they "mispronounced" some words; and in at least one classic case subsequently reported by the United States Civil Rights Commission a white registrar turned away a black applicant because of "mistakes in spilling."

Even more effective were harassments, threats (and some instances) of physical harm, cross-burnings, and rifle shots into the homes of "smart" Negroes. And, again, blacks who attempted to register found themselves suddenly evicted from homes or farms, or deprived of employment, of credit, or of buyers for their produce. Here and there were verdicts of "accidental" injury or even death by shooting.

The Act of 1957, passed after a long and acrimonious struggle in Congress, fell far short of the hopes of civil rights crusaders, but a significant beginning, at least, was made.

THE CIVIL RIGHTS ACT OF 1957[1]

PART I—ESTABLISHMENT OF THE COMMISSION ON CIVIL RIGHTS

Section 101. (a) There is created in the executive branch of the Government a Commission on Civil Rights (hereinafter called the "Commission").

(b) The Commission shall be composed of six members who shall be appointed by the President by and with the advice and consent of the Senate. Not more than three of the members shall at any one time be of the same political party. . . .

Rules of Procedure of the Commission

Section 102. (a) The Chairman [to be designated by the President] at a hearing of the Commission shall announce in an opening statement the subject of the hearing.

(b) A copy of the Commission's rules shall be made available to the witness before the hearing.

(c) Witnesses at the hearings may be accompanied by their own counsel for the purpose of advising them concerning their constitutional rights. . . .

(e) If the Commission determines that evidence or testimony at any hearing may tend to defame, degrade, or incriminate any person, it shall (1) receive such evidence or testimony in executive session; (2) afford such person an opportunity voluntarily to appear as a witness; and (3) receive and dispose of requests from such person to subpoena additional witnesses.

(f) Except as provided in sections 102 and 105 (f) of this Act, the Chairman shall receive and the Commission shall dispose of requests to subpoena additional witnesses. . . .

[1] P.L. 85–135, 85th Cong., H.R. 6127, September 9, 1957; 71 *U.S. Statutes at Large*, 634.

Duties of the Commission

Section 104. (a) The Commission shall—

(1) investigate allegations in writing under oath or affirmation that certain citizens of the United States are being deprived of their right to vote and have that vote counted by reason of their color, race, religion, or national origin. . . .

(2) study and collect information concerning legal developments constituting a denial of equal protection of the laws under the Constitution; and

(3) appraise the laws and policies of the Federal Government with respect to equal protection of the laws under the Constitution.

(b) The Commission shall submit interim reports to the President and to the Congress at such times as either the Commission or the President shall deem desirable, and shall submit to the President and to the Congress a final and comprehensive report of its activities, findings, and recommendations not later than two years from the date of the enactment of this Act.

(c) Sixty days after the submission of its final report and recommendations the Commission shall cease to exist. [Subsequent legislation extended the life of the Commission.]

Powers of the Commission

Section 105. (a) There shall be a full-time staff director for the Commission who shall be appointed by the President by and with the advice and consent of the Senate. . . .

(c) The Commission may constitute such advisory committees within States composed of citizens of that State and may consult with governors, attorneys general, and other representatives of State and local governments, and private organizations, as it deems advisable. . . .

(e) All Federal agencies shall cooperate fully with the Commission to the end that it may effectively carry out its functions and duties.

(f) The Commission, or . . . any subcommittee of two or more members, . . . may, for the purpose of carrying out the provisions of this Act, hold such hearings and act at such times and places as the Commission or such authorized subcommittee may deem advisable. Subpoenas for the attendance and testimony of witnesses or the production of written or other matter may be issued in accordance with the rules of the Commission as contained in . . . this Act. . . .

(g) In case of contumacy or refusal to obey a subpoena, any district court of the United States . . . within the jurisdiction of which . . . said person guilty of contumacy or refusal to obey is found or resides or transacts business, upon application by the Attorney General of the United States shall have jurisdiction to issue to such person an order requiring such person to appear before the Commission or a subcommittee thereof, there to produce evidence if so ordered . . . and any failure to obey such order of the court may be punished by said court as a contempt thereof.

Part II—To Provide for an Additional Assistant Attorney General

Section 111. There shall be in the Department of Justice one additional Assistant Attorney General, who shall be appointed by the President, by and with the advice and consent of the Senate, who shall assist the Attorney General in the performance of his duties. . . .

PART IV—TO PROVIDE MEANS OF FURTHER SECURING AND PROTECTING THE RIGHT TO VOTE

Section 131. Section 2004 of the Revised Statutes (42 U.S.C. 1971), is amended as follows: . . . .

(c) Add, immediately following the present text, four new subsections to read as follows:

"(b) No person, whether acting under color of law or otherwise, shall intimidate, threaten, coerce, or attempt to intimidate, threaten, or coerce any other person for the purpose of interfering with the right of such other person to vote for, or not to vote for, any candidate for the Office of President, Vice President, presidential elector, Member of the Senate, or Member of the House of Representatives, Delegates or Commissioners from the Territories or possessions, at any general, special, or primary election held solely or in part for the purpose of selecting or electing any such candidate.

"(c) Whenever any person has engaged or there are reasonable grounds to believe that any person is about to engage in any act or practice which would deprive any other person of any right or privilege secured by subsection (a) or (b), the Attorney General may institute for the United States, or in the name of the United States, a civil action or other proper proceeding for preventive relief, including an application for a permanent or temporary injunction, restraining order, or other order. . . .

"(d) The district courts of the United States shall have jurisdiction of proceedings instituted pursuant to this section and shall exercise the same without regard to whether the party aggrieved shall have exhausted any administrative or other remedies that may be provided by law. . . ."

PART V—TO PROVIDE TRIAL BY JURY FOR PROCEEDINGS TO PUNISH CRIMINAL CONTEMPTS OF COURT GROWING OUT OF CIVIL RIGHTS CASES AND TO AMEND THE JUDICIAL CODE RELATING TO FEDERAL JURY QUALIFICATIONS

Section 151. In all cases of criminal contempt arising under the provisions of this Act, the accused, upon conviction, shall be punished by fine or imprisonment or both: *Provided however,* that in case the accused is a natural person the fine to be paid shall not exceed the sum of $1,000, nor shall imprisonment exceed the term of six months: *Provided further,* that in such proceeding for criminal contempt, at the discretion of the judge, the accused may be tried with or without a jury: *Provided further, however,* That in the event such proceeding for criminal contempt be tried before a judge without a jury and the sentence of the court upon conviction is a fine in excess of the sum of $300 or imprisonment in excess of forty-five days, the accused in said proceeding, upon demand therefore, shall be entitled to a trial de novo before a jury, which shall conform as near as may be to the practice in other criminal cases. . . .

Section 152. Section 1861, title 28, of the United States Code is hereby amended to read as follows: "#1861. Qualifications of Federal Jurors

"Any citizen of the United States who has attained the age of twenty-one years and who has resided for a period of one year within the judicial district, is competent to serve as a grand or petit juror unless—

"(1) He has been convicted in a State or Federal court of record of a crime punishable by imprisonment for more than one year and his civil rights have not been restored by pardon or amnesty.

"(2) He is unable to read, write, speak and understand the English language.

"(3) He is incapable, by reason of mental or physical infirmities, to render efficient jury service."

The Civil Rights Commission established by the act promptly began, with staff assistance, to conduct studies, surveys, and investigations. Summaries of the data it assembled in impressive quantity were published, usually with the Commission's findings and conclusions, and with specific recommendations for future legislation and administrative action. These publications were to be a major influence in the shaping of public policy and legislation, and in public enlightenment.[1] At this writing, in the winter of 1969/70, the Commission is still vigorously active, and still engaged in collecting evidence and making disclosures and recommendations.

THE CIVIL RIGHTS ACT OF 1960[2]

In 1960 came a second installment on federal civil rights legislation, and again the act that emerged from a sharply divided Congress was a disappointment to the advocates of full justice for blacks. It served chiefly to stop up loopholes left by the 1957 law, but it had also provisions to cope with terrorists who bombed and burned to intimidate blacks; a clause to enlarge the powers of the Civil Rights Commission; and a section providing for unsegregated education of the children of armed forces personnel. The most important effect of the law was to take care of the problem of registrars who resigned on the eve of federal suits (leaving no party to sue), or who refused to make registra-

[1] A list of the Commission's publications up to the summer of 1966, including Statutory and Interim Reports, Clearinghouse Publications, Transcripts of Hearings and Conferences, Staff Reports, State Advisory Committee Reports, and Films is available in United States Commission on Civil Rights, *Publications Catalog* (Washington, 1966).

Examples of important books and booklets published by the Commission since the appearance of the foregoing bibliography are (all published in Washington in 1967) (1) *Education Parks;* (2) *A Time to Listen . . . A Time to Act; Voices from the Ghettoes of the Nation's Cities;* (3) *Racial Isolation in the Public Schools* (two volumes); (4) *Southern School Desegregation,* 1966–67. Some examples of titles issued by the Commission in 1968 (all of them published in Washington) are (1) *Political Participation;* (2) *Agricultural Stabilization and Conservation in the Alabama Black Belt;* (3) *Education and the Mexican American Community in Los Angeles County;* (4) *Employment Practices at Kelly Air Force Base, San Antonio, Texas;* (5) *Toward Equal Opportunity in Atlanta, Georgia;* (6) *Federal Role in School Desegregation in Selected Virginia Districts.* In addition, the Commission has been publishing a series of pamphlets on a wide range of topics relating to civil rights, under the series title of *CCR Special Publications,* and a quarterly magazine called *Civil Rights Digest.*

[2] P.A. 86–449, 86th Cong., H.R. 8601, May 3, 1960; 74 *U.S. Statutes at Large,* 86.

tion and voting records available for the Commission's inspection, and even destroyed such records, as stratagems for frustrating the effectuation of the Act of 1957.[1]

TITLE I

Obstruction of Court Orders
[Reinforces the authority of federal courts by making it a federal crime—punishable by fines not exceeding $1000 or imprisonment for not more than one year, or both—to obstruct any federal court order "by threat or force."]

TITLE II

Flight to avoid prosecution for damaging or destroying any building or other real or personal property; and, illegal transportation, use or possession of explosives; and, threats or false information concerning attempts to damage or destroy real or personal property by fire or explosives.
[Provides for penalties (of fines up to $5000 and/or imprisonment up to five years) for bomb-throwing terrorists convicted of the newly defined federal crime of escaping from the United States or across state boundaries to avoid prosecution or to evade the duty to testify in cases involving the bombing or burning of buildings or vehicles. The section also prohibits both the transportation of explosives across state lines for the purpose of damaging property, and the making of bombing threats by mail, telephone, or telegraph.]

TITLE III

[Assists federal investigators in the detection of voting frauds and discrimination, by requiring state election officials to preserve for twenty-two months, for the inspection by the Attorney General of the United States or his representatives, all registration and voting records in all elections for federal officers.]

TITLE IV

Extension of Powers of the Civil Rights Commission
[Empowers individual members of the Commission to "administer oaths or take statements of witnesses under affirmation."]

TITLE V

Education of Children of Members of Armed Forces
[Guarantees, through action of the Department of Health, Education, and Welfare, uninterrupted education for children of members of the Armed Forces, in areas where desegregation orders have resulted in the closing of the schools.]

[1] What follows is a summary based on the text of the act, as given in RRLR V, 347.

TITLE VI

[*Registration of Negro Voters*]

[Makes available to persons improperly excluded from the franchise a remedy affording a voting-referee procedure enforced by federal courts. The section authorizes the Department of Justice to enter a federal court in behalf of persons who have lodged a complaint with a United States attorney that they have been denied their registration rights in elections, whether federal or state or local. If the complaint is upheld by the court, the Attorney General is given the authority to ask the court to determine whether "a pattern or practice" of discrimination against Negroes exists in that community. If the court determines that such a pattern exists, it is empowered to appoint referees to hear complaints from any other persons who feel themselves so aggrieved, and each such referee may enroll any legally qualified person who can demonstrate that he has attempted to register and has been refused.]

THE CIVIL RIGHTS ACT OF 1964

Most far-reaching of the acts of 1957–1968 was that of 1964, the most penetrating civil rights legislation in the country's history. Originally urged upon the Congress by President Kennedy, and vigorously pushed after the latter's death by President Johnson, it was in part precipitated by the nation's shock and sorrow following the young President's assassination.

It was helped by other pressures as well. Just as the legislation of 1957 had resulted in no small measure from rising public indignation against the extremism of whites who resorted to fraud, chicane, and violence to prevent the implementation of the *Brown* decision, and just as the way for the 1960 Act had been cleared by similar affronts to the public sensibilities, so the effort to enact the comprehensive laws of 1964 and 1965 benefited from the brutalities which the country had witnessed on television newscasts or had read of in the press: the "Battle of Oxford," when James Meredith was admitted to the University of Mississippi; the shooting of Medgar Evers and the release, after two mistrials, of his accused murderer; the impressive March on Washington in August 1963; the bombing of homes of Negro civil rights workers; the 1963 murder, by bombing (still unpunished in 1970), of four Negro children in a Birmingham Sunday school; the excesses of "Bull" Connor in the same city; the harsh treatment of marchers, "freedom riders," demonstrators, and voter-registration volunteers; Governor Wallace's defiant stand in the schoolhouse door; the murder of three young civil rights workers in Mississippi in one grisly episode in 1964; and the killing of Lemuel Penn, Viola Liuzzo, and James Reeb in 1964 and 1965, in three separate crimes, all of whose slayers are still at large in 1970.

The new act outlawed the exclusion of blacks from restaurants, hotels, theaters, and other public accommodations; empowered the Justice Department to bring school desegregation suits; denied federal aid to any program or service which practiced racial discrimination; and forbade racial bias in employment and union membership policies.[1]

Title I: Voting

The purpose of this section is to provide more effective enforcement of the right to vote in Federal [presidential and congressional] elections without regard to race or color. It also speeds up the procedure by which voting rights suits may be decided. The Act: (a) requires that the same standards be applied to all individuals seeking to register and vote; (b) forbids denial of the right to vote because of some minor mistake or omission; (c) requires that only literacy tests that are written may be used as a qualification for voting; and that the tests and answers be available on request; (d) establishes that in voting rights law suits the court must presume that anyone who completed the sixth grade is literate, unless the State can prove otherwise.

In any voting suit brought by the Government charging that there is a "pattern or practice" of voting discrimination, either the Attorney General or the defendant may ask that a three-judge Federal court be appointed to hear the case. Appeals from the decisions of such a court may be taken directly to the Supreme Court.

Title II: Public Accommodations

Discrimination on the basis of race, color, religion or national origin is specifically forbidden in the following places of public accommodation:

(a) hotels and motels, restaurants, lunch counters, movie houses, gasoline stations, theaters and stadiums; (b) any other establishment which offers its services to patrons of the covered establishment; for example; a barbershop or tavern located in a hotel; or a department store in which there is a restaurant: *so long as* the covered facilities either affect interstate commerce in their operations, or are supported in their discriminatory practices by State action.

In addition, discrimination is forbidden in any other place of public accommodation that is required to segregate by State or local laws.

If there are no State or local laws requiring segregation, the Federal law does not cover: (a) barbershops, beauty parlors and other service establishments unless they are located in a hotel and offer these services to hotel guests; (b) retail stores that do not serve food, or places of recreation (except as listed above) which do not serve food; (c) lodging houses, hotels or similar places which take temporary guests if they have fewer than six rooms for rent in a building occupied by the owner.

Places that are actually owned and operated as private clubs are exempted from coverage of this title except to the extent that they offer their facilities to patrons of a covered establishment, such as a country club that customarily allows guests of a hotel to use its golf course.

[1] What follows is a summary of the act, prepared by the United States Commission on Civil Rights, in *Special Bulletin: Summary of the Civil Rights Act of 1964* (Washington, 1964). The full text of the statute is in P.L. 88–352, 88th Cong., H.R. 7152, July 2, 1964; *U.S. Statutes at Large*, 241.

No person may intimidate, threaten or coerce anyone for the purpose of interfering with the rights created by this title.

The provisions of this title may be enforced in two ways:

1. By *individual action* in a civil suit filed by the persons discriminated against, or

2. By *Government action* in a civil suit filed by the Attorney General.

In public accommodations suits filed by individuals:

—the court hearing the suit may appoint a lawyer for the person bringing the complaint and exempt the complainant from the payment of certain costs;

—the court may permit the Attorney General to enter the case;

—if there is a State law or local ordinance that prohibits discrimination, the complaint must first be taken to the State or local authorities, allowing them 30 days to begin a proceeding before suit can be filed in a Federal court;

—once the case is in court, the court can postpone action until the State or local proceeding is completed;

—if there are no State or local anti-discrimination provisions, the court may refer the matter to the Community Relations Service (see Title X) so that it may seek to secure voluntary compliance within no more than 120 days.

The Attorney General may file a public accommodations suit when he believes there is a pattern or practice of resistance. As in Title I voting suits, he may request a three-judge court for this action.

In public accommodations suits brought either by individuals or the Attorney General, the court may issue temporary or permanent injunctions or restraining orders against those found to be violating the law. A person or persons failing to obey such court decrees may be punished by contempt proceedings under the jury trials provision of the law (see Title XI).

Title III: Public Facilities

The Attorney General is authorized to bring a civil suit to compel desegregation of any publicly-owned or operated facility whenever he receives a written complaint of discrimination. He must believe that the complaint merits action and must certify that the individual or individuals making the complaint are themselves unable to take the necessary legal action. State or municipally owned or operated parks, libraries and hospitals are among the facilities covered.

Title IV: Public Education

Under this title the U.S. Office of Education is authorized to: (a) conduct a national survey to determine the availability of equal educational opportunity; (b) provide technical assistance, upon request, to help States, political subdivisions or school districts carry out school desegregation plans; (c) arrange training institutes to prepare teachers and other school personnel to deal with desegregation problems; (d) make grants enabling school boards to employ specialists for in-service training programs;

In addition, the Attorney General is authorized to file civil suits seeking to compel desegregation of public schools, including public colleges.

Before filing such a suit the Attorney General must have received a signed complaint from a pupil or parent and must have determined that the complainant, according to standards set forth in the Act, is unable to bring the action. The Attorney General is also required to notify the school board and give it a reasonable period of time to correct the alleged condition before filing suit.

Title V: Commission on Civil Rights

The life of the U.S. Commission on Civil Rights is extended until January 31, 1968. Since 1957 the Commission's functions have included investigating denials of the right to vote, studying legal developments and appraising Federal policies relating to equal protection of the laws, and making recommendations for corrective action to the President and the Congress.

Title V gives the Commission added authority to:

(a) serve as a national clearinghouse for civil rights information; (b) investigate allegations of vote fraud.

Commission hearing procedures are amended to further protect the rights of individuals who may be affected by Commission proceedings.

As a national clearinghouse, the Commission will provide civil rights information in such areas as voting, housing, education, employment and the use of public facilities to Federal, State and local government agencies and officials, organizations and businesses, and the general public.

Title VI: Federally Assisted Programs

Under this title every Federal agency which provides financial assistance through grants, loans or contracts is required to eliminate discrimination on the grounds of race, color or national origin in these programs.

For example, this title would require the following:

(a) hospitals constructed with Federal funds would have to serve all patients without regard to race, color or national origin; (b) elementary and secondary schools constructed, maintained and operated with Federal funds would have to admit children without regard to race, color or national origin; (c) State employment services financed by Federal funds would have to refer qualified job applicants for employment without discrimination; (d) schools for the deaf and the blind operated with Federal funds would have to serve the deaf and blind of any color; (e) colleges and universities receiving funds for their general operation or for the construction of special facilities, such as research centers, would have to admit students without discrimination; (f) construction contractors receiving funds under Federal public works programs would have to hire employees without discrimination.

Action by a Federal agency to carry out the requirements of this title may include the terminating of programs where discrimination is taking place, or refusal to grant assistance to such a program.

Each agency is required to publish rules or regulations to carry out the purposes of the title. These rules and regulations are subject to the approval of the President.

Compliance actions are subject to the following conditions:

(a) notice must be given of alleged failure to comply and an opportunity for a hearing must be provided; (b) in the event assistance is to be cut off, a written report must be submitted to Congress 30 days before the cutoff date; (c) compliance action may be appealed to the courts.

Social security and veterans benefits, and other Federal benefits distributed directly to individuals are not affected by this law.

Federal assistance in the form of insurance of guaranty—for example, FHA insured loans—are not covered by this title (however, the President's Executive Order prohibiting discrimination in Federally aided housing remains in effect).

TITLE VII: EQUAL EMPLOYMENT OPPORTUNITY

This title establishes a Federal right to equal opportunity in employment. It creates an Equal Employment Opportunity Commission to assist in implementing this right.

Employers, labor unions and employment agencies are required to treat all persons without regard to their race, color, religion, sex, or national origin. This treatment must be given in all phases of employment, including hiring, promotion, firing, apprenticeship and other training programs, and job assignments.

When this title goes into full effect employers will be subject to its provisions if they have 25 or more regular employees in an industry that affects interstate commerce. Generally speaking, labor unions will be subject to the Act if they either operate a hiring hall for covered employers, or if they have 25 or more members who are employed by a covered employer. Employment agencies are also included if they regularly undertake to supply employees for a covered employer.

(Enforcement of the nondiscrimination requirements for employers and unions is postponed for one year. Employers and unions with 100 or more workers will be covered beginning July 2, 1965 and coverage will be extended each year until July 2, 1968 when employers and unions with 25 workers will be covered.)

Not covered by this title are (1) public employers, (2) bona fide private clubs, (3) educational institutions with regard to employees working in educational activities and all employment in religious educational institutions, (4) employers on or near an Indian reservation with regard to preferential treatment of Indians, and (5) religious corporations, institutions, etc., with regard to employees working in connection with religious activities.

When someone believes he has been discriminated against because of color, race, religion, sex, or national origin in any phase of job placement or employment, he may bring his complaint within 90 days to the Equal Employment Opportunity Commission or the Attorney General.

The Commission will handle his complaint directly, unless the State or locality where the alleged discrimination occurred has fair employment laws. If so, the person complaining must allow the State or local officials no more than 120 days to resolve the matter. If there is no satisfactory conclusion within this time or if the State or locality rejects the complaint before the time is up, the complainant may then go to the Commission, which is authorized to settle valid complaints by conciliation and persuasion. Nothing said during the conciliation proceedings may be made public or used as evidence without the consent of the parties.

If the Commission fails to secure compliance within a period of no more than 60 days, the individual may take his case to a Federal court. This court may appoint an attorney and may exempt the complainant from payment of certain costs. The court, in its discretion, may allow the Attorney General to enter the case.

A worker who thinks he has been discriminated against may take his complaint directly to the Attorney General, who may bring the case before a three-judge court if he believes there is a pattern or practice of resistance to this title.

If the court in either action finds discrimination, it will order the employer, employment agency or union to take corrective action, which may include hiring or reinstating employees with or without back pay.

Title VIII: Voting Statistics

The Secretary of Commerce is required to conduct a survey of persons of voting age by race, color and national origin and to determine the extent to which such persons have registered and voted in such geographic areas as the Commission on Civil Rights recommends.

A similar survey must also be conducted on a nationwide basis in connection with the 1970 Census. No person questioned during such survey may be compelled to disclose his race, color, religion or national origin and everyone must be advised of his right to refuse to give this information.

Title IX: Intervention and Removal in Civil Rights Cases

The Attorney General is authorized to intervene in any Federal court action seeking relief from the denial of equal protection of the laws on account of race, color, religion or national origin. If a Federal court refuses to accept a civil rights case and sends it back to a State Court, this action may be reviewed on appeal.

Title X: Community Relations Service

A Community Relations Service is established in the Department of Commerce to provide assistance to persons or communities requiring help with civil rights problems where discriminatory practices impair constitutional rights or affect interstate commerce. The Service is authorized to cooperate with both public and private agencies, either on its own initiative or upon request from local officials or interested persons in situations where disputes threaten peaceful relations among the citizens of a community.

In addition, the Service is authorized to seek a voluntary settlement of public accommodation complaints which may be referred to it by a Federal Court. The Act directs that all activities of the Service in providing conciliation assistance shall be conducted in confidence and without publicity. . . .

THE CIVIL RIGHTS ACT OF 1964: COMPLIANCE REGULATIONS

While public attention was focused on the "Guidelines" for compliance by public schools with Title VI of the Civil Rights Act of 1964, other less conspicuous, but no less significant, regulations were laid down by the several federal agencies to ensure obedience to the statute's sweeping command to abandon discriminatory practices. One such document, for example, that of the Department of Health, Education and Welfare, is typical of twenty-one major federal agencies, including the several cabinet-level departments, as well as such agencies as the

General Services Administration, the Housing and Home Finance Agency, the National Science Foundation, the Atomic Energy Commission, the Civil Aeronautics Board, the Federal Aviation Agency, the Veterans Administration, the Agency for International Development, the National Aeronautics and Space Administration, the Office of Economic Opportunity, the Office of Emergency Planning, the Small Business Administration, and the Tennessee Valley Authority. It may be found, as cited below, with the summary here quoted in part, by which the document is prefaced:[1]

> . . . regulations for the effectuation of Title VI of the Civil Rights Act of 1964 prohibiting federal financial assistance for any programs or activities in which discrimination on the basis of race, color or national origin is practiced. Generally, these rules state their purpose and scope of application, list discriminatory practices prohibited and illustrative applications of the prohibitions, prescribe assurances of compliance to be furnished by applicants for federal financial assistance, provide for compliance reports and investigations of alleged violations, and set up procedures for enforcement of the cut-off provisions of the Title. [Then follow the *Federal Register* citations of the comparable statements of regulations laid down by the twenty agencies and department of which the HEW directive is typical.]

The following "Assurance of Compliance" form is required, as a condition of participation in federally assisted programs, as prescribed by Title VI of the Civil Rights Act of 1964, of thousands of schools; colleges; hospitals; medical and health services; vocational rehabilitation services; old-age assistance programs; assistance grants for the blind, the deaf, crippled children, and mentally retarded; public libraries; water pollution research and treatment; for educational television; public works projects; etc., etc. The form below is prescribed for federal aid grants under the general supervision of the Department of Health, Education, and Welfare. Similar forms are employed by other departments and agencies administering federally assisted services and aids.[2]

HEW 441—Assurance of Compliance Form

ASSURANCE OF COMPLIANCE WITH THE DEPARTMENT OF HEALTH, EDUCATION, AND WELFARE REGULATION UNDER TITLE VI OF THE CIVIL RIGHTS ACT OF 1964 ____________

(Name of Applicant)

(hereinafter called the "Applicant") HEREBY AGREES THAT it will comply with the Title VI of the Civil Rights Act of 1964 (P.L. 88–352) and all requirements imposed by or pursuant to the Regulation of the Department of Health, Education, and Welfare (45 CFR Part 80) issued pursuant

[1] Department of Health, Education, and Welfare, December 3, 1964; 29 *Federal Register*, 16298.

[2] Reprinted in RRLR IX, 1960.

to that title, to the end that, in accordance with the Title VI of that Act and the Regulation, no person in the United States shall, on the ground of race, color, or national origin, be excluded from participation in, be denied the benefits of, or be otherwise subjected to discrimination under any program or activity for which the Applicant receives Federal financial assistance from the Department; and HEREBY GIVES ASSURANCE THAT it will immediately take any measures necessary to effectuate this agreement. . . .

THIS ASSURANCE is given in consideration of and for the purpose of obtaining any and all Federal grants, loans, contracts, property, discounts or other Federal financial assistance extended after the date hereof to the Applicant by the Department, including installment payments after such date on account of applications for Federal financial assistance which were approved before such date. The Applicant recognizes and agrees that such Federal financial assistance will be extended in reliance on the representations and agreements made in this assurance, and that the United States shall have the right to seek judicial enforcement of this assurance. This assurance is binding on the Applicant, its successors, transferees, and assignees, and the person or persons whose signatures appear below are authorized to sign this assurance on behalf of the Applicant.

Dated____________________________

____

(Applicant)

By ____________________________

(President, Chairman of Board, or
comparable authorized official)

____

____

(Applicant's mailing address)

THE PUBLIC SCHOOLS AND TITLE VI: THE "GUIDELINES"

In April 1965, the United States Department of Health, Education, and Welfare, through the United States Office of Education, issued a detailed statement of the standards by which compliance or noncompliance with Title VI of the Civil Rights Act of 1964 by state and local school authorities would be measured by the federal government. Officially entitled "General Statement of Policies Under Title VI of the Civil Rights Act of 1964 Respecting Desegregation of Elementary and Secondary Schools," the document came to be known as "The Guidelines." After several months of experience, the guidelines were revised, and a new statement of policies issued in 1966 to govern the 1966–67 school year. With minor changes, the principles laid down in 1966 remained in force in 1967–1969.

Initial resistance to the guidelines was severe throughout the South. The state of Alabama even went so far as to forbid state and local school officials to obey their directives, but the comparative firmness of the federal authorities (and particularly of United States Commissioner of Education Harold Howe) charged with their effectuation brought the great majority of the nation's thousands of school systems into more or less grudging compliance. It was, however, often little more than a paper concession. Many school systems sought to find the very minimum degree of compliance that would forestall the loss of federal funds, and even then the terms they pledged to abide by were not scrupulously honored.

Critics and outright foes of the guidelines were especially resentful of the energetic Commissioner Howe, and it was partly to conciliate this sentiment that responsibility for administration of the guidelines was soon transferred from the Office of Education to HEW itself, and the somewhat more flexible direction of Peter Libassi, head of the Department's Office for Civil Rights, whose policy seemed to shift the emphasis from quantitative measurement of the rate of desegregation to the more general goal of making bona fide progress toward the reasonably early abandonment of all dual school systems.

Here are reproduced excerpts of major sections of the revised guidelines.[1]

Subpart A—Applicability of This Statement of Policies

#181.1 Title VI and the HEW Regulation

. . . As required by Section 602 of Title VI, the Department of Health, Education, and Welfare has issued a Regulation to assure the elimination of discrimination in Federal aid programs it administers. . . .

#181.2 Compliance by School Systems Eliminating Dual School Structure

To be eligible for Federal aid, a school system must act to eliminate any practices in violation of Title VI, including the continued maintenance of a dual structure of separate schools for students of different races. The HEW Regulation recognizes two methods of meeting this requirement: (1) a desegregation order of a Federal court; or (2) a voluntary desegregation plan.

#181.3 Purpose of This Statement of Policies

This Statement of Policies . . . sets forth the requirements which voluntary desegregation plans must meet for the Commissioner to determine under the HEW Regulation that a plan is adequate to accomplish the purposes of Title VI. . . .

#181.4 Initial Demonstration of Compliance

To be eligible for Federal aid, a school system must first assure the Commissioner that it will comply with Title VI and the HEW Regulation. It must submit the form of assurance that meets its circumstances. . . .

#181.6 Systems Under Federal Court Order for Desegregation

[1] 31 *Federal Register* 5623 (April 9, 1966); 45 *Code of Federal Regulations,* Part 181, p. 398 (revised as of January 1, 1967).

(a) Submission of Order. A school system under a Federal Court desegregation order which meets the requirements of the HEW Regulation may submit, as evidence of compliance with Title VI, a copy of the court order, together with an assurance that it will comply with the order, including any future modification. . . .

#181.7 Systems With Voluntary Desegregation Plans

(a) Submission of Form 441-B. A school system with a voluntary desegregation plan must provide an assurance that it will abide by the applicable requirements for such plans contained in this Statement of Policies. Such assurance may be given by submitting HEW Form 441-B to the Commissioner. . . .

(b) Changing Type of Plan. A school system may change from one type of desegregation plan to another if such action would eliminate segregation and all other forms of discrimination more expeditiously. . . .

(c) Retaining Present Type of Plan. A school system with a desegregation plan accepted by the Commissioner need not resubmit its plan if it intends to continue under the same type of plan. . . .

(d) Initial Submittal of Plans. If no desegregation plan has been submitted or accepted for a school system, HEW Form 441-B and a plan meeting the requirements of this Statement of Policies must be submitted.

Subpart B—Basic Requirements for All Voluntary Desegregation Plans

#181.11 Various Types of Desegregation Plans

It is the responsibility of a school system to adopt and implement a desegregation plan which will eliminate the dual school system and all other forms of discrimination as expeditiously as possible. No single type of plan is appropriate for all school systems. In some cases, the most expeditious means of desegregation is to close the schools originally established for students of one race, particularly where they are small and inadequate, and to assign all the students and teachers to desegregated schools. Another appropriate method is to reorganize the grade structure of schools originally established for students of different races so that these schools are fully utilized, on a desegregated basis, although each school contains fewer grades. In some cases desegregation is accomplished by the establishment of non-racial attendance zones. Under certain conditions, a plan based on free choice of school may be a way to undertake desegregation. In certain cases the purposes of Title VI may be most expeditiously accomplished by a plan applying two or more of the foregoing procedures to certain schools or different grade levels. Based on consideration of all the circumstances of a particular school system, the Commissioner may determine that its desegregation plan is not adequate to accomplish the purposes of Title VI, in which case he may require the adoption of an alternative plan. . . .

#181.12 Student Assignment Practices

Title VI precludes a school system from any action or inaction designed to perpetuate or promote segregation or any other form of discrimination, or to limit desegregation or maintain what is essentially a dual school structure. Any educational opportunity offered by a school system must be available to students without regard to race, color, or national origin. In particular, any academic tests or other procedures used in assigning students to schools, grades, classrooms, sections, courses of study or for any other purpose must be applied uniformly to all students without regard to race, color, or national origin. Curriculum, credit and promotion procedures must not be applied in such a way as to penalize or hamper students who transfer from one school to another pursuant to a desegregation plan.

#181.13 Faculty and Staff

(a) Desegregation of Staff. . . . Each school system is responsible for correcting the effects of all past discriminatory practices in the assignments of teachers and other professional staff.

(b) New Assignments. Race, color, or national origin may not be a factor in the hiring or assignment to schools or within schools of teachers and other professional staff. . . .

(c) Dismissals. Teachers and other professional staff may not be dismissed, demoted, or passed over for retention, promotion, or rehiring on the ground of race, color, or national origin. . . .

(d) Past Assignments. The pattern of assignment of teachers and other professional staff among the various schools of a system may not be such that schools are identifiable as intended for students of a particular race, color, or national origin, or such that teachers or other professional staff of a particular race are concentrated in those schools where all, or the majority, of the students are of that race. Each school system has a positive duty to make staff assignments and reassignments necessary to eliminate past discriminatory assignment patterns. Staff desegregation for the 1966–67 school year must include significant progress beyond what was accomplished for the 1965–66 school year in the desegregation of teachers assigned to schools on a regular full-time basis. . . .

#181.14 Services, Facilities, Activities, and Programs

(a) General. Each school system is responsible for removing any segregation and any other form of discrimination affecting students in connection with all services, facilities, activities and programs (including transportation, athletics, and other extra-curricular activities) that may be conducted or sponsored by or affiliated with the schools of the sytsem. . . .

#181.15 Unequal Educational Programs and Facilities

In addition to the changes made in student assignment practices under its desegregation plan, each school system is responsible for removing all other forms of discrimination on the ground of race, color, or national origin. . . . If the facilities, teaching materials, or educational program available to students in [formerly all-Negro schools] are inferior to those generally available in the schools of the system, the school authorities will normally be required immediately to assign such students to other schools in order to discontinue the use of the inferior school. . . .

#181.17 Official Support for Desegregation Plan

(a) Community Support. School officials must take steps to encourage community support and acceptance of their desegregation plan. They are responsible for preparing students, teachers and all other personnel, and the community in general, for the successful desegregation of the school system.

(b) Information to the Public. Full information concerning the desegregation plan must be furnished freely to the public and to all television and radio stations and all newspapers serving the community. . . .

Subpart C—Additional Requirements for Voluntary Desegregation Plans Based on Geographic Attendance Zones

#181.31 General

A voluntary desegregation plan based in whole or in part on geographic attendance zones must meet the requirements of this Subpart for all students whose assignment to schools is determined by such zones. . . .

#181.32 Attendance Zones

A single system of non-racial attendance zones must be established. A school system may not use zone boundaries or feeder patterns designed to perpetuate or promote segregation, or to limit desegregation or maintain what is essentially a dual school structure. . . .

#181.34 Notice

(a) Individual Notice. On a convenient date between March 1 and April 30 in each year, each school system must distribute, by first class mail, a letter to the parent, or other adult person acting as parent, of each student who is then enrolled, except high school seniors expected to graduate, giving the name and location of the school to which the student has been assigned for the coming school year pursuant to the desegregation plan, and information concerning the bus service between his school and his neighborhood. . . . Each letter must be accompanied by a notice, in a form prescribed by the Commissioner, explaining the desegregation plan. The same letter and notice must also be furnished, in person or by mail, to the parent of each prospective student, including each student planning to enter the first grade or kindergarten, as soon as the school system learns that he plans to enroll.

(b) Published Notice. The school system must arrange for the conspicuous publication of an announcement, identical with the text of the notice provided for under (a) above, in the newspaper most generally circulated in the community, on or shortly before the date of mailing under (a) above. . . .

Subpart D—Additional Requirements for Voluntary Desegregation Plans Based on Free Choice of Schools

#181.41 General

A voluntary desegregation plan based in whole or in part on free choice of schools must meet the requirements of this Subpart for all students whose assignments to schools is determined by free choice. . . .

#181.42 Who May Exercise Choice

A choice of schools may be exercised by a parent or other adult person serving as the student's parent. A student may exercise his own choice if he (1) is exercising a choice for the ninth or a higher grade, or (2) has reached the age of fifteen at the time of the exercise of choice. Such a choice by a student is controlling unless a different choice is exercised for him by his parent, or other adult person acting as his parent, during the period in which the student exercises his choice. . . .

#181.43 Annual Mandatory Exercise of Choice

Each student must be required to exercise a free choice of schools once annually. . . .

#181.44 Choice Period

A period of at least 30 days must be provided for exercising choice, to commence no earlier than March 1 and to end no later than April 30, preceding the school year for which choice is to be exercised. . . .

#181.49 Assignment According to Choice

No choice may be denied in assigning students to schools for any reason other than overcrowding. In cases where overcrowding would result at one or more schools from the choices made, preference must be given on the basis of the proximity of schools to the homes of students, without regard to race, color, or national origin. . . . Standards for determining overcrowding and available space that are applied uniformly throughout the system must be used if any choice is to be denied. . . .

#181.50 Transfer for Special Needs

Each student must attend the school to which he is assigned under the foregoing provisions, except that any student who requires a course of study not offered at that school, or who is physically handicapped, may be permitted, upon his written application, to transfer to another school which is designed to fit, or offers courses for, his special needs. . . .

#181.52 Officials Not to Influence Choice

. . . at no time may any official, teacher, or employee of the school system, either directly or indirectly, seek to influence any parent, student, or any other person involved, in the exercise of a choice, or favor or penalize any person because of a choice made. Information concerning choices made by individual students or schools to which they are assigned may not be made public.

#181.53 Public Notice

On or shortly before the date the choice period opens, the school system must arrange for the conspicuous publication of a notice describing the desegregation plan in the newspaper most generally circulated in the community. . . . Copies of this notice must also be given at that time to all radio and television stations serving the community. . . .

#181.54 Requirements for Effectiveness of Free Choice Plans

A free choice plan tends to place the burden of desegregation on Negro or other minority group students and their parents. Even when school authorities undertake good faith efforts to assure its fair operation, the very nature of a free choice plan and the effect of longstanding community attitudes often tend to preclude or inhibit the exercise of a truly free choice by or for minority group students.

For these reasons, the Commissioner will scrutinize with special care the operation of voluntary plans of desegregation in school systems which have adopted free choice plans. . . .

The single most substantial indication as to whether a free choice plan is actually working to eliminate the dual school structure is the extent to which Negro or other minority group students have in fact transferred from segregated schools. . . .

As a general matter, for the 1966–67 school year the Commissioner will, in the absence of other evidence to the contrary, assume that a free choice plan is a viable and effective means of completing initial stages of desegregation in school systems in which a substantial percentage of the students have in fact been transferred from segregated schools. . . .

In districts with a sizable percentage of Negro or other minority group students, the Commissioner will, in general, be guided by the following criteria in scheduling free choice plans for review:

(1) If a significant percentage of the students, such as 8 percent or 9 percent, transferred from segregated schools for the 1965–66 school year, total transfers on the order of at least twice that percentage would normally be expected.

(2) If a smaller percentage of the students, such as 4 percent or 5 percent, transferred from segregated schools for the 1965–66 school year, a substantial increase in transfers would normally be expected, such as would bring the total to at least triple the percentage for the 1965–66 school year.

(3) If a lower percentage of students transferred for the 1965–66 school year, then the rate of increase in total transfers for the 1966–67 school year would normally be expected to be proportionately greater than under (2) above.

(4) If no students transferred from segregated schools under a free choice plan for the 1965–66 school year, then a very substantial start would normally be expected, to enable such a school system to catch up as quickly

as possible with systems which started earlier. If a school system in these circumstances is unable to make such a start for the 1966–67 school year under a free choice plan, it will normally be required to adopt a different type of plan. . . .

Subpart F—Desegregation Plans Not Reaching All Grades for the 1966–67 School Year

#181.71 Opportunity to Transfer in Grades Not Reached by Plan

In any school system in which, for the school year, 1966–67, there are grades not yet reached by the desegregation plan, the school system must arrange for students to attend school on a desegregated basis in each of the special circumstances described in (a), (b), (c), and (d) below. This opportunity must be made available in such a way as to follow, to the maximum extent feasible, the desegregation procedures in grades generally reached by the plan, according to the type of plan in effect.

(a) Transfer for a Course of Study. A student must be permitted to transfer to a school in order to take a course of study for which he is qualified and which is not available in the school to which he would otherwise be assigned on the basis of his race, color, or national origin.

(b) Transfer to Attend School With Relative. A student must be permitted to transfer in order to attend the same school or attendance center as a brother, sister, or other relative living in his household, if such relative is attending a school as a result of a desegregation plan and if such school or attendance center offers the grade which the student would be entering.

(c) Transfer for Students Required to Go Outside System. A student must be permitted to transfer to any school within the system which offers the grade he is to enter if he would otherwise be required to attend school outside the system on the basis of his race, color, or national origin.

(d) Transfer for Other Reasons. A student must be permitted to transfer to a school other than the one to which he is assigned on the basis of his race, color, or national origin if he meets whatever requirements, other than race, color or national origin, the school system normally applies in permitting student transfers.

#181.72 Students New to the System

Each student who will be attending school in the system for the first time in the 1966–67 school year in any grade not yet generally reached by the desegregation plan must be assigned to school under the procedures for desegregation that are to be applied to that grade when it is generally reached by the desegregation plan.

#181.73 General Provisions Applicable

A student who has transferred to a school under #181.71 above, or entered a school under #181.72 above shall be entitled to the full benefits of #181.14 above (relating to desegregation of services, facilities, activities and programs) and to any and all other rights, privileges, and benefits generally conferred on students who attend a school by virtue of the provisions of the desegregation plan.

#181.74 Notice

Each school system in which there will be one or more grades not fully reached by the desegregation plan in the 1966–67 school year must add a paragraph describing the applicable transfer provisions at the end of the notice distributed and published pursuant to #181.34 above or #181.46 and 181.53 above, as is appropriate for the type of plan adopted by the school system. The text of the paragraph must be in a form prescribed by the

Commissioner. The school system must make such other changes to the notice as may be necessary to make clear which students will be affected by attendance zone assignments or free choice requirements.

In addition, for the letter to parents required in #181.46, school systems with free choice plans which have not desegregated every grade must use a letter describing the plan and will enclose with the letter sent to parents of students in grades not desegregated a transfer application instead of a choice form. For the letter to parents required in #181.34, school systems with geographic zone plans must send to each parent of students in grades not desegregated a letter describing the plan and a transfer application. The text for these letters and the transfer application must be in a form prescribed by the Commissioner.

#181.75 Processing of Transfer Applications

Applications for transfer may be submitted on the transfer application form referred to in #181.74 above or by any other writing. If any transfer application is incomplete, incorrect or unclear in any respect, the school system must make every reasonable effort to help the applicant perfect his application. Under plans based on geographic zones, and under plans based on free choice of schools, the provisions of #181.42 as to whether a student or his parent may make a choice of school, shall also determine whether a student in a grade not yet generally reached by desegregation may execute a transfer application.

#181.76 Reports and Records

In each report to the Commissioner under #181.18, 181.35, and 181.55 above, the school system must include all data, copies of materials distributed and other information generally required, relative to all students, regardless of whether or not their particular grades have been generally reached by the plan. Similarly the system must retain the records provided for under #181.19, 181.35, and 181.55 above, with respect to all students.

By the autumn of 1967 the HEW's Office for Civil Rights (OCR) was for the first time setting deadlines for complete desegregation of particular districts, and intimated that it expected most school districts to finish the process by the fall of 1969. Deadlines varied from district to district, depending upon local circumstances. The shift in policy was precipitated by the manifest failure, in most instances, of freedom-of-choice plans to end the practice of racially separate schools. In such districts, according to Libassi, school officials were obliged, under the penalties provided by Title VI, to substitute other plans that would more effectively close out the dual school system. There were at the beginning of the 1967–68 school year 1238 school districts in the South operating under "voluntary" desegregation plans, most of them on the free-choice model. Approximately one hundred of the districts had suffered the cutoff of federal funds, but of these some forty were soon again receiving money from Washington after complying with HEW requirements.

The OCR's Peter Libassi reported that three-fourths of the black children in southern and border states were in 1967–68 still attending all-Negro schools; and while the shift from the earlier plan of requiring certain percentages of transfers to the newer policy of establishing deadlines was calculated to hasten the end of dual systems, he conceded that the elimination of dualism would not necessarily decrease segregation in the larger southern cities, since Negro children usually attended schools in their own neighborhoods, thus producing (as in northern urban centers) de facto segregation. It was to this problem that HEW would turn its attention for the 1968–69 school year.

THE TWENTY-FOURTH AMENDMENT

The same year that brought forth the Civil Rights Act of 1964 saw also the ratification of an amendment to the Constitution of the United States, abolishing the poll tax as a prerequisite for voting in federal elections.[1]

ARTICLE XXIV

Section 1

The right of citizens of the United States to vote in any primary or other election for President or Vice President, for electors for President or Vice President, or for Senator or Representative in Congress, shall not be denied or abridged by the United States or any State by reason of failure to pay any poll tax or other tax.

Section 2

The Congress shall have power to enforce this article by appropriate legislation.

THE VOTING RIGHTS ACT OF 1965

Prior to the enactment of the Civil Rights Act of 1957 the vindication of the right to vote had relied almost wholly on private litigation. In the 1957 law the Attorney General was given statutory authority to institute suits in behalf of Negroes deprived of voting rights; and the Act of 1960, and Title I of the Civil Rights Act of 1964, strengthened the 1957 measure. Even so, no significant increase in Negro registration occurred.

The white primary was, to be sure, no longer available as a means for the effectual disfranchisement of the Negro. But the literacy test and other devices purporting to screen out incompetents were still making it extremely difficult (and in some counties impossible) for black citizens to qualify officially as voters. Such new powers as the Department of Justice had acquired in 1957, 1960, and 1964 produced little more than protracted litigation which, when successful, reached only limited geographical areas.

[1] *Constitution of the United States of America; Analysis and Interpretation,* 88th Cong., 1st sess., Senate Document No. 39 (Washington, 1967), 74.

Systematic exclusion of Negroes from political party affairs, and from the election of 1964, and the beating of voter-registration workers and demonstrators in 1965, especially at Selma, Alabama, prompted the Congress (which, in turn, had been influenced by rising popular pressures) to pass the Voting Rights Act of 1965.

Its effects were dramatic. The percentage of Negroes of voting age who were now registered as voters promptly rose, for example, from 27 to 53 percent in Georgia, from 19 to 52 percent in Alabama, and from less than 7 to 60 percent in Mississippi, in less than two years. Early in 1967 Negro registration was more than 50 percent of the Negro voting age population in every southern state.

In the 1968 general elections informed estimates reported that 6,300,000 of the 78,964,000 votes cast in the presidential election were those of Negroes, and that in the South about 52 percent of all Negroes of voting age (as compared with 61.9 percent of whites of voting age) actually voted. The gap had been greatly narrowed. In addition to influencing the nomination and election of white candidates, and affecting the policy positions of the parties, this greatly increased black vote was reflected in the election of black officeholders, from minor county officeholders to an increased congressional delegation. By the end of 1969 there were at least 1200 elected black public officeholders in the country, more than 400 of them in the eleven states of the old Confederacy.[1] Some states, like North Carolina, saw the election of the first Negro state legislators in a century. Even in Georgia, no fewer than fourteen black legislators were sent to the state's General Assembly. Much of the increase was accomplished under the supervision of the federal examiners for which the Act of 1965 provided, but far more of it was done under the supervision of the local voting registrars, now convinced that the federal government would no longer tolerate recalcitrance.[2]

An Act to enforce the Fifteenth Amendment to the Constitution of the United States and for other Purposes.

Voter Requirements Outlawed by This Act

No State or political subdivision (counties, municipalities and parishes) covered by the Voting Rights Act may require the use of any test or device as a prerequisite for registration or voting. Tests or devices included in this Act are those which may require:

[1] *The New York Times,* Dec. 30, 1969, p. 18.

[2] P.L. 89–110, 89th Cong., S. 1564, August 6, 1965; 79 *U.S. Statutes at Large,* 437. The summary that follows relies upon U.S. Commission on Civil Rights, *Political Participation* (Washington, 1968), especially pp. 11–13. *See also* U.S. Commission on Civil Rights, *The Voting Rights Act of 1965; CCR Special Publication No. 4,* August, 1965.

1. A demonstration of the ability to read, write, understand or interpret any given material.
2. A demonstration of any educational achievement or knowledge of any particular subject.
3. Proof of good moral character.
4. Proof of qualifications through a procedure in which another person (such as an individual already registered) must vouch for the prospective voter.

Coverage

The Voting Rights Act of 1965 states that no person shall be denied the right to vote in any Federal, State or local election (including primaries) for failure to pass a test if he lives in a State or political subdivision which:

1. Maintained a test or device as a prerequisite to registration or voting as of November 1, 1964.

and

2. Had a total voting age population of which less than 50 percent were registered or actually voted in the 1964 Presidential election.

If the above two factors are present, the State or political subdivision is automatically covered by the 1965 Act. If an entire State meets these qualifications, all of its counties come under the provisions of the Act. If only one county in a State meets them, the single county is subject to the requirements of the law.

States covered by the Act include Alabama, Alaska, Georgia, Louisiana, Mississippi, South Carolina, Virginia, and approximately 26 counties in North Carolina.

A State or political subdivision may be removed from coverage by filing a suit in a three-judge District Court for the District of Columbia. The State or political subdivision must convince the court that no test or device has been used for the purpose or with the effect of denying the right to vote because of race or color during the five years preceding the filing of the suit.

However, if there has been a previous court judgment against a State or political subdivision determining that tests or devices have been used to deny the right to vote, the State or political subdivision must wait five years before it can obtain an order from the District Court for the District of Columbia removing it from the coverage of the Act.

A judgment may be obtained more quickly if the Attorney General advises the court that he believes that the tests have not been used to discriminate on the basis of race or color during the five years preceding the filing of the action. He may also ask the court to reconsider its decision any time within five years after judgment.

Changes in Voting Laws

When a State or political subdivision covered by the Act seeks to change its voting qualifications or procedures from those in effect on November 1, 1964, it must either obtain the approval of the U.S. Attorney General or initiate a Federal Court suit. If the Attorney General objects to these changes, or if they have not been submitted to him for his approval, the new laws may not be enforced until the District Court for the District of Columbia rules that the changes will not have the purpose or the effect of denying the right to vote because of the race or color of any person.

Federal Examiners

Once it is determined that a political subdivision is covered by the Act, the U.S. Attorney General may direct the U.S. Civil Service Commission to appoint Federal examiners to list voters if:

1. He has received twenty meritorious written complaints alleging voter discrimination, *or*
2. He believes that the appointment of examiners is necessary to enforce the guarantees of the Fifteenth Amendment.

The times, places and procedures for listing will be established by the Civil Service Commission.

Authority of the Examiners

The Federal examiners will list (that is, declare eligible and entitled to vote) those who satisfy state qualifications that have not been suspended by the Voting Rights Act. Examples of valid qualifications would be those of age and residence.

The examiners will prepare a list of qualified voters and send the list each month to State authorities who must register them—that is, place their names in the official voting records. This list must be available for public inspection. Each person on the examiner's list will be issued a certificate by the examiners as evidence of eligibility to vote in any Federal, State or local elections.

No person listed by the examiner will be entitled to vote in any election unless his name has been sent to local election officials at least 45 days before that election thereby allowing the State election machinery to run without complication.

Enforcement of Action by Federal Examiners

At the request of the Attorney General the Civil Service Commission may appoint poll watchers in counties where Federal examiners are already serving to observe whether all eligible persons are allowed to vote and whether all ballots are accurately tabulated.

If anyone who is properly listed or registered is not permitted to vote in any political subdivision where examiners are serving, a complaint may be made to the examiners of this denial within 48 hours after the polls close. If the examiner believes that the complaint has merit, he must inform the Attorney General immediately. The Attorney General may seek a district court order to provide for the casting of the ballot and suspend the election results until the vote is included in the final count.

Challenge of Listed Persons

A formal objection challenging the qualifications of a person listed by the Federal examiner may be filed (at a place to be designated by the Civil Service Commission) within ten days after the list of qualified voters has been made public and must be supported by at least two affidavits. The validity of the challenge will be determined within fifteen days after filing by a hearing officer appointed by the Civil Service Commission. The U.S. Court of Appeals may review decisions of the hearing officer.

Until the final court review is completed, any person listed by the examiner is still eligible and must be permitted to vote. If a challenge is successful, the name of the registrant will be removed from the examiner's list.

Withdrawal of Federal Examiners

Examiners may be withdrawn from a political subdivision when the names of all persons listed by the examiners have been placed in the official records and when there is no reason to believe that persons in the subdivision will be prevented from voting. The removal may be accomplished by action of:

1. The Civil Service Commission after it receives notification from the U.S. Attorney General, *or*
2. The District Court for the District of Columbia in a suit brought by a political subdivision after the Director of the Census has determined that more than 50 percent of the nonwhite voting age population in the subdivision is registered to vote.

A political subdivision may petition the U.S. Attorney General to end listing procedures and to request that the Director of the Census conduct a survey to determine whether more than 50 percent of the nonwhite voting age population is registered.

Poll Taxes

. . . The U.S. Attorney General is directed to institute suits against Alabama, Mississippi, Texas and Viriginia which require the payment of poll taxes in order to determine if such taxes violate the Constitution. While a suit is pending, or upon a finding that poll tax is unconstitutional, persons registered or listed for the first time in areas covered by the Act need only pay the tax for the current year. The poll tax may be paid up to 45 days prior to an election regardless of the timeliness of the payment under State law.

Voting Suits

The Voting Rights Act of 1965 gives new enforcement powers to the courts in voting cases. When the court finds that there has been a denial of the right to vote in a suit brought by the U.S. Attorney General, the court must:

1. Authorize the appointment of examiners by the Civil Service Commission unless denials of the right to vote have been few in number, they have been corrected by State or local action, and there is no probability that they will reoccur.
2. Suspend the use of tests or devices in an area where it has been proved that at least one such requirement has been utilized to deny the right to vote because of race or color.

When examiners have been authorized by court order, they may be removed by an order of the authorizing court.

Language Literacy

If a person residing in a State where tests or devices have not been suspended has completed at least six grades in an "American-flag" school (a school in the United States or its territories), his inability to speak the English language shall not be the basis of denying him the right to vote. . . .

Criminal and Civil Penalties

Public officials or private individuals who deny persons the right to vote guaranteed by the Voting Rights Act of 1965 or anyone who attempts to or intimidates, threatens, or coerces a person from voting are subject to criminal penalties. It is also made a crime to attempt to or to intimidate, threaten or coerce anyone who urges or aids any person to vote. Criminal penalties are provided for applicants who give false information about their eligibility to vote or who accept payment to register or vote in a Federal election. The U.S. Attorney General is also authorized to bring action for injunctive relief to restrain violations of the Act.

THE CIVIL RIGHTS ACT OF 1968

After the enactment of the sweeping Civil Rights Act of 1964 and the Voting Rights Act of 1965, a period of mounting civil disorders and increasing demands from the more militant spokesmen in the struggle, as well as a general public weariness over seemingly endless and insoluble problems of race relations, produced a "backlash," and mobilized both popular and congressional opinion against further federal civil rights legislation for the present. A proposed Civil Rights Act of 1966 was transmitted to the Congress by the Attorney General, and its passage was strongly urged by President Johnson in a message to Congress of May 2. The House passed the bill, but it was killed in the Senate. Revived in 1967 and again passed in the House as a mild measure to protect civil rights workers from harassment and reprisal, it was considerably strengthened by a Republican-Democratic coalition, which forced through an open-housing provision, and sent it back to the lower house in greatly expanded form. There, with the House in a more conservative mood, the proposed law might have died had not the assassination of Dr. Martin Luther King on April 4, 1968, generated an enormous surge of indignation against racial discrimination, and of sympathy for the Negro's plight. The omnibus bill, hitherto considered unlikely to pass, was swiftly enacted a week later.

Although Title VIII, on open housing, was easily the most important portion of the act, there were titles dealing with other aspects of minority rights. Portions of the law defined and safeguarded the rights of American Indians; there were two antiriot clauses, and a lengthy section prescribing penalties for interfering, by violence or intimidation or other means, with any person's enjoyment of his federally protected rights. The following are excerpts from the statute's most significant innovations:[1]

TITLE VIII: FAIR HOUSING

Policy

Section 801. It is the policy of the United States to provide, within constitutional limitations, for fair housing throughout the United States.

Sections 802–803. [Concerns certain definitions, and effective date of certain provisions.]

Discrimination in the Sale or Rental of Housing

Section 804. As made applicable by section 803 and except as exempted by sections 803(b) and 807, it shall be unlawful—

[1] P.L. 90–284, 90th Cong., H.R. 2516, April 11, 1968.

(a) To refuse to sell or rent after the making of a bona fide offer, or to refuse to negotiate for the sale or rental of, or otherwise make unavailable or deny, a dwelling to any person because of race, color, religion, or national origin.

(b) To discriminate against any person in the terms, conditions, or privileges of sale or rental of a dwelling, or in the provision of services or facilities in connection therewith, because of race, color, religion, or national origin.

(c) To make, print, or publish, or cause to be made, printed, or published any notice, statement, or advertisement, with respect to the sale or rental of a dwelling that indicates any preference, limitation, or discrimination based on race, color, religion, or national origin, or an intention to make any such preference, limitation, or discrimination.

(d) To represent to any person because of race, color, religion, or national origin that any dwelling is not available for inspection, sale, or rental when such dwelling is in fact so available.

(e) For profit, to induce or attempt to induce any persons to sell or rent any dwelling by representations regarding the entry or prospective entry into the neighborhood of a person or persons of a particular race, color, religion, or national origin.

Sections 805–806. [Prohibit discrimination in the financing of housing and in the provision of brokerage services.]

Sections 807–813. [Provide for certain exemptions for the administration of the act; for the initiation of certain educational and conciliatory activities to promote full compliance with the act; and for its enforcement, both by private persons and by the Attorney General.]

Sections 814–816. [Provide for the expedition of proceedings, define the act's effect upon state laws; and provide for cooperation with state and local agencies administering fair housing laws.]

Interference, Coercion, or Intimidation

Section 817. It shall be unlawful to coerce, intimidate, threaten, or interfere with any person in the exercise or enjoyment of, or on account of his having exercised or enjoyed, or on account of his having aided or encouraged any other person in the exercise or enjoyment of, any right granted or protected by Section 803, 804, 805, or 806. This section may be enforced by appropriate civil action.

(7)

THE FEDERAL COURTS AND THE BLACK AMERICAN, 1954–1970

The role of the courts in advancing the cause of racial equality was somewhat obscured from the public view from 1954 to October 1969 by the more spectacular news from the legislative and executive branches of the government—to say nothing of the turmoil in the streets. It was also diminished by the disposition of judges, notably in the case of the Supreme Court in the afterglow of the *Brown* decision, to "make haste slowly"—to proceed, in short, with the "deliberate speed," the "majestic instancy," which the nation's highest tribunal had itself required of others in the formula for compliance with the *School Segregation* decree. The reluctance of the judiciary to take a firmer line was publicly deplored both by many who were unfamiliar with the interior processes of the federal system and with the complexities and constraints under which the judicial machinery operates, and, as we shall see, by men deeply learned in the law, who saw in the Supreme Court's cautious responses to clear and present urgencies a refusal to commit itself unreservedly to the principle of a thoroughly equalitarian society.

Still others, including the news media and journals of opinion, took less and less notice of civil rights victories in the courts, because of the growing conviction that the triumphs that began in 1938 with the *Gaines* case and culminated in *Brown* and its subsequent applications, still left the mass of Negroes untouched where it mattered: still languishing in second-class citizenship; still badgered by imputations of inferiority; still stamped with the mark of oppression and the insignia of poverty—squalid housing, job discrimination and other economic deprivations and exclusions, grossly inferior schools, decaying standards of health and welfare. Millions of Negroes felt more alienated, more rejected and hopeless than ever, even while the statistics on certain tangible indices of well-being documented steady improvement in their lot.

Conceding that the rate of truly significant social change lagged far behind the progress that judicial decrees seemed to guarantee, defenders of the Supreme Court could point to the judges' growing hospitality to sanctions that reached beyond cold legalism to cope with the realities—the social, psychic, emotional, political, and moral effects of segregation. This gathering trend was stoutly rebuked as high-handed innovation by conservatives who overlooked the fact that the Court was not breaking new ground here, but cultivating a growth that had been in the minds of the framers of the Thirteenth, Fourteenth, and Fifteenth amendments, and had germinated at least as early as 1880 in the *Strauder* case.[1] Restated by Justice Harlan in his *Plessy* dissent in 1896, and sharpened by the Court's judgments in *Sipuel* (1948), *Sweatt* (1950), and *McLaurin* (1950), and then emphatically affirmed in *Brown* (1954), the principle that the *effects* of discrimination, including the "badges of slavery," the heart-wounds and intangible de-

[1] See above, p. 65, and see also G. Theodore Mitau, *Decade of Decision: The Supreme Court and the Constitutional Revolution,* 1954–1964 (New York, 1967), pp. 61–62.

privations it imposed, must be taken fully into account was now becoming judicial orthodoxy, as many of the cases noted below will attest.

The Court was finding, especially in the Fourteenth Amendment's equal protection clause, and in the amendment's conferral upon Congress of "power to enforce, by appropriate legislation, the provisions of this article," ample sanction for narrowing the license of local communities to abridge what states chose (or were obliged by federal constitutional provision) to guarantee. Its definition of "state action" was progressively widened until few discriminatory acts, however remotely they depended upon the public process, were ultimately immune to the judicial negative. Indeed, it went almost the whole way to abolishing the distinction between acts of the state and acts of private individuals, so far as the applicability of the Fourteenth Amendment was concerned. No less fateful for the future was the Court's movement to the position that the equal protection clause not only forbade the states to impose or connive at obstacles to equality, but also laid upon them the positive duty to *remove* such obstacles, and affirmatively to *promote* equality.

More than that, it showed a new receptivity to the view that the Thirteenth Amendment prohibiting slavery extended its caveat also to the "badges of slavery" when (before the Civil Rights Act of 1964 made further insistence upon the point unnecessary) proprietors of accommodations claimed the private "right" to select their clientele. The same extension of the Thirteenth Amendment to outlaw the relics of servitude was at least in part the basis for the 1967 *Loving* decision which found state antimiscegenation statutes unconstitutional.[1] In addition, the ruling in *Jones* v. *Mayer*,[2] in which the Court, coming to the relief of a Negro couple who had been prevented from purchasing a home in a white neighborhood, upheld the Civil Rights Act of 1866 with the unequivocal declaration that "surely Congress has the power under the Thirteenth Amendment rationally to determine what are the badges and the incidents of slavery, and the authority to translate that determination into effective legislation."

The commerce clause was another reservoir of authority into which the Supreme Court lowered its buckets more deeply than heretofore. More and more kinds of commercial enterprise were brought within the reach of the regulatory power of the Congress and of the independent agencies it had created, and hence into the orbit of federal civil rights legislation. More than that, conduct which had the effect of impeding the flow of commerce even at remoter points in the total economy was now construed by the courts as a direct invitation to congressional regulation. The scope of the commerce power was decisively enlarged,

[1] See below, p. 518.
[2] See below, p. 532.

for example, when the Court took official cognizance of the argument that the volume of travel by blacks was measurably reduced all over the country when local eating establishments made them unwelcome, and when it accepted the logic that provision of inferior protection to Negroes discouraged the movement of new industries into an area, and by that token affected interstate commerce in sufficient degree to subject such failures to congressional surveillance.

While the Court tightened the standards of measuring equality and for setting reasonable time limits for achieving compliance with laws and court decrees, it was increasingly pragmatic in judging the legality of halfhearted obedience: freedom-of-choice plans were to be appraised by the single standard of actual performance in eliminating dual school systems; the absence of Negroes on juries was to be checked against the number of available qualified potential black jurors in a community; sophisticated and ostensibly legal devices for defeating the Fifteenth Amendment, or for thwarting black applicants to white colleges, or for evading the duty to admit Negroes to hospitals, playgrounds, swimming pools, and other "places of public resort," were now to be scrutinized by judges with primary regard to their intent and their practical effect, rather than to the technical niceties by which they had been contrived.

Even so, the misgivings of honest doubters must also be set down. In October 1968, Lewis M. Steel, associate counsel of the NAACP, spoke out bluntly in a widely noticed article,[1] in which he took the United States Supreme Court severely to task, charging that it had "never committed itself to a society based upon principles of absolute equality." He was promptly discharged by the association, which emphatically repudiated the attack, and which promptly suffered the resignations of all other members of the association's legal staff in protest to his dismissal.

Speaking for a growing body of dissenters, black and white, Steel declared that the Supreme Court "struck down only the symbols of racism while condoning or overlooking the ingrained practices which have meant the survival of white supremacy in the United States, North and South." Only in the case of the most overt and obnoxious racial barriers has the Court "deigned to move," he charged, and this no less after 1954 than before it. And even when it had moved, it had only followed the lead of other institutions rather than taking the bold initiative that many have imputed to the Court, or it yielded only to other considerations—like winning a war, or relieving a labor shortage, or easing the country's conscience, or quieting the clamor of reformers with half-measures or mere paper reassurances.

[1] Lewis M. Steel, "Nine Men in Black Who Think White," *New York Times Magazine,* October 13, 1968, pp. 15–16, 112, 115, 117, 118, 120, 122.

In some cases, said Steel, the courtroom victories "were directed only at overt discriminatory practices in the southern or border states," and in others have resulted in de facto discrimination at least as reprehensible as the de jure discrimination which the decrees ostensibly reproved. And in the case of protest marchers and demonstrators, Steel argued, the Supreme Court, at first, when demonstrators "were considered to be humble supplicants seeking succor from white America," indulged them; but later, when "Negroes had become assertive in a society which considered such behavior anathema," the Court, again following shifts in the popular mood, moved to the position that "demonstrations and riots were synonymous." Since the Civil War, Steel concluded, "[the Court] has allowed itself to be swayed by the prejudices and mores of whites, and more recently, by their fears that equality for Negroes would adversely affect them."

Whether Steel's readers agreed with the details of his argument or not, few could not find more than a little truth in the proposition that most whites and Negroes were in 1969, in most aspects of their daily lives, almost as separate and as unequal as they were before May 17, 1954. But this writer would argue that such gains as the decade-and-a-half had witnessed, inadequate though they were, were eased into being by the courts. And if after the *School Segregation* cases the Supreme Court had turned a deaf ear to the petitioners, the forces of reaction might well have mounted a counterrevolution that any friend of progressive social change would have found egregiously painful to contemplate.

A. *Segregated Education: The Public Schools*

Recognizing the compelling momentum of the past and the variety of local problems and traditions which United States district courts would encounter in translating the *Brown* decision's command into accomplished fact, the Supreme Court had, in that decree, announced that it would give states and local authorities the opportunity to offer arguments as to the mode of enforcement before the implementing decision would be handed down. New hearings were held before the tribunal in April 1955, when some seventy lawyers filed briefs for an assortment of private plaintiffs, ten states, the District of Columbia, the Department of Justice, and others. Then, on May 31, 1955, the *Brown II* decision was announced.

By ordaining that district courts were to retain jurisdiction throughout the implementation process of the cases coming to them, the Supreme Court established a pattern for the guidance of the lower courts in dealing with the anticipated flood of litigation. They were to scrutinize the desegregation proposals of each local school unit against which enforcement proceedings were instituted, so that, rather than impose an iron uniformity, the judiciary could ease the transition to good faith compliance, in the context of local realities.[1]

Full implementation of these constitutional principles may require solution of varied local school problems. School authorities have the primary responsibility for . . . solving these problems; courts will have to consider whether the action of school authorities constitutes good faith implementation of the governing constitutional principles. . . . The courts which originally heard these cases can best perform this judicial appraisal. Accordingly, we believe it appropriate to remand the cases to those courts.

In fashioning and effectuating the decrees, the courts will be guided by equitable principles. . . . At stake is the personal interest of the plaintiffs in admission to public schools as soon as practicable on a nondiscriminatory basis. [This] may call for elimination of a variety of obstacles in making the transition to school systems operated in accordance with our May 17, 1954, decision. . . . But . . . the vitality of these constitutional principles cannot be allowed to yield simply because of disagreement with them.

. . . the courts will require that the defendants make a prompt and reasonable start toward full compliance. . . . [and] may find that additional time is necessary to carry out the ruling in an effective manner. The burden rests upon the defendants to establish that such time is necessary in the public interest and is consistent with good faith compliance at the earliest practicable date. . . . The courts may consider problems related to the physical condition of the school plant, the school transportation system, personnel, revision of school districts and attendance areas into compact units to achieve admission to the public schools on a nonracial basis, and revision of local laws . . . which may be necessary in solving the . . . problems. They may also consider the adequacy of any plans the defendants may propose to meet these problems. . . .

A few weeks after *Brown II* came further reassurance to uneasy southerners that the *Brown* doctrine, far from forcing full integration upon any school district, only forbade *publicly enforced segregation.* In this action, involving one of the five original *School Segregation* cases, the Court which had first heard the case, and to which *Brown II* remanded it, issued an injunction forbidding school authorities to *require* segregation, and retained the case on its docket to supervise the implementation of its decree.[2]

. . . . [T]he Supreme Court . . . has not decided that the federal courts are to take over or regulate the public schools of the states. It has not decided that the states must mix persons of different races in the schools. . . . What it has decided, and all that it has decided, is that a state may not deny to any person on account of race the right to attend any school that it maintains. . . . The Constitution, in other words, does not require integration. It merely forbids discrimination [and] the use of governmental power to enforce segregation. The Fourteenth Amendment is a limitation upon states or state

[1] *Brown* v. *Board of Education of Topeka,* 349 U.S. 294 (1955).
[2] *Briggs* v. *Elliott,* 132 F. Supp. 776 (E.D.S.C., 1955).

agencies, not . . . upon the freedom of individuals. . . . It is ordered . . . that the provisions of the Constitution and laws of South Carolina requiring segregation . . . in the public schools are null and void because violative of the Fourteenth Amendment.

Remaining doubts that the *Brown* principle applied also to a state's public colleges and universities were effectually disposed of in an action brought by several Negro youths who sought a declaratory judgment by a district court in North Carolina that the University of North Carolina was illegally denying them admission on the basis of race, and that they were entitled to relief by injunction. A three-judge court concluded:[1]

. . . [T]he only defense offered by the defendants in this suit is that the Supreme Court in *Brown* v. *Board of Education* . . . decided that segregation of the races was prohibited by the Fourteenth Amendment only in respect to the lower public schools and did not decide that the separation of the races in schools on the college and university level is unlawful. We think that the contention is without merit. . . . There is nothing to suggest that the reasoning does not apply with equal force to colleges as to primary schools. Indeed it is fair to say that they apply with greater force to students of mature age in the concluding years of their formal education as they are about to engage in the serious business of adult life.

As we have seen, state and local governments and school officials promptly set about contriving stratagems for evading or obstructing the rule that *Brown* laid down. In the flood of litigation by which Negroes pressed for bona fide compliance, the Supreme Court continued to take a soft line, as the states wrestled with the problems with which the decision had confronted them.

The Court in fact carefully sidestepped confrontation that would have compelled it clearly to approve or rebuke the widespread efforts to retard integration, efforts at which many lower courts and local school boards openly connived. But the issue could not be indefinitely postponed. The break came in the Little Rock crisis of September 1957, when Arkansas' Governor Faubus defied the federal courts by ordering state troops to Little Rock's Central High School to prevent the admission of nine Negro children whose request to be enrolled had been upheld by judicial order. This dramatic clash between the nation and a state—the sharpest since 1860—left President Eisenhower no choice but to dispatch units of the United States Army to sustain the authority of the United States.

On September 2, 1957, the governor coolly explained in a television address that he was ordering the state militia to the school to "restore order and to protect the lives and property of citizens." Three weeks

[1] *Frasier* v. *Board of Trustees of University of North Carolina,* 134 F. Supp. 589 (M.D.N.C., 1955).

later, the President, in a national telecast, explained that state and private force was being exerted to prevent the effectuation of the district court's orders, and "whenever normal agencies prove inadequate to the task . . . it becomes necessary for the Executive Branch of the Federal Government to use its power and authority to uphold Federal Courts. . . . This became necessary when my Proclamation of yesterday was not observed. . . ."

Although the federal government had won its point at Central High, the city's school officials asked for permission to suspend until 1961 the gradual-integration plan which it had initiated in 1957, pleading that conditions created by public hostility to integration, and by the unrest of teachers, pupils, and parents, seriously impaired the city's educational program. In June the court granted the petition. A United States court of appeals then reversed the lower court's action in August, but delayed its order, to permit the Supreme Court to act in the case.

The result was a case which compelled the Supreme Court at last to face the sort of enforcement issues that the tribunal had avoided since *Brown II*. The petitioners were Little Rock's school authorities; the respondent-plaintiff was John Aaron, a Negro parent. The Court convened in special term so that the question could be disposed of in time for the school's fall opening, and soon handed down the full text of its unanimous decision. The opinion addressed itself to several aspects of the enforcement question.[1]

[One passage faced the problem of defining "all deliberate speed":] . . . The District Courts were . . . [in *Brown II*] . . . directed to require "a prompt and reasonable start toward full compliance," and to take such action as was necessary to bring about the end of racial segregation in the public schools "with all deliberate speed." Of course, in many locations, obedience to the duty of desegregation would require the immediate general admission of Negro children. . . . On the other hand a District Court, after analysis of the relevant factors (which, of course, excludes hostility to racial desegregation), might conclude that justification existed for not requiring the present nonsegregated admission of all qualified Negro children. In such circumstances, however, the Court should scrutinize the program of the school authorities to make sure that they had developed arrangements pointed toward the earliest practicable completion of desegregation, and had taken appropriate steps to put their program into effective operation. It was made plain that . . . only a prompt start, diligently and earnestly pursued, to eliminate racial segregation . . . could constitute good faith compliance. State authorities were thus duty bound to devote every effort toward . . . the elimination of racial discrimination in the public school system.

[Another passage dealt with the defendant plea that the danger of violence and disorder justified the slowdown of integration:] The constitutional rights of respondents are not to be sacrificed or yielded to the violence and disorder which have followed upon the actions of the Governor and Legislature. As this Court said some 41 years ago in a unanimous opinion . . . in a case in-

[1] *Cooper* v. *Aaron*, 388 U.S. 1 (1958).

volving another aspect of racial segregation: "It is urged that this proposed segregation will promote the public peace by preventing racial conflicts. Desirable as is the preservation of the public peace, this aim cannot be accomplished by laws or ordinances which deny rights . . . protected by the Federal Constitution." Thus law and order are not here to be preserved by depriving the Negro children of their constitutional rights. The record before us clearly established that the growth of the Board's difficulties . . . is the product of state action. . . . [which] can also be brought under control by state action.

[Finally, the court rejected "the claim . . . that there is no duty on state officials to obey federal court orders" on the pretext of the state's reserved rights:] The command of the Fourteenth Amendment is that no *State* shall deny to any person . . . the equal protection of the laws. . . . In short, the constitutional rights of children not to be discriminated against . . . can neither be nullified . . . directly by state legislators or state executive and judicial officers, nor nullified indirectly through evasive schemes for segregation, whether attempted ingeniously or ingenuously. . . .

Article VI of the Constitution makes the Constitution the "supreme law of the land." In 1803 . . . *Marbury v. Madison* . . . declared the basic principle that the federal judiciary is supreme in the exposition of the law of the Constitution. . . . It follows that the interpretation of the Fourteenth Amendment enunciated by this Court in . . . Brown . . . is the supreme law of the land. . . .

It is . . . true that the responsibility for public education is primarily the concern of the States, but it is equally true that. . . . State support of segregated schools through any [means] cannot be squared with the Amendment's command that no State shall deny to any person within its jurisdiction the equal protection of the laws. . . .

An early reliance of segregationist state officials was the appeal to the rule that plaintiffs must exhaust all available remedies before seeking judicial relief. By simply multiplying the number and complexities of administrative procedures, repeated postponements, and snail-paced action, desegregation could be long deferred. A Fourth Circuit Court of Appeals ruling involving a North Carolina county, on December 1, 1955, seemed to give its blessing to this dodge.

The federal courts manifestly cannot operate the schools. All that they have the power to do in the premises is to enjoin violation of constitutional rights in the operation of schools by state authorities. Where the state law provides adequate administrative procedures for the protection of such rights, the federal courts manifestly should not interfere with the operation of the schools until such administrative procedure has been exhausted. . . .[1]

But a year later the same court, in a Charlottesville, Virginia, action, made plain that this principle could not be invoked when it was apparent that administrative remedies would be futile.

Defendants argue that plaintiffs have not shown themselves entitled to injunctive relief because they have not individually applied for admission to

[1] *Carson* v. *McDowell County,* 227 F. 2d 789 (4th Cir. 1955).

any particular school and been denied admission. The answer is that in view of the announced policy of the respective school boards any such application to a school other than a segregated school maintained for colored people would have been futile; and equity does not require the doing of a vain thing as a condition of relief.[1]

Under the Federal Rules of Civil Procedure, "class actions" are permissible only when persons constituting an aggrieved group are so numerous as to make it impracticable to bring them all before the court. Proceedings brought by school boards to prevent class actions in school desegregation suits were thwarted in a South Carolina case in 1962, by the Fourth Circuit Court of Appeals. The action had been brought by forty-two black children of Clarendon County.[2]

The court's consideration of these problems is facilitated by the presence of multiple plaintiffs. The effect of a particular practice or procedure may be determined more readily in the light of its impact upon a number rather than upon one alone. On the other hand . . . a school board may encounter difficult administrative problems as it effects desegregation of its schools, but such problems might be obscured or unapparent if the only question before the court was the possible reassignment of a single pupil.

There being common questions of fact, these multiple plaintiffs were entitled . . . to join in one action.

In the following year the Supreme Court tightened its criteria for determining whether a particular segregation plan met the requirement of "all deliberate speed." Although the plaintiffs in this instance were bringing a class suit to accelerate the desegregation (already under way) of a city's parks and recreation facilities, the case had a bearing upon schools because it provided the Court with occasion to pronounce upon the concept of deliberate speed.[3]

It is now more than nine years since . . . *Brown* v. *Board*. . . . And it was almost eight years ago . . . that the constitutional proscription of state enforced racial segregation was found to apply to public recreational facilities. . . . Given the extended time which has elapsed, it is far from clear that the mandate of the second *Brown* decision requiring that desegregation proceed with "all deliberate speed" would today be fully satisfied by types of plans or programs for desegregation of public educational facilities which eight years ago might have been deemed sufficient. *Brown* never contemplated that the concept of "deliberate speed" would countenance indefinite delay in elimination of racial barriers in schools, let alone other public facilities. . . . The nature of the ultimate resolution effected in the second *Brown* decision largely reflected no more . . . than a concern that delay not be conditioned upon insufficient reasons or, in any event, tolerated unless it imperatively and compellingly appeared unavoidable.

[1] *School Board of Charlottesville* v. *Allen* (1956), quoted in RRLR II, 59.

[2] *Brunson* v. *Board of Trustees of Clarendon County,* 311 F. 2d 107 (4th Cir. 1962).

[3] *Watson* v. *City of Memphis,* 373 U.S. 526 (1963).

Resourceful attorneys for southern cities and states even sought to set the *Brown* decision at nought by arguing that the Fourteenth Amendment was itself unconstitutional because it had been forced upon the states. A United States district court in Tennessee met this bold objection with this reply:[1]

> The Court is asked to go back practically a hundred years . . . and declare that the amendment was not validly adopted in the first instance. . . . Now . . . in Coleman v. Miller . . . the Supreme Court of the United States did substantially indicate its view that the courts do not have jurisdiction to inquire into the manner, means, and methods used to make the Fourteenth Amendment a part of the Federal Constitution. In other words, the adoption of the Fourteenth Amendment was treated by the Court in this case as a political question which addressed itself to the legislative branch of the government and not to the judicial branch. . . . It is a matter over which the judiciary certainly at this date does not have jurisdiction. . . .

Pupil assignment laws to which several southern states looked to preserve segregation[2] were repeatedly challenged. In one landmark case the Supreme Court declined to brand such laws as unconstitutional on their face, whatever might later be said of the manner of their enforcement.[3]

> This present opinion must be limited to the constitutionality of the law *upon its face*. The School Placement Law furnishes legal machinery for an orderly administration of the public schools in a constitutional manner by the admission of qualified pupils upon a basis of individual merit without regard to their race or color. We must presume that it will be so administered. If not, in some future proceeding it is possible that it may be declared unconstitutional in its application.

But on March 2, 1961, a court of appeals looked beyond the substance of the Little Rock pupil assignment law to its effect; and on November 22, a district court in Tennessee went still further to curtail the effectiveness of pupil assignment plans for slowing down integration.[4]

> . . . The obligation to disestablish imposed segregation is not met by applying placement or assignment standards, educational theories or some other criteria so as to produce the result of leaving the previous racial situation existing as it was before. If application of standards and criteria has the effect of preserving a created status of constitutional violation, such application fails to constitute a sufficient remedy in dealing with the constitutional wrong. . . .

[1] *Kelly* v. *Board of Education of Nashville*, Civil Action No. 2094 (M.D Tenn. 1956); reprinted in RRLR I, 1042.

[2] See above, p. 390.

[3] *Shuttlesworth* v. *Birmingham Board of Education*, Civil Action No 8914, May 9, 1956, N.D. Ala.; reprinted in RRLR II, 425.

[4] *Norwood* v. *Tucker*, 287 F. Supp. 798 (1961); *Sloan* v. *Wilson County, Tennessee*, Civil Action No. 3107, November 22, 1961, M.D. Tenn.; quoted in RRLR VI, 999.

The Court cannot approve the Tennessee Pupil Placement Law as a plan for accomplishing desegregation of the schools. This law, as shown on its face, is not a plan for desegregation nor is desegregation a part of its subject matter or purpose. As the Court understands it, its real purpose is . . . to vest in the school authorities the right to transfer and assign students based upon specified factors . . . under an elaborate and complex procedure set forth in the statute.

. . . At best [it] provides a most cumbersome and time-consuming procedure to accomplish transfers of students; and it is not, in the Court's opinion, a "prompt and reasonable start" toward desegregation. On the contrary, it would cause an unreasonable delay in effectuating . . . the Brown [decision].

In view of the fact that defendants have . . . failed to offer a fair, reasonable, or workable plan of desegregation or to make a prompt and reasonable start toward accomplishing such purpose . . . an injunction should be issued.

When plans submitted by school boards as proof of intention to make "a prompt and reasonable start" were challenged by Negro plaintiffs as dilatory evasions, the courts judged the proposals on their individual merits. Nashville's grade-a-year plan, for example, by which one grade per year was to be integrated until total desegregation was accomplished, was accepted by the federal court as satisfactory evidence of good faith compliance.[1]

The Supreme Court of the United States made it clear that adjustment must be made in accordance with the exigencies of each case and that the concept of "all deliberate speed" is a flexible one. . . . Local conditions call for the application of a local remedy.

In approving the present plan no denial of the constitutional rights of the plaintiffs . . . is involved. . . . The plan contemplates their full enforcement . . . in accordance with the time schedule which though protracted for the best interests of the school system as a whole is nevertheless definite and unambiguous. Full desegregation is not denied. It is merely postponed.

Only two years later a similar plan in Delaware was rejected by a United States court of appeals as falling short of all deliberate speed, because circumstances were different in Delaware.[2]

We are aware that strong courts have held in substance that a grade-by-grade integration . . . has met the criteria laid down by the Supreme Court in its decisions in *Brown* v. *Board*. . . . But the all-important issues of integration "with all deliberate speed" and what constitutes a "reasonable start toward compliance" with the ruling of the Supreme Court as required by its Brown decision . . . can be decided only on due consideration of all the pertinent factors. . . .

In short, integration in . . . Delaware, which already has integrated many of its schools, . . . should not be . . . judged by the more restrictive standards reasonably applicable to communities which have not advanced as far. . . .

[1] *Kelley* v. *Board of Education of Nashville,* Civil Action No. 2094, July 17, 1958 (M.D. Tenn.); quoted in RRLR III, 651.

[2] *Evans* v. *Ennis,* 281 F. 2d 385 (3rd Cir. 1960).

Again, as late as 1964, a federal district court took cognizance of the obstacles to rapid desegregation in rural Georgia, and approved a grade-a-year plan:[1]

> The purpose of the schools is to train minds, not to revise customs. Race is not one of the three R's.
>
> The mandate of the Supreme Court must be obeyed, but in making the transition from a racially segregated system to a racially non-segregated system it is important that the change be orderly and effective, with a minimum of turmoil and confusion, lest there be great damage to the system. Intellectual achievement must remain the primary goal. . . .

In some communities the closure of public schools (typically coupled with a scheme of tuition grants to enable white students to attend private schools) was the desperate solution to which last-ditch segregationists turned. The most conspicuous examples were provided by Virginia, notably in eastern cities and counties where Negroes approached 45 percent of the total population, and the proportion of Negroes in the public-school population exceeded 50 percent.

A law of 1956 authorized the state to cut off funds from schools in which it proved no longer possible to preserve segregation, and to divert such moneys for tuition grants to enable white students to attend private schools. (There were no private schools for Negroes.) Acting upon this legislation, Governor J. Lindsay Almond closed nine public schools in September 1958, forestalling the integration of what would probably have been about seventy black students, and incidentally depriving nearly 13,000 white students of public school education, a large number of whom thereupon entered private schools. Many of the latter were makeshift institutions, operated by educational "foundations."

Several of the public schools thus closed were in Norfolk, and here, on October 27, 1958, certain *white* children and their parents filed suit in the federal district court for an injunction against "massive resistance laws," as applied to Norfolk. In granting the writ, the court rejected the reasoning that since the closure deprived *both* races, there was no denial of equal protection. Rather, the fact that both races were deprived in some parts of the state, while both had access to public schools elsewhere, constituted a clear violation of the equal protection clause, in the opinion of the Court.[2]

> . . . Virginia, having . . . assumed the responsibility of maintaining and operating public schools, cannot . . . close one or more public schools in the state solely by reasons of the assignment to . . . that public school of children of different races or colors, and, at the same time, keep other public schools throughout the state open on a segregated basis. The "equal protection" af-

[1] *Lockett v. Board of Education of Muscogee County,* Civil Action No. 991, April 22, 1964 (M.D. Ga.); *aff'd* in part, 342 F. 2d 225 (5th Cir. 1965).

[2] *James* v. *Almond,* 170 F. Supp. 33 (E.D. Va. 1959).

forded to all citizens and taxpayers is lacking in such a situation. While the State of Virginia . . . maintains and operates a school system with the use of public funds . . . no one public school or grade in Virginia may be closed to avoid the effect of the law of the land as interpreted by the Supreme Court, while the state permits other public schools or grades to remain open at the expense of the taxpayers. . . . We do not suggest that, aside from the Constitution of Virginia, the state must maintain a public school system. That is a matter for state determination. We merely point out that the closing of a public school, or grade therein, for the reasons heretofore assigned, violated the right of a citizen to equal protection of the laws and, as to any child willing to attend a school with . . . members of the opposite race, such a school-closing is a deprivation of due process of law.

When, in 1961, a United States court of appeals affirmed a district court's judgment requiring school officials of Louisiana's St. Helena's Parish to go forward with all deliberate speed in enrolling children without regard to race, steps were taken to close the public schools of the parish. Existing legislation combined authorization to close schools by local option referendum with provision for "private" schools, supervised by the state through a grant-in-aid program. When suit was brought in a federal district court to enjoin the use of this legislation, a three-man panel of judges struck down the statute on the grounds that it was a means of continuing segregation in schools already under court orders to desegregate, and that the state could not delegate powers to preserve segregation.[1]

There can be no doubt about the character of education in Louisiana as a state, and not a local, function. The Louisiana public school system is administered on a statewide basis, under the control and supervision of public officials exercising statewide authority under the Louisiana constitution and appropriate state legislation. . . .

At least in the area of declared constitutional rights, and especially with respect to education, the state can no more delegate to its subdivisions a power to discriminate than it can itself directly establish inequalities. When a parish wants to lock its school doors, the state must turn the key.

After a brief experience with school closing, Virginia recoiled from so drastic a measure, but Prince Edward County, one of the defendants originally involved in the *Brown* decision in 1954, chose to cling to it, rather than face court-imposed desegregation. In September 1959, white children were shifted to private schools and black parents were counseled to establish private schools for their children. Except for very light attendance at a few makeshift "training centers," conducted by and for Negroes, the county's black children received no further schooling until the Prince Edward Free School Association, operating for one year on an emergency basis, wholly with private funds, was established in the fall of 1963.

[1] *Hall* v. *St. Helena Parish School Board,* 197 F. Supp. 649 (E.D. La. 1961).

The school-closing scheme sustained a severe blow in August 1961, when a federal district court examined the legality of tuition grants:[1]

> By closing the public schools, the Board of Supervisors have effectively deprived the citizens of Prince Edward County of a freedom of choice between public and private education. County tax funds have been appropriated (in the guise of tuition grants and tax credits) to aid segregated schooling in Prince Edward County.
>
> That, to say the least, is circumventing a constitutionally protected right. We do not hold these County ordinances are facially unlawful. We only hold they become unlawful when used to accomplish an unlawful end.

On August 12, 1963, the Fourth United States Court of Appeals handed down a judgment that the maintenance of a public school system is not per se required by the Fourteenth Amendment as a guarantee of equal protection. But the comfort afforded Prince Edward County's segregationists by this ruling evaporated when the Supreme Court, on May 25, 1964, handed down a decree reversing it. The circuit court had erred, said the Supreme Court, when it had reversed the ruling of the district court in which the action had first been heard, for the district court had been correct in its holding that a state cannot allow a particular county to abandon its public school system as a means of avoiding school integration, so long as public schools are maintained in the rest of the state; and that the closing of Prince Edward County's schools denied the equal protection of the laws to Negro children so long as public funds were used to support schools for white children only.[2]

> Since 1959, all Virginia counties have had the benefits of public schools but one: Prince Edward. . . . Virginia law, as here applied, unquestionably treats the school children of Prince Edward differently from the way it treats the school children of all other Virginia counties. Prince Edward children must go to a private school or none at all; all other Virginia children can go to public schools. . . . Colored children until very recently have had no available private schools, and even the school they now attend is a temporary expedient. . . . The result is that Prince Edward County school children, if they go to school in their own county, must go to racially segregated schools, which, although designated as private, are beneficiaries of county and state support.
>
> A State, of course, has a wide discretion in deciding whether laws shall operate statewide or shall operate only in certain counties . . . , "having in mind the needs and desires of each. . . ." But the record in the present case could not be clearer that Prince Edward's public schools were closed and private schools operated in their place with state and county assistance, for . . . one reason only: to ensure . . . that white and colored children in Prince Edward County would not, under any circumstances, go to the same school. Whatever non-racial grounds might support a State's allowing a county to

[1] *Allen* v. *Prince Edward County School Board*, 198 F. Supp. 497 (E.D. Va. 1961).

[2] *Griffin* v. *School Board of Prince Edward County*, 377 U.S. 218 (1964).

abandon public schools, the object must be a constitutional one, and grounds of race and opposition to desegregation do not qualify as constitutional.

A court decree followed, and the county's Board of Supervisors voted to comply with the federal judiciary's command that they "levy taxes . . . to reopen, operate, and maintain without racial discrimination, the public school system in Prince Edward County like that operated in other counties in Virginia."

That the *Brown* decision required teacher desegregation as well as pupil desegregation was clearly averred in a federal district court ruling:[1]

> The plaintiffs possess the right, arising under the due process and equal protection clauses of the 14th Amendment, to have the public school system operated on a non-racial basis. This includes . . . assignment of teachers, principals and supervisors and supporting personnel on a non-racial basis. . . .
>
> There may be no determinations based upon race or color . . . with respect to the operation of the public school system. . . . The *Brown* case is misread and misapplied when it is construed simply to confer upon Negro pupils the right to be considered for admission to a "white" school.

For a decade after *Brown,* the power vested in local school officials to discharge teachers resulted not infrequently in the dismissal of teachers known to be identified, however tenuously, with civil rights activities. Local courts could be depended upon to deny relief to teachers whom school officials had dismissed as "trouble makers." School boards could also take the easier route of explaining the failure to renew a contract on the basis of "incompetence" or "neglect of duty."

After the enactment of the Civil Rights Act of 1964, however, federal courts were occasionally looked to by aggrieved Negro teachers for relief. Although in 1969 it was still hazardous, in much of the South, for a teacher to throw himself into the civil rights struggle, the protections afforded him by the courts had been notably increased.

A case typifying the newer climate was that of Mrs. Gloria B. Rackley, who was relieved of her teaching post in an Orangeburg, South Carolina, public school in October 1963. The court found no "contention on the part of the defendant school board that she was not a very capable, qualified and competent classroom teacher." She was, however, a leader in civil rights demonstrations in Orangeburg, was an active member of the NAACP, and had on several occasions been arrested for "breach of the peace" while engaging in peaceful demonstrations in places of public accommodation which excluded blacks. The school board made no attempt to conceal the fact that it was for

[1] *Braxton* v. *Duval County, Florida,* Civil Action No. 4598, August 21, 1962 (S.D. Fla.).

her participation in these activities that she had been dropped from the school system.

The federal district court in which the action was tried in 1966 found the plaintiff's activities to be an exercise of constitutionally protected rights, particularly in light of the retroactive effect of the subsequently enacted 1964 Civil Rights Act, and directed that she be reinstated, with back salary.[1]

> [T]he discretion exercised by the school boards [in hiring and discharging teachers] must be within reasonable limits so as not to curtail, impinge or infringe upon the freedom of political expression or association, or any other constitutionally protected rights.
>
> The basic question to be determined by this court is whether or not the defendant Board of Trustees exercised a reasonable discretion in discharging plaintiff for cause. . . . This court is loathe [*sic*] to interfere or override any actions of a public administrative body in the exercise of its discretionary powers and functions except in the clearest of cases. However, after a careful consideration of the record herein and the applicable controlling decisions of the United States Supreme Court and the Fourth Circuit Court of Appeals . . . , this court must conclude . . . that plaintiff was discharged by the defendant board without "good and sufficient reasons for so doing . . . ." Her discharge by the Board and its failure to rehire her were based upon improper illegal and constitutionally proscribed considerations, which resulted in an unwarranted and discriminatory exercise of its discretionary powers.

Gerrymandering of school districts in the North was also held to be a clear violation of the *Brown* ruling, if any portion of its purpose was to inhibit the progress of desegregation. New Rochelle, New York, had for more than thirty years drawn and redrawn district lines which would ensure the confinement of Negroes within one particular school. After the *Brown* decision a small enrollment of whites brought the Negro total down to 94 percent, which the school officials cited as proof that the school was not segregated.

In ordering the board to present a desegregation plan, the federal district court which heard the complaint in January 1961 laid down this dictum:[2]

> The *Brown* decision, in short, was a lesson in democracy, directed to the public at large and more particularly to those responsible for the operation of the schools. It imposed a legal and moral obligation upon the officials who had created or maintained segregated schools to undo the damage which they had fostered. And, compliance with the Supreme Court's edict was not to be less forthright in the North than in the South. . . .
>
> I see no basis to draw a distinction, legal or moral, between segregation established by the formality of a dual system of education, as in *Brown*, and that created by gerrymandering of school district lines and transferring of white children as in the instant case. . . . The result is the same in each case:

[1] *Rackley* v. *Orangeburg County*, 258 F. Supp. 676 (D.S.C. 1966).

[2] *Taylor* v. *Board of Education of New Rochelle*, 191 F. Supp. 181 (S.D. N.Y. 1961).

the conduct of responsible school officials has operated to deny to Negro children the opportunities for a full and meaningful educational experience guaranteed to them by the Fourteenth Amendment. . . . In a community such as New Rochelle, the presence of some 29 white children certainly does not afford the 454 Negro children in the school the educational and social contacts and interaction envisioned by *Brown*.

Having created a segregated school, the Constitution imposed upon the Board the duty to end segregation, in good faith, and with all deliberate speed. It is patently clear that this obligation has not been fulfilled.

The issues raised in New Rochelle were aspects of a wider and deeper dilemma. One of the most stubborn and unmanageable forms of educational discrimination was de facto segregation—the sequestering of schoolchildren resulting from the circumstances that most urban neighborhoods throughout America were either all white or all black, or nearly so; and that schools served particular neighborhoods only. The result was "racial imbalance" in schools, which, even in the absence of explicitly discriminatory programs for pupil assignment or arbitrary enrollment procedures, were attended wholly or almost wholly by members of one race.

One attempted solution was that of mass transfers of white children to "Negro" schools, and black children to "white" schools, until a significantly diminished disparity was achieved. Because these programs required the transporting of children to schools remote from their own neighborhoods, such "bussing" encountered very considerable hostilities, especially from whites, and inevitably gave rise to lawsuits on equal protection grounds.

In Gary, Indiana, for example, when Negro plaintiffs charged the city with de facto segregation, a federal district court ruled that segregated *housing* was the basis of the problem and that the school board had no duty to correct the effects of residential segregation by arbitrary transfer of schoolchildren. The district court's opinion, subsequently sustained by a United States court of appeals, not only did not support the plaintiffs' contention that they had suffered discrimination by being subjected to de facto segregation, but even asserted that the bussing itself would offend the Fourteenth Amendment.[1]

The neighborhood school . . . is a long and well established institution in American public education. . . . In any school system with a large and expanding . . . Negro population, it is almost inevitable that a racial imbalance will result in certain schools. Nevertheless, I have seen nothing in the many cases dealing with the segregation problem which leads me to believe that the law requires that a [neighborhood] school system . . . honestly and conscientiously constructed with no intention . . . to segregate the races, must be destroyed . . . because the resulting effect is to have a racial imbalance in certain schools. . . .

[1] *Bell* v. *School City of Gary,* 213 F. Supp. 819 (N.D. Ind. 1963); *aff'd* in 324 F. 2d 209 (7th Cir. 1963).

Furthermore, requiring certain students to leave their neighborhoods and friends and be transferred to another school miles away, while other students, similarly situated, remained in the neighborhood school, simply for the purpose of balancing the races in the various schools would in my opinion be indeed a violation of the equal protection clause of the Fourteenth Amendment.

In June 1967 came the most far-reaching decision yet to be rendered by a federal court on the prickly issue of de facto segregation, when the United States district court for the District of Columbia (in what *The New York Times* called "a monumental exercise in sociological jurisprudence") delivered a smashing blow at the inequality of educational opportunity that results from residential apartheid. The case was brought in behalf not only of blacks, but of poor children generally, in the public schools of the District of Columbia. Because of its extraordinary importance, it was tried by a judge of the United States court of appeals, J. Skelly Wright, a native of New Orleans, who, in a series of decisions from 1956 to 1962, had ordered that city's schools integrated. Now in a 183-page opinion, he ruled that de facto segregation is no less unlawful than segregation by statute.

The opinion rested on the premises that racially and economically discriminatory treatment within a school system are forbidden by the *Brown* decision; and that the educational and social values of desegregation are of such magnitude as to warrant bussing on a citywide scale if necessary. Judge Wright ordered the school board to begin in the fall of 1967 to bus a substantial number of black children from overcrowded Negro schools to underpopulated white schools. He asked the board to consider installing educational "parks" to pair[1] schools for full-scale integration, and to give thought to a student-exchange program. Faculties must be far more fully integrated, he insisted; and "optional zones" must be abolished because they are in practice available only to whites. He also ventured to say that the "track system," by which students were grouped by ability as shown in standardized tests, was, as currently administered, denial of equal protection of the laws.[2]

The basic question presented is whether the defendants in the operation of the public school system here, unconstitutionally deprive the District's Negro and poor public school children of their right to equal educational opportunity with the District's white and more affluent public school children. This court concludes that they do.

[1] "Pairing" is an arrangement by which two schools, one black and one white—even though separated by considerable distance—are combined in a single unit, in which all the children in certain specified grades attending the hitherto white school are transferred to the hitherto black school, and all the blacks in the remaining grades of the formerly black school are transferred to the formerly white school.

[2] *Hobson* v. *Hansen*, 265 F. Supp. 902 (D.D.C. 1967).

. . . Racially and socially homogeneous schools damage the minds and spirit of all children who attend them—the Negro, the white, the poor and the affluent—and block the attainment of the broadest goals of democratic education, whether the segregation occurs by law or fact. . . . [The] neighborhood school policy . . . effectively segregates the Negro and the poor children from the white and the more affluent children in most of the District's public schools. This neighborhood school policy is relaxed . . . through the use of optional zoning for the purpose of allowing white children . . . to "escape" to a "white" or more nearly white school, thus making the economic and racial segregation of the public school children [still] more complete. . . .

The teachers and principals in the public schools are assigned so that generally the race of the faculty is the same as the race of the children. . . . The median annual per pupil expenditure ($292) in the predominantly (85–100 percent) Negro elementary schools in the District . . . has been a flat $100 below the median annual per pupil expenditure for its predominantly (85–100 percent) white schools ($392).

Generally the "white" schools are underpopulated while the "Negro" schools are generally overcrowded. . . . As they proceed through the Washington school system, the reading scores primarily of the Negro and poor children, but not the white and middle class, fall increasingly behind the national norm. By senior high school the discrepancy reaches several grades. . . . The aptitude tests used to assign children to the various tracks are standardized primarily on white middle class children. Since these tests do not relate to the Negro and disadvantaged child, track assignment based on such tests relegates Negro and disadvantaged children to the lower tracks from which . . . the chance of escape is remote. . . .

Other incidental, but highly indicative, findings are as follows: (a) 55.3 percent of the 18-year-olds from the District of Columbia failed the Armed Services mental test, a higher percentage than any of the 50 states. (b) . . . The District of Columbia spends less per capita on education generally than all states except Arkansas and Tennessee. (c) The . . . District of Columbia spends more per capita on police protection than all states without exception. . . . The inferences, including those bearing on the relationship of the quality of education to crime, which arise from these findings are obvious.

. . . Prejudging, through inappropriate testing, the learning abilities of the disadvantaged child as inferior to the white middle class child; placing the child in lower tracks for reduced education based on such tests, thus implementing the self-fulfilling prophecy phenomenon inherent in such misjudgments; placing inferior teachers in slum schools; continuing racial and economic segregation of pupils; providing textbooks unrelated to the lives of disadvantaged children; inadequate remedial programs for offsetting initial psychological and social difficulties of the disadvantaged child—all have contributed to the increase in crime, particularly juvenile crime.

. . . To correct the racial and economic discrimination found in the operation of the District of Columbia public school system, the court has issued a decree attached to its opinion ordering: (1) An injunction against racial and economic discrimination in the public school system here. (2) Abolition of the track system. (3) Abolition of the optional zones. (4) Transportation of the volunteering children in overcrowded school districts east of Rock Creek Park to underpopulated schools west of the park. (5) The defendants, by October 2, 1967, to file for approval by the court a plan for pupil assignment eliminating discrimination found to exist in the operation of the Washington public school system. (6) Substantial integration of the faculty of each school beginning with the school year 1967–68. (7) The defendants, by October 2, 1967, to file for approval by the court a teacher assignment plan fully integrating the faculty of each school.

The enormous volume of litigation in the decade following the *Brown* decision still produced only token compliance. On its tenth anniversary, fewer than ten percent of the black children in the seventeen southern and border states and the District were attending school with white children. In the deeper South, the proportion was a mere *one* percent. Here matters stood when the Congress enacted the Civil Rights Act of 1964. With this law[1] the federal government's desegregation effort shifted from the courts to the Departments of Justice and of Health, Education, and Welfare. The preceding decade had seen approximately three hundred lawsuits, and it had become clear that the federal courts were simply not equipped to draw up and monitor programs for countless local school systems.

The 1964 Civil Rights Act supplied a new approach. Now for the first time there were federal *statutory* recognition of *Brown* and administrative instruments for enforcing it. Congress took the burden off the courts and shared it with the administration, restoring the judiciary to its traditional role as interpeters of the law. The Attorney General was given authority both to initiate and to intervene in school desegregation suits, in a way that would bring speedier and more extensive integration than had been produced in tiny increments, district by district, by litigants and by school boards acting voluntarily. The heart of the act, so far as school desegregation was concerned, was Title VI, which forbade discrimination in federally assisted programs, and directed federal agencies administering financial aid to promote nondiscrimination by imposing standards for compliance and penalties for noncompliance.

By 1966 federal funds appropriated for local and state school systems in the South exceeded $750 million annually—a factor of such magnitude that school officials could hardly afford to risk the penalty for intransigence. Even so, three principal strategies, usually employed in combination, still thwarted integration. One was the rezoning of attendance areas, a scheme that promised little relief, however, after United States district courts, in 1963 and 1964, held that zone lines could not be gerrymandered to preserve a dual system. Moreover, in August 1964, a district court in North Carolina, in *Wheeler* v. *Durham Board of Education*,[2] had ordered desegregation of the city schools after having found that school lines had "been drawn along racial

[1] See above, p. 405 ff.

[2] Civil Action No. 54-D-60, August 3, 1964 (M.D. N.C.); quoted in RRLR X 656.

residential lines, rather than along natural boundaries or the perimeters of compact areas surrounding the particular school." A federal court of appeals had also insisted not only that the burden of proof is on the school district to demonstrate that lines are not drawn for the purpose of preserving segregation, but also that "disturbing the people as little as possible," and preserving "school loyalties" were not legitimate criteria for drawing zone lines.

Most school districts ostensibly desegregating by geographic attendance zones included some provision for voluntary transfer, presumably limited only by "the capacity of the school selected." A hitherto widely adopted scheme of permitting students to transfer *from* schools which had formerly served only (or principally) students of the other race was rejected by the courts as an unconstitutional device for perpetuating segregation.[1]

A second broad strategy for impeding desegregation, the Pupil Placement Plan, was enacted by all the southern states after *Brown,* but it too had by 1964 been diluted by federal judicial rulings. (See pp. 390 and 436, for a description of such plans, and for cases restricting their effectiveness.) In a Louisiana suit, for example, a United States court of appeals took exception to the state's placement law's provision that students once assigned could not elect another school unless they had submitted to a test.[2]

> This failure to test all pupils is the constitutional vice in the Board's testing program. However valid a Pupil Placement Act may be on its face, it may not be selectively applied. Moreover, where a school system is segregated there is no constitutional basis whatever for using a Pupil Placement Law. A Pupil Placement Law may only be validly applied in an integrated school system, and then only where no consideration is based on race.

The third pattern for preserving tokenism was the freedom-of-choice plan, under which compliance fell so far short of the reality that the Civil Rights Commission found it producing only a tiny measure of integration in the South in 1966–67. The Commission reported in 1967 that free-choice plans were the overwhelming preference of the 1787 school districts under voluntary plans. In fact, *all* such districts in Alabama, Mississippi, and South Carolina, and 83 percent of the districts in Georgia adopted free-choice. In addition, most of the districts desegregating under court orders were also employing it.

In its study of desegregation in the South in the 1966–67 school year,[3] the Civil Rights Commission found that freedom-of-choice failed

[1] *Goss* v. *Board of Education of Knoxville,* 373 U.S. 683 (1963).

[2] *Bush* v. *Orleans Parish School Board,* 308 F. 2d 491 (5th Cir. 1962).

[3] U.S. Commission on Civil Rights, *Southern School Desegregation, 1966–67,* pp. 47–69.

to produce a significant volume of desegregation, thanks to intimidation by violence or economic coercion; harassment by white students; and obstructive conduct on the part of school officers and other public officials. Poverty was another impediment to real freedom of choice, because financial charges for the use of special equipment and services (not available at all in Negro schools) were hard for Negroes to bear, and because indigent parents were reluctant to send children to predominantly white schools without suitable clothes. In districts desegregating under court decree, the orders were themselves so loosely drawn by southern federal judges, or so inconveniently published, as to defeat their pretended purpose.

The lower federal courts continued to try countless cases, and even though their outcome usually whittled at the evasions that skillful lawyers contrived, integration proceeded very slowly. In the North, Negroes remained in their ghetto schools rather than accept the freedom to choose long distance travel and white hostilities and rejections. Compliance with court orders and submission of desegregation plans were slow to emerge, and even when they did, only the barest minimum of the guideline requirements were met.

Another cause of the failure of freedom-of-choice to promote integration was the circumstance that it not only did not eliminate the "racial identity" of the schools, but also placed the burden of transfers upon apprehensive and defenseless black parents and children, rather than upon public authorities. In addition, the Office of Education lacked adequate evaluative procedures and staff for discovering violations of Title VI, so that the "monitoring" of compliance was confined to the investigation of complaints (which Negroes were fearful to press), and to proceeding against school districts which flatly declined to file the assurances of compliance which the 1964 Act prescribed.

The 1966–67 Guidelines established certain criteria for gauging progress under freedom-of-choice. Percentage figures were prescribed as standards, requiring that in districts in which as many as 8 or 9 percent of pupils had been transferred from segregated to desegregated schools in 1965–66, at least twice that number was an acceptable minimum standard for compliance; then, with two intermediate steps requiring a tripling (or more) of the 1965–66 rate, a fourth group, in which no transfers had occurred in 1965–66, was warned that "a very substantial start would normally be expected, to enable such a school system to catch up. . . ." If a school system could not make such a start for the 1966–67 years under free-choice, it would be required to adopt a different plan.

After the enactment of Title VI, there were still not a few instances in which desegregation was introduced or accelerated in particular systems by the former pattern of litigation, with the difference that now an aggrieved plaintiff was often joined by "the United States of America, Intervenor." Such cases often ended with the court's directive to the defendant school district to submit a satisfactory desegregation plan. Once a proposed plan met with the court's approval, it became a court order, and jurisdiction in the cause was retained by the court while the new plan went into effect.

Court-ordered plans were, necessarily, detailed directives, covering such matters as school district boundaries, the specification of dates for the exercise of transfer options, provisions for notification of the public, detailed listings of schools to which children in specified neighborhoods might apply, painstaking description and analysis of the existing plan and the grounds for requiring that it be supplanted, and a discussion of "the conclusion of laws." Also included was a critical review of the existing practices with respect to geographical zoning, speed of desegregation, mandatory exercise of grade level options, transportation, public notices, service facilities, activities and programs, school equalization, compliance reports, desegregation of faculty and staff, school construction, curricula, textbooks, supplies and equipment. The order would usually end with a decree setting forth the specifications for the new plan, with dates for its effectuation.

An order of this kind, typical of hundreds like it, was served upon the school officials of Mobile County, Alabama, in October 1967. Negro students, joined by the United States as intervenor, brought a class action in a federal district court, seeking to require the school board to present a desegregation plan for the court's approval, or to have it enjoined from operating segregated schools. Most of the 10,000-word order was devoted to matters like those described in the foregoing paragraph, and it concluded with the following decree:[1]

It is therefore, ORDERED, ADJUDGED and DECREED as follows:

1. Transfer request forms shall be made available during the transfer request period at the office of the principal of each senior high school of the system as well as at the School Board office and the published notice shall so state.

2. Students in senior high school or who have attained the age of 16 years shall be permitted to pick up forms for their own transfers and the published notice shall so state.

3. The form of notice to parents of action taken upon transfer requests shall be revised in such fashion as will indicate with more clarity the reason for the denial of the transfer request when such request is denied.

4. The published notice as to the transfer request period shall, in addition to information included in past display advertising, contain in general terms the bases upon which transfers shall be granted and shall make specific reference to the granting of transfers to correct past racial assignments based upon

[1] *Birdie Mae Davis and United States, Intervenor* v. *Board of School Commissioners of Mobile County,* 364 F. 2d 896 (5th Cir. 1966); and U.S. Dist. Court, August 24 and October 13, 1967 (S.D. Ala. 1967). See RRLR XII, 1820–34.

residence in a former dual attendance area and the availability of subject matter transfers.

5. Appropriate steps shall be taken to insure as nearly as possible the mandatory exercise by parents of the grade level options where appropriate.

6. The form letter directed to parents with regard to the grade level options shall include therein, prominently, the assurance that additional information will be provided by telephone or in person from the offices of the defendant board upon request. Said letter shall contain the address of the School Board office and the telephone number and extension to be called for such additional information.

7. Parents shall be afforded seven days within which to exercise the grade level option.

8. The defendant board shall procure the publication, annually, prior to the opening of the school year of a map or maps of Mobile County showing attendance area boundaries; location of schools; and anticipated bus routes.

9. The defendant board shall instruct its school personnel, including teachers and principals more adequately as to the provisions of the plan governing initial enrollment, grade level options, and transfer provisions in order that intelligent assistance may be given parents in the exercise of these rights.

10. The practice of the Board in furnishing transportation to eligible students who select a proper optional school shall be written into the plan itself and notice thereof included in the letter to parents regarding grade level options and the display advertising concerning initial enrollment.

11. The plan shall be amended to provide that when the boundary line of any attendance area is altered, any parent or guardian whose residence is placed in a new attendance area as a result of a change shall be entitled to exercise the option provisions of the plan just as if such parent or guardian had moved his residence from one attendance area to another; and the plan shall be further amended to provide that actual notice be given to the parents whose children are known to be affected thereby, by letter, which letter shall include an outline of the options available to the parent and the method of exercising the same.

12. Regular status reports shall be filed with this Court and copies furnished to all parties, as follows:

(A) By June 30 of each year, beginning June 30, 1968, the defendant will file with this Court a report containing the following information:

1. A map showing the name and location of each school planned to be used the coming school year, and the location of all attendance area boundary lines; as well as a description of any changes in attendance area boundary lines that have occurred since the last report to the Court, and any contemplated for the coming school year.

2. A tabulation of the following as they are expected to exist for the coming school year:

(a) The total number of schools and the number of bi-racial schools in the system.

(b) The total number of students in bi-racial schools.

(c) The number of Negro students in bi-racial schools by grade, and an indication of how each has been so enrolled.

(d) The number of white students in bi-racial schools by grade.

3. A tabulation of transfer applications filed during the most recent April 1–15 transfer period, showing with regard to each:
   (a) The name, grade and race of the student.
   (b) The school from which and to which the transfer was requested.
   (c) The action taken on the request, and the reason for denial, as to those denied.
4. (a) The planned faculty assignments for the coming year, listing each teacher by name, race, school and grade or subject taught.
   (b) The number of faculty vacancies, by school, that have occurred since the last report. The name and race of the teacher employed to fill each such vacancy, and an indication of whether such teacher is newly employed or was transferred from within the system. As to transferred teachers, the schools from which and to which transferred.

(B) By September 30 of each year, beginning September 30, 1968, the defendant will file with this Court a report containing the following information:
1. A notation and explanation of any attendance area boundary lines that are in effect, other than as reported on the map referred to in 12 (A) 1 above, with reference to the June 30 report.
2. A tabulation of the information required by 12 (A) 2 above, as it exists after the opening of school.
3. A tabulation of the information required by 12 (A) 4 (a) above, as it exists after the opening of school.

13. Except with respect to any building project already in progress, including the Howard Scarborough, Emerson and Williamson projects, the defendant will, prior to beginning construction of any new school, make a comprehensive investigation as to the advisability and location of such school, and will submit the same to this Court for approval or disapproval.

14. The notice published prior to the opening of school each year, giving notice of the option provisions of the plan, shall contain the statement that information as to the optional schools available will be furnished upon request by the principals of all schools at the time of enrollment, or by telephone or personal request to the School Board Office. And the address, and telephone number of the School Board office shall be given.

15. The plan shall be amended to require that all display advertisement notices published in the newspaper pursuant to the plan, shall be published once a week for three consecutive weeks, immediately preceding the occurrence of the event in connection with which the notice is given.

16. Defendants' desegregation plan filed in this Court on October 19, 1966 meets current constitutional standards and is therefore approved by this Court. In order to insure better operation of the plan the foregoing requirements shall be effectuated promptly.

17. In all other respects, except as to relief included in the interim order of August 24, 1967, plaintiff's Motion for Further Relief as Amended and Plaintiff-Intervenor's Motion for Supplemental Relief are denied.

18. Jurisdiction of this cause is retained to enter such further orders and to take such other proceedings as may be meet and just in the premises.

Entered this 13th day of October, 1967.

On December 29, 1966, the Fifth United States Circuit Court of Appeals (embracing Alabama, Florida, Georgia, Louisiana, Mississippi, and Texas) handed down a resounding judgment that declared war upon tokenism, and bluntly redefined "deliberate speed" so that no one could mistake its meaning. A monumental document of some 40,000 words, it had the effect of approving the Office of Education's Guidelines, including the percentage formula. The action was a consolidation of seven cases arising in school systems in Louisiana and Alabama. Because the case had been heard by a three-judge panel of the circuit, it was, on account of its gravity, subsequently reheard and affirmed by the full court, on March 29, 1967.[1]

[Of major importance was the court's categorical repudiation of the doctrine laid down in 1955 in *Briggs* v. *Elliott*[2] that *Brown* did not require integration, but only forbade enforced segregation:] . . . The mystique that has developed over the supposed difference between "desegregation" and "integration" originated in Briggs v. Elliott . . . 1955 . . . [which held] "The Constitution . . . does not require integration. It merely forbids segregation." . . . This dictum is a product of the narrow view that Fourteenth Amendment rights are only individual rights; that therefore Negro school children individually must exhaust their administrative remedies and will not be allowed to bring class suits to desegregate a school system. [But we now] use the terms "integration" and "desegregation" of formerly segregated public schools to mean the conversion of a de jure segregated dual system to a unitary, nonracial (nondiscriminatory) system—lock, stock, and barrel: students, faculty, staff, facilities, programs, and activities. . . .

As we see it, the law imposes an absolute duty to . . . disestablish segregation. And an absolute duty to integrate. . . . Racial mixing of students is a high priority educational goal. . . .

As long as school boards understand the objective of desegregation and the necessity for complete disestablishment of segregation by converting the dual system to a nonracial unitary system, the nomenclature is unimportant. . . . Decision-making in this important area of the law cannot be made to turn upon a quibble devised over ten years ago by a court that misread *Brown,* misapplied the class action doctrine in the school desegregation cases, and did not foresee the development of the law of equal opportunities.

[Moving on to issues of the most critical purport, the court went on to say:] *The only school desegregation plan that meets constitutional standards is one that works.* By helping public schools to meet that test, by assisting the courts in their independent evaluation of school desegregation plans, and by accelerating the progress by simplifying the process of desegregation the HEW Guidelines offer new hope to Negro school children long denied their constitutional rights. A national effort, bringing together Congress, the executive, and the judiciary may be able to make meaningful the right of Negro children to equal educational opportunities. The courts alone have failed.

Succeeding pages spelled out the sterner new requirements. All school districts must desegregate all twelve grades promptly; and dis-

[1] *United States* v. *Jefferson County Board of Education,* 372 F. 2d 836 (5th Cir. 1966); *aff'd* on rehearing, *en banc* C.D. No. 23345. See RRLR XII, 120.

[2] See above, p. 431.

trict courts which had already approved slower plans must now stiffen them to conform to HEW specifications. The courts would no longer tolerate evasion:

Case by case over the last twelve years, courts have increased their understanding of the desegregation process. Less and less have courts accepted the question-begging distinction between "desegregation" and "integration" as a sanctuary for school boards fleeing from their constitutional duty to establish an integrated, non-racial school system. With the benefit of this experience, the Court has restudied the School Segregation Cases. We have reexamined the nature of the Negro's right to equal educational opportunities and the extent of the correlative affirmative duty of the state to furnish equal educational opportunities. We have taken a close look at the background and objectives of the Civil Rights Act of 1964. . . . Now after twelve years of snail's pace progress toward school desegregation, courts are entering a new era. The question to be resolved in each case is: How far have formerly de jure segregated schools progressed in performing their affirmative constitutional duty to furnish equal educational opportunities to all public school children? The clock has ticked the last tick for tokenism and delay in the name of "deliberate speed."

The decree with which the judgment concluded set forth a detailed program of "affirmative action to disestablish all school segregation and to eliminate the effects of past racial discrimination in the operation of the school system." Section I prescribed that "commencing with the 1967–68 school year, in accordance with this decree, all grades, including kindergarten grades, shall be desegregated and pupils assigned to schools in these grades without regard to race or color."

Sections II–IV carefully itemized the manner in which students were to exercise choices, free from influence, harassment, or reprisal. Section V decreed that every aspect of a school's program, with no exceptions whatsoever, were to be "conducted without regard to race or color," while Section VI called for "prompt steps . . . to provide physical facilities, equipment, courses of instruction, and instructional materials of quality equal to that provided in schools previously maintained [only] for white schools. . . . [and] if for any reason it is not feasible to improve sufficiently any school formerly maintained for Negro students . . . such school shall be closed as soon as possible, and [its] students . . . reassigned on the basis of freedom of choice." Section VII required school authorities to "locate any new school . . . with the objective of eradicating the vestiges of the dual system." Section VIII ordered the absolute integration of faculty and staff of all schools, and Section IX ordered systematic and full reports to the court of progress under this plan toward eliminating the dual school system.

School boards cannot, however, by giving up federal aid, avoid the policy that produced the limitation on federal aid to schools: Title IV authorizes the Attorney General to sue, in the name of the United States, to desegregate a public school system. More clearly and effectively than either of the other coordinate branches of the Government, Congress speaks as the Voice of the Nation. *The National policy is plain: formerly de jure segregated public school systems based on dual attendance zones must shift to unitary, nonracial systems—with or without federal funds.* . . . We read Title VI as a congressional mandate for change—change in pace and method of enforcing desegregation. The 1964 Act does not disavow court-supervised desegregation. On the contrary, Congress recognized that to the courts belongs the last word in any case or controversy. But Congress was dissatisfied with the slow progress inherent in the judicial adversary process. Congress therefore fashioned a new method of enforcement to be administered not on a case by case basis as in the courts but, generally, by federal agencies operating on a national scale and having a special competence in their respective fields. Congress looked to these agencies to shoulder the additional enforcement burdens resulting from the shift to high gear in school desegregation. . . .

. . . In a school system the persons capable of giving class relief are of course its administrators. It is they who are under the affirmative duty to take corrective action toward the goal of one integrated system. As judges Sobeloff and Bell said in *Bradley* v. *School Board of the City of Richmond*, . . . , 1965 . . . *"the initiative in achieving desegregation of the public school must come from the school authorities. . . . Affirmative action means more than telling those who have long been deprived of freedom of educational opportunity, 'You now have a choice'. . . ."* The failure to adopt an affirmative policy is itself a policy, adherence to which . . . has slowed up the desegregation process. . . . The position we take in these consolidated cases is that *the only adequate redress for a previously overt system-wide policy of segregation directed against Negroes as a collective entity is a system-wide policy of integration.*

A few weeks after the original judgment of the three-man court in the *Jefferson County* case came another frontal assault upon tokenism when the Court of Appeals of the Tenth Circuit affirmed the judgment of a district court which had struck down the Oklahoma City School Board's gradual desegregation plan on the ground that it required different standards for transfers for Negro students than were applied to whites. Although holding that neighborhood school attendance policies, when impartially administered, do not per se violate constitutional principle, the school authorities did have the duty—especially since the segregated housing patterns which led to de facto segregation in the schools had resulted from state statutes in the first place—to take affirmative steps toward desegregation.[1] Another case, a suit in which the Alabama tuition grant law was declared unconstitutional, and state officials were ordered to carry out a *uniform statewide* plan for desegregation, applicable to each city and county system not already undergoing desegregation under federal court order, illustrated the new insistence upon positive programs for the reasonably early elimination

[1] *Dowell* v. *School Board of Oklahoma City*, 244 F. Supp. 971 (W.D. Okla. 1965); *aff'd* 375 F. 2d 158 (10th Cir. 1967); cert. denied, 387 U.S. 93 (1967).

of racially identifiable schools. The detailed decree opened with these words:[1]

> It is ORDERED, ADJUDGED AND DECREED that [the state and school authorities of Alabama] shall be and hereby are permanently enjoined from discriminating on the basis of race in the operation or the conduct of the public schools of *Alabama*[2] or in any manner pertaining to the public schools of Alabama. As set out more particularly in this decree, said defendants shall take affirmative action to disestablish all state enforced or encouraged racial discrimination in their activities and their operation of the public school systems throughout the State.

Another strong court ruling which affirmed that the use of tuition grants to enable white children to attend segregated schools was no longer available as an instrument of tokenism was handed down by a district judge in Virginia, in the endlessly protracted litigation with the Prince Edward County school system, one of the original litigants in the 1954 *School Segregation* cases. Citing previous district and circuit court rulings against Prince Edward County's tuition plan, the court on December 4, 1967, declared with some asperity:[3]

> . . . [T]uition grants are not useable in the Prince Edward County Educational Foundation schools so long as those schools refuse to accept pupils on account of race or color. [The Foundation] may advise the Court by appropriate petition that it is now accepting pupils in its schools without regard to race, color or creed. . . . This Court will then determine, upon further hearing, whether any of the defendants in this proceeding may proceed or approve applications for paying tuition grants for use in the said Foundation schools.

Admittedly, the new formula for ending the dual school system, by which the executive, legislative, and judicial branches of the federal government under Title VI were at last embarked upon a coordinated effort to end school segregation, had not by 1968 made a great deal of difference so far as school statistics are concerned. But the new direction of the current was unmistakable. Louisiana, for example, with 3.4 percent of its Negro pupils in integrated schools in 1965–66, jumped to 7.9 in 1966–67; North Carolina advanced from 15.4 to 20.13 in that single year; and Tennessee from 28.4 to 34.4. In the following year the process gathered momentum, and where progress lagged, the penalties began to be seriously applied. In the spring of 1968 federal funds were being withheld from a hundred southern school districts, and more than a hundred others were caught up in various stages of federal enforcement proceedings.

[1] *Lee* v. *Macon County Board of Education,* 267 F. Supp. 458 (M.D. Ala. 1967).
[2] Emphasis added.
[3] *Allen* v. *School Board of Prince Edward County,* Civil Action No. 1366, December 4, 1967 (E.D. Va.). See RRLR XII, 2010.

In the summer of 1968 letters were sent out by HEW to city and county systems throughout the South, announcing the imminent cutoff of funds if desegregation plans were not promptly and very materially revised, with a good faith intention of ending dualism, once and for all. By the fall of 1968 the proportion of Negro children in the formerly all white public schools in the eleven southern states exceeded 20 percent.

Jack Greenberg, Director of the NAACP's Legal Defense and Educational Fund, writing on the new directions in the February 17, 1968 *Saturday Review*, concluded,[1] "From now on [HEW's] policy will be not to focus on percentage, but on the development of comprehensive plans to eliminate dual schools systems. The purpose of these plans will be to avoid the creation of de facto segregation problems in formerly de jure districts. While HEW will not seek the universal abolition of free-choice plans, it would proceed against them on a case-by-case basis where they won't work."

Fourteen years after the *Brown* decision, thirteen hundred southern school systems were relying on freedom-of-choice to slow down integration to the very minimum that the courts would tolerate. On May 27, 1968, however, the Supreme Court issued three simultaneous judgments in which Arkansas and Virginia free-choice plans and a similar free-transfer plan in Tennessee were overturned. The implications of these rulings were clear enough to move Governor Lester Maddox of Georgia (at that time contemplating the awesome decision as to whether or not he was in conscience bound to offer himself as a candidate for the Democratic nomination for the presidency of the United States) to order all flags on state property flown at half-mast, and to issue a proclamation mourning "another black and tragic Monday," which would produce "more assaults, rapes, burnings, deaths and violence in our public schools."

The Court took particular note of the fact that these plans had resulted in the selection of white schools by only 15 percent of Negro children, and of Negro schools by no whites at all. Such plans, said the Court, in yet another expression of the new pragmatism of judging practice by its tangible results, can no longer be accepted as adequate steps to desegregation. The cases were *Green* v. *New Kent County* (Virginia) *School Board; Monroe* v. *Board of Commissioners of the City of Jackson* (Tennesee); and *Raney* v. *Board of Education of Gould City* (Arkansas). The two latter were heard as companion cases to *Green*.[2]

. . . In determining whether respondent School Board met the command [of the School Segregation cases] by adopting its "freedom-of-choice" plan,

[1] *Saturday Review*, 51 (February 17, 1968), p. 58.

[2] *Green* v. *School Board of New Kent County, Va.*, 391 U.S. 430 (1968).

it is relevant that this first step did not come until some 10 years after *Brown II* directed the making of "a prompt and reasonable start." This deliberate perpetuation of the unconstitutional dual system can only have compounded the harm of such a system. Such delays are no longer tolerable. . . . Moreover, a plan that at this late date fails to provide meaningful assurance of prompt and effective disestablishment of a dual system is also intolerable. . . . The burden on a school board today is to come forward with a plan that promises realistically to work, and promises realistically to work *now*. . . .

In three years of operation not a single white child has chosen to attend Watkins school and although 115 Negro children enrolled in New Kent School in 1967 . . . 85 percent of the Negro children in the system still attend the all-Negro Watkins school. In other words, the school system remains a dual system. Rather than further the dismantling of the dual system, the plan has operated simply to burden children and their parents with a responsibility which *Brown II* placed squarely on the School Board. The Board must be required to formulate a new plan and, in light of other courses which appear open to the Board, such as zoning, fashion steps which promise realistically to convert promptly to a system without a "white" school and a "Negro" school, but just schools.

While most of the legal scuffling over desegregation involved southern schools, the overwhelming majority of children in the North and West were also in schools serving primarily (and often only) their own race. The difference was that segregation in the South had long been required by state and local laws; elsewhere it was de facto, resulting from "natural" circumstances or only remotely as a consequence of state action, not directly bearing upon education.

We have seen that the 1961 New Rochelle (New York) case[1] had imposed the first major check upon the protracting of de facto segregation by gerrymandering district lines, and transferring children out of a district into another school of their own race. The two years following New Rochelle produced a freshet of antisegregation suits in the North, and then in the next year the enactment of the Civil Rights Act of 1964 stimulated still more action.

Especially singled out were gerrymandering of districts; transfer policies and "feeder" patterns, by which children moved up from all-Negro elementary schools to all-Negro high schools; the overcrowding of Negro schools and under-utilization of white schools; site selection for new schools, calculated to perpetuate neighborhood segregation; failure to provide Negro schools with special programs available in white schools; bias in the employment and assignment of black teachers; and inferiority of plant, equipment, and instructional programs in Negro schools.

As late as March 1967, the United States Commission on Civil Rights, in a remarkable study,[2] reported that nine-tenths of the

[1] See above, p. 442.
[2] *Racial Isolation in the Public Schools* (Washington, 1967).

children in northern schools were in all-black or all-white schools, or in schools having less than 10 percent of one or the other race, and that the degree of racial isolation in the nation's public schools had not only increased after *Brown*, but was in fact in 1967 *still* increasing.

After the enactment of Title VI, federal courts began seriously to urge the duty of school systems in which racially separate schools resulted, however unintentionally, from neighborhood residential configurations or other factors, to take tangible measures to correct imbalance in the schools. In Springfield, Massachusetts, for example, when Negro children brought suit against de facto segregation where no original intention to segregate could be shown, a district court specifically overruled *Briggs* v. *Elliott*.[1]

> . . . The question is whether there is a constitutional duty to provide equal educational opportunities for all children within the system. While Brown answered that question affirmatively in the context of coerced segregation, the constitutional fact—the inadequacy of segregated education—is the same in this case. . . . It is neither just nor sensible to proscribe segregation having its basis in affirmative state action while at the same time failing to provide a remedy for segregation which grows out of discrimination in housing, or other economic or social factors. Education is tax supported and compulsory, and public school educators, therefore, must deal with inadequacies within the educational system as they arise, and it matters not that the inadequacies are not of their making. . . . This court recognizes that the problem of racial concentration is an educational as well as constitutional problem and therefore orders the defendants to present a plan no later than April 30, 1965, to eliminate to the fullest extent possible racial concentration in its elementary and junior high schools.

A year later, a federal district court in New York dismissed an action which had challenged an attendance zone plan designed to correct racial imbalance in a Malverne, New York, district. Addressing itself to the fascinating objection that publicly prescribed "balance," because it is based on race, is itself a violation of the federal Constitution's equal protection clause, the court replied:[2]

> . . . The emphasis in this case is not on race but on equal opportunity for minority groups. While classifications based on race alone are "constitutionally suspect" under the Equal Protection Clause, such a classification is not proscribed if it is necessary to the accomplishment of a permissible State policy. The [state] Commissioner [of Education] has determined that such classification is necessary to effectuate the State's policy of equal educational opportunities and he has the support of expert opinion and the New York Court of Appeals. . . . Today the Woodfield School is 91 percent Negro. All that is done here is a reorganization of the attendance zones with respect to grades kindergarten through 5 . . . to eliminate excessive imbalance. By the Com-

[1] *Barksdale* v. *Springfield School Committee*, 237 F. Supp. 543 (D. Mass. 1965). See above, p. 431.

[2] *Olsen* v. *Board of Education of Malverne, N.Y.*, 250 F. Supp. 1000 (E.D. N.Y. 1966).

missioner's action, the plaintiff is not required to attend a school which, under similar circumstances, other students, regardless of race, are not also required to attend. The motivation is not discrimination but assistance to minority groups in providing equal educational opportunities . . . not otherwise available.

Meanwhile, some state courts (as in *Tometz* v. *Board of Education of Waukegan, Illinois*[1]) had begun to affirm the constitutionality of state laws requiring the correction of racial imbalance even in the absence of intention to discriminate, and even where such remedies require somewhat inconvenient and awkward rezoning of school districts. Examples in which federal courts sustained such state action also began to accumulate. For example, in *Offermann* v. *Nitkowski,* involving schools in Buffalo, New York, a United States court of appeals again rejected the doctrine that state laws requiring correction of ostensibly unintended racial isolation were themselves a denial of equal protection:[2]

That there may be no constitutional duty to act to undo *de facto* segregation . . . does not mean that such action is unconstitutional. Since *Brown* is the law, some attention to color count is necessary to see that it is not violated, for it affirmatively requires admission to public schools on a *racially* nondiscriminating basis. What is prohibited is use of race as a basis for unequal treatment. . . . Consideration of race is necessary to carry out the mandate of *Brown,* and has been used . . . in cases following *Brown.* Where its use is to insure against, rather than to promote deprivation of equal educational opportunity, we cannot conceive that our courts would find that the state denied equal protection to either race by requiring its school boards to act with awareness of the problem.

At the opening of the school year in September 1968, Berkeley, California, by daily bussing of thousands of children came nearest among the nation's densely populated centers to achieving "balance," when by this policy of deliberate mixing by mass transportation, it had approximately 50 percent white students in all schools and somewhat under 40 percent Negroes, the remainder being accounted for by Oriental and other ethnic groups. The experiment was watched with interest by school officials throughout the land, and no less by HEW and the United States Office of Education.

The problem of de facto segregation in the North and West was, of course, more difficult to solve than was that of the South's legislated dual system. After an abortive cutoff of federal funds in Chicago (restored after four days), the Department of Health, Education, and Welfare did not again before 1968 make a serious effort on its own initiative to enforce desegregation in the North. But in that year, under revised Title VI Guidelines, a new emphasis was placed upon a require-

[1] 237 N.E. 2d 498 (Ill., 1968).
[2] 378 F. 2d 22 (2d Cir. 1967).

ment that all northern school districts reexamine their practices with respect to pupil and faculty assignment, to make sure that they do not promote or preserve segregation. The guidelines did not in fact require northern urban districts to correct school segregation caused by housing patterns, or to take such positive steps as "bussing" and mass transfers of students, to promote integration. Some school systems in northern cities had begun to take such initiative themselves. Chicago, for instance, began on a small scale by bussing two hundred and forty black children to eight white schools on the northwest side, and Berkeley, California, as we have seen, mounted a massive bussing program in 1968.

HEW's opening campaign against northern de facto segregation was directed in 1968 against selected cities of ten thousand to fifty thousand pupils, with the expectation that the effort would move to larger cities later on. In short, the 1968 standards were to be directed to the schools of the nation, not merely to those of the South, to comply with 1967 legislation requiring equal antibias enforcement for schools in all the states. The 1968 regulations set the 1969–70 school year as the deadline for school districts which were desegregating under "voluntary" plans, and, for the nation as a whole, they ordained that eligibility for federal funds would depend upon any district's substantial progress toward eliminating and preventing discrimination in *all* service facilities, programs, and activities, and toward the abolition of student and faculty assignment procedures, of school attendance zones, and of other practices whose effect is to contribute to racial isolation in the schools. Particular examples of practices at predominantly Negro schools which federal authorities would regard as discriminatory were overcrowded classes and activities, assignment of less qualified teachers, expenditure of less money per pupil, and poorer facilities and instructional methods than those enjoyed by whites.

One more augury of future HEW, Justice Department, and judicial pressure on northern school districts to cope with de facto segregation came at the close of the 1967–68 school year with the first school desegregation case brought by the Justice Department in the North, ordering a school in suburban Chicago to stop discriminating on the basis of race. A federal prosecutor warned that other schools in the Chicago area would soon face court action if they did not take "immediate steps" to give full effect to the *Brown* decision. United States District Judge Julius J. Hoffman granted a preliminary injunction restraining the South Holland, Illinois, District No. 151 from discriminating in the assignment of teachers and students in the six schools in suburban South Holland, Harvey, and Phoenix, Illinois. With the order he issued a detailed plan, prescribing the action to be taken immediately in assigning pupils and faculty and in undertaking new school construction. Noting that after fourteen years of "deliberate speed" almost no progress was discernible in South Holland, he said:[1]

> Too often there has been deliberation but not speed. . . . There has not even been a beginning in some cases, despite increasing and well-documented evidence showing that racial segregation in the schools has been detrimental to the Negro child, the white child and to the United States. . . . School segregation, whatever the cause, has the effect of stigmatizing Negro pupils and retarding their educational development. . . . We do not need another fact-finding commission to tell us that something must be done to prevent a school situation which produces apathy and hopelessness that cause a life to be wasted, or frustration and anger that cause it to be risked in public disorders. It is not rational to maintain a situation which is conducive to the kind of behavior that we must prevent or to expect schools to produce law-abiding citizens in a school system that flouts the law. School boards and school administrators have a moral and civic duty as well as a legal duty to end segregation. To fail the Negro child would be to fail the nation.

Brushing aside the plea that the pattern of segregation had emerged originally as an innocent and unintended by-product of neighborhood residential configurations, Judge Hoffman sharply reminded the defendants that they had done nothing, through the years, to resist this unhealthy growth, but had, in point of fact, systematically promoted it. More than that, said the court: the defendants were required by the Constitution to take positive steps to foster racial balance in the schools, and to proceed speedily to ending the dual school system once and for all.

The defendants appealed from the preliminary injunction, but the court of appeals, on December 17, 1968, stoutly sustained the court below in its view that the defendant school authorities' practices with respect to teacher assignments, drawing of attendance zones, bussing students, and selecting school sites had always been and still were clearly motivated by the unconstitutional purpose of maintaining segregation in the schools.[2]

The hard blows struck at the sham of freedom-of-choice in *Green* v. *New Kent County* and its companion cases, *Monroe* v. *City of Jackson* and *Raney* v. *Gould City*[3] were increasingly repeated by federal circuit and district courts in early 1969. In case after case, judges in the southern federal circuits moved, when spurious desegregation plans were challenged by Negro litigants, to bring school districts into conformity with *Green*. School authorities must come to understand, said the judges, that the *Green* doctrine placed local school officials under an affirmative duty to "abolish the vestiges of state-compelled

[1] *United States* v. *School District of Cook County*, 286 F. Supp. 786 (1968).

[2] *United States* v. *School District of Cook County*, 404 F. 2d 1125 (7th Cir. 1968).

[3] See p. 456, above.

segregation and to establish a unitary system which achieves substantial desegregation. . . . At the very least, that means that [a] school board has an obligation to see that schools . . . remain no longer all-white schools enrolling only an infinitesimal fraction of Negro students."[1]

In *Anthony* v. *Marshall County Board of Education*,[2] to take one of many examples, the United States Court of Appeals for the Fifth Circuit insisted that the degree of desegregation in a Mississippi county failed utterly to measure up to the *Green* ruling, and that the "school systems remain dual systems . . . and 'freedom-of-choice' plans have not been effective in eliminating the dual systems, nor do they show any promise of doing so in the future." Furthermore, in this case as in others, the court in firm and measured tones edged with asperity warned that the threat of widespread withdrawal of white students from the public schools in which Negroes predominated was no justification for retaining unconsitutional desegregation schemes. Once more, the burden of coming forward with "realistic and workable plans" for bona fide abandonment of dual school systems was declared to be lodged squarely with the school boards.

Soon after the *Anthony* decision in the closing days of the Warren era, the Supreme Court again came to the aid of school desegregation when it held that a federal district court had properly ordered an Alabama county school board to desegregate school teachers according to a specific mathematical ratio.[3] A 1968 order by a district court for the systematic desegregation of the schools of Montgomery County, Alabama, had been substantially accepted by the county board except that it appealed from the portion of the order relating to faculty desegregation. The order had prescribed that for the 1968–69 school year each school with fewer than twelve teachers must have at least one full-time teacher of a race different from that of the majority of the school's faculty. In schools with twelve or more teachers the ratio was to be at least 1:6. A United States circuit court of appeals struck out the specific ratio as "rigid and inflexible," and required only "substantial" and "approximate" compliance with the formula. The Supreme Court in a unanimous decision now reversed the court of appeals' ruling, insisting upon the right of the district court to prescribe fixed ratios, and concluded: "We hope and believe that this order and the approval that we now give it will carry Alabama a long distance on its way toward obedience to the law of the land as we have declared it in the two *Brown* cases and those that have followed them."

[1] *United States v. Indianola Separate School District*, 410 F. 2d 626 (5th Cir. 1969).

[2] 409 F. 2d 1287 (5th Cir. 1969).

[3] *United States* v. *Montgomery County School Board*, 395 U.S. 225 (1969).

The encouragement that advocates and friends of desegregation drew from the foregoing cases was, however, more than offset by two other developments in late June and early July, 1969. The retirement of Chief Justice Warren in June and his replacement by Justice Warren Burger, a presumed conservative, created widespread apprehension among liberals and civil rights enthusiasts that the movement was entering an era when it could expect far less aid and comfort from the courts than it had enjoyed in the sixteen years preceding.

They saw even more ground for pessimism in the statement issued for the Nixon Administration by the Attorney General and the Secretary of Health, Education, and Welfare on July 3, 1969. The Johnson Administration's policy, clearly enunciated in January 1968, and handed on to the Nixon Administration, had unequivocally called for the end of the dual school system by September 1, 1969. Any school districts not in compliance would on that date suffer cutoff of federal funds, as provided in Title VI of the Civil Rights Act of 1964, except in the case of counties and other political units where Negro students were in the majority or where there were special problems of school building construction, in which case these would be given until September 1, 1970.

Although the Nixon Administration in its opening weeks sought to quiet Negro apprehensions by promising to do more for the Negro than any previous administration, it soon became clear that it was under enormous pressure from conservatives, and particularly from southern voters and political leaders like Senator Strom Thurmond, who had made the President's election possible. After some exchange of charges and rebuttals—some of it within the administration itself—the President authorized a statement blurred with calculated ambiguities, but having the effect of extending the period of grace for recalcitrant school districts, hundreds of which were at the time of the announcement facing a loss of federal funds by September because of their failure to satisfy the courts that they were closing out the dual school system in good faith.

The policy statement, approved by the President before he left for his Fourth of July vacation weekend, was announced in the press on Independence Day, while most of the members of Congress were absent from Washington. It was carefully worded to avoid the implication that the September, 1969, deadline was being sacrificed, but few construed it as anything but a relaxation of the desegregation effort. It was immediately denounced by civil rights leaders, congressional liberals of both parties, and the National Education Association as a capitulation to southern political pressures and as an invitation to refractory school boards to come forward with excuses.

The statement read in part:[1]

This Administration is unequivocally committed to the goal of finally ending racial discrimination in schools, steadily and speedily, in accordance with the law of the land. . . . Setting, breaking and resetting unrealistic "deadlines" may give the appearance of great Federal activity, but in too many cases it has actually impeded progress. . . .

A great deal of confusion surrounds the "guidelines." The essential problem, however, centers not on the guidelines themselves but on how and when individual school districts are to be brought into compliance with the law. . . .

The most immediate compliance problems are concentrated in those states which, in the past, have maintained racial segregation as official policy. These districts comprise 4,477 school districts located primarily in the seventeen Southern and Border states. . . .

A total of 121 school districts have been completely cut off from all Federal funds because they have refused to desegregate or even negotiate. There are 263 school districts which face the prospect, during the coming year, of a fund cutoff by H.E.W. or a lawsuit by the Department of Justice. . . .

[I]t is not our purpose here to lay down a single arbitrary date by which the desegregation process should be completed in all districts, or to lay down a single arbitrary system by which it should be achieved.

A policy requiring all school districts, regardless of the difficulties they face, to complete desegregation by the same terminal date is too rigid to be either workable or equitable. This is reflected in the history of the "guidelines."

Our policy in this area will be as defined in the latest Supreme Court and circuit court decisions: that school districts not now in compliance are required to complete the process of desegregation "at the earliest practicable date. . . ."

In general, such a plan must provide for full compliance now—that is, the "terminal date" must be the 1969–1970 school year. In some districts there may be sound reasons for some limited delay. In considering whether and how much additional time is justified, we will take into account only bona fide educational and administrative problems. Examples of such problems would be serious shortages of necessary physical facilities, financial resources or faculty. Additional time will be allowed only where those requesting it sustain the heavy factual burden of proving that compliance with the 1969–70 time schedule cannot be achieved; where additional time is allowed, it will be the minimum shown to be necessary.

At the opening of the new school year in September 1969, the future of the dual school system was still clouded with ambiguity. It was clear enough that the scheduled *ending* of racially identifiable schools, the announced policy of the Johnson Administration, would be deferred for at least another year or two, perhaps even indefinitely. Desegregation was, to be sure, going forward with gathering speed. The 20 percent of

[1] *The New York Times,* July 4, 1969.

the South's black children in integrated schools in 1968–1969 seemed almost certain to become at least 35 percent in 1969–1970. But few could see what lay farther ahead.

As the statistics on integration climbed, resistance mounted correspondingly. The Nixon Administration, under political obligation to the South (the only major region in the country that had actually given the President a majority in his presidential race in 1968), and eager to build a strong Republican party there, without antagonizing its razor-edge pluralities elsewhere, pursued what many regarded as a vacillating course whose prevailing drift was toward an easing of federal pressures on southern school districts.

On the one hand, the government, on August 1, 1969, initiated legal action against the school districts of Georgia (where in the 1968–1969 school year only 15 percent of the black children were in schools officially listed as desegregated), with the object of desegregating every public school in the state by September 1970. After the initial suit was filed, and Georgia had made its response in court, the government, on September 2, singled out for the first assault nine districts in which previous pledges to desegregate were in default. "School districts cannot," said HEW Secretary Robert H. Finch, "cast aside the commitments they have made to provide equal educational opportunities." Similar action was initiated against Alabama, parts of Louisiana and South Carolina, and most of the South's largest cities. Critics of the Nixon Administration's apparent slowdown were quick to point out that, for all its surface zeal, the action against Georgia was to be based not upon the cutoff of federal funds, but upon the older, slower, and less effective strategy of case-by-case litigation.

Only a few days before the Georgia proceeding was well launched, the government had, in *Alexander* v. *Holmes County Board of Education,* pleaded in the U.S. Court of Appeals (Fifth Circuit) in New Orleans that an earlier court order requiring a number of Mississippi districts to integrate by September 1, be modified to grant three months of delay and an opportunity to present a new plan. "Administrative and legislative difficulties" made the respite necessary, said Secretary Finch; the alternative, he warned, was chaos, confusion, and a catastrophic educational setback for 135,700 children if the schools were hurried through a desegregation plan. The court granted the reprieve on August 28, 1969.

The strategy adumbrated by the July 3 statement made on behalf of the President by Secretary Finch and Attorney General Mitchell, seemed now to become clearer: relaxation of federal pressure; abandonment of HEW fund cutoffs; back to case-by-case litigation as the major weapon for enforcing compliance. The changed program was justified by administration spokesmen on the plausible plea that the more impetuous policy inherited from the Johnson Administration would disrupt and impair the education of the South's children and, would, in addition, deprive Negroes and the poorest whites most of all, since they are the chief beneficiaries of federal funds. An additional justification for the shift was the argument that circumstances differ from district to district, from county to county, from state to state, and that the uniform application of rigid deadlines was therefore unworkable and inequitable.

The administration's request for delay exposed surprising differences inside government circles, even precipitating what amounted to a virtual revolt against their chief, the Attorney General, by lawyers in the Justice Department's Civil Rights Division. Alarm spread through the civil rights movement. If the Deep South's surprisingly liberal Fifth Circuit Court of Appeals (which had in recent years been quick to veto dubious requests for desegregation delays) could give encouragement to districts whose resistance to desegregation had been longest and most adamant, it could hardly be doubted that federal courts throughout the South would soon be flooded with requests for time, and that progress toward eliminating the dual school system would be mired in a swamp of protracted litigation.

The NAACP's Legal Defense and Educational Fund—speaking especially through its chief counsel, Jack Greenberg—had entered the case as friend of the court, and now moved at once for an appeal to the Supreme Court of the United States. Certiorari was promptly granted, and the case was set for oral argument on October 23, 1969.

In the meantime, administration policy, as illustrated by the leniency accorded to the Mississippi districts, drew fire from several directions, and elicited obfuscatory and even contradictory statements from inside the Nixon Administration. Early in September, no less an authority than the United States Commission on Civil Rights, speaking through its forthright chairman, the Reverend Theodore M. Hesburgh (President of Notre Dame University), released a public statement sharply criticizing the administration's "major retreat," as exemplified by the shift from fund cutoffs to litigation, and by a general winding down of the government's desegregation efforts.[1]

Three weeks earlier, immediately after the August 28 circuit court decision, some forty lawyers of the Justice Department's Civil Rights

[1] *The New York Times,* September 17, 1969, gives the text of this remarkable document. An example of the political pressure on the President was the persistent rumor that Senator John Stennis (Dem., Miss.), Chairman of the Senate Armed Forces Committee, threatened to drop the administration's precariously poised Defense Appropriation Bill (including provision for the Anti-Ballistic Missile proposal to which the President was deeply committed), halfway to passage, unless the "heat" was taken off Mississippi's school districts.

Division assembled informally in the apartment of one of the group and drafted an unprecedented rebuke to their superior, the Attorney General, John Mitchell, deploring the administration's break with the Justice Department's fifteen-year-old policy of ending school segregation. The dissident attorneys made especially emphatic their dissent from the abandonment of proven tactics. The real reason for the change, they hinted, was the fact that the older tactics were actually succeeding, and that the Nixon government was fearful of alienating southern segregationists.

Less than four weeks before the scheduled October 23 review of the circuit court's action by the Supreme Court, the President (who made a practice of saying little about the issue, preferring to let Attorney General Mitchell, HEW Secretary Finch, and Vice President Spiro Agnew serve as the administration's spokesmen and lightning rods), in an effort to reassure what he believed to be the country's silent majority, made a "clarifying" statement that was soon to bring him keen embarrassment. At a press conference on September 26, the President declared:[1] "It seems to me that there are two extreme groups. There are those who want instant integration and those who want segregation forever. I believe that we need to have a middle course between these two extremes. That is the course on which we are embarked. I think it is correct."

A month later, by this definition, every member of the Supreme Court was an extremist, including the new Chief Justice whom the President had just appointed presumably in part because of his conservative attitudes on race relations, and who had not yet, as Nixon spoke, heard his first case on the supreme bench. The President's statement did little to clarify disparate voices in his own official family. On September 16, for example, Vice President Agnew assured the Southern Governors' Conference, meeting in Williamsburg, that bussing was no part of the administration's strategy, for the President was committed to "stimulating compliance rather than compelling submission." Five days later HEW Secretary Finch disclosed, on an "Issues and Answers" interview on the ABC Television Network, that "You can't rule out bussing. I mean bussing is there." Reiterating that segregated systems must be ended, he declared that the department would tell local school boards to "rearrange your bussing patterns" to achieve desegregation. "We have insisted that they add buses in order to do this."[2]

When the Court sat on October 23 to hear arguments over the delay granted on August 28 by the court of appeals, the case for granting the postponement to thirty-three Mississippi districts was, ironically, presented by the chief of the Civil Rights Division of the Department of

[1] *The New York Times,* September 27, 1969.
[2] *The New York Times,* September 22, 1969.

Justice, Jerris Leonard, who found himself in the novel position of being the first spokesman of that agency ever to ask for postponement of compliance with the *Brown* decision. Arguing on the same side with him was the country's leading segregationist lawyer, John C. Satterfield, of Yazoo City, the attorney for the Mississippi school districts, and former president of the American Bar Association.

At issue was the question whether the court of appeals had erred in extending until December 1, 1969, for the convenience of thirty-three Mississippi school districts, an earlier order which had set September 1 as the deadline and which the district had originally accepted. The circuit court had granted the breathing spell subject to the condition that the districts take "significant action" toward ending dual school systems during the school year 1969–1970.

It was clear to the most casual observer that much hung in the balance, far more than a mere ninety-day extension for thirty-three Mississippi school districts. Some 1,534 school districts in the South and Border South were at that moment still not formally classified as desegregated. If some of the most recalcitrant districts in the country could win a reprieve from one of the nation's most liberal circuit courts, a turning point in the desegregation drive could be anticipated. Any wavering on the government's part would almost certainly be the cue for a torrent of requests for grace, endlessly renewed. If the government took an ambivalent line, the position of "moderate" and wavering districts would be seriously undercut; if it took a hard line against temporizing, the desegregation process would doubtless be accelerated.

The Court, in a stunning surprise, took a harder line than the country expected. Chief Justice Warren Burger, whom the nation regarded as a conservative on civil rights, carried a unanimous court with him in issuing a brief and unequivocal command that now, at last, "all deliberate speed . . . is no longer constitutionally permissible. . . . The obligation of every school district is to terminate dual school systems at once and to operate now and hereafter only unitary schools."

The complete text of the ruling follows:[1]

[1] *Alexander* v. *Holmes County Board of Education,* 38 LW 3161, 24 L. Ed. 2d 41 (1970). Mr. Jack Greenberg, speaking for the NAACP's Legal Defense and Educational Fund, announced at once that his organization would proceed immediately, without waiting for the end of the semester, to monitor compliance with the order, and to bring suits against every laggard. He did not expect, he said, that the Justice Department would seize the initiative with energy; indeed the Assistant Attorney General and head of the Civil Rights Division himself had said shortly before the decision that the government simply lacked the staff to mount a full-scale effort to achieve Southwide compliance. Asked at a news conference on September 29 what the Department of Justice would do if the Supreme Court rejected his plea for delay in the Mississippi districts, he replied, "Nothing would change," because the department lacked the "bodies and people" to enforce immediate desegregation across the South. *The New York Times,* October 16, 1969.

October 29, 1969

Present: Mr. Chief Justice Burger, Mr. Justice Black, Mr. Justice Douglas, Mr. Justice Brennan, Mr. Justice Stewart, Mr. Justice White, and Mr. Justice Marshall.

632 *Alexander* v. *Holmes Cty. Board of Education,* et al. Per Curiam. These cases come to the Court on a petition for certiorari to the Court of Appeals for the Fifth Circuit. The petition was granted on October 9, 1969, and the case set down for early argument. The question presented is one of paramount importance, involving as it does the denial of fundamental rights to many thousands of school children, who are presently attending Mississippi schools under segregated conditions contrary to the applicable decisions of this Court. Against this background the Court of Appeals should have denied all motions for additional time because continued operation of segregated schools under a standard of allowing "all deliberate speed" for desegregation is no longer constitutionally permissible. Under explicit holdings of this Court the obligation of every school district is to terminate dual school systems at once and to operate now and hereafter only unitary schools. *Griffin* v. *School Board,* 377 U.S. 218, 234 (1964); *Green* v. *County School Board of New Kent County,* 391 U.S. 430, 438–439, 442 (1968). Accordingly, It is hereby adjudged, ordered, and decreed:

1. The Court of Appeals' order of August 28, 1969, is vacated, and the cases are remanded to that court to issue its decree and order, effective immediately, declaring that each of the school districts here involved may no longer operate a dual school system based on race or color, and directing that they begin immediately to operate as unitary school systems within which no person is to be effectively excluded from any school because of race or color.

2. The Court of Appeals may in its discretion direct the schools here involved to accept all or any part of the August 11, 1969, recommendations of the Department of Health, Education, and Welfare, with any modifications which that court deems proper insofar as those recommendations insure a totally unitary school system for all eligible pupils without regard to race or color.

The Court of Appeals may make its determination and enter its order without further arguments or submissions.

3. While each of these school systems is being operated as a unitary system under the order of the Court of Appeals, the District Court may hear and consider objections thereto or proposed amendments thereof, provided, however, that the Court of Appeals' order shall be complied with in all respects while the District Court considers such objections or amendments, if any are made. No amendment shall become effective before being passed upon by the Court of Appeals.

4. The Court of Appeals shall retain jurisdiction to insure prompt and faithful compliance with its order, and may modify or amend the same as may be deemed necessary or desirable for the operation of a unitary school system.

The irony of the situation did not escape Greenberg or his well-wishers. The NAACP's legal arm was, of course, even less adequately staffed than the Justice Department, but this relatively small private organization which had done so much to achieve the Negro's courtroom victories of the past fifty years, was now obliged to plunge into a huge mopping-up operation while laboring under a $250,000 deficit in its $3,000,000 budget.

5. The order of the Court of Appeals dated August 28, 1969, having been vacated and the case remanded for proceedings in conformity with this order, the judgment shall issue forthwith and the Court of Appeals is requested to give priority to the execution of this judgment as far as possible and necessary.

The *Holmes County* ruling was widely hailed as the death knell for segregated schools, after fifteen years of repeated stays of execution. Many began to say openly what they had long felt: that the "deliberate speed" formula laid down in *Brown II*[1] had been a mistake from the beginning, an over-generous indulgence to the South that only invited procrastination. Now, at least so far as the de jure dual school systems of the South were concerned, an era had ended. Far from clear, however, were the implications of the *Holmes County* decree for de facto segregation in the North. There were, in fact, those who predicted that the decision simply would not reach that far.

Southern (and some northern) segregationists' response to the new order brought no immediate surprises. It could only provoke confusion, violence, and damage to public education. "A criminal Act against the people by the federal government. . . . This court is no better than the Warren Court," lamented Governor Maddox. Governor John Bell Williams mourned that the schoolchildren of Mississippi "have been cruelly offered as sacrificial lambs on the altar of social experimentation. [It can lead to] the destruction of public education." Not a few critics predicted that many districts would close down their public schools altogether; others agreed with Alabama's Attorney General that "the public school system will become a colored school system." There was talk of refurbishing the old "Impeach Earl Warren" billboards to read, "Impeach Warren Burger."

While few could foresee, in the immediate wake of *Holmes County*, what its ultimate consequence would be, many insisted that it was the most important civil rights pronouncement from the Supreme Court since it had declared in 1954 that "in the field of public education the doctrine of separate but equal has no place [because] . . . such segregation is a denial of the equal protection of the laws."

Still others, sober students of the integration movement, were more restrained in their judgment. The *Holmes County* decision perhaps did not in point of fact make a great deal of difference. Freedom-of-choice and "deliberate speed" were dead *before* Chief Justice Warren relinquished his office. The new ruling only made plain that the transition from the Warren court to the Burger court would bring no relaxation in the supreme tribunal's determination that the time for obstructionist maneuvers had passed. All that was new was a clearer formulation of

[1] See above, p. 430.

the principle that laggard school districts could no longer rely on the old formula of "litigate now, integrate later"; they must now proceed from the rule "integrate now, litigate later, and expect your litigation to fail."

The demise of the dual school system had in the past been so often prematurely announced on the morrow of stiffly worded pronouncements by the Supreme Court and United States courts of appeals that there was an understandable reluctance in the immediate wake of the *Holmes County* decision of October 1969, to hazard once more the judgment that the days of the dual system were now truly numbered. But in the opening weeks of 1970 events moved with such swiftness and compelling urgency that all but a few skeptics became convinced that the dam had broken, and that the tides of change, pent up for fifteen years, would now roll with such force that no tactic of obstruction or delay could possibly restrain them.

Mississippi was the first of the deep South states to be overwhelmed by the flood. The change-over, when classes resumed after the Christmas holidays, was remarkably peaceful. There was, to be sure, a roar of mingled rage and distress from segregationist whites; there were a few boycotts, mounted by resolute parents who preferred no schools at all to "mixed" schools for their children. There was also a rush to establish private schools in the early weeks of the transition; against which a three-judge federal panel promptly directed a ruling to end tax exemption for such schools, and to deny income tax credits to those who supplied them with funds. But it seemed safe to conclude that at least 80 percent of the 56,000 white students in 30 districts to which the *Holmes County* decision had been addressed would, when the excitement had passed, be in the public schools, and that all of the public schools in the state would by the end of the 1969–1970 school year be genuinely biracial. The percentage of black pupils and teachers in formerly all-white schools would for some time, doubtless, be very small, and the proportion of whites in formerly all-black schools even smaller still. But legal pressures for full achievement of a unitary system would, it was widely assumed, move the proportions closer and closer to racial balance. In many school districts segregated classes promptly appeared in desegregated schools, and this strategy for evasion was also marked for early attack by the triumphant Legal Defense and Educational Fund of the NAACP.

From Mississippi the tide rolled to five other southern states, where again the Supreme Court, on January 14, 1970, denied pleas for extended time, and insisted upon immediate abandonment of the dual system, to be achieved by February 1, in 14 school districts, even if the price was a period of confusion and turmoil in the middle of the school year. In the three-sentence *per curiam* opinion, the Court, by a

6–2 vote, reiterated its determination to adhere to the *Holmes County* ruling calling for immediate and effective measures for replacing dual by unitary systems.[1]

The Justice Department now joined the push for the *Holmes County* ruling's effectuation, presumably with the approval of President Nixon and Attorney General Mitchell. The Legal Defense and Educational Fund vowed an unremitting drive to bring every school district in the country into compliance, and announced its intention to use the January 14 ruling as a fulcrum for a massive thrust for immediate desegregation in at least two hundred cases at that moment pending before the courts. As usual, it was the de facto segregation in the non-South that proved most difficult to cope with, but there also a resolute beginning was planned.

An earnest of the executive and judicial branches' intention to grapple with that problem came on January 20, 1970, when a federal district court judge ordered the Pasadena, California, school system to submit a desegregation plan by February 16, to go into effect by September 1970, in all the schools of the suburban Los Angeles district. The order stipulated that the plan must not permit any school in the district to operate with a majority of nonwhite students, and that it must extend also to teaching assignments, hiring, and promotion practices, and the construction of new school facilities. The action was notable also for the fact that it was the United States Department of Justice, which had so recently argued for delay, whose lawyers now pressed for an immediate end to segregation in the Pasadena schools. The district's school population, incidentally, was approximately fifty-five percent white, thirty percent black, ten percent Mexican, and five percent Oriental.

The case did not in fact raise a clearcut issue of purely de facto segregation, because the plaintiffs took the position that, besides residential patterns, a policy of drawing school district lines and locating new schools had been maintaining racial isolation in the schools of Pasadena. The suit had originally been filed in August 1968, and had been joined by the Justice Department in November of that year, in the closing weeks of the Johnson Administration.

Six other suits against de facto segregation, all but two of which had been initiated by the Johnson Administration, were being pressed by the government in early 1970. They were directed against the school systems in Chicago, Tulsa (Oklahoma), East St. Louis (Illinois), Indianapolis, Waterbury (Connecticut), and Madison County, Illinois.[2]

[1] *Carter* v. *West Feliciana Parish School Board*, and *Singleton* v. *Jackson Municipal Separate School District*, 30 LW 3265, 24 L. Ed. 2d 477 (1970).

[2] *The New York Times*, January 5, 1970, p. 1; January 21, 1970, p. 4.

B. *Segregated Education: Colleges and Universities*

Public Institutions of Higher Learning

Some measure of integration had begun in the South's public colleges and universities by 1936, and on the eve of the *Brown* decision twenty-nine of them were admitting both races. Indeed, as we have seen, the principle that access to state-supported institutions of higher learning without racial discrimination is required by the Constitution had been established four years before *Brown*. Although the courts did not take a stand against separate institutions per se, they did insist that the *School Segregation* decision was as much applicable to universities as to the common schools.

After 1954 the movement of blacks into white institutions was slow, and in the deeper South deferred altogether until militant efforts were exerted. There were for all practical purposes, no state-supported black colleges outside the South—except for a teachers' college or two—but nonsouthern Negro youths flocked to the separate colleges in the South, not only for undergraduate work, but especially for professional training in medicine (at Howard and Meharry) and law (at Howard).

Outside the Deep South the slow traffic was partly explained by the understandable preference of blacks for their "own" schools, rather than face the hostility, the exclusions from campus activities, and the rigorous competition in the classroom, for which their underprivileged earlier education and deprived backgrounds gave them little preparation. Other factors were their failure to meet entrance requirements (which were not always uniformly applied to whites and Negroes); dilatory and obstructionist processing of Negroes' applications; and community antagonisms which denied them adequate housing, dining, and recreational facilities as well as a proper atmosphere for happy and satisfying college life.

The principal conflicts occurred in the deeper South, where the determination to hold off integration as long as possible was bluntly proclaimed by high public officials, spokesmen for the colleges and their communities, students, faculties, and trustees. A week after *Brown*, the Supreme Court made clear its intention that the ruling there pronounced was to be applied also to public institutions of higher learning. In an action commenced before the *Brown* suits, blacks had sought admission to the law school of the University of Florida. When the state's supreme court ruled against the petitioners, they asked the United States Supreme Court for a writ of certiorari. The Court granted the petition, and reversed and remanded the case. The ruling, here reproduced in full, could hardly have been more brief.[1]

PER CURIAM:

The petition for writ of certiorari is granted. The judgment is vacated and the case remanded for consideration in the light of the Segregation Cases decided May 17, 1954, *Brown* v. *Board of Education*, etc., 347 U.S. 483, 74 S. Ct. 686, and conditions that now prevail.

The Supreme Court of Florida, upon hearing the case on remand, concluded to continue the case pending findings on questions of the school's capacity, physical plant, and "other conditions that prevail." A Negro applicant thereupon petitioned the United States Supreme Court to review this action, and although the Court refused to grant the review, it entered a new order which reiterated that *Brown* applied to all levels of education, and that the circumstances justifying delay in elementary and secondary schools which had been recognized in *Brown II* are not involved in graduate and professional schools.[2]

In [*Brown II*] . . . we did not imply that decrees involving graduate study present the problems of public elementary and secondary schools. . . . As this case involves the admission of a Negro to a graduate professional school, there is no reason for delay. He is entitled to prompt admission under the rules and regulations applicable to other qualified candidates.

The number of colleges admitting students on an integrated basis doubled in the first year after *Brown*, and continued to increase at a substantial rate for another year. In the 1957–58 academic year there were 128 desegregated public colleges and universities in the South. By the 1960–61 school year the number had reached 140, and in 1961–62 all but seventy-nine institutions in the Border South were operating on an integrated basis. In 1962–64, forty-five more schools dropped the racial bar.

The last southern states to admit Negroes to formerly all-white public institutions—Mississippi, South Carolina, and Alabama—held off until 1962–63, and then yielded to court orders. Ten years after *Brown*, 197 of the region's 292 public colleges and universities had desegregated, thirty-two of them upon court order, and 165 "voluntarily." The number of black students in biracial schools by 1964 was still small: perhaps 36,000, or about 5 percent of the total student population in the South's public institutions of higher learning. In individual southern states, the proportion was much lower.

National attention was drawn in 1955 to the short-lived enrollment of Autherine Lucy at the University of Alabama, in a state which had thus far preserved absolute segregation in *all* its schools. Miss Lucy, in a class action, filed application for admission (to study library science)

[1] *Florida ex rel. Hawkins* v. *Board of Control of Florida*, 347 U.S. 971 (1954).
[2] *Florida ex rel. Hawkins* v. *Board of Control of Florida*, 350 U.S. 413 (1956).

in September 1952, after graduating from the all-Negro Miles College in Birmingham. When her application was mailed, together with a deposit of five dollars for a room reservation, she was informed that she would be welcomed. A few days later she sent the Dean of Admissions a transcript of her previous college work. He received it on 19 September, but on the twentieth, when Miss Lucy appeared at his office, she was told that she had been rejected. She was offered a refund of her room deposit and urged to seek admission to Alabama State College (for Negroes), at Montgomery.

The federal district court to which the plaintiff appealed ruled:[1]

> This suit arises under the Constitution and laws of the United States and seeks redress for the deprivation of civil rights guaranteed by the Fourteenth Amendment. . . . There is no written policy or rule excluding prospective students . . . on account of race or color. However, there is a tacit policy to that effect. . . . Plaintiffs were denied admission to the University of Alabama solely on account of their race and color. In conformity with the equal protection clause of the Fourteenth Amendment, plaintiffs and others similarly situated are entitled to equal advantages and opportunities available at the University of Alabama at the same time and upon the same terms and qualifications available to other residents and citizens of the State of Alabama. . . . Plaintiffs are entitled to a decree enjoining the defendant, William F. Adams [and others] . . . who might aid, abet, and act in concert with him, from denying the plaintiffs and others similarly situated the right to enroll in the University . . . , solely on account of their race and color.

The ruling was subsequently affirmed by a United States court of appeals. Miss Lucy was admitted to the university, though not permitted to use any dormitory or dining room. Trailed by a policeman assigned to her protection, she sat in class in a row occupied by no others. On the campus, students and outsiders assailed her with verbal abuse, and threatened bodily violence. Dangerous commotion seemed to impend, and after she had attended classes for three days, the trustees suspended her for having publicly charged the board with conspiring with a mob. The court did, however, order her readmission. When the university then took steps to expel her permanently, she again sought judicial protection, but the court declined, on the ground that the board's normal power to expel had not been arbitrarily exercised on the basis of race.

Another break-through, which deserved more public notice than it attracted, occurred in January 1961, at the University of Georgia, which had never enrolled a Negro student in its 175-year history. The admission of two Negro applicants on this occasion marked the first breach in the state's wall of separation, which until that moment had excluded Negroes from white public classrooms, from kindergarten to

[1] *Lucy* v. *Adams,* 134 F. Supp. 235 (W.D. Ala. 1955).

graduate school. Indeed, if (as it should be) the brief fiasco at the University of Alabama in 1955 were to be excepted, the crack in the wall at Georgia was the first in all four of the hard-core, last-ditch segregationist states, where, for years after *Brown,* official spokesmen were still proclaiming that segregation would *never* cross their borders.

Eighteen months of litigation preceded the final admission, on January 9, 1961, of Charlayne Hunter, eighteen, and Hamilton Holmes, nineteen, to the University of Georgia. Both were 1959 honor graduates of Turner High School in Atlanta. Both had been denied admission to the university in 1960, on various pretexts, carefully worded to avoid the appearance of racial discrimination, and relating principally to the plea that limited facilities compelled the university to disappoint many qualified students.

Holmes entered Morehouse College, in Atlanta, and Miss Hunter, Wayne State University, in Detroit; but both continued to press for admission at Georgia, and both were told that now the university was forced, by reason of overcrowding, to deny admission to students who sought to transfer from other colleges. Informed that applications could not, in any case, be considered without a personal interview, the defendants asked for interviews, but were again put off with the reply that overcrowding prevented consideration of their applications for the present.

On September 2, 1960, the two students brought a class action in federal district court, asking for an injunction to restrain the university's officials from refusing to consider their applications and those of other Georgia Negroes on the same terms as those applied to whites. In preliminary hearing the court, instead of granting or dismissing the petition, gave the university an additional thirty days to provide the interview and act upon the applications.

The university granted the interview, denied admission to Holmes on the ground that he was not a "suitable applicant," and declined to consider Miss Hunter's application until the fall of 1961, because of "limited facilities." Following a trial, the court filed an opinion on January 6, 1961, that the plaintiffs had been denied admission solely because of race, and that the university was in fact systematically excluding blacks.

A sample of the evidence is afforded by the following passage from the opinion:[1]

> Apparently the interview was conducted with the purpose in mind of finding a basis for rejecting Holmes. He was asked, in substance, the following questions . . . which had probably never been asked of any applicant before:

[1] *Holmes* v. *Danner,* 191 F. Supp. 394 (M.D. Ga. 1961).

(1) Have you ever been arrested? (2) Have you ever attended interracial parties? (3) What is your opinion concerning the integration crises in New Orleans and Atlanta? (4) Give some insight into the workings of the student sit-in movement in Atlanta. (5) What are some of [these] activities . . . and have you ever participated therein? (6) Do you know of the tea houses (or coffee houses, or Beatnik places) in Atlanta, and have you ever attended any of them? (7) Do you know about the red light district in Athens? (8) Have you ever attended houses of prostitution? (9) Since you are interested in a pre-medical course, why have you not applied to Emory University, since it is in Atlanta?

. . . It is evident . . . that the interview of Holmes was not conducted as the interview of white applicants and . . . that, had [his] interview been conducted and evaluated in the same manner as the interview of white applicants, Holmes would have been found "to be an acceptable candidate for admission to the University."

[A portion of the court's decree follows:]

ORDERED, ADJUDGED and DECREED that the defendant, Walter N. Danner . . . and all persons in active concert and participation with him are hereby permanently enjoined as follows:

From refusing to consider the applications of the plaintiffs and other Negro residents of Georgia upon the same terms and conditions applicable to white applicants seeking admission to said University; and from failing and refusing to act expeditiously upon applications received from [them]; and from refusing to approve the applications of qualified Negro residents of Georgia for admission to said University solely because of the race and color of the Negro applicants; and from subjecting Negro applicants to requirements, prerequisites, interviews, delays and tests not required of white applicants for admission; and from making the attendance of Negroes at said University subject to terms and conditions not applicable to white persons. . . .

The students entered the university on January 9, 1961. On the following night violent demonstrations by students and "outsiders" prompted the university to suspend the Negro students "in the interest of their personal safety." On January 16 a new court order returned the pair to the campus under strengthened security measures. The January 11 disorders led to the arrest of eight Klan members and two students.

A week after the enrollment, when Miss Hunter sought admission to the university's dining halls, state officials asked the federal court for clarification of its original injunction. The district judge, citing *McLaurin* v. *Oklahoma*,[1] held that "with respect to the opportunities and facilities which it extends and offers to white students [the university] cannot deny such facilities and opportunities to plaintiffs solely on the basis of their race and color."[2]

[1] See above, p. 275.

[2] *Holmes* v. *Danner, U.S. Dist. Ct.,* Civil Action No. 450, March 9, 1961 (M.D. Ga.). See RRLR VI, 125.

Hamilton Holmes is now (1970) an Army doctor in Germany, and Charlayne Hunter is a reporter for *The New York Times*. Nine years after their admission, Miss Hunter recalled her first days at the University and contrasted them with what she found on a recent visit to the campus.[1]

Several days after Hamilton (Hamp) Holmes and I entered the University of Georgia in 1961 under court order as its first two black students, I sat in a world-history class, fighting desperately to stay awake and avoid confirming the stereotype that all blacks are lazy. The drowsiness was the result of my first few days on campus when white students, protesting our admission, rioted outside my dormitory. . . .

[T]he girls who lived above me—I was the sole resident on the first floor—continued for a long time to pound the floor, night after night, late into the night, and I suffered the physical and mental exhaustion of those first few days throughout the winter quarter. Somehow, it was always in this mid-morning history class that I would find myself embarrassed as my head drooped and my eyes closed.

Almost nine years later, during my first visit to the campus since graduation, I entered that same classroom—this time wide awake, and found not a course in world history, but one in African history, part of a new black-studies program; and not one exhausted black girl, but five outspoken black men and women among the students and a young black man, with a heavy Afro haircut and wearing a turtleneck sweater, teaching the course. By the end of the hour, as the white students sat quietly taking notes, the black instructor was acting as referee for two of the black students who were engaged in a vehement clash of opinion on the subject of pan-Africanism.

A far more dramatic clash between federal and state authorities accompanied the long-deferred break in Mississippi's segregation wall on October 1, 1962, when James Meredith, the son of a small farmer, was enrolled in the University of Mississippi by order of the federal courts.

Upon graduation from high school, Meredith had volunteered for the Air Force. During nine years of service he had accumulated thirty-four semester credits by attending night courses at the University of Maryland's Far Eastern Division in Tokyo; at the University of Kansas; and at Washburn University. In addition he had taken a number of courses at the Armed Forces Institute. Upon his honorable discharge from the service, he entered the all-Negro Jackson State College, at Jackson, Mississippi, where he was allowed fifty-seven quarter hours of credit for the work he had taken. Early in 1961, when he had reached fourth-year standing, he sought admission at the University of Mississippi, having concluded that Jackson State was "substandard."

The step required no small courage. The only other Negro who had applied for admission at "Old Miss," Clennon King, a history professor

[1] Charlayne Hunter, "After Nine Years—A Homecoming for the First Black Girl at the University of Georgia," *The New York Times Magazine*, January 25, 1970, p. 24. Copyright © 1970. Reprinted by permission of *The New York Times*.

at Alcorn A & M College (Mississippi), had been swiftly repulsed. (King had, incidentally, been so critical of the "radicalism" of the NAACP and the civil rights movement that more than 85 percent of Alcorn's student body—not then noted for militancy—had in 1957 staged a strike, demanding his removal.) In June 1958, he tried to enroll in the university's summer session. As he stood in line with other prospective registrants, he was invited into the administration building, ostensibly to confer with the registrar. Instead, he was ejected from the campus by highway patrolmen, and taken to Chancery Court, where a lunacy warrant was issued. After thirteen days in the state mental hospital he was declared sane, and released. Thoroughly chastened, King left the state for his home in Georgia.

Meredith mailed his application on January 26, 1961, explaining that as a Negro he was unable to furnish as references the required names of six university alumni, because there were no Negro alumni and he knew no white graduates. He sent instead five certificates from residents of Attala County attesting his good moral character.

When the registrar wired Meredith that overcrowding forced the school to discontinue consideration of applications, Meredith wrote to ask that his request be considered "a continuing application for admission during the summer session beginning June 8." The registrar replied that since the university was unable to accept further candidates, his room deposit was being returned. When further correspondence drew no reply, Meredith wrote the Dean of the College of Arts and Sciences asking him what requirements he had thus far failed to meet, and requesting assurance that his race and color were not the reason for his failure to be admitted. Later the university informed him that the school could not recognize credits from Jackson State because its "programs are not recognized." The certificates of good character, furthermore, were not acceptable either, and there was, therefore, "no need for mentioning any other deficiencies."

On May 31, 1961, Meredith filed a class-action complaint with the United States district court, asking for an injunction to restrain the university from limiting admissions to whites. Upon preliminary hearing the court declined to issue a temporary writ, but scheduled a formal hearing. In declining immediate relief, the court ruled that "the overwhelming weight of testimony is that the plaintiff was not denied admission because of his . . . race," but because he had not presented alumni certificates, because of overcrowding in the university, and because the university had decided to raise scholarship standards by accepting credits only from institutions which were members of recognized accrediting associations.

Meredith then turned to the court of appeals for a preliminary injunction requiring his admission by February 6, the beginning of a new semester. Instead, the court ordered the district court to proceed at once to trial, and observed that the lower court had heard the case "in the eerie atmosphere of never-never land":[1]

> Counsel for [the university] argue that there is no state policy of maintaining segregated institutions of higher learning and that the court can take no judicial notice of this plain fact known to everyone . . . Counsel . . . insists . . . that appellant's counsel should have examined the genealogical records of all the students and alumni . . . and should have offered these records . . . to prove the University's alleged [whites-only] policy. . . .
>
> We take judicial notice that the state of Mississippi maintains a policy of segregation in its schools and colleges. . . . We hold that the University's requirement that each candidate . . . furnish alumni certificates is a denial of equal protection of the laws. . . . The fact that there are no Negro alumni . . . , the traditional social barriers making it unlikely, if not impossible, for a Negro to approach alumni . . . for such a recommendation, the possibility of reprisals if alumni should recommend a Negro . . . , are barriers only to [Negroes]. It is significant that the University adopted the requirement of alumni certificates a few months after *Brown* v. *Board* . . . was decided.

But the circuit court concluded also that the evidence had not made clear that Meredith had been refused on discriminatory grounds, and for this reason it directed the district court to proceed promptly with a trial "on the merits." When the district court announced its decision, it reiterated its finding that the plaintiff had failed to meet his burden of proof that he had clearly been denied admission because of his race, and it dismissed both the individual and the class action. Again Meredith appealed to the circuit court, and again it denied the injunction, insisting that it should not issue "without [the court's] opportunity to study the full record and testimony." The circuit court did, however, order that a hearing of the appeal on the merits be expedited so that a decision could be reached before the start of the next college term.

Finally the court of appeals, on June 25, after hearing the case on the merits, reversed the district court's judgment, averring that it had found no evidence to contradict its earlier judgment that Mississippi was maintaining a policy of segregating state schools. Meeting point by point the university's list of reasons for finding Meredith unacceptable (including the insinuation that his habit of sending letters to the university by registered mail exposed him to the suspicion of bad faith; that he had filed false statements on his application papers—which the court, on the evidence, dismissed as "a frivolous defense"; and that he was a "troublemaker" and a "bad character risk"—again, charges which the court found unsupported by the record), the court ruled that Meredith had indeed been denied admission solely because of his race:[2]

[1] *Meredith* v. *Fair*, 298 F. 2d 696 (5th Cir. 1962).
[2] *Meredith* v. *Fair*, 305 F. 2d 343 (5th Cir. 1962).

A full review of the record leads the Court inescapably to the conclusion that from the moment the defendants discovered Meredith was a Negro they engaged in a carefully calculated campaign of delay, harassment, and masterly inactivity. It was a defense designed to discourage and to defeat by evasive tactics which would have been a credit to Quintus Fabius Maximus.

The circuit court now ordered the district court to issue the decree, but it was only after further legal skirmishes in succeeding months that the latter, on September 13, 1962, at last issued a permanent injunction against the university's officials, commanding:[1]

that the defendants . . . and all persons acting in concert with them, are enjoined to admit . . . James Howard Meredith to the University of Mississippi upon his applications heretofore filed and, . . . from excluding [him] from admission to continued attendance at the University . . . or discriminating against him in any way whatsoever because of his race. . . .

Thus far the Meredith case had excited only mild interest in the country. It was in the sequel, witnessed by millions on television, that the real excitement lay. It will be remembered that on the day the injunction was issued, not a single known Negro was in a Mississippi public school, at any level, with whites. The case flamed into a national issue as the governor and legislature moved to thwart the court order. It seems unlikely that state officials seriously expected their defiance to preserve absolute segregation, or that they expected by their obstruction to achieve more than increased popularity with Mississippi's rank and file of voters, and (relying on the reluctance of the Democratic administration in Washington to alienate their party's southern wing) a few more momentary delays.

Moments after the district court's injunction had been issued, Governor Barnett released a proclamation:[2]

. . . NOW, THEREFORE, I, Ross Barnett, Governor of the Sovereign State of Mississippi . . . do hereby proclaim that the operation of the public schools, universities and colleges of the State . . . is vested in the duly elected and appointed officials of the State; and I hereby direct each said official to uphold and enforce the laws duly and legally enacted by the Legislature of the State of Mississippi, regardless of this unwarranted, illegal and arbitrary [federal] usurpation of power; and to impose the State Sovereignty and themselves between the people and any body-politic seeking to usurp such power.

Six days later, a chancery court of Jones County, Mississippi, granted a temporary injunction forbidding Meredith, the Attorney General of the United States, federal marshals, and various state and university officers from "performing any act intending to enroll and register the Negro, James Meredith, as a student in the University of Mississippi; or

[1] *Meredith* v. *Fair, U.S. Dist. Ct.,* Civil Action No. 3130, September 13, 1962 (S.D. Miss.).

[2] RRLR VII, 748.

do any other thing contrary to the laws and the statutes of Mississippi which would aid or abet the integration of any university, college, or common school within the state of Mississippi."[1]

Ten more days of legal wrangling followed. On September 20 the legislature hurriedly enacted "that no person shall be eligible for admission to institutions of higher learning in the State . . . who has a criminal charge of moral turpitude pending against him . . . in any . . . court." On the same day the United States, as *amicus curiae*, petitioned the district court to enjoin the enforcement of the foregoing; and asked for an injunction against the arrest of Meredith on state charges of "false voter registration," of which he had been hastily convicted in a justice of the peace court earlier on that day, at Jackson, and for which he had been sentenced to a year in jail. The court responded by enjoining the arrest of Meredith for what it was convinced was a spurious conviction. The same day also brought an injunction from the United States court of appeals, enjoining the enforcement of the Act of September 20, and estopping all state, county, and municipal officials from "taking any steps to effectuate the conviction and sentence on September 20, 1962, in the Justice of the Peace Court of Jackson, Mississippi, of James Meredith for false voter registration."

Also, at 3:00 P.M. on that day, the Board of Trustees of the state's institutions of higher learning adopted a resolution investing the governor with "full power, authority, right and discretion of this Board to act upon all matters pertaining to . . . the registration of James Meredith at the University of Mississippi." At this point, Governor Barnett, armed with this authority, flew to the campus at Oxford to deal personally with Meredith—despite telephoned admonitions from Attorney General Robert Kennedy, who warned him of the legal implications of his intransigence. By this time uniformed state troopers, newsmen, and television camera crews had converged upon the university grounds to witness the confrontation. Meredith, flanked by federal marshals, marched from his car past jeering students and townsfolk to the university's Center for Continuing Studies, where the waiting governor refused to accept his federal court orders and credentials.

To the question of a Justice Department aide, "Do you realize you are breaking the law?" the governor adroitly replied that it was for a federal judge to say that he was in contempt. The marshal then accompanied Meredith back to the car and drove off with him through a torrent of abuse from the students. Before the day was over, the Justice Department was back in federal court, where the spokesman of the Attorney General secured an order upon officers of the university to "show cause, if any they have, on September 21, 1962, at 1:30 P.M.

[1] RRLR VII, 749.

o'clock in the United States District Courtroom . . . in Meridian, Mississippi, why each of them should not be held in civil contempt by reason of his failure and refusal to obey the injunction of the Court of September 13, 1962."[1]

At the appointed hour on September 21, the district court found the university officers not guilty of civil contempt (they had, to be sure, been relieved of their duties by the governor), and three days later, the governor issued yet another proclamation, declaring that federal action in behalf of Meredith was a "direct usurpation [of the state's reserved] power," and directing the arrest of any agent of the federal government who attempted to arrest or fine any state official in the performance of his official duties.

On that very day, September 24, the court of appeals held the hearing which it had ordered on September 21, following the district court's ruling that the university's officers were not in contempt. The officials now indicated their willingness to comply with district court orders and to register Meredith. The court thereupon (1) ordered the trustees to "revoke and rescind the action of the Board taken on September 20, 1962, appointing Ross R. Barnett . . . as the agent of the Board to act in all matters pertaining to the registration of James H. Meredith"; and (2) ordered the Board to notify all employees of the university "that the orders of this Court are to be complied with in connection with the . . . admission . . . of James H. Meredith. . . ."

The following day, at 8:30 A.M., the circuit court entered a temporary order restraining the governor from "interfering with . . . the performance of obligations or the enjoyment of rights under this Court's order of July 28, 1962, and the order of the United States District Court . . . of September 13, 1962." Mere hours later the trustees revoked their action and instructed all university officials "to register and receive James H. Meredith for actual admission." The governor, however, took the unusual step of directing a proclamation at Meredith, finding his sanction in the state's police power. The bizarre charade was acted out in the corridor of an office building opposite the state capitol, which housed the state college board. Meredith, escorted by two United States marshals, stepped off the elevator on the tenth floor and made his way to the board's office. As he reached the door, it swung open and revealed the governor resolutely stationed on the threshold. "I want to remind you," said one of the federal agents, "that the Circuit Court of Appeals . . . entered a temporary restraining order at 8:30 this morning enjoining you from interfering in any way with the registration of James Meredith. We'd like to get on now, Governor, to the business of registering Meredith."

[1] U.S. Dist. Ct., Sept. 20, 1962 (S.D. Miss.); see RRLR VII, 753.

The governor's reply was to draw his proclamation from a pocket and to read it off:[1]

> I, Ross Barnett, governor of the state of Mississippi, having heretofore by proclamation, acting under the police powers of the state of Mississippi, interposed the sovereignty of this state on September 14, 1962, and in order to preserve the peace, dignity and tranquillity of the state of Mississippi, and having previously, on September 20, 1962, denied to you, James H. Meredith admission to the University . . . for such reasons, do hereby finally deny you admission to the University of Mississippi.

That done, one of the marshals again asked, "Do you refuse to permit us to come in the door?"

"Yes, sir," said Barnett, ". . . . I do that politely."

"Thank you. We leave politely," said the spokesman for the United States.

Before the day was over, the circuit court of appeals, at the request of the federal government, issued an order that "Ross Barnett appear personally before this Court on September 28, 1962, at 10 o'clock A.M. in . . . the United States Court of Appeals . . . [in New Orleans] to show cause . . . why he should not be held in civil contempt of the . . . order entered by this Court this day." A similar order was issued to Lieutenant Governor Paul Johnson.[2]

A few hours earlier Meredith had gone under escort to the university to make another effort to register. Because Barnett's airplane had been detained by bad weather, he sped to Oxford by car, arriving too late to participate in the drama. In his stead Johnson, assisted by several state law enforcement officers and a barricade of police cars, blocked the roadway to the main entrance of the campus.

"We want to take Mr. Meredith into the University under the direction of the Federal Government and have him registered," said a marshal.

"I am going to have to refuse," replied Johnson.

After a brief attempt to push their way through, Meredith and the marshals, hopelessly outnumbered, withdrew.

Both Barnett and Johnson failed to appear at the New Orleans courtroom, and both were declared in contempt of the restraining orders, and ordered to pay very heavy fines unless by October 2, 1962, at 11 A.M., they showed the court that they were fully complying with the court's directives.

The tragicomedy now moved to its conclusion. At the White House, at midnight, September 29–30, President Kennedy ordered Mississippi's National Guard into the federal service, dispatched national troops to

[1] RRLR VII, 759.

[2] RRLR VII, 759.

Memphis to stand by in case they were needed at Oxford, and issued a proclamation calling upon "all persons engaged in such obstructions of justice to cease and desist therefrom and to disperse and retire peacefully forthwith."[1]

The legal battle was over, but resistance was not. In a nationwide television appearance, the President appealed to Mississippians for peaceful compliance, but an excited crowd of 2500 people assembled when Meredith arrived on the campus, on September 30. Bricks and bottles flew through the air; the marshals were menaced by lead pipes, rifles, and shotguns, and defended themselves with tear gas. The rioting went on past midnight, leaving two dead, and more than 3300 (including 166 United States marshals) injured. Three thousand federal troops were hurried forward, and the disorders were quelled only after fifteen hours of tumult, and after 150 persons had been arrested.

But Meredith remained in school under the protection of federal marshals, until he graduated the following June. The color line in Mississippi's educational structure had at last been breached.

Four months later, South Carolina was the next of the last-ditch states to give way, when Harvey B. Gantt was admitted to Clemson College. Gantt's suit was commenced on July 7, 1962; six months later he was enrolled. When his application first reached the college, the school offered a show of resistance, for his admission would signalize the state's capitulation, despite recent boasts of its leadership that "the time for desegregation in South Carolina is NEVER." The state did not want Negroes in white schools, but it wanted even less to risk the disorders that had brought Mississippi into disrepute. Leading citizens of South Carolina in government and business, determined not to scare off industries in search of southern sites, and eager to protect Clemson's rising reputation, were joined by the governor and the school's administration in laying careful plans for Gantt's peaceable reception and for making certain that unauthorized visitors would not stir up strife on the day of the change-over. More than 150 newsmen gathered on the campus to report the historic event—many of them veterans of the "Battle of Oxford"—but they had little to relate on a day that was as momentous as it was uneventful.

There remained only one state where the line still held against successful admission of the first Negro in a white school—Alabama, where, after Autherine Lucy's three-day stay at the University in 1955, official opposition was still overwhelming. But here too, a determined United States Department of Justice faced down an astonishingly stubborn Governor George C. Wallace, when, in June 1963, a Negro matriculated at the university under court order.

[1] John F. Kennedy, Proclamation No. 3497, Septebmer 30, 1962; 3 *Code of Federal Regulations*, 1959–1963 Compilation, 225.

Confronted by a request from Vivian Malone and other Negroes, the school on May 16 asked the federal district court for a clarification of the judgment it had rendered in 1955. The court replied that the earlier ruling which had forbidden the university to deny blacks the right to enroll was still binding upon the successors of the officers it had originally enjoined. On May 24, the federal district court, after the United States had filed a complaint that the governor of Alabama had publicly declared that he would bar Negroes from the institution, entered an order requiring him to show cause why a preliminary injunction should not be issued estopping his threatened obstruction. The governor was unmoved, and on June 5 the court granted the petitioners a writ prohibiting the governor from "preventing, blocking or interfering with, by physically interposing his person or that of any other person . . . the entry of Vivian J. Malone to the campus . . . for the purpose of enrollment as a student." Judge Seybourn H. Lynne concluded his memorandum opinion with these unconventional words:[1]

> It clearly appears that unless an injunction is issued pending submission of this action on the prayer for final relief in a trial on the merits, the plaintiff will suffer irreparable injury resulting from obstruction to the lawful orders of this court and the consequent impairment of the judicial process of the United States.
>
> May it be forgiven if this court makes use of the personal pronoun for the first time in a written opinion. I love the people of Alabama. I know that many of both races are troubled and, like Jonah of old, are "angry unto death" as the result of distortions of affairs within the state, practiced in the name of sensationalism. My prayer is that all of our people in keeping with our finest traditions, will join in the resolution that law and order be maintained, both in Tuscaloosa and in Huntsville.

True to his public pledge ("I shall refuse to abide by illegal court orders to the point of standing at the schoolhouse door"), Governor Wallace ignored the injunction and prepared to put up what he must have known was hopeless resistance. The country, which had witnessed the Mississippi episode with troubled fascination, now stopped to watch the crisis in Alabama.

The governor ordered out a five-hundred-man military police unit to be ready to assist law enforcement contingents in the university area on Sunday, June 9. He had, besides, more than four hundred state troopers and some four hundred revenue agents, game wardens, and other state personnel patrolling the region. On Monday President Kennedy wired the governor, firmly warning him not to carry out his schoolhouse-door vow. On Tuesday the governor stationed himself at the door of the building in which students were to register for the summer session. Federal officials advanced upon the door, while Miss Malone was left

[1] *United States* v. *Wallace,* 218 F. Supp. 290 (N.D. Ala. 1963).

sitting in an automobile, both for her safety and, presumably, to make it easy for the governor to perform his ritual without actually violating the injunction—which only forbade him to block the entry of Miss Malone by interposing his person. As the federal officers advanced within a few steps of the governor, he thrust out his hand and said "Stop!"

What followed was little more than a solemn farce, for few doubted that the students (there were in fact two) would be admitted, that Wallace would not invite a jail sentence, and that the Department of Justice would not unnecessarily goad the South. The dialogue began when Assistant Attorney General Nicholas Katzenbach temperately called upon the governor to "give unequivocal assurance that you will not bar entry to these students."

"We don't want to hear any speeches," snapped the governor, who then proceeded to read a proclamation that began:[1]

> As Governor and Chief Magistrate of the State of Alabama, I deem it to be my solemn obligation and duty to stand before you representing the rights and sovereignty of this state and its people.
>
> The unwelcome, unwanted, unwarranted and force-induced intrusion upon the campus of the University of Alabama today of the might of the Central Government offers frightful example of oppression of the rights, privileges and sovereignty of this state by officers of the Federal Government. . . .

Then, after a brief discourse on federal-state relations, phrased in the logic of the South Carolina Nullifiers of 1828–30, the governor continued:

> I stand here today, as Governor of this sovereign state, and refuse to willingly submit to illegal usurpation of power by the Central Government. I claim today for all the people of the state of Alabama those rights reserved to them under the Constitution of the United States. . . . [I am] raising basic and fundamental constitutional questions. My action is a call for strict adherence to the Constitution of the United States as it was written. . . . My action seeks to avoid having state sovereignty sacrificed on the altar of political expediency . . . I . . . denounce and forbid this illegal and unwarranted action by the Central Government.

When the declamation was over, Katzenbach asked the governor to step aside. Wallace only glared at him. "From the outset, Governor," said Katzenbach, "all of us have known that the final chapter of this history will be the admission of these students."

Still Wallace stood defiantly at his station. "Very well," said Katzenbach, and as he turned away the federal marshal escorted the two Negro students to their dormitories. Katzenbach then telephoned the Attorney General, who called the President, who, in turn, ordered the

[1] RRLR VIII, 457.

Alabama National Guard into the federal service. Later that afternoon, Brigadier General Henry V. Graham of the Thirty-first Infantry, an Alabama Guard Division, strode up to the governor in the doorway, saluted, reported that the Guard had been federalized, and ended saying: "Please stand aside so that the order of the court may be accomplished."

Wallace read a final statement and walked away. Within minutes the two black students were led into the building and were registered. The last total-segregation state had surrendered. And although only two Negroes had as yet crossed the fateful line, the magnitude of this day's business was not lost upon students of America's constitutional history.

As in the case of elementary and secondary schools, colleges and universities accelerated their rate of integration under the prodding of Title VI of the 1964 Civil Rights Act. When compliance officers from the United States Office for Civil Rights (OCR) began visiting campuses early in 1968, they supplemented data already available to them from a nationwide questionnaire survey of 2900 such schools which OCR had conducted in the fall of 1967.

The situation in the 1967–68 school year stood thus, according to figures supplied by the U.S. Civil Rights Commission:[1] approximately a fourth (26 percent) of the southern and border region's 184,600 Negro college and university students were in predominantly white (most of them formerly *all*-white) institutions of higher learning. (Negroes comprised approximately 11 percent of the region's total college population of approximately 1,700,000.) For the eleven southern states the percentage of Negroes in biracial, predominantly white schools was somewhat less: there twenty-one percent of the Negro students were in 414 of that section's 455 predominantly white colleges and universities. There were, of course, wide variations among the several states. In Florida 45.7 percent and in Texas 43.5 percent of all Negro college and university students were in predominantly white schools; in Alabama, Georgia, and Mississippi, the figures were 9.8, 9.4, and 7.6 percent, respectively.

To summarize: 26 percent of the 184,600 Negro college students in the eleven southern states, the six border states, and the District of Columbia were in predominantly white schools in the fall of 1967; 8.5 percent were in all-Negro schools; 65.5 percent were in biracial but predominantly black schools. The last figure fades into insignificance, however, when it is recalled that "biracial predominantly Negro schools" had extremely small white enrollments, sometimes as few as one or two students. Some 70 percent of the 184,600 Negro students were in public colleges and 30 percent in private schools. Moreover, of the 47,918 Negro students in predominantly white colleges and univer-

[1] *Southern Education Report*, III (April, 1968), 40–41.

sities in the southern and border states and the District of Columbia, more than 85 percent were in public, and less than 15 percent in private, institutions.

A new study by John Egerton of the Southern Education Reporting Service, published in the spring of 1969, showed that while 11 percent of the population of the United States is black, no predominantly white state college or university in the country in 1969 had a black enrollment approximating that proportion. In the eighty formerly all-white or nearly all-white colleges and universities surveyed in the study, less than 2 percent of the students and less than 1 percent of the faculty were blacks. In 1969 the institutions which were formerly all black were still largely black, and they still enrolled a majority of the nation's black college students. Some of these latter institutions were, moreover, far more integrated than almost any formerly all-white institution. So new was the movement of black students into predominantly white colleges and universities that early in 1969 half of the black students in these schools were freshmen. The report also emphasized that the slowly gathering momentum of college and university desegregation was beginning in a significant measure to drain off the best students and teachers from the predominantly black schools.

Less than four years after Governor Wallace had unwillingly stepped aside to admit the first Negro as a "permanent" student at Alabama, there were some three hundred blacks among the 17,621 students on the university's five campuses, ninety-three of them at the main campus in Tuscaloosa. A lonely group, ostracized by their white fellows, the black students went quietly about their business, housed and fed in unsegregated dormitories and dining halls, and encountering little serious friction.

This gradual and grudging integration of formerly all-white colleges in fact attracted little public notice after 1964. Far more newsworthy was the militant Black Student Movement that first blazed into prominence in 1967 and 1968. From New York to California, black students, so lately excluded, now denounced the institutions in which they were enrolled, on the ground that the white-oriented education they were receiving had no relevance to their needs, that administrators were obstructing Negro admissions and systematically keeping blacks from achieving places on their faculties.

Sometimes allied with whites who were vociferously demonstrating against the Viet Nam war or for "student control" of the campuses (or both), the Black Student Movement was at many schools vigorously organized and led, based on sustained anger and excitement, and going in some cases to the length of deranging the institutions' entire programs, seizing and occupying offices and buildings, and even holding administrators captive. There was as yet, at the close of 1969, no national organization to coordinate the rebellion; the insurgent groups were typically campus-wide only, and it is doubtful that an actual majority of the black students was actively and enthusiastically (or voluntarily) involved on any of the campuses swept by the revolt.

Some of the groups limited themselves to vague demands that the curricula be made more "relevant," and that black students be given "a piece of the action," but others issued ultimata that contemplated full-scale "black studies" programs, to be taught and administered by blacks only (whose appointment should be partially, if not wholly, vested in students), assisted by black deans of black student affairs. Failure to meet the demands was to court a paralyzing strike and the risk of physical violence to college property, if not to personnel. Especially heavy pressures were exerted for courses in Afro-American history, culture, literature, music, etc., either grafted onto the general curriculum, so that all students, black and white, would "get the picture," or leading to a special degree. Another insistent demand was for courses in the history and culture of Africa, including its history, religion, economics, and languages. Not unusually, the proposals called for autonomous control, by the Negro students, of the black studies programs, independent of the institution's regular administration, and even of its board of trustees. On some campuses the demand was for a department of black studies. At the University of California at Berkeley militant blacks made common cause with Mexican Americans (Chicanos), Asians, and Native Americans (Indians) to press for a College of Ethnic Studies, with departments for each of those groups.

The student rebels could not be ignored. Some of the country's colleges and universities, including Harvard, Yale, Northwestern, Ohio State, Brandeis, and San Francisco State (the latter with little success in preventing campus revolution) had, in fact, begun moving toward meeting the blacks' demands in anticipation of student pressure. Countless predominantly white colleges were by 1968 methodically seeking qualified black students and faculty members— sometimes to the alarm of the country's predominantly Negro institutions who looked upon such "raiding" with mixed emotions. Early in 1969 Harvard was completing plans for what amounted to a full-scale major in black studies.

Prominent among the student black power "peace terms" was an insistence upon greatly increased recruitment of black students, even if this required relaxation of normal admission requirements(which, the rebels argued, were calibrated to white middle class backgrounds and experience); the systematic search for more black athletes; hiring of far more black professors, administrators, counselors, and athletic coaches; special tutoring for blacks; and the outlawing of the term "Negro" in favor of some such term as "Black" or "Afro-American." Particularly startling to many whites who were not familiar with the spirit of the movement was the clamor for separate living quarters (complete with "soul food" in the dining halls) for black students—a shattering repudiation of the older drive for integration and interracial cooperation which the old-line civil rights organizations had so long espoused.

Perhaps nothing in the Negro's struggle in the 1960's so dramatically demonstrated the pace of change as the contrast between the close of the previous decade, when black students were still knocking in vain for mere admission, and a brief half dozen years later when, once inside campus gates, they turned in a towering rage upon the schools to which they had gained entrance, to confront them with the alternative of capitulation to black demands or total disruption of the institution's program.

Private Institutions of Higher Learning

The Civil Rights Act of 1964 placed private colleges and universities under the same requirement as that applied to public institutions of higher learning, by which assurance of nondiscrimination must be filed as a precondition for participating in federally assisted programs. As a result, the barriers to enrollment of qualified Negroes in such private institutions promptly began to fall away, except where, as in the case of some church-related schools, they were willing to forgo the boon of federal funds.

A special problem, however, was that of private schools whose charters, at the instance of founders and benefactors, confined enrollment to whites. The answer, once litigation was instituted, was not long in coming. Two cases in point were those of Rice University in Texas and Sweet Briar College in Virginia.[1]

In the former, restrictions in its original trust and charter forbade the university to charge tuition and to admit Negroes. The Texas courts, the state supreme court affirming, released the university from the restriction on pragmatic grounds. The benefactor of the school had intended, said the court, that it become an institution of highest quality. The enormous increase in the costs of maintaining a university of the first rank, and the "changes in habits, customs, laws and economic conditions of the State and nation," now made it impossible to realize the founder's intention unless the stipulated restrictions be rescinded, because the cost of maintaining the university required that the no-tuition proviso be repealed, and because "under present conditions a university which discriminates in the selection of teachers and students on the basis of race cannot attain or retain the status of a first-class school."

[1] *Coffee* v. *Rice University,* 408 S.W. 2d 269 (Civ. App. Tex., 1966); and *Sweet Briar Institute* v. *Button,* July 14, 1967 (W.D. Va.). See RRLR XII, 1188.

The suit, incidentally, had been brought by the university itself, not by an aggrieved plaintiff. A similar action arose at Sweet Briar College. Here too the school itself brought suit to prevent the state of Virginia from forcing it to comply with a trust provision designating the funds "for the education of white girls and young women." Pointing, as did Rice University, to the impediments that racial discrimination would put in the way of recruiting excellent faculty members and students, and in the way of sharing in federal funds, the college won from the United States district court a ruling that the state could not require compliance with the white-only clause in the founder's will, because such enforcement would be state action forbidden by the Fourteenth Amendment.

More attention was attracted by the "Girard College Case." Established in Philadelphia in 1848 under the will of a wealthy merchant, Stephen Girard, who had specified that enrollment was to be confined to "poor, white, male orphans," the school (in fact a secondary school, not a college) did not enroll a Negro until the autumn of 1968, when several black students were at last admitted.

As long ago as 1855 a Pennsylvania court had denied a petition that the restriction be set aside; and as late as 1956, the 1855 judgment was affirmed upon challenge. Then followed years of legal wrangling. In 1957 private trustees took over the administration of the school from the city of Philadelphia by state court order, after the United States Supreme Court had ruled that the board of trustees was an agency of the state, acting in violation of the Fourteenth Amendment.

Eventually the Commonwealth of Pennsylvania, its attorney general, the city of Philadelphia, and seven Negro male orphans brought a class action in a federal district court against the trustees of the Girard estate, to enjoin the continued denial of admission to blacks. In July 1967 came the court's decision in *Commonwealth of Pennsylvania* v. *Brown*[1] (subsequently sustained on appeal), based on *Evans* v. *Newton,* a 1966 case involving a privately endowed park.[2]

> . . . Girard [College] undeniably performs a service to its students which would otherwise *have* to be performed by the public school system, since students at Girard are, by definition, unable to pay for education. In addition, there is substantial evidence of collaboration between the College and principals at various City public schools. . . . [T]he College relies in part on the resources of the City schools, and the public schools look upon the College as an obvious agency to which to refer "qualified" students, who, by definition, must be "white." . . . Thus, while Girard College is not a facility of general access to the public or even necessarily to the school-age population, it has always held itself out as an institution whose benefits are available to *any* needy, fatherless boy—as long as he is "white." In this sense, the College

[1] 276 F. Supp. 782 (E.D. Pa. 1967).
[2] See above, p. 507.

has become assimilated to a public boarding school or orphanage, "municipal in nature," the sole distinguishing feature of which at the present time is its racial restriction. . . . The Orphans' Court has demanded, uniquely as to this trust, periodic accountings and has, for all the record shows, accepted and approved them. Pennsylvania has overseen and approved both the education and upbringing of students at Girard College and the operation of the institution as a school and as an orphanage, serving an obviously public function. . . . We . . . find it logically and legally impossible to escape the conclusion that racial exclusion at Girard College is so afflicted with State action, in its widened concept, that it cannot constitutionally endure. Since the strictures of the Fourteenth Amendment apply to the administration of the institution, it may no longer deny admission to applicants simply because they are not "white."

C. *The Franchise: Equality in Sight*

Although the Fifteenth Amendment had since 1870 underwritten the Negro's right to vote, its effectuation in much of the country relied almost wholly upon private suits brought by aggrieved Negroes at their own expense, to say nothing of other risks. Some relief came with the Civil Rights Act of 1957, which gave the Attorney General of the United States statutory power to institute such suits in behalf of particular persons. These Justice Department proceedings were often countered, however, by dilatory tactics, and at best a court victory brought redress to only an individual or a small group. And because the courts did not countenance suits against a state or its agents, local registrars could frustrate the proceedings by resigning from office while suits were pending. Moreover, the Civil Rights Commission was gravely handicapped in its investigations of alleged violations, by the refusal of registrars to permit the Commission to inspect voting records, and, in at least one state, by legislation permitting registrars to destroy all past records of registration.

The franchise provisions of the Civil Rights Acts of 1960 and 1964 improved matters somewhat, but, so far as any significant increase in Negro registration is concerned, the results were still negligible. Court cases arising from the legislation were therefore not of landmark importance, because the really effective federal enforcement of the Fifteenth Amendment came with the Civil Rights Act (known as the Voting Rights Act) of 1965.[1]

Before the latter act began producing its dramatic results, there were a few cases that should be noted here. In the first suit under the Act of 1957 its constitutionality was sustained.[2] This action also invalidated

[1] See above, p. 420 ff.

[2] *United States* v. *Raines,* 362 U.S. 17 (1960).

literacy and interpretation tests because of the discriminatory manner in which they were administered. Later that year came a more widely noticed case, which raised a unique issue.

An Alabama statute of 1957, redrawing the boundaries of the city of Tuskegee, substituted "a strangely irregular twenty-eight-sided figure" for what had been a square, for the obvious purpose, and the undisputed effect, of "removing from the city all save four or five of its four hundred Negro voters, while not removing a single white voter or resident." A federal district court and a court of appeals had dismissed the complaint of five Negroes against this astonishing gerrymander, holding that "the power of increase and diminution of municipal territory is plenary, inherent, and discretionary in the legislature, and, when duly exercised, cannot be revised by the courts."

On further appeal, the Supreme Court reversed, and ordered the district court to determine the truthfulness of the allegations in the plaintiffs' original suit. The charges that the purpose and effect of the statute was to deny plaintiffs the right to vote in city elections and to participate in other rights of municipal citizenship, if proven true, would, said the Court:[1]

> . . . abundantly establish that [the] Act . . . was not an ordinary geographic redistricting measure even within familiar abuses of gerrymandering. If these allegations upon a trial remained uncontradicted or unqualified, the conclusion would be irresistible, tantamount for all practical purposes to a mathematical demonstration, that the legislation is solely concerned with segregating white and colored voters by fencing Negro citizens out of town so as to deprive them of their pre-existing vote. . . .
>
> It is difficult to appreciate what stands in the way of adjudging a statute having this inevitable effect invalid in light of the principles by which this Court must judge, and uniformly has judged, statutes that, howsoever speciously defined, obviously discriminate against colored citizens. "The [Fifteenth] Amendment nullifies sophisticated as well as simple-minded modes of discrimination." Lane v. Wilson. . . . [The offending statute was struck down for unconstitutionality, and the trial court subsequently issued an injunction estopping its enforcement.]

One of the most successful devices for frustrating the intent of the Civil Rights Act of 1957 was the mass resignation of registrars, thus leaving the United States no party to sue. A case in point is *United States* v. *Alabama*.[2] Two months before the commencement of the action the allegedly offending registrar resigned, leaving the office vacant. The Justice Department then amended its complaint, naming the State of Alabama and the Board of Registrars as defendants, along with those who had resigned. The district and circuit courts dismissed the case, holding that the resigned registrars could no longer be tried as

[1] *Gomillion* v. *Lightfoot*, 364 U.S. 339 (1960).
[2] 171 F. Supp. 720 (M.D. Ala. 1959).

officials, that the Board of Registrars is not suable, and that the Act of 1957 did not authorize actions against a state. Before the case reached the Supreme Court, however, the Civil Rights Act of 1960 was enacted, expressly authorizing such action against a state, and the case was remanded for further proceedings.

In another series of cases, Negroes stricken from registration rolls by challenge (claiming their ineligibility on one ground or another) were ordered to be restored because the challenges that had producd the erasures had not conformed to procedures prescribed by law; for example, notices had not been mailed to challenged voters, challengers had failed to make affidavits, and notices had not been published in newspapers.

During the years between the passage of the Acts of 1957 and 1965, the most effective means of limiting the right to vote was the "reading-and-interpretation" test, administered, along with other qualification tests, by local registrars in whom wide discretion was vested. Although the Justice Department had power to sue, litigation proved to be extremely protracted and reached only a minor fraction of the counties in which Negro registration was being restrained.

In the first three years after the 1957 Act, in the Eisenhower Administration, only ten voting cases were filed. Then, in the three Kennedy years, nearly fifty more were instituted. Meanwhile, a climate increasingly favorable to more effective civil rights laws was engendered by a number of unpunished brutalities in the Deep South. The murder of Medgar Evers, in Jackson, in the summer of 1963, and the death by bombing of four black children in a Birmingham church a few months later (as well as the assassination of President Kennedy, who had called for stronger civil rights laws), helped to produce the Act of 1964. And then the killing of three civil rights workers in Mississippi, the shotgun slaying of Lemuel Penn on a Georgia highway, the bombing of numerous Negro churches, and the brutal beating of voter-registration demonstrators (witnessed by millions of their countrymen on television newscasts) in Selma, Alabama, expedited the passage of the Act of 1965.

The new measure differed from the federal civil rights legislation of 1957, 1960, and 1964 by providing for direct federal action to enable Negroes, without protracted lawsuits and legal maneuvers, to register and vote. The results were startling. In the counties of six southern states to which examiners had been dispatched, for example, the percentage of Negroes of voting age who were on the registration books immediately before the act's passage was only 17.3. Two years later it stood at 71.6. In Mississippi the figure climbed from 8.1 to 70.9 percent. Two years after the enactment, in every southern state black registration exceeded 50 percent of those of voting age.

This is not to say that all of the newly registered Negroes voted. The

United States Commission on Civil Rights still received reports of threats (and some instances) of violence, reprisal, and economic sanctions. Southern states and counties also resorted to various devices for "diluting the Negro vote," among them such practices[1] as (1) switching to at-large elections; (2) consolidation of counties as a means of gerrymandering; (3) redistricting with a view to minimizing the weight of the black vote: (4) full-slate elections, to prevent "single-shot" and "block" voting. Measures were also found to discourage, and indeed prevent, Negroes from becoming candidates, or obtaining public office: abolishing the offices; extending the terms of white encumbents; substituting appointment for elections; increasing filing fees; adding to existing requirements for getting on the ballot; withholding information, such as the time and place of nominating conventions and party meetings; and imposing barriers to the assumption of office—illustrated by the refusal of the Georgia legislature to seat Julian Bond, allegedly because of his "disloyal" criticism of the Selective Service System and of United States policy in Viet Nam.

Even so, Negro voter participation was enormously increased, and office-holding substantially so. The Civil Rights Commission's report on *Political Participation* (1968) lists more than 250 Negro holders of public office in the South on December 15, 1967, a number that was soon to increase to 400. Included among these were two sheriffs, three state senators, twenty representatives, scores of city councilmen and school board members, and numerous justices of the peace. It was only a very small beginning, but a beginning that few would have dared to predict a decade earlier.

Cases arising under the 1965 Act began to reach the courts almost at once. One such example is the case of the *United States* v. *Ward and Louisiana*.[2]

This action arose in 1963 when a United States district court had found that a state law requiring applicants for registration to establish their identification had been used in a discriminatory manner, requiring more burdensome proofs from Negroes than from whites. The court, by injunction, forbade the practice. Thereupon the Department of Justice appealed to the Fifth Circuit Court of Appeals, alleging that the court below should have employed the "freezing principle," making the standards formerly applied only to whites uniformly applicable to all, instead of using the new and more severe criteria. The court pointed out that the current (new) standards would subject Negroes to stricter requirements than those which at least 1,760 permanently registered

[1] Described in U.S. Commission on Civil Rights, *Political Participation* (Washington, 1968).

[2] 352 F. 2d 329 (5th Cir. 1965). The resulting district court order is Civil Action No. 8547, October 22, 1965 (W.D. La.), and is reprinted in RRLR X, 1697.

whites had been required to meet, at a time when virtually no blacks were being registered. The court then issued the "freeze" order for a *two*-year period.

Soon thereafter the Voting Rights Act of 1965 was passed, and the United States filed a petition for rehearing of the 1963 action in the court of appeals, because the legislation now authorized a five-year "freezing period" in order to allow Negroes to "catch up" with whites who had qualified for registration under the older, more lenient rules. The government also cited the provision of the statute which forbade the use, during this five-year period, of any voter qualification test or device as defined by the act, regardless of whether whites had previously been subjected to them. An order was drawn to that effect and, in addition, detailed specific guidelines for conducting registration were set forth, a procedure for reviewing rejections was prescribed, and written monthly reports, regarding progress of compliance, were ordered filed with the court for the inspection of the United States.

Because it so well expresses the highly significant shift from the older pattern of individual suits brought on the initiative of individual aggrieved Negroes, to the newer tactic of vigilant monitoring of the registration process, the final decree handed down by the trial court upon order of the court of appeals is here reproduced at some length:

> I. This Court finds that the defendants have engaged in acts and practices which have deprived Negro citizens of Madison Parish, Louisiana, of their rights secured by 42 USCA §1971 (a) to register to vote without distinction by reason of race, and that such deprivation has been pursuant to a pattern or practice of discrimination against Negro citizens in the registration processes in Madison Parish, Louisiana. . . .
>
> II. It is ordered, adjudged and decreed by the Court that the Defendant State of Louisiana and the Defendant Katherine Ward, Registrar of Voters of Madison Parish, Louisiana, their agents, . . . and successors in office . . . are hereby enjoined from engaging in any act or practice which involves or results in distinctions based on race or color between Negro citizens and other citizens in the registration for voting process in Madison Parish . . .
>
> III. It is further ordered, adjudged, and decreed by the Court that the Defendant State of Louisiana and the Defendant Katherine Ward . . . , their agents, officers, employees and successors in office . . . be hereby enjoined, for a period of five years after the entry of any final judgment of any court of the United States determining that denials or abridgments of the right to vote on account of race or color through the use of any "test or device" as defined in . . . the Voting Rights Act of 1965, have occurred anywhere within the State of Louisiana, and in any event until the United States District Court for the District of Columbia has determined that no such test or device has been used during the five years preceding the filing of the action for the purpose of denying or abridging the right to vote on account of race or color, from (a) requiring any applicant for voter registration in Madison Parish, as a precondition to such registration, to take or pass any test of literacy, knowledge, or understanding or to comply with any

other test or device as defined in . . . the Voting Rights Act of 1965, i.e., any requirement (including the "good character" requirement specified in Article VIII, Section 1(c) of the Louisiana Constitution and Title 18, Section 32, of the Louisiana Code, except to the extent that these provisions permit disqualification for conviction of a felony) that he (1) demonstrate the ability to read, write, understand, or interpret any matter, (2) demonstrate any educational achievement or his knowledge of any particular subject, (3) possess good moral character, or (4) prove his qualifications by the voucher of registered voters or members of any other class, or (b) rejecting any applicant for voter registration in Madison Parish for failure to comply with any such requirement.

IV. It is further ordered . . . that for the period specified in paragraph III . . . the Defendant State of Louisiana and the Defendant Katherine Ward, Registrar of Voters of Madison Parish, Louisiana, their agents, officers, employees, and successors in office are enjoined from determining the qualifications of citizens in Madison Parish, Louisiana in any manner . . . different from or more stringent than the following:

(a) He is a citizen and will have attained the age of 21 years prior to the next election;
(b) He has resided in the State for one year, the Parish six months and the Precinct three months prior to the next election;
(c) He is not disqualified by reason of conviction of a disqualifying crime.

V. It is further ordered that Defendant Katherine Ward, her agents, employees, and successors, in conducting registration of voters in Madison Parish, Louisiana, are enjoined and ordered to:

(a) Afford each applicant for registration an opportunity to apply to register whether either the registrar or a deputy registrar is present;
(b) Accept from Negro applicants for registration reasonable proof of their identity, such as:
    (1) Authentic licenses or permits issued by any governmental agency or authority, such as driving, hunting, or fishing licenses, library cards, or automobile registrations;
    (2) Authentic military identification documents, such as selective service registration cards, discharge papers, or reserve unit identification cards;
    (3) Authentic records of the possession or ownership of real property, such as rent receipts, deeds or contracts to purchase or lease, receipts for deposits on utilities, or homestead exemption certificates.
(c) Advise each applicant whether [he] is accepted or rejected; if accepted, the applicant must be registered at that time; if rejected the applicant must be informed of the . . . reasons for his rejection and must be advised of his right to apply directly to this Court to be registered as provided in paragraph VI hereof.
(d) Receive and process each applicant as expeditiously as possible to the extent that the physical facilities of the registration office permit but in no case less than [two] applicants at one time; in no case refuse to process fewer than [two] applicants at one time, and take all reasonable steps to insure that, wherever possible, each applicant is processed on the day he appears for registration. The office of the registrar shall be open during regular business hours for registration from Monday through Friday of each week except on holidays.

VI. Any applicant for registration hereafter rejected or not given the opportunity to apply by the Defendant Katherine Ward, her agents, employees, or successors, may in accordance with 42 USCA §1971 (e) apply to this Court, or to a voting referee to be appointed by and in the discretion of this Court, no more than 20 days after receipt by the Court of the first application, to have his qualifications determined. The Court or such referee shall register all such applicants who meet the standards established in this order.

VII. It is further ordered that the Defendant Katherine Ward, her agents, employees, and successors in office shall file a written report with the clerk of this Court and shall mail a copy thereof to the Plaintiff's attorneys on or before the tenth day of each month. Said reports shall state the dates and places applications were received and the hours during which the Registrars were available to receive applications; and also shall contain the name and race of each applicant for registration from the previous monthly period, the date of the application, the action taken on the application, and if the applicant is rejected, the specific reason or reasons for rejecting the application. . . .

VIII. The Defendant Katherine Ward, her deputies, agents, and successors in office shall, until further order of this Court, make the registration records of Madison Parish, Louisiana, available to attorneys or agents of the United States at any and all reasonable times for the purpose of inspection, copying, and photographing.

IX. Jurisdiction is retained of this cause for all purposes and especially for the purpose of issuing any and all additional orders as may become necessary or appropriate for the purposes of modifying and/or enforcing this order.

X. Costs in this Court are awarded to Plaintiff and taxed against the Defendants.

The court did not, in the foregoing case, feel called upon to go to the question of constitutionality of the 1965 Act. That issue was specifically raised in the action now to be examined.

Soon after the passage of the Voting Rights Act of 1965 the state of South Carolina filed a motion in the United States Supreme Court to bring an original suit challenging the constitutionality of the law, and asking for an injunction against its enforcement. The motion was promptly granted, and the case was expedited. After hearing extensive arguments, a unanimous Court (with Justice Black dissenting on some particulars) upheld the act as an appropriate measure for congressional enforcement of the Fifteenth Amendment. The carefully drafted thirty-one page document is summarized below:[1]

Recognizing that the questions presented were of urgent concern to the entire country, we invited all the States to participate in this proceeding as friends of the Court. A majority responded by submitting or joining in briefs on the merits some supporting South Carolina [five southern states] and others [twenty states of the North, West, and Border South] the Attorney General. Seven of these States also requested and received permission to argue the case orally in our hearing. Without exception, despite the emotional overtones of the proceeding, the briefs and oral arguments were

[1] *South Carolina* v. *Katzenbach,* 383 U.S. 301 (1966).

temperate, lawyer-like and constructive . . . and this additional assistance has been most helpful to the Court.

The Voting Rights Act was designed by Congress to banish the blight of racial discrimination in voting, which has infected the electoral process in parts of our country for nearly a century. The Act creates stringent new remedies for voting discrimination where it persists on a pervasive scale, and in addition the statute strengthens existing remedies for pockets of voting discrimination elsewhere in the country. Congress assumed the power to prescribe these remedies from [section] 2 of the Fifteenth Amendment, which authorizes the national legislature to effectuate by "appropriate means" the constitutional prohibition against racial discrimination in voting. We hold that the sections of the Act which are properly before us are an appropriate means for carrying out Congress' constitutional responsibilities and are consonant with all other provisions of the Constitution. We therefore deny South Carolina's request that enforcement of these sections of the Act be enjoined.

. . . Two points emerge vividly from the voluminous legislative history of the Act contained in the committee hearings and floor debates. First: Congress felt itself confronted by an insidious and pervasive evil which had been perpetuated in certain parts of our country through unremitting and ingenious defiance of the Constitution. Second: Congress concluded that the unsuccessful remedies which it had prescribed in the past would have to be replaced by sterner and more elaborate measures in order to satisfy the clear commands of the Fifteenth Amendment.

[The opinion then summarized the history of the Negro suffrage and of the unavailing attempts to insure it, from 1870 to the passage of the 1965 Act, and asserted that:]

The Voting Rights Act of 1965 reflects Congress' firm intention to rid the country of racial discrimination in voting. [Then follows a detailed analysis of the bill's general structure; the coverage formula; provisions relating to the suspension of tests, the review of new rules, and the employment of federal examiners.]

[The Court next proceeded to rebut the plaintiff's argument that the statute was not an appropriate means of enforcing the Fifteenth Amendment, but an unconstitutional extension of the powers of Congress, an encroachment upon powers reserved to the states, a violation of the principle of equality of the states; a denial of due process because it bars judicial review of administrative findings; a forbidden bill of attainder; and an impairment of separation of powers by adjudicating guilt through legislation.]

[Meeting these objections point by point, the Court went on to affirm that:]

Congress exercised its authority under the Fifteenth Amendment in an inventive manner [in] . . . the Voting Rights Act of 1965. First: The measure prescribes remedies for voting discrimination which go into effect without any need for prior adjudication. This was clearly a legitimate response to the problem, for which there is ample precedent under other constitutional provisions. . . . Congress had found that case-by-case litigation was inadequate to combat a widespread and persistent discrimination in voting, because of the inordinate amount of time and energy required to overcome the obstructionist tactics invariably encountered in these lawsuits. After enduring nearly a century of systematic resistance to the Fifteenth Amendment,

Congress might well decide to shift the advantage of time and inertia from the perpetrators of the evil to its victims. . . .

Second: The Act intentionally confines these remedies to a small number of States and political subdivisions which in most instances were familiar to Congress by name. This, too, was a permissible method of dealing with the problem. Congress . . . knew no way of accurately forecasting whether the evil might spread elsewhere in the future. In acceptable legislative fashion, Congress chose to limit its attention to the geographic areas where immediate action seemed necessary. . . . The doctrine of equality of States . . . applies only to the terms upon which States are admitted to the Union, and not to the remedies for local evils which have subsequently appeared.

[After addressing itself to the appropriateness of the several remedies the Act affords, the opinion concludes with the judgment that:]

After enduring nearly a century of widespread resistance to the Fifteenth Amendment, Congress has marshaled an array of potent weapons against the evil, with authority in the Attorney General to employ them effectively. Many of the areas directly affected by this development have indicated their willingness to abide by any restraints legitimately imposed upon them. We here hold that the portions of the Voting Rights Act properly before us are a valid means for carrying out the commands of the Fifteenth Amendment. Hopefully, millions of non-white Americans will now be able to participate for the first time on an equal basis in the government under which they live. We may finally look forward to the day when truly "the right of citizens of the United States to vote shall not be denied or abridged by the United States or by any State on account of race, color, or previous condition of servitude."

The bill of complaint is *Dismissed.*

It would appear that by mid-1969 the federal government possessed at last, in the legislation of 1957–1965, and in the construction the courts have placed upon it, the means for coping with Negro disfranchisement, whether it takes the form of violence, intimidation, and harassment or of devious, fraudulent, or intricately obstructive contrivances.

In its closing days the Warren court handed down a decision extending the protections afforded by the Voting Rights Act of 1965, while the Nixon Administration and congressional leaders were planning to weaken that law presumably to pay off political debts to the South.

The statute, it will be remembered,[1] had suspended the use of literacy tests and other devices in those states or counties in which less than 50 percent of the residents of voting age were registered on November 1, 1964, or voted in the 1964 presidential election. A state or county wishing to reinstate the test or device could do so if in a suit brought before a three-judge federal district court, it could establish "that no such test or device has been used during the five years preceding . . . for the purpose of denying or abridging the right to vote on account of race or color."

[1] See above, p. 420 ff.

On June 2, 1969, the Supreme Court disposed of such an appeal by a North Carolina county, by taking the position that wherever the *effect* of such a test or device was to exclude persons on the grounds of race, however innocent the intention of the test may have been, the test may not be reinstated. Taking recourse again in the Warren court's familiar pragmatism, the judges held, in a 7 to 1 decision, that *past* discrimination in the school system of the county had produced a higher degree of illiteracy among blacks than among whites, and that the literacy test,[1] therefore, in violation of the Fifteenth Amendment, abridged the right to vote on account of color.[2]

The case had first been heard in the District Court of the District of Columbia, which had ruled in favor of the aggrieved black citizen on much the same grounds that the Supreme Court now invoked. Earlier objections to literacy tests had rested heavily upon their unequal administration. Now even their perfectly fair and impartial application could not save them from the judicial negative:

> We conclude that in an action brought under . . . the Voting Rights Act of 1965, it is appropriate for a court to consider whether a literacy or educational requirement has the "effect of denying the right to vote on account of race or color" because the state or subdivision which seeks to impose the requirement has maintained separate and inferior schools for its Negro residents who are now of age. . . .
>
> Appellant urges that it administered the 1962 re-registration in a fair and impartial manner, and that in recent years it has made significant strides toward equalizing and integrating its school system. Although we accept these claims as true, they fall wide of the mark. Affording today's Negro youth equal educational opportunities will doubtless prepare them to meet, on equal terms, whatever standards of literacy are required when they reach voting age. It does nothing for their parents, however. From this record, we cannot escape the sad truth that throughout the years, Gaston County systematically deprived its black citizens of the educational opportunities it granted to its white citizens. "Impartial" administration of the literacy test today would serve only to perpetuate these inequities in a different form.
>
> The judgment of the District Court is
>
> *Affirmed.*

D. *Public Accommodations: Toward Equal Access*

Although federal laws and the Fourteenth Amendment, long before the *School Segregation* cases, had erected a paper bulwark against

[1] Which, incidentally, required only that an applicant, in as much time as he needed, be able to copy one sentence from the state constitution.

[2] *Gaston County* v. *United States,* 395 U.S. 285 (1969).

racial segregation in publicly owned and operated facilities and accommodations, the effectuation of the principle did not begin in earnest until *Brown* v. *Board.* Precisely one week after *Brown,* the Supreme Court remanded to a federal district court in Kentucky a case involving recreational facilities in Louisville. The lower court's judgment (made as long ago as 1951), while holding that the Negro plaintiffs were entitled to the use of facilities equal to those provided for whites, had been, on the basis of *Plessy* v. *Ferguson,* that such facilities might be separate. Now, however, the high court, on petition for certiorari, granted the writ, reversed and remanded, in this laconic judgment:[1]

PER CURIAM:
The petition for writ of certiorari is granted. The judgment is vacated and the case remanded for consideration in the light of the Segregation Cases decided May 17, 1954, *Brown* v. *Board of Education, et. al.,* 347 U.S. 483, 74 S. CT. 686, and conditions that now prevail.

In a similar action the Supreme Court on November 7, 1955, affirmed a decision of a court of appeals that the Fourteenth Amendment's equal protection clause forbade the state of Maryland to invoke its police power to enforce racial segregation on public beaches and in public bathhouses. The court of appeals had held as follows:[2]

It is now obvious . . . that segregation cannot be justified as a means to preserve the public peace merely because the tangible facilities furnished to one race are equal to those furnished the other. The Supreme Court expressed the opinion in *Brown* v. *Board of Education of Topeka* . . . that it must consider public education in the light of its full development and its present place in American life, and therefore could not turn the clock back . . . but must also take into account the psychological factors recognized at this time, including the feeling of inferiority generated in the hearts and minds of Negro children "when separated solely because of their race from those of similar age and qualification." With this in mind, it is obvious that racial segregation in recreational activities can no longer be sustained as a proper exercise of the police power of the State; for if that power cannot be invoked to sustain racial segregation in the schools, where attendance is compulsory and racial friction may be apprehended from the enforced commingling of the races, it cannot be sustained with respect to public beach and bathhouse facilities, the use of which is entirely optional.

On the same day that the Court handed down its *per curiam* ruling in the Baltimore case, it held that the city of Atlanta could not deny the use of its municipal golf courses to citizens because of color. Upon remand the district court in which the case had originated, in obedience to the Supreme Court's ruling that it "enter a decree for petitioners

[1] *Muir* v. *Theatrical Park Association,* 347 U.S. 397 (1954).
[2] *Dawson* v. *Mayor and City Council of Baltimore,* 220 F. 2d 386 (4th Cir. 1955).

in conformity with *Dawson* v. *Mayor and City Council of Baltimore*," issued an order that:[1]

> the defendants . . . are hereby restrained and enjoined from making any distinction on account of race or color . . . in providing opportunities, advantages and facilities for playing the game of golf upon the public golf courses that are . . . provided by the City of Atlanta. . . . It is further ordered that this judgment and decree take effect immediately.

It was soon made clear also that a city could not, by *leasing* recreation facilities, evade its duty to make them available to all persons without regard to color. Dr. George Simkins, a Negro dentist, and five companions were denied access to a municipal golf course which the city of Greensboro, North Carolina, had leased to the "Gillespie Park Golf Club." After tendering the fee, which the course's attendants refused, the Negro golfers proceeded to play the course but were arrested, and later convicted in a state court. When they appealed to federal district court for injunctive relief, the court entered a decree restraining the defendants from discriminating against the plaintiffs or other Negro residents of the city in the use of the course and from disposing of the golf course other than by a bona fide sale. The opinion, later concurred in by the court of appeals, read in part:[2]

> The plaintiffs as citizens of the City of Greensboro are entitled to the equal protection of the law and cannot be deprived of their rights solely on account of color. The doctrine of *Plessy* v. *Ferguson* . . . of equal but separate facilities, has been overruled in *Brown* v. *Board of Education*. . . . The facts show that the City is still "in the saddle," so far as real control of the park is concerned and that the so-called lease can be disregarded, if and when, the City decides to do it. It also lends powerful weight to the inference that the lease was resorted to in the first instance to evade the City's duty not to discriminate against any of its citizens in the enjoyment in the use of the park . . . If the lessee desires to continue to operate the golf course, it must do so without discrimination against the citizens of Greensboro. This public right can not be abridged by the lessee; so long as the course is available to some of the citizens as a public park it can not be lawfully denied to others solely on account of race.

The *sale* of a municipal swimming pool by the city of Greensboro, even though the clear purpose was to relieve the city of the duty to make its recreational facilities available to all without regard to color, was approved by the federal courts, so long as the facility passed entirely out of the city's hands. Constitutional guarantees of equal protection, the courts reasoned, required only that *if* the city maintained a swimming pool at all, it must be opened to white and black patrons alike. The city did not have a duty, however, to own and

[1] *Holmes* v. *City of Atlanta*, U.S. Dist. Ct., Civil Action No. 4621, December 22, 1955 (N.D. Ga.). See RRLR I, 151.

[2] *Simkins* v. *City of Greensboro*, 149 F. Supp. 562 (M.D. N.C. 1957).

operate swimming pools; and if it already had one, it had the right to discontinue its operation and sell it, even if the purchaser intended to discriminate between the races.

Faced with a demand from Negro citizens for admission to its swimming pool, heretofore open only to whites, Greensboro decided to close and sell the pool. The city was then sued by black citizens who asked a declaratory judgment and injunctive relief against the city's refusal to allow Negroes to use a municipal pool and against the sale of the pool to avoid municipal operation. The district court (whose judgment was subsequently affirmed by the court of appeals) declined to issue the injunction.[1]

> The plaintiffs make the . . . contention that the sale could not be bona fide since the Greensboro Pool Corporation publicly announced before the sale that if it acquired title to the pool same would be operated for the exclusive use of the white citizens of Greensboro. This contention is based on the novel theory that municipalities may only sell recreational facilities upon the condition that the purchaser will operate the facility on an integrated basis. No authority is cited in support of this contention . . . [The court's] opinion is limited to a determination of whether or not the completed sale of the Lindley Park Swimming Pool was bona fide in the sense that the city divested itself of all control over the future use and operation of the pool. It is concluded that the plaintiffs have failed to sustain the burden of showing that the sale was not bona fide, or that the City of Greensboro has any agreement of any kind with the Greensboro Pool Corporation relating to the future ownership, use or operation of the pool. It necessarily follows that the complaints should be dismissed and that the plaintiffs should pay the costs of this action. [It is perhaps worth noting here that the city bought back the pool some years later when the citizens of Greensboro had accustomed themselves to a growing measure of integration. Thereafter, of course, the pool was operated by the city on an integrated basis.]

It is not to be assumed that the federal courts' insistence that the *Brown* principle required the end of segregation in city-owned or leased recreational facilities peremptorily ended the practice. Such discrimination was now clearly illegal, however, and aggrieved plaintiffs, if they were willing to go to the trouble, expense, and risk of seeking redress, could usually count upon judgments in their favor, although it might prove necessary to carry their cause as far as the United States court of appeals or the Supreme Court itself. In *Shuttlesworth* v. *Gaylord*,[2] for example, Negro plaintiffs, five years after the Baltimore and Atlanta cases cited above, were still seeking to break up the segregation of public recreation facilities in Atlanta. Here the Fifth Circuit Court of Appeals ruled, *per curiam:* "We have collected many of the cases which now settle the law beyond legitimate debate

[1] *Tonkins* v. *City of Greensboro,* 171 F. Supp. 476 (M.D. N.C. 1959).
[2] 202 F. Supp. 59 (N.D. Ga. 1960).

that enforced racial segregation in the public parks and public recreational facilities of a city are unconstitutional."

Another stubbornly resistant species of segregation was that practiced by quasi-public agencies, but here too the reach of the *School Segregation* cases extended, thanks to the courts' liberalized conception of state action. In the *Derington* case, for instance, Negroes brought suit in a federal district court against the lessee of a restaurant operated in a county courthouse who denied service to blacks. The court found in the Negroes favor, and the court of appeals affirmed:[1]

> If the County had rendered such a service directly it could not be argued that discrimination on account of race would not be violative of the Fourteenth Amendment. The same result inevitably follows when the service is rendered through the instrumentality of a lessee; and in rendering such service the lessee stands in the place of the County. His conduct is as much state action as would be the conduct of the County itself.

In a far-reaching and often cited opinion, the United States Supreme Court, overruling the State Supreme Court of Delaware, ruled that refusal of service to Negroes by a Wilmington restaurant located in a leased space in a public parking building owned by the city's Parking Authority violated the Fourteenth Amendment's equal protection clause:[2]

> By its inaction, the Authority, and through it the State, has not only made itself a party to the refusal of service, but has elected to place its power, property and prestige behind the admitted discrimination. The State has so far insinuated itself into a position of interdependence with [the] Eagle [Coffee Shoppe] that it must be recognized as a joint participant in the challenged activity, which, on that account, cannot be considered to have been so "purely private" as to fall without the scope of the Fourteenth Amendment.

In *Coke* v. *City of Atlanta*, a United States district court had handed down a similar ruling when a Negro passenger, waiting to change planes at the Atlanta airport, was assigned to segregated seating at the Dobbs House restaurant, in the airport terminal located on property owned by the City of Atlanta:[3]

> . . . the Court holds that the conduct of Dobbs Houses, Inc., is as much state action as would be similar conduct of the City of Atlanta itself and that the discrimination practiced by Dobbs Houses, Inc., in refusing to serve Negroes except upon a segregated basis is violative of plaintiff's rights as a Negro citizen under the equal protection provision of the Fourteenth Amendment.

[1] *Derington* v. *Plummer*, 240 F. 2d 922 (5th Cir. 1956).
[2] *Burton* v. *Wilmington Parking Authority*, 365 U.S. 715 (1961).
[3] U.S. Dist. Ct., January 5, 1960 (N.D. Ga.); see RRLR V, 138.

An additional consideration was involved in *privately endowed* public recreational facilities, in which segregation was prescribed. The case we now examine was to establish a precedent. In 1911 a citizen of Macon, Georgia, left to the City as trustee a tract of land for a public park to be used only by "white women, white girls, white boys, and white children of the City of Macon." After operating the park on these terms for several years, the city began to allow Negroes to use it after the Supreme Court had ruled that compulsory segregation of public facilities was unconstitutional.

When white citizens objected, the city sought to resign as trustee and give place to private trustees. After a hearing in a state superior court, the city was permitted to resign and private trustees were appointed. black intervenors thereupon appealed to the Georgia Supreme Court, on the ground that the resignation of the city as trustee had the effect of empowering the trial judge to appoint a successor trustee, thus retaining a measure of state action in the transfer. The State Supreme Court upheld the trial court.

Upon writ of certiorari, the United States Supreme Court reversed. Said Justice Black:[1]

> For years [the park] was an integral part of the City of Macon's activities. . . . [I]t was swept, manicured, watered, patrolled, and maintained by the city as this record shows. There has been no change in municipal maintenance and concern over this facility. . . . If the municipality remains entwined in the management or control of the park, it remains subject to the restraints of the Fourteenth Amendment. . . . [W]e cannot take judicial notice that the mere substitution of trustees instantly transferred this park from the public to the private sector.
>
> The service rendered even by a private park of this character is municipal in nature. It is open to every white person, there being no selective element other than race . . . Under the circumstances of this case, we cannot but conclude that the public character of this park requires that it be treated as a public institution subject to the command of the Fourteenth Amendment, regardless of who now has title under state law. . . . [W]e cannot say that the transfer of title *per se* disentangled the park from segregation under the municipal regime that long controlled it.
>
> Since the judgment below gives effect to that purpose, it must be and is
>
> *Reversed.*

Another landmark decision, this time from a United States court of appeals, related to hospital facilities. (Defendants subsequently appealed to the United States Supreme Court, which, in denying certiorari, gave its blessing to the court of appeals' judgment.)

George Simkins, of Greensboro, North Carolina, joined by other Negro doctors and dentists (who, like him, had sought staff privileges in the defendant hospitals, and had been denied them because of the hospitals' freely admitted racial exclusionary policies), brought a class

[1] *Evans* v. *Newton,* 382 U.S. 296. (1966)

action against two nonprofit, private, state-licensed hospitals in Greensboro, and asked for a declaratory judgment that a federal statute permitting use of federal funds to construct segregated hospitals is unconstitutional. The district court granted the defendants' motion to dismiss; but, on appeal, the court of appeals reversed the judgment, on the ground that defendants' use of federal funds and participation in the Hill-Burton program so deeply involved them in federal and state activities that defendants' actions, which might in other circumstances be considered wholly private, now became the actions of federal and state governments as well. And this was even though the Hill-Burton Act expressly permitted participating hospitals to segregate, and even though defendant hospitals pleaded that they "accepted government grants without warning that they would thereby subject themselves to restrictions on their racial policies."[1]

> . . . we find it significant here that the defendant hospitals operate as integral parts of comprehensive joint or intermeshing state and federal plans or programs designed to effect a proper allocation of available medical and hospital resources for the best possible promotion and maintenance of public health. . . . Having found the requisite "state action," necessarily we must remand to the District Court with directions to grant the requested injunctive relief. . . . Giving recognition to its responsibilities for public health, the state elected not to build publicly owned hospitals, which concededly could not have avoided a legal requirement against discrimination. Instead it adopted and the defendants participated in a plan for meeting those responsibilities by permitting its share of Hill-Burton Funds to go to existing private institutions. The appropriation of such funds to the Cone and Long Hospitals effectively limits Hill-Burton funds available in the future to create non-segregated facilities in the Greensboro area. In these circumstances, the plaintiffs can have no effective remedy unless the constitutional discrimination complained of is forbidden.

Prior to the *Simkins* case, discrimination in medical facilities had stimulated very little litigation, and not much active public attention. Most hospitals in the South and border states had theretofore been segregated by statute, and those in the North and West by local custom, even though in many of the latter states discrimination was forbidden by state law or city ordinance. After *Simkins,* the Civil Rights Act of 1964 was the principal prod to hospital desegregation, but even it met with so much resistance that the Guidelines were given only grudging and token compliance—which dwindled to even less when public and congressional criticism of the Guidelines led, late in 1966, to a reduction of appropriations for Title VI enforcement and a substantially reduced monitoring of compliance.[2] It should also be noted here that the beginning of Medicare payments in 1965 had, for practical pur-

[1] *Simkins* v. *Moses Cone Memorial Hospital,* 323 F. 2d 959 (4th Cir. 1963).
[2] See *The New York Times,* May 26, and files for September and October, 1966.

poses the effect of subjecting nearly all of the hospitals in the country to the *Simkins* ruling.

Although in the decade following the *School Segregation* cases the growing number of states with civil rights laws of their own afforded to aggrieved Negroes a substantially improved prospect for successful litigation, it was the federal Civil Rights Act of 1964 that proved to be the more important conduit of social change toward desegregation of public and private facilities serving the public. Before its enactment, privately owned and operated services—restaurants, hotels, motels, theaters, bars, barber shops, soda fountains, laundries, concert halls, skating rinks, bowling alleys, swimming pools, garages, airports, and the like—were, even where there were state laws or city ordinances to forbid it, still in most cases open to whites only, or available to both but only on a strictly segregated basis.

The Civil Rights Act of 1964, particularly Title II, promptly began to change these long-established and deeply entrenched usages, with astonishing speed, once the constitutionality of the act had been assured. Some establishments did not wait for a court order. "Throughout the South," reported *Time* Magazine, "from Charleston to Dallas, from Memphis to Tallahassee, segregation walls that had stood for several generations began to tumble in the first full week under the new Civil Rights Act."[1] Surprise that so profound a social change could move so swiftly was exceeded only by surprise that it could be done with so little friction.

A few months later, however, resistance stiffened, and it soon appeared that the majority of white public facilities and accommodations in the Deep South (and, to a less extent, elsewhere also, for that matter) would continue to exclude Negroes whether by open defiance of the law or by such stratagems as admitting Negroes to formerly all-white enterprises but serving them in a separate area or section; or by changing the establishments into "private clubs," open to "members" only.

But these devices, however adamant, or however devious, steadily yielded before the pressure of litigation, supplemented by boycotts and public demonstrations. Some gave way only when resistance became clearly hopeless, as in the case of two movie theaters in the strongly segregationist city of Orangeburg, South Carolina. There, when Negroes brought suit, under the Civil Rights Act of 1964, against the operators of the theaters, the federal district court dismissed the action when the defendants demonstrated that, since the suit had begun, they had abandoned segregation.[2] A less pliable owner of a motion picture house in Louisiana in the following year continued his earlier custom

[1] *Time*, 84 (July 17, 1964), 25–26.

[2] *Thomas* v. *Orangeburg Theaters*, 241 F. Supp. 317 (E.D. S.C. 1965).

of excluding blacks from the main floor only, protesting that the Civil Rights Act did not reach him, since he was clearly not operating in interstate commerce. When Negroes brought a class action against him, however, a federal district court enjoined him from further operation of his theater in this manner, and held that his enterprise was in fact reached by the act because the films he customarily showed did move in interstate commerce.[1]

The Justice Department's opportunity to demonstrate its determination that the law be enforced, and to establish its constitutionality, was supplied by Lester Maddox, proprietor of the Heart of Atlanta Motel and of the Pickrick, a fried chicken eating house, and by Ollie McClung, owner of Ollie's, an obscure barbecue house in Birmingham which served whites on the premises but permitted blacks to have "take-out" privileges only. Mere hours after the Civil Rights Act of 1964 became law, an enraged Maddox, pistol in hand, ordered three Negroes away from the Pickrick. Shortly thereafter, United States attorneys sought injunctions against both establishments. The cases involving Maddox and McClung were in litigation simultaneously, but it was the Pickrick affair that caught the country's fascinated attention on the television newscasts, and which Maddox counted upon to strike down at least the public accommodations section of the act, on grounds of constitutionality.[2]

Freely admitting that the Heart of Atlanta and the Pickrick did not and would not serve Negroes, Maddox and his attorney argued that because the act was ostensibly an exercise of the Congress' interstate commerce power, his places of business were clearly not within its orbit, since neither the motel nor the restaurant was engaged in interstate commerce.[3]

To the plaintiff's plea that the act's attempt to regulate a local establishment was an unconstitutional extension of the Congress' power to regulate interstate commerce, the trial court replied that "Congress may use its power under the interstate commerce clause to regulate intrastate activities, when such regulation is an appropriate means of exercising control over interstate commerce." The three-judge court went on to point out that the Supreme Court had long ago made the same determination respecting the Sherman Anti-Trust Act and the National Labor Relations Act, holding that such earlier statutes properly applied to local businesses dealing in products which were obtained within the state but which had previously, or would subse-

[1] *Bryant* v. *Guillory*, U.S. Dist. Ct., Sept. 15, 1965 (W.D. La.); see RRLR XI, 426.

[2] The *McClung* case is considered on p. 513, below.

[3] *Heart of Atlanta Motel* v. *United States*, 379 U.S. 241 (1964); *Willis and Kennedy* v. *Pickrick Restaurant*, 234 F. Supp. 179 (N.D. Ga. 1964).

quently, move in interstate commerce. The court denied relief to the motel and granted the Attorney General an injunction forbidding the plaintiff to refuse persons for reasons of race or color.

In the Pickrick action, the three Negroes whom Maddox had driven from his premises brought suit against the restaurant corporation and its operator, seeking an injunction to restrain the defendant from excluding Negroes. The United States entered the case as intervenor, as authorized by the Act of 1964. Maddox and his counsel were more confident in the matter of the Pickrick than they were in the motel affair that their position could be maintained. The Pickrick did not, they argued, solicit business from interstate travelers, nor advertise in out-of-state publications; it was not recommended by motor associations or by such national groups as Duncan Hines; and it bought its chickens and other foods locally. The government, however, presented evidence that interstate travelers did in fact patronize the Pickrick and that foods used in the establishment came from as far away as Virginia, Florida, Iowa, Louisiana, and California.

In this instance, as in the motel case, the courts upheld the constitutionality of the public accommodations section of the Civil Rights Act of 1964; issued an injunction to restrain further exclusion of black patrons; and stayed the effective date of the order for several days, to allow Maddox to appeal to the Supreme Court of the United States. Maddox appealed, and publicly vowed, "I'm not going to integrate. I've made my pledge. They won't ever get any of that chicken."[1] On August 10, the day preceding the end of the grace period offered Maddox by the district court, Justice Black (as presiding Supreme Court Justice for the Fifth Circuit) refused Maddox's request to stay the effectuation of the district court's desegregation order, and indicated that the Supreme Court would hear the appeal in October.

Shortly after this rebuff, Maddox, tearful and trembling with rage, stood in the door of the Pickrick, and screamed at Negroes outside: "You no-good dirty devils! You've just put sixty-six people out of a job! You dirty Communists!" He thereupon announced the restaurant's closing "for good," and stepped outside to read the Ten Commandments and explain to sympathetic onlookers that segregation is God's way.

Before going the whole length of closing the Pickrick and redeeming his fervent pledge never to integrate, he had denounced Title II and the district court's order as "involuntary servitude," and had invited white sympathizers to help him defend his ramparts by availing themselves of a box of red-painted ax handles marked "Souvenir—Or Otherwise—$2." When Negroes appeared at the Pickrick's door he drove them off

[1] *Time*, 84 (July 31, 1964), 2.

with ax handles and pistol until the district court asked him to show cause why he should not be cited for contempt. Recognizing his defeat, he then closed the Pickrick with a parting volley at the President, the Congress, and the Communists for destroying not only his "childhood dream" but also the "American Free Enterprise System, Private Property Rights, Freedom and Liberty."

Lester Maddox was now out of the restaurant business. Finding himself a hero to Georgia arch-segregationists (and undaunted by a series of earlier defeats in attempts to achieve public office), he made an audacious bid for the Democratic party's gubernatorial nomination, won it, and—to the nation's astonishment—was elected governor of Georgia.

Particularly interesting in both the Maddox and McClung cases is the Supreme Court's assigning to contemporary circumstances the principles for defining the limits of interstate commerce, which had been laid down by Chief Justice John Marshall nearly a century and a half earlier. Important also in both was the Court's judgment as to the effect of discrimination in sleeping and eating facilities upon such commerce. No less noteworthy is the application in these two cases (see, for example, the first quoted paragraph in the excerpt from the *McClung* opinion, p. 514 below) of the "sociological jurisprudence" that had informed the celebrated Brandeis brief in a maximum hours case[1] nearly a half century earlier, and the Court's opinion in the *School Segregation* cases of 1954. The following excerpts are from the *Heart of Atlanta Motel* opinion:[2]

The record of [the Civil Rights Act's] passage through each house [of Congress] is replete with evidence of the burdens that discrimination by race or color places upon interstate commerce. . . . This testimony [before Congressional committees] included the fact that our people have become increasingly mobile with millions of all races traveling from State to State; that Negroes in particular have been the subject of discrimination in transient accommodations, having to travel great distances to secure the same; that often they have been unable to obtain accommodations and have had to call upon friends to put them up overnight; . . . and that these conditions have become so acute as to require the listing of available lodging for Negroes in a special guidebook which was itself dramatic testimony of the difficulties Negroes encounter in travel. . . . These exclusionary practices were found to be nationwide. . . . This testimony indicated a qualitative as well as quantitative effect on interstate travel by Negroes. . . . Uncertainty stemming from racial discrimination had the effect of discouraging travel on the part of a substantial portion of the Negro community. . . . The voluminous testimony presents overwhelming evidence that discrimination by hotels and motels impedes interstate travel.

[Then, after quoting extensively from John Marshall's opinion in *Gibbons*

[1] *Muller* v. *Oregon*, 208 U.S. 412 (1908).

[2] *Heart of Atlanta Motel* v. *United States*, 379 U.S. 241 (1964).

v. *Ogden*, the opinion continued:] In short, the determinative test of the exercise of power by the Congress under the Commerce Clause is simply whether the activity sought to be regulated is "commerce which concerns more than one state" and has a real and substantial relation to the national interest. . . . That the transportation of passengers is a part of commerce is not now an open question. . . .

It is said that the operation of the motel here is of a purely local character. But, assuming this to be true, "if it is interstate commerce that feels the pinch, it does not matter how local the operation that applies the squeeze." . . . The power of Congress over interstate commerce is not confined to the regulation of commerce among the states. It extends to those activities intrastate which so affect interstate commerce or the exercise of the power of Congress over it as to make regulation of them appropriate means to the attainment of a legitimate end, the exercise of the granted power of Congress to regulate interstate commerce.

Thus the power of Congress to promote interstate commerce also includes the power to regulate the local incidents thereof, including local activities in both the States of origin and destination, which might have a substantial and harmful effect upon that commerce. One need only examine the evidence we have discussed above to see that Congress may—as it has—prohibit racial discrimination by motels serving travelers, however "local" their operations may appear.

The separate action involving the Pickrick restaurant had ended earlier, on September 4, when the district court handed down a permanent injunction, restraining the establishment from discriminating among patrons on the basis of color. The grounds for issuing the injunction were substantially those upon which the Supreme Court had rested its *Heart of Atlanta Motel* opinion. At one point in the accompanying opinion the court pointed out that Georgia produced no tea, coffee or pepper, and mined no salt—"items necessary to restaurant operation."

The action concerning the restaurant of Ollie McClung, which the Supreme Court heard as a companion to *Heart of Atlanta Motel*, was resolved on substantially the same grounds as that case, and the two decisions were handed down simultaneously on December 14, 1964. They differed, however, in that Ollie's Restaurant, a family owned emporium in Birmingham, Alabama, was much farther from the main-traveled roads of interstate commerce. Because Ollie's did no advertising, sought no transients, was eleven blocks from the nearest interstate highway, and bought its meat from a packing plant in Birmingham, it afforded the Department of Justice an excellent case for testing the outer reaches of the commerce clause, and by that token, for demonstrating the scope of the 1964 Civil Rights Act. Despite Ollie's remoteness from interstate highways, said the Court, 46 percent of the meat obtained by Ollie's from local packers had, in turn, been procured from outside the state. Moreover:[1]

[1] *Katzenbach* v. *McClung*, 379 U.S. 294 (1964).

The record is replete with testimony [before congressional committees when the Civil Rights Act of 1964 was under consideration] of the burdens placed on interstate commerce by racial discrimination in restaurants. A comparison of per capita spending by Negroes in restaurants, theaters, and like establishments indicated less spending, after discounting income differences, in areas where discrimination is widely practiced. This condition, which was especially aggravated in the South, was attributed in the testimony of the Under Secretary of Commerce to racial segregation. . . . This diminutive spending springing from a refusal to serve Negroes and their total loss as customers has, regardless of the absence of direct evidence, a close connection to interstate commerce. . . . In addition, the Attorney General testified that this type of discrimination imposed "an artificial restraint on the market" and interfered with the flow of merchandise. . . . In addition, . . . there were many references to discriminatory situations causing wide unrest and having a depressant effect on general business conditions in the respective communities.

Moreover, there was an impressive array of testimony that discrimination in restaurants had a direct and highly restrictive effect upon interstate travel by Negroes . . . because discrimination practices prevent Negroes from buying prepared food served on the premises while on a trip, except in isolated and unkempt restaurants and under most unsatisfactory and often unpleasant conditions. This obviously discourages travel and obstructs interstate commerce, for one can hardly travel without eating. Likewise . . . discrimination deterred professional, as well as skilled, people from moving into areas where such practices occurred and thereby caused industry to be reluctant to establish there.

. . . we must conclude that [Congress] had a rational basis for finding that racial discrimination in restaurants had a direct and adverse effect on the free flow of interstate commerce.

In a purely legal sense, the *Heart of Atlanta Motel* and *McClung* decisions only reasserted the ancient rule that the commerce clause gives the Congress sweeping powers to regulate any activity affecting interstate commerce, however remotely. But the implications for race relations were stupendous, for a Negro could now travel anywhere, and stop at any hotel, motel, or eating establishment, in the secure knowledge that the law of the land—whatever the propensity of the proprietor—stood squarely behind his request to be served.

Although the immediate and potential effect of Title II was truly momentous, its provisions did not, as some supposed, direct their commands to every form of public accommodation. That all publicly owned facilities were forbidden to discriminate on the basis of race or color had, of course, been established long before 1964. But privately owned enterprises covered by the 1964 Act were confined to the list catalogued in Section 201(b) of the Title. This list was comprehensive, and its wording sufficiently commodious to embrace most suppliers of what are commonly considered public accommodations; but it was not complete. One evident exception, at least for the present, was the category of bars, taverns, and nightclubs where only liquor was dispensed.

In *Cuevas* v. *Sdrales*, a Negro had brought suit in a federal district court, alleging that a Utah tavern proprietor, in refusing him service, had violated the public accommodations section of the Civil Rights Act of 1964. The court dismissed the complaint on the ground that because the defendant's tavern sold only beer and incidentals associated with beer, it did not come under Section 201(b). On appeal, the Tenth Circuit Court of Appeals affirmed. Noting that the statute applied (among other named accommodations) to "any restaurant, cafeteria, lunchroom, lunch counter, soda fountain, or other facility principally engaged in selling food for consumption on the premises," the court held that:[1]

> Beer, and similar drinks, might in some instances be classed as food, as they supply some nutriment to the body, but generally, beer is considered a drink, and although it may be served in eating places, a place serving only beer is not considered a restaurant, cafeteria, lunchroom, lunch counter, or soda fountain. . . . If the legislation were intended to cover such places as bars and taverns, where the sale of drinks is the principal business, Congress would have specifically included them. Furthermore, the Department of Justice of the United States, in an analysis of Title II . . . says "A bar or tavern which serves little or no food is not covered."

In view of the resourcefulness of segregationists in devising stratagems for defeating the intention of the *Brown* decision, it is hardly surprising that the Civil Rights Act of 1964 should have evoked some elaborate schemes for evasion. One such improvisation was the "restaurant club." (The "club" concept was applied to other kinds of accommodations as well.)

The Department of Justice found, for example, a cluster of more than ninety restaurants operating in northern Louisiana practicing this dodge. Briefly stated, the restaurants served only "members"; but white persons seeking to be served were admitted as a matter of course, and issued "membership cards" (in some restaurants upon payments of a fee of ten cents) "without any requirements or conditions whatsoever." Admission to service in the restaurant was by "membership card only," and in no case was a Negro issued a card, despite repeated requests. Said the United States District Court in issuing an injunction requiring an immediate end to the practice:[2]

[1] 344 F. 2d 1019 (10th Cir. 1965).
[2] *United States* v. *Northwest Louisiana Restaurant Club*, 256 F. Supp. 151 (W.D. La. 1966).

FINDINGS OF FACT

[After a detailed description of the club and its operations:]

15. The defendant Northwest Louisiana Restaurant Club and its voting members have engaged in acts and practices which constitute a pattern and practice of resistance to the full and equal enjoyment by Negroes of the goods, services, facilities, privileges, advantages and accommodations of the places of public accommodation owned or operated by such members, without discrimination or segregation on the grounds of race or color. This pattern and practice is of such a nature as to, and is intended to, deny the full exercise of such rights. . . .

CONCLUSIONS OF LAW

7. The acts and practices of the defendants, as set forth in this Court's findings of fact, constitute an unlawful deprivation of the rights secured to Negro citizens to the free and equal use and enjoyment of public accommodations as guaranteed by Title II of the Civil Rights Act of 1964.

8. This deprivation, resulting from the acts and practices of the defendants, has been and is pursuant to a pattern and practice of resistance to rights within the meaning of . . . the Civil Rights Act of 1964. . . .

9. The plaintiff is entitled to a permanent injunction as a matter of law.

The defenses against such evasive maneuvers as those employed by the Northwest Louisiana Restaurant Club were still further reinforced in one of the last decisions to be rendered by the Warren court.

The Lake Nixon Club, a privately owned recreation center near Little Rock, Arkansas, with swimming, boating, miniature golf, dancing facilities, and a snack bar, admitted only whites to membership. A twenty-five-cent membership fee was charged to those who sought to use its accommodations. Whites were routinely enrolled, but blacks were categorically excluded. The fact of such exclusion was not denied by the management, who took the position that the club was not a place of public accommodation covered by Title II of the Civil Rights Act of 1964.

The Supreme Court, reversing the decision of a lower federal court, held that at least one of the operations of the facility, the snack bar, was run for profit, and, moreover, served food "a substantial portion" of which had moved in interstate commerce and thus came within the reach of Congress' power to regulate interstate commerce.[1]

Petitioners argue first that Lake Nixon's snack bar is a covered public accommodation under Section 201 (b) (2) and 201 (c) (2), and that as such it brings the entire establishment within the coverage of Title II. . . . Clearly, the snack bar is "principally engaged in selling food for consumption on the premises." Thus it is a covered public accommodation if "it serves or offers to serve interstate travelers or a substantial portion of the food which it serves

[1] *Daniel and Kyles* v. *Paul*, 395 U.S. 298 (1969).

> . . . has moved in commerce." [The quoted passages are from the 1964 statute.] We find that the snack bar is a covered public accommodation under either of these standards.
>
> The Pauls [the proprietors] advertise the Lake Nixon Club in a monthly magazine called "Little Rock Today," which is distributed to guests at Little Rock hotels, motels, and restaurants, to acquaint them with available tourist attractions in the area. Regular advertisements for Lake Nixon were also broadcast over two area radio stations. In addition, Lake Nixon has advertised in the *Little Rock Air Force Base,* a monthly newspaper published at the Little Rock Air Force Base in Jacksonville, Arkansas. This choice of advertising media leaves no doubt that the Pauls were seeking a broad-based patronage from an audience which they knew to include interstate travelers. . . .
>
> The record, although not as complete on this point as might be desired, also demonstrates that a "substantial portion of the food" served by the Lake Nixon snack bar has moved in interstate commerce. The snack bar serves a limited fare—hot dogs and hamburgers on buns, soft drinks and milk. The district court took judicial notice of the fact that the "principal ingredients going into the bread were produced and processed in other states" and that "certain ingredients [of the soft drinks] were probably obtained . . . from out-of-State sources." . . . There can be no serious doubt that a "substantial portion of the food" served at the snack bar has moved in interstate commerce. . . .
>
> The snack bar's status as a covered establishment automatically brings the entire Lake Nixon facility within the ambit of Title II.

A variation on the private-club theme was the community-owned recreation center, typically a swimming pool, in which residents purchased shares, to form a "neighborhood association." These sprang up in hundred of communities throughout the country in the 1960's. In the Virginia-Maryland suburbs clustered around the national capital there were at least 130 such centers in 1969. In December of that year such arrangements were put on notice by the Supreme Court that as devices for screening out persons on the basis of race they were illegal.

One such center, in Fairfax County, Virginia (a swimming club called Little Hunting Park) had among its shareholders one Paul E. Sullivan, a white employee of the Pentagon. In 1965 he purchased a second house in the community, leasing the first to Theodore R. Freeman, a black economist in the Department of Agriculture, turning over to him also his right to join the "club." The club sought to dissuade Sullivan from transferring his share, and when he persisted it suspended him, reimbursed him for both his cancelled shares, and denied Freeman access to the pool.

Freeman meanwhile had been transferred to Tokyo as an American Agricultural aide, and had leased the house in question to Air Force Sergeant James T. Malloy, another black. When Sullivan brought suit to vindicate his right to transfer his membership to Freeman as incidental to the transfer of his home, the Virginia Supreme Court of Appeals sustained a lower court's ruling that the facility was a private club and therefore beyond the reach of civil rights laws. The United States Supreme Court, however, reversed, pointing out in its crisp ruling that the association's claim to be a private club was a transparent subterfuge, for it employed "no selective element other than race," and that it was, moreover, "a device functionally comparable to a racially restrictive covenant," long since outlawed in *Shelley* v. *Kraemer*, and more recently in *Jones* v. *Mayer*.[1]

The status of bona fide private clubs from which persons are excluded on the grounds of race remained ambiguous, but increasingly on the defensive. And, once again, a courtroom triumph de jure was not followed by a de facto gain for equality of protection and opportunity. As in so many other instances, the technical victor, in this case Sergeant Malloy, hesitated to appropriate its benefits at once. "There is a very unhealthy atmosphere here," he said, "and I know my children won't be welcome at the pool."[2]

E. *Miscellaneous Discriminations and the Federal Courts*

Racial Intermarriage: Ending the Ban

In view of the intensity of public passion surrounding the issue of racial intermarriage, it may well be doubted that any new Supreme Court ruling in the decade and a half after the *School Segregation* cases signalized a more profound social change than did the 1967 judgment which struck down state laws forbidding the "mixing" of races.[3] It was a Virginia statute that the Court invalidated, but similar laws (by now confined to fifteen other states) fell with it, and for the first time in the nation's history there were no legal impediments to the intermarriage of whites and blacks, anywhere in America.

> There can be no question but that Virginia's miscegenation statutes rest solely upon distinctions drawn according to race. . . . Over the years, this Court has consistently repudiated "distinctions between citizens solely because of their ancestry" as being "odious to a free people whose institutions are founded upon the doctrine of equality." . . . If they are ever to be upheld, they must be shown to be necessary to the accomplishment of some permissible state objective, independent of the racial discrimination which it was the object of the Fourteenth Amendment to eliminate.
>
> There is patently no legitimate overriding purpose independent of in-

[1] See above, pp. 78 and 130.

[2] *Time*, Vol. 94 (December 26, 1969), p. 23. The Court also based its judgment on the finding that the Civil Rights Act of 1866 outlawed the conduct against which the plaintiff had brought suit. *Sullivan* v. *Little Hunting Park*, U.S. Supreme Court, No. 33, October term, 1969 (December 15, 1969); 38 LW 4059.

[3] *Loving* v. *Virginia*, 388 U.S. 1 (1967).

vidious racial discrimination which justified this classification. The fact that Virginia only prohibits interracial marriage involving white persons demonstrates that the racial classifications must stand on their own justification, as measures designed to maintain White Supremacy. . . . There can be no doubt that restricting the freedom to marry solely because of racial classifications violates the central meaning of the Equal Protection Clause.

These statutes also deprive the Lovings of liberty without due process of law. . . . The freedom to marry has long been recognized as one of the vital personal rights essential to the orderly pursuit of happiness by free men. . . . The Fourteenth Amendment requires that the freedom of choice to marry not be restricted by invidious racial discriminations. Under our Constitution, the freedom to marry, or not to marry, a person of another race resides with the individual and cannot be infringed by the State.

These convictions must be reversed.

Public Transportation: The Death of Jim Crow

The legal standing of segregated public transportation, already fatally weakened before *Brown,* tottered and collapsed in the post-*Brown* decade. Typical of court actions speeding the demise of Jim Crow travel was a 1956 case in a federal district court in Alabama, in which black citizens of Montgomery brought suit against state and city officials, and the company operating local buses. Said the court:[1]

. . . In fact, we think that *Plessy* v. *Ferguson* has been impliedly, though not explicitly overruled, and that, under the later decisions, there is now no rational basis upon which the separate but equal doctrine can be validly applied to public transportation within the City of Montgomery and its police jurisdiction. The application of that doctrine cannot be justified as a proper execution of the state police power.

. . . We hold that the statutes and ordinances requiring segregation of the white and colored races on the motor buses of a common carrier of passengers in the City of Montgomery and its police jurisdiction violate the due process and equal protection of the law clauses of the Fourteenth Amendment of the Constitution of the United States.

Shortly thereafter came a *per curiam* judgment from the Supreme Court to affirm the foregoing: "The motion to affirm is granted and the judgment is affirmed. *Brown* v. *Board of Education* . . . *Mayor and City Council of Baltimore* v. *Dawson* . . . *Holmes* v. *Atlanta* . . ."[2]

In February 1962, the United States Supreme Court had before it a case appealed from a district court, in which Negro citizens of Mississippi had brought a class action against the city of Jackson, state and local government authorities, and named transportation agencies, from enforcing segregation on common carriers. Its language could hardly have been more categorical:[3]

[1] *Browder* v. *Gayle,* 142 F. Supp. 707 (M.D. Ala. 1956).

[2] 352 U.S. 903 (1956).

[3] *Bailey* v. *Patterson,* 369 U.S. 31 (1962). But see *Thomas* v. *State* below, p. 523.

We have settled beyond question that no State may require racial segregation of interstate or intrastate transportation facilities. *Morgan* v. *Virginia* . . . , *Gayle* v. *Browder* . . . , *Boynton* v. *Virginia* . . . . The question is no longer open; it is foreclosed as a litigable issue.

The Assault upon the NAACP

Although the United States Supreme Court in *NAACP* v. *Alabama,*[1] on grounds of freedom of association as protected by the Fourteenth Amendment, dissolved a contempt citation fine levied against the Association for its refusal to disclose its membership lists to state authorities, the Arkansas legislature (among others) some months later (as we have seen[2]) enacted a statute declaring: "It shall be unlawful for any member of the National Association for the Advancement of Colored People to be employed by the State, school district, county or any municipality thereof, . . . so long as such membership is maintained." In the same spirit, an Alabama state circuit court, in December 1961, permanently enjoined the NAACP from doing business and from recruiting members in the state, but the decree was struck down by the Supreme Court of the United States:[3]

> There is no occasion in this case for us to consider how much survives of the principle that a State can impose such conditions as it chooses on the right of a foreign corporation to do business within the State, or can exclude it from the State altogether. . . . This case, in truth, involves not the privilege of a corporation to do business in a State, but rather the freedom of individuals to associate for the collective advocacy of ideas. "Freedoms such as . . . [this] are protected not only against heavy-handed frontal attack, but also from being stifled by more subtle governmental interference." *Bates* v. *City of Little Rock,* 361 U.S. 516, 523.

Sit-ins and Demonstrations: Qualified Support

The Montgomery bus boycott of 1955–56, the first successful concerted effort to force abandonment of Jim Crow by a particular enterpriser, did not touch off a wave of protest effort. It was the lunch-counter sit-in at the Woolworth store in Greensboro, North Carolina, beginning on February 1, 1960, that ushered in the era of demonstrations and other forms of direct action, dedicated to a reliance upon passive, nonviolent resistance.

The new strategy evoked, as we have noted, a spate of new statutes and ordinances, and reinvigoration of old ones, to forestall or contain what opponents of these tactics regarded as trespass, disorderly con-

[1] 357 U.S. 449 (1958).
[2] See above, p. 385.
[3] *NAACP* v. *Alabama,* 377 U.S. 288 (1964).

duct, or disturbance of the public peace. Within six months after the beginning at Greensboro, the sit-ins and similar pressures had produced desegregation in at least some of the eating facilities in several cities in Virginia, Texas, North Carolina, and Tennessee; and thereafter more or less peaceable demonstrations multiplied throughout the South and the nation at large, directed toward other forms of segregated public facilities as well. State and local courts proceeded somewhat cautiously to restrain the movement, but federal courts were, understandably, more indulgent. The North Carolina Supreme Court, for example, upheld trespass convictions in a series of lunch-counter sit-in cases arising in the cities of Durham, Raleigh, and Monroe. Said the court in the Raleigh incident:[1]

> To test the right of an operator of a private mercantile establishment to select the customers he will serve in any particular portion of the store, defendants seated themselves at the lunch counter and demanded service. . . . Despite repeated requests to leave the enclosed area, they remained and persisted in their demand for services until arrested by city police and charged with violating G.S. 14–134, the trespass statute.
>
> Defendants contend a merchant who sells his wares to one must serve all, and a refusal to do so is a violation of the rights guaranteed by the Fourteenth Amendment to the Constitution of the United States. The contention lacks merit. The operator of a private mercantile establishment has the right to select his customers, serve those he selects, and refuse to serve others. The reasons which prompt him to choose do not circumscribe his right. . . . The Constitution of North Carolina['s] . . . . guarantee against imprisonment except by the law of the land was not intended to protect trespassers from prosecution or to prohibit a private property owner from selecting his guests or customers.
>
> Since defendants had no constitutional right to remain on private property over the protest of the lawful occupant, it follows that the refusal to leave when requested was a violation of the statute.

State courts were usually, in such cases, careful to point out also that statutes directed against trespass and breaches of the public peace are not based on race.

Two years after the North Carolina action—in a judgment fairly representative of others it previously and subsequently rendered—the Supreme Court of the United States, on First Amendment grounds, set aside the sentences of 187 Negroes for breach of the peace in connection with a parade protesting segregation. The demonstrators were convicted by a magistrate's court (which the South Carolina Supreme Court affirmed). Evidence had been presented that the defendants, and their sympathizing on-lookers, had impeded traffic, before the defendants were ordered by police to disperse. From that moment the demonstration had become more boisterous.[2]

[1] *State* v. *Fox*, 254 N.C. 97, 118 S.E. 2d 58 (1961).
[2] *Edwards* v. *South Carolina*, 372 U.S. 229 (1963).

. . . It is clear to us that in arresting, convicting, and punishing the petitioners under the circumstances disclosed by this record, South Carolina infringed the petitioners' rights of free speech, free assembly, and freedom to petition for redress of their grievances.

It has long been established that these First Amendment freedoms are protected by the Fourteenth Amendment from invasion by the States. . . . The circumstances in this case reflect an exercise of these basic constitutional rights in their most pristine and classic form. The petitioners felt aggrieved by laws of South Carolina which allegedly "prohibited Negro privileges in this State." They peaceably assembled at the site of the State Government and there peaceably expressed their grievances "to the citizens of South Carolina, along with the Legislative Bodies of South Carolina." Not until they were told by police that they must disperse on pain of arrest did they do more. Even then, they but sang patriotic and religious songs after one of their leaders had delivered a "religious harangue." There was no violence on their part or on the part of any member of the crowd watching them. Police protection was "ample." . . . These petitioners were convicted . . . upon evidence which showed no more than that the opinions which they were peaceably expressing were sufficiently opposed to the views of the majority of the community to attract a crowd and necessitate police protection.

The Fourteenth Amendment does not permit a State to make criminal the peaceful expression of unpopular views. . . . As Chief Justice Hughes wrote . . . "The maintenance of the opportunity for free political discussion to the end that government may be responsive to the will of the people and that changes may be obtained by lawful means, an opportunity essential to the security of the Republic, is a fundamental principle of our constitutional system." . . . For these reasons we conclude that these criminal convictions cannot stand.

Later in the same term, the United States Supreme Court reversed several convictions for trespass and inciting to trespass, of persons who had taken part in sit-in demonstrations in Alabama, Louisiana, North Carolina, and South Carolina, on the ground that the lunch counters' operators were compelled by city ordinances or other official directives to exclude Negroes, and that their conduct was, for that reason, a form of state action forbidden by the Fourteenth Amendment. In one of these actions, in 1963, involving the exclusion of Negroes from the lunch counter in a Kress store in Greenville, South Carolina, the Court spoke plainly:[1]

The evidence in this case establishes beyond doubt that the Kress management's decision to exclude petitioners from the lunch counter was made because they were Negroes. . . . It cannot be denied that here the City of Greenville, an agency of the State, has provided by its ordinance that the decision as to whether a restaurant facility is to be operated on a desegregated basis is to be reserved to it. When the State has commanded a particular result it has saved to itself the power to determine that result and thereby "to a significant extent" has "become involved" in, and in fact, has removed that decision from the sphere of private choice. It has thus effectively determined that a person owning, managing or controlling an eating place is left with no

[1] *Peterson* v. *Greenville*, 373 U.S. 244 (1963).

choice of his own but must segregate his white and Negro patrons. The Kress management, in deciding to exclude Negroes, did precisely what the city law required. . . . When a state agency passes a law compelling persons to discriminate against other persons because of race, and the State's criminal processes are employed in a way which enforces the discrimination by that law, such a palpable violation of the Fourteenth Amendment cannot be saved by attempting to separate the mental urges of the discriminators.

In the North and West demonstrators had the protection of state laws and city ordinances *forbidding* discrimination, which, though poorly (if at all) enforced, at least rendered demonstrators relatively safe from convictions for trespass or public disorder when they made collective demands to be served.

With the more highly organized—and more widely publicized—"freedom rides," directed against segregated transportation, and calculated, through that symbol, to strike at the whole fabric of apartheid, the exasperation of the Deep South not infrequently spoke from the bench. Early in 1964, for instance, the Supreme Court of Mississippi twice unanimously sustained convictions of Negroes who defied state statutes prescribing separate bus seating and waiting rooms for the races. Said the court in one of these actions, reviewing the conviction for disorderly conduct of a Howard University student who had participated in the spring, 1961, freedom ride organized by the Congress of Racial Equality:[1]

We hold that the constitutional rights of defendant were not violated by his conviction for disorderly conduct. The state's interest in preventing violence and disorder, which were imminent under the undisputed facts, is the vital and controlling fact in this case. . . . He and his associates participated in a highly sophisticated plan to travel through the South and stir up racial strife and violence. All of their activities were broadcast in a manner to create the greatest public commotion and uneasiness. . . . There is no evidence that the police did anything other than keep the peace. . . . This Court cannot escape the duty to accord to police the authority necessary to prevent violence, and this is true whatever the motives of those who are about to cause the violence, or to precipitate it. In the situation the police found themselves, it was reasonable to require defendant to move on to wherever he wanted to go.

Similarly, the North Carolina Supreme Court sustained the conviction for trespass of a Negro who refused to leave a "white only" restaurant upon the demand of the proprietor:[2]

The defendant contends that G.S. 14–134, which in pertinent part reads: "If any person after being forbidden to do so, shall go or enter upon the lands of another, without a license therefor, he shall be guilty of a misdemeanor," is unconstitutional by reason of conflict with Article I, Section 17 of the Constitution of North Carolina and the Privileges or Immunities, Due

[1] *Thomas* v. *State,* 160 So. 2d 657 (Miss. 1964).
[2] *State* v. *Davis,* 261 N.C. 463, 135 S.E. 2d 14 (1964).

Process and Equal Protection Clauses of the Fourteenth Amendment to the Constitution of the United States. . . . . [W]e hold that where a person without permission or invitation enters upon the premises of another, and after entry thereon his presence is discovered and he is unconditionally ordered to leave the premises by one in the legal possession thereof, if he refuses to leave and remains on the premises, he is a trespasser from the beginning.

. . . We further hold that the provisions of G.S. 14–134 do not conflict with . . . the Constitution of North Carolina or with . . . the Constitution of the United States.

After the enactment of the Civil Rights Act of 1964, convictions for trespasses and disorderly conduct on the part of sit-iners and demonstrators became less common. Indeed, the Supreme Court canceled trespass convictions—as in the case here cited—even though the conduct upon which the conviction was based occurred before the passage of the Act.[1]

Now that Congress has exercised its constitutional power in enacting the Civil Rights Act of 1964 and declared that the public policy of our country is to prohibit discrimination in public accommodations as therein defined, there is no public interest to be served in the further prosecution of the petitioners. And in accordance with long-established rule of our cases they must be abated and the judgment in each is therefore vacated and the charges are ordered dismissed.

But the Supreme Court's record with respect to the rights of sit-iners and demonstrators suggests a degree of ambivalence. It preferred to deal with individual cases, on their particular merits, and persistently avoided the basic Fourteenth Amendment issues raised by sit-in and similar cases. Such seeming irresolution has been construed by some critics as deference to the anxieties and property interests of whites. In the earlier phases of the sit-in movement—so runs the argument—when the demonstrators were in the posture of entreaty, and when they had broad public sympathy, the judiciary saw no offense to the laws in their conduct; but when the demonstrations developed more muscle the judges took alarm.

An apparent shift came in the middle 1960's. In 1964, for example, in *Bell* v. *Maryland*,[2] the Supreme Court was confronted with black sit-iners who had been convicted of criminal trespass. The Justices were in fundamental disagreement over the issues, and, taking advantage of the accident that the state had, pending the review, adopted public accommodation laws, the Court remanded the cases to the state courts for consideration of the effect of the new legislation. Later in the same year, in *Cox* v. *Louisiana*,[3] the Court reversed the conviction of Negro demonstrators but warned that the right to protest could be

[1] *Hamm* v. *Rock Hill*; and *Lupper* v. *Arkansas*, 379 U.S. 306 (1964).
[2] 378 U.S. 226 (1964).
[3] 379 U.S. 559 (1965).

limited: ". . . there is," said the tribunal, "no place for violence in a democratic society . . . , and the right of peaceful protest does not mean that everyone with opinions or beliefs to express may do so at any time and at any place."

Then, in *Adderley* v. *Florida* the Court handed down a judgment in which some critics have seen judicial solicitude for white anxieties. In this action the Court ruled that a completely peaceful protest outside a police station could be legally dispersed.[1]

. . . Nothing in the Constitution of the United States prevents Florida from even-handed enforcement of its general trespass statute against those refusing to obey the sheriff's order to remove themselves from what amounted to the curtilage of the jailhouse. The State, no less than a private owner of property, has power to preserve the property under its control for the use to which it is lawfully dedicated. For this reason there is no merit to the petitioners' argument that they had a constitutional right to stay on the property, over the jail custodian's objections, because this "area chosen for the peaceful civil rights demonstration was not only 'reasonable' but also particularly appropriate. . . ." Such an argument has as its major articulated premise the assumption that people who want to propagandize protests or views have a constitutional right to do so whenever and however and wherever they please. That concept of constitutional law was vigorously and forthrightly rejected [by us in] *Cox* v. *Louisiana*. . . . We reject it again. The United States Constitution does not forbid a State to control the use of its own property for its own lawful nondiscriminatory purpose.

The Court emphatically affirmed in a 1967 ruling that it did not side with demonstrators who deliberately violated legitimate local laws. In 1963 a state circuit court had issued a verdict of criminal contempt against Dr. Martin Luther King, Jr. and seven other Negro civil rights leaders for defying an Alabama state court's injunction against a civil rights march in Birmingham. The group had been forbidden to parade by the notorious "Bull" Connor, at that time Birmingham's commissioner of public safety. The injunction had been based upon a city ordinance forbidding persons to engage in or to incite others to engage in mass street parades without permits. The state circuit court's judgment was appealed to the Alabama Supreme Court. When it affirmed the ruling, the petitioners carried their case to the Supreme Court of the United States. Said that tribunal:[2]

The petitioners . . . claim that they were free to disobey the injunction because the parade ordinance . . . had been administered in the past in an arbitrary and discriminatory fashion . . . They did not apply for a permit. . . . Had they done so, and had the permit been refused, it is clear that their claim of arbitrary or discriminatory administration of the ordinance would have been considered by the state circuit court.

[1] 385 U.S. 39 (1966).
[2] *Walker* v. *City of Birmingham,* 388 U.S. 307 (1967).

This case would arise in quite different posture if the petitioners, before disobeying the injunction, had challenged it in the Alabama courts, and had been met with delay or frustration of their constitutional claims. . . .

[The] precedents clearly put the petitioners on notice that they could not bypass orderly judicial review of the injunction before disobeying it. Any claim that they were entrapped or misled is wholly unfounded, a conclusion confirmed by evidence in the record showing that when the petitioners violated the injunction they expected to go to jail.

The rule of law that Alabama followed in this case reflects a belief that in the fair administration of justice no man can be judge in his own case, however exalted his state, however righteous his motives, and irrespective of his race, color, politics or religion. . . . One may sympathize with the petitioners' impatient commitment to their cause. But respect for judicial process is a small price to pay for the civilizing hand of law, which alone can give abiding meaning to constitutional freedom.

Affirmed.

Fair Trials: Narrowing the Gap

Some of the most conspicuous gains the Afro-American made in the three decades after 1938 were won in court actions and in civil rights legislation, both of which—while they hardly improved his housing, his job, or his education in the ghetto—nudged him further down the road at least to the political and civil equality that the Constitution guarantees him. But, ironically, it was precisely in the field of law and administration of justice that he continued to be most frequently foiled.[1]

Although this indictment is usually framed in terms of southern practice, it applies—if not in degree, at least in kind—to the rest of the country as well, wherever blacks are massed in considerable numbers. In 1970 it must still be recorded that murders of civil rights workers go unpunished in the Deep South, even though hopes for more evenhanded justice were stirred when a white youth was sentenced in Mississippi to life imprisonment for raping a black girl, and in Georgia eleven Negroes sat on a jury to try the black killers of a white police officer.

The southern courthouse continues to be the sign and seal of white power over blacks. The symbol is a bastion compounded of laws and ordinances against "disturbing the peace," frankly intended to keep the black community under control; ill-educated justices of the peace, paid on a per-conviction basis; a lack of Negro lawyers—in many counties a total lack; a bail system calculated to keep accused Negroes in their segregated jails until they come to trial; poverty that keeps adequate legal counsel beyond a black's financial reach; courthouses where everyone except the janitor is white, from the judge and

[1] *Time*, 87 (April 15, 1966), 46.

juror and prosecutor down to the lowliest clerk; an etiquette, adapted from slavery days, that permits judges and attorneys to address a Negro witness as "boy," and to refer to the accused as "this nigger."

But most of all, despite the accumulating laws and judicial rulings to the contrary, the chief barrier between the black defendant and justice in the courts continues to be the all-white jury—or, occasionally, ten or eleven whites and one or two intimidated or obliging blacks. (Jury commissioners indicted for violating the 1875 federal statute against systematic exclusion of Negroes from juries would only be tried by white juries, with reasonably predictable results.) Not only does the white jury all too often convict the Negro with unseemly zeal; it breeds injustice in other ways: Negroes convicted of crimes against other Negroes are too casually judged; whites committing crimes against blacks are even more leniently dealt with; and blacks committing crimes against whites are punished with startling severity.

A trend to correct these ancient abuses is unmistakable in 1970, but it cannot as yet be characterized as more than a trend.

Although the bulk of litigation in which the United States Supreme Court was confronted with appeals from accused blacks who complained of unfair treatment continued, as in the previous decades, to turn upon charges of systematic exclusion of Negroes from juries, the empaneling of biased jurors, and confessions obtained under pressure of threatened or actual violence, the bench's increasing solicitude for fair play on the black man's day in court was illustrated in the 1960's by further refinements of older rulings on these issues. Not only were the judges more insistent now upon impartial selection of jurors, and upon the more obvious protections which federal and state constitutions guarantee to the accused; they were also more vigilant with respect to less conspicuous denials of due process.

In one case, for example, the right of black defendants to courtesies long denied them in court was pointedly asserted. One Mary Hamilton, in a hearing for a writ of habeas corpus, refused to reply when she was addressed as "Mary," and declared that she would answer questions only if she was called "Miss Hamilton." Fined for contempt of court and sentenced to five days in jail, she was denied rehearing by the Alabama Supreme Court.[1] Upon her petition of certiorari to the Supreme Court of the United States, however, that tribunal responded *per curiam* with a twelve-word judgment: "The petition for writ of certiorari is granted. The judgment is reversed."[2]

In another surprising opinion, a United States court of appeals held that a Negro had been denied equal protection of the laws in the

[1] *Ex parte Hamilton,* 275 Ala. 574, 156 So. 2d 926 (1964).
[2] 376 U.S. 650 (1964).

deliberate *inclusion* of Negroes on the grand jury that had indicted him.[1]

> A Negro is entitled to the equal protection of the laws, no less and no more. He stands equal before the law, is viewed by the law as a person, not as a Negro. . . . An accused cannot demand a mixed grand jury, some of which shall be of his same race. What an accused is entitled to demand under the Constitution is that in organizing the grand jury there shall be no discrimination against him because of his race or color. . . . The only list of importance to the decision of this case is the list of twenty from which the foreman was selected and the other eleven grand jurors drawn. Six Negroes were deliberately included in this list of twenty because of their race. When to this circumstance is added the . . . facts then known to the jury commissioners that the grand jury to be chosen from that list . . . was to consider whether to return an indictment against Collins, and that no other case was scheduled . . . , the conclusion becomes inescapable that in the organization of the grand jury which indicted Collins there was discrimination against him because of his race or color. . . . The judgment must be reversed and the cause remanded to await a possible reindictment and retrial of Collins.

The black man's right to be selected without bias for jury service, and, by that token, to be tried by his peers, was still far from secure in 1970. Although the Supreme Court did[2] strike down some of the more brazen procedures for keeping blacks off jury lists, that tribunal was still upholding schemes which, while on their face not discriminatory, were in practice almost insuperable barriers to the selection of more than an occasional token black juror.

On January 19, 1970, for example, the Court handed down two opinions in which it declined to repudiate vaguely worded jury-selection laws which Negro litigants contended had been used in Alabama and Georgia to keep many blacks from jury rolls. In the action challenging the system prescribed by state law in Alabama, black appellants submitted impressive evidence to show that state laws as drawn made it extremely easy for officials charged with keeping jury lists up to date to "overlook" eligible blacks, or to have prospective black jurors disqualified on the ground that they did not meet the law's vague and subjective requirement that jury commissioners may select as jurors only those persons who are "generally reputed to be honest and intelligent and . . . esteemed in the community for their integrity, good character and sound judgment." The state's statutes also placed the jury selection procedure in the hands of a three-member jury commission for each county, appointed by the governor. The litigants complained further that the governor made a practice of appointing only whites as commissioners. They pointed out that blacks made up three-

[1] *Collins v. Walker*, 339 F. 2d 100 (5th Cir. 1964).

[2] As in *Avery* v. *Georgia*, 345 U.S. 559 (1953), and *Whitus* v. *Georgia*, 385 U.S. 545 (1967).

fourths of the population of their county, and that while fifty percent of the white male population in a recent year found its way to the jury roll, only four percent of the Negro males did so.

Still, although the Court found "overwhelming proof" that the law had been abused, it held that it would be improper to conclude that the statute itself was so clearly discriminatory in its *intent* that judicial interference with the state's prerogatives to regulate its own jury selection was justified.[1]

The Georgia case arose in Taliaferro County, where although sixty-two percent of the population was black, no Negro had ever served on the school board, a body which, in turn, was appointed by the county grand jury. The grand jury list for January 1968, numbered 130 of the county's citizens, but only 11 of these were blacks. It was this gross underrepresentation of blacks on the grand jury upon which the appellants centered their attack. Again, as in the Alabama case, the Georgia statutes greatly facilitated the elimination of Negroes as potential jurors by reason of "poor health or old age," and more particularly on the slippery grounds of not conforming, in the judgment of those charged with making the selections, with the requirement that jurors be "discreet," and "upright," and "intelligent."

Again the Court, in declining to intervene, took the position that while the laws upon which the jury selection system rested might be abused, they were not "inherently unfair."[2]

> Georgia's constitutional and statutory scheme for selecting its grand juries and boards of education is not inherently unfair, or necessarily incapable of administration without regard to race; the federal courts are not powerless to remedy unconstitutional departures from Georgia law by declaratory and injunctive relief. The challenged provisions do not refer to race; indeed, they impose on the jury commissioners the affirmative duty to supplement the jury lists by going out into the county and personally acquainting themselves with other citizens of the county whenever the jury lists in existence do not fairly represent a cross-section of the county's upright and intelligent citizens.

Increasingly typical during these years, however, of judgments for the relief of blacks protesting unfair trials was the finding in the following case, in which two blacks, convicted of murder in a North Carolina court, objected that Negroes had been systematically excluded from the grand jury by which they had been indicted. The North Carolina Supreme Court had refused, on the evidence, to find systematic exclusion, but the same data when submitted on a writ of certiorari to the United States Supreme Court brought this blunt retort:[3]

[1] *Carter* v. *Jury Commission of Green County,* 38 LW 4082, 24 L. Ed. 2d 549 (1970).

[2] *Turner* v. *Fouche,* 38 LW 4090, 24 L. Ed. 2d 567 (1970).

[3] *Arnold* v. *North Carolina,* 376 U.S. 773 (1964).

In support of their motion to quash the indictment because of consistent exclusion of Negroes from grand jury service, petitioners, both Negroes, offered testimony . . . showing that the tax records of the county . . . revealed 12,250 white persons and 4,819 Negroes in the county, with 5,583 white men and 2,499 Negro men listed for poll tax. In addition, the clerk of the trial court testified that. . . . in his 24 years as clerk he could remember only one Negro serving on a grand jury.

The judgment below must be reversed.

One issue that civil libertarians were eager to hear the Supreme Court pronounce upon was the question whether the prescribing of the death penalty for rape was not, de facto, a denial of equal protection, because it was selectively enforced to the Negro's very great disadvantage. In the state of Georgia, for example, of sixty-one persons executed for rape from 1930 to 1962, all but three were Negroes. The Court was willing to take up the issue in 1966, but the occasion to do so was withdrawn under these circumstances: On June 20, 1966, the Court granted certiorari, in the case of *Sims* v. *Georgia,* to consider five questions raised by that controversy by its outcome in the state courts. One of them read, "Where a Negro defendant sentenced to death in Georgia for the rape of a white woman offers to prove that nineteen times as many Negroes as whites have been executed for rape in Georgia in an effort to show that racial discrimination violating the equal protection clause of the Fourteenth Amendment produced such a result, may this offer of proof be disallowed?" The petitioner eventually elected, however, not to raise this issue in his brief, preferring to rest his hopes on other grounds.[1]

Housing: Leveling the Ghetto's Walls

Some small progress toward fair housing was made by Executive Order 11063, issued by President Kennedy in 1962, banning discrimination in housing insured by agencies of the federal government, and by older statutes and orders relating to public housing;[2] but discrimination by private owners and their agents was more stubborn. There were, to be sure, cases in which state antidiscrimination laws were sustained in state and federal courts, and in which violators were convicted, but they were few and, proceeding suit by suit, their reach was extremely limited. The ghetto is still a hard reality, perhaps the most *conspicuous* fact, of Negro American life. In 1970 the contribution of fair housing provisions to racially balanced neighborhoods and to free access to all neighborhoods unhampered by racial considerations was still

[1] Thomas I. Emerson, David Haber, and Norman Dorson, *Political and Civil Rights in the United States* (third edition, 2 vols., Boston, 1967), II, 1823.

[2] See above, p. 395.

all but invisible. Moreover, such litigation was often expensive; it exposed Negroes to harassment and intimidation, and, even when successful, defeated its purpose, because the movement of a black family into a neighborhood often resulted in the flight of whites. The ultimate result was only another black neighborhood. Indeed real estate brokers were quick to profit from such panicky propensities on the part of whites, and they soon were deliberately spreading alarm in white communities and buying up property at distress-sale prices and selling them at inflated prices to blacks. Such "block-busting" soon became the object of legislative restraint.

Two landmark decisions of the United States Supreme Court in the fair housing field which came in 1967 and 1968 seemed to have wide implications for the future. Two years after the adoption of "Proposition 14," which, by popular referendum, became Article I, Section 26, of the California constitution and by whose terms the state was forbidden to abridge the right of owners or their agents to sell or rent, or refuse to sell or rent, to whomever they chose, a Negro couple whose efforts to rent an apartment had been repulsed brought suit, alleging that the clause violated the Fourteenth Amendment. Denied an injunction by a state superior court, the couple appealed to the state's supreme court, which reversed, and sided with the plaintiffs. "When the electorate assumes the law-making function," said California's highest court, "the electorate is as much a state agency as any of its elected officials." Defendants appealed to the United States Supreme Court. That tribunal, sustaining the state supreme court, found that such exclusion of Negroes was a denial, by *state* action, of equal protection of the laws.[1]

The judgment of the California court was that [section] 26 unconstitutionally involves the State in racial discriminations and is therefore invalid under the Fourteenth Amendment.

There is no sound reason for rejecting this judgment. . . . The right to discriminate, including the right to discriminate on racial grounds, was now embodied in the State's basic charter, immune from legislative, executive, or judicial regulation at any level of the state government. Those practicing racial discrimination. . . . could now invoke express constitutional authority, free from censure or interference of any kind from official sources. . . . Only the State is excluded with respect to property owned by it.

. . . Here we are dealing with a provision which does not just repeal an existing law forbidding private racial discriminations. Section 26 was intended to authorize, and does authorize, racial discrimination in the housing market. The right to discriminate is now one of the basic policies of the State. The California Supreme Court believes that the section will significantly encourage and involve the State in private discriminations.

[That Court's judgment is] *Affirmed.*

[1] *Reitman* v. *Mulkey,* 387 U.S. 369 (1967).

More far-reaching in its effects was an action in which a Negro and his white wife who had been denied the opportunity to purchase a thirty-thousand-dollar home in a new St. Louis development sued the developer. Their attorney cited, among other legal sanctions, the Civil Rights Act of 1866[1] (ignored since the Civil Rights cases of 1883), which declared that *all* citizens of the United States shall have the same right, in every state and territory, as is enjoyed by white citizens thereof, to inherit, purchase, lease, sell, hold, and convey real and personal property. The United States district court and the circuit court of appeals had dismissed the complaint. The United States Supreme Court, however, reversed. After a searching analysis of the history of the 1866 statute, and of the intention of its framers, the Court, speaking through Justice Potter, concluded:[2]

> . . .Surely Congress has the power under the Thirteenth Amendment rationally to determine what are the badges and the incidents of slavery, and the authority to translate that determination into effective legislation. Nor can we say that the determination Congress has made is an irrational one. For this Court recognized long ago that, whatever else they may have encompassed, the badges and incidents of slavery—its "burdens and disabilities"—included restraints upon "those fundamental rights which are the essence of civil freedom, namely, the same right . . . to inherit, purchase, lease, sell and convey property, as is enjoyed by white citizens" . . . Just as the Black Codes, enacted after the Civil War to restrict the free exercise of those rights, were substitutes for the slave system, so the exclusion of Negroes from white communities became a substitute for the Black Codes. And when racial discrimination herds men into ghettoes and makes their ability to buy property turn on the color of their skin, then it too is a relic of slavery.
>
> Negro citizens North and South, who saw in the Thirteenth Amendment a promise of freedom . . . would be left with "a mere paper guarantee" if Congress were powerless to assure that a dollar in the hands of a Negro will purchase the same thing as a dollar in the hands of a white man. At the very least, the freedom that Congress is empowered to secure under the Thirteenth Amendment includes the freedom to buy whatever a white man can buy, the right to live wherever a white man can live. If Congress cannot say that being a free man means at least this much, then the Thirteenth Amendment made a promise the Nation cannot keep.

The two foregoing decisions, taken together, are, again, part of a remarkable pattern of extraordinary judicial solicitude for the weak and the defenseless against the strong who use their power for their own ends. In *Reitman*, the Court brushed aside a state constitutional provision (adopted by referendum, 4,526,460 to 2,395,747) to safeguard the citizen from state encouragement of private discrimination. The doctrine of state action had come a long way since the days when only overt action by the state itself could invoke the force of the Four-

[1] See above, p. 46.
[2] *Jones v. Mayer*, 392 U.S. 409 (1968).

teenth Amendment. And in *Jones* v. *Mayer* came at last an unequivocal application of the full strength of the Thirteenth Amendment, which the courts had long declined to read as very little more than a prohibition of chattel slavery. Now it would be not only slavery that the amendment estopped, but also its "badges," the stigmata that persisted a century after the peculiar institution's demise.

Employment: New Gains for Equal Opportunity

Various state and federal laws—chief among them Title VII of the Civil Rights Act of 1964[1]—prohibit discrimination in employment, both public and private. That very substantial gains have been made in recent years in widening job opportunities for Negroes in *public* jobs would perhaps be almost universally conceded. That they are, however, still effectually fenced out of jobs of nearly every sort in nongovernmental employment, in every section of the country, is equally plain. Such discriminations range from categorical exclusions to subtle partialities. The Negro is still, typically, the last to be hired, the first to be fired, and is rarely promoted over a white fellow worker's head. Millions have little more than a choice between menial work or no job at all.

In periods of recession the unemployment rate among black workers is distressingly high; and even in times of "full employment" the rate for Negroes is commonly from three to five times as high as the presumably "normal" unemployment of three to five percent for the country at large. Pay rates for the race tend to fall very substantially below those for whites performing the same tasks, and labor organizations have often compounded the black worker's misfortunes by excluding him from membership and from apprenticeship training. Employment agencies have helped to perpetuate the invidious differentials by discriminatory referral of applicants.

There have, however, been a few court victories in recent years for the principle of fair employment, a brief sampling of which is worth noting here. In 1963 the United States Supreme Court sustained a state commission's cease and desist order, even though it clearly involved *interstate* commerce, in an area of employment traditionally closed to Negroes. A Negro had filed a complaint with the Anti-Discrimination Commission of Colorado, alleging that Continental Airlines had denied him employment solely on the ground of race. After lower court proceedings, the state supreme court held that the state has no power to regulate employment practices of an interstate carrier, because interstate travel requires uniform regulation, by a single authority. The

[1] See above, p. 409.

United States Supreme Court reversed, declaring that (1) prohibition of racial discrimination in employment in interstate commerce does not unduly burden such commerce; and (2) the Colorado statute was not nullified by federal preemption of regulation of interstate carriers, because the state law did not frustrate any part of the purposes of existing federal laws and regulations.

Recalling two older Supreme Court cases which seemed to sustain the Colorado Supreme Court's position (*Morgan* v. *Virginia* and *Hall* v. *De Cuir*), the Court reasoned:[1]

> The Court in *Morgan* v. *Virginia* . . . held that a Virginia law requiring segregation of motor carrier passengers, including those on interstate journeys, infringed the Commerce Clause because uniform regulation was essential. The Court emphasized the restriction on the passengers; freedom to choose accommodations and the inconvenience of constantly requiring passengers to shift seats. As in *Hall* v. *De Cuir,* the Court explicitly recognized the absence of any one, sure test for deciding these burden-on-commerce cases. It concluded, however, that the circumstances before it showed that there would be a practical interference with carrier transportation if diverse state laws were permitted to stand. . . .
>
> We are not convinced that commerce will be unduly burdened if Continental is required by Colorado to refrain from racial discrimination in its hiring of pilots in that State. Not only is the hiring within a State of an employee, even for an interstate job, a much more localized matter than the transporting of passengers from State to State but more significantly the threat of diverse and conflicting regulation of hiring practices is virtually nonexistent.

In an interesting parallel to *Smith* v. *Allwright,* in which the Supreme Court had held in 1944 that primary elections, having become an integral part of the electoral process, had therefore come within the reach of the equal protection clause, the Supreme Court now held in the case before us that labor unions could, in some circumstances, be subject to a similar rule, where they were an integral part of recruiting employees for governmental construction work. Here three black workers, claiming that they had been denied employment on federal construction projects as a direct result of the total exclusion of Negroes from membership and apprentice training in an iron workers' union, brought a class action. The result was a Court order directing the union's committee on apprenticeship to admit them as members and to employ them as apprentices.[2]

> The Union and the Joint Committee are, on the basis of the facts here, an integral part of a Federal and State project. A private citizen or organization, to the extent that their activities remain entirely private and unrelated

[1] *Colorado Anti-Discrimination Commission* v. *Continental Airlines,* 372 U.S. 714 (1963). For the Morgan and Hall decisions, see above, pp. 63 and 285.

[2] *Todd* v. *Joint Apprenticeship Committee of Steel Workers of Chicago,* 223 F. Supp. 12 (N.D. Ill., 1963).

and non-dependent upon the sovereign, cannot be charged with denial of equal protection of the law. However, we have more. The Federal government through two of its agencies and the State through one of its agencies, is at the very least passively assisting, aiding and making it possible for the defendant Union and Joint Committee to realize and perpetuate their discriminatory practices. The defendant agencies in practice and in effect are permitting the Union and the Joint Committee to practice racial discrimination and by so doing if not directly at least indirectly are denying plaintiffs their constitutional rights.

Finally, *Bell* v. *Georgia Dental Association* illustrates the beginning of the end of barriers which had long narrowed the opportunities of black professional men. Here, Negro dentists sued in a federal district court, seeking to compel the state's dental association and its affiliates to admit Negroes as members. The defendant associations moved to dismiss the action on the ground that they were voluntary associations whose conduct, therefore, does not constitute state action. The court took another view of the matter:[1]

The Georgia legislature . . . by giving the Dental Association the right to nominate members of three state agencies [Board of Dental Examiners; Georgia Board of Health; and the state's Hospital Advisory Council] . . . made it an agency of the State of Georgia to that extent. The Dental Association by excluding Negro dentists from its membership thereby deprived them of the right to vote in connection with the nomination of dentists to fill places on the three boards mentioned, one of these boards having the responsibility of examining applications for a license to practice dentistry in Georgia. The result of such action therefore is that only dentists approved by those of the white race can be elected to such offices and Negro dentists can have no voice in their selection. This seems to be a clear violation of the Equal Protection Clause of the United States Constitution.

As the crusade pushed on, whites weary of the commotions it stirred and irritated by what they considered the ingratitude of blacks, whose demands rose after every success, frequently asked in exasperation when the black petitioners would at last be satisfied. The writer of a letter to the editor of *The New York Times Magazine* suggested the answer in a parable:[2]

. . . An innocent man was once condemned to life imprisonment. He took his case to the highest courts, wrote letters to the authorities, went on hunger strikes and finally became violent. He protested against everything: the prison conditions, the wardens, and of course, his life sentence. After years of disgraceful behavior, the prison authorities gradually and reluctantly made some concessions toward improving prison conditions. The prisoner's cell was heated when the outside temperature dropped below 40 instead of 20 degrees; he was given two solid meals a day instead of one; he was also given a

[1] U.S. Dist. Ct., Civil Action No. 7966, Feb. 3, 1964 (N.D. Ga.). See RRLR IX, 327.

[2] October 13, 1968, p. 320 The letter is signed, "Jacques Preston, New York."

second blanket. You will notice that in each case there was 100 percent improvement in living conditions. Surprisingly enough, the prisoner continued his protests. The prison officials became indignant and threatened him with severe reprisals, and finally, exasperated beyond endurance, they asked how many more improvements they would have to make, and at which point would he desist from his extremist behavior. The answer, of course, is simply when his sentence is vacated and he is compensated for the time spent behind bars.

INDEX OF CASES CITED

SUBJECT INDEX

ELGIN COMMUNITY COLLEGE LIBRARY
Elgin, Illinois